GETTING U S INTO WAR

By PORTER SARGENT

HANDBOOK OF AMERICAN PRIVATE SCHOOLS
    25TH AN. ED., 1941

WHAT MAKES LIVES, 1940

THE NEW IMMORALITIES, 1935

SPOILS, FROM A CROWDED LIFE, 1935

HANDBOOK OF NEW ENGLAND
    3D ED., 1921

GETTING US

INTO

WAR

BY

PORTER SARGENT

PORTER SARGENT
11 BEACON STREET, BOSTON, MASS.

COPYRIGHT, 1941, BY
PORTER SARGENT

TABLE OF CONTENTS
INTRODUCTORY

WHY THIS BOOK 11
TO MEET A DEMAND—I COULD "DO NO OTHER"—WHAT IS HISTORY?—
IS HISTORY BUNK?—THE CULTURAL APPROACH—MOTIVES CANNOT BE
IGNORED—THE VICTORS WRITE THE HISTORY—THE ROAD WE HAVE
COME OVER—INTELLIGENCE

WHAT FEAR DID 19
TIPPING THE BALANCE—TORY JITTERS—WELCOMING FASCISM

THE APPEASERS 27
FRIENDS OF GERMANY—BLESSED ARE THE PEACEMAKERS—CAUSES
WORKING FOR WAR—IF WAR COMES—WHAT DUTY DID—LET US NOW
PRAISE GREAT MEN—THE END OF APPEASEMENT

WINNING AMERICA OVER 41
VANSITTART DISAPPEARS—AN ANCHOR TO WINDWARD—SECRECY
ESSENTIAL—A GOOD INVESTMENT—IMPROVED TECHNIQUE

PRESIDENTIAL PROGRESS 49
"ARMS AND THE MEN"—THE FOOLS' GOLD SPEECH—DEFEAT—HOWE
—FRUSTRATION—SOME REMARKABLE COINCIDENCES—QUARANTIN-
ING AGGRESSORS—FUTILITY—SALVATION

TOWARD WAR 61
SECRET DOINGS—MUNICH AND AFTER—WHOSE FOREIGN POLICY?—
SHIFTING FRONTIERS—IF WE DON'T HAVE WAR

PREACHING PEACE 69
WEANING US FROM NEUTRALITY—PACIFYING THE 'ECONOMIC ROYAL-
ISTS'—COORDINATING AND ORGANIZING—STRATEGY—INSURING RE-
PEAL—THE EMBARGO IS KILLED

'SHORT OF WAR' 77
WHO'S BEHIND—HARVARD PROMOTES WAR—THE WHITE MACHINE—
HOW IT FUNCTIONED—ASSOCIATED ORGANIZATIONS

'ALL OUT' 83
CONCEALED OBJECTIVES—BY EASY STEPS—IT'S OUR WAR

THERE'LL ALWAYS BE AN ENGLAND 87
ENGLAND FAREWELL, 1913—ENGLAND REVISITED, 1933

THE SARGENT BULLETINS

THE BULLETINS—HOW THEY STARTED—QUESTIONING MOTIVES . . 95

WAR PROPAGANDA—HARMLESS EXPOSED—PETERSON RECAPITULATES—
ROGERSON ANTICIPATES—ENGLAND APPEASES—AMERICA HATES . 97

TO BRING US INTO THE NEXT WAR—NYE DISCOVERS ROGERSON—NEWS-
PAPERS POOH-POOH PROPAGANDA—INVESTIGATION DEMANDED . . 102

PROPAGANDA FOR WAR—PREPARING CIVILIAN AMERICA—CIVIL LIBERTIES
IN ENGLAND—VANSITTART COORDINATES PROPAGANDA—MILLIONS
FOR PUBLIC OPINION—AMERICA ASSUMES BRITAIN'S BURDEN . . 104

BRITISH PROPAGANDA 1939—BRITAIN WOOS AMERICA—MENCKEN ON THE
"MORAL ALLIES"—FOREIGN DEVILS—WHOLLY UNNEUTRAL . . 113
BRITISH PROPAGANDA AND AMERICA'S FOREIGN POLICY—FROM THE ECO-
NOMIC TO THE MORAL—INFLUENCE OF EMOTIONS—WAR FEVER . 118
BRITISH PROPAGANDA RESULTS—STEPS SHORT BUT SURE—STALIN LAUGHS
—INTIMATE SKETCHES—MADE OPINION—30 YEARS MORE? . - . 120
BRITISH PROPAGANDA: PROGRESS REPORTS—AMERICA DISAPPOINTS—NEU-
TRALITY MISMANAGED—WASHINGTON BETRAYS—ROYALTY ON PARADE 122
BRITISH PROPAGANDA IN AMERICA: IMPROVED TECHNIQUE—REMOVING
THE ODORS—OPPOSITION TO REPEAL—MECHANIZED WHALES—HOW
TO FILL WAR COFFERS—NEUTRAL AGAINST WHOM? .   .   . 126
IS THERE BRITISH PROPAGANDA IN AMERICA?—MIGHT AND RIGHT—EN-
TANGLING EMOTIONS—HITLER SERVES BRITAIN—BELLING THE PRO-
PAGANDISTS—WORLD IN REVOLT—ODDS 10 TO 1 WE'RE IN . 131
NOTES ON A MORAL WAR, by H. L. MENCKEN—PRETENSIONS EXPLODED
—RATIONAL, NOT MORAL—HEADACHE OVER ALTRUISM—MULTIPLY-
ING THE BILLIONS—DIVIDING THE SPOILS—AMERICA'S BIG JOB . . 137
THE DREAM OF CECIL RHODES—UNION NOW—OF THE SATISFIED COUN-
TRIES—THERE'S A JOKER—LION AND THE LAMB—LAST WILL AND
TESTAMENT—MILNER'S "KINDERGARTEN"—LEAD KINDLY STREIT . 143
COMMENTS—INTERESTED—AMAZING GRASP—ABLE AND ERUDITE . . 151
ARE WE "THE BEST INFORMED PEOPLE IN THE WORLD"?—STARVING FOR
FACTS—FED ON EMOTIONS—BOOKS ON PROPAGANDA—MOST POWER-
FUL MAN—DECLINE AND FALL—LET THEM HAVE WARS . . 155
SOURCES OF INFORMATION FOR AMERICANS—VIOLATING TABUS—WOMEN
SCORNED—MEN SCORNED—EDUCATORS TAKEN IN . . . 160
MORE BOOKS THAT INFORM—BEWARE BEST SELLERS—PROPAGANDA—RE-
VOLUTION—TWILIGHT AND FUTURE—WHY MEDDLE? . . 162
MORALITY—INTERNATIONAL AND ACADEMIC—UNCTUOUS CONCERN—
PSITTACISM—POLLY WANTS MORALITY—CONANT RESENTS—"CRIM-
SON" ATTACKS—PITIFUL AND PITIABLE—PRIESTLEY REMEMBERS . 164
RECENT RESPONSES—HARVARD STRAINED—PRESIDENTIAL FREEDOM . 171
OUR PHONEY NEUTRALITY—REPEALING EMBARGO—LOBBYISTS SWARM—
SUBMARINES AND VOTES — DANGEROUS QUASIFATALISM — POROUS
LEGISTATION—TRANSFER OF REGISTRY—THEY PLANNED IT THAT WAY 172
'WAR AND PEACE' PROPAGANDA—ACCENT ON PEACE—FASHIONS IN PROP-
AGANDA—LAMONT LAMENTS—MILLIS RECANTS—THE PEACE OF 1944 178
HELL IS PAVED WITH GOOD INTENTIONS—MOTHERS' SONS—UNENDURA-
BLE VIOLENCE—SECRET AID TO FRANCE—WILL MORALITY BE SACRI-
FICED? 184
THE FINNISH FLARE-UP—FEVER MOUNTS—ROOSEVELT REBUFFS CRITICS—
THE WATER, NOT THE LAND—MANNERHEIM SLAUGHTER—THREAT-
ENING PETROGRAD—MURMANSK TO ARCHANGEL—LAST STRAW TO
BRING US IN 187

THE PROPAGANDA WAR GOES ON ON ALL FRONTS—WAR OF NERVES—
PROPAGANDISTS AS PROTAGONISTS—LOTHIAN COCKTAIL—ENGLAND A
NIGHTMARE—HOLLAND TERRORIZED—ITALY FATTENS . . . 195

BLOOD, OIL, AND DOLLARS—LAST DROP OF BLOOD—FOR OIL—DIE WACHT
AM RHEIM—DISSENSION AMONG THE LORDS—THE WAY OF ALL GOLD 213

OUR 'NEUTRAL' NAVAL EXPANSION BELT—WHY ONLY TWO OCEANS?—
THE KING'S DIVING BELL—ECONOMIC SUICIDE—GIRDLE ROUND ABOUT
THE EARTH—THE GOLD-PAVED ROAD TO WAR 219

COMING EVENTS CAST THEIR SHADOW—WAR AND THE TORIES—JITTERS IN
ENGLAND AND FRANCE—THE VOICE OF LOTHIAN—SNUBBERY AND
SNOBBERY—OUT OF OUR TREASURY—EDISON POLISHES THE HANDLE 231

100 BRITISH PROPAGANDISTS IN AMERICA—BRITAIN INTENDS NO PROPA-
GANDA—PROPAGANDISTS UNREGISTERED—LECTURERS ON CALL . . 241

AN INTIMATE LETTER TO READERS—EXPOSING BUNK—NOT PROPAGANDA
PROOF—STILL TIME TO CRITICIZE—IT'S ALL IN THE PAPERS . . 244

WHAT WAR HAS BROUGHT TO CANADA—BUSINESS AND SACRIFICE—
"EVERY TWENTY YEARS"—WILL CANADA HOLD THE BAG?—RECRUIT-
ING THE UNEMPLOYED—DISSENTERS FACE THE BARS—ROYAL FAVORS 247

A CANADIAN VIEW—IF HITLER'D GONE TO ETON—PLOW UNDER, PLOW
UNDER 252

EMBROILING THE NEUTRALS—PROFUSION OF CONFUSION—CHERUBIC
CHURCHILL—HORSETRADING YANKEES NOT SO SHREWD—FOOLS OVER
GOLD—HOGS, TOBACCO, AND ORANGES—LUMBER FOR FINLAND . . 255

STRANGLING, STARVING, FALSIFYING,—FOR POWER—SINISTER PLOT—
PLUMP LITTLE CLERGYMEN—A GOOD WAR AT LAST—BLOODTHIRSTY
PREACHERS—OIL IS POWER—FOR RIGHTEOUSNESS' SAKE . . . 263

THE THREAT TO OUR 'CIVIL LIBERTIES'—"FORTUNE'S" ROUND TABLE—
MUDDYING THE STREAM—A NOBLER UNITY—GIRDED FOR THE FIGHT . 272

THE COMING RED DRIVE—BOSTON RAIDED—BOMBS IN NEW YORK—
YANKEE GOVERNOR SPEAKS—OUT OF IGNORANCE GROWS HATE—
SCIENTIFIC PERIODICALS CUT OFF—ANTI-ALIEN BILLS . . . 280

INTERNATIONAL INANITIES—A CONTINUOUS PERFORMANCE—SCRAPING
THE BOTTOM—ARSENAL OR TARGET?—ROVING AMBASSADOR WELLES
—SEARCHING THE MAILS—VIOLATING THE NEUTRALITY BELT . . 285

ON TO DICTATORSHIP—BLANK CHECK POWERS—'SEALED ORDERS'—RED
RAIDS—VIGILANCE AND LIBERTY 290

THE GOLD MENACE—WE STILL HAVE THE BONDS—FINANCING THE
U.S.S R.—THE AVALANCHE OF GOLD—A $15 DUTY—SUBSIDY FOR WAR 295

OUR FRIENDS REPLY—UNIVERSITY PRESIDENTS—COLLEGE LIBRARIES—
PRIVATE AND PUBLIC SCHOOLS—ARMY, NAVY—FROM EAST TO WEST . 301

OUR SECRET ALLIANCE WITH GREAT BRITAIN—"JOINT ACTIVITY" IN THE
ORIENT—PACIFIC ISLES—AN ACT OF WAR—WATCHDOG IN THE PACI-
FIC—SECRET COMMITMENTS—AMERICA IN IGNORANCE . . . 305

FINLAND'S DEBTS AND CREDITS—MOSTLY DEBTS—BANKERS' WON'T LEND
—HURRICANE LUMBER—ANOTHER SOILED WHITE PAPER . . . 313

A TIME TO BE ON GUARD—DEMOCRATIC PROCESS—POPULAR PROTEST—
    THREE TIMES REBUFFED—PAMPHLETEERING REVIVED—CROMWELL
    TRIAL BALLOON—KEYNES PLAN—MENDICANT MOTHER COUNTRY   . 320
OBJECTIONS RAISED BY CORRESPONDENTS—THE OTHER SIDE—NOT JUDI-
    CIAL—PROPAGANDA PROOF—GERMAN PROPAGANDA .   .   . 326
WHAT THE LAST WAR COST—SOIL AND OIL—LABOR AND LIVES—FREEDOM
    AND FRUSTRATION—COST OF SOULS—WERE THEY RIGHT? .   . 328
HOW MUCH SHALL WE WASTE ON THIS WAR?—FORCE WITH FORCE—
    JUGGLING THE BILLIONS—PROFITS VS. WAGES—SWEAT AND BLOOD . 336
A FOUR BILLION DOLLAR ELECTION FUND—DEFENSE APPROPRIATIONS—
    AGAINST HITLER OR WILLKIE?—ROOSEVELTIAN PERFORMANCE .   . 339
FOR WHOSE RELIGION—GOD'S WORK CUT OUT—ALL CLAIM HIM—UNI-
    VERSITIES FIRST—ROOSEVELT AND VATICAN—RELIGIOUS "GABBLE" . 342
WITCH HUNT AHEAD—CIVILIZED VENEER—FREEDOM SUBVERTED—PRESI-
    DENTIAL SENSITIVENESS TO OPPOSITION—BRITISH FIFTH COLUMN . 346
WILL BRITAIN WIN OUR ELECTION?—UNTAPPED RESERVOIR—"TOO
    MANY GERMANS?"—AMERICANS HAVE TO BE SCARED   .   . 349
100% (ANGLO-) AMERICAN (IMPERIALIST)—UNIVERSITIES PROMOTE
    WAR—UNDERGRADUATES RESIST—CLARK LAUNCHES CONSCRIPTION
    —OL' BILL WHITE'S COMMITTEE—"CURSED WITH A CLEVER PEN"—
    LYNCHING BEE HATRED—WOODRING OUSTER   .   . 352
40 MILLION CONSCRIPTS—THE NEW DISCIPLINE—FIRE POWER OR MAN
    POWER—PARADE-GROUND TRAINING?   361
THE BUILD-UP FOR WILLKIE—BUILDING ON BUNKUM—THE LANDON
    MYTH—WHICH GRASS ROOTS?—MEN IN THE BEDROOM—SECRET
    MEETING—PROFESSIONAL TALENT—STRUGGLE FOR POWER   .   . 366
NO MORE MILLIONAIRES—"PROFITS OR PEACE"—"PATRIOTISM IS NOT
    ENOUGH"—"WHO BETRAYED FRANCE?"—UNUSED TANKS—BRITISH
    PROFITS—EXCESS TAX JOKER—SCANDAL IN ENGLAND   .   . 372
IS WILLKIE'S WHITE BLACK, AS PAINTED?—"REVERENCE FOR WHITE"—
    "UNITE WITH BRITAIN"—WILLKIE'S WHITE CONNECTION .   . 379
DOCTORING THE MONROE DOCTRINE—SUBSIDIZING DEMOCRACY—"YAN-
    QUI IMPERIALISMO"—FASCIST TRADE—CANNING DOCTORED MONROE
    —UBIQUITOUS DR. HULL—CARTEL CONTROL 386
CONSCRIPTION IS OPPOSED—ALL OVER, IN THE HEADLINES—GRENVILLE
    CLARK PROMOTES—CONSCRIPTION SLOWS PREPAREDNESS .   . 396
FROM OUR CORRESPONDENTS—SHARING IDEAS—ON PRESIDENT AND PRESS
    —"UNTHINKING ACCEPTANCE"—WAR MONGERING .   .   . 402
QUICKSTEP TO WAR, BY H L MENCKEN—BLATHER ABOUT PERIL—
    BRITISH INVASIONS—THE REAL OBJECTION TO ROOSEVELT   .   . 405
$500,000,000 FOR SOUTH AMERICA—A HALF BILLION IN NEW CHIPS—
    SUBSTITUTE FOR CARTEL—BAIT OR BRIBE?—"BUYING FRIENDSHIP" . 408
HULL'S HAVANA TRIUMPH—A MORAL SUCCESS—SUPPRESSING DISSENSION
    —TRADE VS. SENTIMENT—FREE HAND FOR AGGRESSION .   .   . 411

WILL THE DRAFT BE HONORED?—DRAWN ON FOR 12 MILLION—NO RE-
FERENDUM ON CONSCRIPTION—PLANNED SINCE 1918—NEWSPAPERS
DELUDE—PREDICTING POLLS—VOLUNTARY SYSTEM UNTRIED . . 415

WAITING FOR WILLKIE—EIGHT YEARS OF CHARM—POLITICAL DYNAMITE
—A THREE-POINT FLOP—PRESIDENTIAL PAREGORIC 421

UNITY THROUGH CONSCRIPTION—UNITED AGAINST IT—PRESS AND POLLS
DISTORT OPINION—CONSCRIPTING WEALTH 424

THE TIDE TURNS AGAINST CONSCRIPTION—PASSING THE BUCK—PROTEST
UNLEASHED—"PLAYING POLITICS WITH THE WAR"—PRESIDENTIAL
POWERS—CONSCRIPTION 'DEMOCRATIC'—TOWARD DICTATORSHIP . 426

'AMORTIZATION AMELIORATION'—COURTING THE ECONOMIC ROYALISTS—
PRESENTS FROM THE PEOPLE—FATTENING AIRCRAFTERS—PROTECT-
ING STOCKHOLDERS—KNUDSEN'S EMBARRASSMENT—CORPORATIONS
STRIKE—SCANDAL IN ENGLAND—INSURED AGAINST RISK . . . 432

THE PRESIDENT'S PREDICAMENT—THE "COUNTRY SQUIRE"—EXCESS ADUL-
ATION—FAMILY BACKGROUNDS—SPENDING AND DEFENSE . . . 439

CONSCRIPTS OR VOLUNTEERS—'CANNON FODDER'—FOR REGIMENTATION
—"TO OUTDISTANCE HITLER"—HALFWAY DOWN NIAGARA . . 442

THE VOTER'S DILEMMA—'CONVICTIONS'—THE WILLKIE MYTH—ASTROLO-
GICAL FORECASTS—"WHILE YET THERE IS TIME TO THINK" . . 447

THE PRESIDENT'S SECRETS—"OPEN COVENANTS"—OVER-AGE DESTROYERS
—LONG ARM OF COINCIDENCE—OBSOLETE PROFESSORS . . . 450

PROTECTING WAR PROFITS—"EXCESS WAR PROFITS"—THE TAX LOBBY—
"THE MOST COMPLICATED BILL"—INCENTIVE OF PROFITS . . . 461

WEALTH CONSCRIPTION HOAX—VOTES MEAN POWER—THE 'DRAFT IN-
DUSTRY' MEASURE—WILLKIE EXPLODES 467

MORE AND MORE MYSTERIES—SENATOR LUNDEEN'S DEATH—PACIFISTS
BEATEN UP—"GUILTY MEN"—"SEVEN MYSTERIES OF EUROPE" . . 469

HELL BENT FOR ELECTION—"SWEAT, TEARS, AND BLOOD"—VOTERS LIKE
TAFFY—"BUM'S-RUSH TO WAR"—POTENCY OF FEAR . . . 471

DICTATORSHIP TODAY—90% MAJORITIES—"NEW INSTRUMENTS OF
PUBLIC POWER"—"MANUFACTURED EMERGENCIES"—THE "CONFER-
ENCE" METHOD—"A DISASTER WORSE THAN WAR" 476

IN HITLER'S FOOTSTEPS—"DRIFT TOWARD COLLECTIVISM"—THE ART OF
RULING—POLITICAL ABSTRACTIONS—"UNFIT FOR LIBERTY"—AMERI-
CAN ROOTS OF FASCISM—BORROWINGS FROM GERMANY—"FREE ELEC-
TIONS"—ROOSEVELT PLEDGES—"SHORT OF DICTATORSHIP" . . 489

BUILDING A LOYAL OPPOSITION—"UNITY" OR "EUNUCHY"?—"A FEELING
OF ANXIETY"—"ETERNAL VIGILANCE"—OPPOSITION SPEAKS UP . 512

PRODDING JAPAN INTO WAR—CHINA TRADE AND LOWESTOFT—BRITAIN'S
EASTERN INTERESTS—"OUR STAKE IN THE ORIENT"—THE OPEN DOOR
—SCRAP IRON AND OIL—PROMOTING IMPERIALISM—RUBBER QUININE
TIN—ANNAMESE DEMOCRACY—"RETREAT OF THE WEST" . . . 525

How Come France Collapsed—Military Lessons—Fear of Change
—Diary to Dunkirk—Deepseated Rot—Who Betrayed?—"Sui-
cide of a Democracy" 545
Why Germany Wins—"Why" Implies Planning—Technological
History—"Infinite Capacity for Taking Pains"—Civilian Inven-
tions—The "Mostest There Fustest"—"Does Hitler Represent
Germany?"—Surprise and Psychology—New Economics—The
Financial Revolution—Let's Understand the Process . . 563
The Road We Follow—Defense Euphemism—"Morally Unpre-
pared"—'Lease Lend' Bill—What Objectives?—Swimming Pools
and Defense—Cool Heads in Washington—New Financial Sys-
tem—German Necessity—American Assets—American Indebt-
edness—Government Never Pays—The Steps Along the Road . 582
Whose 'New Order'?—Wilson's League—Utopias—Paving the Way
—Apostles of Racism—The Value of Space—Lothian's Fore-
sight—Regionalism—Wisdom of the Body 609
Adjustment and Change—Perpetual Revolution—An American
Conception—Recognition of Social and Economic Change—
Our Present Pre-Revolutionary Condition—Nothing New . 615
Errata 618
Index 619
List of Publishers 636
Announcement of Books 637

WHY THIS BOOK

Now on the verge of war, the way lies straight ahead, but it may help to recall something of the road we have come over. Even on the rim of hell I shall want to know how I got there. The rapid tide of events has confused most of us and dulled the sharpness of first impressions. It's understanding, not confusion, that contributes to morale.

This volume is little more than a scrapbook, a selection from voluminous files of clippings and comments on events domestic and international, and notes on articles and books of the past few years. This contemporary running summary, with later notes bringing the topics up to date, and introductory chapters which endeavor to give in narrative form something of the background, may prove clarifying. The 100 Bulletins which form the core of the book must at times show the heats and fevers of the day, but may have as much value because of this as the more careful accounts which will be the aftermath of the present excitement.

TO MEET A DEMAND

The Bulletins, sent out approximately weekly, were widely distributed, first to private school and college people on my regular mailing list, and later only to those who asked for them or were recommended The flood of letters that came in response showed how seldom recognized were British propaganda methods even by supposedly well-informed Americans. So I felt obliged to continue to supply so far as I was able this demand for suppressed information.

The making of this book has been the part-time avocation of a man past the university retirement age, who finds twenty-four hours a day, seven days in a week, too brief a time to carry on his regular work of publishing, maintaining an advisory service for schools, and helping to solve the educational problems of over a thousand families yearly. The reading and the research have been done chiefly when honest men were in bed and others in night clubs. The compilation was dictated in snatches in intervals of a busy day, fitted to the limits of a stencil and mailed out still moist.

This was not my job though it is true that each year I have made it my business to bring to the attention of discriminating parents and readers, as well as to educators, current matters that seemed of importance to the future of their children and the country. And in my privileged and detached position of what for a quarter of a century I have described on

my letterhead as "Adviser·fo Parents and Schools", I have not hesitated
to speak out boldly. Of late it has seemed that nothing could be of more
importance to my clients that what might happen to their children
through the possible coming of war, and that it was time to speak up
about plans that were being made for us in other countries.   ·

I could not stand idly by while my countrymen, through misleading
teaching, were again being brought to that state of disastrous idealism
which might result in such hysteria as I had witnessed in the war twenty-
two years before. Unless someone better qualified stepped forward, I
had to carry on.

I COULD "DO NO OTHER"

This book is the work of a man who is not a joiner, who represents no
organization or group, who holds to no 'isms', not even pacifism. Born
to Republicanism and Presbyterianism, he has endeavored to avoid
forgery of other fetters. He belongs to no political or social organizations He is not a clubable man. He has maintained membership in one
University and two Harvard clubs, but has found few men in such environment with whom to share interests. Living on both the Atlantic
and Pacific coasts, teaching since the age of eighteen, eye glued to a
microscope for ten years, another ten years in Europe and around the
world studying and interpreting human cultures, European social and
political systems, Buddhism, Sung art,—interests have been many.

When World War I broke out my interests had been for some years
chiefly in Chinese art, and my purpose at that time was to help to interpret the East to the West The sudden shift of interests was attributed
somewhat resentfully to the action of the Czar and the Kaiser. Five years
in Europe and five trips around the world, more under the British flag
during the ten years than under the American, had given me opportunity
to see the British Empire in all its aspects and rather spoiled for me the
idea that we were promoting democracy by going to war.[1]

In the present situation I have believed as did Lord Lothian that we
Anglo-Saxons should stop meddling in Europe. So though a great admirer of President Roosevelt during his first term, I have been unable to
follow him in his foreign policy with equal appreciation.

Scientific training and travel experience have increased my reliance on
observation and deduction, decreased my confidence in opinion. The
moving scene has been too rapid to admit of settled opinion. Usually I
rejoice in the joyous detachment of my ancestors who swung by their

tails (let us hope they were prehensile) from the treetops and viewed the scene below with ever increasing interest. But now in these troubled times, hopes and fears rise, for my gaze is fixed on my own, my native land, and on my own people though all their gods are not my gods.[2]

WHAT IS HISTORY?

What a book this might have been had it been undertaken by a learned, scholarly professor of history whose interest was chiefly in events of the past (how quickly they are past). Occupying a comfortable chair in a great university, working in a secluded cubicle in a great library with all materials at hand, he might have made it a work of scholarship. But this was produced in no such ivory tower.

The nearest approach to what this might have been is Richard Heindel's study of the influence of America on England opinions from 1900 to 1914 It is an admirable example of the scientific method. (cf p 149) Directly from the mouths of English public men and from the writings of English journalists and publicists, he takes the live and pulsating prejudices or attitudes of the day.

What is history if it doesn't give you the 'feel' of the time, some understanding of how men lived, some comprehension of how real people behaved and why they acted as they did.

The memory of man is short. To lengthen it men devised means of keeping records,—graven in stone Later kings had chroniclers to record their valiant deeds and triumphs. Still later cloistered scholars working over the old records wrote histories of the doings of kings and their viziers Eventually Greene demonstrated how a history of the people of England might be written. Once we thought of history as written once and for all. Then we came to realize that it must be rewritten for each generation, and later we faced the fact that each nationality wrote history in its own way. This rather demeaned the dignity of academic scholars, so they invented the myth of objectivity which still lingers in cloistered academic circles. [3]

As the market for historical writing has broadened with increased literacy and intelligent awareness, history has come to be set down in many different ways for many different audiences by different types of minds An observer of the activities of an ants' nest could report it in many different ways depending upon his training, backgrounds and interest How many more diverse ways then there must be of reporting on the activities of men under varied social systems, men under the age long influence of Confucius or Buddha, or bitten by these modern doctrines of democracy or sovietism.

IS HISTORY BUNK?

The academic historian has a violent prejudice against vivisection. He prefers the autopsy. He still insists on having the cold facts laid before him. Which facts he selects will depend upon his former training and future hopes. So we have histories social, economic, and everyday life. The facts selected within any of these categories will depend upon the slant of the historian and of those to whom he looks for patronage and pensions So in lengthening the memory of man the historian may stretch it in some particular direction and put the spotlight on some events in such a way as to benefit those whose interests he feels it desirable to protect.

The nature of the records that are used has been questioned as to their authenticity, which usually meant their antiquity. There is generally failure to realize that most contemporary records were propaganda of the time, written in praise of a conquering hero, or in the midst of intrigue and struggle to blacken the reputation of the opponents of the writer's patrons. And if the patron did not prove to be victor, what was so written was very wisely destroyed.

Most of our historians are in subsidized institutions. Others to get a public must pander to a popular taste. Here again there is influence from higher up which determines what may *not* be published. Writers who conform are not necessarily consciously dishonest. Because of their training or conditioning they may have blind spots as they look at the social scene. All this was once unrecognized and is still denied by many occupants of university chairs of history.

"Any selection and arrangement of facts pertaining to any large area of history . . . is controlled inexorably by the frame of reference in the mind of the selecter and arranger". Charles Beard declared in his presidential address to the American Historical Association in 1933. This denial of the objectivity of the historian, was then met with contempt

THE CULTURAL APPROACH

At the 1939 meeting of the same Association, papers on the cultural approach to history were presented, later edited by Caroline F. Ware,

Columbia University Press. She wrote, "In recent decades . . . the sight of historians becoming propagandists in war time cast doubt not only on the individual historians but on the possibility of real objectivity. The scientific approach no longer inspired . . . confidence" especially when we saw university scientists exhibiting the most violent partisanship.

The new history has demanded of the historian that "he must be a good psychologist, anthropologist, economist, sociologist, geographer, political scientist, biologist—in short, a specialist in every field whose work was throwing light on the nature of man and society",—a prescription so exacting that "it had only limited reflection in either the writing or the study of history".

The anthropologist has shown in his studies of primitive societies the necessity for the new cultural approach to the history of a people. The nature of their culture or 'pattern of social behavior' can only be seen from a detached point of view which historians in the past have not been able to take, but which avoids the biases of the older historians.

This cultural approach to history is still one in which few writers of history are competent to exploit the possibilities. They don't know enough. They have been bred in water-tight compartments. It makes history a study of human behavior, of individuals and groups under varying geographic, economic and political conditions. It involves an understanding of the "ritual, mythology, and belief" of each people, of the influences to which the younger have been subjected. Psychology and psychoanalysis aid in the understanding of adult character (Geoffrey Gorer, ibid). Moreover, there has been "little conscious collaboration between historians and psychologists. Both are engaged primarily in the observation and interpretation of human behavior." This is due to the "regrettable barriers which commonly separate our academic fields". (Goodwin Watson, ibid)

MOTIVES CANNOT BE IGNORED

Men's motives are protected by one of our most sacred tabus, in the U. S. Senate by a rule never broken. But motivation in the perspective of history still reflects the "psychology of the Age of Reason which culminated in the French Revolution", writes Watson. History ignores the result of injustice and frustration. "Show me a gentle person", writes Kenneth Burke, "and I'll show you one who, when balked or warped, will do the most thorough job of brutality."

"Do our homes and schools give more reward for acquiescence or for initiative? . . . If our educational institutions are primarily concerned with the production of docile employes" then there is relatively little danger that there will be many of these propaganda snoopers.

In dealing with children psychologists "have learned the futility of inquiring 'Who started this fight?' " We look for "persistent patterns of frustration. . . . The study of war should be subordinated to the study of frustration and consequent aggression. . . . If men are asked to fight only for their own economic advantage, they can too easily decide that the game is not worth the candle. When their cause is felt to be supported by God, by Nature, by social evolution and right and justice, men will endure all and accept no compromise." (Watson, ibid)

THE VICTORS WRITE THE HISTORY

The history that is being made every day may, like the sound of the waterfall where there is no ear, or the flower that blushes unseen in the desert, never be known   The victors usually have a way of destroying, modifying or distorting the record. For history is written by the victors, or at their order, to enlarge upon their greatness and to cover up their defects. No one was left to write the history of the tribes that Caesar in his conquest of Gaul so ruthlessly eliminated to the last individual. To reconstruct the life of the vanquished, one must go with the archaeologist to the ruined cities and dig in the debris and filth heaps of the past.

But history may be controlled at the source in the writing of news and the making of records. As the existence of any government and those who control it depends upon the success of their propaganda, enormous amounts of taxpayers' money is spent for this purpose. With the great volume of information transmitted by the improved facilities today, this control of news has become more than ever important and propaganda has become the greatest of the arts.

It follows that the academic historian is wise in avoiding the dangers of inquiry and analysis of political doings as reported unless it is in the interest of those in power. So in our endowed institutions, there is little hope that the gift horse will be looked in the mouth. Those who do are denounced as propaganda snoopers and worse may happen to them.[4]

This book is largely a compilation of items of hot news still palpitating. It takes propaganda right off the griddle, hot air right out of the mouths of the orators, excerpts from editorials written close to the 2

A M. deadline, often written under the influence of stimulated fear of airplane or submarine attack. Such bits from various pens, tongues, propaganda organizations, put in such position, reveal an incongruity sometimes humorous, sometimes ominous. While we have not hesitated to draw inferences from facts given or to interpret trends when the data was sufficient, we have avoided expressing opinions, having little respect for opinions, our own or any others.

Opinion implies a conclusion, the matter closed. Opinion hardens into belief, fossilizes in creed. The scientist, on the other hand, from such data as he has, builds an hypothesis, knowing it is a mere scaffolding for some future approach nearer to the truth. The scientific spirit is grateful to the keener critic who finds a defect, brings the scaffolding down, destroys the hypothesis. The scientist then searches for more materials, and builds a better higher scaffold on which to hang his Haman.

THE ROAD WE HAVE COME OVER

It has been a tortuous road we have followed these past two years that has led to many positions not anticipated by those who now occupy them. It has taken skilful strategy on the part of those guiding our destinies to bring us so far along, for the great mass of people were stubbornly set against following any such road as they had traversed twenty-two years before. But fears presented, lures offered, have brought us along.

Beneath the higher intonations of 'peace', 'defense', 'no mothers' sons' blood on foreign soil', there has been the intermittent rumble of "ancestral voices prophesying war". The people have been confused. So keen a mind as Cardinal O'Connell as late as March 29 expressed a feeling of "distrust" at "things going on behind the scenes".

When war comes we are supposed to put up our mental shutters, close our intellectual shop and stop thinking When the time for action comes it is the road ahead that concerns those who get the order "forward march".

Morale, however, is all important for those who are to move forward as the striking force. Confusion will interfere

INTELLIGENCE

The intelligence department is essential in military affairs. Morale and munitions will be of no avail if we do not know where and how to use them,—what is ahead. The French and Italians have recently demonstrated this. The better the map of the road we have come over, the more able will we be to foresee with some understanding the road ahead. If we have forgotten the way we have come, if we have become confused amid its twistings and turnings, we can hardly go straight. If we are to make utmost use of our man power and the patriotic drive that actuates us, then we must have full confidence in our intelligence department, in the staff and strategy that direct our march ahead   If the information on which they plan is false, incorrect, then munitions may be abandoned and morale broken in the rout.

In this book we have attempted to glance back at the road over which we have come. If it helps to a clearer vision, that should help in the success of the next move forward.   '

NOTES

(1) Something of the cause as I saw it I explained in a letter published in *Time*, Dec. 2, 1940,—"That is the trouble with the Germans—they work when others loaf. In ten years' travel around the world before War I, I saw lit up, until near midnight, the German offices in Hong Kong, Bangkok or Bombay The British, already then largely Scotch, closed their offices at two or three for the races, later to sit around their clubs cursing the swine who were stealing their markets. Worse still, those damn Germans adapted the stuff they tried to sell to the natives' needs and desires. Such betrayal of European standards was just too much for the British merchants. So the Germans had to be knocked out and now we have got to do it again "

(2) Cf "The New Immoralities", by Porter Sargent (1935),—"An American Goddess", "The Great American God", pp 62-3.

(3) "Not only up to the middle of the eighteenth century was history merely the biography of might, it has been so since, and is so this day. . . . The stronger individuals caused the weaker to provide them with the favorable conditions of existence indispensable to them. . . . Parasitism proved by experience to be the easiest form of adaptation.   . This parasitism on the part of the strong is the object—the obvious or occult, direct of indirect—of almost all the institutions that have arisen in the course of centuries, and represent the framework, even the substance, of civilization. . . . Externally, then history is a melodrama on the theme of parasitism, characterized by scenes that are exciting or dull, as the case may be, and many a sudden stage-trick." (Max Nordau, "The Interpretation of History")

(4) "Voltaire's comment (April 14, 1732) to M. Bertin de Rocheret. 'Who writes the history of his own time must expect to be attacked for everything he has said, and for everything he has not said: but those little drawbacks should not discourage a man who loves truth and liberty, expects nothing, fears nothing, asks nothing, and limits his ambition to the cultivation of letters.' " (Schuman, "Night Over Europe")

WHAT FEAR DID

The British plans for bringing the United States into the next war, so fully explained in Rogerson's book, were a shock to the few Americans who learned of them. Generally disillusioned in the last war, we had tried to forget, and when the revisionists again brought the war and its blunders to our consciousness, we came to the firm decision that "never again" would we take part in a European war. Absorbed in the ventures of the New Deal, intent on building our own country, the thought came angrily to many,—why should there be another war?

TIPPING THE BALANCE

"It can be stated very simply. Britain's policy has always been to support the second strongest power on the continent." That was the answer, given straightforwardly by Winston Churchill at a forum meeting in Chicago in 1938. Canning a century before had put this policy in writing but it had been followed by Britain for more than two centuries, during which the English had held the world in the hollow of their hands. Referred to as the "balance of power", it brings to mind the scales of justice, but Britain's practice has been to weight the scale surreptitiously with a thumb, that was diplomacy,—or in crisis by throwing in a military force. [1]

"The policy of 'divide and rule' has forced the growth of rivals competing industrially with England and with one another—and has brought all Europe, including England, to the edge of destruction", writes Jerome Frank in "Save America First" (Harper, 1938). "It was not liberty that England sought—except incidentally and accidentally; it was continental anarchy."

After the war the continent was dominated by France, with the greatest army in the world at a high state of efficiency. Germany had been completely disarmed and denuded of all surplus and material for armament, reduced to impotence. The Versailles Treaty had provided that the other powers too should gradually reduce their armaments. France, nervous for her security and complaining that the United States had not lived up to her expectations in guaranteeing the Treaty, with loans and in connivance with the international armament clique, armed the buffer states by which Germany had been encircled. [2]

England viewed France's aggressiveness with anxiety which increased when France occupied the Ruhr and entered into alliance with Russia in 1932. England, following her traditional policy of tipping the balance against the strongest, strengthened Germany by a treaty permitting her to build a navy 35% as strong as England's, though this, the French claimed, violated agreements with France.[3]

TORY JITTERS

However, it was the Soviet success with their five-year plans, their growing industrial power and the increasing strength of their army that gave the Tories the jitters. The Russian Revolution had been the greatest shock to the established world since the French Revolution a hundred and thirty years before. The British Tories watched too with anxiety the growth in Germany of the Communist party.

When, after the Armistice, the Spartakus Communists had been suppressed, Ludendorff approached Foch with the suggestion that the German and French armies march on Russia and put down the Bolsheviks. Foch proposed the plan to the Versailles conference.[4] For two decades it continued to reappear as the 'Nazi Rosenburg Plan' or the 'Four Power Pact' by which Germany and Italy were to be used by Great Britain and France to aid in suppressing communism. (cf p 190)

In the early twenties, England spent four billions in promoting the invasion of the Soviet territory by the forces of seven nations It was Churchill who after the Armistice by his urging brought Wilson into this adventure. Deterding, then "The Most Powerful Man in the World", thwarted by the Bolshevists in his attempt to control Baku oil, vengefully continued through his lifetime to spend hundreds of millions for sabotage in the Soviet Union. Deterding, a citizen of Holland, was a Knight of the British Empire but later took up his residence in Germany when Hitler came in. ("What Makes Lives", 59-62)[5]

WELCOMING FASCISM

Mussolini had been welcomed by English and Americans as one who had thwarted the communist threat. American millionaires fawned under his flattery. Thomas Lamont praised him and through the House of Morgan helped to float a hundred million dollar bond issue which insured his grasp of power.

"Fascism appeals to a wealthier class", Geoffrey Garratt writes in

"Mussolini's Roman Empire" (Bobbs-Merrill, 1938). "The authoritarian gospel attracts the successful businessman, the keen Catholic, the man of leisure and a certain type of intellectual. . . . Ultra-Conservatives and business interests . . . find a natural basis for working with the Catholics in their common distrust of socialist experiments and in their desire for an 'ordered society', which to their minds means a state where the lower orders are well-disciplined and kept in their place."

Hitler was shrewd enough to play up to the part assigned him, the White Knight who was to save the world from the oncoming tide of communism (cf p 100). Montagu Norman and Hjalmar Schacht had long been friends and arranged in 1934 for the Bank of England to loan Hitler 750,000 pounds Community of interest between German and English industrialists and bankers grew and has continued. In a conference in Germany a few years ago arrangements were made to divide the South American markets between them. There was much visiting back and forth of the leaders of the governments of England and France, and when von Ribbentrop became ambassador to London he was a guest of Lord Londonderry and made a great splurge, capturing the whole Tory set.

The fear of bolshevism, however, was always behind this love of the Nazis, and Von Ribbentrop was skilful in cultivating it. In London October, 1936, he said, "The Fuhrer is convinced that there is only one real danger to Europe and to the British Empire as well, that is, the spreading further of communism, the most terrible of all diseases —terrible, because people generally seem to realize its danger only when it is too late." (Toynbee, "Survey of International Affairs", 1936)

Hitler became for the Tories their bulwark against Communism and brought no protest from them when he reoccupied the Rhineland, March 4, 1936. In justification Hitler "claimed that France's alliance with the Soviet Union had violated the Locarno Pact Besides being an excuse, this also was a reminder to timid British Conservatives of dreaded Moscow." (Friedrich, "Foreign Policy in the Making", Norton, 1938)

Lloyd George asked the skeptics, "If the Powers succeeded in overthrowing Nazism in Germany, what would follow? Not a Conservative, Socialist or Liberal regime, but extreme communism. Surely that could not be their objective. A Communist Germany would be infinitely more formidable than a Communist Russia."

HELPING HITLER

English statesman recognized that German expansion was inevitable. Philip Gibbs had asked, why shouldn't England divert Germany toward the East? If there must be war, why not on the Russian steppes rather than again on the shores of the English Channel?[6] The people wanted peace and security and neutrality. The possessors of wealth feared for the loss of their property and were terrorized by the Bolshevists, the Red Menace. The politicians, the brokers for both, sought to strengthen by reenforcing the "Anti-Comintern" totalitarians, hoping they could be turned against the soviets, as Schuman makes clear in his "Night Over Europe". To make this possible, Czechoslovakia, the fortified bastion which commanded the two routes to the Ukraine through Poland and down the Danube, must be demolished.

In acceding to "the domination of Central and Southeastern Europe by Germany . . . Chamberlain has done no more than carry to completion the policy which Sir John Simon and Mr. Baldwin consistently followed from 1934 onwards."[7] The appeasers are not "consciously pro-Fascist . . . it is rather that they have great possessions" and are "stampeded into a kind of anxiety-neurosis at the mention of Socialism or Russia." So wrote Graham Hutton, an English barrister on the inside, editor of the London *Economist*, in the *Atlantic*, Jan 1939.[9]

"Who finances Germany? Without this country as a clearing house for payments and the opportunity to draw on credits under the standstill, Germany could not have pursued her plans. We have been so ready to sell to Germany that the question of payment has never been allowed to interfere with the commercial side," lightly commented the London Stock Exchange *Gazette* in 1935.

NOTES

(1) This policy was first enunciated in 1513 by Cardinal Wolsey, "In Europe never throw your power to the side of the strong, but create disunity, create a balance of power by siding with the weak".

On the eve of the second Hague conference for the limitation of armaments, Henry White, sent by President Theodore Roosevelt to London to see Balfour, engaged with him in the following conversation as recorded by Allan Nevins in "Henry White, Thirty Years of American Diplomacy":

Balfour (somewhat lightly). "We are probably fools not to find a reason for declaring war on Germany before she builds too many ships and takes away our trade." White: "You are a very high-minded man in private life. How can you possibly contemplate anything so politically immoral as provoking a war against a harmless nation which has as good right to a navy as you have? If you wish to compete with German trade, work harder." Balfour: "That would mean lowering our standard of living. Perhaps it would be simpler for us to have a war." White: "I am shocked that you of all men should enunciate such principles." Balfour (again lightly): "Is it a question of right or wrong? Maybe it is just a question of keeping our supremacy."

(2) "The French desire is purely a desire . . to be Grandma, the female counterpart of the head of a French family council . . . whom all other members of the Continental family would always consult before presuming to act . . . As the Germans were continually accused by the French of bad faith in the execution of the military clauses of the Treaty of Versailles, so they were long accused of wilfully abstaining from the payment of reparations", writes Montgomery Belgion in "News of the French" (Faber and Faber, 1938).

"We created Hitler at the instigation of France. . . . It cannot be too often repeated that Hitler is a direct product of the policies of Downing Street and the Quai d'Orsay. . . . Round Germany . . from France, from Italy, from England, from Russia, Czecho-Slovakia, Poland, Yugo-Slavia and all the rest of them, pointed immense howitzers, forests of bayonets, the guns of mighty fleets The neighbouring skies were thick with planes. At every vantage point towered soldiers, representing armies which were reckoned by millions. That was twelve years after we had signed a pledge to disarm." (Beverley Nichols, "News of England", Jonathan Cape, 1938)

Lord Lothian saw the situation realistically and revealed it clearly in numerous articles and addresses. At Chatham House on June 5, 1934, he said, "France set to work not only to modernise her own army, but to organize and equip the armies of Poland, Czechoslovakia, Roumania and Yugoslavia, and to enter into military alliances with them, in order to give her overwhelming military preponderance. . . European realities were nakedly revealed when France . . . entered the Ruhr in 1923, alone and contrary to the advice of Great Britain. . . . They have resisted disarmament by themselves or re-armament by Germany on the ground that the Treaties of Peace were the public law of Europe . . . They (the British) have felt that the Treaties of Peace were both dictated and severe, and required some, though not much, revision by agreement. . . . They have become more and more convinced that there could be no lasting peace in Europe except on the basis of 'equality' in armaments for Germany."

Again, April 2, 1936, at Chatham House, he said, "The entry into the Ruhr probably did Germany more harm than her defeat in the War; it ruined the middle class, and raised the suicide rate to prodigious heights Therefore, Germany feels that the Locarno Treaty, to a considerable extent, was also a dictated treaty, because it was the price she paid, and then willingly paid, as a guarantee against a second Ruhr occupation." A year before, Feb. 1, 1935, he had written the London Times, "National Socialism is the outcome of a four years' war, the Ruhr, inflation, and two revolutions in 20 years."

(3) It was Palmerston who said, "England has no eternal enemies, only eternal interests". Up to the defeat of Napoleon the strong power on the continent had been France, the enemy of England for two centuries In the '80's the French navy was becoming too powerful to please England In the '90's British and French imperial interests in Africa clashing at Fashoda on the upper Nile threatened war.

(4) This plan Clemenceau and Lloyd George were regretfully compelled to dismiss as inexpedient at the moment. President Wilson laughed in Marshal Foch's face Col. House declared, "The United States is not at war with Russia. There is no ground for supposing that it will ever take part in any action directed against that nation." But within two years American troops were invading Russia from Archangel and Siberia from Vladivostok, and the stars and stripes floated on gunboats in the Caspian in the unavailing attack on Baku, center of the oil industry (cf pp 189, 268).

(5) Glyn Roberts in his life of Sir Henri Deterding, "The Most Powerful Man in the World" (Covici Friede, 1938) tells us, "After the Nazi failure in the 1923 putsch . . . Deterding had placed at Hitler's disposal, while the party was 'still in long clothes' . . . four million guilders. . . . In the Presidential election of 1932, in which the two leading candidates were . . . Hitler and Paul von Hindenburg, Deterding was accused, as Edgar Ansell Mowrer testifies in his 'Germany Puts the Clock Back', of putting up a large sum of money for the Nazis on the understanding that success would give him a more favored position in the German oil market. On other occasions, figures as high as £55,000,000 were mentioned." In 1936 "Deterding did *not* lay off the Nazis; he did *not* cease to praise their aims and achievements in public and in private, and he did *not* cease to assist them financially " (cf p 158)

Littlepage, the American mining engineer, in his "In Search of Soviet Gold" (cf Bul#39) throws much light on the intrigues stimulated by foreign gold to bring about sabotage of Soviet industry, and how this led to the purges and trials which, as reported, so shocked the world.

(6) That "the Western appeasers were basing their calculus on the hope of a Fascist-Communist clash and on the expectation of a German attack upon the U.S.S R." was clearly emphasized as a theory by Frederick L Schuman in his articles in *Events* and the *New Republic* and later in his "Europe on the Eve". Of this he reminds us in his "Night Over Europe" (Knopf, 1941). This thesis met with ridicule as unduly suspicious. But today it is generally acknowledged. In *Events*, Nov. 1938, Schuman wrote "The last time the Teuto-Slav conflict broke out, Britain and France were dragged into it. . . . If this ancient feud flames up again, it would be well to deflect it into those regions where it can do least harm."

Time, November 14, 1938, remarks, "That Dictator Stalin may attempt and may succeed in compromising with Dictator Hitler and making friends somewhat as Dictator Mussolini has done, is the startling alternative theory now being plugged by famed Russian observer Walter Duranty. According to him, anti-

Semitism, the card which Benito Mussolini played in Italy to win Adolf Hitler's favor, is already being played by Joseph Stalin. Cabled careful Mr. Duranty from Paris: 'When you come down to brass tacks, there is no obstacle now to Russo-German friendship, which Bismarck advocated so strongly, save Hitler's fanatic fury against what he calls "Judeo-Bolshevism". But Hitler is not immortal and dictators can change their minds and Stalin has shot more Jews in two years of the purge than were ever killed in Germany.' " .

Charles Benedict in the *Magazine of Wall Street,* Dec. 21, 1938, wrote, "It is now very clear — if ever there was any doubt before — that it was a deliberate decision on the part of Chamberlain and the ruling powers in England to throw their lot with the Nazis against what they believed was to be the other alternative — communism. . . . Actually, the nazism of today is the communism of tomorrow! Together with fascism, these three dictatorships are equally red, and have their roots in the Lenin theory of totalitarianism The differences are only of method."

"Kipling in his 'Truce of the Bear' had presented the nightmare that was Russia to a previous generation. Of course, it may be that Hitler is the perfect fool that the British Tories think. It may be that Stalin is a Mongolian idiot, as the Tory theory requires It may be that on the steppes they will strangle each other while the Tories gloat in glee . . . They may die in a death struggle, or weakening, survive mere puppets of the great British raj, which goes on exploiting the world and holding America in leading strings for future generations. But *Fortune* doubts this." (quoted from the still unpublished "Course of Human Events", 1938, by Porter Sargent)

Though "communism and fascism have many points of difference there is no reason to suppose that Hitler and Stalin (or their successors) may not reach an agreement to emphasize their likenesses and trade with each other. In the improbable event that the religious *mystique* has not gone out of fascism and communism by then the conservative West may well tremble. For with a peacefully disposed Russia at its back door, Germany could afford to turn on France." Hitler, come to power, "showed a grasp of foreign affairs that was truly Bismarckian " The course he laid down in "Mein Kampf" "corresponded to the dictates of German character as shaped by German geography; it was as simple as that (*Fortune,* Dec 1938)

(7) When Stanley Baldwin was turned out of office in 1924, a year after he became premier, the first Labour Government came in It was friendly to the Soviets, which stimulated the Tory fear of bolshevism. "Five days before the date fixed for the election England was startled by the disclosure of the notorious 'Zinoviev Letter'. Its authenticity remains in doubt, but there can be no dispute that it was in any case *ben trovato.* The inevitable result of the disclosure, coming when it did, was to ensure the return of a Conservative Government to power, and the treaties were incontinently scrapped " This is quoted from "A Short History of International Affairs, 1920 to 1938" (Oxford, 1938), published under the auspices of the Royal Institute of International Affairs, and

written by G. M. Gathorne-Hardy, a member of the editorial board of the Royal Institute's quarterly, *International Affairs*, who understandably presents the Tory attitude. (cf p 124)

With the return of Baldwin to power, in the next five years the Kellogg Pact was killed by British reservations, the Geneva naval conference wrecked, labor war gains deflated in the General Strike in England and in the Boston police strike, and the League degraded. (cf p 159) The story of how Boston was made the Belgium in this anti-labor war, how this was part of the British plan propagated here in America through the House of Morgan, has never been adequately told, though it has been written up from the newspapers of the time.

(8) Douglas Reed writes, "Many people in England toy with the pleasant delusion that you can use Germany, Germany who wants your colonies, as a bulwark against Bolshevism. Germany, who covets your backyard, is to be your armed doorkeeper." ("Insanity Fair", Cape, 1938)

Geoffrey Garratt says, "It is clear that Göring and Ribbentrop succeeded in persuading the whole of that ignorant and gullible section of the English comfortable classes that the Nazis were the last bulwark of capitalism and of the rich against the growing forces of Communism " ("What Has Happened to Europe", Bobbs-Merrill, 1940)

H. N. Brailsford, English journalist, wrote of the English and French leaders, "Neither Premier is a man of big caliber, and both were surrounded by comfortable, rich men who dread 'bolshevism' (as they call it) more than they fear fascism This inner governing class does not yet wish to abandon democracy at home, because it is justly confident in its own practiced ability to manage the people for its own ends. But it decidedly prefers fascism, at the safe distance of Rome and Berlin, if the alternative is the ascendancy of the Left in any form." (*New Republic*, Nov. 6, 1938)

Edward Thompson reminds us that the word of terror to Englishmen "used to be Jacobin, then Republican, then democrat, then chartist, then Radical, then Socialist . . . now it is communist or Bolshevist. In the Manchester *Guardian*, Mr J. L Hammond wrote 'Today there is a large class of Englishmen who in their dread of Communism think that the success of Franco in Spain, of Mussolini in Italy, and of Hitler in Germany is so important that the fate of British power in the Mediterranean is a secondary matter.' " ("You Have Lived Through All This", Victor Gollancz, 1939)

Quincy Howe writes, "A time may come when both England and France would be only too delighted if they could appease Hitler at the expense of the United States. [France seems to be doing this now. Are we sure England is not?] What is really worrying the leaders of those two countries . . . is the fear that the outbreak of a general war in Europe will lead at once to social revolution." ("Blood is Cheaper Than Water", Simon and Schuster, 1939)

THE APPEASERS

Some of these English statesmen were declared fascists. They feared British labor and its communistic tendencies, and they hated communism with an abiding fear. If Germany could be lured eastward, England would be freed from a lot of commitments to protect a lot of silly little nations. So there was little doubt in the minds of these Tory statesmen what horse to put their money on.

FRIENDS OF GERMANY

The Anglo-German Fellowship, organized in England after Hitler came to power to cultivate friendship with his regime, included 27 Members of Parliament and 28 Lords, among them Lord Londonderry, the great coal magnate and host of Von Ribbentrop; Lord Nuffield, England's Henry Ford; the Marquess of Lothian. Lord Halifax cannily was not a member, though he was the society's guest of honor. The great bank, insurance, munitions, transportation, and oil companies were well represented. The Friends of Italy and the Friends of National Spain, similarly organized, had many of the same members.[1]

Lord Londonderry had for years urged Anglo-German understanding as a fundamental of peace, and advocated a conference of the four European powers, Britain, Germany, France, and Italy. Londonderry House in London, center of Tory entertaining, which dazzled MacDonald into becoming pro-German and into making Londonderry Air Minister in 1931, frequently saw Chamberlain. As Air Minister under Baldwin up to 1935, Londonderry had sought to avert or postpone the time when Germany might, as he wrote, "strike out along a course of *Weltpolitik* frankly antagonistic to Great Britain and her many imperial and commercial interests".

With Chamberlain as Prime Minister, Londonderry again became "a potent behind-the-scenes figure in Prime Minister Neville Chamberlain's policy of appeasing the dictators. . . . Nazi Germany has had no stauncher friend in England than the tall, handsome, 60-year-old Marquess of Londonderry", who numbered among his personal friends Führer Adolf Hitler, Propaganda Minister Joseph Goebbels, Minister for Aviation Hermann Göring, Foreign Minister Joachim von Ribbentrop. (*Time*, Dec. 26, 1938) Londonderry visited the Reich twice in 1936 and twice in 1937, arranged for Lord Halifax' visit in November, 1937, and was present at the Munich Conference.[2]

Londonderry, in his book, "Ourselves and Germany", (Robert Hale, 1938) wrote, "I was at a loss to understand why we could not make common ground in some form or other with Germany in opposition to Communism. . . . Herr Hitler's conciliatory gestures have been disregarded and his offers brushed on one side, and German armaments have been rapidly and efficiently built. . . . Herr Hitler has repeatedly solicited the good will of England. . . . I have made every effort to convince the people of this country of the value and importance of a friendly understanding between Britain and Germany. . . . The robust attitude of Germany, Italy and Japan, which wholeheartedly condemn communism and bolshevism . . . is an attitude of mind which is not properly appreciated in this country. . . . Bolshevism is a world-wide doctrine which aims at the internal disruption of all modern systems of government. . . . The treatment of Germany since the Great War deserves the severest criticism and is responsible to a very large extent for the present unhappy international situation . . . They are as proud of their country and their people as we are here, and they have a full belief in their future and a determination to establish the position which they feel they have a right to claim"

BLESSED ARE THE PEACEMAKERS

The Chamberlain policy was shaped "in accordance with ideas enunciated" months before by "Lord Lothian, once well-known as Philip Kerr, who, as Lloyd George's private secretary and alter ego, carried the Foreign Office round in his attaché case for two or three years after the War" (Willson Woodside, *Harper's*, Dec. 1938).[8]

Lothian as early as 1934 had said, "My own view is that, if only we do not interfere, Europe will rapidly establish a regional security system of its own, which may well prevent war and lead both to appeasement and to some measure of limitation of armaments in a system of balance before many years are past." (Chatham House, June 5) Some months later Lothian revealed his wisdom in a letter to the London *Times*, "War comes far more frequently from inability to change out of date political arrangements in time than from direct aggression" (Feb. 1, 1935).

In the spring of 1936 he reiterated, "I am inclined to think that Europe will never make peace within herself until we leave her to her own work. I am not sure that Europe might not come to peace if it were made quite clear that no group in Europe could hope for a military alliance with us, that we were not concerned in that aspect of the European game at all." (Chatham House, April 2, 1936)

To the House of Lords in 1937 Lord Lothian explained the difficulties of Europe that were working toward war "The fundamental reason for that is not the ambition or the malignity of any particular race or people, it is the fact that today it is divided into twenty-six sovereign States. The difficulties of Europe are far greater today than they were in 1914. Then there were seventeen sovereign States. . . . If we withdraw from Europe, it is the best contribution we can possibly make to the peace of Europe today."

"The argument that the nations who are satisfied with the status quo should enter into something like a military alliance in order that they may be overwhelmingly and collectively stronger than any nation that seeks to alter the status quo—is nothing else than the modernisation of what in my view has been the fatal policy which has been maintained by the French Government since 1920. That is a policy which in the first fifteen years of peace concentrated on keeping Germany without arms and encircled, and which is now concerned in building up a system of armed alliances about it, a policy, I may add, for which we and the United States of America must bear our full share of blame." (House of Lords, March 2, 1937)

CAUSES WORKING FOR WAR

"The easiest solution of the economic problem for Germany would be special economic arrangements in Central Europe. Germany and the smaller countries to the east and south are largely economically correlative, and the present excessive economic sub-division of Eastern Europe cannot be permanent." This Lothian wrote in an article in *The Nineteenth Century and After* (Jan.-June, 1937). And at Chatham House, June 29, 1937, speaking of the smaller nations of Europe, he said, "Their greatest need is that Central Europe should settle down, and that is only possible in my view under German leadership. . . . I think it must be admitted that National Socialism has done a great deal for Germany. It has undoubtedly cleaned up Germany in the ordinary moral sense of the word. . . . It has given discipline and order and a sense of purpose to the great majority of young people who in earlier days did not know what they were living for."[4]

Under the title "The League Contract — Dealing with the World Today", Lothian wrote in an article to the London *Times*, Sept. 10, 1937: "I am not against collective action by the League against an international wrong. Quite the contrary. But such action must be subject to two conditions. The first is that we do not direct it to the maintenance of a status quo which is out of date, but recognize that changes are both just and necessary and that unless the League can bring about these changes by its own action they will inevitably and rightly be brought about in other ways. . . . There is a good chance these adjustments can be made without war and without international injustice."

IF WAR COMES

To the House of Lords March 2, 1937, Lord Lothian, anticipating war, said, "The only possible cause we could be fighting for would be to insist on the maintenance of the anarchy of Europe. . . . I venture to think that this is not a cause for which it is worth laying down the lives of British men." And a year later to the Royal Institute, March 24, 1938, after the occupation of Austria, Lothian said:

"The whole post-War attitude of the Allies, of the small nations and France and the Great Powers, has been an attempt to stem one of the vital forces of history. And now Hitler, by methods which we cannot help deploring because of the shock they give elsewhere, has at last realized the dream of the German people — the dream they have dreamed for three hundred years, to be a united people, as Italy is a united people, and France is a united people and England is a united people and every other race in Europe is a united people except the Germans.

"I have felt for the last three years that the most imperative thing was to go and have a real talk with the Germans as to what the basis of a lasting peace should be. Perhaps it was because I felt that they had legitimate grievances which had to be removed before there could be peace. . . . But what stood in the way? That Great Britain was committed to . . . the sanctity of the Paris system of treaties through the League of Nations.

"If another war comes and the history of it is ever written, the dis-

passionate historian a hundred years hence will say not that Germany
alone was responsible for it, even if she strikes the first blow, but that
those who mismanaged the world between 1918 and 1937 had a large
share of responsibility for it. I say this unpalatable thing because I
think it is necessary to a balanced view and is a corrective to the natural
instinct of hatred and indignation which springs up when we see what
is going on." (Chatham House, March 24, 1938)

WHAT DUTY DID

In these addresses and articles through the years Lord Lothian was
speaking to his peers, his own people, of his own class. One of the
forgers of the Versailles Treaty, he was one of the first to demand its
modification. He continued to advocate that England pay her war
debts. Lothian, from his broad experience, wide travels, contact with
many peoples, had that valuable capacity, that trait that is so modern
but has always come out in the greatest men, of being able to understand other people. That means ability to get inside their skins, look
out through their eyeholes, suffer their fears, see the world as they see
it. But basic to that modern acquisition was his brutal British sense of
duty. Duty has driven the best meaning men to kill, to beat their
children, to persecute their fellows, convinced they were right and the
others were wrong.[5]

In "What Makes Lives" a year ago I presented Lothian from quite
another point of view, as he revealed himself in the *Round Table*, a
propaganda quarterly for the English speaking world, and later as Ambassador to the United States. In this other role he was performing a
duty to his country. Knowing that England could not win without
allies, that the gestures toward Russia were hopeless, that the United
States was essential, in loyalty to his country and from that sense of duty
so highly prized by us English, he came to this country to bring us in
as participants. He well knew that the war was due to the blundering
of his colleagues, their stupid failure to see the light as he pointed it
out. With tact and skill he won us over to a war that he knew in his
heart was needless and harmful.

Senator Lundeen in September, 1940, just before his death in an airplane crash, addressed the Senate on Lord Lothian's former attitude,
quoting extensively from his speeches through the year. Later these

speeches, edited by James Burr Hamilton as "Lord Lothian vs. Lord
Lothian" were published by Flanders Hall. This forced the ambassador
to privately re-explain his position to his friends, which to him was not
so much an embarrassing as a soul-trying experience. On his return
from bomb-shattered London, where his own house had been hit, he
understood too well the desperate task allotted him. His inner conviction remained unchanged, but stern duty, as he conceived it, compelled him to exert all the skill and tact and vitality he had to win us
over. And he died.

On such loyalty and duty we English pride ourselves. Churchill not
long ago, when reproached for attempting to appease godless Russia,
said that he would enter a compact 'with the devil to save England'.
Lothian would never have said that, though he might have done it [6]
from a sense of duty. We have the same thing in our English-American
stock, heads of universities, leaders of public thought, like Conant
who at the Harvard Tercentenary outlined a future for the world so
different from the one that he is now helping to create. [7] Because of
pressure of events and that strong sense of duty which survives from
the English Puritans, he and hundreds of others have been forced by
internal and external forces to stand for things that would have shocked
them a few years ago. It takes a strong man indeed to stand out against
these racial and atavistic tendencies, and such are usually torn limb
from limb if they stand too long against public opinion.

But to understand what makes men act as they do, from a sense of
duty, for righteousness' sake, or to put down what they conceive evil, —
that's the great problem before us. There is no one solution. The
change in Roosevelt from his 'fool's gold' speech to his present intense
religious zeal to preserve morality and put down evil arises from quite
different factors. He is no Puritan. His ancestors came from the Low
Countries.

LET US NOW PRAISE GREAT MEN

Winston Churchill in his book "Great Contemporaries" wrote of
Hitler, "The story of his struggle cannot be read without admiration
for the courage, the perseverance, and the vital force which enabled
him to challenge, defy, conciliate or overcome all the authorities or
resistances which barred his path." In his speech of November 11,

1938, Churchill stated, "I have always said that if Great Britain were defeated in a war, I hoped that we should find a Hitler to lead us back to our rightful position among the nations." And just before the outbreak of war, warning him not to jeopardize his great gains, Churchill reminded Hitler of all he had done in raising Germany from frustration and defeat. (cf p 197) [8]

Sir Nevile Henderson, British ambassador to Berlin, as late as September 20, 1939, wrote, "It would be idle to deny the great achievements of the man who restored to the German nation its self-respect and its disciplined orderliness . . . Many of Herr Hitler's social reforms, in spite of their complete disregard for personal liberty of thought, word and deed, were on highly advanced democratic lines. The 'Strength through Joy' movement, the care of the physical fitness of the nation, and above all, the organization of the labour camps, are typical examples of a benevolent dictatorship. Nor can the appeal of Nazism with its slogans so attractive to a not over-discerning youth be ignored Much of its legislation in this respect will survive in a new and better world. . . . I should like to state here, parenthetically but emphatically, that Herr Hitler's constant repetition of his desire for good relations with Great Britain was undoubtedly a sincere conviction." [9]

The late Lord Rothermere, brother of Lord Northcliffe, in his "My Fight to Rearm Britain" (Eyre and Spottiswoode, 1939) quoted the above from Henderson, and added, "What Sir Nevile, with his close experience, expresses in those passages about the German leader who had forced us into war, I felt from almost the first days of his regime. In the relatively few letters which Hitler sent to me, his desire for Anglo-German friendship was insistent, and, as Sir Nevile Henderson testifies, undoubtedly sincere."

"To deride the German Führer because he was once a poor housepainter, and to make that a reason for believing him devoid of culture — in our English sense of the word — is about as sensible as to deny culture to Shakespeare because he was once a horse-holder in the gutters of Bankside, or to denigrate Mr. Wells because he was once a shop assistant, or to deny that James Thomson was a poet because he was once an army schoolmaster. The circumstances of his rise and origin tempted his foreign neighbours to regard him as a shallow fanatic, unstable, ready to use the most ruthless means to attain his ends. But the man who could so command the imagination of his race, and transform so successfully the German system of government without disaster, was obviously something different from this." [10]

THE END OF APPEASEMENT

The government and the majority of the leading men of England continued to work toward peace and appeasement with Germany. Meantime Chamberlain and Halifax were working with the Vatican toward the same end. The preceding January they had visited the late Pope Pius XI, less than a month before his death. Other elements in England were all for courting the Soviets.

Sir Samuel Hoare, March 10, 1939, had told the world that "Five men in Europe — three dictators and the prime ministers of England and France — if they worked with a singleness of purpose and unity of action, might in an incredibly short space of time transform the whole history of the world. These five men, working together in Europe, and blessed in their efforts by the President of the United States of America, might make themselves the eternal benefactors of the human race." Hoare continued to send up brilliantly colored balloons of peace and prosperity, while Chamberlain optimistically portrayed a five-year peace.

It was the next day that Stalin turned all these plans sour by his speech ridiculing the Tory scheme to embroil Germany and the Soviets. Hitler, on the same day, viewed as a "not unpleasing sign that the people in Great Britain recognize and directly admit what worthwhile opportunities the western powers neglected for bringing about arms limitation", and referred to "declarations of President Roosevelt, designed doubtless to aggravate the situation". (N. Y. *Times* wireless, March 11, 1939)

Chamberlain, as late as June 9, 1939, announced that Britain "still is ready to discuss round the table the claims of Germany or any other country. . . . Such a settlement must be obtained by negotiation, not force." And Halifax, June 12, spoke optimistically of "a fair settlement by negotiation".

London financial circles still hoped for a gentlemanly deal, which was natural as the magnates of British and German industry and finance had many investments in common. Even as late as July 23, 1939, there were rumors in the press of a British disarmament loan of a billion pounds to Berlin, denied the following day by Chamberlain telling the Commons "there is no proposal of a loan to Germany"

The same day British cooperation with Tokyo was announced by the government. Chamberlain had continued to appease Japan in spite of President Roosevelt's opposition "Downing Street apparently hoped for American acquiescence in the impending Oriental Munich in view of the fact that the President on July 18 had accepted defeat at the hands of Congress of Administration efforts to remove the arms embargo provisions from the Neutrality Act and to impose restrictions on the sale of war supplies to Japan. Machiavelli must have roared with laughter from his grave at the spectacle of London and Washington pretending to oppose the Japanese conquest of China while 75% of Japan's imports of war supplies came from American and British sources." (Schuman, "Night Over Europe")

The President, smarting from the defeat of his neutrality measures by Congress, slapped Chamberlain in the face by suddenly abrogating, July 26, 1939, our long-standing 1911 trade treaty with Japan. (cf p 123, 307)

After Congress and Parliament had both adjourned early in August, announcement of the Soviet-German pact brought consternation. The *Round Table* in its September issue predicted repeal of the embargo. Senator Byrnes at the behest of the President polled Congressmen and found that the Neutrality Law could be repealed. (cf Bul #22) The President, September 21, called a special session for that purpose In France appeasers were still saying, "Danzig is not worth a war". Poland was invaded September 3. Censorship was clamped down in France, appeasers imprisoned.

Appeasement in the past year has been made a hateful word in America by the President, who little more than a year ago was all for peace. Appeasers are looked upon as traitors, betrayers of England. But the desire for peace through appeasement still lingers in England. Many of the property owning class, influential with the government, look at the situation realistically, and can see only a stalemate ahead with no possible results worth the great sacrifice of wealth and lives.

Lord Halifax, still Foreign Minister in the British Government and now Ambassador at Washington and lobbyist for the 'lease lend' bill, (cf p 312) on his arrival was greeted by Henry Ehrlich in the Boston *Herald* as "remembered here primarily as an appeaser, the man who flew with Chamberlain to Munich, the man who stood consistently in the path of an Anglo-Russian alliance. . . . The President will find that he has himself many of Halifax's landloving attributes, that both are essentially country squires. With Vice-President Wallace he will share an extreme piousness, an intense religious conviction, and with Secretary Hull he will find a common bond of moral fervor, high principle and earnest integrity." [11]

Lord Halifax was foremost among the appeasers of Hitler and haters of the Soviets until the war broke, as is shown in his "Speeches on Foreign Policy" (Oxford Univ. Press, 1940). [12] In an address to America, Oct. 27, 1938, he said, —

"We have learnt by bitter experience that, however righteous the cause, war is likely to leave a legacy of greater difficulties than it can resolve, for the heat of conflict is fatally apt to blur the issues, and the evils of war drag on into the peace that follows."

"It is not enough to devise measures for preventing the use of force to change the status quo, unless there is also machinery for bringing about peaceful change. For a living and changing world can never be held in iron clamps, and any such attempt is the highroad to disaster " (June 29, 1939) [13]

NOTES

[1] Lord Mottistone of the Friends of Italy, addressing the House of Lords against supporting the Ethiopians, said, "It is a wicked thing to connive at sending arms to these cruel, brutal men while denying them to others who are playing an honorable part." (Theodore Dreiser, "America Is Worth Saving")

[2] "Lord Londonderry is a potent friend because he is chairman of the Conservative Party." (*Time,* Dec. 26, 1938) After Baldwin had thrown out Londonderry as Air Minister in 1935 when his program failed, Neville Chamberlain restored him to good standing as Chairman of the Conservative Party, the highest honor the Tories can bestow. Londonderry's philosophy is like that of his grand uncle Castlereagh, who at the Congress of Vienna in 1815 participated in the partition of Europe and determined the course of empire On the back of the dedication of his book is a quotation from Castlereagh, "It is not our business to collect trophies, but to try if we can bring back the world to peaceful habits."

Londonderry's chief contribution to history may perhaps be his blocking, at the Disarmament Conference, of the resolution to do away with the bombing plane, because he asserted it was necessary for policing the "outlying districts", to which the Turkish delegate replied, "What are the 'outlying districts' of this great round world?"

[3] Former Ambassador Dodd in his "Diary" for February 12, 1936, reports

that William Bullitt, then ambassador to Russia, said he didn't believe England could work in alliance with France and Russia. "He said Germany would capture Austria and Czechoslovakia in two weeks' time and quickly bring all Europe under her control. I questioned: Do you think this would be good for the United States and England? He cared 'not a damn' for England and reported that both Lord Lothian and Lloyd George are against the English, French, Russian cooperation. . . . He added that Lothian preferred to let Germany go on her conquering way towards European domination rather than to impose limitation upon Germany by his country "

(4) "The Versailles settlement was based on the theory of the sole responsibility of Germany for the Great War. I do not think anybody who has made a serious study of pre-War history, or even of the events which immediately preceded the War, can hold that view today . . On the strength of it Germany was deprived of one seventh of her European territory, she was deprived of her colonies; she was unilaterally disarmed, and she was compelled to demilitarise the Rhineland. . . There was placed upon her a burden of reparations for which I do not suppose to-day there is a single advocate.

"In January 1933, Germany was promised equality in a regime of security. But . . Sir John Simon, after consultation with his French friends . . . announced at Geneva in October 1933 that, in effect, no practical steps in the direction of conceding equality to Germany could be taken for four more years, and M. Paul Boncour added that, even at the end of four years, it would be necessary to take the political situation into account. . . . The episode led . . . to the conviction that what counts in international affairs is not the force of your case, but the strength of your armaments." (Lothian, June 29, 1937)

(5) "Duty is a sadistic wench who has led many a good man astray. How the rod was laid on the backs of children by generations of pedagogs impelled by duty' . . . Sporadic crime results from impulse. The great crimes against our fellow men, war and punishment, today as always spring from a sense of duty. Humanity has made progress only through those who were strong enough to defiantly repudiate their duty " ("The New Immoralities", Porter Sargent, 1935)

(6) "Great Britain knows her men better than they know themselves If the United States should now adopt the European war in a total manner and save England, the claim of Lord Lothian to the highest niche in Great Britain's gallery of diplomats could hardly be disputed. As a propagandist he had the art to make people intellectually grateful. They were obliged to him for putting their thoughts in order — their own thoughts, as it seemed to them, returned to them in historical perspective . . . He could make Americans believe their Monroe Doctrine was a borrowed plume, and that for a century of success, freedom and security they were indebted to the British navy and to a ring of benign fortresses, named Britain, Gibraltar, Cape Town, Suez, Singapore and Australia.

"He was neither a pacifist nor an appeaser. His one soul was British His mind and his way of seeing were his own . . It is true that Lord Lothian did say, in 1938, that if the war came and the history of it were ever written, no dispassionate historian would blame Germany alone, even though she had struck the first blow. Here one must remember what his passion was. To confine the war to Continental Europe, to let Europe find her own balance, in any case to keep England out of it — that was his passion, and it was founded on the fear, or the vision, that the policy England was pursuing, and did still pursue, would bring to pass her own downfall " (*Sat Eve Post,* Jan. 18, 1941)

(7) *Current Biography,* March 1941, gives a two page sketch of Conant, from which we quote. "At the 1936 Harvard Tercentenary President Conant fearlessly demanded that we 'build an educational basis for a unified, coherent culture suited to a democratic country in a scientific age " There are "those who feel that President Conant's liberalism has grown somewhat less ardent since that time. Another critic went so far as to write that Conant, 'enthusiastic in 1935, became cautious in 1937, fearful in 1938, despairing in 1939, tyrannically jittery in 1940." (cf Bul #16, and Handbook of Private Schools 1936-37, 1937-38, 1938-39, 1939-40)

(8) Reviewing René Kraus' "Winston Churchill" (J. B. Lippincott, 1940) Ferdinand Kuhn, Jr., writes, "It is strange to read that he was once an admirer of the Kaiser's Germany, and that in 1908 he fiercely attacked Lord Cromer for 'alarmist warnings of coming dangers from Germany' He even tried to coax Germany into an anti-Communist front after Versailles Just before the Nazis came to power he urged that British help to France should be kept 'short of war', and his arguments of those days have an oddly familiar ring today."

(9) "One cannot, just because he is a dictator, refuse to admit the great services Signor Mussolini has rendered to Italy; nor would the world have failed to acclaim Hitler if he had known when and where to stop; even, for instance, after Munich and the Nuremburg decrees for Jews." (Nevile Henderson, "Failure of a Mission", cf *Life,* March 25, 1940)

(10) In his *Daily Mail,* Lord Rothermere, May 1938, said, "Great numbers of people in England regard Herr Hitler as an ogre, but I would like to tell them how I have found him He exudes good fellowship. He is simple, unaffected, and obviously sincere He is supremely intelligent."

In his *Daily Express,* Lord Beaverbrook, in October, 1938, wrote, "We certainly credit Hitler with honesty and sincerity. We believe in his purpose stated over and over again, to seek an accommodation with us and we accept to the full the implications of the Munich document."

(11) Lord Halifax was still a member of the British Government, Foreign Minister, when he took up residence in Washington as Ambassador. A correspondent of the *Chr Sci Monitor* spoke of him as "not high-powered mentally". He was preceded by publicity reproductions in color, a full length portrait showing him in the white satin pants and robe of a Knight of the Garter with the coquettish dangling garter. He had become an embarrassment to the Churchill government, and there was popular demand for his removal. The solution was to foist him on America. A high churchman, medieval in his mind and outlook, Jesuitical in his methods, autocratic, aristocratic, he is in close touch with God with whom he is said to communicate several times a day

Louis Bromfield, author of "The Rains Came", in "England A Dying Oligarchy", (Harper, 1939) tells of a witticism said to have been born in the Foreign Office, which "concerns Lord Halifax, the High Church leader and Minister of Foreign Affairs who prays long and earnestly and with such futility before dealing with Hitler and Mussolini Of him it is said 'Rien comprendre c'est tout pardonner' (To understand nothing is to pardon everything)." Bromfield quotes the two following bons mots attributed to the late Lord Birkenhead, —"Although it was said first, centuries ago of Erasmus, 'The trouble with Sam Hoare is that he is descended from a long line of maiden aunts'. For Sir John Simon, Birkenhead went back to Dean Swift when he said, 'Simon has a smile like the brass plate on a coffin'."

Bromfield, who has lived much in England and in India, studying the English character under varied conditions, writes of it illuminatingly. "Anglo-Saxon hypocrisy is something unique . . . calculated but uncynical, and very often it deceives its perpetrator far more profoundly than it deceives those at whom it is aimed. . . . Upon an extreme hypothesis let us suppose that an Anglo-Saxon decided to murder his mother to gain an inheritance The first stage in the mental attitude of the murderer is to understand that he is about to commit an unspeakable crime; nevertheless he decides, with a cold-bloodedness unknown to any other race, to go ahead with the crime. The next stage is to find a justification for the crime — a justification which is unselfish, which will permit him not only to evade all reproach, but will react to the credit of his own honor and virtue and to the benefit of humanity The third stage is to convince himself that his aged mother is a shrew, a witch, a burden not only to himself but to the whole human race (for the Anglo-Saxon is always thinking of the human race) and the profit he can make out of it. Once he is convinced of the evil qualities of his mother, he then considers what he will do with the money. Well, he will buy himself a fine house and a great many new clothes, not because these things give him any selfish benefit or pleasure but because such action will put money into circulation and benefit his fellow men and especially benefit trade. He will give a certain amount of the gains by murder to charity, perhaps even to educational institutions, again for the good of humanity. By the fourth day he will have convinced himself that the murder of his mother will confer a great benefit on the human race (and on trade) and therefore it is his duty to act. On the fifth day he will take up the axe and set to work on his aged mother not only with a clear conscience but with a sense of virtue, and when the reckoning comes he will face the world with the impregnable sense of integrity which saved Lizzie Borden from the noose."

(12) Halifax had collaborated with Lord Lloyd in a book "The Great Opportunity", setting forth their idea of a totalitarian regime. He made it clear that both were extreme rightists and stood for a Catholic fascist society. From his writings one gathers democracy is a silly abstraction, a sop thrown to the masses. As Lord Irwin, Viceroy of India, he jailed Gandhi and 47,000 Indian Nationalists whose greatest crime was they wanted democracy in their own land. Ehrlich reminds us that Halifax at the end of the last war "was among 200 Conservative notables who demanded the imposition of stiffer terms on Germany."

Lord Lloyd, who died Feb. 4, 1941, at the age of 61, was then British Colonial Secretary and Government Leader in the House of Lords. As Governor of Bombay from 1918 to 1923, he once had Gandhi arrested As High Commissioner of Egypt and the Sudan, he ruthlessly suppressed rebellion

Lord Lloyd's "The British Case", published after the outbreak of war, was hailed by Halifax in the name of the British government. Lloyd had been staggered by the Russo-German pact he called "Hitler's final apostasy. It was the betrayal of Europe " Lord Lloyd's last great labor was to hold Rumania for England His publicity agents discovered that Rumania was a republic, and their build-up of Carol made him a heroic figure. (cf pp 148, 190-1)

(13) In his *Weekly Foreign Letter*, March 6, 1941, Lawrence Dennis tells us "All thinking Americans, including Harry Hopkins and F.D R." as well as enlightened British, realize that there must be a new order in Europe, and that the Germans are the organizing people who have got to put it across. First we must knock out Hitler, then put in the right men who will do what they are told and be nice Germans and reorganize Europe But this idea can't be sold to the moralistic, idealistic American people. "It seems to us an awful lot of killing and expense just to substitute one gang of Germans for another. In our simple way, it seems to us that if some crew of Germans has to run a Continental system in Europe, and if some crew of yellow men has to boss the Far East, it is not worth our fighting over to decide what crew it shall be. Then, too, the trouble with fighting to oust one gang of foreign despots for another, the Kaiser for Hitler, for example, is that one can never be sure what the successors will be like. Our interventionists believe in the Devil theory of war and human ills."

"After the War: A Symposium of Peace Aims", edited by William Teeling (Sidgwick and Jackson, 1940) presents contributions of fourteen influential publicists, mostly members of Parliament and mostly appeasers. Sir Richard Acland, who distinguished himself at the recent Malvern religious conference with his demand for a new order in England and the British Empire, writes a letter which he would have sent to all German soldiers. He would admit the past crimes and abuses of the Empire and British governments and offer to share, internationalizing all colonies and internationalizing all armed forces. "Don't you think, you German soldiers, that you and we could get on rather better living in the same barracks than living in opposite trenches?"

WINNING AMERICA OVER

When Chamberlain succeeded Baldwin as Prime Minister in May, 1937 and appointed the chief appeaser, Halifax, his Foreign Minister,[1] it made impossible the position of the Permanent Under-Secretary, Sir Robert Vansittart, who "loves appeasement not" (*Time*, Sept. 4, 1939).[2] Vansittart's responsibility for foreign policy had led to the Hoare-Laval mess which had raised such a storm of popular protest that his retirement was demanded by the press. However, to dismiss the head of the Foreign Office is almost unprecedented.

VANSITTART DISAPPEARS

It was given out that Vansittart had retired and that Chamberlain himself would take a more intimate interest in foreign affairs. He disappeared almost wholly from the political scene and was rarely mentioned in the press. It was almost a year before Chamberlain in response to a Parliamentary inquiry let it be known that Vansittart was acting in an advisory capacity. In the 1939 Whitaker's Almanac, Vansittart was listed as "Chief Diplomatic Adviser to the Foreign Office", a new title, non-existent in 1938 when he was listed under the title of "Permanent Under-Secretary", with the same salary, £3000.[3]

Vansittart's new activities were carefully guarded. Not only was news kept from the newspapers but sophisticated editors knew that here was something that was to be left alone, protected. But putting together the little bits of news from the back pages of newspapers, newsletters and clandestine sources that have slipped by censors and editors, one gets occasional glimpses of his new activities. (cf p 100)

"There's a reason why Sir Robert Vansittart has rarely been heard from since his 'eclipse' in the British Foreign Office. The fact is that he's busy handling one of the nation's most delicate problems—how to combat Nazi and Fascist propaganda abroad." This item in *Newsweek*, November 28, 1938, attracted little attention, nor did the surmise of one of the writers of the *Fortune* article, Dec., 1938, that Chamberlain had "politely kicked Sir Robert Vansittart into an upstairs job". (cf "What Makes Lives", p 163)

The new job was to build in secret a great organization to control all information that went to the United States. To insiders this organization was referred to as the "Bureau for anti-Nazi Propaganda in Neutral Countries". Actually its chief function was to make Americans hate Hitler and all his works as Vansittart did so sincerely.[4]

AN ANCHOR TO WINDWARD

But why should the British government be interested in making Americans hate Germany? Britain's foreign policy, consistently followed, has been to have allies to do as much of the fighting as possible in any war on which she embarks. More than fifty nations of the world were enlisted in the last war to put down the central powers. But Britain's record of gratitude for help, of gobbling up the spoils, and of matching one power against another, was becoming too well known.

The encircling buffer states, less willing to act as buffers, were only too anxious to remain neutral and so remain alive. France was not to be counted on to the bitter end, and the Soviets were even more doubtful. America was essential. Her resources, her money, her man power only could save the British. But it was not alone love of England that would bring us in, it must be hatred of evil. A devil must be created to arouse our moral purpose.[5]

It was rather embarrassing to Britain in the last war to have to call on us for help even though their 'backs were against the wall', and they have since been a bit reluctant to admit their dire need. Churchill and others have not hesitated to say we should have minded our own business and stayed out, that we were late coming in, that Uncle Shylock made billions out of the war, that the money we had given did not compensate for the lives they had sacrificed.

That had been the policy under Baldwin, but under Chamberlain, who had been put into power by the "City", represented by Montagu Norman, it became the purpose not only to appease Hitler but to win over America as the need for an ally again became apparent. Following his occupation of the Rhineland, Hitler's armed strength continued to increase, and while the Tories still hoped this would be turned against the Soviets, it seemed wise to cast an anchor to windward should Hitler fail them. Moreover, if Americans could be brought to hate Hitler, that would make it easier and cheaper for the English to cultivate friendship with him.

Americans were already suspicious of British propaganda methods, and the plans set forth in Rogerson's book didn't make Vansittart's task any easier. Towards Germany since the war America had felt increased interest and kindliness. Our boys had fraternized with the Heinies. On the Rhine they had been popular, and many a doughboy had brought home as wife a German fraülein. Moreover, after the war we made large investments in Germany, encouraged by Britain, for it enabled Germany to better pay reparations. The Dawes and Young Plans successively resulted in further investment in Germany as our industrialists bought up German plants at bargain prices Four billions of dollars of American money went into Germany, about half of which came back to France and England as reparations.

SECRECY ESSENTIAL

New and improved techniques were essential, but no man could be better equipped than Vansittart, and the facilities of the British Empire were his. The British Intelligence Service, which ramifies elusively from the Foreign Office, "covers the world in the service of the City and British interests". Its function is "to disseminate information, meaning propaganda and occasionally lies", writes Roberts, the biographer of Deterding.[6]

A passion for anonymity as with President Roosevelt's executive secretaries is essential for the members of the permanent government and especially of the Foreign Office and its Intelligence Services. Not elected, they do not need votes, and so do not receive publicity. Vansittart, a poet, esthete, highly intelligent, was especially retiring, though his influence was all pervading through a succession of ministries, as is fully explained in "What Makes Lives" where he is described as "the brains of the Empire", "the torch-bearer of a tradition associated with such names as Nicolson, Crowe, and Tyrrell" (Abshagen).

A cloak of secrecy had covered the propaganda organization and methods in the previous war.[7] Not until the participants began to write their memoirs some years after did we begin to understand the influences that had been brought to bear to change our opinion. C.F G Masterman organized the first and most successful propaganda at Wellington House. But his activities were unknown to intelligent Englishmen and not even suspected in America His widow, in her recent biography of her husband, emphasizes the secrecy with which all this was conducted. "So well was this secrecy achieved and maintained that of all the books on propaganda that I had read for the purpose of this memoir only Mr Duane Squires in his Harvard Essay has more than a passing reference to Masterman."

If Great Britain had spent ten times the hundreds of millions of pounds she has used to produce today's result, it still would have been the best investment that could have been made. "The funds for British propaganda were mostly taken from the general vote of supply for 'His Majesty's Foreign and other Secret Services' ", Lasswell tells us in his "Propaganda Technique in the World War". In his later "Propaganda and Promotional Activities" he says, "After the World War the unpopularity of 'secret diplomacy' led to the inclusion of various secret funds in regular government budgets."

A GOOD INVESTMENT

Propaganda has been Britain's best paying export. There has always been a demand for it. Americans lap it up, pay for it, and derive a sense of morality, religious exaltation and self-righteousness after gobbling it down. It was five or six years after the first World War before our university professors began to feel the first pangs of pain from their gullible gluttony. So secret and unsuspected have been the methods this time that it may take even longer. They were not immunized but apparently left even more susceptible. For again temperatures are rising Is it a relapse, or is this war fever endemic in the university soil, or recurrent in the individual, or chronic in some cases?

Winston Churchill, who occasionally frankly blurts out state secrets, wrote in his "World Crisis 1915" (Scribner, 1923) of bringing Italy into the last war, "With their very existence at stake neither Britain nor France was inclined to be particular about the price they would pay for the accession to the alliance of a new first class power."

With no other allies to be counted on this time, it was worth any possible expenditure Britain could make to again bring America with all her resources to her aid. Hundreds of millions of pounds have gone into building up Britain's secret services, but the returns from America have already been in billions of dollars.[8]

IMPROVED TECHNIQUE

The propaganda methods developed and used during the last war have been fully explained in the memoirs of the participants, in the treatises of Lasswell and Peterson and scores of others.[9] Lasswell's bibliography on this subject ran to thousands of titles (cf p 97). Rogerson deals with the methods, generally known to the man in the street, to be used to bring America into this war.

The Ministry of Information [10] in the early days of this war used those methods and at the time of the Finnish flare-up put forth canned propaganda prepared in advance, the falsity of which was soon recognized. But even these well known methods have been improved and refined. (cf p 193) [11]

The methods of Vansittart's secret organization have not yet been revealed. They are still unsuspected by the majority of the victims and consequently have proved effective, for propaganda once discovered is harmless.

News of events is still the chief material of the propagandist. It must be slightly twisted, colored, given a slant to produce the desired emotional reaction. Effective use is made of the direct testimony of people from the enemy country, to tell of brutalities, persecutions, in the public prints, in articles and books, or on the radio and the platform. Germans who were not wanted in their own country have been afforded every facility for reaching America in person, by voice or in print.

The intensity of the dose of hate they administered was graduated from the early poetic, nostalgic Nora Waln style to the later brutal, sadistic reminiscences of the former communist spy, Jan Valtin, much of which reads like the testimony before the La Follette Committee of Texas Ford workers and the California Okies. As hatred rose, we could take stiffer and stiffer doses, like the Darre speech which *Life* printed, implying that it was privately made and side-stepping all responsibility as to its authenticity. Such methods were effective with the millions after they had been worked up, but were too crude to have emanated from an artist like Vansittart.

THE VANSITT ART

The art of influencing people is as old as human nature, but the great effort and vast sums spent on technical improvements have made it perhaps the greatest of the arts. In advertising, which is to influence people to buy something, three to four billions are spent in this country and great talent employed. It is great art to make people give up their money or their lives. Patriotism is not enough. "A propagandist must always be alert to capture the holy phrase which crystallizes public aspiration about it", writes Lasswell. The conscript or taxpayer must be given a 'moral stake' in the war, a 'moral responsibility' to 'put down evil'. But to influence other nations to become your allies, to espouse

your cause when that has become desperate, is a still greater achievement To accomplish it a second time within a generation has required
a directing brain fired by a great emotion,—a great artist

"All art", said Michelangelo, "is the expurgation of the superfluous". The most effective propaganda presents, with convincing candor, the story of events in part, the information selected and expurgated
to accomplish its purpose The way to measure art is by its effect. Do
you pass the painting unnoticed? Does the music leave you cold?
Then it is not art for you. Do newspaper and radio accounts of events
and personal messages from the enemy country produce a change in
your emotions and reactions? If the answer is yes, then it may be the
result of the propagandist's art. For these are the media that he must
use If in the music, the painting, the story, you see the technique, the
evidence of effort, then the thing is a failure. You treat it with contempt
and laugh at it as you do at German propaganda.

Everybody has seen the great change in the emotional attitude of the
American people since 1937, and most believe it due to events It has
been the function of the unseen British propaganda organization to so
present these to us as to bring about the emotional result that has been
planned. The artist in propaganda paints, on the minds of people, with
selected and slightly distorted stories, the pictures he has conceived in
order to affect emotions and to bring about the action desired. And the
technique has been so perfect that we do not detect the art. It seems
to us reality.

Sir Robert Vansittart is an artist, a poet and a playwright, but cynical
and hard bitten, hard hating. He may now sit back complacently as he
contemplates Americans hysterically squandering their wealth and
their future in a desperate attempt to destroy Hitler to save the Empire,
while he thinks to himself with a wry smile, "I planned it that way"

NOTES

(1) "Lord Halifax, Chamberlain's Foreign Secretary, has little flair for consecutive thought about English balance-of-power history or the ethics of treaty
breaking. . . . Critics have joked about Lord Halifax's ignorance of Central
Europe." (*Fortune,* December, 1938)

(2) Eddie Rickenbacker, America's ace, on fraternal terms with the German
aces, in 1922 visited Germany and dined with Göring, Milch, Vandlend and
Udet. These down and outers told of their hope and plans first to teach gliding
as a sport, then build commercial aviation, then a skeleton military airforce.

At that time "Hitler was an unknown, neurotic vagrant", Germany "a ragged tramp, a bum, among the nations". In 1935 Rickenbacker, then a leader in American aviation, returned and found that the German aces had made good. "What Eddie saw was a revelation He visited the Junkers factory where 20,000 men, working day and night, were turning out planes for the new Germany. . . . Rickenbacker moved on to England. There, at a dinner at Lord Beaverbrook's, he met Sir Robert Vansittart, Permanent Under-Secretary of the British Foreign Office 'When will they be ready?' asked Vansittart. Rickenbacker told the gathering that 'they' would be ready within a maximum of five years, a minimum of three Vansittart, agitated and gloomy, said no, the estimate was too hopeful so far as England was concerned; the Germans would be ready within two years, surely. But Lord Beaverbrook, who was to pay for his skepticism by a summer of Herculean work in 1940, laughed. So did the politicians in Washington when Rickenbacker came home, even as they laughed at Lindbergh later on." (*Fortune*, March, 1941, p 64)

(3) His former deputy, Sir Alexander Cadogan, became Permanent Under-Secretary. He "had long been a counselor in the permanent organization. He had specialized on League of Nation affairs and had conducted many important negotiations. He had served as ambassador to China from 1928 to 1935 and then had been called back to be second to Vansittart " (Eugene J. Young)

(4) Capt. King-Hall, in the Sunday *Times,* knowing Vansittart's hate, recently declared, "We tell the Germans that this war will go on until the Nazis are extirpated. Incidentally, how does one recognize that Nazis are extirpated? Which Nazis? All members of the party or whom? The Nazis naturally say, 'If we disappear the British will give you hell and the Treaty of Versailles will be a feather-bed compared to a Treaty of Berlin drafted by Sir Robert Vansittart.'" (*Uncensored,* Feb. 15, 1941)

(5) John Foster Dulles, Princeton-Wall Street lawyer, in "War, Peace and Change" (Harper, 1939) writes, "The background of history is written and taught in terms of the melodrama of nation-hero versus nation-villain Superimposed upon this is the contemporary portrayal by the press and radio of foreign news, which is selected largely to fit into and accentuate some preconceived nation-villain concept."

"Once the principle of the criminal nation is established, once the moral duty of the United States to share in the restraint of a 'guilty people' is accepted by the American people, then it must be clear that Uncle Sam is in a fair way, not, as in 1917, to be taken for a ride in Europe alone, but to be presented with a commutation ticket for travel in three continents." ("John Bull's Holy War" by the late Frank H. Simonds, *Sat Eve Post,* December 21, 1935; cf "What Makes Lives", p 126)

(6) "The B.I.S. always works behind the scenes, giving people deep convictions on subjects favorable to British interests for the moment without the people's even knowing just how they arrived at those convictions—but they are always convictions involving the highest 'moralistic' and 'enlightened'

palaver. It is a system that has usually worked in the past", writes Burton Rascoe. (*Newsweek*, Aug 22, 1938)

(7) "When propaganda must be carried on in secrecy, the utmost ingenuity may be shown in developing flexible and effective forms of organization and procedure. During the period of neutrality before the United States entered the World War, the English had six or eight different offices in the United States, so that no one man, in or out of the service, knew all the secrets." (H. D. Lasswell, "Propaganda Technique in the World War")

(8) Up to 1935 Britain had appropriated annually about £178,000 for Secret Service. After that the appropriation increased for 1936, 349,000 pounds; 1937, 350,000 pounds; 1938, 450,000 pounds. In response to a question in Parliament by Cecil H. Wilson, M. P., the government replied, "Britain . . . employs 271 spies today for every 100 she had working in her behalf in 1929".

John T. Flynn tells us " 'the British used $150,000,000 to get us into the World War and thought it money well spent' ". He "says that the sum already allocated for English propaganda in this war is no less than $165,000,000". . . . After the war Congressman Calloway revealed exactly how some of the biggest newspapers of America had been bought for England with American money." (Dreiser, "America is Worth Saving")

(9) An earlier review of the propaganda, its personnel, its methods, the books on the subject, will be found in the Handbook of Private Schools, 1935-36 edition. "How We Get Our Ideas" pp 33-40, which tells of how Ambassador Bacon in 1914 decided we should go into the war, returned to America to capture and control the press; "Why We Think So" pp 77-86, which reviews books on propaganda and "Distorting History". Cf also 1937-38 edition pp 105-7 ff.

(10) "The government's intention of going ahead with the establishment of a Ministry of Information was disclosed tonight by publication of a supplementary estimate calling for an appropriation of £40,000. A total of £300,000 is provided for propaganda activities. A fund of £110,000 has been set aside for foreign publicity, of which £10,000 will be spent by the Foreign Office and the new foreign news department and £100,000 through diplomatic and consular representatives abroad. The British Council, which operates under government auspices, will receive £150,000 to extend its work of sending out British lecturers and entertaining visitors to England " (July 12, 1939, London dispatch)

(11) In America, our forums and Town Meetings had been infested with ardent pro-British who popped up repeatedly. They were gradually weeded out, though occasionally a well-meaning Sir George Paish would get by and would have to be suppressed (cf p 243). But eliminated were "the 'Colonel Blimps' of the Tory party—the rotund walrus-mustached retired army officers with 'eyes like affronted oysters' who figure in Low's diabolically clever cartoons" and are "certain that Russian communism . . . is the devil". (*Fortune*, Dec. 1938)

PRESIDENTIAL PROGRESS

During his first term President Roosevelt became the idol of the American people and reflected our attitude of hatred toward war. We had learned that the sole guilt for the World War did not rest on Germany, that there had been deceit and blundering, and that the world had not been made safe for democracy.[1]

"ARMS AND THE MEN"

Gradually there had come to light from the archives of foreign governments and from the records of great munitions industries the story of how French and German industrial magnates had worked together to prolong the war. Quincy Howe had published much on this in the *Living Age* while he was editor, which was utilized for the article "Arms and the Men" (*Fortune*, March, 1934) Senator Borah brought this to national attention in a Senate speech and had it reprinted in the *Congressional Record*. (cf p 158)

In response to popular call for Congressional investigation, Borah recommended Senator Nye, who as chairman made front page headlines for a year, revealing the sinister methods of the bankers and 'merchants of death'. The persistent popular demand that the munitions industries be nationalized was skilfully sidetracked by the President's alternative suggestion that we 'take the profits out of war'. The American Legion had for some years proposed that if men were drafted capital should be too, and tax bills had been introduced to take up to 96% on profits during war time. *Fortune* for a time promoted this demand and spent much money on investigations which were finally suppressed. Powerful commercial organizations through skilled publicists were at work to prevent the public getting foolish ideas.[2]

Hitler in his fourth year, in the spring of 1936, had occupied the Rhineland. That summer war broke out in Spain and the President through the State Department, to please the British Foreign Office and appease the Catholic vote, immediately applied an unofficial embargo, which hampered only the Loyalists as the Nationalists were receiving their munitions through Germany and Italy.

THE FOOLS' GOLD SPEECH

Opening the campaign for his second term at Chautauqua in August, 1936, the President won the confidence and votes of the nation by declaring his love of peace and hatred of war and his desire to maintain "neutrality regardless of any pressure that might be exerted abroad or at home . . . If war should break out again in another continent, let us not blink the fact that we would find thousands of Americans who would be tempted for the sake of fool's gold to break down or evade our neutrality.

"They would tell you, and unfortunately their views would get wide publicity, that if they could produce and ship this and that and the other article to belligerent nations, the unemployed of America would all find work. They would tell you that if they could extend credit to warring nations, that credit would be used in the United States to build homes and factories and pay our debts They would tell you that America once more would capture the trade of the world.

"It would be hard to resist this clamor, it would be hard for many Americans I fear to look beyond to realize the inevitable penalties; the inevitable day of reckoning that comes from false prosperity To resist the clamor of that greed, if war should come, would require the unswerving support of all Americans who love peace. If we face the choice of profits or peace, the nation will answer, 'we choose peace'." [3]

The nation resounded with enthusiastic applause and approval, for the people were determined that "never again" would they enter upon a European war [4] This could not have been better expressed than by Gen. Charles P. Summerall, former Chief of Staff, before the Union League Club of Chicago, Nov. 11, 1939. "Not one cent; not one soldier. . . . Let the American people resolve never again to engage in wars not made upon them. . . . There can be no greater fallacy than to say we should save others from defeat. We cannot settle their quarrels nor maintain the balance of power in Europe." In return for aid in the last war we had "received little from them but criticism, abuse and contempt".

DEFEAT

During the latter part of his first administration, the President's reform legislation had created intense hatreds on the part of his fellow Harvard alumni, the Wall Streeters and those he denominated 'economic royalists'. On the eve of the 1936 election, which brought him the greatest vote ever polled for a president, referring to the difficulties he had mastered in his first term, Roosevelt defiantly announced that in his next he hoped to "show them who is master" Immediately after his second inauguration the President to carry out his ambitious plans introduced into Congress a series of bills which included provision for seven divisional TVA's This brought great elation to his followers, but to his opponents increased intensity of fear and hatred.

In February, 1937, he launched his campaign against the "nine old men" of the Supreme Court who had struck down seven out of nine important New Deal measures, including the two major pillars of the Recovery Program, the NRA and the AAA

There was no such court as this in England to undo the work of Parliament which could make judges more or less as it pleased. In January the British Government had sent to Washington "hard headed Walter Runciman, proprietor of the Isle of Eigg and President of the British Board of Trade" Little publicity was given to the visit though Runciman spent "the weekend quite unofficially at the White House". "What understandings were reached, the world was left to guess", *Time* reported February 1, 1937. What ideas he imparted to the President no one knows. Runciman spent the following summer of 1938 in Czechoslovakia with results that we do know.

The President's effort to 'pack the Court' met with the strongest opposition. "Factions and interests, antagonized by the President's attack upon them from the 1932 to the 1936 campaign, and alarmed by the directions taken by the Recovery Program, recovered from their earlier rout and pressed in open resistance against the New Deal " (Beard and Smith, "The Old Deal and the New")

The President met with bitter defeat and the Democratic Party was split At the same time he was pestered by the conflict between labor and capital which caused him at a press conference on June 29, 1937, to explode, "a plague on both your houses". John L Lewis, who had been a stalwart supporter, became his bitter enemy An enormous burden had been put on the President's able leader in the Senate, Joseph T. Robinson, and his death on July 14 was a tremendous loss to an already harassed and frustrated man in his hour of defeat.

HOWE

"The court bill proved a fiasco for lack of able lieutenants. The battle was trickily, even stupidly, launched and badly fought." The President's most spectacular failure is attributed to the illness and death of his shrewd, gnome-like little adviser, Louis Howe.

Since 1910 when "the handsome, aristocratic young Franklin Roosevelt came up to the New York Senate after a victory at the polls in traditionally Republican territory", Howe, then political correspondent of the N. Y. *Herald,* had acted as his political mentor. The significance of this relationship at this time is dwelt on by John Keller in "Franklin's on His Own Now: The Last Days of Louis McHenry Howe" (*Sat Eve Post,* Oct. 12, 1940).

For twelve months Howe had been in bed first in the White House, later in the naval hospital. All through the winter during the Supreme Court fight he kept sending messages to Roosevelt. "It is a safe bet that, had Howe been there, the story would have been different. Not that he would have balked at the bill He would have had no misgivings about constitutionality. 'The people', he used to say, 'do not bunk well on the constitutional issue'. .. Louis Howe would have perceived, and could have made the President perceive, what Roosevelt was eventually to learn by hindsight—that victory could be had without pressing for victory. It is impossible to sum up in any one way the loss which the President suffered in Howe's going. . . .

"Howe was a master of trickiness and connivance, which for an undercover man were highly useful attributes. But Roosevelt learned too well to relish, and cultivate, the shifty and the tricky. In the case of the court bill, this betrayed him . . . Roosevelt's fault as well as virtue as a pupil, one guesses, was that he was too apt. . . . ·In retrospect, it is clear that a whole series of opportunities for salvaging the objective of the bill without loss of face were muffed by the badly integrated New Deal leadership."

FRUSTRATION

The President's attitude after the Supreme Court debacle is perhaps best reflected in Rex Tugwell's rather guarded report of a luncheon conversation with him in the summer of 1938, reported May 13, 1940 in the *New Republic.* Tugwell had sought to dissuade him from the decision which rumor reported he had half formed not to run for a third term. "The impulse which had brought him to the verge of decision was not difficult to understand. . . . He had, against bitter opposition, righted some of the worst wrongs and corrected a few of the worst maladjustments. . . . I had suffered myself, in a small way, and I had seen Mr. Roosevelt suffer, from unfair attacks on his integrity in the press." (cf p 123)

Tugwell referred to the "wearing fight", to the "terrible central responsibilities of a time not only of trouble but of recrimination", to the "reverses inherent in a position so carefully checked and balanced" that "had brought a refining caution which was almost physical". Tugwell told the President no one "could wish to see him condemned to another four years of such immolation. Those privateers of business . . . had fostered what hatred and distrust they could, and that was a good deal."

The President, "constantly checked and frustrated by legislative reverses . . . had never been able to establish the commodity dollar he said he wanted; he had seen his industrial and farm policies repudiated; he had never been permitted to gauge the national need for purchasing power and to supply the deficiency in time to be effective. His TVA idea had been grotesquely distorted."

SOME REMARKABLE COINCIDENCES

Runciman's ostensible mission to Washington was "to pose some vital questions . . whether Britain can afford to make a trade agreement and become dependent upon the U S. for supplies which will be denied her by U. S. neutrality laws if an enemy attacks her" (*Time*, Feb. 1, 1937). But so skilful an under-cover worker, who always got results, would hardly have been called from retirement for so minor a task Subsequent international affairs would indicate that he put the President in touch with the plans and desires of the British Government.

Within a month, in March, 1937, Britain occupied Canton and Enderbury Islands. A year later the United States seized these islands, an act of war, but it resulted in a joint agreement the following August (cf pp 61, 306-7). May 12, George VI was crowned. On the 28th Chamberlain became Prime Minister. During the summer, Japan and China having engaged in war, Roosevelt was proposing Anglo-American-Soviet blockade of Japan and Germany (Flynn).

"There followed some remarkable coincidences which it is hard to believe were entirely fortuitous", A. Whitney Griswold wrote in *Events*, Nov. 1937. Without invoking the neutrality laws, the President, Sept. 14, placed an embargo on the use of government owned vessels carrying munitions to either belligerent. And at Hyde Park he talked belligerently of a long range economic boycott of Japan.

September 19 Foreign Secretary Anthony Eden over an international

broadcast "revived hopes for the conclusion of the languishing Anglo-
American trade pact. . . The next day Sir Frederick Phillips, Under
Secretary of the British Treasury, gave point to the Foreign Secretary's
remarks by opening a series of discussions with Secretary Morgenthau
on Anglo-American financial and commercial relations". The same day
the United States accepted the League's invitation to act as a non-voting
member of the Far Eastern Advisory Committee of the League.

"This deferential gesture to the wishes of London may well have
inspired—or been inspired by—Mr Eden's solicitude for the Anglo-
American trade pact. Speaking on the same program as had Mr. Eden,
and again, the next day, before a large Boston audience, Secretary Hull
reaffirmed his faith that both his own commercial policy and the principles enshrined at Geneva could and would prevail. American diplomacy seemed to be moving in the direction of London and Geneva."
It was spoken of as a 'parallel action'. September 22 the State Department in a 'strongly worded' note objected to the Japanese Government's
warning to foreigners to take shelter.

"Meanwhile, the British public was described by the strongly Anglophile American press as aflame with indignation, and there was talk of
a British boycott of Japan. There was no concealing the fact that Japanese military operations against cities in the Yangtze Valley had
touched Great Britain on an economic nerve center, and that she was doing her best to arouse the rest of the world, especially the United States,
against Japan. .. While Admiral Yarnell and the American military
and naval forces in China continued with apparent singleness of purpose to perform their non-political duties, the words, if not the deeds,
of their superiors in Washington gave cause for doubt as to how long the
United States would remain neutral. . . . While the American press
played up the irresponsible British talk of a boycott of Japan, it tucked
away inconspicuously the news that the British Government was appre-
hensively discouraging this talk. . . . On October 4 Great Britain made
the most determined of all her recent efforts to maneuver the United
States . . . to share a greater measure of responsibility for the League's
decisions." (Griswold, *Events,* Nov. 1937) [6]

QUARANTINING AGGRESSORS

The President the following day delivered his famous belligerent
'quarantine' speech before a great Chicago audience, advocating a

'strong-arm policy' and summoning the 'peace loving nations' to restrain
the lawless tenth of the nations intent on war.[6] He implied dissatisfaction with the restraints imposed upon him by the neutrality laws.
"By implication he denounced Japan, Italy and Germany as dictatorial
states threatening the peace and safety of mankind, and suggested a
union of democratic nations in a quarantine against them. In a flash this
address to mankind crowded 'the Black affair' into an obscure place in
the newspapers. One Roman holiday was substituted for another"
(Beard, "America in Midpassage")

"The sensitive antennae of foreign offices across the seas had picked
up the overtones of Mr Roosevelt's speech. These statesmen understood that the president of the United States had in effect declared war.
His Chicago listeners   would have said that the only war implied was
moral war. The chancelleries of Europe and Asia, more skilled in
reading the full score, knew that Mr Roosevelt had taken the first irre-
vocable step by which the nations are drawn into conflict." ("And So
To War", Hubert Herring, Yale, 1938)

It was apparent that the President was about to seek new satisfactions
in foreign fields, in fighting for right and morality and saving western
civilization.[7] From this time domestic affairs ceased to hold his interest. The cartoonists pictured him at a desk with telephones labeled
London, Paris, and other foreign capitals. His latest cause of domestic
annoyance had been the tremendous outburst of antagonism to his appointment of Senator Black to the Supreme Court. "A tremendous diversion of popular interest to some other theme was necessary" to allay
the antagonistic public excitement and restore his falling prestige to the
high pinnacle where he loved to see it. "Willingly or not the President
made the decision." (Beard, "America in Midpassage")

The 'economic royalists' in their hate had unwittingly perhaps ex-
patriated the President, driven him to Whitehall. Among the Anglophiles of Wall Street or his fellow Harvard alumni there may have been
guiding minds who desired and were elated to see the skilful British
diplomats take advantage of a frustrated and defeated President.

FUTILITY

A copy of the President's quarantine speech was in the British Foreign
Office before the address was made, the N. Y. *Herald Tribune* reported

October 6. "London and Paris were seemingly prepared to push action [on Japan]. It was anticipated that the United States would cooperate in the name of the 1922 treaty, if not in the name of the League Covenant . . . No other power was as yet willing to supply the force." (Schuman, *Events,* Nov. 1937)

"At the time Great Britain and France were more keenly concerned in Europe . . . were inclined against adventures in the Far East and not averse to an 'understanding' with Japan." At the Brussels conference, Nov. 3, 1937,[8] delegates "offered the badge of the world's policeman to the United States and then recessed. The President was disappointed by this maneuver. At home the rising protests against the quarantine speech disconcerted him. . . .

"He ignored the proffered role of world policeman but in January, 1938, sent a special message to Congress calling for an enormous increase in armaments . . . Throughout the whole period from the seizure of Austria to the outbreak of the war, the President and the State Department pursued the policy of collective internationalism. They were encouraged in this by the strong sentiment among the American people against Hitler's ruthless course. Americans were horrified at the cruelties of the Nazis against the Jews in Germany and against others in German conquered territories." (Beard and Smith, "The Old Deal and the New") [9]

Perhaps the American idealists, who have more difficulty than the British in distinguishing between the Oriental and Central European fascists, were rendered a bit more skeptical of accepting the role of knight errant in the East because of Lord Halifax' visit Nov. 17, 1937 to Hitler "with the aim of discovering the German objectives and, if possible, striking some peaceful settlement. The evidence would indicate that Halifax returned deeply impressed with the magnitude of the German program, especially in central and eastern Europe." (Langer's Revision of Ploetz, Houghton Mifflin Company, 1940)

SALVATION

In the approach to war of Wilson and Roosevelt, an "historical parallel" is seen by Matthew Josephson ("The President Makers", Harcourt, Brace, 1940). Wilson had bogged down after a big program of reform legislation. The country would take no more. Business was on the decline, the President's prestige was shattered and his re-election doubtful. But a foreign war was waging to which he turned the attention of the country, created new emotional outlets and led his country in a crusade to "make the world safe for democracy".[10]

Franklin Roosevelt, like his chief of earlier days, Wilson, found that his program on domestic issues had bogged down. "Early in the second term of President Franklin D. Roosevelt, toward 1938, the movement of progress showed signs of reaching its natural limits, halting before apparently insurmountable obstacles, in a manner nearly identical with the stoppage of President Wilson's New Freedom program. The forward movement under Wilson, had it continued at its swift, initial pace, would have confronted quickly the tormenting problem of economic inequality. There are now clear enough signs that the Wilsonian movement, at first so immensely promising, halted before the first World War was upon us, rather than because of the coming of war. . . .[11]

"Under the second Roosevelt, in a later phase of our economic development, very imposing social gains had been registered. We were, by 1937, the time of the President's contest to 'liberalize' the Supreme Court, farther along the road of social progress than ever before. We had departed boldly enough, as a government, from the policy of laissez-faire so that one out of every six Americans was supported by government aid. Some constructive ideas were in the air; new methods were being mastered, beginnings were being made at the management of giant public projects by devoted and patriotic young public servants of a new type. There was bustle and hope again, and a new human prosperity. . . .

"Then, very markedly, the advancing movement, which hoped-to conserve and increase human and natural wealth alike, came to a halt. Once more, by a historical 'coincidence', in the midst of domestic crisis, unfinished and-unsolved, we turn as a nation to confront the world's wars, the dangers and the opportunities they offer." (cf p 332)

Battered by the 'economic royalists', the Democratic Party split by the Supreme Court battle, the President found himself in the predicament of needing new issues and new allies with which to restore his prestige Big business lacked confidence. The House of Morgan was on the decline. People lacked jobs. The old sources for spending had dried up. No longer would the local communities support by taxation the swimming pools and playgrounds that the federal government prof-

fered them. (cf Buls #82, 98) Blocked, thwarted by people of his class
who should have been helping him, Mr Roosevelt saw no recourse but
"to busy giddy minds with foreign quarrels", as Charles Beard reminds
us Henry IV advised his son Harry (*Harper's*, Sept 1939).

The fear of war stimulated new emotions, aroused new impulses.
It tapped new sources for money to support government effort for defense. War offers escape, excitement. Everyone likes war, the speeding
up of industry, jobs for all, the increased importance of youth, the marching feet, bands playing. We are thrilled, our pulses beat faster. And
our President has always been interested in the implements of war and
especially of sea war. The smiling approbation of Britain's skilful diplomats, the appeal of royalty for help, was balm to a bruised ego.

NOTES

(1) "By 1935 the revisionist view of the World War of 1914-18 had become
the majority view", writes Frederick Lewis Allen in his "Since Yesterday"
(Harper, 1940). "According to this version, there has been guilt on both sides,
not simply on the German side, and the United States had been unhappily sucked
into participation in the war by British propaganda and its economic stake in an
allied victory."

(2) "The first trick was turned in December 1934. At that time, the investigators were probing deeply into the affairs of the powerful duPonts, and Senator
Nye had roused a formidable demand throughout the country for nationalization
of the munitions industry", Hanighen tells us in "The Munitions Makers Triumph". "In the face of this threat, the government acted. President Roosevelt
produced the famous red herring of 'taking the profits out of war', a far better and
more practicable scheme—it was suggested—than buying out munitions plants.
This diverted public opinion from the subject of nationalization for some months
while committee experts worked out a war-profits plan. When the experts finally
reported their plan, they demonstrated that their measure was grim and drastic
Another shift was necessary. Public opinion was cleverly focused on another
matter. The war-profits scheme was shelved and neutrality legislation became the
favorite"

(3) Who wrote the Chautauqua speech, how much of it was the President's
own, remains unknown, but the attitude expressed he put across at that time with
apparent sincerity and conviction Raymond Moley, in "After Seven Years"
(Harper, 1939) tells a good deal about how the President's speeches were written
It was his habit to have scripts for his speeches drafted by members of his entourage. Often he would have more or less incongruous elements from several such
drafts combined in order perhaps to appeal to different groups. On Harry Hopkins' return from his trip to England a Washington correspondent reports that

the President's first question to him was who writes Churchill's speeches? The President at present is relying largely on MacLeish, it is generally reported

At Buenos Aires, on December 1, 1936, he had declared, "We know, too, that armament work . . . builds no permanent structures and creates no consumers' goods for the maintenance of a lasting prosperity. We know the nations guilty of these follies inevitably face the day when either their weapons of destruction must be used against their neighbors or when an unsound economy, like a house of cards, will fall apart."

In 1938, the Administration protested and recovered for the sinking of the Panay though it "had been convoying Standard Oil tankers—in other words, had been engaged in just the sort of enterprise which the neutrality advocates of 1935 had sought to eliminate as a possible *casus belli* . . . At about the same time the Administration used its political influence with Congress to bury in committee the Ludlow Resolution which would have required a national referendum to get the United States into war; this measure, it is said, would 'cripple any President in the conduct of our foreign relations'." ("Since Yesterday")

(4) The Democratic platform of 1936 which as Charles Beard points out (*Harpers,* Sept. 1939) Roosevelt "made his own office" declared, "We shall continue to observe a true neutrality in the disputes of others, to be prepared resolutely to resist aggression against ourselves; to work for peace and to take the profits out of war, to guard against being drawn, by political commitments, international banking, or private trading, into any war which may develop anywhere "

(5) The League Advisory Committee's October 5 resolution expressing disapproval of Japan was opposed by China and the Soviet Union, Frederick L. Schuman tells in *Events,* Nov 1937, apparently because they saw in it "a parallel to the situation of 1931-1933 when the problem of checking Japan was futilely tossed about from one body to another without effective action of any kind resulting".

When in January 1932 our Secretary of State Stimson, invoking the Pact of Paris against Japan's invasion of Manchuria, was snubbed by Simon, "On that dark January morning England told the world that . . . the League of Nations offered no protection to its members, unless they were exactly the right color.
. The Chinese were too yellow, later the Ethiopians were to be too black, and later still the Spanish too red." (Geoffrey Garratt, "Conscript Europe")

(6) "At Chicago in October, 1937, Roosevelt said that 'the moral consciousness of the world . must be aroused to the cardinal necessity . . of putting an end to acts of aggression', added that an 'epidemic of world lawlessness' was spreading, and that 'when an epidemic of physical disease starts to spread, the community approves and joins in a quarantine' " (Allen, "Since Yesterday")

(7) "America's Far Eastern policy was moving yet more rapidly away from detachment and the protection of nationals toward the sirens of intervention, anti-war crusades and other risks of involvement in the affairs of foreign nations from which the American people, as represented by the last Congress, fondly

imagined they had been guarding themselves with Neutrality Laws. With Congress out of town, the President had removed the cotton from his ears, harkened to the sirens and headed for the same reef that had wrecked the New Freedom of Woodrow Wilson ... White House aides, and a handful of loquacious Senators interpreted it as the signal for an attack on the Neutrality Laws." (A. Whitney Griswold, *Events,* Nov 1937)

(8) In August, 1937, "Anthony Eden, the British Foreign Secretary, told questioners in the House of Commons that consultation with the United States was very much on his mind.... War scare headlines swept the country" (Griswold). "Mr Anthony Eden told the House of Commons, 'I would go from Melbourne to Alaska to get the United States to the conference'. But it was not necessary for Mr. Eden to overwork himself. 'It is not of record', wrote Mr. Edwin L. James in the N. Y. *Times* (Nov. 21, 1937), 'that Britain, or anyone else, forced us to inspire the calling of the sad Brussels conference. It was our idea; it was our party.' Brussels was dismal. The British tried to push Mr Norman Davis out into the spotlight, to let the United States take the bow as the Lochinvar out of the West." (Herring, "And So To War", Yale Univ. Press, 1938)

(9) "Clearly, it had never occurred to Roosevelt or Secretary Hull to raise the question why treaties were being broken throughout the world—to forego a wringing of hands over the breaking of treaties and to inquire why treaties were so brittle. American foreign policy up to October, 1937, was like nothing so much as a penology that considers only the apprehension and punishment of criminals without a thought of what makes people criminals   our continuous harping on the sanctity of treaties which established existing world boundaries actually seemed to strengthen the German and Italian governments at home. It made it possible for them to tell their people that the United States was allied with those determined that there should be no readjustment." (Moley, "After Seven Years")

(10) "We shall fight", said Wilson, "for the things which we have always carried nearest our hearts—for democracy, for the right of those who submit to authority to have a voice in their government ... for a universal domain of right by such a concert of free peoples as shall bring peace and safety to all nations and make the world itself at last free." Roosevelt has sung the same tune, writes Herring in 1938, and "has gone farther toward war in six months than Wilson did in two years. Just as Wilson insisted that his every move was dictated by the love of peace, so does Mr. Roosevelt affirm that his heart is set on concord."

(11) Charles Callan Tansill, in reviewing the process by which 20 years ago "America Goes to War" (Little, Brown, 1938), writes, "There is not the slightest evidence that during the Hundred Days that preceded America's entry into the World War the President gave any heed to demands from 'big business' that America intervene in order to save investments. ... Colonel House and Secretary Lansing had far more influence than the House of Morgan", while "it is well known" that Lansing "was at times in sympathy with the viewpoint of 'big business' " and it is "conceivable" that House "had similar inclinations".

TOWARD WAR

However much the President hated war, it was evident from the time of his quarantine speech that he hated neutrality more. Every move of the Administration was calculated to bring greater and greater support to Britain. In his message to Congress in January, 1938, he appealed for a big navy. Alarmed at this straight drive to war, former President Hoover began his series of warning broadcasts to the people to avoid alliances and to keep out of war, and presented his case in "Shall We Send Our Youth to War?" (Coward-McCann, 1939).

SECRET DOINGS

In August, the President dramatized the fear of imminent danger by assuming the defense of Canada. "I give you my assurance that the people of the United States will not stand idly by if domination of Canadian soil is threatened by any other empire."

This same month, a joint communique of Great Britain and the United States anounced "that the two governments had agreed to set up a regime for the use in common" of Canton and Enderbury Islands. That the preliminary steps had been taken the year before at about the time of the President's 'quarantine' speech remained unknown until revealed a year and a half later by George Holden Tinkham, Representative from Massachusetts, in a speech fully documented with correspondence with the State Department (*Congressional Record*, March 21, 1940). (cf pp 305-312, 455 and "What Makes Lives", p 160)

That same summer of 1938, Tinkham cabled from Europe to the President and Secretary Hull, charging that the Administration, then following a policy of 'parallel action', was in secret collusion with Britain, and demanding action. In a release January 29, 1940, he charged, "They sent American officials to Czechoslovakia in 1938 to support Great Britain in the political crisis there which eventuated in the Munich Settlement, and again the United States was involved in the humiliating and disastrous denouement." (cf p 312)

MUNICH AND AFTER

Lord Runciman, this same August, 1938, had settled down in Prague, for some months deep in diplomacy. "They sent out the Runciman Mission to see if there was not some 'painless' way of prying the Sudetenland from Czechoslovakia. . . . It was Chamberlain, not Hitler, who

first officially proposed this solution, and Chamberlain who forced it
on the French and the Czechs", writes Willson Woodside, a Toronto
journalist, in *Harper's,* December, 1938. Describing Runciman as a
"one-man European power", *Time,* August 8, 1938, adds, "British public opinion will never support the use of arms to aid Czechoslovakia if
the recommendations of Lord Runciman are against it". Eventually it
became evident that Lord Runciman was not against it and had other
ways of settling things than by use of arms.[1]

The American public was greatly aroused by the alarmist radio reports of European events at this time. "Then came Munich, and whatever the merits and necessities of that settlement in Europe, the effect
on American opinion was like the Hoare-Laval deal intensified, there
was a throwback to disillusionment and insulation. To counteract these
effects, Anthony Eden made a hurried trip to the United States." (Canham and Harsch, *Chr Sci Monitor,* May 6, 1939)

After the Munich Conference "the majority of Americans became
convinced that another general war could not be avoided", though in
January, 1938, "the Gallup poll showed two-thirds of the American
people favoring stricter neutrality legislation. . . .

"Roosevelt took advantage of this . . to launch a drive against the
Neutrality Act or, indeed, any legislation designed primarily to keep
America out of war. . . . Within less than two years after this Act went
on the statute books, American public opinion was becoming more and
more . . convinced . . . that their national interests should lead them to
oppose further expansion by Germany." (Quincy Howe, "Blood is
Cheaper Than Water", Simon and Schuster, 1939)

As early as November 1938, Washington correspondents were aware
of the President's intentions to get rid of the hampering neutrality bill
which Congress had passed in spite of him. "The President will propose
amendment of the neutrality act, doubt it not. He needs more power,
but Congress will be reluctant to give it without defining close limitations A compromise substitute is likely to be adopted, the scope of
which is not foreseeable yet." (Paul Mallon, Nov 10, 1938)

WHOSE FOREIGN POLICY?

"After Munich Roosevelt at once summoned home our ambassador to
Berlin. There were consultations with Ambassadors Phillips, Kennedy,
and Bullitt The consensus seems to have been agreement that the time

had come to do 'something practical' to stop Germany, Italy and Japan, and to assist England and France. That 'something' was to be a revision of the Neutrality Act to permit France and England to buy guns and munitions in this country", Moley tells us in "After Seven Years".

Alsop and Kintner, in "American White Paper" (Simon and Schuster, 1940) give an intimate inside story of this period in which America's foreign policy was being reformulated by the President in consultation with Hull, Welles, Berle (cf pp 332-3). "From the Munich crisis through the spring of 1939, American policy was ingenious rather than forthright It was ersatz; the best substitute the President could improvise for the more positive policy he was debarred from following."

The aim was "to prevent war if possible, and if war proved inevitable, we must do our best to assure victory for the other democracies". The authors find it "irresistible to speculate on what might have happened if the President had dared . to present the issues of American foreign policy squarely to the people . . warned them of the approach of war. . . The President has not repudiated the possibility of naval and aerial participation It may be assumed that there are no limits to Roosevelt's determination to see an Allied victory." (*Uncensored*, May 4, 1940)

"A vague four-point statement of American policy was given the press", Moley tells us, "a statement which left the Senate, the newspapers, and the country cold because it did not explain the bungled plane deal, it did not make clear what American interests were so endangered that the facts must remain a secret, and it certainly did not convince reasonable people that the Administration was not up to its neck in the game of power politics." By January, 1938, "a policy of active, though unacknowledged, 'cooperation' with England . . was under way.

"Observers recognize . signs of a State Department campaign to 'educate' the American public to the need for a stronger foreign policy."[2] It had started a year before "when Secretary Hull spoke of 'collaboration' along 'parallel lines' to prevent the spread of 'the contagious scourge of treaty breaking and armed violence'. . . In the autumn it seems to have been given impetus with the mysterious spread of fear-provoking stories out of Washington." Moley lists seven such stories.[3] Submarines were sighted off the coast of Florida. This technique was repeated whenever a doubtful issue arose, as when the vote on embargo repeal was about to be taken (cf Buls #8, 9).

During this period Hitler was conciliatory in his speeches, and the English leaders including Lothian were working for appeasement, critical of our belligerent baiting of Hitler.[4] But Roosevelt would have none of it. Not satisfied with the way his domestic reforms had gone he was now ready to assert, we are reminded by the N. Y. *Times*, July 4, 1939, "that prevention of war in all parts of the world was the first policy of his administration".

SHIFTING FRONTIERS

The President in his message to Congress January, 1939, emphasized "there are many ways short of war, but stronger and more effective than mere words". All these he continued to use, as Moley remarks, in the 'educational' campaign to bring the people closer to war.

"Later that month (January, 1939) a Douglas attack plane crashed at Los Angeles, and soon it was discovered that the passenger in this plane built to United States Army specifications had been a Frenchman; obviously France was being permitted, with the Administration's blessing, to order good new American fighting planes   (cf Bul #20)

"Then the President held a long secret session with the Senate Committee on Military Affairs, and after this meeting came senatorial rumors—which were sharply denied—that the President had said if war came, America's frontier would be in France." ("Since Yesterday")

While the President was threatening and using these methods "short of war", the Tories continued to propose peace plans. Chamberlain and Halifax were working with the Vatican toward appeasement. (cf p 33)

"There is little reason to believe that our intervention in Europe to date [1939], for all its lofty motives, has suceeded in doing more than (1) to wangle the United States into a position where Prime Minister Chamberlain can and does act as though the British might be willing to cooperate with us in our war with Germany, and (2) to throw the United States athwart those belated forces for appeasement whose earlier appearance would have made the growth of fascism impossible in the first place." (Moley, "After Seven Years")

IF WE DON'T HAVE WAR

The country was flooded with British propagandists and lecturers, but the people still remained oblivious of the European situation. With his usual sense of timing (cf p 339) and the dramatic, the President called

the attention of the nation to the oncoming war with his farewell words
on leaving Warm Springs April 9, "I'll be back in the fall if we don't
have war" (cf pp 120, 184).

In England there was growing dissatisfaction with the appeasement
policy of the Chamberlain government, and Churchill was gaining in
power. Three years before, Churchill, then in the opposition and crying
for rearmament, had confided to Gen. Robert E. Wood, the General
testified in the Senate hearings Feb. 1941, "Germany is getting too
strong. We must smash her." (cf Bul #98)

From his European advisers the President had doubtless learned that
the British had so speeded up their armament program that they would
be ready for war by September.

At a newspaper conference April 11, the President for the first time
came out for war, going out of his way to endorse an editorial in the
Washington *Post* that had been written by Felix Morley, which implied
that "it was now up to the U. S. to take the lead in halting the dictators
—by threat and, if that failed, by war" (*Newsweek*, April 24, 1939).
Three days later, in addressing the representatives of twenty-one
Latin American nations, the President declared that he was prepared
to use force "to defend American peace" (cf p 332). "Rarely, if ever,
had a President of the United States lashed out so severely at the governments of countries with which his own was at peace and with which he
affirmed his purpose to remain at peace. . . . Neither house of Congress
was in session at the time . . . but a number whose names or opinions
had news value to the press gave interviews and voiced their alarm. . . .
Within a few hours, however, Mr. Roosevelt had circumvented much
of this criticism by" dispatching personal telegrams to Hitler and Mussolini. (Whitney H. Shepardson and William O. Scroggs, "The United
States in World Affairs", Harper, 1940)

He asked the dictators to refrain from attacking thirty-one specified
countries, Danzig not mentioned, for a period of from ten to twenty-five
years, and offered as a "friendly intermediary" to call a conference. The
President, as *Newsweek* (April 24, 1939) remarks, had "long since
disqualified himself as a possible arbiter by his strong language and his
undisguised partisanship". "Many observers felt that the plea had been
weakened in advance by too much loose anti-Nazi talk by American officials", observed *Harper's* editor, Frederick Lewis Allen.

As the President had transmitted copies of this to all other governments and had had the message broadcast in six languages and rebroad-
cast from London in German and Italian, direct replies were slow in
coming Five days later Mussolini referred rather contemptuously to
"Messiah-like messages" Hitler announced that he would reply April
28, after receiving answers from the states Roosevelt had mentioned.

Schuman ironically comments, "This masterpiece of Hitlerical oratory
achieved several purposes at once. By exposing the hollowness of Roosevelt's words and contrasting American professions of purpose with
American deeds, it demonstrated the absence of any American foreign
policy." Even Winston Churchill, then in Opposition, referred to the
"tactless phrases" in Roosevelt's appeal, but expressed fear lest the dictators accepted his terms. Laborite M.P., John Morgan, on the other
hand, seemed to be afraid they wouldn't. "The attitude of the people of
the United States is bringing upon us the calamity we all dread."

The scorn which greeted Mr. Roosevelt's last attempt at appeasement[5] fixed his zeal to put down what seemed to him evil. The foreign
situation became simplicity itself, "to side with good, i. e., Britain, versus, evil, i. e, whatever. Britain may be fighting", writes Lawrence
Dennis in his *Weekly Foreign Letter,* January 2, 1941.

NOTES

(1) An editorial, "shown to the German Embassy before publication", was pre-
maturely published in the London *Times* weeks before Munich, while Runciman
was in Czechoslovakia The *Times,* which had stood all along for giving the
Sudeten area to Hitler, advocated the dismemberment of Czechoslovakia, which
was repeated in "a New York paper" and later at the protest of Chamberlain
repudiated by the London *Times* But ten days after its publication the Chamberlain Government had overtly adopted its policy. (Willson Woodside, *Harper's,*
December, 1938)

Anticipating and re-enforcing Runciman's decision that Czechoslovakia should
be broken up, there was published under the auspices of the Royal Institute of
International Affairs, otherwise known as Chatham House, of which Astor is
Chairman of the Council, "Czechs and Germans: A Study of the Struggle in the
Historic Provinces of Bohemia and Moravia", by Elizabeth Wiskemann (Oxford).

(2) "The change desired by President Roosevelt may be slow in coming. The
instinct of isolation in America is still deep-rooted", Sir Frederick Whyte, director of the American division of the British Ministry of Information, declared.

"Those who lead us into war have first the task of persuasion, or 'education',
as Robert Lansing put it. They must take people who do not want to fight and
make them want to fight They must take peace-loving people and convince them

that the war is a just war, a generous war, a war for their own good and for the
ultimate good of future generations. This was what Woodrow Wilson did for
us in the years 1914-17." And many of those who had supported Roosevelt were
beginning to distrust him for the same reason. (Hubert Herring)

"A large part of foreign policy is conducted by executive and administrative
action—that is, without consulting either the people or their representatives. If
American policy was pushed too far or too fast into world politics, so as to arouse
domestic opposition, it was usually a simple matter to drop the objectionable
procedure, fall back on the non-political, and thus unobjectionable form, for a
fresh start as soon as the home protest died down. Certainly it confused the
American people, the vast majority of whom were for 'peace' in the general and
yet found their country moving deeper into the dangerous shoals of world politics . . . Thus a masterful strategy was evolved for casting the weight of the
United States into world politics without seeming, apparently to do so." (Beard
and Smith, "The Old Deal and the New")

(3) This "foreign danger blackmail" as the French call it, Montgomery Belgion
tells us in "News of the French" "is not new: Napoleon III was accused of re-
sorting to it in 1870 and the late Mr. Doumergue of doing so on the wireless
when he was Prime Minister in 1934" The British, when they used it in the
fall of 1938 in digging up Hyde Park and distributing gasmasks, had learned it
from the French. It's an old French custom.

"This gag of fetching the boobs by discovering and scotching bugaboos beyond the seas is an old one, and has been resorted to by more than one hero of
the Republic. . . . Samuel Johnson entertained the boozers in a London tavern
with a very tart characterization of its practitioners, now accessible in all books of
quotations." (H. L. Mencken, *American Mercury*, March, 1939)

"Emanating from him or quarters close to him came pronouncements and declarations that were of the old, inflammatory type Typical of such matters was
the alleged sighting of submarines off the coasts of New England and of Alaska,
reported by the President himself Yesterday he admitted that the reports had
not been verified But such stories thrown into the charged atmosphere of war
had done their damage in helping to destroy the restraint and balanced temper
upon which neutrality depends." (Editorial, Boston *Transcript*, Sept. 30, 1939)

"The President began a fire as soon as the war started. He gave out alarms
about spies He had the Attorney General go on the screen. . . . He notified the
country of submarines off our coast. He made speeches describing how Hitler
could come here by the air. . The effect of this attack upon the mind produced
the inevitable result—a condition of terror, growing alarm that it is only a question of a little time when we shall have to meet the Nazi terror in our own streets
and our own homes. The President started this fire and it sped around the land
until the public mind was a conflagration of fear" (John T Flynn on "War
Hysteria", *New Republic*, Nov. 11, 1940)

Hitler's "psychology of terror" is a technique in which the President is well
versed. "The President appears to be making the most of that fear which he had

held to be a needless factor in the lag in our economic recovery" (Editorial, Springfield *Union*).

(4) "Perhaps it would be too much to say that there has been deliberate exaggeration of the points of friction by American officials, but certainly there has been no tempering of American protests against German actions. Here are some of the sore spots. First, Germany is the only country in the world to which the United States denies most-favored-nation treatment in the application of reciprocal trade agreements Secondly the United States is taking the lead in the refugee conference at Evian, an activity which is directly critical of German policy. Thirdly, the United States has refused helium to German dirigibles, after having passed a special act of Congress to permit such export, on the specific ground that it might be used for military purposes. Next, a spy plot in the United States, involving the indictment of 18 Germans, was played up by the Government with zest and thoroughness, even more, perhaps, than the occasion warranted. The cases may drag on indefinitely. Finally, public officials are increasingly critical of Germany in their speeches, and no effort is being made to smooth over these affairs—which could be done quite easily. In short, it has become good politics to be anti-German " (Lothian, *Round Table*, Sept. 1938)

The late great English liberal Parliamentarian and labor leader, George Lansbury, in "My Quest for Peace" (Michael Joseph, Ltd , 1938) tells of his interviews with the leaders of the European countries and America in an effort to bring them together in a peace conference. "During the more than two hours" with Hitler "his whole conversation was impersonal and understanding and clear-cut. . . I imagined myself listening to speeches that I had heard in our House of Commons defending concentration camps in South Africa and the actions of the Black and Tans in Ireland. Policies of repression may differ in their form and expression, but in essence they are the same. . . . At the end Hitler . . . agreed . . .: 'Germany will be very willing to attend a conference and take part in a united effort to establish economic cooperation and mutual understanding between the nations of the world if President Roosevelt or the head of another great country will take the lead in calling such a conference.' " (pp 138, 9)

Senator Nye, in a letter to the N. Y. *Times* in September, 1940, attributing the outbreak of war to American meddling, said that "we sold out, by deliberate falsification, the two European nations with which we had the closest ties. We sent France to her death and have brought England perilously close to it."

(5) Relating how the "President Backed Hitler", the *People's Lobby Bulletin*, January 1941, reminds that it was on the insistence of the President that Congress retained the embargo on Loyalist Spain, "which was attempting to put down an insurrection fomented by Hitler and Mussolini", and gives as the first of four reasons for the President's insistence, that "it conformed with Britain's policy of 'appeasement' of the Axis powers, a word for which the President has only recently acquired distaste".

PREACHING PEACE

"Through all the centuries and down to the world conflict of 1914-18, wars were made by governments. Woodrow Wilson challenged that necessity. . . . It is but an extension of that challenge of Woodrow Wilson for us to propose in this newer generation that from now on war by governments shall be changed to peace by peoples." When President Roosevelt during his first term wrote this in his second book "On Our Way", the people generally knew that they had been fooled in the last war. Wilson, disillusioned at Versailles, in his St Louis speech, almost his last, acknowledged that it had been an economic war for plunder. *che* Two years before, Eugene Debs, for the same statement had been sent to prison

WEANING US FROM NEUTRALITY

This Wilsonian attitude was so popular at the time that Roosevelt naturally espoused it. The political vote getter must "take care of the appeals to patriotism and peace . . . In 1936 the President pledged to keep America at peace by keeping America neutral. In 1937 he proposed to keep the world at peace by means of quarantine In 1939 he decided that two billion dollars' worth of armaments offered the United States its only protection against aggression. . . . At the beginning of 1939 he believed just as firmly in peace by rearmament as he did in peace by neutrality at the end of 1936 or in peace by quarantine at the end of 1937. At all times war was the last thing he wanted. But the course of events coupled with the policies that he had pursued, made it necessary for him to accompany his pleas with stronger and stronger appeals to patriotism and bigger and bigger armament bills." (Quincy Howe, "Blood is Cheaper Than Water", Simon and Schuster, 1939) (cf p 490)

The President was driven successively and successfully to oppose the Ludlow referendum for a vote on war, to turn aside the Legion's insistence that capital be drafted if men were, to check the Nye investigation of how the war came about, and to stifle the popular demand that munitions manufacture be nationalized (cf pp 157-8, 376-7). Instead he suggested that we 'take the profits out of war', and then all bills to that end, it was seen to, were pigeon-holed

The first Neutrality Resolution in 1935, Beard reminds us in "Midpassage", "was in large part an outcome of the munitions investigation and was thoroughly disliked by President Roosevelt and Secretary Hull. Although Roosevelt signed the Resolution, he resented the spirit and letter of the Neutrality Act and clung tenaciously to the idea of intervening in the controversies of Europe, despite the abstention and equality of treatment stipulated in the Act."

On the outbreak of the Spanish War in the summer of 1936, the President by proclamation established an unofficial embargo on exports to Spain. A year later with the Neutrality Law again before them, Congress yielded to the President authorizing at his discretion the 'cash and carry' sale of other than munitions.

When in May, 1939, the 'cash and carry' plan was about to automatically expire, the President, still irked by restrictions on his foreign policy, laid his plans to kill the embargo on munitions. American resources, it was well understood by those on the inside, were essential if Britain were to successfully engage in war with Germany. At whatever cost, American opinion must be won over to make it possible to do away with the embargo. In April it was learned from London that Lothian was to come to us as ambassador[1]. The King and Queen were to drop in on the President shortly after.

PACIFYING THE 'ECONOMIC ROYALISTS'

'Peace' was the keynote in the propaganda which flooded the country. It emanated both from the Administration and from organization committees. In order to preserve peace and keep out of war, we were told that the President must be freed from the restrictions of the current neutrality laws. The change could only be effected if presented as promoting peace, to which the people were devoted as shown by frequent polls. Peace gestures continued to come, too, from Continental sources,[2] but after the President's telegrams to Mussolini and Hitler in April, 1939, later proposals were considered by the State Department not "feasible".

Business organizations like the National Association of Manufacturers opposed the President, fearing a war economy. But his foreign policy met with the approval of other of his former hated 'economic royalists' who had so bitterly opposed the New Deal domestic policies. It was not that they loved the President more but that his purpose of supporting Britain was dear to their hearts and not unconnected with their purse strings. Nor did the terrors of war cause them to flinch.

So it behooved those acting for the British to do all possible to promote peace and harmony between the Administration and the 'economic royalists'. As the ostensible purpose in removing the embargo was to promote peace, it was appropriate that the international peace foundations, as in the last war, should early be brought into action (cf pp 180, 183-4) The great peace, philanthropic and educational foundations had on their boards representatives of the financial and British interests, the same 'economic royalists' who had been so at variance with the President.

The World Peace Foundation, in Boston, Edwin Ginn's endowment, dominated by Harvard's President Emeritus A. Lawrence Lowell, went on record September 30, 1939, in favor of repeal of the arms embargo The Carnegie Endowment for International Peace, closer to Wall Street, was even more responsive to British interests. It is presided over by President Butler of Columbia and a board of directors whose loyalties to all that is financial and British are "expressed in a complex network of interlocking directorates".[3] Centering about it are a group of philanthropic and educational organizations of great influence, served by able and effective men. Prominent among them are Clark M. Eichelberger (cf pp 130, 354, 457), Director of the League of Nations Association, and James T Shotwell, Director of the Carnegie Endowment.

Mr Shotwell was chairman of the Commission to Study the Organization of Peace inspired by Thomas W. Lamont in the late summer of 1939.[4] Its worthy ends drew to the directorship college presidents of liberal and pacifistic tendencies like William Allan Neilson, Frank Aydelotte and Virginia C. Gildersleeve. Clarence Streit was included to promote "Union Now", and Clark Eichelberger for his executive drive. The Commission organized radio forums and study groups for which they put out "educational" material. The general conclusion of the commission was that to be received at the peace table we would have to contribute to the war.

COORDINATING AND ORGANIZING

With the arrival of Lord Lothian in September, 1939, on the outbreak of war, Mr. Eichelberger became even more active in organizing and coordinating the forces favoring all aid to Britain and in creating opinion for the repeal of the embargo so essential to British success. During the summer he had organized and was chairman of the American Union for Concerted Peace Efforts, of which Mr. Shotwell was honorary vice president, the purpose of which was to bring all peace societies to a 'unified

front' in support of collective security   The Non Partisan Committee
for Peace Through the Revision of the Neutrality Law was now organized, with Mr. Eichelberger as director, "under the auspices of the
Union", as its first letterhead announced. The offices of all these organizations were convenient to the British propaganda centers.

Early in the fall Mr. Eichelberger had taken and publicized a poll
which showed Columbia and Teachers' College instructors opposed the
embargo. On October 11, 1939 (cf p 167) he "announced the results of
a poll among college presidents and deans in which 90% of them
favored President Roosevelt's neutrality program" (*Uncensored,* Oct.
14). Eichelberger's comments were so unctuously phrased that those
who were not already on the bandwagon made a rush for it. "This can-
vass of college and university leaders gives further indication that the
well-informed elements of the community are overwhelmingly in support of the President's peace stand. This committee has found that
clergymen of all faiths, editors and other well-informed persons generally are in support of the President. We believe that public opposition
while undoubtedly including many who are sincere, appears much more
numerous than it actually is because of the noisy tactics of small but
highly organized groups."

To the preceding release was appended as an apparent afterthought the
simple statement, "William Allen White is Chairman of the Committee". *Time,* August 19, 1940, tells of the negotiation necessary, "William
Allen White was drafted by stages to take an active part in converting
opinion into action. When the Congressional debate on repeal of the
Neutrality Act was at its height, his old friend Clark Eichelberger . . .
called him from Manhattan, asked him to head a committee to advocate
repeal of the embargo Editor White steadfastly refused, but Eichelberger induced other friends to press him, and White finally made
several speeches. In Emporia when repeal was certain, he received a two-
word telegram from Franklin Roosevelt: 'Thanks, Bill'."

STRATEGY

The intelligent public had little knowledge of how these committees
operated, for whom or for what purpose. Their ramifications reached
through interlocking directorates of the philanthropic and educational
foundations to the great banking, insurance and industrial corporations
and into the boards of the universities. Working with the Administra-

tion and Whitehall for a common purpose, with control of information through the means of communication, the press and radio, those in ultimate control, acting through these committees, were able to bring about the change in public opinion necessary to do away with the restrictive embargo on munitions.

In the name of Mr. White, who wrote chattily and optimistically, and occasionally visited New York headquarters, Mr. Eichelberger could now push the organization program with vigor. Offices were opened in every city and town and eventually in every ward, and mass meetings and telephone campaigns were organized. Money was available for the initial steps, and as the more socially acceptable were drawn in and the movement became fashionable, abler assistants were engaged.

The names of key men on the committee then 'in process of formation', were listed on the first letterhead to the number of several hundred. Nationally prominent people were strategically selected to avoid as far as possible a Wall Street-Whitehall flavor. Though the names often suggested Park Avenue, the purpose was to present it as a popular movement from the grass roots.

The publicity was skilfully handled by the John Price Jones Corporation. Jones and Lamont had both been to Exeter and Harvard, concerned in promoting Liberty Bond sales and later in raising the twenty million Harvard endowment. (cf p 530) Some of the committee objected to the whacking fee Jones asked for his services, but Mr. Lamont let it be known they were to "take Jones and pay his price". Later when the public learned of this it was given out Jones had withdrawn.

The publicized aims appeared at first sight to be of the noblest, though to some it seemed that if we were to defend America only by giving Britain weapons, it was like hiring a gunman. Later we were told 'this is our war' but that we did not have to fight,—to which some Englishmen came back, "Then if we do the fighting you should pay us better". (cf p 321) But the strategy worked. It concealed the real purpose and fooled a confused people.

INSURING REPEAL

The long drawn out battle between the President and Congress finally ended in July when the Senate adjourned without renewing the 'cash and carry' clause of the Neutrality Act. During the summer, smarting from the Senate rebuff, the President took every precaution to reverse this defeat and insure repeal of the restrictions placd upon him.

Lord Lothian's scholarly quarterly, the *Round Table,* in its April issue had announced, "The Administration intends to seek amendment of the act". In the September issue, an article "America and the World Crisis", prepared at least a month earlier, prophesied, "If war is actually precipitated, President Roosevelt will call a special session of Congress . . . and will seek the practically guaranteed repeal of the arms embargo. . . . The full economic, industrial, agricultural resources of the United States would then be at the disposal of Great Britain . . though perhaps on a cash and carry basis." (cf pp 122-123)

How close was the coordination between the White House and Whitehall at this time we can only surmise until the memoirs are published But it's evident that the Foreign Office with the aid of Britain's financial agents in New York and skilled propagandists in this country were working subtly for the removal of the embargo so essential for their success. Certainly the course the Administration was to pursue was better known by the English leaders than by the American people

The *Round Table* in its December, 1939, issue stated, "Before the Congress met in September, the President had Senator James F. Byrnes, a skilled and highly popular negotiator, poll his colleagues at their homes in all parts of the country by lavish use of the long distance telephone" (cf pp 130, 204-5). Senator Byrnes was then able to report to his chief that he had obtained ample commitments to repeal the arms embargo, an "astute job of political management".[5] This result, known in London's inner circles long before it was even suspected in this country, led to the anticipation that America would come into the war promptly.[6]

THE EMBARGO IS KILLED

The American press, which had so long and so bitterly opposed Roosevelt's domestic policies, became strong supporters of his foreign policy to aid Britain We were constantly told that the removal of embargo restrictions was the only sure way of keeping us out of war, of preserving peace through honest neutrality. The Boston *Herald* editorially complained at the delay "The matter has been exploited so thoroughly that there would seem to be little necessity of a long special session." It voiced its irritation and fear at popular protest, explaining (Sept. 20) that the President and his advisers had prepared "for the speediest possible action. . . . Unless they get the matter to vote in the Senate soon or the trend of letters flooding the Capitol changes materially, the Administration might find itself faced soon with an extremely difficult situation in its effort to change the Neutrality Law."

So in the face of rising popular opposition which twice halted its progress, the amended Neutrality Act lifting the arms embargo passed Congress November 3, 1939, and was signed by the President the following day. Proclaimed a measure to insure peace and prevent war, it successfully demonstrated that public opinion can be changed through control of the means of communication It gave the Administration confidence in its ability to bring Congress to heel through a new kind of patronage, to allure and control the legal profession and the investing public through new sources of profit Prestige for the socially ambitious, ostracism for honest opponents was meted out in ways the British had learned from Eastern nabobs. It was a great triumph for the President's political skill and for Lothian-Lamont-Eichelberger propaganda.

It was just as President Roosevelt had foreseen at Chautauqua "We would find thousands of Americans who would be tempted for the sake of fool's gold to break down or evade our neutrality". (cf p 50)

NOTES

(1) Lothian, with his broad acquaintance among the leaders of America and especially in the universities, was the ideal man for the purpose However, he took the job only from a sense of duty (cf pp 23-31) for he knew well, as he had said at the Royal Institute, April 2, 1936, "The United States has made up her mind, once and for all, that her intervention in Europe in 1917 was a waste of effort, that somehow or other Europe must solve her own problems and that she is not going to be associated, in any way, with European commitments " In the *Observer*, Feb. 26, 1939, he referred to "the inveterate suspicion in the United States that every British proposal is designed to induce the United States to underwrite British interests—a suspicion which rests on the fact that Anglo-American cooperation obviously operates to the benefit of the British Commonwealth and not so obviously to the benefit of the United States We long ago realised that the best and cheapest way of assuring our own security was to encourage other nations to fight for their own security "

(2) The Duke of Windsor, May 8, 1939, in a broadcast from Verdun, made a plea for peace, condemning alike "aggression" and "encirclement". An American poll in October, 1939, reported about seven out of ten to be in favor of a conference "to end the war and settle Europe's problems". Hitler in November, 1939, again made a peace proposal, one of his recurrent offers, which was scoffed at as when after reoccupation of the Rhineland in 1934, he offered to guarantee a twenty-five year peace.

(3) Butler presides over The Pilgrims, whose executive chairman is Thomas W
Lamont, an organization of highbrow Anglo-Americans of which the English
Speaking Union is the lowbrow branch to accommodate larger numbers. (cf
Quincy Howe, "England Expects Every American To Do His Duty", Simon and
Schuster, 1937, pp 47-75; Lavine and Wechsler, "War Propaganda and the
United States", Yale, 1940, pp 72-84). Their annual dinner in New York in
1939 was addressed by Lothian, in 1941 by Halifax,—"In this war Great Britain
seeks no selfish end. Its immediate cause, as in 1914, was the German breach of
a treaty on the one hand, and the fulfilment of a treaty by Great Britain on the
other."

(4) Thomas Lamont is for peace, if it is the British peace. November 15, 1939,
addressing the Academy of Political Science, he declared, as summarized by the
N. Y. Times, "The Allies must win the war", Britain's "sea power and France's
'wonderful army, magnificently equipped and led, and backed by the calm determination of the whole French people, so clear to the world', would bring victory".
(cf pp 180, 183) When Lamont is not at hand to guide, J. P. Morgan lets it be
known that his firm are British agents. Arriving in America, September 5, 1939,
driven from his grouse-shooting in Scotland, he told reporters, "It would be a
natural thing if they wanted an American agent, that they would call upon us to
repeat our performance".

(5) "On the evening of July 18, 1939, on the President's invitation, a number of
Senate leaders gathered in the upstairs study of the White House to discuss the
situation For an hour Roosevelt repeated the arguments in favor of the immediate repeal of the arms embargo. When McNary asked if he believed in the proba-
bility of war before the next session of Congress, the President replied that he was
certain there was 'a very strong possibility' " (Schuman, "Night Over Europe",
p 214) September 3, 1939, the President addressed the nation by radio. He "repeated old platitudes in praise of morality and in condemnation of force. He
warned against propaganda and rumor. . . . He intoned clichés in order to calm
hysteria and afford time for opinion to solidify in favor of lifting the arms embargo." (p 448).

(6) Uncensored, Oct. 7, 1939, relates, "In a private conversation in Washington
last week, Assistant Secretary of State Adolph A. Berle was confronted with the
question, 'Do you think we will be in the war by January?' Before he thought
twice Berle replied, 'Not that soon'. From a steadily increasing number of sources
that claim inside information, the most persistent report is that the Administration expects the country to be at war in six months In no case is the prediction
longer than nine months." Kiplinger, Washington financial agency, in November, 1939, was reporting that in Washington and Canada they expected us to be
in the war in four to six months. England looked upon it as a certainty.

'SHORT OF WAR'

With the people so strong for peace no elected official dared advocate war (cf p 487). Even as late as March, 1941, a Gallup poll showed 83% opposed to foreign war. Before election all rearmament was for defense and all measures proposed were to be 'short of war' (cf p 509).

WHO'S BEHIND

The winter of "hibernating" war, as the English termed it, which to the Americans had seemed "phoney", proved to be for the Germans a period of intensive preparation. The spring of 1940 brought the British fleet into the neutral waters of Norway. Then followed the rapid German thrusts north and west.

Meantime, in this country, the agents and friends of Britain were planning behind the scenes for war. Mr. Lamont's group, which had met without publicity late in April (cf pp 352, 357, 368, 379), were men of like mind who represented British and French interests. They were public spirited men who, while working for their own interests, sought to preserve what seemed to them essential to our 'way of life'. Some had played an active part in promoting 'the war to save democracy'.

Had this meeting not been held, Willkie might still have raised the millions to run for president, Harvard alumni might have successfully promoted conscription, and White might have acted as front for the "Committee" that brought us along toward war. But without the alliance between our federal Administration and the once hated 'economic royalists', the British Empire might have gone down.

"The hatred of Roosevelt which had burned for years in the hearts of big business men was already dying. . . . Some of the once-indignant . . . were even beginning to like Roosevelt now—for his foreign policy." The "long quarrel between the TVA and Commonwealth & Southern" had been settled for a price the taxpayer was to pay as a result of the strenuous work of its Morgan appointed president (Allen, "Since Yesterday").

HARVARD PROMOTES WAR

The Associated Harvard Clubs' annual meeting in May, 1940, in New York City turned out to be of political and historical importance. Thomas Lamont, most influential of Harvard alumni, always plays an important part.[1] Grenville Clark (cf pp 359, 363, 397, 425), most prominent member of the Harvard Corporation, and chairman of the American Bar Association's committee on civil liberties, had taken a leading part that spring in organizing the Military Training Camps Association (cf pp 361, 397, 400, 444). On May 18, just before the meeting of the Harvard Clubs, he had published in the New York *Times* his long, rambling, but much reprinted letter (cf p 353) urging universal conscription. It was almost the first public pronouncement on the subject and received wide publicity.

At the Harvard Club the drive for conscription was launched under Mr. Clark, Gen. John F. O'Ryan, Lewis W. Douglas, Henry L. Stimson, Robert P. Patterson, Elihu Root Jr., and Julius Ochs Adler. The publicity on these matters was of course well managed. It was not until the fall of 1940, after the story had been printed in the *Congressional Record,* that the Harvard *Alumni Bulletin* presented a brief statement of the part Harvard men had played in promoting conscription.[2] The University made an award of distinction to Grenville Clark for his patriotic work for the conscription bill during the long hot summer

At the meeting signatures were secured of a score or so members of the class of 1917 to a letter which echoed the note Mr. Lamont had previously accented at Exeter and in the Harvard *Alumni Bulletin* (cf "What Makes Lives" p 191), regretting the irresponsibility of the younger generation The Harvard undergraduate publications had opposed the war mongering of President Conant who was gradually bringing his faculty to heel (cf pp 165-6) This complaint that "the irresponsibles" were "distrustful of all words and distrustful of all moral judgments" became the theme of the prize song of Archibald MacLeish.

Up to this time any Harvard alumnus who manifested sympathy with the policies of President Roosevelt had been almost an outcast, so great had been the hatred of the President displayed by the more influential Harvard men Now, due to the influence of a few Harvard men at this spring meeting, Harvard alumni were brought in line with the program of the President so far as it affected foreign policy and expenditure for defense. This coalition of forces to preserve the British Raj if not the British Pax was a triumph for the British agents and representatives in this country And the President, through his popular appeal, soon found ways and means of rewarding those who served.

THE WHITE MACHINE

In the legislative battle to do away with the embargo on munitions the
previous fall, the suspicion that the direction and impetus came from
Wall Street had stimulated popular opposition (cf pp 130, 241, 245,
320). So William Allen White (cf pp 354, 358, 360, 379) and his
skilled pen, had been enlisted to remove the unfortunate suspicion

Too much Harvard would be just as harmful in a popular movement
More "grass roots" were called for, so Mr. White of Emporia was
again played up to make it seem that he had originated the whole
thing [3] *Time* reported August 19, 1940, "On May 19, when Germany
had broken through the Low Countries, he telephoned Eichelberger 'I
think it's about time to act'. His appeal went out to 60 men—governors,
college presidents, editors, a sprinkling of actors, lawyers, writers."
Telegrams of acceptance poured into the Emporia *Gazette* office.[4]

Publicity releases came from the "White Committee" in the name of
Mr. White, but the directing genius, the driving force of the Committee to Defend America by Aiding the Allies was Mr. Eichelberger
He played his part well, as on a little higher level did great men like
President Butler, old guard attorneys like Henry L. Stimson, newspaper
men like Frank Knox and Julius Ochs Adler In the publicized lists
some who had been active from the first, like Coudert and Lamont, were
kept as much as possible in the background. Committees were set up,
for historians by Charles Seymour of Yale, for the theater by Robert
Sherwood (cf pp 355, 380, 383).

Through well-managed publicity and subtle propaganda, public
opinion was created in support of measures that would be of aid to
Britain. The President was only too ready to put these measures into
effect as soon as might be possible. The Committee was acting as Mr
White described it in a radio address of August 22 as an "engine of
publicity and propaganda". He referred to himself as "only the rooster
on the cowcatcher crowing lustily sometimes at the crossroads".[5]

HOW IT FUNCTIONED

By September, 662 local chapters had been organized with more than
100,000 members From the first White Committee were carried over
many who had proved their worth through their activities or prestige.
Added were key men from the upper strata of our social system,—

presidents of universities, influential writers, representatives of most of
the professions, the press, screen, stage, radio, church, even labor leaders,
and some liberals who if neglected might have been critical. Omitted,
except for a few to direct and leaven, were most of the Harvard group,
and those who had been active in promoting conscription. The selection
was made so as to attract and not repel the hesitant.

A detailed study of the organization was made by Charles G. Ross
(cf p 357), contributing editor of the St. Louis *Post-Dispatch,* (Sept.
22, 1940) and reprinted in the *Congressional Record,* Sept. 23. Ross,
though he calls it an "inside story", does not attempt to go behind the
scenes. He begins with the joining of the Committee by White, who
he assumes organized it. An advisory policy committee was in formation at the time Ross wrote his article, on which in addition to Thomas
Lamont and Frederic R. Coudert were included important university
presidents like Conant of Harvard, Graham of North Carolina, Seymour
of Yale,—ardent Hitler haters like Frank Kingdon, Freda Kirchwey,
Robert A. Millikan, Robert Sherwood. Ross carries the story up to
the then most recent demand of the Committee for twenty-five "flying-
fortresses" for Britain (cf p 452).

"Chief among all the agencies at work to break down the instinctive
American aversion to implication in the present European conflict is the
Committee to Defend America by Aiding the Allies", wrote the *Christian
Century,* Nov. 6, in an article well summarizing Ross' study. The
editors later (Nov. 20) answering a correspondent who questioned the
"justification for your implied charge that there is something shady and
reprehensible about the course of White, Miller, Van Dusen and their
associates", stated they thought it important their readers should know
"how a great organization for propaganda purposes comes into existence, how it functions, how its decisions with regard to policy are
reached".

ASSOCIATED ORGANIZATIONS

About the White Committee there grew up through creation or
cohesion subsidiary and associated groups and organizations. Early in
June a group of 30 citizens signed a public statement urging immediate
declaration of war. Some of these were members of the White Committee. Six of them later appeared as members of the Miller group.

Late in June some of the ardent members of the White Committee met to devise ways of aiding Britain. Lewis W. Douglas early in July entertained this group at a luncheon at which it was decided to formulate a program for immediate help to Britain. Francis P. Miller was suggested as the man to head such a group. He secured "leave of absence from the Council on Foreign Relations, another link in the Carnegie Endowment network", and opened an office on July 22. This "informal thinking and finagling" group on the 25th "met at the Century Club in New York and hammered out the detailed plan for the drive to send destroyers to Britain. . . It persuaded three Willkie supporters—White, President Conant of Harvard and Lewis W. Douglas—to solicit signatures for an 'unqualified endorsement' of the deal." (*Uncensored*, Sept. 28, 1940) [6]

Early in August they "descended on Washington", as Ross puts it, "to overcome the 'lethargy' of the President". Mr Miller induced John Balderston to come from Hollywood to New York to issue a confidential 'wire letter' twice a week to fifty newspapers, known as the 'William Allen White news service' (cf pp 452, 457-9).

"A member or members of the group helped to sound out Wendell Willkie on the destroyer deal Though he declined to commit himself publicly in advance, he indicated that he approved it", Ross tells us. September 3, 1940, the President announced the destroyer deal a 'fait accompli', which St. Louis *Post-Dispatch* declared (cf p 503) "an act of war" by "America's first dictator".

NOTES

[1] "Of Thomas W. Lamont, Ferdinand Lundberg said that he 'has exercised more power for 20 years in the Western Hemisphere, has put into effect more final decisions from which there has been no appeal, than any other person. Lamont, in short, has been the First Consul de facto in the visible Directory of post-War high finance and politics, a man consulted by president, prime ministers, governors of central banks, the directing intelligence behind the Dawes and Young Plans'. . . . With the actual coming of World War II Lamont almost immediately affirmed his belief that the United States should avoid armed conflict. . . . In April 1940 he again urged that the United States remain aloof from the European War, although his participation in the founding of the Committee to Defend America by Aiding the Allies created a little suspicion that he was not quite on the isolationist side." (cf *Current Biography*, Oct., 1940) Cf also, for Thomas Lamont's relations with Harvard, foundations, publications, etc., "What Makes Lives" pp 171-2, 202-4, "Human Affairs 1938" pp 77-8.

Mr. Clark, a leading member of the N. Y. bar of the firm of Root, Clark, Buckner & Ballantine, addressing the American Newspaper Publishers' Association on "The Relation of the Press to the Maintenance of American Civil Liberty", warned, "The tendency to abuse of governmental power has been repeatedly revealed in recent years and has not yet been discredited to the extent that it should be." (Boston *Globe,* Dec. 1937)

(2) The Harvard *Alumni Bulletin,* after all had come out, related briefly with apparent frankness and candor the large part taken by Harvard alumni in promoting conscription If Mr. Clark with some others had written the Conscription Bill why not, why make a row about it?

(3) The same motive influenced the selection of his successor. "Both Mr. White and Mr Gibson are essentially country folks, Emporia having a population of some 14,000, Brattleboro of about 9,000, and Londonderry, the Vermont habitat of the senator's senatorial father, of only a few hundred" (Boston *Herald* editorial).

(4) White naively "outlines the job of his Committee after the war is over, win, lose or draw 'We shall try then to give to American youth the same joy and enthusiasm for freedom of speech, peaceful assemblage, free conscience, trial by jury and the benefits of personal freedom that the Germans have put into their youth by teaching them national pride, race arrogance, and international hatred.' " *(Time,* August 19, 1940)

(5) "Roy Howard, of the Scripps-Howard Newspapers, sent a telegram to William Allen White asking him to define the position of his committee on war Mr White replied from Emporia, saying: 'The only reason in God's world that I am in this organization is to keep this country out of war ' . . . He begged that his committee be not condemned because there were some martial-minded people in it, and added that 'Any organization that is for war is seriously playing Hitler's game.' . . . (cf p 382) The only thing its strategist could do was to repudiate the chairman's statement and theatren to repudiate him. . . . He received violent telegrams, calling him pallid and ineffective and wishing him happiness in the embrace of the appeasers. What other pressure came upon him we do not know. We know only that two days later another message was sent to the President, saying there were a few names to be added to the petition urging 'Everything that may be necessary to insure the defeat of the Axis Powers', and among the names thus added, in an obscure position, without comment or adjunct, was the name of William Allen White." *(Sat Eve Post,* Feb 1, 1941)

(6) An interesting study could be made of the pressures that have brought the change in Conant to the "all out" advocate of war from his liberal attitude of 1935, when he demanded that "We must examine the immediate origins of our political, economic, and cultural life . . . as fearlessly as the geologist examines the origin of rocks". (cf pp 165-6 Cf also *Current Biography,* March, 1941; Handbook of Private Schools, 1936-37 ed., pp 57-59; 1937-38 ed., pp 57-78; 1939-40 ed., pp 181-212.)

'ALL OUT'

"The natural love of our people for peace" to which the President referred in his Jackson Day speech March 29, 1941, had to be overcome before we could be brought to war It is easiest to do this on moral grounds, to show that the enemy follows outrageous, to us unfamiliar, customs, that he breaks tabus which to us seem sacred.

"So great are the psychological resistances to war in modern nations that every war must appear to be a war of defense against a menacing, murderous aggressor There must be no ambiguity about whom the public is to hate", observes Lasswell in "Propaganda Technique".

CONCEALED OBJECTIVES

The President in the same speech denounced those who "have tried to shatter the confidence of Americans in their Government". 'Government' seems in his mind synonymous with president, as it is very nearly today, as it was for Louis XIV. "L'etat c'est moi."

The venerable Cardinal O'Connell warned the same day, "The trust of the people in their Government is a dangerous thing to toy with. There is a distinct feeling that things are going on behind the scenes, unknown to the people. This is the sort of distrust that brought about revolutions in Europe—the distrust of the people in their government."

The strategic management of all the propagandists' propulsions have, however, allayed the suspicions of most and brought us to the verge of war. The technique and publicity methods by which our intellectuals have been brought to serve the purposes of the Tory crew that is ruining the British Empire is worthy of the greatest admiration. Pearson and Allen in their column, and Senator Wheeler in a radio address late in March, 1941, have given some admiring recognition, as has Garet Garrett, editorialist for the Sat Eve Post, who, Feb 1, 1941, expounds,—

"It was perfect strategy. . . . The and-America strategists who controlled the war propaganda knew better than to name their objectives in the beginning. Therefore, they advanced under such hypnotic phrases as 'measures short of war', and 'defend America by aiding the Allies', which gathered up in one emotional mass all the hatred of Hitler, all the natural feeling among us for Great Britain, all the abhorrence of war and all the hope there was of keeping the war away. On the ground they occupied they could not be attacked precisely for the reason that it was false ground. Anyone who challenged their slogans had to prove a meaning that was not literally there and one which they plausibly disclaimed. Measures short of war were to keep the country out of war. If you doubted it you were fascist, fifth columnist or appeaser."

BY EASY STEPS

At Chautauqua five years before the President had warned us that if we watched the "small decisions of each day", we could keep out of war (cf p 594) He proposed that we take the profits out of war, that we maintain our neutrality, that we modify the neutrality law in order to prevent our getting into war.

"Peace" was the objective, announced in the title of the first Eichelberger Committee. The second Committee put "defend America" in the title and 'defense' became the theme to the tune of scores of billions. "Short of war" was the apology of the President for inciting acts, but after election it was "all out".

Promoted by members of the same Committee, 170 prominent citizens signed a message urging the President in his next fireside chat to declare it "the settled policy of this country to do everything that may be necessary to insure the defeat of the Axis Powers". January 2, 1941, fifty-three, most of whom had signed the earlier telegram, sent a second telegram urging unstinted aid to Britain. They represented the extreme war group. Their signals the President has heeded.

No one may now advocate 'peace' till 'orderly processes' are brought about everywhere, till every little Hitler is put down in every country. We were led on,—the Allies will win,—we have got to hurry to get in,—there will soon be revolution in Germany,—the people are not with Hitler,—all we need to do is give Britain a little help to tide her through the winter,—she will be stronger in the spring,—fifty destroyers will save the British Empire,—and then some more.

Now the Committee, again acting as his advance agent in breaking and making public opinion, calls for convoys and recruiting in this country for foreign armies and announces, "We are opposed to appeasement" or "a negotiated peace" (*Sat Eve Post,* Feb. 1, 1941), and the President makes 'peace' sound like treason and calls pacifists "dupes of the Axis", though during the election he announced, "I am a pacifist".

England, like France, was not ready for war. It was suicide for the one, it may be for the other, but if so we all go down together We have failed to watch the "small decisions of each day".

OUR WAR

With our help the British won last time. Their victory has not benefited the world very much. All was settled at Versailles,—Germany disarmed, surrounded by armed buffer states We English speaking peoples for 200 years have been the dominant force in the world. Since the defeat of Napoleon, England has held the world in the hollow of her hands, shaping it to her own desire, building buffer states to confine central Europe, rewarding her satellites with fat empires.

Halifax recognized the responsibility of Britain for the peace of the world when September 27, 1934, he said, "We certainly have no excuse for being under any delusion as to the greatness of the contribution we ought to have it in our power to make. . . . It is no exaggeration to say that in these days, with our standards of thought and our code of international dealing, the future of the world in a very great measure depends upon us."[1]

Lord Lothian for years urged his country to leave Europe alone to solve its own problems. The leading statesmen agreed with him and the English people were all for peace. But it could not be. We interfered We are now interfering. This is our war.

THE CARROT AND THE GOAD

This art of managing men, of influencing human behavior, is the greatest of all the arts and yields the largest rewards. Ancient in its origins, it has increased in importance as technique has improved. Modern means of communication bring a flood of information through print and film and over the air to eye and ear. Control of this makes it possible to produce changes in the mental content of whole peoples over great areas in brief time Our emotional reactions and our opinions are based on the knowledge we have, which comes to us as it may have been planned by a school board, a propaganda organization, a dictator.

Events, most of us believe, are what determine all this. But few of us experience events. What we experience is our reaction to the news we receive about them. This has been carefully selected, slightly distorted, arranged to produce the effect desired by the propagandist. Such information is the soil from which grow our fears and hatreds. Let me write the songs of a people and I care not who makes the laws, wrote the poet. Let me present events through newspaper, film and radio, and I can make the people hate and fight whom I please and when, say the propagandist and dictator.

But this propaganda is only part of a whole. Fear may be so stimulated that little men, college professors, bank officers, while unconscious of it, feel a desire to join up, to get on the bandwagon. Or fear may be only slightly accented and the desire greatly stimulated,—for prestige, through association with the right group and the hope of getting a share of whatever comes to the leaders.

This hope of achieving position which insures getting a share of perquisite, privilege, prestige, pelf or plunder, may be even more powerful than fear. Acquisitiveness may be an instinct as some claim, but in any case it can be stimulated in most of us. The carrot often brings results with the donkey when the goad has failed. The man who would revolt at the thought of anything so gauche as accepting a bribe will lick the blacking off the boots of someone whom in his heart he despises, in order to get recognition in certain circles, or if he is an ambitious young attorney in the hope that a receivership or a reorganization may be thrown his way (cf p 359). In the subtle technique of influencing behavior, the adjustment of the monocle or the raising of an eyebrow may among British of the ruling class prove a more effective means of compulsion than the carrot or the goad.

NOTES

(1) "For fully sixteen years, France and Great Britain enjoyed that superiority. They had only to raise a finger to hold German revenge in check. . . . France was in a position to give a new lease of life to the Europe of 1919. . . . Neither France nor Great Britain has shown herself morally and materially fit to keep alive the Europe they themselves had created at a gigantic expense of blood and treasure." ("The Safety of France" by Pertinax, *Atlantic*, Jan , 1939)

"Three generations of liberal intellectuals had pointed the road toward a democratic collectivism which alone offered hope of abolishing poverty amid plenty and meeting the crisis of a sick capitalism in a fashion suited to the needs and hopes of the masses . . . The last leaders of the West preferred to seek economic security for their class (and, if possible, for all) by clinging to dead magic and dying gods . . Those who were summoned to risk their lives . were called to arms only in defense of what was, what had been, and what they half-knew could never be again. Under such leadership the cause they fought for was self-defeated " (Schuman, "Night Over Europe", pp 444-5)

THERE'LL ALWAYS BE AN ENGLAND

Lest the conclusion be drawn that I am not an Anglophile, not a lover of England, as I am, I here emphasize my record for nearly thirty years and thirty generations back. With William the Bastard when he came over to conquer England were Sarjents. Some still remain in Normandy. Since 1630 Sargents have been New Englanders. I have known England intimately since 1899, and from 1905 to 1914 I spent more time under the British flag than the American, coming to know the Empire in five trips round the world.

In these two poems from "Spoils, from a Crowded Life 1935", each written aboard ship after a protracted sojourn in England, it is apparent that I leaned on Shakespeare and Wordsworth. Eric Bell, Aberdeen Scotsman, old Public School boy, president of the Mathematical Association of America, now professor at Cal-tech, writes, "If 'England Farewell, 1913' was written *in* 1913, it is a most remarkable forecast. But anyone since 1900 might have seen the same—only few did."

In England during the summer of 1935 I saw through Baldwin's trickery in defeating the overwhelming vote for peace promoted by Lord Cecil, and wrote, "The sinister crew who represent the heavy industries and manipulate the puppets of the British ministry, by clever political manipulation utilized this passion for peace to perpetuate their control and increase their profits and plunder. Standing for righteousness they magnified the League to win an election. Now, rearmament and huge profits assured, they are ready to wreck the League and deliver Abyssinia to Mussolini" This was in the 1936 Handbook of Private Schools (pp 47-48). And in the 1938 edition under the title "The Wreckers" I quoted from far-sighted Englishmen who foresaw 'the desperate incompetence' of 'the crew that controls England' (pp 115 ff).

The British Empire, with all its faults and crimes, and the Pax Britannica, have been a blessing to the world But the Empire cannot last forever without change There will always be an England, but not the England of Arthur or Alfred or Harold, who were conquered. England always conquers her conquerors and of them makes better Englishmen. And drawing sustenance from English soil and blood, they are still English in America, Australia, or New Zealand And it is there that the English should be not merely defended but brought to fuller flower

ENGLAND FAREWELL, 1913

Afloat once more upon the salted seas
Where still Britannia holds the trident,
I see the long and jagged range of cliff and coast
Where thy white horses ceaseless toss their ragged manes
That long have held thy shores
'Gainst lands less happier than thine.
The coast of England dims in distance,
The rocky heights of Wales are lost in haze.
So once again, old England, 'tis good-bye,
This dear old England that my forebears bore.
Leaving, I feel the pang of blood-bond severed.

Yet shall I return again to sense
The welcome of the land that gave my fathers birth,
To feel the tie that all we English speaking know,
To feel my heart expand at all the glory
English arms have won in every clime,
To sense the beauty of this lush green isle,
To know myself of this same English breed,
To learn still more of how my heritage has come;
Again to drink the air of Devon moors,
Or dwell in thatched and oak-beamed cottage
At Clovelly, nestled in a combe beside the Cornish sea
Perhaps the same that sent forth men
With Raleigh, Hawkins, Drake,
The breed that set Spain at defiance,
Mocked her Armada, singed her monarch's beard,
Or looted galleons on the Spanish main.
Here virile virtues still breed men,
And send them forth frontiersmen of the world.
Or may I wander mid the English lakes,
That wondrous færie land of beauty,
Whose scars and meres still haunted seem
By Celtic elfin hordes, when the moon's light
Plays along the shadowed sward.
This land hath nurtured Wordsworth,
Taught him contemplation of Nature's milder moods
To voice them in sweet, simple fancies
With here a nobler granite ruggedness,
Like thy sharp scars rising above thy soft secluded vales.
Nor can I pass the Yorkshire dales
Whose springtime loveliness refutes
The tumbled, windswept barren moorlands,

Under whose brows they hide
Nor its race of men, open, broad, sincere
Concealing tender vales of sentiment.
Nor shall I miss the Surrey hills
Where Meredith, thy Cymric seer,
Learned to interpret Earth and Man
And formed his thought in verse,
And yet shall be to all philosophy a mine.
And London, sink of a vast empire,
Great treasure house of the world's spoil,
Massed hoard of superwealth and art,
The nations gave in tribute to thy power—
London will call.

I love thee, England, with a grandson's reverence.
Thou hold'st the second place in my allegiance;
And I mourn to know thy vigor failing,
To foresee the doom of thy dominion
Yet I know those same unchanging virtues
Which hereto brought thee wealth and power
Now hold you bound for younger nations to outstrip.
Oh, could you cast your shackles off
And hold your place for centuries to come
Among the nations of the earth, I should rejoice.

Time and the world have never offered
Fairer opportunities than your highbred
Now spurn in senseless apathy.
No high aims, no new ideals,
Can touch these island Pharisees.
A privileged aristocracy in medieval pride,
Incapable of breeding leaders,
Idly sees rural England crumbling to decay
And poverty festering round the pillars
Which the material greatness of the land support.

But still you sit complacently, in pride,
Holding in honor your idle landed lords
Who hog the bounteous beauties of your land
For wasteful wanton pleasures
While patient wealth creating millions,
Spawning on fitful factory industry,
Crowd monotonous long rows of tenements
In sordid sooty towns

And soak and blacken sense and soul in city slime
How can your peasantry, from the land divorced,
Lacking the sense of ownership of humblest cottage
Or tiniest plot of land they till,
In cheerless hopelessness of unremitting labor
On a scant weekly sixteen shilling wage,
Retain the virile virtues needful for a nation?

Vain hope and pride that what was once the best,
If it remain unchanged, shall still be best,—
For time moves on, is rotten ripe for change,
And other peoples taught by what you once achieved
Attain new heights of right and justice.
Privilege entrenched in medieval strength
Forces your workers in trade union bonds
To band for that should be theirs willingly,
And thus is fostered sloth and inefficiency.
How comes it, England, you who led the world
In freedom's growth, in constitutional advance,
Are sunk in sloth, while others march straight on?
You alone untouched by conquests,
Wherewith Napoleon overturned the sod
Of long established institutional privilege,
Yours were more firmly rooted by immune success
An old, mad, blind, despised and dying King,
Princes, the dregs of their dull race—
Your ruling aristocracy with arrogance unchecked,
More firmly gripped the reins of power,
Crushed the humble under burdens—
Inspired to revolt the high-spirited
Byron, Shelley, Landor.
Cant and hypocrisy stagnated morals and religion,
Your landed lords, fattened on high rents,
And scarcity of corn,—cruel with fear
As every thought of change,
Sent the panic and terror through them;
And to Tories coerced the timid
Wordsworth, Southey, Coleridge,—
Thus were such leaders lost.
A nation of traders, of the middle class,
The industrial revolution left you
Manufacturers and factory workers,
And brought new greed for gold.
So while the people sang Rule Britannia

The Britons were enslaved
By blighting home-grown tyranny.
Only one in thirty held the franchise,
The rich in Commons held their seats as private property,
The social organism seemed deadlocked.
And still you bear the curse of that smug time
Though a starved and outraged people, forced to riot,
At length broke through impregnable power
And won reform in thirty-two

O England,
Again thou art a fen of stagnant waters
And thy sons have forfeited their ancient English dower.
All are narrow, stupid, selfish men—
Save for a few clear-visioned prophets
Who with the pen invoke thy torpid brood
To break the corruscating curse conservative
Of Tory apathy that keeps thee marking time.
Prophets of Celtic, Cymric blood have sought to stir you,
But Ruskin's words were raving in your ears
And Carlyle preached work to idle, empty oafs
The serious melancholy note of Arnold
Found no responsive chord.
And Meredith, your sanest seer,
Loving his England with a love as sweet and sure and strong
As Shakespeare's, wore life proudly,—
The world for these held purport, none ye know.
Your bubble-pricking, hidden-truth-revealing Shaw,
Sincere to seriousness, you deem a mountebank,
Your Wells of deepest insight and prophetic foresight
Is but an intellectual toy to your ennui,
Your Watson cries realities in a wilderness unheard.
Thou art become a welter and a chaos,
A roaring reach of life and death,
In which dim hordes of disinherited conspire,
Multitudinous ranks of toilers labor sullenly.
Perhaps some cruel blow, perhaps invasion,
Yet may wake your latent strength,
Shake your full pride,
And stir your sluggish blood to new endeavor,—
That you may search your soul and find
Where you are wanting

But all things on this earth must pass,

Senility must follow vigor,
Dominion passes on.
So if you cannot stir yourself
To shake off old time custom,
To bring your institutions into consonance with new ideals,
If no great man can bring your torpid brood to see new light—
Rejuvenate your blood and breed—
Then may at least your aged decline be glorious,
Hailing on the newcomers in the strife,
As an old grandsire, hoar and mellow.
And may the might of this great England
In leavening thought, in bringing on the world
In future time, in other tongues reverently be spoken,
As is the glory that was Greece,
The lamp of Renaissance it was Italy's pride
To hold to light all Europe.

And in decline still shalt thou be a shrine,
A mecca for the coming peoples.
Still will proud Nature fling
The splendor of her dawns and sunsets
Upon a land of radiant beauty.
Deep rivers flowing twixt old stone mill and parish church,
Thatched, half-timbered cottages and gardens green,
Manorial mansions set mid bosomed oaks
Where sloping swards look out to sea,
Long stretches of quiet down,
Standing white and clean from the surrounding blue,—
All this shall still proclaim thy peerless beauty
And bring thee homage.

ENGLAND REVISITED, 1933

Again I tread the soil of this old England,
Again behold the pleasant country side,
Where sheltered by billowing elms or sturdy oaks
Villages stand bold upon the open wold
Or nestle in the hills, or beside sweet flowing river—
Thatched villages unchanging as the sod.
Again to let the eye dwell on these scenes,
Again to know this noblest breed of men
That from thy womb have sprung,
Men who have faced indomitable odds
With steadfast purport, clear of vision,
And changed the course of empire;

Poets whose burning lines have fired youth
To aspiration or revolt in other lands.
Again in this dear land that speaks of forebears
To tread the soil that reeks of English blood,
Shed to defend the freeman's right
Against the might of feudal lord
And right divine of king.
This sheltered land set in a stormy sea,
Whose waves beat on the feet of white chalk cliffs
And from the shore send back an intermittent roar,
To warn the envious and keep thee free
From foreign war's infection.
This dear, dear land our Shakespeare knew and loved
And sang and praised and heralded to all the world,
Where the blind Milton from his thatched cot
At Chalfonte in St Giles upheld the right of man
As more divine than might of king
This England whose champions
First shook the shackles from the slave,
Whose adventurous youth
Opened the seven seas to trade,
Whose breed has planted all the western world.
How comes it, England, that you've broke your stride,
Become a sodden laggard, lost your pride?

At Framlingham and Colchester and many another spot
An ancient feudal castle speaks of men-at-arms,
Of war and of defence in troublous times,
Stout hearts and virile men,
And stirs the heart and makes the blood run red.
The walls, yea every stone a story tells
That he who runs may read

At base the Roman work, alternate ashlar and red brick tile,
Set in cement more time resisting than the stones they hold,
The thin red tile uncrumbled with the years,
Sharp edged as when set by Roman mason slaves.
Above a Saxon course of smaller stones
Laid in the crumbling mortar of a feebler time.
But the looming mass of wall and keep
Tells of a sturdier Norman race
Who built to hold in fief their conquered realm
Against the jagged blue a broken Tudor battlement.
And in every crevice where there is a toe hold
For tiny seed or root, valerian, magenta, pink or white,

And caper and many a dainty trailing plant
With tracery enamel the crannied wall.
While overgrowth of lush luxuriant ivy, purple-berried,
Has here or there thrust destroying root
And brought to tumbled ruin a valiant tower

As are these castles, so is your social system,
Its structure of diverse racial elements
Upon a base of feudal privilege and might
Castle and custom tell the tale of conquerors
Who've held and passed but left their stamp
Upon this glorious isle.
Donjons of monopolistic greed stand staunch and firm
Upon their ancient base, defiant of every modern need,
Ignoring all humanitarian advance
That Christianity has brought the race
But there are hard-won breaches in these walls of law
That hedge hereditary rights of favorites
And pimps of former kings.
And here some fast growing tree has reft apart
With socialistic roots what once defied
Assault of arméd host and catapult.
And communistic need in many a place has thrown
A gracious mantle of green ivy over the crumbled stone,
And glorious growth and bright blossom of valiant deed,
To meet the social need, conceals the blunt injustice
Which the crumbling rubble still protects.
However grateful to our beauty hunger,
These ivy-clad and crumbling walls hold no hope,
Afford no firm foundation on which to build the future.

No heaven piercing steel constructions here shall rise,
No modern adaptations to man's needs on these shall stand
The fiefs, liens, tithes, monopolies are but the quicksand
Left from feudal times.
And though o'erlaid with boons and sops thrown in
To hold the mob in check, shall not avail
To find foundations here to build the future
You must clear away the debris of what's been
Since Rome built on the ancient British strongholds.
You must get down to the underlying flints
Which still tell the story of primitive man's
Hundred thousand years, to which this little tale
Is but a passing hour.

THE BULLETINS

These Bulletins which cover a period just short of two years, from Memorial Day, 1939, to the end of March, 1941, were stimulated by Senator Nye's speech in which he disclosed Rogerson's "Propaganda in the Next War". As the newspapers gave it little notice, it seemed imperative that something should be done to make the book more widely known. I immediately ordered and received a copy from the London publisher, Geoffrey Bles. Later on the supply was shut off.

It was late May before I could get 10,000 copies of Nye's reprint to send out to my mailing list of private school people, college presidents and school superintendents with a simple one-sheet mimeographed statement, Bulletin #1.

Since then my readers have insisted on having bulletins once a week and that has kept me reading, during my free hours from 11 P M. to 2 or 3 A M., the great quantities of material that comes to me in print, and dictating and redictating the results to secretaries in the spare moments of a busy life, while carrying on many other already previously assumed activities and responsibilities. This sloppy output has been hammered into shape, duplicated, mimeographed, lists compiled and mailed, and the resulting voluminous correspondence attended to with the assistance of eight or nine of an already occupied staff.

The Bulletins have taken up matters of domestic and international concern that seemed immediate and have attempted to present what might not otherwise have come to my readers   They have dealt with contemporary affairs, often with what now seem trivialities but which at the moment were difficult to distinguish from what was vital   Behind the noisy battles over 'peace', 'cash and carry', 'short of war', 'defense', 'lease lend', larger movements were going on dimly discerned by few"

Written often in the heat of action, confusion and conflict, these Bulletins may sometimes seem to have taken a sardonic tone "in praise of folly". The purpose, however, it is apparent, was to attract attention to what was little known or to what had been distorted or concealed, to endeavor to arrive at some understanding of what was underlying and to detect the general trend

Let no one believe that he finds here evidence of adherence to any ism. I have no belief or confidence in any ready-made panacea for human ills, though I realize that man has always sought and will con-

tinue to hopefully wish for an easy plan of salvation. But that has not
been Mother Nature's way. My scientific training, paleontological vision
and biological trend of thought leads me to always question and challenge, to search for the yet undiscovered data and when accumulated,
to formulate an hypothesis and then to welcome the critic who can
destroy it.

Consequently I have no opinions. I endeavor to observe especially
what has not been generally detected and to deduce from such observations some temporary conclusion. This is referred to as the scientific
method. It was the method of primitive man who inherited it from
his simian ancestors. Human tradition, principle and institutions have
led to distortion and corruption It is the method of the past to which
we must revert. It is the method of the future which offers the only
hope for the realization of the possibilities of the species.

Events in human affairs, aside from an occasional earthquake or tidal
wave, are the results of the acts of men who are actuated by motives,
who have immediate objectives in view. Did the man murder his wife?
The detective, the judge and the jury search first for the motive Did
the statesman embroil us in war? We don't look for motive. We may
question the motives of the child, the criminal, our inferiors. We dare
not challenge the motives of our superiors.

As yet we have little understanding of who control events and how,
and only a glimmering as to how they control the reporting of events
We must go further and understand the motives that move such. Then
we may learn something of how we get our opinions, why we believe
as we do, and why we act as we do. That is primary to intelligent, conscious control of the welfare of peoples, to the waging of war, the
maintenance of peace. But the motives of those who control are kept
covered, protected, by tabus which we dare not violate. The fear of
those who control is the beginning of wisdom,—but not the end.

In events as reported, as summarized in these Bulletins, there has
been a desire to untwist the twisted report, to understand by whom
and for what purpose the news of the events was modified.

Some of the Bulletins have been reduced to mere Notes, ephemeral
material omitted. On the whole, the Bulletins have been little edited
The Notes elaborate on cryptic statements or justify rash prognostica-
tions. Statements that at the time seemed daring now seem conservative.
Anticipations have in general been disappointingly realized.

WAR PROPAGANDA

Exposed, it's harmless. When dead, academic scholars will dissect the carcass.[1] Lasswell and Casey 1935 bibliography lists 4500 titles. Nearly all on international propaganda were published after 1932.

"Propaganda For War", by H. C. Peterson, just published, (U. of Okla Press) explains vividly the technique of British propaganda which brought us into the last war 'to save democracy'.[2]

"Propaganda In The Next War", by Capt. Sidney Rogerson, ed. Capt. Liddell Hart, published last fall by Geoffrey Bles, Manchester Square, London, 5s., describes realistically the improved technique.[3] The cynical chapter on the methods now in use in America was inserted by Senator Nye in the *Congressional Record*. We quote:

"In the next war the result will probably depend upon the U.S.",—"reaction of her public to propaganda properly applied",—"more susceptible than most peoples to mass suggestion" "Atrocity propaganda will be less effective in the next war",—Japan "more easily saddled with atrocities,—a cynical observation".

"For obvious reasons" Rogerson avoids mention of the official agencies "to coordinate propaganda, with Sir Robert Vansittart, chief diplomatic adviser to the Foreign Office, as chairman", disclosed by Chamberlain to the House of Commons, February 7, 1938.[4]

In England, Hitler is cultivated, strengthened, 'appeased'. Books and articles recently published present Germany favorably,—[5] Domville-Fife's "This Is Germany", 1939, etc [6] Unfavorably reviewed in the London *Times* are books such as Erika Mann's "School For Barbarians" [7] In America, England stimulates hatred of Germany so that Hitler values England's friendship and 'appeasement' is cheaper.

Headlines and lead paragraphs in our newspapers showed a change after Feb-Mar '39 visits to publishers by C. S. Kent, "business director" of London *Times*, just as after Northcliffe's visits in 1917.[8]

News censorship in London has been relaxed since Stalin, Mar. 11, threw the Tories into confusion and reversal of their 'appeasement' policy by ridiculing the Tory plot to embroil Germany and Russia [9]

England sends her most skilful and diplomatic to persuade America in the subtlest and most flattering ways that our cooperation is needful for the preservation of 'democracy and civilization', i.e. the British

Empire. Eden prepared the way for the parade of royalty. The Marquess of Lothian comes as 'follow-up' man.

Senators Borah, Nye, Walsh, Reynolds, Johnson, Bone; Representatives Tinkham, Casey, Holmes, and others are actively opposing British propaganda and the Administration's war policy

A 'National Committee to Keep America Out of War' organized by Congressmen aims "to counteract the inspired propaganda emanating from the White House", "check the propaganda of all foreign nations", "take the profit out of war"

British propaganda, because unsuspected, has succeeded in making us hate, in making our participation in war seem inevitable   Disclosed, it need not continue to be successful, nor war inevitable.

It is difficult to hate what you thoroughly understand
Memorial Day, May 30, 1939

NOTES

(1) Not until 1925 was the stench from the dead propaganda that brought us into the last war so strong that it attracted the attention of the academic scholars who, as Sir Gilbert Parker relates, had been the first and easiest mark of his propaganda   It was German scholars who first investigated and wrote about the war propaganda in which the British had proved their superiority.   These researches are alluded to in Lasswell's "Propaganda Technique in the World War", published in 1927, the earliest thorough-going analysis in English.   But his book remained little known and it was not until 1933 that Frederick Lumley's "The Propaganda Menace" was reviewed in the 17th edition of the Handbook of Private Schools   In the 20th edition ("How We Get Our Ideas" pp 33-40, "Why We Think So" pp 77-86) I reviewed a number of the more notable titles. O W Reigel's "Mobilizing for Chaos", J Duane Squires' "British Propaganda", Leonard W Doob's ' Propaganda, Its Psychology and Technique".

British propaganda today is very much alive, and as it gives off no stench, its existence is denied   Moreover, its importance in the last war is now decried even by writers like Walter Millis who were foremost in uncovering it.   So far has this tendency gone that late in November, 1940, the President and the N Y. *Times* simultaneously were speaking of the propaganda of the last war as a 'myth'.

That's part of the game of helping the new unseen propaganda to bring us in again as explained in the Handbook of Private Schools, 24th edition, pp 131-194 Here the subject is treated as a phase of education, the imparting of mental content in our schools and universities.

(2) Through investigations in London Peterson discovered much new material, notably "The American Press Résumé". This was prepared secretly by Sir Gilbert Parker's organization in the United States for the British Foreign Office and

Ministers "The traditional information agents, ambassadors, and consuls, naturally sent in regular reports In addition, the Morgan firm kept British officials informed as to conditions in the United States."

"Emotional appeal was made in every major section of British propaganda," writes Peterson "A most important phase of this technique was the practice of exploiting idealism. The British did all they could to identify British and American ideals and to picture German actions as attacks upon democracy—the symbol of American idealism The almost hysterical reaction in the United States to British propaganda demonstrates very clearly the effectiveness of such appeals.

"The fact that it was especially influential among the highly educated seems to indicate that learning is not an impregnable defense against appeals made to the emotions " (cf "What Makes Lives", pp 149-150)

(3) Rogerson's book was one of a series "The Next War" edited by Captain Liddell Hart written for the English people. Though Nye attracted attention to it the following spring, I didn't receive a copy until May 25, and was unable to get reprints of Nye's speech until a few days later. With all our information agencies, correspondents, newspapers, periodicals, how did it come about that these generally accepted plans for our entry into the war, promoted among the people of England, remained wholly unknown in this country and are yet but little apprehended. Captain Sidney Rogerson was in the propaganda service of the Foreign Office during the last war, but without giving away inside information he tells cynically what the English believe must be done to bring America into the next war. "The next war will be billed as a fight between democracy and dictatorship We shall almost certainly represent the struggle in the propaganda we shall be compelled to do toward France, the United States of America and our own Empire as democracy and freedom versus dictatorship and persecution.

"It will need a definite threat to America, a threat, moreover, which will have to be brought home by propaganda to every citizen, before the Republic will again take arms in an external quarrel. The position will naturally be considerably eased if Japan were involved and this might and probably would bring America in without further ado At any rate, it would be a natural and obvious object of our propagandists to achieve this, just as during the great war they succeeded in embroiling the United States with Germany.

"Of the world Jew population of approximately 15,000,000, no fewer than 5,000,000 are in the United States. Twenty-five per cent of the inhabitants of New York are Jews During the Great War we bought off this huge American Jewish public by the promise of the Jewish national home in Palestine, held by Ludendorff to be the master stroke of Allied propaganda " Writing before Hitler through his ejection of the Jews had magnified their importance, Rogerson emphasizes the necessity of winning them to the British cause, and the difficulty in view of the fact that they were fooled last time.

(4) At the time this sheet was prepared to accompany Sen Nye's reprint of Rogerson's chapter, Sir Robert Vansittart had for some years disappeared from the public print. Never widely publicized, for the head of the Foreign Office

works in secrecy, he had become an even more mysterious figure at this time. For some years I had been following the work of Sir Robert Vansittart and collecting material, part of which was published in the spring of 1940 in the Handbook of Private Schools, 24th edition, and much of which will be forthcoming in a book entitled "The Course of Human Events". (cf pp 106, 111)

(5) In their fear of Russia, the Tory element of England sought to build up the power of Germany as a bulwark against Bolshevism and to cultivate Hitler as the White Knight to save Western civilization. Hitler had many supporters and friends among the English upper classes. The group that gathered about Lady Astor for weekends at Cliveden were almost exclusively pro-German, out of which came an organization of public men and people of title known as the Friends of Germany Among these Lady Astor had long sponsored her friend Philip Kerr, later Lord Lothian. "Lothian Once Liked Hitler" was the headline of an article in the Boston *Herald,* Dec. 13, 1940, on Lothian's death. "At one time, this bitter opponent of Nazism had believed in Hitler and he even went so far as to criticize Anthony Eden for blocking the German Fuehrer's moves. . . Even before that time . it was no secret that he had felt Versailles had crushed Germany much too heavily." Lothian's regard for Germany and sympathetic understanding of Hitler is shown in his addresses and writings published in the *Round Table* and *International Affairs* from 1934 to 1938. These have been collected and published by Flanders Hall, Scotch Plains, New Jersey, 50¢.

(6) The Marquess of Londonderry, friend of Hitler, Goering and Von Ribbentrop, had visited the Reich twice in 1936 and twice in 1937, and arranged for Lord Halifax' visit in November, 1937. In his "Ourselves and Germany", in which he collaborated with Lady Desborough and Mr. G. Ward Price, he confessed, "I was at a loss to understand why we could not make common ground in some form or other with Germany in opposition to Communism".

It was easy at that time to get published in England books favorably presenting Germany,—Sven Hedin's "Germany and World Peace" (Hutchinson, 1937), George Lansbury's "My Quest for Peace" (Michael Joseph, Ltd., 1938), Rupert Croft-Cooke's "The Man in Europe Street" (Rich & Cowan, 1938), C. W. Domville-Fife's "This Is Germany", Foreword by Lord Queensborough, G B.E. (Seeley Service, 1939)

"Germany Speaks", presenting in their own words the aims, purposes and ideals of the leaders of the German government, was translated and published in England. Hjalmar Schacht, the friend of Montagu Norman of the Bank of England, wrote on "Germany's Economic Position". British propaganda in the United States at the same time was creating in the American mind the idea that these men were gangsters

In "I Loved Germany" (Michael Joseph Ltd., 1940) Sir John Evelyn Wrench writes, "Immediately before the Great War I had seen with my own eyes the steady advance of German shipping in five continents, and the mounting total of German exports in both hemispheres. Germany applied great imagination in her drive for world trade. I had talked to many British Consular officials in my travels and there was no doubt that unless Great Britain drastically overhauled her methods of salesmanship over seas she would be relegated to a secondary position in the export field. With everything in her favour it would surely be lunacy for Germany to involve herself in a world struggle But I was wrong In the years that led up to the triumph of Hitlerism I argued that Nazism was the inevitable reaction of the German people to the errors of Versailles, and that the regime was so deeply absorbed in tasks of social reconstruction that the Fuhrer would never go to war if Germany's major grievances were settled "

(7) During 1938 there was much published in England in praise of the German system of education, even expressions of over-admiration of things German and building good will for Hitler, still the White Knight Books like Erika Mann's, if reviewed or noticed in England, were deprecated, while in America they were being exploited Miss Mann's intense hatred for what's doing in Germany and especially of the 'evils' of German education is not due to direct observation as she has not been able to return to Germany for six years or more. There are many sound books by unprejudiced Americans on German education (cf Handbook of Private Schools, 21st edition, pp 88-89). A thorough-going and objective study is presented in "The Educational Philosophy of the Third Reich" (Yale University Press, 1941). The author, George F Kneller, a thirty year old Englishman, has lived in America nineteen years, studied at fourteen universities and visited Germany five times This was a Ph D thesis which made the news. Behind their present educational practice, leaders in Germany have a definite plan, vision, conception, philosophy "dominated and dictated by circumstances under which they live and must live". Circumstances geographical, economical and political make them pragmatists. Their educational philosophy was determined long before there was a dictatorship which these leaders would regard as "a temporary expedient necessitated by present conditions and pressure from without". (cf *Newsweek,* June 24, 1940, p 48)

(8) Lord Northcliffe established two principles, "First, it should be truthful, and secondly, it must always be linked to a definite policy, and whenever possible precede it", Rogerson tells us Northcliffe was "a 'news' man and his propaganda was based on hard facts, tellingly expressed, instead of appeals to history, to law, to humanity or high Heaven" (p 16) H. G. Wells, working with Northcliffe, laid out a plan to win the war by propaganda. "The design of the Allies is not to crush any people, but to assure the freedom of all on a basis of self-determination   It follows that one of the first requisites is to study and lay down the lines of a practical League of Free Nations", said Wells This not only succeeded in infecting Woodrow Wilson,—it intoxicated him,—he thought it was his own.

The Northcliffe-Wells propaganda was creative It stimulated the imagination Rather than inciting hate, it gave discontented and unhappy people a vision of freedom and greater happiness that might be achieved Few if any then recognized this as propaganda. It was a living force, just as the improved propaganda today. while it is an activating force unrecognized, is not traced back to its carefully concealed sources. We don't know that our feelings and actions have been planned in distant offices.

(9) The agreement between Russia and Germany brought about great confusion in British policy and embarrassment to the Friends of Germany. The relaxation of the censorship which brought America news before cut off was only temporary The friends of the Soviet now exerted pressure on the government, and from that time on there were spasmodic attempts to appease Stalin and form some alliance against Germany. In August the announcement of a non-aggression pact between Hitler and Stalin produced even greater confusion in the British Government policy.

BRITISH PROPAGANDA TO BRING US INTO THE NEXT WAR

Subtle, working from the top down, through President, State Department, universities, intellectuals, it is suspected by few,—we are unaware As in 1914-18 we think we are responding to our sense of right, and on high moral ground taking action against the forces of evil

April 25, 1939, Senator Nye inserted in the *Congressional Record* the chapter from Captain Rogerson's "Propaganda in the Next War", explaining the technique by which America was to be brought into the war. This went unnoticed by our press, which was still writing editorials and lead paragraphs as instructed by the British propaganda agent who had recently visited this country for that purpose

May 7, newspaper reports of a Coughlin broadcast first brought this to the attention of the public   Later in May the *New Yorker* printed a paragraph about the book, and New York newspapers reported that the book had been suppressed in England. May 25, copies of Rogerson's book were received in Boston. Senator Nye had reported only one copy was in this country.[1]   May 30, to 10,000 educators and others throughout the country, I sent out a brief bulletin and Nye's reprint of Rogerson's chapter

June 5 an editorial in the Boston *Transcript* quoted from Rogerson as printed in the *Congressional Record,* and pooh-poohed the possibility of "bamboozling the American people" as was done twenty years before. The same issue of the *Transcript* [2] carried an anonymous letter which belittled Peterson's "Propaganda For War", pointing out that its importance was "largely documentary". "It would be the height of folly to attempt to draw any close parallel between the position of the American people in 1914 with that in which we find ourselves today",—

and recommended Streit's "Union Now", which proposes in effect that we unite with the British Empire.

June Commencements—British publicists and churchmen get the headlines, repudiating 'self-sufficiency', 'mind your own business', advocating union of 'democratic' and 'spiritual forces' against the 'forces of evil' (obviously German). French bestow "Palmes Academiques" and other decorations upon school heads and college teachers.

Responses to demand for Congressional investigation:[3] Rep George Holden Tinkham, May 13—"I am wholly in agreement . . . I only wish that there could be an investigation of British propaganda in this country which, of course, is very aggressive, but quite subtle and well done Perhaps we can succeed in having such an investigation". Sen. David I Walsh, May 6—"What you say about British propaganda is unfortunately all too true and I hope sooner or later something may be done. . . . I shall continue to do what I can."—Sen. Gerald P. Nye, May 19—"Work of this kind will save us from terrible disaster,—help mightily in keeping us out of other people's wars."

John Dewey, May 29—"You are doing a unique work,—hope your material about British propaganda will receive the attention it deserves." Charles Beard, May 24—"You are doing good work on the war propaganda racket. Your very presence in this vale of tears gives me courage." *June, 1939*

NOTES

(1) There was a good deal of mystery about Rogerson's book. It was difficult to obtain. Baker and Taylor, largest New York book jobbers, reported early in June "no copies available". There was confusion and change doubtless in censorship regulations in England. In this country there was evidence of a campaign to suppress the book and to belittle the idea that there was British propaganda. Propaganda hunters were pooh-poohed by college professors, by editorial writers Consequently, it seemed necessary to send to those who had responded so cordially to my first mailing this second, which we called Bulletin #2. This was put out with no intention of continuing. But again the response was such that by June 15th it seemed essential to attract the attention of the increasing number of interested correspondents to new things that had appeared.

January 16, 1941, Baker & Taylor Company wrote,— "We wish to advise Rogerson's "Propaganda in the Next War", pub. by Geoffrey Bles, London, 1938, is not for sale in America."

(2) Much light could be thrown on American journalism by a study of the

Boston *Transcript* over the past two years With essentially the same staff, enlightened, public spirited, hard working, straining at the leash, the policy of the
paper has changed,—at times over a week-end,—first critical, then no word
against the Administration, again pointing out the danger of propaganda, later
making fun of its possibilities, and finally for Willkie and against Roosevelt.
It would seem as though orders had come from outside.

(3) In February, 1939, I wrote to a number of senators including Nye and
Walsh attracting their attention to British propaganda in this country. Early in
May again I wrote, "Can't we have a Congressional investigation of the British
propaganda in this country? It's subtle, skilful, more highly organized, technically more perfect than it was in the last war. It's so good that people don't
recognize it All they hear is the lumbering of the German propaganda machine,
and much of that is due to the skill of the British Foreign Office. The key man
is Sir Robert Vansittart But watch our new ambassador, Lord Lothian, and
Lord Baldwin (American disguise for Earl of Bewdley) Why wait, as we did
last time, to investigate after all the damage is done? I have collected a lot of
data that the magazines and newspapers will not publish" Later Senator Clark
introduced his resolution calling for such investigation, which was promptly
pigeon-holed, though repeated attempts were made to develop interest in it.
Since then we have written repeatedly to Congressman Dies, with no response,
attracting his attention to our accumulation of material on propaganda which we
offered to put at his service. The same offer made to J. Edgar Hoover of the
F.B.I. brought very polite acknowledgment,—"Please be advised that this Bureau
has no information concerning the subject matter of your inquiry." Later we
learned that this attitude of the F.B I. was due to instructions received from the
State Department, which is the right hand of the President.

PROPAGANDA FOR WAR

"Preparing Civilian America for War", by Harold J. Tobin, professor
of political science, Dartmouth, *Foreign Affairs* (pro-British) [1] July
issue, 1939, describes in detail the organization planned for a major war,
based on a "force of 1,000,000 men, capable of expansion to 4,000,000
men". This can have only one purpose,—to again smash Germany in
support of the British Empire. Public Relations Administration plans
"involve no sharp departures from World War practice". (Conscientious objectors were hung by their wrists to their cell doors, working men's
meetings raided and members herded in boiler rooms at a temperature
of 140°, for expressing unpopular opinions, prison terms of twenty to
forty years meted out to some.)

Full support of the American people is assumed. "However, in case
co-operation is given reluctantly, the Government must possess the

power to coerce." Radio[2] and motion pictures[3] will be "completely dominated". Should Congress fail to give full "war powers to the Executive immediately" the President "could broadly interpret the authority already granted". "For example, Wilson created the whole system for mobilizing industry which centered around the War Industries Board on no more authority than the Overman Act permitting the reorganization of the Executive branch."[4]

"The fear is frequently expressed that . . this Plan would inevitably create just that sort of totalitarian regime which we now so vigorously condemn." But we are comfortingly assured that provision has already been made to discontinue this system after hostilities are over.

"Civil Liberties in England" is discussed in the *Virginia Quarterly*, June, 1939, by D. N. Pritt, M.P., a barrister and member of the National Council for Civil Liberties. "In Great Britain . . . the distinctions of wealth and power are grotesque and horrible . . . economic difficulties are growing . . . so it is inevitable that the ruling class seeks to 'tighten up' and to add to the restrictions on liberty" and "can no longer run the risk of leaving economic and political agitation free to run". The Emergency Powers Act, the Trade Unions Act, the Incitement to Disaffection Act, give the government dictatorial powers. The latter makes it a crime to have in your possession any document the dissemination of which would tend to "seduce any member of His Majesty's forces from his duty or allegiance". In the year ending June, 1937, there were 320 prosecutions for opinions disliked by the government.[5]

"British News Controls", by Sir Arthur Willert, now in Washington, formerly Chief Press Officer of and for fourteen years with the British Foreign Office, in the same issue of *Foreign Affairs* that carries Tobin's article, admits with Baldwin's naive blundering frankness the "deliberate assaults upon the liberty of the press and other organs of public opinion" in England, and that " 'the censorship mind' dominates at Whitehall". Willert explains other repressive acts in addition to those enumerated by Pritt. The 1920 Official Secrets Act "hampers the use of official documents or information which might be considered confidential. Two writers of books have been prosecuted since 1920 for publishing confidential documents or information."

Explaining the extraordinary powers granted by Parliament, Willert assures us they are being used with discretion. He deprecates "the tendency of foreigners to impute to British Governments an aptitude for Machiavellian propaganda . . one of the most curious of contemparary myths". But he admits, "We were not bad at it towards the end of the Great War". With disarming naiveté, he concludes "downright political censorship" could hardly happen in Britain "even in wartime", because "British democracy" would find "means of protecting" itself.

June 13, 1939, London AP cable tentatively announced, "The British government was reported reliably today to be setting up machinery for a propaganda ministry to combat foreign propaganda and promote the British view in other countries . . . no official announcement. . . . This would be Britain's first such agency in peace time . . . There would be no peace time censorship."

June 15, London cable states Mr Chamberlain announced in Commons that "the new organization will be called the Foreign Publicity Department of the Foreign Office   to co-ordinate and extend the existing forces . . . that the Earl of Perth, recently Ambassador to Rome (and as Sir Eric Drummond, from 1919 secretary to the League of Nations while its powers were being undermined) would head the Department and that Home Secretary Sir Samuel Hoare was preparing plans for turning the Department into a full Ministry in wartime."

All these obviously frank disclosures screen the actual propaganda machine, which has been directed by Sir Robert Vansittart, since 1930 head of the Foreign Office and who, since Chamberlain came in, as Chief Diplomatic Adviser has devoted his talents to building an 'Anti-Nazi propaganda bureau for foreign countries' [6]

February 7, 1938, Chamberlain disclosed in Commons under pressure of inquiry that the Government had formed a committee "to co-ordinate propaganda, with Sir Robert Vansittart, chief diplomatic adviser to the Foreign Office, as chairman". (*Journalism Quarterly,* Dec. 1938)

October 6, 1938, during the Czech crisis, the World Press News (London) revealed that a Ministry of Information had been prepared "in shadow form", Sir Stephen Tallents, public relations director of the British Broadcasting Corporation, to be director-general

The British propaganda technique has functioned so smoothly as to change public opinion in the United States in the last two years. Without the U. S. A. or the U. S. S. R., all know that England can not possibly win in a war to again smash Germany. [7] The best of British brains are going into propaganda and no effort or expense can be too great to win America's support.

British Parliamentary appropriations for 'Secret Service' were, in pounds sterling: 1935,—178,000; 1936,—349,000; 1937,—350,000, 1938,—450,000 (Nofrontier News Service). 1938 expenditure for "censorship and propaganda" estimated at 651,654 pounds (Newspaper World, August 6, 1938). The totals are probably much larger.[8]

When in 1917 Lord Northcliffe came here to reorganize Sir Gilbert Parker's propaganda, he remarked, "They dress alike, they talk alike, they think alike. What sheep."[9] And he may well have added, "It's an easy job we have here". It was, and it is today. With better technique, the method is the same,—from the top down, President, State Department, university heads, newspaper publishers, and gradually the people. In two years since his Chautauqua speech Roosevelt has gone farther and faster than Wilson in the same time [10]

Is "American public opinion" a "cockleshell floating helplessly and unconsciously in the wake of the British man-of-war", as Professor Lasswell picturesquely phrases it?

"America and World Affairs", by Joseph Hilton Smyth, *North American Review*, Summer, 1939, tells us our foreign trade yields but 5% of our income. 95% comes from home sales For this 5% we have since the war appropriated hundreds of millions to build a merchant marine to carry that trade and we have put billions into armaments to protect that merchant marine and trade (and the British Empire). The money comes out of the worker who produces, but it leaks to those who have government contracts

Only 1% of our foreign investment is in China. "Americans owned ... 6 per cent of the total foreign investments in China in 1931, as compared with Britain's 36 per cent ... Japan's 35 per cent " (Griswold, "Far Eastern Policy of the United States", p 469) [11] (cf Bul #95)

"In 1935, on behalf of our Far Eastern policy, the United States spent $601,439,792 ... Our $750,000,000 stake in the entire Orient—of which a little more than one-fourth is invested in China proper", including missions,—is about what the American people spend annually on football and other sports (Walker Matheson, "Our Stake in the Orient", *North American Review*, Winter, 1938-39). (cf Bul #95)

June, 1939, The *Round Table*, British-American propaganda organ, until recently edited by the Marquess of Lothian, our new ambassador, in an anonymous article states, "The U. S. Government cannot give a hard-and-fast guarantee that its fleet will protect Malaya and Australasia. Public opinion will not support guarantees. But . . . there is little doubt that part of the American fleet would move into Singapore in the event of a Far Eastern threat . . . against the Dutch or British possessions in Malaya "

Lothian's skill in affecting "public opinion" may yet result in our fighting to protect British and Dutch tin and rubber monopolies and exploitation of cheap labor in Malaya   Bolivian tin and Brazilian rubber, without British interference, would supply our needs. [12]

The American fleet was sent to the Pacific, ostensibly to protect our Eastern trade, actually to intimidate Japan and prevent her joining the Axis, soon after Stalin's speech of March 11.

The Administration, through Secretary Hull, "prodded by a coterie of State Department advisers" (N. Y. *Times* dispatch, June 14, 1939) insists (*Times* dispatch, June 13) that our neutrality laws be so framed that we may without stint continue to support the British Empire.

Eventually we shall have Congressional investigations, after the damage is done   Why not demand such now to inform us what our foreign trade yields over what it has cost?—what it has cost us to support the British Empire, its trade and monopolies? [13]   The figures are astounding. We should know the present commitments of our Administration to defend Dutch and British possessions in Malaya   Instruct your Congressman how far you wish to go in continuing our support of the British Empire.

June 15, 1939

NOTES

[1] Quincy Howe, in his "England Expects Every American to Do His Duty", devotes a chapter to the British network   "The Council on Foreign Relations, organized shortly after the war, . . . illustrates . . clearly the pro-British bias of most well-to-do Americans."   It calls itself "non-partisan and non-commercial". Its membership includes "a real cross section of political and economic opinion". Its quarterly organ, *Foreign Affairs,* prints a varied assortment of articles   "But on the board of eighteen directors we encounter many of our friends of the English-Speaking Union . . . the League of Nations Association and the Foreign Policy Association" (pp 60-61).   The editor of *Foreign Affairs,* Hamilton Fish

Armstrong, "is also the author of that effective piece of British propaganda entitled 'We or They?' "

(2) Radio played a small part in the last war. In every emergency recently it has been the effective thing. "Paul F Lazarsfeld, director of the Office of Radio Research at Columbia University . . . received a grant from the Rockefeller Foundation to survey public opinion regarding radio . . . In 'Radio and the Printed Page' he reports that "in the field of foreign news and comment, radio covered about twice as many items as the newspapers'." (Quincy Howe, "The News and How to Understand It", Simon & Schuster, 1940)

"Under the present system of government supervision, wave lengths are assigned to individual stations. The radio industry lives in fear of the FCC . . . a three-man board appointed by the President", Howe explains. It "assigns licenses" which expire every six months and are renewed almost automatically Radio has greatly increased the interest in foreign news, and consequently it has become increasingly important for foreign or international propaganda. The big radio chains insist on retaining control over many of the so-called 'educational' features, like 'America's Town Meeting of the Air', which could easily be sold to a sponsor.

"Rockefeller and Morgan money provided most of the original financing for the National Broadcasting Company, owned by the Radio Corporation of America which makes radio sets. NBC also ties in with General Electric and Westinghouse, each of which owns a station David Sarnoff [is] chairman of the board of NBC and president of RCA. . . . The other directors of NBC, however are better known for their industrial and banking connections. They have an educational expert in the person of ex-President James Rowland Angell of Yale, who belongs to the great tradition of academic conservatism " Columbia Broadcasting System has as directors representatives of General Electric, Brown Bros. and Lehman Bros , as is evidenced by its news commentator, H V Kaltenborn Mutual Broadcasting System is dominated by Bamberger and Macy.

(3) How the movies are used to turn peace loving peoples to haters, to create that kind of 'idealism' which prepares the way for the top sergeant to stimulate the bloodlust of youth to get the bayonet into the other fellow, is made clear in the review of the subject in the "American Yearbook," 1940.

A vivid documented account of how the movies have been debased is given by Winifred Johnston in "Memo on the Movies, War Propaganda 1914-1939" (Cooperative Books, Norman, Oklahoma, 1939). "For almost twenty-five years the screens of the world have been filled with pictures of hate For twelve years the real issues have been ignored and evaded by a censorship which bans all treatment of 'social, political, or economic problems'. .

"Motion picture history from 1914 to 1939 becomes understandable only when its incidents are considered as a series of moves in this deadly game." When "the last group of pictures begins to appear depicting the villain for the people to hate, the interests back of the industry are usually on their road to war."

With a domestic revenue of over a billion dollars, the movies are big money even to the big bankers   During the last war, the Chase National Bank, Standard Oil, and the Rockefeller-controlled American Tobacco Company, as well as the Du Pont interests got into the game

(4) For the enormous expansion of the president's powers in the last twenty-five years, see "The President, Office and Powers" by Edward S Corwin (N. Y. Univ. Press, 1940)   (cf also Buls #38 and #94)   "Taken by and large", says Corwin, "the history of the Presidency is a history of aggrandizement, but the story is a highly discontinuous one.   Of the thirty-one individuals who have filled the office, only about one in three has contributed to the development of its powers"   The character of the incumbent has been more important than his party affiliation

The President in declaring a state of emergency in the fall of 1939 granted himself large additional powers but modestly termed it a "limited" emergency   The law which grants him these emergency powers makes no question of "limited" emergency

How completely we are mystified and fooled by the President is illustrated by persistent rumors in Washington in December that the President would, after his return from inspection of the "Caribbean fishing stations" (Boston *Herald*, Dec 9, 1940) declare an emergency that would give him war powers

Uncensored, Dec 14, 1940, points out that "the U. S is now living in an emergency declared by the President on September 8, 1939   The emergency is not 'limited', as the President told newsmen it was on the day of its declaration   The word 'limited' did not appear in the official proclamation.   Legally speaking, there is no such thing as a 'limited' emergency.   The President possesses all emergency powers short of certain powers reserved for him in war, or for a time when war is imminent.   Among his present powers, is the authority to issue executive orders regulating the movement of 'any vessel, foreign or domestic, in the territorial waters of the United States,' and to 'take possession' of such vessel in order to secure U S rights.   This sweeping authority is conferred by the so-called Espionage Act of June 15, 1917, which was cited when the President first issued his 'Proclamation of National Emergency'   The act was designed to cover occasions when the U. S. was neutral as well as when it was at war

"If this power should be invoked, the German and Italian vessels presumably would not be commandeered and handed directly to Britain or Canada—which could be called an overt act of war.   A degree of finesse would be employed. The foreign ships would replace U. S. ships on coastal, inter-coastal and hemisphere runs   Then U. S ships would be sold for trans-Atlantic service.

"A less cautious prediction is that the U. S. Navy might convoy cargo ships half-way across the Atlantic where they would be met by British warships.   In Washington they remember that in the course of the press conference at which the President spoke of a 'limited' emergency, he also startled newsmen by saying that U. S territorial waters extended 'as far as our interests required.' "

(5) A brave show of maintaining civil liberties has been kept up in the House of Commons and at Hyde Park Corner, but with increasing fear of German in-

vasion only in those show places   Popular indignation rose to great heights against the house to house questioning instigated by Duff Cooper to test British loyalty   Twenty thousand foreigners were swept into alien camps, against the protest of H. G Wells and others   In his book "War by Revolution", quoted by *Life* (Dec. 2, 1940), Francis Williams, former editor of the Laborite *Daily Herald,* suggests that some of these Central Europeans be released and trained as a Fifth Column to sabotage the Central Powers.

(6) Sir Robert Vansittart is one of the most mysterious but "behind the scenes" influential personalities in recent British history.   As head of the Foreign Office for twenty years, he more than any other was responsible for formulating Britain's foreign policy.   When Chamberlain became Prime Minister in 1937, Vansittart was given the important task of organizing and coordinating British propaganda in America, then disappeared from the public prints.   Something of the subtle skill with which he re-educated Americans, changing their opinions and attitudes in the course of three years, is told in "What Makes Lives" (pp 154-164).   Sir Robert Vansittart, hard bitten, cynical, may well sit back complacently and smile as he contemplates American hysteria rising as in 1917 and say to himself, "I planned it that way".   With Churchill's accession Vansittart, having accomplished his great task and with lessened responsibility, again appears in the press with a poem expressing hatred at the disloyalty of the French.   Dec. 2, 1940, the short waves brought his voice.   "His theme was that the war of 1939 was no more an accident than those of 1914, 1870, 1866, 1813, or even the wars which Charlemagne fought.   From German historian Treitschke to Nazis Von Schirach and Dr. Ley all Germans believed in their divine right to rule, according to Vansittart, who never changes his British-Isles attitude, and views continental Europe merely as a British impediment."

(7) This seemingly rash and forehanded prognostication was based on knowledge of the great effort and expense to which the British Foreign Office, policy maker for the Empire, was going to enlist the sympathy, interest and later participation of the United States.   As soon as they were aware that their long cultivated plans for embroiling a strengthened Germany with a weakened Russia had fallen through, the task of bringing the U. S to the support of the Empire became all important.   However, this was not generally recognized in America until late in 1940 when on their return from England both Ambassador Kennedy and Lord Lothian made it clear that without U. S. help England could not win. (cf Bul #93 and Notes)

(8) Even more closely guarded than the organization and personnel of a government's propaganda is the amount of money available to them   It will be many years after the war, not until those active write their memoirs, that detailed information will be revealed   They who are about to die sometimes confess the truth

(9) Later Northcliffe in England and Sir Gilbert Parker, too, remarked that the Americans were more gullible than any people except the Chinese. And Americans, especially in our universities, continue to prove it.   That we are sheeplike, we put proudly another way.   We pride ourselves on doing as others do, keeping

up with the Joneses, being in fashion, doing it promptly and keeping up to date And we are urged by our leaders to conform. The mob is incited to suppress minority and dissident opinion and our great leaders call for unity of thought

"Our bankers, 'small town boys who made good,'—our diplomats, North Carolina 'tar heel' or Tennessee mountain feudist,—our statesmen, former cattle rustler or silver miner,—all are good at the great American game of poker. So to them the international game looks easy. Such naive confidence makes these idealistic optimists easy picking. The easy mark for the gambler is the man who has made easy money The gambler never gambles He doesn't have to. He has a sure thing Europeans generally look on America as a land of easy money. While they were working at the old diplomatic game, gaining political experience, we have been busy pioneering, and making easy money in the exploitation and waste of a new continent. We immigrants before we came over were the politically unsuccessful,—that's why we left,—the discontented, the nonconformist, the indentured servant, the outcast, that the older countries threw off to make for them the new Unsophisticated colonists and emigrants we Americans still seem to the English and French The politically successful stayed behind and bred their kind, the politically experienced. The financiers and statesmen of England come from that line" This is quoted from "America the Gullible" planned for publication next year in "The Course of Human Events" (cf also "What Makes Lives" pp 145-6)

(10) This back-sliding 'pilgrim's progress' of the President up to the year 1938, chronicled in Hubert Herring's "And So To War", is continued in the introduction to this present book, "Getting U S Into War".

(11) Our stake in the Orient has been enormously exaggerated by those who are interested in their own investments, ship's subsidies, protecting British interests, a deception which has cost the American people billions, as enlarged upon in Bulletin #95 and Notes

(12) Robert Aura Smith, in "Our Future in Asia" (Viking, 1940), tells us that Bolivia in 1937 exported only one-third the amount of tin the U. S. uses and adds that if the British tin syndicate had not need of the Bolivian ore to mix with the Malayan to facilitate the process of smelting, it might have been even less. Enrique de Lozada, formerly a member of the Bolivian diplomatic staff and now a professor at Williams, points out that the idea that Bolivian tin ore could not be smelted without mixing with the Malayan is a myth.

In 1935 an investigation by the U. S. Congress proved that Bolivian tin could be successfully smelted and refined without mixing. Patiño controls the Bolivian product though there are many independent producers. He is a member of the international tin pool. All Bolivian tin ore is shipped to Liverpool for smelting with Malayan ore So all refined tin that is shipped back to the U. S pays an extra profit to the British. But American industrialists who use tin, American Can and others, are holders of stock in the British pool while the Patiño and British interests are shareholders in American Can and similar companies. So none except the impotent American consumer and the independent Bolivian producers are interested in American smelting and cheaper tin for America.

During the fall of 1940, Patiño spent much time in New York and Washington There was much activity and rumor of American smelters being established. December 9, Paul Mallon reported from Washington, "Construction of a tin smelter has been held up by a row over what kind of a smelter it is to be. The Jones group in RFC wants a small and cheap one. The War Department has been trying for two months to get a synthetic rubber project started, involving construction of 10 plants Their plaint is that the price could be reduced within reason by such large scale operations and the plants could be built in a year and a half. The project has been held up in RFC " Just how the British tin monopolists control our State Department in such matters, it would be interesting to know. (cf Bul #95 re: embargo on scrap iron to Japan) (The RFC has plenty of money,—if it isn't inimical to British interests)

(13) Some idea of the billions that it has cost the American people to support the British Empire, of the wealth that has been taken out of America to maintain the British way of life among the upper classes, (and do they know how to live! thanks to India) of the contributions we have made to restore and reconstruct the devastations caused by the failure of their diplomats, may be learned by consulting Leigh's "Conscript Europe" and Cless' "11th Commandment".

BRITISH PROPAGANDA 1939

"Britain Woos America", the latest timely Bulletin, June 10, 1939, of the Institute for Propaganda Analysis, reviews Captain Rogerson's "Propaganda in the Next War" at some length. "The British would probably like the United States to repeal the Johnson Act, to amend—if not repeal—the Neutrality Act.[1] Britain would like to borrow from us and to buy munitions from us, and it can do neither if those acts remain in force."

Duff Cooper, *Herald Tribune,* May 17, claims the royal visit was due. to fatigue,[2] for rest and recreation, not propaganda. The Institute points to the connection of Munich, rearmament, and the royal visit. "When they came, propaganda came with them. Nor will it leave when they do "

H. L. Mencken, in the *Baltimore Sun,* in an editorial on "The Third Term Campaign,"—"Their Britannic Majesties . . . did not come unaccompanied, but brought along a formidable entourage of high-pressure lovers of humanity, and others were already at work in Washington. While King George suffocated in his heavy English underwear . . there were plenty of confidential conferences out in the garage . . . all based on the theory that when, as and if the war comes at last, the United States will do its duty. . .

"If the Russians can be roped by the Moral Allies, war will become a possibility at any moment, and the English will probably be able to choose the time for it. It is hard to imagine them overlooking, in that event, the domestic convenience of their American friends, who in any case will have to find the money for the show. If they can do anything to keep Roosevelt and company in power, they will undoubtedly do so."

A Washington financial service reports, "Publicity keynote just now" of Administration "is world affairs, 'foreign devils' . to distract public attention from domestic issues and failures.   They call it 'good strategy'. You must look behind the publicity front . . . to motives. Otherwise government manipulates your thinking."

Roosevelt immediately after the Royal visit "insisted" on his kind of a neutrality law. June 20 he made this "must" legislation. We "must" be ready to bring aid and comfort to our British cousins   We used to have a name for it. Ambassador Page, who worked with Lord Grey to bring us into the last war, has been accused of treason.   But Ambassador Kennedy, because of his Boston Irish background supposedly proof against English influence, has been even more completely captured.[3] Earl of Bewdley confers (*Newsweek*, June 19) LL D from Cambridge University.   Other LL.D.'s have been bestowed by the Universities of Bristol, Dublin, Edinburgh, Manchester, Liverpool and Oxford.

A joint resolution for "genuine neutrality", "impartial treatment of all belligerents" was introduced by Congressman Tinkham, May 15, 1939   This is the policy that kept Holland and the Scandinavian countries out of the last war and will keep them out of the next, again to their profit.[4]   Tinkham charges that Roosevelt and Hull "are now committing acts of political intervention in Europe which are wholly unneutral, and at the same time, for purposes of their own, have brought great fear of war to the U. S".   "Without reason and without intelligence", with "abusive and threatening language, vilification, and aggressive and hostile acts", they are "encouraging and promoting war "

War Insurance Bill, an Administration measure introduced by Rep Bland of Virginia, (N Y. *Times* dispatch, June 17, 1939)—"This insurance would cover war risks on American vessels, their cargoes, their crews, and 'foreign' vessels 'engaged in the foreign or domestic trade of the United States', as well as their cargoes and crews."   This means that the American taxpayer will recompense any owner of whatever nationality for his boats and cargoes sunk or injured in carrying munitions, and seamen injured would receive benefits up to $5000 each.

Japan "could not have fought the war against China at all without American scrap iron and munitions paid for out of the silk trade" (John T. Whitaker, Boston *Transcript,* June 18, 1939). The British, too, refuse to cease their profitable trade with Japan.

Tientsin—William H. Stoneman cables from London, June 17, "What the British actually will dare to do if the Japanese force the issue, will depend upon how much co-operation they can expect from the United States." Gen. Hamma, Japanese commander at Tientsin, AP June 19, says British reprisal "will be worthless unless America co-operates". Chamberlain, AP June 19, said Britain was maintaining "close touch with the French and American Governments".

In Singapore a great meeting of all naval commanders of the East is now on. The American fleet has not been reported since it passed the Panama Canal. Lothian (see Bul #3) expects Singapore to be its headquarters. Where is the fleet? Is the news censored?

"General Semantics and Propaganda", (*Public Opinion Quarterly,* April, 1939) by Dr S. I Hayakawa of the University of Wisconsin,— The primitive habit of mind which, satisfied with verbalizations, responds emotionally to words that have been surcharged with prejudice, is the result of a "complete conditioning". The words bring a definite reaction. "Hun" arouses hate "Jew" stirs prejudice. "Flag" brings cheers.

> "And others, when the bagpipe sings i' the nose,
> Cannot contain their urine for affection,
> Mistress of passion, sways it to the mood
> Of what it likes, or loathes."

"Such 'unconditional responses' are not sane." It is the purpose of the propagandist to produce this type of insanity,—to condition us to step on the gas whenever the green light shows, even if another car is in the path.

Millions are being spent on propaganda to influence American opinion, to bring us to the support of the British Empire.[5] Of the world's earnings 40% is being put into preparation for destruction. There is a huge margin of profit for some. You would not condone it if a large investment had not been made in propaganda to create hatred. You can't hate what you understand.

John D. Rockefeller, Jr. is circulating Harry Emerson Fosdick's sermon suggesting "that we do good to those who hate us". Instead "we ape the enemies we hate". "Jesus' ethic is preposterous" to those who want "their own prestige, personal or national, their gain and profit, their vengeance even, or their private conquest".

If you wish more and later bulletins on this subject, write.[6]

June 23, 1939

NOTES

[1] Ways have been found around both the Johnson Act and the Neutrality Act to get money to the British, and the President has proved clever in creating money where there was none. He wishes a decree that we shall pay some billions more to the British and Jewish owners of South African gold mines for the product of their indentured black labor and immediately announces a profit on the gold already on hand   From that stabilization fund he has now assigned through banker Jones, who finds that China like Great Britain is "a good risk", 50 millions to China and 50 or 60 millions to Argentina, accompanying this paper money by some Export and Import Bank money

But the real products, munitions and trucks, that these countries get in exchange for that money, will require real labor and sweat in mine and blast furnace and mill. The manufacturers will be paid in real money and it is the taxpayer who will pay them with the result of real labor   Such matters do not concern our great President. With a wave of his hand, he bestows an additional 2 billions on Great Britain denouncing his wife's project of donating cash as banal Removing the dollar sign, he takes us now to higher spiritual realms, but after all the munitions are only to be lent or leased he assures us.

[2] Duff Cooper did not increase his own popularity or that of the royalty in his addresses during his extended tour of the United States

[3] The English influence to which Kennedy was subjected was that of Chamberlain, Lady Astor, and their set who could see how disastrous war would be and wished to preserve England from catastrophe. After Munich, Chamberlain got the jitters and guaranteed Poland without any means of making good. Lloyd George denounced this as impossible of accomplishment. When Roosevelt's influence had undermined the Chamberlain policy, the war mongers came in Kennedy, loyal to his chief, Roosevelt, still sought to conciliate and save   Since his return in the fall of 1940, he has been "helping the President keep out of war". Our apologies go to Mr. Kennedy for misunderstanding his attitude

[4] Some college professor with hackles rising will moronically reply that this policy did not save Holland and Scandinavia this time. He, impressed with the morality of the British raj, will give no credence to the evidence that the British in self defense were about to occupy these countries   If they were not, they were stupid   They had not hesitated to so protect Belgium in 1914, and again in 1940. Fortunately, it has not been necessary so far for either Great Britain or Germany to completely occupy America to protect it

(5) "Beware British Propaganda" by Porter Sargent, Harvard *Progressive*, Cambridge, Nov, 1939, reminds how Robert Bacon changed public opinion twenty-five years ago, and the part Presidents Roosevelt, Conant and Seymour have played to bring us from "never again" to "it's inevitable", not as the result of events but because of the way they have been interpreted.

"Watch British Propaganda" by Porter Sargent, *Common Sense*, Nov., 1939, describes the effective propaganda machine that brought us into the last war, Lord Milner's "kindergarten", and how Vansittart and Lothian with a great staff of lecturers and journalists are changing public opinion today

(6) The responses that were received at this time to these Bulletins surprised me. The following were enclosed with Bulletin #4 and these in turn encouraged others to write. There was no intent to continue but as intensity increased and some formerly open minded closed up and supporters fell away under pressure, it became encouraging to those who stood fast to hear from others.

Raymond Pearl, June 20, 1939—"The Bulletins on propaganda are grand! Keep it up. . . . What of a word on local aid and comfort to British propaganda arising from desire to perpetuate Roosevelt dynasty?"

Alfred M. Bingham, *Common Sense*, June 20, 1939—"On British propaganda to line us up in a coming war . . we should have our eyes open to what is going on, so that if we make a choice it will be as nearly a free choice as possible."

Gerald P. Nye, June 15, 1939—"Your follow up . . interested me more than a little. How I wish there were more like yourself helping people to see with clarity the one way open to America in these times."

David I. Walsh, June 9, 1939—"I commend you for the good work you are doing on the question of neutrality."

E. A. Ross, June 17, 1939—"Exceedingly good stuff. . . . I feel about the British endeavor to entrap us into another war to preserve the British Empire just as you do. I was in Australia for 15 weeks last spring and summer and was much entertained to see the way in which the British Garrison handled the Australian newspapers so as to make them think that all that happens in this country are lynchings, crime, race riots, labor troubles, and divorces. Every Australian I met who had been in this country was amazed at the contrast between what he saw and what the Australian newspapers—deriving their American news through British channels—had led him to expect"

Harlow Shapley, June 14, 1939—"You have quite thrown my mind off of your observations on things academic by including with your letter of June 12 a page on 'War Propaganda'. . Keep your scratchy pen flowing down the groove where the fox-hunting English are again attempting so actively to trick their leading trade rivals—the American merchants and mariners. . . I am not much prejudiced against the English and their present activity in the interest of the British Empire, but I am continuously annoyed at the apparent blindness of the American public. The newspapers, of course, are bribed, and perhaps not with money—the worse luck!"

E A Hooton, June 18, 1939—"Read with the greatest interest your bulletin on British propaganda. I am pro-British by education and by taste, but my Anglophilia is wearing thin British national behavior seems to reach a new low day by day. Undoubtedly you are doing a public service by bringing out these bulletins "

Most Americans, like myself, are Anglophile by association and tradition. But the term is more often applied today to those on whom the propagandists of the British ruling class have put something over, so that they have become bootlicking traitors, as was our war time Ambassador to England, loyal not to England or America, but to the wrecking crew that flattered him

"The English people are sound. . . . But what has been done to England in these last hundred years, and more especially in these last twenty years since the World War is mortal sin . . this system of privilege and protection and preference. . ." (Douglas Reed, "Disgrace Abounding", Jonathan Cape, 1939)

BRITISH PROPAGANDA AND AMERICA'S FOREIGN POLICY

The propagandists' best trick is to shift attention from the economic to a moral basis A moralistic people, our hate is easily aroused.[1]

"Our Foreign Policy" was discussed before the Economic Club, New York, March 22, 1939. James P. Warburg, admitting that "in all our thinking about foreign policy we are influenced, consciously or unconsciously, by emotions of terrific force," still believed, "the nature of the struggle which is going on in the world today—though probably economic in origin—transcends the mere matter of territorial or economic adjustment It has become a struggle of conflicting theories "[2]

John Foster Dulles, senior member of the law firm Sullivan and Cromwell, trustee of many foundations, counsel to the American Peace Commission at Versailles, 1918-19, Member Reparations Commission, 1919, author of "War, Peace and Change", (Harper, 1939) warned

If we go into war, "it will be because we have caught the war fever. . . . Every pretext has been availed of to arouse by provocative words the emotions of the American people. . . . We talk only . . . of 'sanctity of treaties', 'law and order' and 'resisting aggression' . . . which are always used by people who desire to hold their position intact, without concession to the inevitable requirements of change . .

"If our policy were based upon a genuine understanding of the causes of the present crisis and was intelligently designed to achieve a world order whereby recurrent crises might hereafter be avoided", demand for action might be justified

"Unfortunately this prerequisite to affirmative action seems . . . to be non-existent. . . . I do not find in our public opinion, official or private, any comprehension of the true nature of the problem. Our reactions seem to me to be impulsive and emotional, wholly lacking either that intellectual content or that idealism which alone would justify the risks which would be involved . . .

"The goal of our policy seems to be to regain the power to make over again the same mistakes." We should not go into war to "repress a revolt which the policies of the democratic powers have made inevitable, and which a continuance of those policies will make recurrent".

Senator Burton K. Wheeler foresaw: "If the U. S gets into another world war, we will come out . . . with an absolute loss of democracy.

"France and England . . . having refused to make concessions to what was then a democratic Germany . . now say, 'We want you to save us again'. There will be terrific propaganda in the United States of America to get us into that war. It isn't a fight between dictators and democracies over there at all. It is an economic fight, a fight over trade opportunities. It isn't our fight. I am not so worried about the loss of our exports as I am about the loss of our sanity."
August, 1939.

NOTES

(1) As if to justify this, Presidents Seymour and Conant sounded off at the opening of the academic year 1939-40 on the note morality and religion (cf Bul #16), which was taken up in academic centers of less prestige and soon was chorused up and down the land It was as if the program outlined by Rogerson was being guided by some central agency The alumni, led by the most prosperous with Wall Street or Washington-Whitehall connections, came rapidly. It took more time for the faculty to realize how their trustees and foundation directors stood and to learn which side their bread was buttered on, but by the fall of 1940 they were worked up to a proper moralistic state of hysterical hate. By mid-winter the undergraduates were coming rapidly, but some of them were still only half-baked

(2) The propagandist must always accent ideologies. It's the evil in other men coming out on the surface that he combats He does it for their good. We don't hate the Germans until we get a little scared that we can't lick them At first it is only their vicious beliefs, later their gangster leaders, finally it's every blessed Hun whom we would exterminate. The sequence is always the same It's the reverse of how our theories, ideologies, philosophies of democracy or morality or whatnot are formed Man behaves in certain ways. We observe the acts of others We are envious, jealous, or don't approve We formulate codes Soon

we have an ideology of society or a code of morality or a system of theology. We have to have a basis for excusing our acts and condemning others. An ideology, a philosophy, a theology is a kind of screen, a camouflage It enables us to adopt a superior attitude.

BRITISH PROPAGANDA RESULTS

Now we know what Roosevelt meant when, bidding his Georgia friends farewell last spring, he uttered the startling and cryptic "I'll be back in the fall if we don't have war" By telephone he had learned from Kennedy England would be ready for war late in the summer.[1]

Since that time it has been the part of our administration, working with the British propagandists to prepare American opinion to bring every aid and comfort to Great Britain by "measures short of war",— the same measures which gradually, inadvertently, unintentionally brought us into the last war. Not entirely successful with his policies in this country, Roosevelt has turned his attention to foreign power politics, which wrecked Wilson.[2]

It was in March, after Stalin in his speech before the Soviet Congress laughed at the Tory plan of embroiling Germany and Russia,[3] that Chamberlain's appeasement policy was abandoned. The Tory group that runs England had been strengthening Hitler hoping he would weaken Stalin British policy since 1919 has been to destroy the growing strength of Russia.

The "Influence and Power of the English Upper Classes" and those who control imperialist foreign policy are revealed by Karl H. Abshagen in his "King, Lords and Gentlemen", (Heinemann, London, 1939). Intimate sketches of the imperialists and propagandists, Lothian, Lloyd, Vansittart, are here given for the first time in print.

British propaganda under Vansittart has used the best brains and unlimited money, and every articulate hater that can be enlisted. For two years it has been directed toward arousing our emotions, our sense of righteousness. Roosevelt has come to the British point of view more rapidly than Wilson His ambassadors, Kennedy and Bullitt, have worked more effectively for the British and French than Wilson's Page and Bacon

H. G Wells in "The Fate of Homo Sapiens", just published, doubts if "the President and Mrs Roosevelt . . . these two fine, active minds have ever inquired how it is they know what they know and think as they do.

They have the disposition of politicians the world over to deal with 'made' opinion. They have never inquired how that opinion is made."

To "see it through" Britain needs our resources of men and money as never before. It's the task of Great Britain's propagandists to make us believe that we should fight to prevent a United States of Europe.

Once we are in, there will be nothing to prevent American and British troops going through Holland and Belgium, their neutrality already violated by British planes. Russia, willing to see Great Britain weakened, cannot afford to see Germany too much humbled. To put down this rebellion against the imperialistic democracies which have so long prevented a strong Central European economic union, we may have to fight Russia, too. Turkey, its boundary marching a thousand miles with the Soviet, will listen to the voice of Stalin. Japan is already making advances to renew her old alliance with England So again American troops may be invading Siberia with the Japanese as twenty years ago.

Prof. Carl Friedrich of Harvard in his "Foreign Policy in the Making", (Norton 1938), suggested the world had already embarked on a new Thirty Years War.[4]

Does the Administration realize what it is taking us into?
September, 1939

NOTES

[1] A year and a half later, just returned from two weeks in the Caribbean, the President in bidding farewell at Warm Springs to ninety polio patients with whom he had had a turkey dinner, again ominously said, "I hope to be down here in March if the world survives".

[2] Josephson in his introduction to "The President Makers" points out the "historical parallels" in Wilson's and Franklin Roosevelt's administrations. The New Freedom, like the New Deal, stemmed from the Square Deal of Theodore After a time the first two bogged down Simultaneously the House of Morgan was at a low, in the first case after the Pujo money trust investigation, in the second following the Nye munitioneering and profiteering investigation. Moreover, in both periods the British Empire was threatened by a strengthening Germany In both cases a frustrated and blocked president needed a spending program to unite his party and the country and to bribe the recalcitrant money brokers with profits. And again there was a Germany to smash. At both periods the solution was war. (cf p 57)

[3] As early as January, 1939, *Dynamic America* reported, "Soviet trade with Nazi Germany grows steadily in volume and the number of trade attachés in the

Berlin Amtorg is reported quadrupled . . Cynics are beginning to raise their eyebrows and speak of a coming Nazi-Soviet rapprochement "

(4) In the writing of this book Friedrich saw contemporary events in Europe as part of a great world pattern of change.   Later in common with other members of the faculty of the great universities and especially Harvard which is used by the pro-British and financial powers as a spearhead to get us into war, he succumbed to the pressure from Whitehall and Wall Street and has become one of the most conspicuous exhibitionists among the hysterical   This shift was perhaps the more necessary for him who came to this country as a visiting German student after the last war and now has to make good as an American

BRITISH PROPAGANDA: PROGRESS REPORTS

The *Round Table*, founded by British imperialistic members of "Lord Milner's Kindergarten", edited until recently by Lord Lothian, our present ambassador, is apparently a scholarly quarterly devoted to the interests of the Empire   "America and the World Crisis" in the September, 1939, issue which has just arrived, makes clear how far America disappointingly still fails to meet the requirements of one of the Commonwealths of the British nation.   Ostensibly written from America by an American, one can imagine Lothian writing or supervising it just before he left for America to present himself as ambassador propagandist   It reveals that though we are gauche, inexperienced, we have something the British value.

"If war is actually precipitated, President Roosevelt will call a special session of Congress . . . and will seek the practically guaranteed repeal of the arms embargo .   . The full economic, industrial, agricultural resources of the United States would then be at the disposal of Great Britain . . . though perhaps on a 'cash and carry' basis . . .

"How, when, or whether the United States would actually be drawn into the conflict is, naturally, a question that cannot be answered, but if one is estimating the probabilities they are that the history of 1914-17 would be foreshortened and repeated . .

"The neutrality law is a sort of fiction, not applicable at present . . . almost certain to be repealed by the time it could legally be applied

"The American people   . are emotionally unneutral, far more so than in 1914   But they also are against sending an expeditionary force abroad.   Therefore the precise pattern of participation might be very different from that of 1917, but it might be none the less effective   . .

"The drive for a new neutrality law was deplorably mismanaged by the Administration.   A dozen minor 'ifs' might have altered the result. The fight . . . was in the hands of Representative Sol Bloom. Had almost any other Democrat been in the post the revisions of the Neutrality Act might well have gone through Congress Now, how did Sol Bloom get on this important committee, anyway?" And the author tells "an American political anecdote" which "perhaps readers will not object to".

How unsatisfactorily to the British we are running our affairs is thus made clear   Apparently there is every reason for 'union now',—they could do it so much better for us.   Furthermore, America at times shows a traitorous tendency to keep its plans secret from Downing Street and Whitehall until they have been already acted upon

When a resolution was introduced by "Senator Vandenberg, one of the Republicans who voted against action on the neutrality law", to denounce the 1911 U S. trade treaty with Japan, "President Roosevelt and the State Department, not willing to let a Republican get ahead of them, speedily . . . gave notice of termination of the 1911 treaty. They did not even let Downing Street know ahead of time . . . News cables . . . carried   British disappointment at not having been forewarned."[1]

Termination of the treaty "was a purely executive act . . . but the Senate beamed approvingly .   a shamefaced reaction from the prior refusal to act on neutrality. It gave Senators a chance to approve the line of action which they had just blocked but in which they really believed "

No blame, however, is attached to Roosevelt and Hull   "It is important to record that President Roosevelt and Secretary Hull were not trying to startle the British. They were trying to be helpful . . . Thus is the United States doing her bit, taking care of her assignment, in the informal and unofficial alliance of the democracies . . .

"The late unlamented session of Congress was completely rebellious." But "whatever President Roosevelt's domestic difficulties, he can count on rising at least a little way above them when he operates with a sure touch in the foreign field . . . The party struggles that have so damaged President Roosevelt's domestic prestige need not necessarily block his foreign program."

Of the royal visit, "a much pleasanter subject", the author says, "Its effects remain as an important factor operating upon American public opinion toward the world problem today

"Never has a ceremonial visit gone more satisfactorily . . . British policy and in a sense Great Britain itself were rather under a cloud in American eyes. The abdication crisis . . . Mr. Chamberlain's policies . . . Sir John Simon's tenure of the Foreign Office in 1932" combined to create a "composite picture . . . in which the British 'ruling classes' came off very poorly indeed.

"The King and Queen almost completely reversed this picture . . . Americans saw that they should amend their judgments about the abdication crisis. Viewing the queenliness of the Queen, they realized what unspoken motives had been involved in the British decision . . . In sum, the royal visit may be said to have rehabilitated British character in American eyes. And that is no small achievement . . .

"Nothing was overdone about the trip . . . The absence of all outward propaganda efforts was entirely correct. All the same, Great Britain got more propaganda, more favorable publicity, spread over the United States than she has had since 1918."[2]

International Affairs, published bi-monthly at Chatham House by Royal Institute of International Affairs, which announces itself as "an unofficial and non-political body, founded in 1920 to encourage and facilitate the scientific study of international questions", in the May-June issue of 1939 carries propaganda articles by Lionel Curtis on "World Order" and by Lord Lothian on "The United States and Europe".[3]

Publication of a *Foreign Affairs Memorandum* which provides the "most complete study of the European situation available" has been inaugurated by the Imperial Policy Group, 13, Old Queen Street, Westminster, London, S.W.1, headed by Lord Phillimore.[4] "Completely independent . . . unofficial and free from all restriction . . . the Committee has gradually improved the technique of production . . . The *Memorandum* contains no propaganda and is a pure statement of fact." The views of investigators in various countries are presented through British eyes. $10 00 pays for 12 issues.

These scholarly media bring us British propaganda in its most insidious form, which profoundly affects our intellectuals. British propaganda always begins at the top, working down until the back stretches of the country, which hold out longest, finally capitulate. We have no equivalent publications in America. We lack foreign interests to protect, and the political sense of the British.

September 15, 1939

NOTES

(1) There was some reason for this complaint. Senator Holt told the Senate that the N Y *Herald Tribune,* Oct. 6, 1938, reported that "the Outer Bridge speech of the President of the United States, about quarantining nations and engaging in war, was given to the British Foreign Office before he delivered the address". This subservience to the British was matched only by the contempt toward the Germans. On the occasion of the Hitler speech, Sept. 1939, which Roosevelt dodged comment on by saying he had not heard it all nor read it, a Washington correspondent reported, "In general the attitude among officials here toward it was one of reserve They wanted opportunity to study the complete text and to await what Prime Minister Chamberlain will say to the House of Commons tomorrow before attempting to estimate possibilities." (Boston *Herald,* Sept 20, 1939)

(2) "The Roosevelts tactfully made the most of this opportunity to cement the bonds of Anglo-American amity and erase whatever unfavorable memories lingered from *l'affaire Simpson*—and from Munich. Their reception of their royal guests was carefully arranged to be both dignified and heartily American, with more than a touch of the military.   Ten 'flying fortress' bombing planes roared over the route of the procession to the White House, and the cars in which rode the King and the President, and the Queen and Mrs. Roosevelt, were preceded by sixty businesslike-looking baby tanks . .   At Hyde Park   . they consumed hot dogs and beer   (The King could have dodged the hot dogs   . but he knew well that a hot dog eaten smilingly in America might we worth a dozen battleships) . . . A few weeks after this success, the President tried hard to get Congress to rewrite the Neutrality Act and do away with the mandatory ban on the export of arms and munitions to warring countries. Not yet, however, was Congress ready to take this leap", writes Frederick Lewis Allen in "Since Yesterday" (pp 341-343)

(3) *International Affairs* since the war has been published at Balliol College, Oxford. The article by Lord Lothian referred to was delivered as an address at Chatham House, March 14, 1939, and is perhaps the last signed article published by him as a free speaking Englishman before it became his duty as ambassador to bring us into the war. Referring to Quincy Howe's "England Expects Every American to do His Duty", he says, "That is just about the attitude of every Englishman. Yet the Americans know quite well that when we urge the United States to do the world's work, she will, if she accepts our advice, be picking our British chestnuts for us out of the international fire."

Lothian who had recently returned from America said, "Of the President himself there is no doubt whatever where his own sympathies lie. . . . In addition to that he is, I think, a good diplomatic poker player" President Roosevelt believes that "to prevent the war happening . . . it is in American interests, as well as in the interests of democracy, to assist France and Great Britain to buy in the United States all the armaments they need in order to strengthen their own defences, because the stronger France and England are, the less likely is war in itself, and, if war comes, the smaller will be the contribution which it will be necessary for the United States itself to make if it wants the democracies to win. There is now a proposal before the Congress to amend the Neutrality Act."

Lord Lothian as Rhodes Scholarship trustee had visited the United States sixteen times since the last war and more recently had been promoting "Union Now", Streit's book, before it was printed in America. In his speech he refers to this project so dear to Cecil Rhodes. He declares, "I am a cautious optimist about the future, though there may be future changes and shocks before we get back to the bedrock of the democratic cooperation for which the new world system must be built."

In the same issue, Lionel Curtis in his address on "World Order" said that while he was in New York in January, 1939, "Mr. Clarence Streit of the New York *Times* called to see me. He had been on President Woodrow Wilson's staff at Paris and had for years represented the New York *Times* at Geneva. In watching the League at work he had seen how unstable a system based on compacts between sovereign States must be. He had then discovered and read 'The Federalist', which had shown him why this must be so .. Mr Streit . afterwards put in my hands an advance copy of his book 'Union Now', privately printed at Geneva, but due for publication in February." (cf Bul #11)

(4) Imperial policies, cultural relations or British propaganda are maintained and carried on by a great complex of societies and agencies privately conducted by the aristocracy, some of which originated in Parliament and the whole more or less coordinated by the mysterious Foreign Office. A simplification of all these complexities is presented in "What Makes Lives", pp 151-164.

To many of these groups and agencies, Viscount Astor acts as patron and presiding officer. This family, almost as long British as it was American, was little more than a century ago German. His somewhat cosmopolitan view is that "America was beginning to see that never again would there be a world under the 'Pax Britannica', and that she would have to play a part in world affairs for her own interests" (*International Affairs*, May-June, 1939) .

BRITISH PROPAGANDA IN AMERICA· Improved Technique

Denial that there is any British propaganda in this country should be recognized as part of the propaganda,(1) which is useless if detected. Lord Macmillan announces, September 27, "The policy is that there shall be no propaganda in the United States of America".

The recently set up and publicly announced propaganda machine of Lord Macmillan rumbles clumsily in the old ruts, suppressing, twisting the news, reviving atrocities, but not yet portraying Germans making soap from battlefield cadavars as in 1916.

Look for British propaganda in editorials, articles, and the flattery of officials, where it is most effective. Be on the lookout for subtle new tricks for discrediting those who oppose endeavor of the Administration to bring our resources, money, and men to the support of the privileged group that profit from British Imperialism.[2]

Here's a new one, less time worn, brought out as a counter measure to the flood of protests reaching Congressmen against repeal of the arms embargo [3]

A New York *Times* (pro-British) dispatch, September 24, from Washington with an air of sinister mystery, announced, "The government has come into possession of various wireless and cable messages from Germany and Russia to persons in this country which officials hold may lead to the source of many of the letters and telegrams now raining on Congress in opposition to President Roosevelt's proposal for repeal of the embargo".

These messages, it was said, were signed with code names, but identification of the addressees (if any) was withheld   In the next column a Washington dispatch headed "U. S Invokes 1917 Spy Act" tends to arouse alarm and suspicion.

Two days later it became known to Washington correspondents that the mysterious cables referred to had "fallen into the hands of Ambassador Kennedy in London".   If the British censor had not intercepted them, then the British propaganda agency might well have invented them.

The effect is to give pause to those public spirited individuals and groups of citizens who are writing Congressmen to "Keep Out of War", —to create suspicion of the anti-war worker who requests someone to sign a postcard to a Congressman.   He's likely to be greeted with, "Oh, you're one of those German spies I read about!"

'War scares', long a Continental method of controlling people, are being worked on us   The President announces mysterious submarines off Alaska and Nova Scotia coasts   Further questioned, he suggests they may be "Swiss" or "Bolivian".   Later we learn, not from him, that the Alaskan is one of the numerous fleet of Russian submarines based on Vladivostok.   The other, seen in the fog of the Grand Banks, possibly German (or more likely a belated summer sea serpent), has already been reported half a dozen times since we got the war jitters [4]

The closing of the White House grounds, the increase in armed guards about the President, his talk about spies, the increase in the number of spy hunters and armed forces, his complaint of a "foreign conspiracy" he "discovered" mysteriously buying up our scant reserves of ferro-manganese and chrome, all tend to magnify this feeling of impending menace.

The Tax Research Institute of New York City, supported by practically all the larger corporations, to aid in tax evasion, has published "Adjusting Your Business to War", $6.50, introduction by Assistant Secretary of War Louis Johnson [5] Mr. Roosevelt said he had "not heard of it until 45 minutes before the press conference" at which he was questioned. The book tells how to promote war business and prints many of the secret bills drawn up by the War Department which are to be enacted the moment we enter the war, and will make the President more powerful than Hitler.

A bill which passed the House last May and awaits action in the Senate carries a clause that anyone saying or having anything in his possession written or printed that would decrease the morale of those who are or are about to be enlisted in the armed forces, shall be sentenced to two to ten years. In England the Commons passed a bill in which the identical provision makes the penalty ten years. Daladier's decree for the same offense prescribes the guillotine

To hand picked supporters in secret conference the day before Congress assembled, the President made it clear that he wanted a 'free hand' to help Britain and France and indicated surprise when "Senator Pittman bluntly said that such a proposal would not get five votes in the 23-member Foreign Relations Committee" (*Chr Sci Monitor*).

In his address to Congress, September 21, he referred to the "age-old and time-honored doctrine of international law". Charles A. Beard in his syndicated analysis promptly made this look silly. International law is largely the creation of the British with the acquiescence of their satellites to foster British ends and embarrass rebel peoples.

Boston *Transcript* comments editorially, "The President's reverence for the traditional in international practice may evoke some slight amusement. More than once during the last seven years the President has derided those conservatives who called for a return to the 'tried and true' principles of orthodox economic practice. To these petitions, the President has more than once scoffingly pointed to the 1929 depression as the fruit of these 'tried and true' methods. No less now, we point to

America's entrance into the World War as the fruit of those 'tried and true' principles of international law."

The President would like Congress to "adjourn partisanship", "to stop debate". Apparently he expects to have his Congress do his bidding as Hitler does his Reichstag. In closing he said·

"In a period when it is sometimes said that free discussion is no longer compatible with national safety" (this is the third time the President has looked forward to wartime limitation of free discussion), "may you by your deeds show the world that we of the United States are one people, of one mind, one spirit, one clear resolution" (this reminds one of Hitler's 'Ein Volk, Ein Reich, Ein Fuehrer'), "walking before God in the light of living." (He has caught the Kaiser's trick of ending so as to convey the inference that the one mind and voice are his and he speaks for God).[6]

Senator Holt remarked, "The President could have said in a sentence, 'Give me the power and go home' ". Senator Clark declares it the "duty of Congress to remain in session . . . during the duration of the national emergency" which the President has declared. "This is and should remain a government by law and not by decree."

The President warns us the only time we had an Embargo, in 1812, the British burned the Capitol, the house he now lives in, so that it had to be painted white. Does he believe we are afraid of that now?

"Sure we're neutral. But whom are we neutral against?" was the reply of the Irish official to the grounded aviator. For Americans the question has been decided by those who are guiding and creating our public opinion.

Senator Elbert Thomas of Utah impatiently stated the real position of the 'neutrality revisionists',—"Let us give up this dream of impartiality. It is better to take sides and fight."

Senator Nye, September 26, summed it up: "The Administration is willing to give anything and everything in exchange for the abandonment of the embargo". It is yielding to "pressure" from England and France, who are now only playing a "checker game". They would not fight, he said, until assured of American support "first with materials, second with money and then with our sons".

Senator Pat McCarran predicts they will win the battle to prevent change in the embargo. Speaking in New York on the "cash and carry" plan, he said, "Once before we put up the cash, and we've been carrying it ever since". England wants us to pay for the war as we did the last, even more generously.

September 28, 1939

NOTES

(1) No propaganda that acknowledged itself as such would be worth spending money or effort on. When recognized or suspected, it becomes necessary to deny its existence That not proving effective, beginning in the spring of 1940 it was generally insisted by college professors that the importance of propaganda in changing opinion was greatly exaggerated. It was events, not knowledge of them or news of them that caused the change. Late in 1940 it was given out by the President and the colleges that the idea that propaganda had in any way affected opinion in bringing us into the last war was a myth, that there was danger of such a myth being revived. It must be destroyed if unity of thought and opinion was to be achieved. It was hoped at that time that the Council of Democracy would "crystallize" American thought

(2) When this warning was issued there had already been planned in London as forecast by Lord Lothian in his Chatham House address of March (cf Bul #7) ways and means of changing our Neutrality Law The British Government and Foreign Office, during the spring and summer of 1939, had apparently made plans to begin the war against Germany in September and to bring America in. To this end, Lothian was selected to replace Lindsay. In the September, 1939, *Round Table* (cf Bul #7) we find all these plans set forth. At the time of the issue of Bulletin #8, Lothian had already arrived and the Non-Partisan Committee for Peace Through Revision of the Neutrality Act had been planned by Lothian and Lamont, or those associated with them under the aegis of Butler and the direction of Eichelberger, who hit upon Emporia as the place to have it originate (cf pp 69-76)

(3) The popular protest to Congress delayed and embarrassed the plans of the British and the President. Inside circles in London in September had understood that America would be in the war by the first of the year. The President, before he issued his call for a special session of Congress Sept. 21 to carry out this program, had Senator Byrnes poll the senators and was assured of the necessary votes The protest not only greatly delayed action but postponed indefinitely our participation in the war Then came the Finnish flare-up with publicity again calculated to bring us in.

(4) Reporting and anticipating, the President has made great use of war scares for which he has been twitted and criticized in the press, but it has worked. He understands the psychology of the American people. Today within the walls of our universities, in the country houses and walled gardens of our wealthiest people there is fear of imminent perils that he has hinted at or described.

(5) Louis Johnson's plans were for a highly mechanized army of trained spec-

ialists, such as in small numbers with relatively few casualties so easily overcame the great conscripted mass armies of France. Because his plans did not fit in with the later ones of regimenting the people, he and Secretary of War Woodring were kicked out.

[6] Hate, like love, is a passion that may dominate lives. The woman scorned cannot dismiss from her mind the object of her passion and her every thought and act is turned to hate. The man who hates with sufficient intensity cannot rid his mind of the object of his hatred and unconsciously in his acts reflects those of the hated one. (cf Bul #93)

IS THERE BRITISH PROPAGANDA IN AMERICA?

There is no British propaganda in this country, and no need of it. It would be of no avail,—we are assured from many sources.

In "The Issue of Might and Right", (Boston *Herald,* Oct. 1) a gentleman prominent in Wall Street, Harvard, and directorates, asserts that 'the emotional reaction to undeniable facts is not the effect of propaganda'. He should remember that the job of the propagandist is to so present the facts as to arouse the desired emotional reaction. [1]

Herbert Hoover, who lived twenty years under the British flag, knows that this is not true. In the August *American Magazine* he declares that "the first and most important danger of our being dragged into the war" is "foreign propaganda to inflame our emotions", adding as second and third dangers "preachments of our officials and steps by our Government to entangle us". [2]

These two contrasting statements show that one is likely to hold to what fits his emotional attitude which has been determined by propaganda. Mr. Hoover has seen Germany smashed and lacks faith that that is the cure for the world's troubles Moreover, he is not directly dependent on the favor of our foreign bank affiliates

Our news from Germany comes over cables owned by the British, or by radio which could be blocked if the British so desired. But Lord Macmillan, explaining that there is no British propaganda adds, "Hitler is our best propagandist".

Discontented expatriates, women scorned, and fugitives[3] from foreign governments have readily disposed of their copy to our periodicals and have influenced our opinion. Most newspaper correspondents must serve their masters to sell their copy.

Rogerson, in his "Propaganda in the Next War", published last fall and now extremely difficult to obtain, remarks, "We shall, as before, send over the leading literary lights and other men", and then he bemoans that it will be difficult to find men that were as good as those of 1916—Kipling, Barrie, Galsworthy, Wells, or Gilbert Parker.[4]

But there is a flood of English speakers, humorists, aristocrats, publicists, correspondents[5] with whom one may get in touch to address your club or forum. Have you a little English speaker in your town? Write the State Department and ask if he is registered, as the law provides

The propaganda coming from Washington is the most effective. The English are a wonderful people. They have political sense, and know how to handle functionaries and diplomats.

Through his secretaries or personally, the President is promoting war scares,—announcing to correspondents mysterious submarines at all points on our coasts. It is the season of whales and sea serpents, but perhaps the Admiralty has helped with a disappearing submarine.

Sir Gilbert Parker, in charge of propaganda here in 1916, after the German U-53 had sunk four merchant vessels off Nantucket, wrote his government confidentially as revealed recently by H. C. Peterson in his "Propaganda for War", "It frightened a good many people rather badly, which was the desired result. I wish the Germans had thought of something of that kind before".

A primary principle of propaganda is, "Show your enemy on the run." That holds wavering old allies and brings new ones Nothing is so satisfying to the mob as the manhunt.

The Nazi chieftains, we are told from London, are all planning to flee, and have planted millions all over the world,—where the British can seize it. The mysterious agency whose remarkable investigation revealed this could only have been the Bank of England The San Francisco bank of the Sumitomo Branch, Ltd of Osaka, Japan, interrogated, officially replied, "We are only a foreign branch. We don't accept deposits." No report has come of any of these funds having been seized, though Goebbels offered 10%

"Allied propaganda to convince us of what is loose in the world is wholly unnecessary," writes D. A. Fleming in October *Events*.

It is coming to be recognized that "what is loose" is more than a mere rebellion of "have nots" against the imperialistic democracies.[6] From the Rhine to the Pacific there are no more large incomes. Even in France and England, now girded for totalitarian warfare, they are rapidly being reduced. Drucker, "End of Economic Man", MacMurray, "Clue to History", and Dulles, "War, Peace and Change", see in this a social revolution

"Revolution of Nihilism", Rauschning calls it in his book, now actively promoted. A former economic royalist, he knows it is revolution but can find no pattern. A member of the German Freedom Party, anonymous author of "Hitler Calls This Living", he complains there are no profits, incomes are decreased and laborers are pampered with luxuries, music, tours, vacations.

The Soviet newspaper "Izvestia" asserts that the "British war to exterminate Hitlerism makes us return to the gloomy Middle Ages. Ideas are impervious to fire and sword. One may respect or deny them but to begin a war to annihilate them is to admit criminal silliness". This gives color to the fear that "socialistic ideas might cross frontiers". (*Transcript,* Oct 10) But some are jittery, even criminally silly. President Conant, replying to Mr. Landon seems to feel "modern civilization will be jeopardized by totalitarian defeat".

Revolutions are seldom recognized by contemporaries. The American Rebels, to the British, were confiscators of Loyalist property. Their leader, Washington, had a price on his head like any gangster. The bloody atrocities of the French Revolution blinded the English to what was happening. Now the French Revolution reaches feudal Poland. "Immediately after the conquest and Russian occupation of Poland, Russia gave the peasants in the Polish Ukraine authority to go after landowners with pitchforks". (*Transcript,* Oct. 5)

"The majority of people don't want war but will be overcome by the organized pro-war groups who are entrenched, and are seeking to inflame public opinion to make us war-minded", declared Senator Walsh (Boston *Herald,* Oct. 10) pointing to the selfish organized interests in Washington He prophesied, "Odds are 10-1 that we'll be in unless the majority of American citizenry organize more effectively than to date."

The British newspaper publisher, Lord Beaverbrook, formerly Max Aitken, woodpulp millionaire of Nova Scotia, arrived in America September 30. October 10 he was reported to have had lunch, "just a gossip" with Mr. Roosevelt. He is quite capable of acting the part Lord Northcliffe played in 1916, in bringing the press more completely to the aid of British propaganda.

Who is behind these bulletins? and why? is asked. 20,000 have been distributed independently. The work and expense are mine. The purpose is not to express opinion or pass judgment but merely to attract attention to the subtler, generally overlooked phases of foreign propaganda that have been and are tending to bring us into war. The noisy German propaganda, if overlooked, would be brought to our attention by the British propagandists.

All responses have shown keen appreciation, save two, which come from Germans in universities who are in a precarious position and who oppose the regime in their own country (See Bulletin #4 for others,— Alfred M. Bingham, Raymond Pearl, Gerald P. Nye, David I. Walsh, Harlow Shapley, E A. Hooton, etc.) I quote:

From journalists: Burton Rascoe—"You are doing a magnificent service." H. L. Mencken—"Immense interest". Franklin Roudybush —"I like your material   Anxious to receive all." Harry Elmer Barnes —"In hearty sympathy with your plan to expose British propaganda". Stuart Chase—"Delighted when Senator Nye told me you are broadcasting British propaganda material".

From educators. E. A. Ross—"The parallelism of your thought and mine is really extraordinary." Edwin M. Borchard—"The information you digest is very useful and I am glad to see that something is being done along these lines." J. G. Umstattd—"I very much enjoyed the broadcast . . . training your guns against war hysteria". Francis M. Froelicher—"Much interested in your bulletins about British propaganda   I hope this sort of publicity will reach a great many people. Many are afraid to be neutral because they fear others will consider them pro-Nazi." T. C. Grier—"I used your article 'Made Opinion' in chapel this morning. It is quite in keeping with my own personal opinion." A. B. Faust—"Your sheet on propaganda is very enlightening." Joseph Brewer—"I think it is wonderful that you are going to straighten out the international muddle for us " Dixon Wecter—"Because of their tonic good sense and their brilliant audacity, your propaganda interested me greatly." A. Gordon Melvin—"The work you are doing is very valuable " Harry A. Peters—"Thank you for the interesting material about propaganda. . . . We need enormous energy to fight the feeling that we are certain to get into war." Howard H. White— "I value as a Discovery the finding of two of your bulletins in the Maynard Public Library." A woman dean—"A swell job. Keep it up." Carleton Washburne—"The best statement of my own position". *October 10, 1939*

Notes

(1) Jerome Greene, Harvard '96, Secretary to the Corporation and Overseers, foundation director, and graduate of Wall Street wrote: "If the United States is drawn into the war it will not be because of foreign propaganda. . . . Passions may be aroused by facts no less than by propaganda. . . . To say that the well-nigh universal reaction to these undeniable facts is the effect of propaganda is nothing short of nonsense."

Einstein has written, "Experience proves that it is rather the so-called 'Intelligentsia' that is most apt to yield to these disastrous collective suggestions, since the intellectual has no direct contact with life in the raw but encounters it in its easiest synthetic form, the printed page."

Mr. Greene's "facts", of course, are Einstein's "printed page". Few 'facts' have been so 'undeniable' as the Belgian atrocities, supported by hundreds of affidavits and certified to by Lord Bryce, whose integrity was undoubted by all Americans. We now know them to have been manufactured lies.

'Events' are the raw material of propaganda Selected, interpreted, slightly twisted and distorted, the reports of events may be used to excite emotions Any power, Great Britain or Germany, which fails to so report events as to suit their ends will be remiss.

The most effective propaganda is that "of the deed, not that of the word", and "when events do not serve their purpose they (propagandists) create them. Many of the news events about which we read are deliberately staged by the governments in the interest of propaganda," E L. Bernays, the highest paid propagandist ("public relations council") in this country, pointed out to the *Guardian* Midwinter Conference on "Propaganda" ("What Makes Lives", p 189)

(2) Hoover was never a Morgan promotion (Josephson), but when Hoover was in office Morgan had access by telephone He was a Rockefeller promotion and Rockefeller and Morgan have always been just a little like the Guelphs and the Ghibellines, like the Higginsons and the Kidder-Peabodys in Boston

(3) Hermann Rauschning shows frustration and disillusionment in the photograph *Time* published Dec 23 listing the year's best sellers An East Prussian Junker, former officer, and landowner of the conservative and nationalist tradition, he joined the Nazi movement believing that it would produce not only the "rebirth of the nation" but would save his own class (land, money, position) from the maw of the underprivileged. He became the Nazi President of the Danzig Senate but, greatly disappointed, yielded his position to Albert Forster, and in 1935 fled to Paris Disappointed economic royalist that he is, he sees that what is going on in Germany is a "revolution of a new and extreme type". Many emigrés, he points out, fail to realize that the situation in Germany is

actually revolutionary. But it is from men like him and Otto Strasser, along with the woman scorned by Hitler and Erika Mann, that we derive 'information'.

Rauschning, in a remarkable summary "The Lessons of the First Phase of the War", *Unity,* Dec 2, 1940, recognizing the economic and cultural world revolution now underway, writes without hate or propaganda purpose: "The secret of Hitler's success is clear enough. He always sailed with the tide On the flood of a new, irresistible urge he was borne along—not on his own personal qualities but on the extraordinary forces which he has been in a position to manipulate. . . . His acuteness of perception into the real situation most of all accounts for the mastery he has attained over its development. How the world should develop was not merely a question of reconciling totalitarian dictatorship with democracy, as has been represented so often." Rauschning's third book is entitled "The Redemption of Democracy", Alliance, 1941. *Time,* March 3, 1941, reviewing it speaks of the author as a "former East Prussian officer and *Junker,* a deserter from the Nazis". His first book "described the proletarian nature of the Nazi revolution". In his last, he attempts to make clear that "World War II is a social revolution . . . the last tremor of the 500-year-long revolt of the masses. Formerly the ancien régime, the old order, kept the masses in check. But skeptical humanism has sapped the faith of the masses in the old order while it sapped the faith of the old order in itself. Rauschning's voice sounds like that of a prophet, sometimes like that of a clever Junker He has little use for forces which most people are used to calling progressive."

(4) "We shall as before send over our leading literary lights and other men with names well known in the United States to put our point of view over the dinner table. Our trouble here will be to find men with equally commanding reputations to step into the shoes of such as Kipling, Barrie, Shaw, Galsworthy, and Wells."

Peterson quotes John Masefield, one of the 1916 contingent, as having written to Sir Gilbert Parker, in charge of propaganda in this country, "I have the honor to present to you my report of things noticed during my stay in the United States between the 13th of January and the 18th of March." Peterson explains, "The immediate task of British propagandists was to make an ordinary political power struggle appear to be a fight between the forces of good and evil. . . . Starting as early as August, 1914, prominent men of America hastened to join a cause that was intellectually fashionable. . . . College professors and school teachers repeated with a great show of wisdom the arguments which had originated in Wellington House or in *la maison de la presse* "

In the horde of propagandists that have been sent over recently to 'explain' to us, the best they have been able to marshall have been Baldwin who early retired, Duff Cooper who fell flat, Anthony Eden advance agent for royalty, and Lothian who has passed In the literary field, J. B. Priestley has gradually warmed up on the radio and H. G. Wells, though he said he would be damned if he would, is doing something half-heartedly on the American lecture platform where his weak voice makes him ineffective.

(5) "The British are coming to Washington at a rate that almost amounts to a second invasion. Even in 1814, when the Redcoats burned the Capitol, their force was scarcely more impressive. Actually there are 430 representatives of the British government in Washington today—130 members of the Embassy staff, 300 members of the British Purchasing Commission and British Air Commission. The figure includes everyone—officers, clerks, messengers, and chauffeurs The British Embassy and Chancery now is the largest diplomatic establishment in Washington, but it is not large enough. An annex has been added to care for an overflow of coding clerks and officials of the office of Economic Warfare. Meanwhile, the two British commissions occupy space in four other buildings. They started out in modest quarters in the Hibbs Building, expanded to the entire top floor of the Willard Hotel, added further space in the Adams Building, and most recently have taken over Andrew Mellon's old apartment at 1785 Massachusetts Avenue to accommodate the Air Commission. These are the British in Washington alone In addition, the New York office of the Purchasing Commission numbers 1,000 persons, plus 500 inspectors who travel about the country testing the wide assortment of articles, from ships to airplanes, which are being purchased in the United States " (Pearson and Allen, Dec 5, 1940)

(6) Recognition that a great world revolution was on came slowly but by the spring of 1940 had been widely recognized, so much so that it became the function of the propaganda centers to pooh-pooh this idea and emphasize that the Empire was engaged merely in a policeman's job to put down gangsters.

NOTES ON A MORAL WAR
by H. L. Mencken

"The English are in the war for a simple and single reason, to wit, their desire to prevent the rise of a powerful rival in Europe, offering an inevitable challenge to their general supervision of the world. That is why they went to war the last time, and that is why they go through the motions of being at war today. It is a rational reason, but it is as devoid of moral content as a theorem in algebra or a college yell. If the English, with the help of French, American and other mercenaries, manage to scotch Hitler, and Poland is restored, they will try to operate it as a puppet state, just as they operate Egypt and Iraq. And if Hitler turns out to be unscotchable they will gladly let him collar as many Polands as may be needed to quiet and content him, just as they let him collar Czecho-Slovakia when Czecho-Slovakia seemed enough.

"That the majority of Americans appear to have fallen more or less for the English pretension to altruism, and even favor supporting it with munitions and money, not to say men, is only one more proof that human beings learn little by experience. Certainly, anyone who sets the full powers of his intellect to the job must be able to recall what happened the last time. When the war was over England had the loot and the United States had a headache and a huge file of bills. In Congress the other day a Congressman, whose name I forget, was trying to figure out the sum total of those bills   He concluded that, with pensions and other trimmings added, they have run to more than $60,000,000,000 to date — with new ones still coming in every day

"This calculation, it seems to me, was extraordinarily modest.   For one thing, it took no account of the useful lives lost, the young men crippled and ruined, the wreck of families, the huge destruction of earning power. . . .   What did we get out of it?   The most I can think of is the pleasure of looking at an American Legion parade once a year. All our professed objects in the war failed   The chief product of the salvation of democracy was the creation of the Russian colossus — the most formidable enemy to democracy that has been seen on earth since the fall of the great Asiatic empires of antiquity. . . .

"England got more, in fact, a great deal more.   It not only gathered in millions of square miles of new territories, and an almost endless store of miscellaneous loot; it also made secure—or, at all events, apparently secure — its hegemony throughout the world   International law, at the end of the war, was hardly more than a series of decisions by English prize courts   No other country had any right that England admitted itself bound to respect.   It owned and operated the sea, and owning and operating the sea, it had a firm grip upon the land.   It ran Europe, it ran Africa, it ran more than half of Asia, and at both ends of the Americas it was triumphant and dominant.

"The United States not only acquiesced in this huge access of power; it even promoted it, and at no cost to the beneficiary.   We acted precisely like an English colony; indeed, we were even more complacent than any actual English colony of ponderable importance, for both Canada and Australia hastened to get something for themselves, and so did South Africa.   In Europe France rebelled very quickly, and was slapped down only with difficulty: it is a forced and unwilling ally at this moment, and may be trusted to prove it if the war goes on.   Russia got off the reservation by 1920 and Italy by 1923   Germany, by 1930, began to prepare darkly for a new *Tag,* and Japan was ready to throw off the yoke in Asia by 1935. But the United States, despite an occasional groan over the unpaid war debt, continued idiotically in the English orbit, and there it is today.

"Worse, we are now asked to strengthen our bonds with more money and more blood Once again, it appears, the world is to be made safe for democracy. Once again the wicked Kaiser, in the person of his even more wicked heir and assign, is to be prevented from ravaging our coasts, burning our cities and selling our people into captivity. Once again we are to fall for the old hooey, and hail with hosannas a return engagement of the old bills. It sounds incredible, but there is the plain fact. Let it revolve a bit in your mind.

"I am the last man on earth to object to the English effort to preserve and extend their great empire It is a magnificent edifice, and no rational people, having once erected it at large cost and made it pay, would willingly let it go. To be sure, a great deal of sharp dealing and worse went into its erection, and it is maintained today only by a constant resort to brigandage and false pretenses. But it is clearly absurd to hold great states to the simple morality of private men, beset alike by the police and the fear of Hell.

"But why should the United States dedicate itself to the dirty work of another country, traditionally our enemy and only transiently, and for revenue alone, our contemptuous, patronizing and dead-beat friend? Why should we convert our own country into a mere client and goon of England, and waste our men and money protecting and augmenting England's empire and fighting England's rivals? Why should we denounce and threaten the Germans because they object to being hedged in and ruined by English bribery and intrigue, or the Italians because they rebel against living in an English lake and under English guns, or the Japs because they believe that the affairs of China, which lies at their very gates, are of more concern to them than to the English, 10,000 miles away?

"The answer we get is that England is a great Christian nation, the guardian of civilization, the consecrated fosterer of "morality and religion," radiating a special and incomparable virtue, and with a special mission to protect the United States.

"That answer is buncombe. England is a country exactly like all the

rest, no worse and no better. Its one aim and purpose is to promote its
own interest; it has no other whatsoever. It was willing and eager, only
six weeks ago, to embrace Comrade Stalin as a brother, and it is trying
to buy him back even now, just as it is trying to buy Mussolini, Franco
and the Turks. So long as the Japs kept their paws off China it was
their ally and buddy, and if Hitler manages to survive the present moral
crusade it will make terms with him quickly and gladly — at the expense
of France, even at the expense of the United States.

"To admire such a great and successful nation is one thing, and quite
reasonable; to fall for its Pecksniffery, pay its bills, and tote its slops is
assuredly something else again."

The above editorial from The Baltimore *Sun*, Oct. 8, 1939, by H. L.
Mencken, is one of a series of rollicking, exhilarating outbursts by the
incorrigible Boobophobe of Baltimore,— long may he wave o'er the
land of the free and the home of the brave which the lovers of moral
bunk are seeking to reduce to a vale of tears

October 13, 1939

NOTES

These weekly sermons of Mr. Mencken have appeared regularly in the Sunday
Baltimore *Sun*. In anticipation of war, we have been turned back to thoughts of
the moral life by our President and the great university presidents have followed
religiously in his footsteps. Mr. Mencken's preoccupation with the moral life is
evident by the titles of his sermons,—"The Call of Service", April 21, 1940,—
"Onward Christian Soldiers", May 19, 1940,—"Idealism Marches On", Oct 15,
1940. But an end must come to all things. January 27, 1941, he writes me, "In
a week or so you'll receive my last Baltimore *Sun* article. The paper has gone
over to Roosevelt and Willkie in a large and vociferous way, and my continuance
on the editorial page begins to seem an affectation. Whether I'll do any writing
on the war any other place remains to be seen—probably not. I have two books
in hand, and they are keeping me jumping My belief is that trying to argue with
the American people is completely hopeless They think with their midriffs, and
have an insatiable taste for demagogues"

Of his native city, we read in the Sargent Handbook of Private Schools (1938-
39 ed), "Famous for its markets and good living, its terrapin, and America's
most articulate boobiphobe, H. L. Mencken, Baltimore is a city of distinctive local
color, customs, and cuisine." Mencken, from his father's house where he still
lives as in the "Happy Days" of his youth, writes me of this "I think 'boobiphobe' is a capital word, and I shall take the liberty of borrowing it I have only
one suggestion to make, and that is that the 'i' be changed to 'o'. For some reason

'boobophobe' seems to me to be a shade more euphonious than 'boobiphobe'. But I leave it to your prayers ... You are free to use anything of mine as you please ... How long I'll be able to go on in the *Sun* remains to be seen. There are already many loud protests from readers   If, when and as Roosevelt horns into the war, it will become completely impossible to write any intelligent thing. Your Bulletins are really grand   I read them with delight."

He does not hesitate to preach to the President as on Sunday, Oct. 1, 1939, "A President of the United States like any other citizen, has a plain right to an opinion about the rights and wrongs of this or that foreign war, and in his official capacity he may also have a right, and even a duty, to indicate that opinion to the people, though on this point learned counsel are far from unanimous. But neither he nor any other man has any right to pretend to neutrality when he is in fact bitterly partisan, nor to talk loftily against war when he is notoriously planning to promote it. Of the first of these improprieties the Hon. Mr. Roosevelt proved himself guilty in every one of the notes he addressed to Hitler, Mussolini and company before the war actually began, and in all his speeches on the subject after his Chautauqua speech. Of the second he convicted himself in the very message to Congress which contained his plea for peace."

On his 'gift of prophecy' he goes on to say, Sunday, May 19, 1940, in biblical phrases which come easily to his tongue in dealing with mundane affairs,—"I have little gift for prophecy and none at all for figures, but if the deficit for the calendar year 1940 does not smash all records I'll certainly be surprised, and if the national debt isn't above $75,000,000,000 by the time civilization is saved again I'll be glad to put on a dunce cap."

Supplementing Bulletin #10 we printed an editorial "America's Big Job" by J. R Burrow, President of the Central National Bank and Central Trust Company, Topeka, Kansas, an old friend and client of mine, approaching the problem from a more practical and less moral point of view. This elicited high praise and many copies were called for. We here reprint an abbreviated form   "America's big job is to save itself, not Europe. To sacrifice humanity and wreck our own chance to survive by going to war would be folly bordering on insanity. The civilization of Western Europe, being precisely the result of civilizing influences working thru all past time, is the most precious heritage of mankind. The French, the German and the English peoples are the most glorious products of that civilization. .. These peoples at home or abroad developed law, philosophy and science.

.. They raised the standard of living of the common man to a degree hardly comprehensible to our generation, the poor of which were born rich in comforts as compared even to our own fathers, let alone to our grandfathers

"Yet the French, the English and the Germans are now fighting among themselves to the death ... The very finest flower of civilization is destroying itself before our very eyes. Why should America enter that gruesome alliance for suicide, and do likewise?

"That the peoples of England, France and Germany do not want war is, thank God, admitted by everybody this time. Must it not inevitably follow that they are unable to control their own politicians? (Can we control ours any better?) If the people of Western Europe—the most intelligent, civilized and noble the race has produced—cannot keep their own governments from waging a self-destroying war the people do not want, can we, the American people, keep them from doing so? We can't elect men to office who can be counted on to keep their word. We can't devise a political party that will do in office what it promised to do if put into office! Even our cities can't rid themselves of bosses all decent people hate, or gang rule and racketeering that make life itself unsafe and the word 'government' a joke! Somewhere along the way the democratic idea took the wrong fork in the road, proceeding in the direction of increasing the relative effectiveness of the voice of the ignorant and inexperienced elements of society instead of moving toward the reduction of the power of government over the lives of the people. Building the political power of the masses makes it easier for governments to dominate them, not vice versa, so that now with the mass mind everywhere carrying every election, peoples cannot keep their governments from going to war The mass, thinking it was becoming freer, became enslaved. Who are we either to jeer at Europe's peoples for their failure to make their governments fulfill their true wishes or to seek to do that for them?

"No, America, your job is not to save Europe Your job is to save yourself. You have a long way to go to do that You must establish a government here that all men can trust—a government that knows its place and stays in it—a government that is proud to occupy a servant's place—to be the people's servant and not seek to become its master. If you can and do accomplish that, America, then your name will be blessed. But if you enter the war you will destroy your own freedom and your opportunity to serve either yourself or humanity. . . .

"I yield to no man in my love for England and all the gorgeous things she stands for in the lives of all true Americans and of civilized people everywhere. But I love America more than I do England, and entering the war would be the end of American destiny. We would merely become another dictatorship country with bloody revolution just around the corner. . .

"To sacrifice humanity, wreck a national social structure, a national economy and the only representative form of government that has a chance to survive by going to war in Europe after the kind of musical comedy statesmanship that has prevailed in the former Allied countries since the war, would be folly bordering onto insanity."

Bulletin #70, July 26, 1940, reprinting additional selections on 'morality' from Mencken's sermons, we said, "Every Sunday, H. L. Mencken bursts into full bloom in all the gorgeousness of his colorful language These blossoms were culled from his editorials in The Baltimore *Sun,* July 21 and 7, respectively and respectfully". We here further abbreviate.

Writing on the President's management of the Chicago Convention and his acceptance speech, he wrote July 21,

"The Great Croon of Croons proceeded early Friday morning, on the dramatic contrast between its pious denunciation of dictators and the hard reality that stared them in the face They had spent the whole week flat on the ground, with the aforesaid steam roller bumping over them. Every sign of opposition, however rational, was instantly slapped down—or anticipated and circumvented All orders came from the White House, and from nowhere else

"The Croon of Croons made many things plain. It not only elucidated at length the theory of the Indispensable Man, it also indicated clearly the program of the campaign. That program will have the one end of keeping the boobs alarmed They will be terrified and lathered by an endless series of nightmares. One day Hitler will be coming by air from the eastward, and the next day the Japs will be coming by water from the west And on all days Fifth Columns at home will be carrying on a sinister war upon religion, morality, and all the rest of it, and only the ceaseless vigil of One whose soul is all sacrifices will be potent to save.

"This, of course, is the buncombe that demagogues have ladled out at all times and everywhere since the earliest dawn of human society. First set up a bugaboo —and then give chase to it with loud yells. First scare the boobs out of their pants, and then rush up to save them. . .

"The Croon of Croons was, on all counts, a masterly document. It established firmly—at all events, for vote getting purposes—the dogma that the long and devious campaign for the third-term nomination was never made at all, and that the candidate had to be drafted in the end And it launched the theory that the conflict now joined is not one between the usual gangs of politicians, eager only to grab places at the public trough, but one between the hosts of Heaven, sweating innocence and righteousness, on the one hand, and the scabrous rabble of Satan on the other . . ."

THE DREAM OF CECIL RHODES

Clarence K. Streit's "Union Now",[1] (Harper, 1939), which naively proposes that we give up our sovereignty, is being actively promoted.[2] It has given rise to the "Federal Union", formed simultaneously in London and New York, a "National Organizing Committee" with branches in 190 cities, and the "Union Press", National Union Building, Washington, which issues the monthly *Union Now Bulletin*. Lord Lothian has all this under his watchful eye. In a full page article in the *Chr Sci Monitor,* illustrated with American patriotic pictures, a beautiful piece of propaganda, he magnifies "Union Now" as a book that will make history as did Adam Smith's "Commonwealth of Nations".

Unlike H. G. Wells' proposal for a 'World Union' of all countries,[3] Streit's plan is to unite the fifteen satisfied countries.[4] These possess half the habitable world and control half of its inhabitants, and it is claimed could easily suppress other rebellious states. Italy, Russia or Germany would not dare to rebel as now.[5]

The control of the "Union" is to lie in a House of Deputies and a Senate. With one deputy for each million inhabitants the United States would have 124 to the United Kingdom's 46. That seems like a great advantage.[6] But the British have superior political sense. They have had experience controlling other peoples. Let us see how it works out Where is the joker?

If to the United Kingdom's 46 votes are added the Commonwealths' 30 votes and the 58 votes of the buffer States, (Holland, Belgium and France, whose colonial possessions are dependent on the British navy), it gives a total of 134. Add the Scandinavian countries 17 votes, which England could control, and the total becomes 151 to the United States' 124 That is the little joker. The big one is in the Senate.[7] Each country is to have 2 senators except France and England who each have 4, and the United States more generously 8. That is the 'come on'. England, with her Commonwealths would have 14. Add the buffer states' 8, add the Scandinavian countries' 8, and Britain would have 30 votes to the 8 of the United States. But supposing we won the votes of Canada? England could immediately give Commonwealth status to India and would then have 350 additional deputy votes

Trust the British! Giving up our sovereignty for "Union" would mean something to us — nothing to Great Britain. The lion and the lamb — there is the joker!

Streit's idea is naively announced by its promoters as 'new and audacious'.[8] It dates from 1877 when it was brought forth by W. T Stead[9] and has since received its fullest elaboration in Lionel Curtis' 1000-page book, "World Order" (Oxford Press, 1939).

Cecil Rhodes, in correspondence with W. T. Stead from South Africa during the '80's, developed great plans for "The furtherance of the Empire". Stead tells us in his book, "Last Will and Testament of Cecil J. Rhodes", p. 61, that "Rhodes planned a secret society, patterned after the Jesuit Society (he had always admired Ignatius Loyola) which should have its members in every part of the Empire working with one object and one idea. They should work to advocate the closer union of England and her colonies to crush all disloyalty and every movement for the severance of the Empire."[10]

Rhodes' last and sixth will, published by the Rhodes Scholarship Foundation, is discreet. In his first will, written at the age of 24, he dedicated his yet unmade fortune to—"The extension of British rule throughout the world . . . the occupation by British settlers of the entire continent of Africa, the Holy Land, the Valley of the Euphrates . . . the ultimate recovery of the United States of America as an integral part of the British Empire . . . and finally, the foundation of so great a power as to hereafter render wars impossible and promote the best interests of humanity." ("Cecil Rhodes", by Basil Williams, Holt, 1921) [11]

After the Boer War, the first threat to British Empire Security, Lord Milner, government representative in South Africa and later executor of Rhodes' will, gathered about him a group of brilliant young Oxford men, later known as "Milner's Kindergarten", whom he inspired and trained in Rhodes new imperialism.

Milner's young men, builders of empire, reconstructed South Africa, strengthened the British Empire, improved its finances. Lloyd saved India and Egypt to the Empire. Tweedsmuir in Canada and Lothian in the United States are bending their best efforts to the final unaccomplished phase of Rhodes' imperialistic dream, "The ultimate recovery of the United States as an integral part of the British Empire" [12]

Neville Chamberlain has repeatedly announced that he is carrying out the unchanging, traditional foreign policy of England That policy is formulated by the permanent staff of the Foreign Office. It is the policy of 'divide and rule', unite with those you cannot subdue, destroy all troublemakers. Couched in moralistic terms, that policy was perhaps best formulated by Sir Eyre Crowe in 1907, at that time head of the Western Department of the Foreign Office, in a confidential memorandum upon Anglo-German relations, which according to Harold Nicolson in "Diplomacy" (1939) "embodies a careful definition of the historical principles of British policy". "British policy must therefore maintain the open door and must at the same time display 'a direct and positive interest in the independence of small nations'. Great Britain must therefore recognize herself as 'the natural enemy of any nation which threatens the independence of smaller countries She must be opposed to the political dictatorship of the strongest single State or group of States at any given time ' "

The smaller nations referred to are those that cannot be subdued, annexed or protected by Great Britain but might be absorbed by some other country They include the buffer states which have been set up to protect Britain or to embarrass her enemies.

Under the guidance of the now mature and somewhat desperate British imperialists of "Milner's Kindergarten", the unification of the British empire goes on, led by the great band of deluded peace-loving Americans, prayerfully chanting "Lead Kindly Streit Amid Encircling Gloom", "Union Now, Union Forever" [13]

October 16, 1939

NOTES

[1] Streit's book was promoted by the Right Book Club which is sponsored by the Royal Family. It promoted another book by an American author, Eugene Lyons' "Assignment to Utopia" which is bitterly anti-Soviet.

[2] "During the Napoleonic wars, when it seemed that the conqueror was to extend his influence to this hemisphere, Thomas Jefferson proposed a 'union' with Great Britain (he even went so far as to propose a 'marriage'). And when the Monroe Doctrine was promulgated by the U. S. in agreement with the British Government, James Madison said· 'With the British power and Navy combined with our own, we have nothing to fear from the rest of the world, and in the great struggle of the epoch between liberty and despotism, we owe it to ourselves to sustain the former, in this hemisphere at least.' " ("Plan for Union", Robert E. Sherwood, *Life,* Oct 7, 1940)

President Seymour of Yale, September 16, 1940, attempted to revive this matrimonial idea. He thinks it necessary America "marry itself to the British fleet and nation". Seymour, who would doubtless like to be best man at the ceremony, to sanctify the situation, would unite us in the holy bands of matrimony, to "love, honor, and obey". For the wedding march, let there be no hunish thing like Lohengrin Let it be "Rule Britannia" This suggestion of legitimatizing the illegitimate strikes a responsive chord in a number of hearts. William Allen White gives it his blessing,—"I like it. I shall watch its progress with pride and delight." Says Dorothy Thompson, "It is a program for saving democracy." And Alexander Woollcott is "tremendously impressed". No telling what issue may come out of this liaison of Uncle Sam with Britannia What will happen to the children worries Missouri's Senator Clark. "Americans would relinquish the guardianship of their most priceless treasure, the heritage of human liberty. They would be sharing this guardianship with the peoples of empires, monarchies, and other government forms" (*Rotarian,* Oct. 1940) Quincy Howe predicts trouble in the family "If the United States wishes to avoid picking up another war where the last one left off and to steer clear of a grand crusade against social changes that are overdue in both Europe and Asia, she will preserve an attitude of rigid isolation toward any such scheme as Mr. Streit suggests" (*Forum,* July, 1939).

That unsentimental New Englander, Richard Olney, Secretary of State under Cleveland in 1895, declared "any permanent political union between a European and an American state unnatural and inexpedient"

"Let the United States and Great Britain assume responsibility and leadership for the whole world, except that part of it at present under the heel of the totalitarians. Let these two great repositories of democracy pool their leadership in brains, vision and courage. Let them participate jointly in such economic, industrial and cultural activities as may grow out of this common undertaking." This astonishing proposal is made by the *New Republic* early in January, 1941. Oswald G. Villard, commenting on it in La Follette's *Progressive,* Jan 4, says, "During many long years of journalism I have read astounding proposals, but this I think takes the cake for wildness, for absurdity, for a counsel of despair. What it would mean, of course, would be the hauling down of the American flag, not merely Clarence Streit's 'Union Now', but a merging of the United States and Great Britain to rule the world If that came to pass can anyone doubt it would be a short time before the Union Jack would be flying over this country again?"

"What William, Cardinal O'Connell calls "exalted hysteria,' burned high at Mecca Temple, in New York. The wick was Clarence K Streit's Union Now, which at first was propaganda for a confederation of Western democracies and turns out to mean simply Anglo-American union. There are Americans who have an expatriate passion for it Somerset Maugham was there. As a British subject, serving his government here, he was for it. He had been converted. How astonishing! Henri Bernstein, the French playwright, was there He denounced American isolationists .. We would remind him that freedom of speech is a right that belongs only to an American citizen. To the guest it is a privilege, and may be very easily abused. And we say the same to all the eminent literary persons who presume upon the amenities of their social welcome to be acting among us as foreign agents and propagandists, besides having the bad manners to tell us how we ought to think and feel and behave " (*Sat Eve Post,* Jan 25, 1941)

(3) Wells advocated a world federation in his famous "Outline of History", and has sung the same theme song in much of his more recent published material, reaching a symphonic climax in his "A New World Order". Unite the world, says Wells, not just part of it à la Streit.

(4) Changing conditions and the elimination of many once 'democracies' caused the Streit Plan to be quickly remodeled, just as the White Committee to Defend America by Aiding the Allies dropped all reference to 'Allies' after Great Britain's heroic withdrawal of her troops from the Low Countries and France. With eight of the original fifteen now hanging in a state of suspension, Streit proposed "that the United States Government invite the British democracies to sign another Declaration—this time a joint Declaration of Interdependence" (*Rotarian,* Oct. 1940)

"Definite disunity exists inside the 'Union Now' movement, although the leaders are trying to keep it quiet", commented the *Nation,* Sept 23, 1940. "The dispute is chiefly over how hard to press for 'Union Now', with Britain virtually the only nation left to unite with " Why snub Greece? Perhaps at that time we didn't know Greece was a 'democracy'. Shortly before under Lord Lloyd Rumania had been declared a republic and cemented its bonds with Britain. About the same time the Administration had come to agree with the economic royalists that this country was a republic, not a democracy. That left Great Britain about the only 'democracy', under a dictatorship.

(5) The designer of "Union Now" hastens to assure us that "it is wrong, all wrong to conceive of Union as aimed against the nations of the Triangle". But peaceful and humble in spirit as the Union professes to be, it asserts that "the democracies can secure world control overnight", and adds cynically, "If we think it wise to warn the world that we will fight for our freedom, is it not still wiser to add the warning that we will begin to fight for it on its European frontiers?"

(6) Under the revised conditions, union would now be governed by an Inter-continental Congress composed of deputies and senators   On the basis of one to every million of population, representation in the lower house of the congress would be as follows: Australia 7, Canada 11, Ireland 3, New Zealand 2, South Africa 7, United Kingdom 46. These total 76 votes against the approximately 130 votes for the United States   Commonwealth status given to India and the resulting additional 350 votes would quickly neutralize America's momentary advantage.

(7) The senatorial votes line up Australia 2, Canada 2, Ireland 2, New Zealand 2, South Africa 2, United Kingdom 4   This totals 14 votes for the British Empire as against 8 votes for the United States   When Congress was debating the League of Nations, Viscount Grey said, "Let America come in with its reservations We will construe their reservations." Those who can 'construe' reservations can probably count votes.

(8) Audacious, perhaps, but hardly new. Three hundred years ago Henry IV of France conceived the idea of a federation of states. And along about the same time one Abbé de Saint Pierre had a similar dream. In line with good twentieth century methods, the Abbé sent out a questionnaire and from Cardinal Fleury, whose wisdom was equalled by his sense of humor, he received this reply, "You have forgotten a preliminary condition. . . . You must begin by sending a troop of missionaries to prepare the hearts and minds of the contracting sovereigns."

Federation is a familiar idea in the British Empire. You may have heard of the Federated Malay States, where indentured labor flourishes Tamils and Chinese have been brought in, to the disgust of the prouder and less tamable Malays. As the British learned that the Malaya Peninsula was especially valuable for the grow-ing of rubber and rich in tin, they became interested in the half score or more sultanates that controlled this region and the jungle people. They 'federated' them   In each the sultan or rajah still has his court and his harem and is main-tained as a puppet, just as in Java the sultanates have been 'federated' by the Dutch But at each court there is an English resident who is an autocrat and con-trols all matters of taxation and matters of exploitation of monopolies, economics, —anything that yields profit.

The Federated States of Europe and America could be well administered by executives trained in the Federated Malay States. We might not like it, but perhaps we would not be as submissive as the Tamils.

(9) Richard H. Heindel, who laboriously and painstakingly searched the output of English minds and mouths from 1900 to 1910, in his scholarly work, "The American Impact on Great Britain 1898-1914" (University of Pa. Press, 1940), writes on this subject of 'union'·

"The prophetic Stead went so far as to write the 'Americanization of the World' (1902) in which he spoke of our emergence as 'the greatest political, social, and commercial phenomenon of our time'. . . . Rosebery . . . did not believe we would quietly accept retaliation. 'Why, they are the most pugnacious nation that exists!' Winston Churchill extended the argument, 'The union of the Anglo-Saxon race was a great ideal, and if ever it was to be achieved it would be by increasing and not diminishing the friendly intercourse of trade.'

"The *Economist* declared in 1906, 'We doubt if the general public, and even some financiers in the U. S , fully recognize how deeply rooted is the distrust in this country, not of the general honesty of the American people, but of the business methods of many of the great industrial undertakings.' *Punch* ridiculed our bumptiousness in a poem, 'Morituri Salutant!'—'What is the hope, then, for civilization? 'What is the cure for a century's tears? 'What—save the mighty American Nation? 'That is the obvious answer, three cheers!' "

(10) "Learn to think imperially; the day of small nations has passed away, the day of empires has come", said Joseph Chamberlain, the dynamic Colonial Secretary whose "accession to office was marked by speeches breathing a new spirit of imperial consolidation"

(11) Ernest R. Trattner in his "Architects of Ideas" (Carrick and Evans, 1938) says, "In his 'Last Will and Testament' Cecil Rhodes, in a rhapsody of race-thinking, declared for 'the furtherance of the British Empire for the bringing of the whole uncivilized world under the British rule, for the recovery of the United States, for the making of the Anglo-Saxon race but one empire. What a dream! But yet it is probable. It is possible.' "

(12) "Britain is looking toward America", wrote Mallory Brown (*Chr Sci Monitor*, July 12, 1940), "for a new business partner to replace its former ally, France".

"If Great Britain falls, it is very likely that the same bitterness now existent between France and Britain would break forth to ruin relations between Great Britain and the United States It will take years for the French to forget that Great Britain did not come to their assistance in their hour of need. Already a somewhat similar resentment, whether justified or not, prevails in England toward the United States. One of the factors which created bitterness in France was Winston Churchill's 11th hour offer of a union between France and Britain. It came as France was crumbling, as her last ray of hope was vanishing. So Churchill's offer met with jeers Remembering the tardiness of Churchill's proposal, various American leaders, both inside and outside the Government, have discussed and urged the idea of proposing such a union between Great Britain and the United States immediately. Such a union, they urge, would give immediate courage to the British to carry on." (Pearson and Allen, July 13, 1940)

However magnanimous such a suggestion may have made the United States feel, Britain didn't seem to like it. "The New York Committee of the Federated Union Movement, which is among the foremost champions of help for Britain, pleads for an actual union with Britain on the lines proposed by Mr Churchill to France, on the ground that then, 'no matter how the Government of the British Isles changes, it can no more surrender the naval, air, or armed Forces than the Government of New York can surrender any of the armed Forces of the American Union'. The suggestion is, of course, gratuitous almost to the point of being insulting", wrote the English magazine *Truth,* August 23, 1940.

The erstwhile liberal journalist, H. N. Brailsford of the Manchester *Guardian* and the *New Republic,* sounds a frantic appeal for aid, "From England to America" (Whittlesey House, 1940) He would scare America into moving toward union, assuring us that we can't count on the British fleet defending us unless we participate in the war. And then he lets the cat out of the bag, declaring that Britain is no longer strong or rich enough to reconquer Nazified Europe. Only the U. S. can, and that means an expeditionary force.

That Britain needs something more than a substitute for an ally was recognized in 1893 by Andrew Carnegie, who showed how and why Britain needed America for her very own—to have and to hold. Said the canny Scot ironmaster, "The only course for Britain seems to be reunion with the giant child or sure decline to a secondary place and then to comparative insignificance".

(13) "Judging by press releases of the past few months and public utterances of government officials in high places, the movement has gained such headway as to receive official sanction and advocacy," stated Senate Document #182, April 15, 1940, discussing Streit's proposal for a British-American Union.

June 4, 1940, Churchill dramatically declared in the House of Commons that the British Empire and the United States "will have to be somewhat mixed up together in some of their affairs for mutual and general advantages. Even if—which I don't for a moment believe—this island or a large part of it, were subjugated and starving, then our Empire beyond the seas, armed and guarded by the British fleet, will carry on the struggle until in God's good time the New World, with all its power and might, sets forth to the liberation and rescues the old " And he cried out, "No one can stop it ' Like the Mississippi, it just keeps rolling along Let it roll ' Let it roll on full flood, inexorable, to broader lands and better days."

August 20, 1940, "Leslie Hore-Belisha, former Secretary of War, raised in Commons the possibility of an eventual union between the United States and the British Empire" (AP), while *Time,* Sept. 30, 1940, reports, "a tacit London-Washington axis is already a fact"

The Anglo-American joint control is to extend to water power "Last week President Roosevelt told a questioner at his press conference that discussions were under way with Canada, looking toward development of the power aspects of the scheme." (CP, Sept. 20, 1940)

"Both President and Mrs Roosevelt" according to *Newsweek*, Sept 30, 1940, "are deeply interested in the general idea of some eventual alliance and have had several private discussions with Clarence Streit, author of 'Union Now'. Naturally, however, the Administration would not openly broach the subject until there had been long public discussion and much further decline in isolationist sentiment." Not by any single act is this British-American union being put into effect. We give the British food, supplies, ammunition, 'obsolete' guns, 'obsolete' destroyers, 'obsolete' tanks, 4/5 of our airplane output, the use of our naval bases, the use of our Navy, the use of our manpower, defend their interests in China, occupy their Singapore base, build strategic airplane lines to New Zealand and Australia, unite with them in defending their territory. And so we find that we are doing all that Whitehall wishes without any formal act of union Again we are under the control of London, more completely than we were before '76

November 5, 1940 (NNS), "Senator Homer T. Bone in a flippant mood remarked that he was organizing a Society for the Promotion of Dominion Status for the United States. British-American relations are becoming so close, in the western Senator's judgment, that such a society will be necessary if we are to preserve our American identity For $1,000, he says, an American may become a belted earl or a bearded duke For $50, he can become a baron and work his way up." This of course will necessitate diadems and coronets for the Senate and ermine and crowns (half crowns perhaps) in the White House.

COMMENTS

Witter Bynner, Santa Fe, N.M., Oct. 6—"I have been immensely interested in your sound anti-propaganda bulletins. I have written our Senators and Congressmen that I am convinced that our participation in the World War, giving victory to one European side over the other when a stalemate would have been healthful, has been the prime cause of the present war, and I feel again that American participation now, if it should bring about over-advantage to the allied side, would prove in the end equally catastrophic to future peace " [1]

Stephen Bradley, Pittsburgh, Pa., Oct. 30—"Congratulations on your mimeographed leaflets which seem to have an amazing grasp on the complex incidents that are taking place all about us these days . . . I can't help feeling a little concern over the Senate's repeal of the embargo For a while it was difficult to arrive at any decision concerning the advisability of retention or repeal. I finally concluded that if we were to repeal it instead of shutting it up even tighter we would in a large measure be responsible first, for prolonging the war over there and, second, we would be the responsible party for a victory peace and a revenge treaty and a third world conflagration I cannot see either side winning this. Should Germany win I don't see how it could avoid avenging itself for the Treaty of Strangulation and the hopeless years that followed. Should England emerge triumphant wouldn't she be apt to wipe out this menace once and for all? How can any American with a grain of conscience wish to be a party to either condition? Yet if we start supplying materials are we not doing just that?"

Dixon Wecter, San Marino, Cal., Oct. 17—"Thank you heartily for your kindness in sending more of your able and erudite bulletins on world news. Although I cannot always share your estimate of the Machiavellian character of the British and a few other judgments of yours, honest and straightforward though they are, I am always keenly interested and shall be grateful for more bulletins." [2]

Chester Maxey, Walla Walla, Wash., Oct. 17—"Keep my name on your mailing list, to receive the bulletins on British propaganda in America I could disagree with all you say, and still appreciate the value of your bulletins. I believe all propaganda should be thoroughly exposed, and you seem to be about the only one interested in exposing the British variety. I am glad to have somebody constantly jogging my elbow with regard to what I read in the papers."

George H. Cless, Jr., Glens Falls, N. Y., Oct. 25—"Your bulletin #11 was a pippin. Great work! Send bulletin #9 to my friend . . . who is tremendously interested.

Herman Wittmeyer, Germantown, Pa., Oct. 20—"I appreciate receiving your spirited bulletins. I shall be eager to read them."

Dr. Lyman Richards, Boston, Mass , Oct. 25—"I enjoyed reading your bulletins very much and would be inclined to think that what you are doing in the interests of truth should be a very good influence in a world so full of inaccuracies and deception."

Lloyd Morain, Los Angeles, Calif., Oct. 15—"Your informative propaganda bulletins have precipitated and stimulated several activities. The members of the scientific group have been much interested."

A Government Official, Oct 31—"I am really a little worried that you should be, as you say, 'afraid' to send me your series on British propaganda. I'll be glad to keep on getting them. Of course, I'm on the President's side in this Neutrality fight. . . Beyond that my present convictions stop—as I truly believe the convictions of practically everybody in Washington stop. . . . So I'm quite willing to have my eyes kept open—and I enjoy your stuff for its saltiness, irrespective of whether I agree with it."

A University Professor, Oct. 31—"I have looked in vain to see if you were going to make some comment on the visit of Duff Cooper The invasion of America by this well known British sadist and glib-tongued propagandist has seemed to annoy me more than many things. . . . To my inquiry as to why Duff Cooper should not be stopped at Ellis Island, as would Dr. Goebbels or Emma Goldman, Mr. . . . writes, to my surprise, 'We weren't able to do anything with Duff Cooper but I passed your suggestion along to . . .' They got busy at once and were responsible for the demand made upon the State Department for a statement of the status of Duff Cooper as a foreign propogandist. . . . I had not seen anything in the papers about this. With thanks for Sargent Bulletin No. 11, which I expose to the young innocents in our reading room."

A Washington Commentator, Oct. 12—"I want to tell you how much I enjoy your bulletins, and I think they are of immense value in these troubled times I have been astonished by the subtlety of the British propagandists in this country. As you probably know I have a wide acquaintance among journalists and feature writers and most of them are pro English. . . . Most of these important writers have been taken in by the British propagandists. They systematically work on them by offering them trips to the war front, special privileges in London and put them up at the best clubs, etc. . . . It is outrageous how these foreign lecturers come over here, and lay the law down to us like we were a group of country yokels. . . . Some of the worse propaganda today is carried on in American colleges by these exchange professors. Some of them are really spies or clandestine propagandists. There is a bureau in London that routes them about in this country, and gives them fantastic amounts of money for entertainment. There is one in each important college. They win over the professors and their wives—and they work on the students and the community."

An International Journalist, Oct. 25—"I have just finished your article in *Common Sense,* and it is a patriotic service to give the American people the truth about British propagandists. . . Here in Washington I have seen them work—Sir Willmott Lewis, Willert, Kent, the managing editor of the London *Times* who spoke at the National Press Club, and then made a tour of the editorial offices of the country We have seen Max Aitken bob in and out of the White House. I am particularly glad you mentioned the house organ of the House of Morgan *Foreign Affairs* and the Foreign Policy Association which is nothing but a pro-English committee. Many of these people consider their American citizenship just a formality and act as though they were really Englishmen. This Anglo-American tie-up has lines into the most inner secrets of our Government. . . . Lord Cecil is a great friend of the Roosevelt family, and when he comes to the United States, he stays at Hyde Park. Interesting point—the President's brother James was first secretary of the American Embassy in London when Lord Salisbury was Prime Minister, was the head of the League of Nations Association in Great Britain. In the past Hyde Park has been sort of an English Hotel for visiting propagandists."

October, 1939

NOTES

(1) As a result of the artfully selected and slightly distorted news that was fed to the American people, rapid change of opinion was going on as illustrated in the following letters written a year later. Witter Bynner writes, "I am not so sure as I was that America's changing attitude is due mostly to British propaganda. Self-preservation is a prime instinct amongst all peoples; and there are too many obvious reasons why we should be feeling that instinct for me to feel its stirring is due to clever manipulation."

(2) Dixon Wecter writes on Oct. 8, 1940, "Frankly I ought to tell you that the continuance of my name on your mailing list is not, from your point of view, a very good investment. I should prefer to see such sums as these bulletins cost go to the British Red Cross rather than be wasted upon such stony soil as your present correspondent. I began to disagree with you a good while ago Just a year ago I recall writing you that I was interested in comments on the international situation, but that I could not share your suspicions about the direfulness of British propaganda. It is possible that your views have remained consistent and unchanged; I know at any rate that mine are clearer and warmer than they were a year ago. Your treatment of the Finnish episode was perhaps the first major irritation to me. Then in the spring, after the German offensive swept over Western Europe, your apparent admiration for men like Shipstead, the late Lundeen, and Rush Holt—whose speeches and views you helped to circulate—left me with a dubious taste in the mouth To my way of thinking these men, both the quick and the dead, symbolize scoundrelism of the first order, rivalled only by the instance of Colonel Lindbergh. I believed, and hope I still believe, that you are honest and acting according to your lights. But I disagree with

your invariable description of any aid to Britain as 'hysteria', your sardonic attitude toward the President, . . . To my view, the destroyer deal was the finest coup in American statesmanship since the spring of 1917. I should not be sorry to see total intervention by the United States upon the side of England; until public opinion has reached that stage of enlightenment, I cheer for every ship, bomber, or tank that we can send to the most gallant struggle this modern world has yet seen, under the leadership of the man whom I most admire today, Winston Churchill "

ARE WE "THE BEST INFORMED PEOPLE IN THE WORLD"?

Americans are kept ignorant of essential facts. England controls news as in last war. German broadcasts come with semblance of freedom, for Chamberlain reiterates "Hitler is England's best propagandist".

British journalists, C. S Kent, managing editor of the London *Times,* Lord Beaverbrook (Max Aitken) in editorial, bankers and White House conferences have done the work Lord Northcliffe did in 1916 to bring the American press to the support of the Empire.

Writers and commentators can sell only what editors believe will feed popular prejudices. Gunther tactfully lets out that this is a war for power. There is no periodical that will print factual observations of unprejudiced travelers. No impartial investigation or report on European affairs is available to the American public. [1]

Books previously mentioned in these Bulletins have been eagerly ordered and read. Of these additional recent books, Rogerson, Abshagen, some others, are, or may be suppressed. "Prohibition against statements or writing 'false or otherwise' which may cause disaffection" or "prejudice recruiting" is provided in the bill which passed the House last May and now awaits Senate action (cf Bul #8). The penalty is 2 years in the U S, Canada 5 years, England 10 years, in France the guillotine. In Canada, "Mounties" raided a "home in Toronto and made five arrests under the new clause" (*Nation,* October 28, 1939).

Has Improved British Propaganda Technique Affected Our Opinions? "Propaganda in the Next War", by Capt. Sidney Rogerson (Geoffrey Bles, London, 1938), reveals plans by which America is to be brought into next war. (Reprint from *Congressional Record* on request) The secret Vansittart organization and technique are not mentioned.

"Propaganda for War: The Campaign Against American Neutrality, 1914-17", by H C. Peterson (University of Oklahoma Press, 1939), forecasts what later revelations will show of what has been going on these past three years in this country. It includes recently discovered secret British Press Resumé of propagandists in America.

"Propaganda Technique and the World War", by Harold D. Lasswell, Assistant Professor of Political Science, University of Chicago, first published in 1927, and republished by Peter Smith, New York, 1938, gives insight into the improved technique of recent years.

"England Expects Every American to Do His Duty", 1937, "Blood is Cheaper Than Water", 1939, by Quincy Howe (Simon & Schuster). Closest American student of our foreign policy, who as editor of the *Living Age*, inspired *Fortune's* article [2] on international collusion for profits during the War, which resulted in the Nye Investigation, here brings the story of the 'British network' in America up to date with names and particulars. Plain speaking, hard hitting.

Who Are the Current Zaharoffs? "The Most Powerful Man in the World: The Life of Sir Henri Deterding", by Glyn Roberts (Covici-Friede, 1938). A former secretary reveals astonishing inside workings of the British Empire, the greatest trading organization in the world, and the personalities and profits of associates and successors to the great Shell Oil magnate. [3]

Is the Government of Great Britain Democratic? "King, Lords and Gentlemen: Influence and Power of the English Upper Classes", by Karl H. Abshagen (Heinemann Ltd., London, 1939). Intimate particulars of personalities and powers that control.

"The Tragedy of Ramsay MacDonald", by L MacNeill Weir (Secker & Warburg, London, 1938). Government opposition prevented publication for years of this revelation by a former Parliamentary Secretary of the inside workings of the British Government and how MacDonald taken in by the Tories, became a puppet and a broken man. [4]

"The Decline and Fall of the British Empire", by Robert Briffault (Simon & Schuster, 1938). Reveals the current and historic myths that support the empire and protect profits.

Is Our American Foreign Policy Over-Influenced by Britain? "The Far Eastern Policy of the United States", by A. Whitney Griswold (Harcourt, Brace, 1938). A Yale professor shows how our "Open Door" policy was sold to us by the British and has been maintained at great expense by us for the benefit of England. [5] "Giddy Minds and Foreign Quarrels", by Charles A. Beard (Harper, 1939). The folly of our Administration, universities, peace societies, in interfering "in foreign controversies everywhere".

Do Bankers and Munitions Makers Promote or Prevent War? "The Pressure Boys: The Inside Story of Lobbying in America", by Kenneth G. Crawford of the Washington Press Corps (Messner, 1939). "Wall Street Under Oath", by Ferdinand Pecora (Simon & Schuster, 1939). The inside of banking as revealed to the Congressional Committee

Is the Coming War Part of an Inevitable Social and Economic Revolution? (cf Bul #9) Frank S Hanighen (*Atlantic,* April, 1939)— "It is a real revolution". Crane Brinton, Harvard author of "The Anatomy of Revolution", recognizes this as an "advanced state of revolution". Even in Japan the militarists are putting an end to the profit system, Oland D. Russell tells us in "The House of Mitsui" (Little, Brown, 1939).

"War, Peace and Change", by John F. Dulles (Harper, 1939) (Bul #5). War results from opposition to inevitable change. "The Clue to History", by John Macmurray (Harper, 1939), going back to Christ, finds that the European dualism is approaching its end. "The End of Economic Man", by Peter Drucker (John Day, 1939), recognizes the end of the profit system from Rhine to Pacific.
November 3, 1939

NOTES

(1) Dr Hans Zinsser in his autobiography "As I Remember Him", speaking of the "intellectual 'Sturm und Drang' in the German youth" of the 19th century, says, "If one studies it, — even superficially, — one is strongly impressed by the intellectual and spiritual interdependence of England, France, and Germany. One gains the conviction that, given half a chance, reasonable freedom from the economic hardship and the propaganda which breed misunderstanding and political perversion, science and intellectual cooperation might again draw them all together, at least sufficiently to act as brakes on international greed. One cannot, of course, hope ever to eliminate entirely the avarice of commercial competition between modern nations largely composed of shopkeepers. But the little average butter-and-eggs men who compose the bulk of population want nothing more than to be left alone to the enjoyment of their nether senses, and the big fellows — the international, super-butter-and-eggs men — might, in the end, be held reasonably in check by a growing educated class under the leadership of intellectuals civilized to the appreciation and admiration of scientific discovery, spiritual nobility, or artistic distinction, wherever or by whom produced "

(2) In *Fortune* in its March issue, 1934, is told the story of munitions profiteer-

ing in the last war, based largely on Quincy Howe's investigation previously printed in *Living Age*. The article was rewritten largely by Archibald MacLeish The American munitioneers were given scant notice. ". . . only 15 words to the Du Ponts, America's leading merchants of death, who were at exactly the time of *Fortune's* story secretly smuggling armaments to Hitler in violation of international law. . . .

"*Fortune* knew that numerous authors were preparing books exposing the munitions traffic, that these books dealt largely with U S. steel, Bethlehem Steel, Anaconda Copper, the 23,000 millionaires created during the World War, the subsidizers of the Navy League, the corrupters of government, the sinister forces which were responsible for bringing America into the war. . . The Nye-Vandenberg investigation shortly afterward took up the industry, filled thousands of pages with its disclosures, and incidentally proved that the House of Morgan . . . had much to do with getting the U.S. into the war. . . .

"*Fortune* . . . announced. '. . a greater campaign on this subject, let this article, then, be considered as no more than an opening gun' . . . *Fortune* sent Hilton Howell Railey to Europe for material . . . Railey piled up documentation proving, he later wrote, that 'the blackest sins alleged against them (munitions makers) were probably pale reflections of the truth' (p 240, Railey's memoirs, 'Touched with Madness,' Carrick & Evans, 1938)." *Fortune* suppressed all this as told by Seldes in *In Fact*, December 16, 1940.

(8) Early in 1940 the British Government announced its intent (*Newsweek*, Feb. 5, 1940) "to turn over the production of all their interests to the British-controlled Royal Dutch Shell in order to present a united front against the Rumanian Government comptroller". This is the company of Deterding, which is now more powerful and more active than in the last war.

"The greatest empire the world had ever seen had recognized in Deterding one of the masterful go-getters of the age." Sir Henri Deterding has been called by an anonymous American writer "the last living representative of the one-man super-trust". Ivar Kreuger and Alfred Lowenstein are dead, wrote Roberts, "but we still have with us such colorful and unresigned gentlemen as Fritz Thyssen of Germany's steel trust, Lord McGowan of Britain's I C. I, Henry and Edsel Ford, Japan's Mitsuis, Dannie Heinemann of the Belgian public utilities octopus, the 'Sofina', Don Simon Patiño of Bolivia and some others".

Shell and Standard were long great rivals. Deterding came to New York and entered into an arrangement with Teagle of Standard Oil to control the oil of the world and regulate the price He made a deal with the Russian government for the exploitation of Baku oil. But the Bolsheviks came in and interfered. As a result, Great Britain spent four billions after the Armistice, Deterding hundreds of millions of his own money, and forced Churchill to force Wilson to send American forces to carry the American flag into Murmansk, the White Sea, Siberia, and the Caspian Sea. But they failed to get oil.

Such men as Deterding have a great stake in the Empire, and the Empire has a great stake in them. If Deterding had become converted to bolshevism, it would probably have deprived the Empire of oil.

"If Sir Henri Deterding, most international, most energetic, most aggressive and forthright of big business men, may reasonably be labeled 'the most powerful man in the world', it is not because of any inherent, God-given qualities in himself or even because of an insurmountable power he has built up around him," his secretary writes.

"It is because he has succeeded in making millions of nervous, amiable, anxious and ordinary little men believe that he and his friends are their advocates . . . that civilization goes when capitalism goes. . . Sir Henri can boast that the propaganda that his class pumps out through its friends and hirelings and tools, through newspapers, sermons, magazines, films, radio bulletins and talks and mouth-to-mouth pep talks, has had a good deal of success. The static type of propaganda, directed to the end that nothing shall be done, as distinct from the dynamic kind which demands action, has had a . . high degree of success in America and the British Empire . . .

"The Deterdings . . . are powerful . . only because our ignorance or cynicism or stupidity or apathy give them power. Their power has no relation whatsoever to their inherent ability or right to rule. Their capacity to tackle economic and financial problems as they arise is pitiably inadequate, blazingly meager. Already the world is in the hands of forces they do not understand and cannot control."

Something of Deterding's Armenian successors who control the world's oil, and other forces behind the British Government, the motives and methods of these most powerful personalities is told in "What Makes Lives", pp. 59-62.

(4) Weir tells the story of the rise of Labour to power after the last war while the greater political sense and experience of the Tories undermined the loyalty of Labour leaders It brings to mind Matthew Arnold's "ebb and flow of human misery that brings the eternal note of sadness in" When Stanley Baldwin, a year after he had become Premier, was turned out of office in 1924, the first Labour Government came in, which was wrecked by the forged Zinoviev Letter, and Baldwin returned to power. In the next five years the Kellogg Pact was killed largely by British reservations, Mussolini boosted in Albania, the Geneva naval conference wrecked, the League degraded. Then came the deflation of labor in England and America, culminating in the General Strike which Baldwin by skilful handling brought on in 1926 and from which labor has not yet recovered.

With the coming of the world depression in 1929 Baldwin shrewdly stepped aside to let the Labour Party bear the onus. The decrease in business, the decline of British exports, the shrinkage of overseas investments and the increase in the dole presented an opportunity which the Tories were quick to seize upon to discredit the Labour Government on the ground of extravagance, and forced it to 'go to the country'

Then the intrigue that set up the 'National' Government was put through. In the 1931 election campaign it was represented that the extravagance of the dole had brought the country's credit so low that they could not borrow money.

MacDonald in his campaigning flaunted worthless German bank notes, prognosticating that British pound notes would be equally worthless unless he and his associates were 'returned' to power and stuck to gold. The electors, filled with fear that the country was on the verge of bankruptcy, voted in the Coalition. Baldwin dominated, but to preserve the appearance of a Coalition the King appointed MacDonald Prime Minister. MacDonald, who had known poverty and lonesomeness, won over by snobbery, pageantry, flattery from the peerage, was now a traitor to his former colleagues. Philip Snowden, tense crusader for Labour, who had stood by gold, was given an earl's robe and sent to the Lords. And immediately the Government went off gold.

MacDonald's "act of political apostasy unparalleled in British history" saved the Tories and gave them a new lease of power. Weir tells us that this was "the greatest disaster that has befallen this country, and indeed the world, since the War It is comparable in its course and consequences with the setting up of the Nazi regime in Germany, for which this Government, too, must bear a major responsibility. . . . Since the advent of the 'National' Government the foundations of democracy have been attacked and Britain's historic freedom has been undermined" (p 565).

This brief story as taken from Weir and other sources, how Baldwin, finally discredited after his hypocrisy as to the state of England's armament, by the discovery of the Hoare-Laval conspiracy of Abyssinia, restored himself to favor by skilful arranging and managing the abdication stunt, and went out in a blaze of glory, leaving the mess in Chamberlain's hands, is told in detail in the chapter "Unknown History" to be published next year in "The Course of Human Events".

(5) An article later by Griswold in *Harpers* for August, 1940, brings the story up to date (cf Bul #95).

SOURCES OF INFORMATION FOR AMERICANS

Welcome criticisms suggest these Bulletins are not judicial. We hope not. The 'other side' means little to one who sees many sides. Here are no attacks, only such explanations as we can find. Yes, we violate tabus in considering motives of those who manufacture and distribute 'news'. Our purpose is to inform, to present the neglected and unseen.

The propaganda fodder that the American people have been fed on, —selected and censored in London, written by exiles, women scorned, discontented expatriates, dispossessed 'economic royalists' (German Freedom Party),—is arousing resentment, even among 'intellectuals'.[1] Expelled journalists are seldom as sympathetically explained as in *Unity*, November 6,—"Edgar Ansel Mowrer, experienced and highly trained correspondent as he is, is yet notoriously anti-Nazi. He has suffered at the hands of the Nazis, and has reason for his hate. Can any man wholly divorce his judgment from his emotions?"

The Jews deserve understanding as well as sympathy. Their vocal justified hate should not mislead us. They are being exploited, they may later realize, for selfish and imperialistic interests.

Royalty, earls, marquesses, statesmen, politicians, authors, humorists, scientists, lecturers, Britain's cream, have come to worship at American shrines, to flatter us with gracious words, to strengthen the 'ties that bind' to 'explain' the peril of 'the democracies',—but not in India.

Our Administration and State Department, ambassadors, college presidents, have been 'taken in', overwhelmed with attentions, just as twenty-five years ago when last we were worthy of British consideration, before they abused us for 'coming in late' and wanting our money back [2] Leaders, national and university, who should be protecting, informing and advising us in international affairs have been transformed into ever-flowing founts of imperialistic propaganda, pleasing to Lord Lothian and Britain's financial agents and those who look to them.

Tactful reiteration that we are "the best informed people in the world" has convinced us. But three years of secret subtle propaganda has brought us from the attitude of "never again" to "now it's inevitable".

That "World War II" is on has been assumed and promoted While the conflicting powers continue diplomatic sparring, the campaign to 'bring us in' goes relentlessly on. The British Tories have discovered that they can declare war without fighting, just as the Japanese militarists earlier showed that they could fight without declaring war.

Our newspaper and periodical press has had its pro-British policy fixed by Kent of the London *Times* and Lord Beaverbrook (Max Aitken) as by Lord Northcliffe in 1917. Directors and affiliates of Morgan supervise, and crash down on offenders, as in *Harper's* for the September issue.

The Private News Letter, due to justified lack of confidence in our press, has become a significant phenomenon of the times. Now censored in England and Canada, in the U. S. the following are important· *Week by Week*, 3034 P St., N.W., Wash , D. C. $5 per year. *Weekly Foreign Letter*, 515 Madison Ave., N. Y. $24 per year. *Uncensored*, 112 E. 19th St., N. Y. Weekly. $5 per year.

November 13, 1939

NOTES

(1) Sometime after the war, investigators will perhaps probe into the motives that lead expatriots, correspondents and commentators to promote the hate which made possible this war. Most will have been found to be sincere. The way was easy for the hate promoters, difficult for those who would stay the hysteria. Some yielded to pressure, some to bribes.

(2) From early spring until fall, 1940, it was fashionable in academic circles to emphasize that there was no British propaganda, no need of it, that we were sophisticated and that events speak for themselves. Ambassador Page, Colonel House, Sir Gilbert Parker, H. G. Wells and innumerable other participants in the propaganda of 1916-18 in their memoirs had told frankly of their part. This was attributed to vainglorious boasting Late in the fall a new fashion was introduced Simultaneously from the professors of Harvard and other great universities that act as sounding boards, and from President Roosevelt himself, came the information that unfortunately a "myth" had grown up that Americans had been misled in the last war, and this was accompanied by denunciation of those who would dim the luster of those who had labored to bring us into that war and served through it.

MORE BOOKS THAT INFORM

Beware of promoted best seller propaganda books written by the haters, and those who pander to established prejudice These suggestions of honest books are supplementary to those recommended in Bulletin #13 and preceding.(1)

Exposing Propaganda for War: "Words That Won The War", by James R. Mock and Cedric Larson (Princeton U. Press, 1939), tells of the Creel propaganda in America twenty years ago. Look for improved technique in the repetition soon to come "And So To War", by Hubert Herring (Yale U. Press, 1939), traces the change in Roosevelt's views and utterances from peace toward war. "When War Comes: What Will Happen And What To Do", ed. Larry Nixon (Greystone Press, 1939). The bill for the next war, 'win or lose'.

Light on the Current World Wide Social and Economic Revolution: "The Ending Of Hereditary American Fortunes", by Gustavus Myers (Julian Messner, Inc., 1939); "The Evolution Of Finance Capitalism", by Geo. W. Edwards (Longmans, 1939); "Business And Capitalism", by Prof. N. S. B Gras, Harvard Graduate School of Business Administration (F. S. Crofts & Co., 1939); "Business And Modern Society", by Dean Wallace B. Donham and the Harvard Business Faculty (Harvard University Press, 1938).

The Future of Man, optimism from present pessimism: "Twilight Of Man", by E. A. Hooton, Harvard anthropologist (Putnam, 1939); "The Fate Of Homo Sapiens: An unemotional Statement of the Things that are happening to him now, and of the immediate Possibilities confronting him", by H. G. Wells (Secker and Warburg, London, 1939).

Other Recommended Books: "Rain Upon Godshill", by J B. Priestley (William Heinemann, 1939). A long chapter on the state of England. "Duplicity in high places and stupidity in low ones. Our national life . . . riddled with complacency, snobbery, hypocrisy, stupidity. Not only have we had, for years, a rich-tired-old-man government, but behind that government there has been a rich-tired-old-man mentality. For the last twenty years we have been governed for the benefit of the City."

"Disgrace Abounding", by Douglas Reed (Jonathan Cape, 1939), assails the stupidity and venality of England's leaders who in control of the world have brought it to its present state. "Light Out Of Darkness", by Clarence C. Hatry (Rich and Cowan, London, 1939). The great English financier, after ten years of contemplation in prison, outlines a plausible plan to bring peace to Europe "Our Present Discontents", by W. R Inge (Putnam, 1939); "Democracy And World Dominion", by E. D. Schoonmaker (Richard Smith, 1939); "The Deadly Parallel", by C. Hartley Grattan (Stackpole, 1939); "Why Meddle In Europe?" by Boake Carter (McBride & Co., 1939).
November 14, 1939

NOTES

(1) Other books have been suggested in connection with Bulletins #13, #22, #71. There is no intent to make this a bibliography, but to mention only books pertinent to the subject or important books that were overlooked or have been suppressed.

The most recent book on propaganda is "War Propaganda and the United States", by Harold Lavine, editorial director of the Institute of Propaganda Analysis, and James Wechsler, published by Yale University Press, 1940. It brings the subject up through the early months of 1940

Peter F. Drucker's "The End of Economic Man" is mentioned in Bul #13, Lawrence Dennis' "Dynamics of War and Revolution" in Bul #71.

E. A Hooton's latest book, "Why Men Behave Like Apes and Vice Versa", a revision of his 1939 Vanuxem lectures at Princeton on body and behavior, was published by the Princeton University Press, 1940

George F. Kneller's "Educational Philosophy of the Third Reich", an important, detailed and exhaustive study, is to be published by the Yale University Press early in 1941.

S. H. Hauck at Scotch Plains, N. J., publishes the "Flanders Hall" series of paper bound books at from 50 cents to 75 cents Some of the titles already issued are. "The Scarlet Fingers", "Lord Lothian vs Lord Lothian", "It Happened Again", "Democracy on the Nile", "Inhumanity, Unlimited", "The Hapless Boers", "The Greatest Crime in History", "Misadventure in Scandinavia", "War Against Women and Children", "Doublecross in Palestine", "The Slave Business". Some of these books, of which no editions are available in any American library though once published in England, have had to be re-translated. An interesting study could be made of books that have been removed from libraries, books whose sale has been quietly suppressed through the intervention of foreign intelligence services.

It is difficult to get books published at the present time This "Getting US into War" would probably not be accepted by any publisher. It hasn't been offered to any. George Cless, Jr., whose "Eleventh Commandment" (Mind Your Own Business), published three years ago, would have saved the U S. billions of dollars had it been more widely read and its counsel heeded, has just completed another book, "America's Rendezvous with Destiny" (Look Before You Leap). One of the largest and most enterprising publishing houses, after carefully considering it, writes him:

"Sorry to report that after many and careful readings of 'America's Rendezvous With Destiny' we have decided that we cannot make an offer of publication. Paradoxically enough, we feel this is a highly publishable book but that it would be too much of a gamble, since we could probably not get it out before the early part of next year at which time there is every possibility that we will be at war. To you I know that this is just dousing gasoline on the flames, because your hope is that the publication of this book will help in the fight to forestall the war."

MORALITY—INTERNATIONAL AND ACADEMIC

"Principles of international morality"[1] are the unctuous concern of Yale's President Seymour. And Mr. Roosevelt has a "craze for what he so humorously calls 'religion and morality'", to quote Mencken, the great American boobophobe "His gabble for 'religion and morality' . . . may give the judicious pause."[2]

Let's have 'religion and morality', and 'democracy' too, the more the better. But to any God-fearing man the kind now trailed about with fish-horn publicity is blasphemous. It leaves an odor of 'Bombay duck'. This hypocrisy stems from the Kaiser's "Gott mit uns", through Chamberlain, Lothian, Hull Now our university presidents parrot it.

Fear that "the hope of free institutions as a basis of modern civilization will be jeopardized" if British imperial power is diminished, has put lines in the face of President Conant of Harvard. He fears too we may "handicap those who are fighting for ideals we share". Is he thinking of Britain and India? J. B. Priestley in his latest, "Rain Upon Godshill", writes of England, "We are not a democracy, but a plutocracy roughly disguised as an aristocracy".

Conant resents that it should "be taken as a premise that the only matter before the country is how to keep the United States out of war". The Harvard *Crimson* (undergraduate daily) replies that Seymour and Conant "are earning an unenviable place in the road-gang that is trying to build for the United States a super-highway straight to Armageddon". "We refuse to fight another balance of power war. We intend to resist to the utmost any suggestions that American intervention is necessary to 'save civilization' or even to 'save democracy and freedom'."

"The lofty positions of these men give their words weight beyond their worth." Their moralistic propaganda is "far more dangerous than any emanating from overseas". They are using the "lever of their prestige to force the unwilling door of public opinion", says the *Crimson*.

It was these same people of position that the British propagandists went after first twenty-five years ago. Sir Gilbert Parker, who directed the English propaganda drive on the U. S. in 1914-1917, wrote, "Beginning with university and college presidents, professors and scientific men and running through all the ranges of the population . . . We . . . established association by personal correspondence with influential and eminent people of every profession in the United States "[3]

Among congratulatory letters to the *Crimson* on its "sound" position one alumnus pointed out Conant and Seymour were "associated on their own university boards with directors of financial institutions, members of Morgan, the British agents and affiliated concerns. They must necessarily stand in with their associates, whether they like it or not

"Seymour has long been conditioned to the attitude of the House of Morgan, acting as apologist for British and American financial interests . . . Conant, just out of the laboratory, showed in his speeches of 1935-36 the broad, liberal mind of a scientist. . . . He has found it difficult to raise the necessary money to make up the Harvard deficits and at the same time fight the powers that be.

"Both are in a position pitiful and pitiable. Be gentle with them."

President Conant's irritable and arbitrary reactions, his jitters amounting almost to a neurosis, have resulted in confusion and rebellion among students and the younger members of the faculty.[4]

The Student Union, new student organizations, undergraduate publications, younger members of the faculty are bitter in their criticism of tyrannical and moralistic internal and international attitudes.[5]

Petitioning undergraduates and protesting faculty committees have been autocratically snubbed and insulted. The powers that hold the money bags must be pleased. 'Let others be damned'. It's a sorry world, my masters! It's almost like a bad dream of legionnaires purging the dissidents or of sadistic cossacks riding down rebellious students.[6]

Freedom of speech is still permitted, to those whom the administration likes! Permission already granted a speaker is revoked because of a phoney action brought as the result of Texas Dies' 'witch-hunt'. Why so sensitive about indictments? Harvard-Morgan men have been indicted; others have escaped. Richard Whitney resigned his Harvard function on going to Sing Sing, where he is now serving as instructor.[7]

The popularity of the Social Sciences and the neglect of the Classics and Humanities were deplored a few years ago in his annual report by Conant. Now he has emasculated the Social Science departments.[8]

On the faculty, men once bold and free, occupying comfortable chairs and looking forward to pensions, are careful to take no stand, to utter no statement that would not be favorably received in Morgan offices [9]

No clear-sighted analysis, no aid in solving problems may be looked for from them. Professor Fay, erudite historian, once bold investigator of war causes, tells us we went into the last war not because Morgan, duPont, and the British hoodwinked us, but because of Shakespeare, Wordsworth, Dickens. "Those whose memories are good know that this idealism . . . was a very real thing."[10]

J B Priestley,[11] a free man with no hope of pension, remembers this and more that Fay forgets. "In 1914 Asquith and Grey may not have been crusading for 'gallant little Belgium'; but the people were, for I was one of them myself and I know. What the world often fails to realize is that we are a nation of idealistic simpletons frequently governed and manipulated by cynics. (We share this strain of thoughtless but genuine moral idealism, of course, with the Americans)"

Clark M. Eichelberger, National Director of the League of Nations Association, Inc., and active interventionist, on October 11 announced that a poll among college presidents and deans showed 90% favoring President Roosevelt's neutrality program. The unfortunate 10% will not be favorably looked upon by their trustees who have to look to our financially minded for funds.[12]

"Newspaper editors have long regarded 'polls' taken by pressure groups as one of the cruder forms of propaganda." (*Uncensored*, Oct. 14, 1939)

It is this financial shadow of imperialism, the need of war to crush those who challenge British trade or profits, that falls athwart our universities, that has made "cowards of us all".

Who is the most powerful man in America? The Marquess of Lothian should be the best pleased. He is getting what he wants.
November 15, 1939

NOTES

[1] "The function of force in human affairs is to give moral ideas time to take root", sagely remarked Mahan, inspirer of the gospel of American imperialism. C E M Joad in his "Journey Through the War Mind" (Faber and Faber, 1940), discussing the amorality of the state, notes that Curry's "The Case for Federal Union" quotes statesmen to make this point. Lord Salisbury, thinking of Russia, says, "Let those take who have the power, let those keep who can, is practically the only rule of Russia's policy", and comments, "Wherein I am bound to add she does not differ widely from many other States". He might have dispensed with the 'm'

[2] Until he transferred his first allegiance from Americans to the British, Mr. Roosevelt had little to say about religion. *Time*, January 16, 1939, remarks that though he "is an Episcopal churchwarden and an occasional worshipper . . he has never been so prone to invoke his Maker as were Calvin Coolidge and Warren G. Harding To many devout churchmen he appeared to have the failings of most modern political liberals—a secular conception of political morality, an indifference about religion's place in the modern state "

From Whitehall, relayed through Wall Street to university presidents and from Washington to the people, various notes have been sounded from time to time First it was a better peace, and how to win a place at the peace table, —then it was democracy and civilization,—more recently 'religion' is accented.

Walter Lippmann, loud-speaker for the House of Morgan, who, though he is not Christian scarcely deserves *Time's* designation, Jan. 16, 1939, "a typical agnostic moralist", similarly declared that "to dissociate free institutions from religion and patriotism is to render them unworkable".

The 'religion' served up this way is a false article, a fake line of goods, to help sell participation in the war to a moralistic and idealistic people. Lord Halifax, when hotel rooms were scarce in London, preserved a separate room for use as chapel for his devotions. (cf Bul #97)

(3) "Why college professors are more susceptible to hate psychoses than are the 'uncultured masses', Einstein attempts to explain in a letter to Freud, quoted by Hogben in his 'Dangerous Thoughts'. 'Experience proves that it is rather the so-called 'Intelligentsia' that is most apt to yield to these disastrous collective suggestions, since the intellectual has no direct contact with life in the raw but encounters it in its easiest synthetic form, the printed page'

"With the revelations of Parker and many other participants before us, we now know whence come the 'disastrous collective suggestions' to which Einstein refers. It will be interesting to attempt to gain some understanding of just how these are propagated and spread in a great university, and by what forces " (cf "Universities Promote War" in "What Makes Lives", pp 181-194)

(4) Some explanation of the pressure that has been applied to bring President Conant from his free liberal attitude at the Tercentenary into line with the views and purposes of Wall Street and Whitehall will be found in the introductions to the Handbook of Private Schools, particularly the 21st and 22nd editions, in "What Makes Lives", pp 181-214, also in the Harvard undergraduate monthlies.

(5) These recently appointed salesmen, university presidents, meet sales resistance and accuse youth of having "no moral sense". "A moral sense is a primary emotional conviction .   that it matters whether a line of conduct is right or wrong. . . . The majority of the peoples of the earth do not have what we call a moral sense at all .   . Bringing children up thus to have a moral sense is a special invention, characteristic of European-American culture and very seldom found in other parts of the world. The real danger to our Democracy lies, not in those who are just growing up, but in all of us—and because we have a moral sense. . . . But these younger people of today are the only ones . . . who have first been taught it was moral to work hard for success, and then have been given nothing to do Moral as they were and are, they are placed in a position in which they cannot do what they have been taught is right. And they have been carefully brought up to feel miserable and guilty unless they do do right. . . . If our moral sense is strong enough to make us feel guilty, but not strong enough to make us criticize ourselves, we may drive the next generation, who also have a moral sense and also want to be right—at least part of the time—into the fold of totalitarian leaders" (*Harper's*, Jan., 1941, pp 134-5, Mead).

(6) A cheerful, optimistic Harvard professor writes me, Nov. 20, 1940,— "You work yourself up into a state of extraordinary exaggeration when you write of a similarity, even remote and bad-dream-like, between the present conditions at Harvard and 'sadistic Cossacks riding down rebellious students'. Probably good sound American hyperbole is as good a weapon as any against the pious internationalists like Streit and my colleagues of the Department of

Government at Harvard. But American exaggeration and humour is such a great thing in itself that I hate to see it wasted on politically unimportant people. I think you are wasting good ammunition. Specifically I feel—though memory and other forms of distortion may play me false—that even at Harvard the movement towards intervention in Europe is not nearly as important and effective as it was when I was an undergraduate in 1915-17. As far as undergraduate opinion and opinion among graduate students and the instructing staff under thirty-five years of age, I am almost sure of the above. At Harvard active interventionists are almost entirely confined to the Government Department." Since then the infection has spread and 80% to 90% of the faculty are rabidly foaming at the mouth, or pretending to, as a means of self-protection.

(7) The most outspoken defense of civil liberties of recent time is that of Wendell Willkie on "Fair Trial" in the *New Republic* in the winter of 1939-40, in which he tells as nowhere else in print just how phoney and flimsy were the cases brought by the government against Earl Browder and Fritz Kuhn, and contrasts the much heavier penalties given them than to Richard Whitney and to Judge Manton, who, in the next highest judicial position in the Supreme Court of the United States, sold justice to his great enrichment, which riches he will soon be free to 'enjoy'.

The precarious position of those on high make them an easy mark for the satirist as in "Jonathan Wild". "Marry, your hero guts an exchequer, while your thief disembowels a portmanteau; your hero sacks a city, while your thief sacks a cellar; your hero marauds on a larger scale, and that is all the difference, for the principle and the virtue are one, but two of a trade cannot agree: therefore your hero makes laws to get rid of your thief, and gives him an ill name that he may hang him; for might is right, and the strong make laws for the weak, and they that make laws to serve their own turn do also make morals to give colour to their laws . . . One is crowned for that for which another is tormented. . . . A poor sheep-stealer is hanged for stealing of victuals, compelled peradventure by necessity of that intolerable cold, hunger, and thirst, to save himself from starving but a great man in office may securely rob whole provinces, undo thousands, pill and poll, oppress *ad libitum*, flea, grind, tyrannize, enrich himself by spoils of the commons, be uncontrollable in his actions, and after all, be recompensed with turgent titles, honoured for his good service, and no man dare find fault, or mutter at it."

(8) Robert K. Lamb, formerly on the faculty of Harvard and later at Williams, in his article on "Starving the Social Sciences", *Nation*, May 15, 1937, deals with the situation at Harvard (cf also Handbook of Private Schools, 22nd edition, pp 57-60).

In the Harvard *Guardian*, Nov. 19, 1939, the then editor-in-chief, Ward Hussey (cf Bul #62) presenting the best possible case for the Administration endeavored to show that it was not motivated by the desire "to make the instruction in.. . . social sciences so poor that the recent trend of undergraduate concentration will be reversed". In the same issue, president Enno Hobbing, and managing editor, William Dale, after making the indictment that the Administration's triumph in the ten year case would mean that teaching would be "severely injured" in fields affecting about one-half the undergraduates, go on to say that "It is idle to ascribe any malevolent intent to the Administration Against its will, the Administration was forced to damage Harvard education "

Explaining "the unsuitableness of Harvard government" historically, Hobbing and Dale show how "as the University came to depend on gifts" it "assumed the structure of a modern corporation" and "combined financial control with power over educational policy". "The power of the President has led to the neglect of faculty opinion. . . As long as the faculty was growing comfortably it . . . was content to let the Deans, the departments, etc., advise the President on appointments and on minor matters of policy However, the present issues are so broad as to require faculty participation in dealing with them. This is clear from the failure of autocratic control to serve education "

(9) In the Fall of 1940 the faculty of Harvard fell in line for the march to war and gave voice to their hysteria in unmeasured terms. In December however Professors Hocking, Holcombe and Shapley jointly wrote a letter to the *Crimson* warning Harvard men not to lead President Roosevelt to break his solemn promise during the campaign that he would keep us out of war.

An anthropologist's point of view as to the susceptibilities of academic faculties is taken in the 23rd edition of the Handbook of Private Schools, pp 67-118 (cf also "The Sterility of Scholarship", by Porter Sargent, *American Teacher,* March, 1939).

(10) "Professor Fay probably has no need to consult the scholarly Shakespeare Yearbook published in Germany, hundreds of pages of fine print telling of productions and editions, to know that there have probably been more Shakespearean productions in Germany since the war than in all the English speaking world. If that was the result of war, then the war was a success and no need for another for the same purpose Anyone who has been in Germany recently knows that even in the small provincial towns there are several Shakespearean productions each month." ("What Makes Lives", p 190).

About the great Shakespeare festival at Heidelberg in the summer of 1939 and the elaborate production of King Lear planned for performance in Berlin in 1940, Mr. Fay may not have known. Such matters are superfluous to the propaganda picture that is being painted by our periodical press (cf "What Makes Lives", p 154).

(11) This was written when J. B. Priestley was living in the United States, more than half Americanized and hoping to be completely so. The outbreak of war found him on the Isle of Wight absorbed in making manuscript. By the spring of 1939 he was actively opposing Chamberlain's appeasement and he has since become England's most important broadcasting propagandist to the United States

(12) This was one of the first steps toward modifying our Neutrality Law and bringing all aid to Britain. Eichelberger, who seems to be a sort of grand

vizier for Nicholas Miraculous Butler, who in turn seems to be the academic representative of the British raj subservient to its financial agents in lower New York, has been the active organizer of both so-called White Committees, so active in modifying the Neutrality Law in giving away all possible to our one ally, and now in December, 1940, has started a new organization, France Forever (cf 383).

RECENT RESPONSES

Faculty members at Harvard, where the situation is strained, must remain anonymous. Brickbats are scarce.

"Many statements seem to be probably untrue and I should think some of them might be libelous. Your opinion that the American people are being 'led by the nose' into a war which they do not desire seems to me pure fancy. I see no evidence of dangerous war propaganda at the present time." C.P., Nov. 20.

"You are right about the foreign propaganda but I am sure you are too violent on the Harvard situation." H E., Nov. 21. "Thanks for bulletins coming regularly. Enclosing a check for postage. You can't expect me to agree with everything you say, especially as God, Nature or a permanent appointment at Harvard has made me more of a middle-of-the-road man than you." B.C., Nov. 20. "The situation here is so complex that it would take a book rather than a letter to describe my reactions. Certainly, nothing quite like it has happened at Harvard before As for the outcome, however, I am afraid it will probably be the old story in the long run." S.J E , Nov 21. "I agree in general with what you say about the situation at Harvard. I have been interested in the bulletins." M.B.K., Nov. 20. "The bulletins have come and I have read them with interest. Will you please continue sending them? Enclosed are some stamps which will help." C.B.W., Nov. 21 "Your bulletin, as always is interesting " H.N.A , Nov. 22.

University Presidents write with more freedom,—"As you report to be the case at Harvard, it is certainly our undergraduates, as a whole, who are most dubious about the wisdom or effectiveness of going to war to save religion, democracy, England's trade routes, or anything else." Valentine of Rochester, Nov. 20. "Thank you for the bulletins. Don't stop! It is so easy for us to sympathize with England that we particularly need to be put on our guard. You are doing this admirably." Brewer of Olivet, Nov 21. "Yes, I value the bulletins you have been sending and should like to continue receiving them." Kent of Louisville, Nov. 20. "Enjoy your publications and find them most interesting." Dykstra of Wisconsin, Nov. 21. "Please do not cease firing." Hutchins of Chicago, Nov 20.

University Professors,—"I enjoy and value the bulletins. You are doing a superb job at battling the propaganda." Raymond Pearl, Johns Hopkins, Nov. 21. "I have appreciated and hope you will continue sending the bulletins I am not at all surprised at the growth of war feeling in the East. The same thing was prevalent in the last war. Much of the feeling here has died down." H. C. Peterson, U. of Okla , Nov. 21. "Yes, I should like to receive your bulletins regularly." Richard Heindel, U. of Pa., Nov. 21.

Senators, representatives, editors, authors, also cheer.

November 24, 1939   .

OUR PHONEY NEUTRALITY

"Repeal of the Neutrality Act in the U S.A. reopens for the Allies the doors of the greatest storehouse of supplies in the world", Chamberlain frankly assured the English "Thús the aggressors are penalized, and that is the policy President Roosevelt has been aiming at", crowed the London *Sketch. Le Petit Parisien* exulted, "To moral support already so precious, will come material support which hasten the hour of victory".

'Bloom-Baruch' Bill they call it, now that so many know it's a fake. It was planned by skilled attorneys for chicane, in the interest of profiteers, munitioneers, and the British imperialists.[1]

Lobbyists swarmed. "Bill Shearer came back to town in connection with cash-and-carry", Eliot Janeway tells us, *Nation,* Nov 11, and "the other ship lobbyists have been operating in the Senate".[2] To get votes for it in the House, patronage was distributed with the President's backing, by Garner's aides. Hundreds of patronage appointments for key positions in the 1940 Census have since been announced.

Lothian, who had deplored Bloom's mismanagement of the bill (cf Bul #7), anxiously promoted the bill. Lothian conferred almost daily with Administration officials, Borah charged, for "repeal of a law he so early and so boldly denounced".

The President, just before each vote, announced the discovery of German submarines alarmingly near our coasts Before the final vote,

British freighter Coulmore on a dark and stormy night within a few hundred miles of New York sent out an SOS, 'Submarine attacking'. These submarines are jokingly admitted today to have been clever bits of propaganda.

When after the final vote in the Senate, Walsh sought to preserve in the preamble the boast that this act was passed 'to keep us out of war', the Administration's Connally angrily objected that it 'could not be foreseen what the country would do'. In Conference the Administration's innocuous platitudes, devoid of promise, were preserved. *Newsweek* said, "This quasifatalism is the greatest potential danger today".

The people, 95% against war,[3] were led to believe the bill the work of Hull. No separation of the "embargo" and the "cash-and-carry" plan was permitted by the President as pleaded for by Senator Tobey. The bill was fully understood and explained by Representative Vorys. "The new part is not neutral. The good part is not new. The new bill does not provide 'cash and carry'. The President has full power to make the cash and carry principle effective right now, under the present law."[4]

The Act does not require cash, nor prevent carriage of munitions in American bottoms, nor transshipment of cargoes, nor transfer of registry. The Act does permit unlimited credit. Only governments buying arms need pay cash. Nothing prevents DuPont or Bethlehem Steel extending unlimited credit to Imperial Chemical Industries Ltd., or to Vickers.

The President is given thirteen discretionary powers to be unneutral. His proclamation makes it possible for American ships to carry munitions to neutral ports for transshipment. The little fishing town of Bergen, 300 miles from Scottish ports, is becoming important. American ships discharging at Bilbao are less than 100 miles from the French border, at Corunna about 500 miles from England.

The administration of this "porous piece of legislation" has been arduous. The barbed wire mazes about the well designed holes have been a source of headaches for State Department and Customs officials.

Roosevelt, Hull, and senators have been at loggerheads on the legality of transfer of registry.[5] Standard Oil tankers were transferred before and since. The timing of the President's proposed transfer of twenty year old ships of the U S. Lines to Panama registry, like the French plane deal of last February, shows the President's ardor to assist the Allies. Hull's reversal of his position on the legality, senators' opposition to transfer, reveal ignorance of the holes, and conflict among those who are backing the several factions. So many quarterbacks in this game that it is more like "Button, button"!

Our State Department protectively long refused to release the list of American ships detained in British and French ports. Now they are known to be more than fifty, some held unreasonably long Some have had their cargo, such as phosphate rock, unloaded, confiscated, and sold. From two steamers more than 1000 bags of mail were taken without explanation or report. Our State Department protests, but gently.[6]

Freedom of the seas for Britain extends into every American port, for her warships to refuel and provision.[7] Our harbors are busy with her armed merchantmen entering and leaving at will, while a hundred American ships are tied up idle and thousands of American seamen are denied the freedom of the seas.

It was advertised that the Allies had seven billions in gold and securities in this country to pay for purchases, that a billion dollars in orders would be placed immediately. Few believe that now. There is great disappointment at sharp bargaining, short purchases, stock prices.

The Federal Reserve bank, a department of a neutral government, is facilitating financing of purchases For publicity purposes the President cautioned Morgan against ostensibly acting as purchasing agent.

Discontent with our neutrality is daily becoming evident. Allen W. Dulles, who with Ham Fish Armstrong, both Wall Street foreign affairs experts, in their recent book promoted the repeal of the Embargo. Now, Nov. 21, Dulles discovers the act "full of holes as a piece of Swiss cheese" Sen. Glass, who helped put it through, now says the law "is disgraceful" and expresses wishful thinking about its repeal.

Academic idealists who boosted the bill have their heads in the sand Late November, the N. E. Conference on Foreign Affairs at Smith College held their noses, dug their knuckles in their eyes, passed a resolution approving this act 'to keep us out of war' But they approved, too, Streit's plan to surrender our sovereignty to the British Empire.

And what of the Democratic process?[8] Roosevelt calls six hundred legislators together, gives them instructions. For six weeks they debate while lobbyists toil and a hundred million people attend. Millions of words, thousands of tons of news print, and it all comes to nothing.

The "navicert" on one side, the "magnetic mine" on the other, make all this palaver about 'neutrality', until "unendurable violence" comes, —seem foolish, except to the few to whom it brings profits because they planned it that way.

But the Act was a success. The President, master of political maneuver, regained control of his party,—and Lothian what he wanted. *November 24, 1399*

NOTES

(1) Kenneth Burke in "a not altogether solemn dissertation" on the "Embargo" in *Direction,* November, 1939, indignantly sputtered, "Cash and carry",—"without the delicate little loopholes that make it too easy for the Anglophiles to extend the definition of 'cash', first to ninety-day credit, and then gradually to indefinite credit . Don't get the idea, however, that a 'cash and carry' policy, even if carried out, would keep us from footing the bill. It is our function, as a province, to foot the bill—and we will.

"For one thing, we'll so gear our productive plant to the war's markets that we are subject to them, cash or no cash

"For another thing, we can pile up all the gold in the world, like savages (my apologies to savages. I never heard of savages so idiotic)—and then, when the war is over, the gold myth will simply be abolished. The British will decree any new basis of currency they prefer, and we'll obey the decree . . . there'll be the Bigger and Better Dust Bowl. There'll be the ghastly increase in the rate at which the fertility of our soil is carried off by erosion. Long after the human blood has ceased to flow in the protection of the British Empire's booty, the blood of our soil will go on leaching, being sucked out by leeches. Who said ideas were weak? Why!—a few bad ideas on the nature of human purpose have proved strong enough to rip and tear and squander a continent, to throw its richness down the sewer, while millions skimp."

(2) In 1929 while President Hoover was preparing for the London Naval Conference, items appeared in the newspapers that William B. Shearer had sued shipbuilding companies for unpaid fees for his services at the Geneva conference two years previously That let a large cat out of the bag. Hoover, who was then seeking to limit naval auxiliaries as capital ships had been limited at the Washington conference, took advantage of the publicity to suggest that a Senate committee go "to the very bottom" of the business The Beards, telling this story in "America in Midpassage", comment that, "All except freshmen in international politics knew very well that the British navalists had been hardnecked at Geneva, that the British government would never rip into British interests through a persistent and comprehensive parliamentary inquest, and that the revelations of a Washington inquiry would be confined to American operations. Yet if Hoover was not to be balked in his foreign policy, something had to be done to counter opposition at home." (Beard, p 384)

Court testimony showed that Shearer had been employed at a large salary with a large expense account to wreck the peace conference,—inveigle, entertain and dissuade delegates. Shearer won his suit and was paid. Bethlehem Shipbuilding Company, and Newport News Shipbuilding and Drydock Company which Shearer sued have gotten dividends, $1,560,020,880 in contracts guaranteed against loss by the government and assured a large margin of profit.

The publicity caused by the Shearer suit perhaps more than anything else led to the Nye investigation of the munitions profits, lobbying, etc. which was set up in April, 1934   "The Shearer investigation had unfolded a certain degree of affiliation between navy officers and propagandists engaged in discrediting arms limitation. By the Nye inquiry knowledge of such relations was greatly amplified, if still inadequately." (Beard, p 404)

(3) "About six months ago, 35 per cent of the people believed that the Johnson act, forbidding loans to nations which have defaulted in the payment of their war debts, should be repealed. Last month the percentage was 54   At present, it is 55. In New England and the middle Atlantic states only 32 per cent desired repeal last May   Now (in January, 1941) the figure is 57." (Boston *Herald*)

(4) "In the last twelve months, 44% of all U S. exports valued at $1,740,000,000 went to the British Empire. In August 1940, 65% of total U S exports were going to the British Empire. In September, British countries took approximately 66% of all U S. exports." (*News Bulletin,* Youth Committee Against War)

(5) Charles William Taussig, one of the original brain trusters of the New Deal, Chairman of the National Advisory Committee of the National Youth Administration, writing on "Toward a More Dynamic Democracy" in the volume "American Youth: An Enforced Reconnaissance", edited by Thacher Winslow and Frank P. Davidson (Harvard University Press, 1940), points out that public opinion is however becoming increasingly important. Its increasing influence on legislation was shown in "the almost instantaneous response in the matter of transferring American ships to Panama after the passage of the Neutrality Act of 1939. It has been estimated that over 100,000 national and local discussion groups and forums scattered all over the country participated in the debate on the Neutrality Bill. Almost every phase of the question was literally and figuratively aired—except the quiet work of the shipowners' lobby to evade the proposed restrictions on American shipping. Congress had adjourned when the proposal to transfer the American ships to Panama was made. Within forty-eight hours a substantial number of congressmen and senators representing all parties had telegraphed or telephoned the Executive Branch of the government their opposition to the proposed transfer They had heard in no uncertain terms from their constituents. . . .

"The entire episode of the Neutrality Act was perhaps the first completely successful case where the people directed legislation while it was on the floor of Congress." As President of the American Molasses Company, using tank ships in the shipment of molasses, Taussig was in a position to know. He failed to add, however, that since that flare-up, the transfer to Panama registry of Standard

Oil tank ships and other vessels has been quietly arranged in opposition to the people's wishes and without congressional authorization so far as known. About the only information that has leaked into the press in regard to this has been an occasional brief notice that submarines have sunk some of these ships under Panama registry. It is obvious the Administration was not in a position to make a fuss "United States Lines transferred five freighters, averaging twenty years in age and 6,000 tons, to its Panama subsidiary so that they might carry munitions to England ." (*Newsweek,* Feb 17)

"The United States has supplied . . . cargo ships since Oct. 26, 1939 . . . making a total of 755,602 tons directly to the British flag. From American to alien registry . . . friendly to Britain . . transfers . . . approximately 1,200,000 tons. All of these transfers were made after approval . . by the United States Maritime Commission, the last transaction involving 12 ships . . . of 107,061 tons . . . consummated Jan. 23 . . . the price . . . being $2,779,600. . . . Jan. 31 . . . transfers approved . . . included more than 300 vessels". 20 have been transferred to Brazil registry, 10 to the Greek, to Peru 7, to France 19, to Belgium 9, and others to Honduras, Portugal, Estonia, Cuba, Norway, Thailand, Uruguay, Venezuela and Mexico. (N. Y. *Times,* Feb. 15)

"The American merchant marine is in the war. American ships have been sunk with several American casualties." The Maritime Commission in its January 27 report "lists more than three million tons of merchant shipping sunk", but "U. S. shipping losses are hidden" under "the Commission's figures for other countries—notably those of the Republic of Panama." A fleet of twenty Standard Oil tankers, registered under the name of the Panama Transport Company, carries oil not only to the British, "but it has also supplied the Axis powers. The Standard-owned *W. H. Libby* has on two successive voyages brought oil to Freetown, a British-controlled West African base, and to Teneriffe in the Canary Islands " They supplied waiting German and Italian tankers. Another Standard Oil tanker, *Charles Pratt,* was sunk and two American seamen drowned. "Over eight million tons of British shipping now work the profitable neutral trade routes to South America and elsewhere. Yet the United States permits almost unrestricted sale of American ships to Britain on the ground of "all aid to Britain". "The present British domination of American and world shipping is actively aided by American interests." "Directors of the I M.M. Co. for 1940 include Vincent Astor, who represents one of America's three largest fortunes, 'who is also director of the Chase National Bank, reputedly the bank of the Rockefeller families; Elisha Walker, partner in firm of Kuhn-Loeb & Co. which, with the House of Morgan, controls more than 88 per cent of American railroads; Harvey D. Gibson . . . John Franklin' " (report of the National Maritime Union). Kermit Roosevelt's "financial connections were important enough to make him forswear his American citizenship".

"The first signs of a new scandal in shipping are looming at this moment. They are to be found in the brief 1940-41 report of Comptroller General Lindsay C Warren, who had discovered several 'irregularities' and 'discrepancies' in the books of the Maritime Commission. The report charges that 'one of the debtors (ship operator) has made no payment on its notes amounting to more than five million dollars ' " (*Friday*, Feb. 21, 1941)

(6) Occasional items in the newspapers have continued to report for the past two years the removal of mail from the American clippers and steamers that stop at Bermuda and to tell of the arrival of hundreds of additional Censors from England to continue the practice. It was reported that Secretary Hull protested again and again during the long period. At one time he even suggested that the Bermuda stop be omitted, but no change was made and it is evident that Hull's protests were for home consumption to quiet the American people while they were becoming conditioned to British ways.

(7) The President in his lend-lease bill has finally provided that our Navy yards be made available for the repair of articles of defense, including British battleships, as Stimson has long been advocating.

(8) "These wide-spread discussions on active issues of public policy are of great significance   They may well develop into a new type of democratic technique" ("American Youth"). The handicap to this is the great difficulty of organizing such public expression, of creating a government organization of volunteers to meet emergencies, to fight against and counteract your elected representatives who can be directly and secretly approached by lobbyists interested in passing the measure the people wish to oppose, and influenced by the pressure that the Administration through its patronage system can bring upon legislators to conform. A senator from Georgia may be elected with the connivance or at the direction of a few important men in Georgia. It takes only a few thousand votes   George was elected by one-fifth of 1% of the population (2% of 10%, cf Bul #94)

"The important thing" says Taussig, "is not only to educate the citizen, and particularly the young citizen, to a sense of responsibility toward his country, but to make him conscious of his own civic potency." (This will probably not be very impressive in Georgia)   "We must, however, be alert to detect efforts to destroy democracy under the guise of movements to change or even to maintain our present economic system   Indeed, capitalism is as good a camouflage for subversive activities as socialism. The unemployed, young or old, who submit to the indignity of enforced idleness without complaint, without active effort to change the system that is responsible for their condition, are not exercising their citizenship. They too are the enemies of democracy"

'WAR AND PEACE' PROPAGANDA

'Blessed are the peacemakers' for they shall call themselves the children of God, and shall inherit the earth.   "Once more we deplore, we deplore and abhor the German attacks on our worth   It is cheek, but the meek turn the cheek ev'ry week and hope to inherit the earth." (Douglas Reed, "Disgrace Abounding", Cape, 1939).

"A new and better peace" is the keynote of the current propaganda to lead us on to war.[1]   It tends to establish the idea not merely that world war is on now but that America has a part in it and so may take part in the peace. Mr. Roosevelt and Mr. Chamberlain are all for peace, later not now, and at their own price. And we bumptiously assume that we can do better than Mr. Wilson with his shipload of experts. "Vanity of vanities", all is Propaganda.

"World War II",[2]—this phrase has served its purpose in referring to the 'weird word war' that so wears on Western Europe's nerves. It is wishful wording, the substance of things hoped for. Its constant reiteration for months has conditioned us to the belief that war for the whole world is inevitable. That takes us in   It is effective propaganda.

But with more than 90% of our people increasingly declaring against being drawn into the war, those who are endeavoring to guide us toward assuming a share in cleaning up the present imperialistic mess, now evasively declare that "the Get-in-or-Stay-out-theory" has "had its day".

So the trick now is to put the accent on peace. We have been invited to the party. If we call the tune we must pay the fiddler   We did before. And we are paying for this war,—not the four billions going into armament for so-called "defense", which realists know is to strengthen the British and threaten their enemies,—but we are being taxed today to pay in part the sixteen billions for the extraordinary profit on gold. We give of our resources for this useless gold. Graham and Whittlesey described this as the "Golden Avalanche". (Princeton U. Press, 1939)

Propaganda slogans change with the emotional weather. The old tripe about "democracies" and "aggressors", "religion and morality" brought contemptuous rebuttal. We were told there was no British propaganda.

Now a horde of propagandists have come from England to tell us what is 'right' and 'wrong'. But our university professors assure us there is no danger from propaganda because of our heightened "moral and intellectual preparedness",—that we are 'propaganda proof'.

Its importance in the last war, they tell us, has been overestimated It was idealism that led us in   But that's the purpose of propaganda to stimulate idealism in the young and in the unsophisticated, the feeling that they must uphold and fight for the right. And in the righteous that promotes hate for what they are led to believe is 'evil' But whence emanate these fashions in propaganda? Who starts them? Who prompts the writers and speakers? Let us now praise great men.

Lord Lothian warned his countrymen (London *Observer*) that if the U.S suspected it "was being maneuvered into commitment to war by foreign intrigue, or for reasons of politics or finance, it might-swing back violently to the ultra-isolationism of the Ludlow amendment".

He is not likely to fall into the error of Sir Gilbert Parker, who spoke of the Americans, victims of his persuasive guile in 1914-17, as "next to the Chinese perhaps, the most gullible sheep in the world".

Lord Lothian late in October tactfully asked the American people, "What do you think should be the settlement we should aim at?"

That was a skilful move to enlist our participation. The cue was promptly taken by Thomas Lamont,—head and brains of J. P. Morgan & Co., agents for the British government,—who devoutly believes we should lend our aid to the maintenance of the British Empire. He sounds off,—

"What of the peace? . . . There can be no world economic stability without continuing American cooperation to help bring it about and sustain it. . . . Does it not follow that America's role is clearly not to enter the war but to make a great and valuable contribution to the peace?"

The Herald *Tribune* editorially summarizes Lamont's view that foreign economic stability after the last war was based "on the assumption that the American loans would continue   They did not", the crash followed. The inference is that Mr. Lamont feels we should continue to lend money (that's his business) to the British Empire (he's their agent). "Had he made the same speech in mid-September senators and editors would indubitably have screamed to high heaven that the House of Morgan was once again plotting to get America into war", *Life* comments, Nov. 27.[8]

The liberal, public spirited Mr. Lamont, his partners and colleagues, exert a great influence on public opinion through our university teaching and the printed word. They are the influential directors of our philanthropic, eleemosynary, and educational foundations.

"Probably the single most influential individual" in publishing, Mr. Lamont testified ("Midpassage", p 196) "the connections of the House of Morgan or its partners with men who happened to be in politics or the publishing business were incidental to financial transactions and in no way designed to influence political or editorial policies".

But this influence is increasingly apparent in periodicals and books. Writers once bold and free subserviently take their cue as do Lothian and Lamont from 'The Foreign Office'. Only undergraduates and men who have neither salary nor hope of preferment or pension dare speak out.

Walter Millis, whose "Road to War" before publication was expunged of reference to the part Morgan played in bringing us in,—now avoids such censoring. In *Life*, Nov. 6, he writes the problem is "not how to 'keep the country out of war' " but what kind of a Peace the Americans want and "how much they are willing and able to do toward securing it".

This same attitude is now promoted by the presidents of our great universities. From above, it percolates down to the college professors and teachers at the bottom of this pyramid of power.[4]

Editors and publishers cannot ignore the influence of Kent and Beaverbrook. Nothing is printed, however factual or documentary, which would not be agreeable to the great men we here praise.

A tamed and subservient press and platform has been taught to proclaim the "striking proof that the nation has recovered from its keep-out-of-war hysteria of two months ago".

The talk is of the Peace, assuming that the war is to go on and we are to go in,—a "second Thirty Years' War", Mr. Lamont announces, which began in 1914. If we keep our eye on the Peace in 1944, we will go forward more thoughtlessly to the four years of fighting and paying. *December 1, 1939*

NOTES

[1] William James, just before the last war in his "The Moral Equivalent of War" (1910) wrote, "England and we, our army and navy authorities repeat without ceasing, arm solely for 'peace', Germany and Japan it is who are bent on loot and glory. 'Peace' in military mouths today is a synonym for 'war expected' The word has become a pure provocative, and no government wishing peace sincerely should allow it ever to be printed in a newspaper. . . . It may even reasonably be said that the intensely sharp competitive preparation for war by the nations is the real war, permanent, unceasing; and that the battles are only a sort of public verification of the mastery gained during the 'peace'-interval."

Peace as a war aim is the subject of a careful, cautious study by a Swiss neutral at Harvard, William E Rappard, "The Quest for Peace Since the World War" (Harvard University Press, 1940). It is an example of liberal scholarship, which means that he is working with words from words, words of statesmen (front men, puppets) in speeches (to persuade, to conceal, to disguise), in state documents (planned by trained bureaucrats to deceive, intimidate, bluff, conceal). Official documents, old propaganda, old political speeches, old befuddling Parliamentary speeches, diplomatic declarations and memoranda, protocols, diplomatic correspondence, minutes of the League of Nations, (greatest center of hypocrisy for twenty years), U. S. Department of State (God save the King!),—these are the material, accepted without understanding, without criticism, and worked over in words and phrases such as can be safely used. True, to this he adds many valuable memoirs, alibis, apologies and self-defenses. A few years ago an instructor at Harvard, wanting to write something on Russia, when he suggested going to the Russian archives, was told by his superiors, "that's just Russian propaganda". We can see it with other archives, not with our own or France's or Britain's.

Rappard is dealing with the words of statesmen who talk about peace, who want peace There is some analysis, not very searching, of what this abstraction peace stands for, how different statesmen used it, but there is not much psychology in it, not much understanding that everybody wants peace, except as they start ructions themselves, nobody wants to be irritated or disturbed or deprived.

There is careful tracing of how Wilson's peace idea was promoted by Sir Edward Grey as early as 1915 Sir Edward was all for peace by "cooperation". He wrote to T. Roosevelt, Oct. 20, 1914, that if the U S had acted with England they might have preserved peace and looked forward to that cooperation "in securing permanent peace afterwards". August, 1915, he wrote to House along the same line, suggesting League of Nations. Tyrrell, secretary to Sir Edward, acted for him. September 22 Grey wrote House, "How much are the U. S. prepared to do in this direction? Would the President propose . . . ? So the idea of the League of Nations was sold to Wilson and participation in the war to put the League across. Then after the war nobody wanted the League. It was a bait. Peace as a war aim? Peace as a red herring!

Another notable attempt to be open-minded about "Conflicting Strategies of Peace Since Versailles" is "Britain and France Between Two Wars" (Harcourt, Brace, 1940), written under the aegis of Yale International Studies in the same series with Whitney Griswold's "Far Eastern Policy". Though his conclusions will be almost distasteful to some who finance Yale, the author, Arnold Wolfers, like Rappard ignores whole tracts of facts that are in *Hansard,* perhaps because they lead to difficult ground The play he presents is one in which the actors, the front men, write their own lines, out of their own heads, determine just what part they will take, act as individuals. The scenery is merely labeled France, England, Parliament. There is no understanding shown of conflict of powers, of forces behind the scenes, of the fact that these men are talking rather than someone else because they serve some group that has power or because they have capacity to fool voters and so get votes

"Skeptics could point to the fact that the British collectivists, who were the champions of high moral principles in the conduct of foreign affairs . . . were in favor of organizing overwhelming force, only in their abstract terminology it was to be that of the peace-loving nations arrayed against the potential aggressors", writes Wolfers

"Experience since Versailles does not suggest the existence of. any objective standard of justice. . . . Fortunately, such standards are neither necessary nor relevant. All that matters is whether Britain and France and Germany can agree on a particular solution." As a temporary solution Wolfers hopefully suggests a new "balance of power". "The difference between the old balance, which was mainly a tool of British diplomacy, and that of the future lies only in the fact that instead of balancing the others all of Britain's weight must now be put into the scales. . To create a new balance of power does not solve the question of European peace; it is not a 'peace plan', but merely one necessary element of an agreement on Europe's crucial problem, Germany's place and power."

(2) Churchill told the Commons, Aug. 21, 1940, "This war is, in fact, only a continuation of the last" (cf Bul #87)

(3) Whenever the way seems long or our hearts begin to fail, which is about every six months, Mr Thomas Lamont makes another speech in which he sounds the pitch The theme is always the preservation of the British and Morgan empires Immediately the little Harvard professors, first one choir and then another, chant their hymns of hate hoping they will reach Mr Lamont's ear. Such was the case with Mr Lamont's speech, before the Merchants' Association of New York, January 28, 1941. He pointed out with some satisfaction that "public opinion as to the war has undergone a vast change in the last year". "All Americans loathe war" and hope for peace on their own terms which cannot be obtained today by "appeasement". As to war aims, he could not "ask for anything better" than those outlined by Lord Halifax which would insure such "political, social and economic" bonds on a resentful, restive and expanding people "that there will not be another war". The exact terms of these are hideous to contemplate. He was "against stripping England of her liquid assets", better to use America's and tax the people for it as in the past. So that is the song the university choirs will now sing.

(4) Peace foundations like educational institutions were once voluntary, the result of private initiative Elihu Burritt, the Connecticut learned blacksmith, was the great promoter of peace foundations a century ago. Then great peace lovers and philanthropists like Edwin Ginn left endowment. The endowment had to be invested to return an income. As financial advice in regard to investments becomes essential, financiers edge into the control As the strong man of the institutions pass, those who succeed lick the hand that feeds them. The staff avoids trouble, looks for security And so from the 'root of all evil', they went 'the way of all flesh'. Soon they have sold their souls

The Carnegie Peace Foundation has from the first been under the control of Miraculous Butler who lifts his eyes up unto Wall Street and Whitehall whence cometh his strength Through interlocking connections, 'Policy Associations', 'Committees to Defend the Allies', it has served to preserve the British Empire system. Ginn's "World Peace Foundation" in Boston, fallen under the influence of Abbott Lawrence Lowell, is satisfied to maintain peace among it own staff.

HELL IS PAVED WITH GOOD INTENTIONS

"Problems connected with the War Department occupied Mr. Roosevelt until the moment his special train left Washington. Louis Johnson, Assistant Secretary of War, conferred with the President aboard his private car, and did not leave the train until it was pulling out."

Arrived at Warm Springs, Mr. Roosevelt referred jocularly to his spring farewell, "I'll be back in the fall if we don't have a war". He had heard from Kennedy Great Britain would be ready for war in September. Hitler was expected to bomb London. That would bring us in.

"We have had war", said Roosevelt to the children, and he went on, —"I believe in war",—against paralysis. This may have seemed a bit light-hearted from one who holds the power of life and death over millions of "sons of American mothers", whom defensively he says he does not "intend to send overseas". A month before, denouncing the anti-war "breast beaters" and "dishonest fakers", he had assured us "The U.S. is neutral and does not *intend* to get involved in war".

But there are those who feel that we are not neutral and already at war. Rep. Vorys has been unkind enough to remind the President that he did not intend to run up the debt to more than 40 billions.

When Senator Walsh attempted to introduce into the preamble of the new "neutrality" act that the U. S. "desires to serve notice to the world that it intends to keep out of participation in the war", Senator Connally, acting for the administration, angrily shouted that they didn't "Want to tell the world what we are going to do".

Only "unendurable violence", the headlines announced, can force America into war. Assistant Secretary of State Messersmith, Roosevelt spokesman, addressing the Boston Chamber of Commerce thus assured us late in November, of our 'neutrality'. (But who is to determine what is "unendurable"?)

Of Messersmith, December *Fortune* tells us "Washington wags have dubbed him the Dorothy Thompson of the State Department".[2] He "yields to no man in his hatred" of Hitler. "In 1935 he predicted that Hitler would be overthrown within a year. . . . His views that we must fight Germany . . . undoubtedly carry weight in Administration circles "

After the crash of an airplane in Los Angeles last spring revealed the President's secret aid to France, the Committee on Military Affairs visited the President at the White House. What the President said has never been revealed. But Senator Lundeen on the floor of the Senate declared, "If the American people ever learn what was said, then the nation would be shocked and stunned". Another Senator, correcting Lundeen remarked that the facts would "shock and stun the world".

Representative Short of Missouri inserted in the *Congressional Record*, April 25, this quotation from Boake Carter's syndicated column (Minneapolis *Journal*, Apr. 18), "It was at that conference that Mr. Roosevelt intimated that the best thing that could happen to the world would be for some one to assassinate both Hitler and Mussolini."

Are Roosevelt or Messersmith sufficiently judicial and unprejudiced to have in their hands the decision of life or death for thousands of American youth? Who is to determine what is "unendurable"?

No man in an electoral position can be foolish enough in the face of the people's wish to declare for war. And perhaps the President's more recently declared intentions are sincere. A monetary war between the Americans and British is now on in China. The British are supporting the Japanese controlled Chinese dollar in opposition to the American backed Chinese dollar of Chiang Kai-Shek.

Roosevelt, in the horse's mouth speech prepared in Washington during the summer which Grew recently delivered to the Japanese, hits out at the British. It is rumored that irked by British demands he is beginning to loathe Lothian. Kennedy, 'sick' of his job, is coming home.

The Commander of the Army and Navy (he's strong for the Navy), has through the 'neutrality' legislation again come to the command of his Party. He may sacrifice his idealism for "religion and morality" and the British Empire and "keep us out of war". He may,—

If the American people are warned against our college presidents, professors, speakers and writers, who having swallowed British propaganda are hysterically pushing us on to a new and better Armageddon.

Hundreds of letters insist on these bulletins continuing. Scores give us courage. Here are a few, more to come,—"What we need in this country are more one-man powerhouses to keep us out of war. Organizations are all very well but the individual who knows where to strike and when is still the mightiest force in the world. Sincerest congratulations." Harvey O'Connor, Chicago, Nov. 13.

"Your bulletins are not only terse and to the point, but maintain a high degree of accuracy. I have made a study of British propaganda for many years. I was once an Englishman myself, with a father attached to the British Foreign Office. I used your piece about Cecil Rhodes in my column recently, giving you credit." Boake Carter, Nov. 28.[2]

"I am heartily sympathetic with the viewpoint which you represent because I cannot see that we in America or we who look forward to a more peaceful and cooperative world order have anything much to gain by the victory of one side rather than the other in the present conflict. I share your contributions with my class in Psychology of Social Change." Goodwin Watson, Columbia Univ , Nov. 29.

"I always get a big shock of satisfaction and wonderment out of anything you send me and hence I am glad to hear from you anytime It is encouraging that undergraduates are putting the brakes on the belligerent swivel-chair makers of history!" Charles Beard, Nov. 27.

"Frank statements of fact regarding the British, when so many are being impressed with their propaganda, is of vast importance to the Nation " George S Parker, Salem, Mass , Nov. 14.

"Continue to send me your admirable material dealing with foreign propaganda. . . . The more people you can reach with such information the better." Joy Elmer Morgan, Washington, D. C., Nov. 28.

"An excellent and much needed piece of work " James Warbasse *December 2, 1939*

NOTES

[1] "The errors, the wrong principles of passionately sincere good men, have done infinitely more of harm to the world, than the acts of bad men acting against a code which they knew to be wrong, crimes which the world had agreed were crimes " (Sir Norman Angell, "Peace With the Dictators", p 89, Harper, 1938) "The evil that men do lives after them, the good is oft interred with their bones."

[2] The Messersmith name and hate seems to have disappeared from the news column. Perhaps this is because his German relative has made his name so prominent in aviation Still burns brightly, however, in her column the hatred of Miss Thompson (Mrs Lewis, Frau Bard) It is a very personal hate for Hitler. It may be explained psychiatrically as the result of a great passion on the part of a woman scorned The high temperature may be due to similarity in temperament Both are mystic, passionate, given to rages, sudden and intense hates. It isn't the first time that a woman's hate has driven a people towards war and changed the course of history.

(3) December 3, 1940 Boake Carter wrote, "For Heavens' sake don't tell me that your magnificent work is coming to an end? It simply cannot be Yours has been one of the most forthright and shining lights pointing down the true road for America amid a fog of propaganda, hysteria, smearing, name-calling, intellectual dishonesty, mental sophistry and immoral talk For the love of Saint Peter, keep on."

THE FINNISH FLARE-UP

The pressure in Washington to bring us into participation in Great Britain's troubles had weakened in November. In England and Canada where they had been led to expect that we were coming in, there was the beginning of sad disappointed recrimination.

Finland, flaming across the newspaper pages, has turned the tide.[1] And ally sentiment is stronger than ever, a nationally distributed financial advisory letter confidentially tells his clients. Due to the war excitement the $500,000,000 additional for defense asked by the President will meet with popular and Congressional approval.

There is inside understanding that the President is heading us toward war. In his press conference, Dec. 5, it was reported in the Boston *Herald,* Dec. 6, the President was ready to "rebuff critics of his foreign policy. He said objection has come from statesmen in Russia and Germany, from the publicity director of the Republican National Committee—whose name he said he could not remember—and from a small number of politically-minded persons in the House and Senate."

In his speech to Congress, Sept. 21, he had declared, "In a period when it is sometimes said that free discussion is no longer compatible with national safety, may you by your deeds show the world that we of the United States are one people, of one mind, one spirit, one clear resolution, walking before God in the light of the living." (cf p 129) The Finnish mess makes this threat to our Civil Liberties imminent.

Our admiration goes out to the Finns, for their runners, for their great master Sibelius and his patriotic tone poem "Finlandia", for their valiant and vigorous defense of freedom. We owe them inspiration for our skiing, for our cooperatives, which some of our Liberty Leaguers still denounce as "Communistic" and "undermining the established economic structure" (*Chr Sci Monitor,* Dec. 6).

Russia and all it stands for, on the other hand, has been exploited to create fear and hate in the American people, further fanned by the Dies

Committee. The resulting emotional reaction is proving a great help to pro-British propaganda which must rely on aroused emotions based on idealism to bring us in. Factual backgrounds must be obscured. Understanding might lessen our hate.[2]

"About 1160 . . . in the guise of a crusade . . . Finland was entirely subjugated" by Erik the Holy "and for 650 years formed an integral part of the Kingdom of Sweden". ("Sweden", 1938, published "with the economic assistance of the government", by the Swedish Traffic Association.)

In 1710 Peter the Great, having founded St. Petersburg, seized Finland, explaining it was "the water, not the land" he wanted. Not until 1809 after the Treaty of Tilsit was it created a Grand Duchy.

From 1900 under the Czars there was rebellion. On the abdication of the Czar, March 15, 1917, the House of Representatives of Finland (which had been established in 1906 by the Social Democrats) declared Finland's independence which the December following was recognized by Russian Bolshevik Government under Lenin and confirmed by treaty March 1, 1918, two days before the Brest-Litovsk Treaty between Russia and Germany. March 7 Germany signed a treaty with the Finnish Whites.

The Kaiser's government as an ally sent an army of 12,000 under General Count von der Goltz, which was "soon joined by numbers of White Finns under the leadership of General Mannerheim, a former officer of the Russian Imperial Guards. . . . Supported by the steady drive of the Germans, Gen. Mannerheim and his White Finns" drove the Red troops into U.S.S.R. ("The Origins of American Intervention in North Russia (1918)", Princeton U. Press, 1937, fully documented, by Leonid I. Strakhovsky a participant in the expedition, now an American, professor at U. of Md.)

Baron Gustav Mannerheim, a cavalry officer in the Czar's forces in the Russo-Japanese War, was sent into Finland to put down rebellion. Encyclopedia Britannica states, "15,000 men, women, and children were slaughtered, and by June 27, 1918, 73,915 Red rebels including 4600 women were prisoners of war". A writer in *Life,* Nov. 20, tells us that the Finnish Information Center in New York, maintained by the Government, claims that 10,000 of the 15,000 died in prison for lack of food. This "permitted the government of the Kaiser to exercise pressure on the Moscow government as their strategic position twenty-five miles from Petrograd constituted a perpetual threat to that former Russian capital. It's occupation could have been effected without much difficulty." It was "a constant Damoclean sword over Petrograd". (Strakhovsky)

Hindenburg wrote of the great importance of gaining "a foothold at a point which immediately menaced Petrograd". Ludendorff said, "It will at any time enable us to advance on Petrograd". (Strakhovsky)

American and British troops in the fall of 1918 from Murmansk and Archangel, and American and Japanese from Vladivostok, supported this thrust and threat. June 22, 1918, Winston Churchill then British Secretary of War had written the Imperial War Cabinet, "We must not take 'no' for an answer either from America or from Japan. We must compel events instead of acquiescing in the drift" After much pressure Wilson in July finally authorized this move. (Strakhovsky)

Since the formation of the Finnish Republic in 1918 Mannerheim has been a power, now designated as head of the Defense Council. The Statesman's Yearbook, which lists the Minister of Defense, does not mention Mannerheim. In 1920 the Soviets ceded to Finland the province of Petsamo, giving them a port on the Arctic, but claimed the province of Karelia as a part of Russia. From 1921 to 1923 this latter claim was before the League of Nations.

It was to this government that America made the loan which has been in part repaid, and the balance of which it is now proposed to remit. Helsingfors, the capital, has made a bright and pleasing picture to visitors. The Finnish government has sedulously built good will in America and has recently been seeking a new loan of $25,000,000 for strategic railways and additional fortifications.

The U.S.S.R. for some months has been negotiating with the Finnish government for withdrawal of troops from their fortified line in Karelia, twenty-five miles from Leningrad. Finally the Soviet demanded that the Finns get rid of their "false leaders".

Premier Cajander and Foreign Minister Erkko resigned. But the German Junker Baron Mannerheim of the Czar's Imperial Guard still remains. The retention of Mannerheim and the maintenance of the Hindenburg threat recent dispatches have attributed to "her imperialistic masters", variously named as England or Germany. Between them they have shared almost equally the monopoly of Finnish trade, and until last March they have been in accord in opposing the U.S.S.R.

This Mannerheim a few days ago issued the appeal so stirring to idealistic Americans, calling on the Finns to defend their "freedom".[3]

Bernard Shaw says the invasion of Finland is "perfectly simple". "She should have accepted the Russian offer for readjustment of territory. . . No power can tolerate a frontier from which a town such as Leningrad could be shelled when she knows that the power on the other side of that frontier, however small or weak it may be, is being made by a foolish government to act in the interests of other and greater powers menacing her security."[4]

"Perhaps the Kremlin feared an anti-Comintern peace in the West— a peace in which Germany, Italy, France and Great Britain would join together against the U.S.S.R —and was merely strengthening Russia's land and sea approaches against the day when the 'land of workers and peasants' would have to be defended unto death," remarks *Time,* Dec. 11, and also suggests that Stalin's purpose may have been merely to regain lost Russian territory, Bessarabia to come next.[5]

Such a combination against Russia, long known as the Four-Power Pact, was first proposed by Ludendorff. During the early '20's it resulted in the invasion of Russia by seven nations, during which Great Britain spent four billions to overthrow the Soviets.

Samuel H. Cross,[6] Professor of Slavic Languages at Harvard, in an interview Dec 1, told the Boston *Transcript,* "The Soviets are still fearful of some deal between the British and the military party in Germany." It is "just another step toward making the Soviet Western frontier airtight. . . . The defense of Leningrad against attack by sea and land is a serious problem. Before the present war, the Germans made no secret of their eventual intention of attacking Leningrad by a military advance northeastward through the Baltic States simultaneously with a naval offensive through the Gulf of Finland It is a known fact that there are more aerodromes in Finland than the Finnish air force could possibly use. . . . Both Mr. Chamberlain and Mr. Daladier have made it clear in their latest speeches that the Allies would not try to break the Seigfried Line, but that the war will continue and that there is no telling in what direction hostilities may spread."[7]

If Russia were attacked, the dagger thrust at Leningrad would consitute the northern point of the pincers, Rumania the southern.[8] Lord Lloyd, busy in Rumania with contracts, loans and promises, has discov-

ered that it is a "republic" and its playboy Carol a hardworking statesman.[9]   Turkey has been neutralized with a loan of 60,000,000 pounds

Finland's new People's Government is headed by the old revolutionary Kuusinen who "left Finland 20 years ago during the White Guard
Terror", *Time,* Dec. 11, tells us. It immediately issued a declaration to
"the entire Finnish people . . . for the overthrow of . . . the reactionary,
avid plutocracy which in 1918, aided by the troops of foreign imperialists, drowned democratic freedom of the Finnish toiling people in a sea
of blood, transformed our country into a White Guard hell for toilers."
The new Government's program calls for state control of banks, an
eight-hour working day, confiscation of large estates

Evidently this Finnish situation is complicated and involved for
American comprehension. But what an opportunity for propagandists
to inflame idealistic emotion![10]   The last straw to bring us in?[11]
December 8, 1939

NOTES

[1] The *Round Table* summarized, "while British and French propaganda has
bogged down, while Americans continued—more or less—to maintain their
desired aloofness toward the main war, they indulged in an emotional orgy over
the Baltic sideshow . . . the day of greater American participation—if and when
the need becomes acute—has become a great deal nearer. It is in this sense that
the Soviet attack on Finland may be called one of the great historical 'accidents'
of our time." (Lavine, p 334)

[2] There were violent polemics from all sides as Lavine and Wechsler point
out, which for the most part only contributed to obscuring issues The purpose
of this Bulletin was not to act as apologist for Russia, but to attempt to quiet the
emotions that seemed to be tending to bring America into war, by putting before
the American people information to counter-balance the propagandized information most frequently and effectively presented to them, from Washington and
Whitehall, through the daily press and over the radio

[3] "Democracy is on the side of Finland, civilization is on the side of Finland,
and Finland is on the side of God," proclaimed La Guardia. "God is not necessarily on the side of the heaviest typewriter battalions," write Harold Lavine and
James Wechsler in "War Propaganda and the United States" (Yale U. Press,
1940), reviewing "Finland vs Russia". "When evenly matched armies clash,
the propaganda artillery may help to resolve a stalemate; it did in 1918, it may
do so again. But when 4,000,000 people combat 180,000,000, Baron Munchausen plus Baron Mannerheim are not enough . . .

"History written after an event rarely discovers a case of unsullied good fighting unmitigated evil. But to contemporaries a war frequently assumes that

coloration   To most Americans viewing the war in Finland, in the twilight of Russia's oft-proclaimed policy of nonaggression, it seemed momentarily as if history had finally been reduced to simplicity.   Here, at last, was virtue against villainy, in the primitive terms of Hoboken drama "

(4) H. G. Wells on his arrival in New York in October, 1940, in a newspaper interview defended the Soviet attack on Finland.   "He asked Americans to suppose that some foreign power was situated on Staten Island, 'a harmless little neutral state'.   'But this little state', he continued, 'was armed to the teeth with powerful guns that commanded the Narrows and you had a theory that this country might be used as a spearhead of attack against the United States.   I ask you what Uncle Sam would do?   I am sure he would dismantle those batteries and I am afraid he would act almost as dreadfully as Russia did.' "   Subsequent advance by the Russians led F. P. A. to insert in his column this "geography lesson", "Probably Finland wishes it were more inland".

(5) "Soviet Russia's invasion of Finland is one more phase in her apparent program to re-establish domination over the 277,148 square miles of territory stripped from her after the world war", commented the AP early in the war. "Here is what she lost in the war settlements: Finland 133,000 square miles, Estonia 16,955 miles, Latvia 24,400 square miles, Lithuania 36,500 square miles, Poland 49,150 square miles, Bessarabia (to Rumania) 17,143 square miles." She has recovered all of her territories now except part of Finland and Poland.

(6) Cross shortly after changed his tactics and soon became one of the leaders in the movement to promote British interests at Harvard, which as the Student Union says is being used for trial balloons.

(7) March 6, Ralph Barnes cabled the *Herald Tribune* from London: " 'Exasperation' is the term used in news dispatches reaching London from Helsinki to express the feelings of the Finns at the failure of 'their friends' abroad to forward the military assistance which, it is said, was promised earlier.   Undoubtedly the Anglo-French allies are among 'the friends' referred to."   (Lavine)

(8) While England was courting Stalin in the spring of '39, there was indication that Russia expected trouble might be hatching in Finland and that that had something to do with her rejection of England's proposal.   Harold Denny, May 11, 1939, wirelessed from Moscow, "Izvestia rejects the statement of Prime Minister Chamberlain in the British House of Commons yesterday that, in defending Poland and Rumania, Britain and France would, in fact, be defending the Soviet Union's western border.   In the first place, says Izvestia, Poland and Rumania do not cover all the Soviet's western border—which is true, because there are Latvia and Estonia, not to speak of Finland and Turkey, all of which might become involved if a general war in eastern Europe broke out."

(9) From Bucharest, Dec 5, 1939, the N. Y. *Times* learned by telephone that "Great Britain today sent a note to the Rumanian government asking it to stop deliveries of raw materials and goods to Germany. . . .   It was emphasized that Rumania was ready to sell her products to anyone who paid a fair price, and to carry out her engagements with Germany and Great Britain alike.   Rumors have

been circulating that Britain has threatened to withdraw the guarantee given to Rumania."

With the collapse of the Rumanian house of cards, Carol disappeared from the press. Then later he was reported having crossed out of Rumania, his car riddled with bullets. Then the stories of graft began to appear in the papers, of a kingdom looted, of great deposits of cash in British and American banks.

(10) "The Finnish cause in the United States was espoused by personalities as diverse as President Roosevelt and ex-President Hoover, Father Coughlin and Elsie the Cow; at Finnish benefits Broadway stars contributed songs and Dorothy Lamour her sarong; the American Institute of Public Opinion reported that 88 per cent of America was rooting for Finland, only 1 per cent for Russia", write Lavine and Wechsler. That there was much propaganda was admitted later by those who were most zealous in spreading it.

During the long cold winter every effort was made to use Finland to win American sympathy to the Allied cause, as Belgium had served in World War I. Women throughout the country were knitting for the Finns. Professor Frederick L. Schuman of Williams was stumping for a more aggressive foreign policy and a "conservative" defense loan of 500 million dollars to Finland. Congress debated the question of a loan, and Dorothy Thompson proclaimed that unless such a loan were made it would show that we were "scared".

Dorothy Thompson wrote March 22, "Several facts emerged when the noise of battle died down on the Russo-Finnish front which matter greatly to the situation of Europe. One is the strength and importance of the Russian army about which most journalists, including this columnist, have been ill-informed. It is a factor to be reckoned with, a big factor."

It was later discovered that the pictures of destroyed houses used in the preliminary propaganda were prepared, before the trouble began, in London from northern France pictures of 1914. Likewise faked were the pictures of Russian troops frozen with their limbs in the air. James Aldridge of the N.A.N.A. cabled December 24, "As if the men had suddenly turned to wax there were two or three thousand Russians and a few Finns, all frozen in fighting attitudes."

Lavine and Wechsler tells us that "In response to inquiry from the Institute for Propaganda Analysis, several scientists and officials of the New York Academy of Medicine all concurred in the view that instantaneous freezing is, as one expert put it, a 'Munchausen tale familiar in Europe for the last two centuries'. It just doesn't happen." No one in dying of freezing would be frozen in an attitude like Laocoon. They would collapse. They would inevitably assume the cuddled folded up primitive foetal position to conserve the maximum of warmth   How were those pictures created? Cadavers were collected and posed in such positions, and after a fresh snowfall photographed. But they were very striking and played an important and dramatic part in the propaganda.

December 26 Leland Stowe cabled a gripping story of "a Finnish soldier . . . armed with only a knife" after his pistol had become "so hot that it broke to pieces". Sergeant Corrah, U.S.A. informed *Collier's,* who published this item,

"Generals, majors, colonels, and enlisted men can fall to pieces if the heat is strong enough, but not a pistol."

Fortune, January, 1941, surveying the course of public opinion over the past year, finds that "as the Russians thrust clumsily into central Finland and battered at the Mannerheim Line, the people of the United States felt their first surge of genuine sympathy for a European nation". Under the barrage of propaganda "the first tremble of terror ran through the United States. But it was as nothing compared to the effect of the invasion of the Lowlands and the fall of France. A whole generation's concept of security crumbled in a few days. . . . The minority of less than 20% who had thought the United States should give more aid to the Allies suddenly found itself an overwhelming majority made up of better than 70% of the people."

(11) In April, 1940 *Direction,* George Seldes writes, "Finland . . . was not betrayed in March, 1940, but in 1925, and in 1930, and in 1935 . . . by the British when she permitted herself to become a base for war, when the Mannerheim Line was first proposed, and finally built, at a cost which drained the wealth of the nation. The Mannerheim Line was a British idea, carried out by British army men, and paid for by the Finns. During the many years of its construction there were also under way airplane fields for 2,000 planes Finland never had more than 150, and could not have afforded thousands, but the bases were prepared. The preparations all pointed towards the Russian frontier. They contemplated an enormous army, a great air fleet, and Britain knew the secrets. Obviously Britain was to supply the men and planes."

Seldes quotes Ludwell Denny, Washington correspondent, that it would be better for the Allies "to sell their war to us on facts rather than on hypocrisy. . . . When empire interests are believed to be at stake, the British government does not hesitate to ditch democracy. . . . This may seem sordid . . ". Truth frequently is.

On the appointment of Sir Stafford Cripps as British ambassador to the Soviets, a Boston *Transcript* editorial writer wrote June 8, 1940, of his boldness in defending labor and opposing appeasement. "Particularly unpopular was his analysis of the Russo-Finnish War, which pointed out its necessity, affirmed considerable faith in the integrity of Russian intentions But no one wanted to hear that Ryti and Mannerheim were renegades, using their own people as pawns, taking blood money from British capitalists, building Mannerheim lines with 'loans' from the Bank of England."

"What Stalin sought from Finland in inviting negotiations on October 5, 1939, was not the annexation of the Republic nor the extinction of its independence nor even a mutual assistance pact, though the latter proposal had been originally made and then withdrawn Stalin sought to strengthen the Soviet's strategic position with respect to the Gulf of Finland, the Red naval base at Kronstadt and the city of Leningrad." "In return Moscow offered to grant Finland permission to fortify the Aaland Islands, providing that no foreign Power, including Sweden, should have anything to do with them, and proposed to cede to Finland

5,529 sq km. of Soviet territory in central Karelia about midway between Lake Ladoga and the Arctic " "Moscow hated and distrusted Mannerheim who was a Germanophile, a cruel and inveterate anti-Bolshevik, and an ex-officer of the Tsar who had massacred fifteen thousand or more Communists in 1918 and had sought to lead the Finns in an attack on Red Petrograd. The Kremlin later alleged, without ever adducing any proof predating the Soviet attack, that Finland was 'backed' by Britain and France for purposes hostile to the U S S R " (Frederick L. Schuman, "Night Over Europe", Knopf, 1941)

ON ALL FRONTS

Why this "hibernating war", as Sir John Simon calls it? Why doesn't Britain bomb Berlin as Bernard Shaw demands? Why doesn't Hitler attack? The next move is so important, all hesitate. It's "After you, Alphonse."

The Allies expected Poland to resist through the winter. They did not expect Russia to move so soon. Preparations had been made for resistance in the Mediterranean, and now they find activities unexpectedly transferred to the Baltic. They had prepared for a 'Blitzkrieg' and to take the shock stoically. Now they are wearing themselves out waiting for events that do not happen. "The German attack is far more insidious. . . . Her aim is to undermine Western Europe economically and socially" as they "concentrate all their efforts on armaments . . . until the whole capitalist system was exhausted". "The new plan of campaign" must cut down on expense, push normal trade, maintain the good will of neutrals (Robert Sencourt, *Commonweal*, Dec. 15).

The present impasse resulted when the patience of both Hitler and Chamberlain was exhausted. In this international game of jockeying for position, power, profits, there always comes a time when bluff, cloaked as diplomacy, breaks down. Someone fails and becomes angry. Then the military are called and the blood-letting usually begins

This time the stakes are so big those who stand to win or lose are keeping a hand on the controls,—no chance for Haigs or Ludendorffs. Hore-Belisha, in control of the military, understands Liddell Hart's thesis in his "Defence of Britain",—"Our chief risk of losing a war lies in trying to win the war". He is convinced as was Clemenceau that now "war is too serious a business to be left to the generals".

The Propagandists are now the protagonists. Seldom seen is the hand of the puppeteer actuating statesmen. Unseen, too, is the source of the "public address system" whose loud speakers are heard in our forums, classrooms and churches.   More obviously operated is the miraculous Charlie McCarthy of our great peace foundation.

Great is the art of influencing people and making them your allies. Vansittart, who so mysteriously 'retired' as head of the Foreign Office when Chamberlain came in three years ago, has with secrecy built a great propaganda machine to change American opinion, and with subtlety improved the technique.   Now he may sit back as he watches his apparently self-actuating puppets perform and say, "I planned it that way".

Selected facts replacing the cruder lies are given a slight twist to bring out the moral flavor desired, just as the bartender with a twist brings out the lime flavor in the gin rickey. [1]

The formula and flavor, always suited to the "gout americain", has been changed lest the taste become jaded. 'Democracy', 'gangster', 'aggression' cocktails have been served with the cherry of 'religion and morality' or the olive of 'a new and better peace'.   Insidiously we have been brought to a state of righteous exaltation.   .

Lothian, the master mixer, serves a 'federation' cocktail concocted from the Rhodes, Milner, Lionel Curtis distillation.   This is guaranteed to contain 'no British propaganda' and to be an antidote to the 'Keep out of war hysteria', even for those who are 'propaganda proof'.   He has served this federation cocktail to MacNutt, the "war monger," whom he would not be averse to seeing president.

Lord Lothian keeps in the public eye by grace of King John's bargain with the barons, [2] at the Gridiron dinner and the National Press Club (return engagement), all of which helps Streit, his chief salesman.

Our university presidents and professors and all the lesser members of the tribe have become inveterate bibbers. Ecstatic inebriety has spread from above downward through the ranks of the intellectuals.

President Roosevelt in this state of exalted exhilaration was inspired in a 'Fireside Talk' to denounce 'breastbeaters' and 'dishonest fakers' and to righteously deny that he 'intends' to send 'sons of American mothers' across the sea   Lord MacMillan in London produces a cruder brew for the common people which makes them red in the face with moral indignation.   But in a sober moment, may we not blow away the smoke of propaganda and take a glimpse behind the screen of censorship?   Let's look.

Germany is presented as on the verge of revolt. Maj. Percy Black, attache of American Embassy at Berlin for three years, arriving in New York, Nov. 29, said "reports of German dissension are largely exaggerated. . . . The German people, from top to bottom, are more afraid of another treaty of Versailles than anything else. They feel that if . . . beaten, it will be the end of Germany".[3]

Villard, in his formerly liberal *Nation*, (Nov. 25) now vituperative in its hatred, writes from Berlin of the "great efficiency". "The reservoir of man-power seems nothing less than extraordinary. . . . One sees countless young men of military age still in civilian clothes . . As for life in Berlin . . you would not know a war was going on. There are no gas masks, no shelter trenches, and so few sandbags that they hardly attract attention. . . . There is sufficient food, though there is a shortage of fat, eggs, and meat. . . . Plenty of vegetables and fruit."[4]

The propagandist makes his cause attractive by enlarging on the troubles and difficulties of his enemies, and suppressing news of his own. It is his duty to present a picture of Germany to Americans that will be unattractive, however distorted. Wishful thinking of disgruntled expatriates and disappointed Junkers is enlarged upon.[5]

Until Stalin on March 11, 1939 exposed the Tory plan of egging Hitler on against Russia, England dilated on the virtues of Germany in articles and books, few of which have reached America (cf Bul #1). An exception is Yeats-Brown's "European Jungle", published Dec. 5 by Macrae-Smith, Philadelphia. The Bengal Lancer tells of Hitler, "His power is based on shrewd common sense and judgment of character".

Chamberlain had faith in Hitler, and Lothian and Halifax praised him. Nevile Henderson, too, "praised Hitler for restoring Germany's self-respect and for introducing many excellent social reforms" (White Paper of Oct. 17). Churchill, in farewell, reminded Hitler of all he had done "in raising Germany from frustration and defeat".

Field Marshal Lord Milne says, "The youth of Germany are thoroughly behind their leader". The London *Economist* in November states, "A blockade could never win a war for England." In a long war it would result in closer economic cooperation and improved communications so that "the German-Russian pact then would become what it is not today—an instrument for rendering Germany blockade-proof".

Britain's blockade, meantime, is ineffective. It has not prevented

German ships from emerging, and the great "Bremen" and "New York" from returning. Cotton is reaching Germany from Spain, the Caspian, the Balkans, and Turkestan. Essentials of high value, like American molybdenum, Chinese chromium, Russian platinum, or Zeiss lenses, can well afford to pay the freight by way of Japan.

Our purpose, remember, is not to be judicial, nor to present the 'other' side, but many sides, to reveal what has been suppressed and to disclose the untruth of what is generally accepted   Our newspapers do not permit us to know what is happening in England and France.   "This England is a nightmare,[6] like the early stages of a Wellsian fantasy", writes Kingsley Martin from London to The *New Republic,* Nov. 29.

The London *Times* weekly Educational Supplement, the London *Journal of Education,* The *New Era* (an educational magazine which reaches us with a censor's permit number) have been filled for months with complaints of the educational chaos,—no schools open, laboratories stripped for offices, millions of children taken from their homes, welcomed at first, now wearing on their hosts, vain attempt of the government to collect from the parents six to nine shillings a week for board, school buildings evacuated for hospitals, and nurses and doctors waiting for casualties forbidden to carry on normal practices.[7]

Putting the best possible propaganda front on the Evacuation, The *Round Table,* Dec. 1939, (p 97) says, "One of its weakest features was the requisitioning" of great public schools, hotels, spas, "for the thousands of civil servants . . . while hutments were in course of erection".

No mass bombing could have effected the disorganization and loss of morale that the ineptness of the Government has brought about so easily. J. B. Priestley makes this clear in his "Rain Upon Godshill".

Bernard Shaw writes, Englishmen "are enduring all the vagaries . . . of the ineptest Military Communism   Powers which no Plantagenet king or Fascist dictator would dream of claiming have been granted to any unqualified person . . . Whatever our work in life may be, we have been ordered to stop doing it and stand by   Wherever our wives and children are they have been transported to somewhere else

"Grievance week" in the House of Commons gave opportunity for bitter complaints on loss of civil liberties, irritating suppressions and controls,—wives of soldiers selling their clothes for food. Parliament's function is to do nothing and talk about it (*Newsweek,* November 13).

Chamberlain admits, "People are sometimes apt to get a little restive when, as they put it, nothing happens. So I welcome the war-time luncheons you are arranging."

Hyde Park orators and Sir Oswald Mosley's fascists are advertised as evidence of 'freedom' and 'democracy'. But Sir John Anderson, who was in control of the 'Black and Tan' in Ireland and suppressed the rebels in Bengal, promulgated regulations that authorize prosecutions for the expression of opinions "likely to be prejudicial to the defense of the realm or the efficient prosecution of the war" and suppression of any action or propaganda that might cause "disaffection" in the fighting services. In the house even the Tory benches rose in rebellion.

Behind the scenes War Minister Hore-Belisha and Overseas Commander General Ironside fight it out. "With the British Army in France", William Stoneman reports "grousing". But Philip Gibbs presents a cheering picture as he did in the last war until it was all over, when he decided "Now It Can Be Told". That's his job

England's daily cost of the war is $30,000,000. Living costs have risen 2.5% in one month. Sir John Simon reports war bill will amount to nearly 10 billions a year, an increase of 66⅔% over the cost of peace Why fight for peace if you can get it at a discount of 66⅔%?

England's imports amount to 15 million dollars a day. If only 1/10 are cut off, that would be a million and a half But the cost of preventive patrols and mine sweeping and losses, curtailment of shipping, business, and commissions would bring the total to 4 or 5 millions a day. A capital levy will soon be necessary.

The British Tories have decided to go down fighting. They are jittery, as they may well be. With the world in the hollow of their hands they have made a mess of it There is no hope of cleaning up without the help of Cousin Jonathan. And already there is resentment at our slowness in coming in

But in spite of the Johnson Act and our Neutrality, our President has found ways of spending American money for the benefit of the British Raj. It goes through the RFC and the Export Bank. Our taxpayers buy Kaffir gold at a huge profit to the producers We lent money to Finland. There is no reason why we shouldn't lend it to Canada. It all serves the same purpose.

In France the penalty for transmitting forbidden news is the guillotine.. "France at War", *Round Table*, December, 1939, guardedly tells of thousands of evacues from the German border, prices down and no markets, Draconian regulations, pessimistic fatalism.

A sixteen-page letter from an American friend resident near Paris who finally escaped from Bordeaux by S. S. St. John, planned for Cape Cod Canal traffic, tells dramatically of trains running all night five days before the war on ten-minute headway moving troops to front, of tension, no sleep, air raid alarms, no mail, all held thirty days. "Not a new war at all . . . same war as the last time. . . . All are 'starting' this war tired, very tired, and in the same mood as they 'finished' the last one. Everyone—stricken just as if each had lost his own mother that morning. No speech. No smiles. Just staring blankly ahead or reading papers and tears in many eyes. The soldiers sitting on their horses looked so sad . . . everywhere . . . resolute . . . But they see the futility . . . and they feel betrayed. . . . They had a duty they would do, but they seemed to feel it should not have been allowed to become necessary. Many blamed England . . . a punishable offense. . . . Some say, 'Ten men made this war, ten million will die for it' . . . But the man who says he will not fight . . . instantly shot. . .'. There will be no ending England's game of playing balance of power unless some force brings about unification of Europe. . . . England's dog in the manger policy of the little clique who rule. . . . In France no confidence in newspapers . . . know they are bought. . . . I heard . . . 'How do we know Hitler is bad? Perhaps he is, but how do we know it? . . He is known to us only through the capitalist press'. The situation is dangerous. I would not be a bit surprised to see all western Europe go Communist if this war goes on".

Serious disaffection is suggested in Daladier's speech insisting on the continuance of his dictatorship as reported in an inside page story in the New York *Times*. Daladier told Bullitt that unless the Allies could win some success he saw no reason to continue the war and is ready and willing to turn over the government to Bonnet, who represents pro-German interests (*Week by Week*, Dec. 9).

The war is not popular. Morale is low. Discontent among the troops in the wet, damp underground fortifications has resulted in the return of some hundreds of thousands of fathers to their homes. Numbers are increased or dismissed for publicity purposes. At mobilization it was given out that 4 to 8 millions were called. Dispatches say 4 million are still in line. "It's a Military Impossibility", according to Lowell Limpus, *Forum,* Dec. 1939.

A drastic decree empowers prefects of the departments (there are more than 70) "to remove from their homes persons considered 'dangerous to national security' and, if necessary, to fix a place of residence for them" (French for concentration camp). "The decree also declares that such persons may be called upon to perform work for the national defense" (in Germany it is 'forced labor'). Thousands of Germans and other foreigners are now experiencing what E E. Cummings described in "The Enormous Room". Hundreds of thousands of Spanish refugees are still half starved behind barbed wire.[8]

Members of the Chamber of Deputies belonging to the Communist Party, French pacifists, intellectuals, idealists nonconformists, are in prison. These were men who a year ago denounced the Munich settlement of Bonnet and Daladier. Imprisoned or merely 'taken into custody' because of advanced age (the last three over 70) are Jean Giono, whose film "Harvest" is now being shown in this country, Marcel Déat, leader of the Socialist Party, Minister for Air in 1936, Prof. Félicien Challaye, who wrote on how French imperialism in Equatorial Africa had reduced a native population of 40,000,000 to 2,500,000, Victor Marguerite, army officer turned pacifist novelist, Alain (Prof. Emile August Chartier), author of "Les Propos d'Alain" (*Uncensored,* Dec 2).[9]

Hushed up are the acrimonious disputes between French and British leaders on war policy. High French government circles are opposed to the Simon and Hore-Belisha policy of 'let the war go on but do nothing' and say that in a waiting game Germany may be able to wait longer than France, because of its stronger industrial position For France lives on supplying the world with luxuries. The world can not afford luxuries French business and trade languish. Meantime, the British have taken over control of French ships, French trade, and are pooling their resources and purchases, with headquarters in London. Hitler is shrewd enough to know that if he leaves them alone they may destroy themselves as a potential invading enemy.[10]

In Spain the Phalangists and Suner, the fascist brother-in-law of Franco, are still struggling for position, with explosion imminent. Coming is the devaluation of the peseta, of vital importance to British financial, mining, and export interests.

Holland is terrorized. Her economic life is completely disorganized on two fronts, commerce off 70%. "Fat, feeble, and defenceless", she is easy plucking. Major Angas, the British stock market adviser, tells us (Digest No 49, Nov. 28) Hitler can easily take Holland, Belgium and Denmark to use as trading pawns when it comes to settlement. Then with England's marine depleted, industrial centers and navy weakened by airplane attacks, Schoolmaster Chamberlain might call it a day if the low countries were given back.

Holland would give Hitler airplane bases half an hour's flight from England and not only bases for submarines but shipbuilding plants to build more. Japan simultaneously would take the Dutch East Indies, rich in oil, rubber, tin, coffee.

Why doesn't Hitler attack? When Holland yields too much to British interference with trade, Hitler threatens. The popular group, which includes the Catholics, is for social reform and resistance. Then Wilhelmina and Leopold offer mediation, for they with the bankers and conservatives believe it wiser to give Hitler submarine and air bases and avoid bankruptcy and ruin.

Van Paassen, recently visiting his birthplace, writes of "subordination of every phase of life to imperialist considerations . . . exploitation of tens of millions of human beings in the Indonesian colonies in the interest of a small coterie of regents who own the banks, the oil wells, the rubber plantations, and the means of production in general"

Finland (Bul #21),—the 'build-up' was well planned weeks in advance, and Oct. 23 and 30 *Life* printed eleven pages of pictures and material evidently straight from the Finnish Information Center at Rockefeller Center   The *Herald Tribune's* Forum contributed to this 'build-up', featuring Lord Lothian and the Polish and Finnish ministers

The correspondents of the London *Times* and Swiss papers, and the Finnish radio, said nothing of the killing of civilians at Helsinki, while the British and American newspapers were flaunting it as a massacre. The photographic publicity of ruins in the British newspapers was obviously faked, Claud Cockburn tells us in The *Week*, December 6, No. 344, American edition cabled from London, $10.00 a year, published at 20 Vesey Street, N. Y C. Well informed London conservatives in late November, The *Week* tells us, were offering even money that the finances and forces of the United States and Sweden would be engaged against the Soviets by spring. The aim was to destroy the chief industrial center of the Communistic world.

The *American Observer,* Washington, D. C., December 11, recognizes "that a strong foreign power might use Finland as a base from which to attack the Soviet Union, especially the city of Leningrad, with a population of 3,500,000, which is only a few miles from the Finnish frontier. ... The Russians demanded .. that Finnish troops be withdrawn 12 to 15 miles from the frontier".[11]

London had a bad moment when the Finnish Delegate in Moscow, Paasikivi, was about ready to reach an agreement. With the British backing, Tanner was substituted The Soviets' left to the jaw dislocated British plans. (The *Week,* 20 Vesey St., N. Y. C.) When on Soviet demand the Premier resigned, a British knight, head of the Finnish bank, was appointed.

Rumania will soon lose Bessarabia,[12] which she seized in the early '20's when the Soviets were in trouble. And Bulgaria will retake the Dobrudja, as Russia has agreed. That will release frightful stories, now prepared in London, of Bulgarian and Russian atrocities in Rumania.

Lord Lloyd in Rumania is promoting the idea of a Danubian Kingdom under the Hapsburgs,[13] F C. Hanighen reports on arriving on the S. S. Manhattan late in November Duff Cooper on his arrival opined that "very likely there will be a monarchial revival", with a merger of Catholic Bavaria and Catholic Austria under Otto von Hapsburg, whom he described as "a very nice young man"

Perfect unity and amity is still lacking in the Balkans. "Inside word is that the idea of a Balkan Union is a flop. Yugoslavia is cold to the plan. ... It is a deep dark secret but the wealthy classes in Rumania are moving their families and their valuables to British possessions in the Mediterranean" (*Week by Week,* Washington, D C , Nov. 25)

The lower Danube valley and its upper industrial reaches are naturally and economically supplementary. But a strong administration rather than intrigue is needed to bring prosperity. P. J. Philip, March 25, in the New York *Times* wirelessed, "Beneath all diatribes against the immorality, brutality, illegality and so forth of German methods, there is the secret admission that central and eastern Europe, which have been lame and sick ever since the war, may become again well ordered, productive, solvent and possibly more peace minded."[14]

Italy's neutrality is proving profitable,[15]—transmitting Franco's American cotton over the Brenner to Germany,—bargaining with England. She needs such easy money as Turkey has gotten from England, variously reported as 240 or 750 millions. Italy holds out for more than Tunisia and the 360 millions reported offered according to recent dispatches. Mussolini, naturally delighted to see British activity transferred to the Arctic, sends 50-80 planes, refueled by Germany, to keep things stirred up in the north. Thus he achieves greater freedom in "mare nostrum".

The Vatican is economically sensitive. Father John J. Boardman bemoans that countries now at war which once sent "millions of dollars" are now sending "scarce a penny" to the Pope. "Where else on earth can he look for assistance, save only to us in America?" The Nazi government is temporarily withholding 15 of the 40 million annually paid to the priests and Catholic Church (J. T. Whittaker, *World Telegram*, Nov. 17).

On the American Front—The *Round Table*, British propaganda quarterly for the academic and scholarly, in the December "Special War Number" just received gives us a 'Whitehall view of our affairs in the article "America and the War" This purports to be by an American, who wisely remains anonymous, for his allegiance is evidently to the British Empire, in whose interests he has been spying out the country, about which he writes with shrewdness and naivete He reports, "The writer has just returned from a 9,000-mile trip to the Pacific coast and the north-west, endeavoring to assess the state of affairs.

"When the war broke out, the average comment of the average American was: 'How soon will we get in?' The estimates of shrewd students of affairs ranged from ninety days to a year." This anticipation was wrecked by "the furious war of propaganda which was waged against repeal. . . Nine out of ten—and perhaps nineteen out of twenty —of these appeals were against lifting the embargo. Thousands of appeals would come to a single Congressman from his constituents within a few days . . . Realistic methods were necessary. . . . Repeal of the arms embargo . . . probably never would have prevailed without a comprehensive and astute job of political management . .

"In September, the President had Senator James F. Byrnes—a skilled and highly popular negotiator—poll his colleagues at their homes in all parts of the country, by lavish use of the long-distance telephone. Striking early, Senator Byrnes obtained ample commitments to repeal of the embargo before ever the Senators returned to Washington for the special session. Similarly, practical methods were employed in the House, where the 'solid south' of Democratic representatives and the machine-controlled city blocs of representatives were all whipped into the party camp. . . .

"It was a triumph of sanity and legitimate political organization . . . Meantime, the Administration is going ahead . . He at once materially increased the size of the Army, the Navy, the National Guard, and the Marine Corps. . . . The 'safety zone' set up by the Declaration of Panama, while perhaps outraging the international law conventions of a sea Power like Britain, is actually a great practical advantage."

Ships now "cannot leave port even to ply between American harbors. Meantime, the right of Britain or France to have access to their possessions in the Americas is untouched, and their naval bases may be used as freely as ever. The situation may be entirely illogical and contradictory, but the fact remains that, unless stupidly mismanaged, the Allies can turn it greatly to their advantage. . . .

"The importance of the American rearmament program is perhaps most valuable in the Far East, where the bulk of the fleet remains, constantly pushing outposts beyond the Hawaii line. . . . A Russo-Japanese deal . . . would be catastrophic to British interests in the Orient. . . . Whether the United States could stomach the probable kind of British-Japanese deal is open to question". If "Russian diplomacy" scores, "the United States will accept Far Eastern responsibilities a bit more fully, and thereby ease pressure on Britain."

But "continuity of foreign policy may be assured" only if Mr. Roosevelt wins a third term. This is likely if there is a period of crisis. One may gather that such crisis may be created in the interest of the Empire, as just before the final Congressional vote on the embargo, when we were startled by the report of submarine attack on the Coulmore just off New York. And the *Round Table* writer is optimistic.[16]

All want peace but on their own terms. Neither Chamberlain nor Daladier dares stop. Demobilization would bring worse troubles. Hitler and Stalin must for propaganda purposes say that they want peace, but as they are the proponents of revolution, which is accelerated in time of disturbance, and as they are evidently winning the war internally in France and Britain as it is, their desire for peace except on their own terms must be discounted.

Capitalist imperialism is now face to face with socialistic imperialism. Individual imperialism up against totalitarian imperialism on equal terms hasn't a chance of winning, our capitalist imperialists know. Those who want peace most are those who have the most to lose. (cf *Weekly Foreign Letter,* Nov. 24, 1939).

This view is gradually winning acceptance. Even the old Boston *Transcript* points out the more successful Britain's blockade, the more Communistic will Germany become, and the more closely allied with Russia. "For the first time in the world's history, it has become unsafe for capitalistic nations to prosecute a war as hard as they can. Modern society has generated conditions that automatically constitute a counter-force to war. Both the traditional ruling classes of Britain and Germany must realize that every successful pressure they bring against each other in this war strengthens their foe . . . The ruling classes of Britain are keenly alert to such a danger" and the need of conserving "their resources against Communism".

Now comes Kennedy with the current word that England expects little of 'Uncle Sam Shylock'. The British government "does not have the slightest belief that this country will get into this war in any way", he reports, though Englishmen "find it difficult to comprehend how we can sympathize with their cause and not take part in it". Wasted by long hours of work in the gloom, he is pessimistic as to the way the battle goes.

"There is no place in this fight for us", he said "We must stay out. . . As you love America, don't let anything that comes out of any country in the world make you believe you can make a situation one whit better by getting into a war. . . . The American people ought to refuse to listen to generalities . . We should not let our emotions rule. . . If the United States were foolish enough to get in . . . I am quite distressed by what might happen to the economic, financial, and social positions of the United States, and I want to safeguard the country."[17] The real story the Ambassador probably reserved for the President.[18] Perhaps he revealed greater naval losses than have been made public. Perhaps he told how the continuous bombing of the Shetlands had sent the British navy to other hideouts.

From across the seas continue to come hordes of statesmen, lecturers, authors,—to tell us with sad recrimination of what is 'right' and 'wrong' and of our lack of moral responsibility The propaganda resources of the British Empire are at the service of insuring a third term for our pro-British President, who is their white hope.[19] [20]

In this present confusion, the propaganda 'stars' hold the whip hand while America bares its back for the 'stripes',—now paying taxes on 44 billion from the last war and paying 3 to 4 billion this coming year toward the new war. And our money is desperately needed not merely for war but to win and hold new allies,—Turkey, Italy.

Meanwhile the British take our ships where the President has forbidden them to go, loot them, confiscate the mail, demand more money and castigate us for our lack of devotion to 'morality and religion'.[21] The 'Stars' and 'Stripes',—Forever?

In late November, before the Finnish flare-up, those in Washington, who size up the international situation and contribute to the confidential financial private letters, estimated the odds on our getting into the war at about 2 to 3. Now our sympathy for Finland has reversed the odds. This is the time to intensify the propaganda campaign and to win us over for War. And so the War goes on, on all fours. "Fore!" calls out Chamberlain. "Fore!" cry Hitler, Stalin, Mussolini, each planning a long shot.[22]

December 15, 1939

NOTES

[1] Recipes for news cocktails will be found in Quincy Howe's "The News and How to Understand It In spite of the newspapers, In spite of the magazines, In spite of the radio" (Simon and Schuster, 1940)

[2] The Magna Carta, one of the several extant copies which had been enshrined at the World's Fair, was, at its close in the fall of 1939, placed in the Library of Congress alongside the Declaration of Independence. It was a master stroke of propaganda admirably managed by Lord Lothian. The brief remarks in accepting it of the newly appointed Librarian MacLeish, reflecting his former proletarian sympathies, "were worthy of the occasion" The barons of the early 13th century, he said "were less concerned for the rights of the people of England than for the privileges they had planned to pocket for themselves". Lord Lothian agreed "the barons were more concerned to preserve their own rights, and privileges than to extend the liberties of commoner and villein" But, intent on his propaganda, Lothian added, "Inscribed on the musty parchment before us we see the nucleus of most of our liberties, of trial by jury, of habeas corpus,

of the principle of no taxation without representation, of the bill of rights, and of the whole constitutional edifice of modern democracy"

MacLeish in rebuttal remarked, "Government by the people's representatives may, from time to time, mistake for true defenders . . . the demagogues, the same in every generation, who appeal to liberty in order to destroy it. Government by the people's representatives may, from time to time, substitute inquisitions and espionage for the equal protection of the laws, and may permit the inquisitors, in their reckless search for enemies of liberty, to break down liberty. . . . History has many curious and circuitous passages, many winding stairways which return upon themselves—but none, I think, more curious than the turn of time which brings the Great Charter." Then "MacLeish dropped the key into his right pants pocket and smiled", the Boston *Herald* reported, Nov. 29, 1939.

(3) Col W. Stewart-Roddie, formerly of British Intelligence Service, *World-Telegram*, Nov. 1, reported, "saw no immediate hope that the morale of the German people would crack to the point of revolt". At the New York Harvard Club, he said "It was clever direction to reduce the standard of living long before the war. This not only permitted the nation to store enormous stocks of food, it accustomed the people to rationing, which has lessened fear of a food shortage."

(4) Villard, who hates the Nazis, was "amazed at the freedom with which people . . . spoke out" and that none of his dispatches were censored. He reports little evidence of war hysteria and no great shortage of food, gasoline, or war materials Lothrop Stoddard from Berlin in a syndicated article (NANA), contradicting recently published propaganda, reports Berliners well fed, well dressed, free from hate, exceedingly kind. "There isn't much censorship", the son of William Allen White tells in the Washington *Star*, Dec. 9, ("Industrial Control Reports", Dec 16).

W. Y. Elliott, Harvard government professor, in an address reported in the Boston *Herald*, Dec. 18, asserted the Reich had "immense stores of aluminum and molybdenum" to last two years. American exports in October to Russia increased from a monthly average of 3 to 8 millions, with re-exports of rubber and copper accounting for 3 millions. England has been selling rubber to the Soviets, which goes to Germany. The past few months U. S shipped nearly a million pounds of rubber to Norway In September imports doubled from U. S. to Scandinavian countries, whose trade with Germany is unimpeded. (Newspaper reports).

Germany's shortage of oil and the impossibility of deliveries from Russia is enlarged upon by Paul Mallon in his syndicated column, Dec. 13. He reports that in the first six months of 1939 Hitler got only 26,000 of 557,000 metric tons of crude oil exported from Rumania and is getting less now. But an AP dispatch, Dec. 14, from Bucharest tells of Rumania's agreement to increase oil shipments to Germany and to give them better exchange. Dec. 20 she agreed to double her shipments to Germany.

(5) Arrivals from central Europe frequently get across to the ship's reporters fresh and vital information. It is strange that after they have been on American

soil they pipe down. Dodds, our misfit ambassador to Berlin, who sputtered and fumed, came home, got into trouble and died, was succeeded by Hugh Wilson who was recalled and shut up. Cudahy in London could tell the truth about behavior of the Germans in Belgium. Arrived here, he too was shut up and the ambassadorship at St. James dangled before him. Kennedy returns, is tamed, breaks forth, offers resignation, which is not accepted so as to keep him in ambassadorial fetters.

If Mr Kennedy has indeed been cleverly gagged, Representative Rogers and Senator Vandenberg of the House and Senate Foreign Affairs Committees, in calling him to testify, have "found a way to remove the obstruction In any case, the country needs the diplomat's counsel and ought to have it" (Editorial, Boston *Transcript*, January 16, 1941). Senator Wheeler after an hour's visit with Joseph P. Kennedy, January 17, 1941, challenged the President to make public reports from Kennedy and Bullitt or to give them to the Senate or the Foreign Relations Committee in executive session. George Seldes in the Jan. 15, 1941, issue of "In Fact" quoted extensively from Kennedy's unpublished and still held secret report to the State Department of last October.

Joseph Kennedy, Jan. 18, 1941, in a radio address to the nation declared that national unity cannot be maintained when "the motives of patriotic men are indiscriminately assailed. . . . Many Americans, including myself, have been subjected to deliberate smear campaigns merely because we differed from an articulate minority" As ambassador, he maintained, that it was his duty "to report the facts to his government as he saw them" He asserted that the British should pay for munitions so far as their assets would permit He told the people he had "opposed the war" but believed that we should help England to win But he did not believe that there was an emergency that required us "to confer upon the President authority unheard of in our history".

AP dispatch from Washington, Jan. 20, 1941, states "the State Department would reject legislative demands that the department make public the diplomatic reports of Joseph P Kennedy and William C Bullitt". Kennedy was 'accused' of "disingenuity" by his classmate, Professor Samuel H. Cross who since the Finnish flare-up has been prompt to see the thing that would be welcomed by influential Harvard alumni of Wall Street. He disagrees with Kennedy's statement "that England was fighting its own war".

Wallace R. Deuel, Chicago *Daily News* correspondent, returning after years in Germany, January 13, 1941, to get the press has to meet the American taste, but reminds us "The German people are tired, as few people have ever been tired without breaking down. In a single generation, they have gone through a major war, a starvation blockade and a catastrophic defeat, they have had two revolutions; they have had their currency wiped out altogether once and have been seriously threatened with the same fate again, they have had the same exhausting and disillusioning experiences of the depression the rest of the world has had; and now they have entered a new war."

(6) Early in December, after the election, the British censors permitted a much

more realistic presentation of the state of Britain and the bombardment of London,—this preliminary to a more pressing appeal for help.

(7) On the outbreak of the war millions of children and mothers were evacuated from the great cities to the country, and each has learned how the other half lives. A little girl sends a postcard to her parents, saying where she is, people put on a different dress to sleep in at night, and now she has one (*Survey*). In another village the women of the thatched cottages have a horror of vermin. A committee has set up a clinic in the schoolhouse where boys and girls are inspected and heads shaved or treated with a fine tooth comb and gasoline. These city children cry for "fish and chips",—the usual food of the slum people, bits of fish and sliced potato fried in fat brought home in a paper bag This, like the eating of "winkles", is a caste custom, *Mass Observation*, Blackheath, S.E. 3, London, showed in a survey late in 1939.

(8) To refute the false picture of the French "place of residence" given in the N. Y. *Times* of Nov. 26, 1939, and by Edgar Mowrer in the N. Y. *World-Telegram* of Nov. 6, Gustav Richter writes in the *Nation* Dec. 16. Secretary of the largest organization of Austrian political refugees in Paris, he tells us he has been confined with 16,000 anti-Nazis, including 12,000 Jews, for "two weeks in an open-air football stadium, sleeping on stone seats and narrow wooden benches ... no warm food .. twenty-eight lunches and suppers . . of bread and liverpaste, nothing more",—then "removed to an open field" where "flimsy tents" allowed "sleeping and living space six feet long and fourteen inches broad on the wooden floor, covered with a little straw. . . Each man . . had only one pint of water daily to drink and use for washing himself and his dishes." These men are writers, journalists, artists, including Konrad Heiden, "author of the best known Hitler biography". Richter is one of a few dozen to have been released All these prisoners are in charge of the Minister of Justice, Bonnet, the same who went to Munich and who represents a European cartel of munitioneers with German connections

Spanish refugees in France, military and civilian, the *Survey Midmonthly*, October, reports, number 315,000, with another 10,000 in Algeria. 70,000 of them are children 167,932, are former Spanish Republican soldiers. The rest are women and older men. They are living in "frightful squalor" upon "meager subsistence" In Britain 6,000 alien suspects were locked up within twelve hours after the beginning of the war, the N. Y. *Times* reports Dec. 12 "Thousands of Germans have been interned in the British African territories", the *Chr Sci Monitor* notes Nov. 18.

Members of the French military and naval missions to London (AP, July 9, 1940) were "being 'held for repatriation' . . virtual internment", lest they communicate information about military and naval forces At the same time Brian Carroll, treasurer of the British Union of Fascists, and Admiral Sir Barry Domvile, age 62, former director of British Naval Intelligence, and Lady Domvile were taken to Holloway Prison

"The present Government of England is hard to distinguish from that of a

Nazi concentration camp, and when the time comes to make terms with Hitler it may go the rest of the way   No Englishman of any sense actually believes in democracy. If he gabbles about it, as all English politicians do, it is only as a means of hoodwinking the vulgar." (H. L. Mencken, Baltimore *Sun,* July 7.)

(8) "Apparently censorship, which was to have been discussed at the secret session, was shelved, for it was announced that this week the Chamber will openly debate the doings of France's Services de l'Information, de la Propagande et de la Censure .   .   Meanwhile last week French Military Courts prepared to try 44 Communist former Deputies on minor charges of 'illegal activities', punishable by not more than two years in jail and loss of civic rights   Incensed was Moscow when major charges of 'treasonable activities', punishable by death, were lodged against nine Communist former Deputies, including Maurice Thorez, the French Earl Browder." (*Time,* Feb. 19, 1940)

(10) "Foreign observers in France today frequently remark that Hitler, if he is wise, will refrain from launching an offensive and wait for discontent to rise to formidable proportions within France. . . The war simply can't be popular with a shopkeeping nation like the French. . . . The government undoubtedly realizes that accumulation of these discontents over a quiet winter would aid Hitler's strategy.   . The Communist Party . has been working in secrecy— circulating an illegal edition of Humanite, distributing anti-war leaflets and carrying on a defeatist campaign by word of mouth." (F. C. Hanighen, *New Republic,* Dec. 20). Elliott Paul, author of "Life and Death of a Spanish Town", just back from Paris, reports that "Daladier knows his government would collapse in a month if he really started to fight" (*Unity,* Nov 20).

(11) "Obscured . . by . moral indignation . . . is one plain strategic fact The Baltic States, including Finland, are primarily buffers between the two big Baltic powers Germany and Russia   Buffers can also be jump-off points for invasion, and in invading Finland, Joseph Stalin was clearly protecting himself." (*Time,* Dec. 18)

(12) "A Bessarabian peasant's income averages $2 or $3 a month. Illiteracy runs about 40 per cent " (*Newsweek,* Dec 18, 1939)

(13) "The stories about talks among the French government, Otto Hapsburg and Starhemberg for the installation of a new Central European Federation under Hapsburg control have considerable foundation" (F. C. Hanighen, *New Republic,* Dec. 20, 1939). This idea for a restoration of the Hohenzollern and Hapsburg dynasties was a pet since 1927 of the late Lord Rothermere's, British press tycoon who controlled the London *Daily Mail, Evening News* and *Sunday Dispatch* (*Time,* Nov. 20, 1939).

(14) According to the Christian Science *Monitor* (March 24, 1939) the treaty signed by Rumania with Germany March 23, "gives Germany the right to develop Rumania's entire economic structure—agricultural and industrial—according to the needs of both countries, and to develop the transport systems on land and water".

"Britain" the Boston *Herald* commented, has not "been in any position to offer

Rumania markets to compensate for the greatly increased markets in Germany, acquired under the present agreement   The British are understood to have indicated this as late as last weekend, when Rumania asked if they could recompense her if she refused to sign the present agreement.   Also, Britain's present leaders have generally recognized the Reich's 'natural interests' in eastern Europe "

"If it were not for the fact that present Germany is an openly aggressive Power", the *Herald* comments, "there could be no legitimate objection to the present agreement.   In 1937, Germany furnished 30 per cent of Rumania's imports and bought 20 per cent of Rumania's exports   The same year Britain furnished only 10 per cent of Rumania's imports, and bought only 9 per cent of her exports. . . .   Britain and France together were not as important to Rumanian trade as the Reich."

[15] Roudybush in his "Washington Diplomatic Letter", Dec. 16 and 24, 1940 told us that Goering, with his brother, owns important munition plants in Italy, and exports Skoda products stamped "Made in Italy" to the Balkans and South America.   He is interested with Flandin in aviation.

[16] It is well for an American to read the British *Round Table* if he wants to find out in advance what is going to happen in America.   "Future American policy depends in its articulation upon the next occupant of the White House, and hence the third term issue is of immediate importance   President Roosevelt is today following the policy of the Great Neutral who leans weightily toward the forces of order in the world, and seeks to create his role in history in the peacemaking.   But if the war continues for another year, Mr. Roosevelt will have to obtain a third term in order to secure any such role.   Continuation of crisis conditions would of course assist the President greatly, particularly if in the intervening months he had administered a popular and cautious course of neutrality.   American opinion is profoundly distrustful of continued personal power in the hands of one man   Yet the needs of the crisis may overrule such emotions.   If they do, continuity of foreign policy may be assured." (*Round Table,* Dec. 1939)

[17] The London *Spectator*, Dec. 15, (UP), says the English press received with something of a shock Ambassador Kennedy's advice to his country to stay out of the war "at any cost".   "Not, of course, that we ever expected America to come in, unless the situation changes catastrophically.   But it would seem there are plenty of eminent persons in the United States to give isolationist advice without the Ambassador to the Court of St James's, knowing all our anxieties, all our ordeals, finding it necessary to join himself in that number."

[18] Pearson and Allen, Dec. 14, say "the confidential report . . . Kennedy brought to Roosevelt was anything but optimistic . . business was going to pot in Europe and . . . the present capitalist system was in grave danger   He did not deny the possibility of revolution behind the lines if the war drags on."

[19] Secretary Wallace was rebuked when he sounded off for a third term. But no rebuke was forthcoming to Ambassador Davies when, returning, he joined with Kennedy in saying that only Mr. Roosevelt was "blessed with the necessary experience", he was the best fireman to save the world from the flames.

(20) The President's naval enthusiasm and "Neutral Belt" was recently celebrated at a great dinner in Washington. The menu was headed: "National Press Club Navel Expansion Program". "The menu cards expounded a 'National Press Club navel expansion program', including 'neutrality eggs in sixteen-inch shells, hors (du combat) a la dictator, kedgeree of destroyers in drydock with high gravity and cracked sternposts, and hemisphere on ice with raspberry sauce an essence of good neighbor' " (AP, Dec. 7, 1939). Aldous Huxley on arriving in Los Angeles last February was surprised to hear men say that the transients had "come to pick our navels" (*Harper's*, Nov. 1939)

(21) To dampen enthusiasm for this War for 'Religion and Morality' read: "What Will Happen and What To Do When War Comes", edited by Larry A. Nixon (Greystone Press, New York, 1939)—it'll make you shudder; "Keep America Out of War", by Norman Thomas and Bertram D. Wolfe (Frederick A. Stokes, 1939)—it tells you how.

(22) Bulletin #23 was made up of items of correction and addenda which have been incorporated in preceding notes. It explained how the propagandists, to stimulate emotions, rely on crooked thinking They conceal failures on their side and enlarge on the dire straits of opponents It is the function of these Bulletins to bring out what has been hidden so as to enable the reader to straighten out what has been distorted. A financial writer in the Boston *Transcript* remarks, "You never know what's going on behind the news".

No statement put forth as ours in these Bulletins has been denied A few have written that our facts were wrong, without specifying which. Unfamiliar or previously unrecognized facts are usually regarded as wrong. Specific criticism is invited, lest we become careless, as recent errors due to haste give evidence.

BLOOD, OIL, AND DOLLARS

"We will fight to the last drop of blood",—and to the last dollar. Whose blood? Whose dollar? French? American? But some blood must be bought. And that takes dollars. Lloyd has been buying Rumania. Francois-Poncet has been dickering with Italy, the cash consideration not revealed. (*Time*, Jan. 1).

Three-quarters of a million was the price to the Turks, as it was originally reported. From Moscow, whence always first comes such news, we learn by radio, Dec. 14 (UP), of a secret clause in the Turkish treaty which provides for an army of 500,000 Turks, 400,000 French, 80,000 British, to invade Russia.

An Allied Expeditionary Force of over 200,000 has been quietly assembled in the Near East basing on Syria under General Weygand These are hardened colonial units drawn from French and English garrisons of Northern Africa and India (without consent).(1) It will operate with the Turkish army of 160,000, which can be increased to 700,000   Russia has been massing troops in the Caucasus and on the northern frontier of Iran. (Saville Davis, *Chr Sci Monitor,* Dec. 28).

The oil of Mosul must be defended, and the oil of Baku is what attracts this swarm. Look to the oil magnates as in the last war for the driving, directing force. Then they centered about the Dutchman Deterding in London and his henchmen and successors, the Armenians Hacobian and Gulbenkian. (Roberts, "The Most Powerful Man In The World", Covici-Friede, 1938).

Propagandists belittle the strength of the enemy by showing him short of essential supplies,—consequently the conflicting reports of Germany's oil   "With all the reports in the newspapers about the dire need of the Reich for oil, it would almost shock the credibility of an American to learn that Germany is actually exporting oil to Bulgaria . . reported in the last issue of *"Business Week"* (*Week by Week,* Dec. 2). Mihail Pizanty, member of the Rumanian Petroleum Institute, quoted in the *Chr Sci Monitor,* Dec 26, reports, "First six months of 1939, Germany took   . 30.5 per cent of our exports or a total of 2,231,091 tons". Latest Rumanian-German agreement reported calls for 190,000 tons a month at a 20% discount and a 6 cent rise in value of the mark.

The Polish gold reserve of 80 millions, with its custodians, by devious routes finally reached Paris   The new Polish government has been set up at Angers. A Czechoslovakian government (National Committee) has been set up by Benes at Paris and recognized by Halifax, Dec. 21 (UP). The treaty signed by President Hacha in Berlin has been declared null and void. The 'build-up' for this, in long cables from Paris, Dec. 21 (UP), told of the terrible torture put upon Hacha in Berlin. The French "Yellow Book" builds up indignation.

This will yield more drops of blood   Now both Polish and Czechoslovakian governments may conscript their nationals in France, England and their dependencies. "It is hoped here that they will eventually be able to call up Czech and Slovak citizens in the United States", cables James B Reston, Dec. 20, from London to the N. Y. *Times.*

$50,000,000 more for Finland,—that's about what the 'build-up' justifies. This will make our permanent investment in Finland $77,376,-890 (cf Bul #22)   Congress will oppose the loan, Rep. Ham Fish threatens. But with extraordinary powers granted in more than a hundred Acts (*Uncensored*, Special Supplement, Dec. 23), as Atty. Gen. Murphy reported, our President may find a way of 'scraping the bottom' of other reservoirs than RFC and Export-Import

Representatives of the Finnish government which is now headed by a British-knighted banker as Prime Minister, unsuccessful in obtaining a loan in Wall Street, have been lobbying Congressmen (AP, Dec. 21).

A Finn military mission, headed by General Menonen, directed by Baron Mannerheim, accompanied by the leading Finnish steel manufacturer, has been contacting our War and Navy Department, securing prior rights on equipment (N. Y. *Herald Tribune,* Dec. 21).

Further 'build-up' on Baron Mannerheim, "the George Washington of Finland", tells he was a page boy at the Czar's wedding His three chief generals, Oesterman, Oesch, and Ohquist, German trained, fought in the German Imperial Army and against the General Mannerheim of the Czar's army. Other Finnish generals, Hanell and Ario, are French trained (Leland Stowe, Boston *Transcript,* Dec. 22). Perhaps it is the rather innocent looking Finnish peasant, President Kallio, who directs this hard-boiled, cosmopolitan crew. Perhaps it is London.

Plans have been in the making for this loan for months, to prepare for the 'jump-off' in the spring from the Mannerheim Line and through the Gulf of Finland to take the great industrial center of the Soviets. Meantime the Finnish campaign diverts Russian munitions and supplies that might have gone to Germany, amounting to a blockade of her Eastern front. In the air, German as well as Italian pilots battle the Russian airmen (Pearson and Allen, Dec. 28).

The resourceful fighting of the valiant Finns, aided by old Boreas, helps the propagandists to enlarge upon the victories which makes easier the money raising But when the brave Finnish soldiers have been slaughtered, watch who runs off with the money bags. Remember what happened in Poland

Lord Strabolgi told the Lords, Dec. 7, "There is talk in certain neutral capitals, and also in restricted circles in this country, that we should make an alliance with Germany quickly to attack Russia. That policy will not carry much weight with the mass of the British people, and it would split the country in two", Ralph W. Barnes cables the N Y. *Herald Tribune,* adding, "No one here is making a secret of the hope that the United States, which is not involved in the struggle with Germany, will give of her immense resources to assist the Finns."

"Now neutral nations can help Finland with arms or men without violating international law" (*Life*, Dec. 25). Instigated by the Red-baiting South American countries at the prompting of Great Britain, the vote of expulsion from the League was taken 'sitting' to make it easy for weak-kneed neighboring nations. *Life* intimates nausea. "Nobody had the stomach to stand up as Russia's champion in that tense room." No delegate rose to oppose.

The sacrifice of 1/10 the League's revenue, $500,000 annually contributed by the Soviets, made the more abundant American money easier. Result was the discharge of 220 employees. "Theirs not to reason why."

"The Rhine shall ours be ever",—how odd it will seem to hear it sung in French or Senegalese[2] by those who hold "Die Wacht Am Rhein". "When one is the master of the Rhine, one is the master of all Germany", Foch proclaimed. Stanley Baldwin and Franklin Roosevelt have echoed, "Our frontier is on the Rhine". The Allies announce this as an essential part of their peace plan (J. T. Whitaker, Boston *Transcript*, Dec. 23).

The French in the Ruhr gave the Germans their Horst Wessel hero and song, Black troops on the Rhine commandeered German women— and the iron was thrust deep into the German soul.

Our own doughboys in their "Wacht Am Rhein" fraternized with the Bosch and courted the German maidens. We lent Germany the money to pay our bill of expense, $225,000,000. Did we get paid? 'La Belle France' was right there, and needed it. Moreover, she had prior claims for billions, and for millions of cattle and tons of coal. So she still has our money.

German products necessarily go down the Rhine to the Dutch ports at the mouth   (Imagine the French still holding the mouths of our Mississippi,—the Mexicans blockading.) The English blockade destroys this transshipment business and livelihood of the people of her buffer state.

Kemp Tromp, arriving Dec. 20, told a New York reporter that while the Zaandam was held by the British at the Downs, he thought much of his ancestor Admiral von Tromp, who swept the English from the seas and with a broom at his masthead sailed up the Thames and fired on London.

"Hitherto British war policy had been based on the assumption that time and the blockade were on the side of the Allies and that under modern conditions only a defensive war could be waged successfully" (*Newsweek*, Dec. 25, 1939). But "Lord Strabolgi told the House of Lords that the Government departments had succeeded in blockading Britain more effectively than the Germans could possibly hope to do" (*Fortune*). "With the British trying to corner world markets to keep Germany from getting supplies, it is the United States that is actually more affected than the Reich" (*Week by Week*, Dec. 23). To bring Germany to her knees by starvation may prove hard on the other nations less prepared.

In the House of Lords, Dec. 13, the Earl of Darnley, Lord Arnold, and the Bishop of Chichester maintained "Britain should take up the offer of mediation made .. by King Leopold and Queen Wilhelmina". Darnley declared "he was 'opposed to the defeatism of those who thought there was no remedy except war' ". Arnold "voiced a fear that Communism would be the ultimate victor and 'we should have paid a terrible price in vain'. When Lord Halifax rose to reply, his long, ascetic face was grave: 'I think this has been an unfortunate debate. . . . I can imagine no more unfortunate impression being created than that it should go out that this country is not substantially united ' " (*Newsweek*, Dec 25).

At Parliament's first secret meeting of the present war, Dec 13, "criticism . . came from all sides" of "bungling the production of arms and munitions and with setting up 'controls' of raw materials which allowed bureaucrats to run the nation's life" (*Newsweek*, Dec. 25)

Lord Halifax has recently emphasized, the British must export to live. *Fortune*, Jan., 1940, tells how difficult it is to maintain British trade, which has declined enormously since 1914, and still more in the past two years Meanwhile, to the rationing of butter and bacon has been added, beginning Jan. 8, meat and sugar limited to 12 ounces a week per person. Business is dislocated, some stagnant, some booming with huge profits in steel helmets, blackout materials, small arms. The increase in profits amounts in some cases to 300%. And old ships bring fabulous prices (*Fortune*, Jan., 1940). . . .

Between the belligerents trade still goes on, direct or through neutral countries (cf Bul #22). The *Iron Age*, Dec. 21, tells of an arrangement for exchange of 4 million tons of "Belgian coal" for 6 million tons of "French iron ore" Belgium is here the intermediary between France and Germany Copenhagen correspondent who reports adds, "Other trade (machinery, tools, implements, etc.) via Belgium between France and Germany has recently been confirmed by Belgian sources".

"Before Americans embark on any fresh moral crusades for any European Powers, we would do well to ascertain just how moral are the crusades", writes "Uncle Dudley" in the Boston *Globe*. "Whoever wishes to pursue the study of these unedifying transactions, which seem to reduce valor to idiocy and human begins to the level of vermin" should read Bernhard Menne's "Blood and Steel" and *Fortune* for March, 1934.

To the imperialism of the Allies and the blessings of war, now add totalitarianism. London now directs French shipping, purchases, economics, and seeks to fasten her hold on the Balkans and the Near East. An Anglo-French-Yugoslav agreement proposes that Balkan exports of minerals be sent to Hungary to be returned as manufactured goods (N. Y. *Herald Tribune*, Dec. 13). London, too, also controls U S. shipping and confiscates our mail. Mr. Streit's followers advocate making the control more complete. "Federation" is the magic word.

But Britain needs American help, our money and resources, more than ever before. Last time they paid us with gold bonds. We marked them down. We reduced the interest. We still have the bonds, not one cent of principal paid. This time they are paying us with gold. We now have most of the world's gold, and it is piling in on us. We will soon have practically all. And we will keep it. Nobody will want it

The last war cost us more than it did France, more than it did England. Our total cost has been variously estimated by ex-President Coolidge, $100,000,000,000, to which the Monopoly Committee has added recently 2 or 3 hundred additional billions. At present we are paying taxes on $44,000,000,000 of that cost. The coming war, centering in Asia, will cost more. How much should we contribute? (cf Buls #49, 50, 53)

Read "The Golden Avalanche" just published by Princeton University Press by two Princeton professors of economics and banking.

How the U. S has in five years contributed ten billions to the rearmament of the European countries and how this coming year we will contribute not less than four billions is explained in a coming bulletin (cf Bul #39)

Our year end good will message was stopped by a feeling of suffocation as we read the supposedly Good Will messages put forth by platitudinous divines and guileful politicians which thinly covered underlying hates. The more candid, vicious animosity of frustrated statesmen seemed less painful. But we still believe there can be no hate where there is understanding, and no peace where there is hate. Our purpose is to bring light to the dark places. God's first commandment was

"Let there be light".

December 29, 1939

NOTES

(1) In January, 1941, it was reported that General Weygand who in June had flown from Syria to take command of the army in France and later been put in charge of the North African armies, had in addition again taken over command of the Syrian army

(2) The Senegambians, so effective in trench warfare with their knives, were as great a handicap under the Stukas and against the tanks as the fugitives.

OUR 'NEUTRAL' NAVAL EXPANSION BELT

The President's great enthusiasm for boats is proving contagious. Up pipes a Congressman suggesting 65,000-ton battleships. Another goes one better and calls for 80,000-tonners   Chairman Vinson of the Naval Affairs Committee calls it a "pipe dream" (N. Y. *Times,* Dec. 31). The largest battleship afloat is 35,000 tons. We heard Japan was building 45,000-tonners, so we are building two at a cost of $70,000,000 to $80,000,000 each   65,000-tonners would cost $130,000,000 each, 80,000-tonners close to $200,000,000 each. But we are all for defense.

We will soon have a two-ocean navy   But why only two? There are seven seas, are there not?   And our State Department head announces that it is our function to "maintain orderly processes everywhere".   .

Ninety-five additional warships and 3000 more navy planes are called for at an added cost of $1,300,000,000 in the bill introduced by Chairman Vinson on which hearings were begun Jan. 3 (AP, Jan. 4).   Ten battleships and scores of other vessels have already been authorized by

Congress, to be completed in five years. But Admiral Stark plans to hasten the pace of construction (AP, Jan. 2).[1]

Secretary of the Navy Edison, on being sworn in, Jan. 2 (AP), soberly announced that the Navy was actually preparing to submit information on battleships of 65,000 tons. He had previously championed the building of twenty-three fast motor torpedo boats of British design and an additional sum for naval research.[2]

Edison deserved promotion. Three weeks before he had written and transmitted a bill to Speaker Bankhead which, on the opening of Congress following his promotion, was presented to the Appropriation Committee for immediate action. This bill, "of less than a dozen printed lines", restores to the President the wartime emergency powers which expired March 1, 1918 (L. C. Speers, N Y. *Times,* Jan. 3). It gives "the President the power to commandeer factories, ships and materials, to cancel or modify the existing contracts or agreements, and to exercise other far-reaching powers in 'a national emergency'. Under existing law, the President is empowered to exercise such authority in time of war." This includes (*Chr Sci Monitor,* Jan. 4) the power to set aside labor contracts, fix reasonable prices. Now, though no reason is given, the President wants immediately the power denied to Wilson after March 1, 1918, during the war. This is in addition to the hundred or more special powers which Atty. Gen Murphy reported the President already held.[3] At the hearing urging the bill, Edison said "no implication should be drawn that we fear being drawn into war. But if in ten or twenty years we should happen to get into war . "

The British disapprove our building so big. The summed-up opinion of British naval experts (London, AP, Dec. 22) was "By all means build more battleships but smaller ones, not larger". They are much interested in how we spend our money. Washington "official champions" (AP, Dec 29) think this ridicule is due merely "to the annoyance of Great Britain" at the idea of our having a bigger navy than hers.

Meantime we are still reconditioning eighty long idle World War destroyers to reinforce the Atlantic squadron. The *Round Table,*— founded, till recently edited, and probably still controlled, by Lord Lothian,—jibes at our 'neutrality belt' and the President's antiquarian interest in old boats. An anonymous writer, presented as an American, in the December issue, superciliously anticipates this emergency meas-

ure of the President's, "He recommissioned scores of old naval destroyers and set them to work patrolling the coast-line and far out to sea".

A ship may be commissioned and not conditioned. In England the
jibe is the King asking for a diving bell for Christmas (in anticipation
of inspecting the sunken but still commissioned British ships). The
Germans recently announced that they had torpedoed the H.M.S Kes-
trel, still commissioned, though the name is now applied to a naval
training station.

The great advantage to Britain of America's accepting the burden
of defense of the Far East is recognized by the *Round Table* writer with
satisfaction that "an American aircraft carrier started for the first time
for the Philippines, to be followed shortly by several flights of heavy
bombers from Hawaii out along the stepping-stones to the Orient".

The President's naval expansion is to cost us a pretty penny. He has
only $275,000,000 for the 'emergency' (AP, Dec. 31). But popular
enthusiasm for policing the waters adjacent to our continents leads him
to look forward hopefully to Congressional appropriations. He hopes
Congress will tend strictly to business,—appropriations, and go home
promptly. The European war has greatly increased the President's
chances for a third term. Talk in Congress can't help. (*Fortune,* Jan)

We are to spend only $8,000,000,000 this coming year it is proposed,
$3,000,000,000 more than we can collect. This will be about one-eighth
of our national income. But France is spending three billions more
than her total national income. At the same rate we might multiply our
expenditure ten times Paul Mallon, Jan. 2, remarks sagely that France
and Britain have an economic stranglehold on Germany but that they
also have a financial stranglehold on themselves.

It was at Panama in the sweaty humid days of September that the
'astute', 'suave', immaculately white clad Sumner Wells first announced
his purpose to "put a girdle round about the Earth in forty minutes".
He won the consent of the assembled swarthy delegates, condescend-
ingly designated "good neighbors", to his modest plan of drawing a line
about the American continents three to five hundred miles off shore.

Within this girdle there was to be no rumble of war. Any warship
or submarine that crossed the thousand miles of ocean, once it nosed
against this 35,000-mile line was to turn back. If trouble occurred
within, it was up to us and our "good neighbors". No one with less

aplomb than our Anglicized Grotonian-Harvard Undersecretary could have put this over, even upon these easily obfuscated Latins.

The cooler tweedy British responded with tolerant contempt. "The neutrality patrol is a good illustration of the pragmatic paradox of American policy", remarks the December *Round Table,* reviewing the President's policy "to keep the war from coming to the Americas" as he had phrased it, and reciting with satisfaction that "while perhaps outraging the international law conventions" it would prove of great advantage to Britain   (cf Bul #22)

The dynamite, the Providence *Journal* says, lies in this 'neutrality' pact: "An attempt to prevent searches, seizures, commerce raiding and other belligerent activities in this zone would be made " Britain makes good use of our folly. Within this safety zone are British and French colonies and naval stations. Their warships may ply to and fro for new supplies of ammunition. Uncle Sam protects them, by barring German boats even if armed only with "boxing gloves".

So this 'neutrality belt' has made us a most unneutral nation. The British have not been able to establish a blockade belt in the North Sea to prevent the exit of battleships and submarines or the return of the great Transatlantic steamers like the Bremen. But we have made our neutrality zone fatal to German merchantmen and warships. Hitting below the 'neutrality belt' seems to be the 'neutral' thing to do.[4]

The wearing of the belt has offered problems of style and adjustment. It has been advertised as having virtues greater than those of the elastic and electric belts for obesity and lack of virility once advertised in the backs of magazines. It was just too much for the President of Panama. He finally died The news of his death reached the State Department at 3 A M The opposition party had vowed that Vice President Boyd, who was acting as ambassador in Washington, should never return to Panama. At 3 A M our State Department got him on the phone, provided a fleet of bombing planes to take him back, and the opposition was squelched Such is democracy in the United States and the "Republic" of Panama. So is the "philosophy of force" set aside in emergency under the presidency of its great opposer.

Mr Hull wears his 'neutrality belt' with an attitude of righteousness and dignity Mr. Welles' supercilious nonchalance permits him to get away in his own estimation even with this ill adjusted belt. The President makes good use of the belt to cover his "naval expansion".[5]

Our State Department has optimistically misrepresented to the American people the attitude of Argentina toward us and the hope of trade with us. Dependent on British trade and financing, she hung back at Panama. When German raiders in the neutral zone interfered with her beef and wheat ships, she seemed to think Uncle Sam should make good. Argentine newspapers are bitter against the U S. for its "selfish and one-sided" proposals " 'without even considering' Argentina's need". So there is little hope of improving our trade (N. Y. *Times,* Jan. 3). "The Argentine is so certain that negotiations are dead that . . . Torriani . . . who has been in charge of negotiations with the United States, is sailing for Japan . . . to negotiate a new trade treaty with the Japanese government." These backgrounds explain in part the prejudice and unneutral way that the incident of the Spee has been reported to us

A hundred days at sea, three months in tropical waters, the growth of barnacle and seaweed had slowed down the Spee. She was under orders to return to her base in January (J W White, N. Y *Times,* Dec. 26). Short on ammunition, "Early on the morning of Dec 13 . . . the Graf Spee sighted a fat little cottontail, the 9,975-ton French steamer Formose, tripping along with no escort in sight. . . Before the Graf Spee caught up, however, . three British cruisers were climbing up the horizon" (*Newsweek,* Dec 25). "The Formose may have been deliberately sent out by the British as a decoy" (Saville Davis, *Chr Sci Monitor,* Dec 15). The British ships, cleaned and refitted at nearby bases within the 'neutral zone', could run circles around the Spee.

In the final encounter in the dusk within the three mile zone, the Spee's fighting power was finally destroyed. "The ship showed the marks of seventeen hits. The fire-control tower was damaged, and both catapult planes destroyed. One gun turret was overturned." She retreated "slowly up the treacherous, silt-filled channel stern-first to keep the sea out of a gaping hole in her bow" (*Newsweek,* Dec. 25).

"The newspapers missed the importance of the fact that the fire-control tower of the Spee was put out of commission   The damage to her fire control tower, nerve center of her whole firing system, rendered her 11-inch guns useless. That was why she wanted to lay up in Montevideo for repairs. That was also why she was scuttled If she had ventured out to meet the British cruisers, she would have been lost. For her system of controlling her giant guns was gutted" (Pearson and Allen, Dec. 23).

Captain Langsdorff in his protest to Uruguay claimed, "To sally onto the high seas would mean . . . negligently endangering a crew composed of more than a thousand men . . . danger due not to any action of the enemy, but only exclusively to the general dangers of navigation" (AP, Dec. 18). "There is strong pressure on both Argentina and Uruguay to change their more or less impartial neutrality into the United States variety of pro-Ally neutrality" (Davis, Dec. 15, *Chr Sci Monitor*).

"Britain had a stranglehold and used it: the British Minister presented a note saying that unless the Graf Spee were forced to put to sea, Britain would stop buying Uruguayan meat and grain. . . . When it seemed likely that the German Government would ignore Uruguay's demand, representatives of eleven American republics—including the United States—met in Montevideo . . . and informed Berlin that their governments backed Uruguay's decision. . . . The combination of Pan-American neutrality sentiment and British economic threats persuaded Uruguay to set an important precedent in this war" (*Newsweek*, Dec. 25).

"Diplomatic sources of high authority disclosed today the United States, Argentina and Brazil had offered armed aid to Uruguay for ejection of the German pocket battleship . . . that in the last tense hours . . . the United States assumed a leading role in the firm stand taken by representatives of the Washington, Buenos Aires and Rio de Janeiro Governments in a meeting here" (AP, Dec. 20, from Montevideo). This the State Department denied (AP, Washington, same date).

It is natural and desirable that British propagandists should so shape such events as to reflect contumely upon their enemy the Germans In a totalitarian war for power, chivalry has no place. But American newspapers and periodicals have swallowed the bunk, and attempted to make a mystery of why the Spee was ordered sunk. Characteristically the *New Republic* in jejune treatment refers to the Spee's plea of unseaworthiness as "lame indeed" as she "had been seaworthy enough to race (sic) into the harbor".

Neither is there any mystery as to why its honorable captain killed himself The Japanese can understand it as a noble protest,—committing hara-kiri on the "good neighbor's" doorstep Once when we were a free and independent people, we could publicly recognize heroism and gallantry, but today we heap contumely. Major Eliot superciliously remarks, "In Germany, no doubt, the act of the captain of the Spee in destroying his ship will be portrayed as an heroic gesture in the finest tradition of the German navy." The captain had reason to believe that his crew, without a ship, would be treated according to precedent.

Germany protested to Argentina, "When in the world war the German submarine 9 sank the three British cruisers Aboukir, Hogue and Cressy in 1914, the Germans point out the crews were landed in Holland and immediately afterwards released by the Dutch government" (N. Y. *Times* wireless, Berlin, Dec. 21). "The Government at Buenos Aires said the points of law had been carefully examined beforehand" (Boston *Transcript*). Had they been British sailors, they would doubtless have been well treated.

The Columbus, returning from a West Indies cruise with American passengers from New York about September 1, on Chamberlain's declaration that a state of war existed, and short of oil, discharged her passengers at Havana, whence they were transported at steamship line's expense to New York. Too large to enter the harbor of Vera Cruz, the Columbus lay outside in the roadstead for more than three months, subject to hard weather. On hearing by radio that British warships were headed south for the Spee and that the Bremen and New York had successfully made their way through the British blockade to their home ports, provisioned and oiled for forty-five days, she headed for the Mid-Atlantic. Two American destroyers followed her, relieved from time to time and necessarily using their radio, so that British boats could listen in. The cruiser Tuscaloosa later was substituted, more suitable to take off the crew. Less than three hundred miles from Nantucket, a British destroyer heard the Tuscaloosa communicating with the Columbus and inquired, "What ship is that?" The reply was "Find out for yourself". They could ask no more.

When Mr. Roosevelt held the Bremen in New York for the British to 'come and get it', the vigilance and skill of the German captain frustrated this proffered gift. The Columbus, too, narrowly escaped the British. Its captain, within one minute of sighting the British destroyer so expeditiously started the sinking and abandonment of his boat as to prevent the British from boarding her.

Most astounding is the lack of animus and good nature of Captain Daehne of the Columbus in telling the story and acknowledging the good will farewells of the commanders of the destroyers who had been set to spy upon him (N. Y. *Times*, Dec. 21). The cost to the American taxpayer of this destroyer trailing and pointing comes out of the $275,-000,000 appropriated for maintaining our 'neutrality' in the 'neutral belt,' for Mr Roosevelt's 'limited emergency' measures. But the expense is not only in dollars. It's to our standards of what is 'fair'.

The unarmed German freighter Arauca left Vera Cruz just before the Columbus, and made the harbor of Fort Lauderdale, Florida, chased by the British H.M.S. Orion, which "dropped shells 2½ miles off our coast.... This caused quite a stir in the State Department when officials actually discussed the use of naval force" (*Week by Week*, Dec. 30).

The German freighter Dusseldorf, captured off the coast of Chile and manned by a British prize crew, holding the German crew prisoners, passed through the Panama Canal, Dec. 25. Though the agent of the line and the German consul protested "that the ship was in neutral waters and relied upon the international ruling which forbids conveying a prize of war through such waters" (AP, Dec. 26), the protest was not "entertained" by the U. S. army commander of the Canal Zone, making this a well-timed Christmas present to the British Empire. The City of Flint, in charge of a prize crew, entering a Norway port on plea of necessity to land a sick American seaman, was freed and the German prize crew interned (AP, Dec. 25).

The quality of our neutrality and mercy could hardly be more strained than in permitting these German seamen thus to be taken prisoners to Jamaica. No note of indignation appeared in any American publication. Kipling had taught us that in Britain's imperial affairs in bringing about "the Utterly Absurd", "the Patently Impossible and Vain", "ten to one was always fair".

Following all these violations of our 'neutral zone', Secretary Hull "indicated at his press conference today that the American republics might consult" (Dec. 14, N. Y. *Times*). Dec. 17, (AP, Montevideo) Uruguay suggested that "the Pan-American Conference make representations to Great Britain and Germany". Dec. 20 (UP London), the British press took the position that the safety zone could not be maintained. The London *Evening News* described it as "a flop".

Meantime the U. S. protests of Dec 8 against the seizure of German exports to neutrals, and of Jan. 2 against seizures of 1700 sacks of U. S. mails to neutral countries, were "in due course pigeon-holed" (AP,

London, Jan. 2). These protests, represented for home consumption as "stiff", were gently phrased, and we swallowed the contempt and insult of the British graciously as we had been trained to do.

In the last war British propagandists included the first men of the realm, the best brains. Lord Grey had for his first victims our Ambassadors Page and House, who were so imbued with his sad, regretful attitude and devotion to morality and righteousness that they could not think of Great Britain as influenced by trade, profits, added territories, peoples to exploit. And so they proved traitors to their country and cost us millions through their deceit.

The more skilful propaganda of Sir Robert Vansittart today has worked insidiously upon the most important and influential. Mr. and Mrs. Roosevelt, well meaning, high minded, have been completely changed by propaganda since the President's "fool's gold" speech of 1936. They hold strongly to opinions of what is "right" and "wrong". But as H. G. Wells has said, "These two fine, active minds have . . . never enquired how it is that opinion is made".

"They are more pro-Ally than they have dared announce" (Paul Mallon, Dec. 1), more unneutral than they dare say. While they and their political family have put up a front of "neutrality", it is evident that what they consider 'wrong' has led them to be as unneutral as they thought the people would condone. Unappreciated at home, they have been obsequiously and flatteringly praised by British diplomats.

Of Roosevelt's recent message to Congress, David Lawrence dares to say it was "hardly neutral in spirit". It was "a tragic confession of failure" (T. Dewey), "a beautiful smoke screen that the Commander in Chief of the Navy threw about his battered political policies in the home line of battle" (N. Y. *Tribune*). To his English admirers, it was a success. The London *Daily Telegraph,* with the usual phrases about "human freedom and totalitarian despotism", hailed this "voice" from "the great neutral republic" as an "oracle". The London *Times* accepts this as the view of America recognizing "the rule of law and . . freedom of peoples and individuals" and invites us to be "an active participant".

"An intellectual insult", Rep. Tinkham calls it. "Straight down the road to war", remarks Sen. Lundeen. It is a tragic thing to see this man of high ideals and great enthusiasms cover up his domestic failures by preachments and scoldings to foreign peoples. To unite the Party he has split, he must rely on a fake 'Neutrality' Bill which caters to international munitioneers (Bul #18). Meantime we continue to gather the world's gold, in exchange for our labor and resources, a policy forced upon the Administration, which it is now afraid to reverse (cf "The Golden Avalanche", Princeton University Press). And this may prove the "fool's gold" of which he prophesied.

Just as the President proclaims 'neutrality' while unneutral, he denounces totalitarianism while putting across this fascistic Navy Bill. It was the wise-guy demagogic Huey Long who said,—'When fascism comes to America it will come in the guise of anti-fascism'. The Boston *Transcript* remarks editorially, Jan. 4, "The drastic Navy Department Bill just released shows what dangerous practices might flow from a certain kind of 'national unity'." It is this reiterated threat of the need of "national unity" that is most ominous,—not the conscription of men and money and industry, but the conscription of ideas, the threat to those who "muddy the stream of our national thinking". "We must combat them as we would the plague". Japan has been successful in suppressing "dangerous thought". Are we to go that way?

All this can be but to one end, to put "mother's sons" across the seas. There has been no pledge from the President for a year that this will not be. There have been expressions of "intent" and "expectation". He recognizes that the "overwhelming majority . . . do not abandon . . . hope" and he "can understand the feelings of those who warn the nation that they will never again consent". He adds insultingly, "But, as I remember, nobody has asked them to consent". And this is democracy?

"Now, if ever, America requires an outspoken, responsible but not obstructionist opposition", editorializes the Boston *Transcript*, Jan. 5. "Let us talk our heads off, let us crab every act we do not approve. There is yet time for this display of democracy." But where will this be displayed? In our universities? Our newspapers? Our periodicals? *January 5, 1940*

NOTES

(1) The law has until recently required that at least half of our fighting ships be built in the eight existing government yards. But when contract awards of nearly four billions for two hundred warships were announced September 9, "it was discovered that about three-fourths of the shipbuilding business was to go to private companies", thus fattening "the private shipbuilders whose excess World

War profits the government is still trying to recover".

This "was all the more surprising because their yards were already surfeited with orders ... Just prior to the awards, the New York Shipbuilding Company reported unfilled orders sufficient to keep it operating at capacity for eleven years. Yet, instead of expanding the government-owned yards," the Navy Department, Oct 9, announced that 76 more millions had been granted as special subsidies to the private firms "to increase their output with government-owned facilities". All this is told in "The High Cost of Ships" in the *New Republic,* January 6, 1941, by Melvin M Fagen, political scientist, and Benjamin Post, economist, both engaged in studies of phases of national defense.

In 1933, "at prices that then seemed to the Nye Committee to carry an exorbitant profit, aircraft carriers could be bought for $19,000,000, cruisers for $12,000,000 and destroyers and submarines for $3,000,000". Battleships 20 years ago were $403 per ton, today, $2,543   "In 1919, the 33,400-ton battleship Idaho was completed by the New York Shipbuilding Company at a total cost of $13,470,000. Now that same company is building a 35,000-ton battleship at a total cost of $88,997,000. The three battleships now being built in private shipyards ... will cost more than did all the fifteen battleships ... now in our fleet", though the three weigh only about one-fourth as much as the fifteen

"Asked last January why destroyers cost four times as much now as during the World War, when steel prices were about twice as high and labor costs greater, Admiral Robinson said: 'Well, everything in the whole United States seems to be increasing in cost... I cannot account for it.... I suppose it is largely due to the increase in labor costs basically' " But the authors, Fagen and Post, point out that while labor-materials costs have increased only 34% since 1933, costs per ton of aircraft carriers, destroyers, cruisers, have increased 90% and 83%.

"Greater speed, striking power and defensive strength" might justify these excessed costs. But "since the navy has announced that it is expediting shipbuilding by eliminating innovations, the carriers ordered in September ... will simply be larger and later editions of the older vessels with no radical changes in design."

The ratio between Navy calculations of excess expenditure and the private companies' share of the naval-expansion appropriation gives some indication of "the magnitude of what one shipbuilder neatly characterized as 'plunder' ... If we assume that in the base year 1933 the shipbuilders were at the very least making the 12 percent return then permitted by law, their total profit on the recent two-ocean-navy awards should approximate one billion dollars   Easy money, when you consider that in effect all risks of loss are borne by the government and that the extra equipment needed is on the house."

The Nye Committee found in 1936 that "the navy has never examined the underlying costs or profits of the private builders... It makes no pretense of doing this .. has no staff for it." Of course, the authors point out, "by using the existing navy yards as a yardstick, the government could know when and for how much it was being held up. But the Navy Department does not seem to want to know, though it has plenty of evidence in its files." Questioned by a

House sub-committee, Admiral Land "replied with poetic imagination: '. . . the fluctuations of the curves of comparison are like the waves of the sea. In many cases they reveal higher costs in navy yards, and in a few cases they reveal lower costs in navy yards. . . . The balance is, so far as cost is concerned, in favor of the private yards ' Six virtually identical 35,000-ton battleships are now under construction, three at government-operated and three at private yards The average cost of hull and machinery for each government-built ship is $41,237,000; for each privately constructed ship, $61,391,000 . .

"It is probably most unreasonable to ask why since 1933 the cost of destroyers built by private enterprise has been allowed consistently to average almost 20 percent higher than exactly the same types of ships produced in government yards." What prevents any "reforms, as Senator Bone reminded the Senate Naval Affairs Committee last May, is not so much the influence of the private shipbuilders as of their partisans and protectors in the Navy Department itself. In 1937, when Bone introduced a bill for the expenditure of only $27,000,000 to expand the navy yards, he was told by the admirals that it was 'contrary to our policy of national defense' to take such a step. It would be unfair to assume, however, that the navy has not struggled to expedite ship building. Last May it sponsored a measure to relax the profit limitations on naval contractors." But about the same time Captain Fisher "zealously advocated the 'temporary sacrifice' for the 'duration of the crisis' of all efforts to 'prevent undue profits, to prevent exploitation of labor, to destroy monopolies and to better sociological and economic conditions in the country. . . .' " So when the time comes when we may have to consider "any insufficiency of our navy", we can console ourselves with the thought that "in spite of hell and high water, 'we have, Mr. Chairman, made government business most attractive ' "

(2) Admiral Stark, chief of naval operations, testified before the House naval committee Jan 9 that the Navy might favor battleships of 50,000 to 52,000 tons, but they regarded the proposed 62,000-tonners as "either too big or not big enough" (Boston *Herald,* Jan. 10, 1940). Even for the 50,000-tonners we would need a new Panama Canal, new harbors, new docks The severest strain on the nation would perhaps not be the President's naval but his cranial expansion.

(3) "Perfectly startling", Borah said of the proposal. "There was plenty of opposition in evidence to Secretary Edison's suggestion" Boston *Transcript* reported. This naval expansion bill was a trial balloon for the lend-lease bill introduced in Jan. 1941, which grants the President opposition claims, dictatorial powers For further discussion of the President's power, cf Bulls #38, #92.

(4) Within the neutrality belt the British have long continued to blockade Martinique, with American destroyers on watch assisting. For a time before election all news was suppressed Eventually we were permitted to know more about how we were serving the British November 14, AP dispatch from San Juan, Porto Rico, reported that "war ships of the U. S. Neutrality patrol have taken over from the British West Indies squadron their mission of patrolling French possessions in the Caribbean. . . ."

It has been suggested that we relieve England of the necessity of taking over the west coast ports of Eire by extending our neutrality belt.

Helen Kirkpatrick of the Chicago *Daily News* cables from Belfast, Jan 28, 1941, that Ulster has a "fifth column of 500,000", the Catholic two-fifths of the population, who will rise up and welcome Hitler.

"The Irish are annoyed at the London newspapers for urging the government to go over and take the ports they need in Eire. This kind of thing, the Irish say, will give the Germans the same kind of excuse they used for invading other countries—the excuse that the British were going to do it anyway. But about 99 per cent of the Irish people want neutrality and they laugh at a threat of German invasion The Germans, they say, never could get an army into Ireland past the British fleet, and if they did the fleet would cut off the army's supplies. Besides, there is a British army of about 250,000 in Northern Ireland ready for action if the enemy should overrun Eire." (Pearson and Allen, Jan 14, 1941)

"Liam O'Flaherty, Irish author and patriot, charged yesterday that England's proposal to take over Irish seaports was an attempt to involve Ireland in the war on her side, and thus influence the 30,000,000 people of Irish blood in America to demand that the United States enter the conflict. During a visit here, O'Flaherty also attacked 'propagandists in America, who are urging the United States government to bring pressure on Ireland, even to help England to invade us, to surrender those ports . . . We know our neighbor very well after 700 years of forced association with her, and we want to tell the American people that this campaign carried on by our neighbor to force us to surrender those ports is an attempt to involve us once more on her side in this war as a belligerent in order that she could use us in the United States, where there are 30,000,000 people of our blood, to bring America into the war and save her tottering empire from destruction ' " (Boston *Herald*, Dec. 29, 1940)

(5) "Wits referred to the zone as a 'chastity belt' or a 'prophyl-Axis' and predicted that it would fail of its purpose. . . . By October 4 Secretary Hull was explaining that the 'patrol service', in which United States war vessels were already engaged, was for 'information' only and that no effort would be made to compel belligerents to respect the zone. . . . The liner Columbus, fleeing from Vera Cruz, encountered a British destroyer 400 miles off the New Jersey coast and was scuttled by her commander. In no instance did any of the belligerents pay the slightest attention to the Declaration of Panama." (F. L Schuman, "Night Over Europe", 1941)

COMING EVENTS CAST THEIR SHADOW

American sympathy for the Finnish people is genuine. The honesty of the popularly elected but unimportant President Kallio is undoubted. He reports that 234 civilians have been killed in one month (AP). Mannerheim had a higher record, he killed 15,000 (cf Bul #21).

"Finns Erase New Division",—reports of Red armies defeated, tabu-

lated by date and place and added, would result in astounding figures.[1]
Paul Mallon is the only one who seems to have cast doubt upon these
figures in the public print   He modestly estimates the exaggeration at
about 300%. When 25 Reds are captured, 75 more are annihilated in
the propaganda news. To make this skepticism more palatable, he re-
peats the myth that Finland "pays its debts".

The recently appointed Premier Risto Ryti, British knighted head of
the British-Finn bank, reporting Finnish funds "sinking rapidly", asks
for new "foreign credit", promising to meet obligations "as faithfully
as we have done up to now" (AP, Helsinki, Jan. 9).

Finland "pays its debts", constantly repeated, has been effective.
Finland now owes us $27,376,890. The total credits in twenty years
amount to $623,110 (cf Bul #22). Recently the Red Cross has given
$250,000, and Hoover has raised as a gift $500,000.

" 'Finland Will Pay', last week the wily Finns" announced in "scattered leaflets offering deserting Russian soldiers . . . 150 rubles for a
rifle . . . 10,000 for a tank . . . 1,000 American dollars for each airplane
received undamaged" (*Time*, Jan. 15).

The 'build-up' on Finland is proving successful. The manufactured
"news" served up in our papers has served its purpose. The purpose is
becoming more obvious to the American people. In November the hope
was for a modest loan of $25,000,000 for armament and strategic rail-
ways (cf Bul #21). By late December demand for $50,000,000 seemed
to be justified. Sen. Brown of Michigan proposes a $60,000,000 RFC
loan. Sen. Pittman, who has managed successfully the subsidy to the
silver mining interests and who floor-managed the fake 'Neutrality' Bill
(cf Bul #18) predicts immediate loan of from $50,000,000 to
$100,000,000. Sen. Carter Glass suggests "government borrowing for
the purpose". And Rep. Dingell has introduced a bill authorizing the
sale to Finland at $1 each of 10,000 of our new Garand semi-automatic
rifles. We have only 55,000, manufactured at a cost of about $100 each.

The President at his Jan. 9 press conference evaded committing himself until "next week". For Finland he had 'scraped the bottom' of the
Export Bank, which now asks Congress for $100,000,000 more (AP,
Jan. 3). A loan to Finland is essentially a loan to the Allies, Washington
wiseacres know, and that is practically a gift. "Credits made available
to Finland can be of use to the Finns only if they are able to convert it

into arms" (W. H. Stoneman, cable from London, Jan. 5).

So it is suggested that as we are short on arms we sell Finland our surplus lumber, to be shipped to England and France, which need it. Then the money we loan Finland would be sent to England and France to pay for it, and they would take care of supplying Finland with armaments. England and France will get the money and the lumber they need, and it is hoped the Finns may get what they need. The sixty millions will come out of the American taxpayer, as usual. Those who bought up hurricane lumber and surplus Southern pine will favor this.

Chamberlain announces Britain intends "to afford the Finnish Government all the assistance she is in a position to give",—the same assistance she gave the Poles and Czechs, perhaps (*Time,* Jan. 15).

The Tories didn't want this war. It was forced upon them. Chamberlain was doing a good job in appeasing Hitler. The Tories know that Russia is England's great opponent, as always, and they are still hoping to use Germany against Russia

The shrewd profiteers and international munitioneers don't want war. Armament means profits. But war brings increased taxation. With continued war, capital levies are inevitable. Already totalitarianism is changing the economy of England and France, and of this country in advance of mobilization as rapidly as the President can achieve it.

Capital has everything to fear   Other powers will prey upon established privileges, upon trade and foreign markets. The 'dog eat dog' policy will prevail. Britain is planning not merely to starve Germany but to cut in on American trade. No trade secrets are safe She searches our ships, our mails, seizes our remittances and our exports. The last war showed she knew how to use what she thus gained.

As England becomes more totalitarian, British ship owners complain at "the straitjacket of Government control" in taking over all of British shipping, which will "cause enormous dissatisfaction . . . more red tape . . . scandal" (AP, Jan. 5). The censor stifles any complaints from French ship owners, who have pooled their shipping with the British.

The outburst over the dismissal of the popular "friend of the Tommies", Hore-Belisha, gave some indication of the general dissatisfaction with the Government's management of the war. Hore-Belisha was all for building a Defense Ministry combining Army, Navy, and Air Force under one direction (*Time,* Jan. 15). But brasshats Ironside and Gort would lose prestige. And Hore-Belisha's bumptious superiority was insufferable to the stolid Tory aristocrats. Moreover, he was a follower of the strategy of Liddell Hart, best military mind in Great Britain, who does not advocate the use of British troops in France in "The Defence of Britain". Hore-Belisha is opposed to sending great masses of troops until trained. His propaganda pamphlets assure Englishmen that fighting on land is unnecessary, all they have to do is avoid defeat. ·

This cabinet shake-up, forecast in Bul #22 and apparently so mystifying to American newspaper writers, is not complete. Fierce antagonisms and conflicts go on not only among the actors on the stage but between the forces behind. With the people, it is a conflict of civil and military, the progressive and the old aristocratic control.

From propaganda control, Lord Macmillan, grumbling, was ejected, for Sir John Reith who, as in his former job as head of the BBC, refuses to see journalists (N. Y. *Times* cable, Jan. 8).

The 'victory diet" will "make a thinner and a fitter nation". The King and Queen, and U S. diplomats waiving their privileges, are issued ration coupon books (AP, Jan. 8),—weekly four ounces of bacon, of butter, and twelve of sugar.

The shift in the army control is ominous. The wise ones believe that neither the British nor the French army could stand the slaughter of attempting to break the Siegfried Line,—there would be mutiny. Eventually they hope by propagandizing to increase the morale (hate) of the army rank and file so they may go through.

The Tommies fought for the King in the last war. Since then they have seen politicians debase a king and make another, who advises them to "Take the hand of God". They know a little more, not much, of what Lloyd George had in mind when he said, "If the people knew how they were ruled, they would rise in rebellion".[2]

The jittery feeling of insecurity is well based. The German command of the air and "the waters under the earth" may prove more effective than the British surface blockade. Churchill and Chamberlain utter brave words, but their anger shows that they lack confidence.

Here's the reason for the drastic uniform clause in the decrees and laws of England, France, Canada, and the Smith Bill which passed the U. S. House last May, against "incitement to disaffection". The great fear of those who possess is loss, of those who control, Revolution. But in spite of all the Inquisition could do, as Galileo muttered coming from his torture, the Earth still revolves.

Insecurity in France, hysterical tyranny of dictatorial control, complaint of the people, grumbling of troops, have lead to sending home of hundreds of thousands (cf Bul #22). The French government demands more British troops. Less than 200,000 are spending the winter grousing on the Belgian frontier. The French asked for 200,000 of the English unemployed, which is greater than at the outbreak of the war, reported Nov. 13 as totaling 1,402,588 (London, AP, Jan. 8.) But British workers rebelled at French wages and hours The difference in pay and food of French and British air pilots has also made for conflict.

Broadcasting in French, Minister of Supply Burgin, Jan. 8, anticipating results from the change in army control, triumphantly declared the present B E.F. is only the "advance guard". "You will soon see column after column" (R. Daniell, N. Y. *Times* cable, London, Jan. 8). Winston Churchill was touring the French frontier. Gen. Gamelin was conferring new decorations on Gort and Ironside.

The British blockade of Germany seems to be futile. The French claim to have halted ten German merchant ships (AP, Paris, Jan. 4). And the two German pocket battleships unapprehended seem to have returned to their bases. The Germans have reconnoitering command of the seas about England. British capital ships, to avoid plane and submarine, are reported concentrating at Halifax, which is to be a contraband station to which American vessels may be taken for search.

"The forcible diversion of American vessels to those belligerent ports which they are by the laws of the United States prohibited from entering" led Hull to write a note to Lothian that Britain would be held responsible for damages Such claims for damages as we have made against Great Britain haven't troubled her since the days when our last great Adams was ambassador and collected the Alabama claims. Our protests are now made for home consumption. The note, written Dec 14 but not released until Jan. 5 after the British had defied it by seizing and taking into Kirkwood the American steamer Moormacsun led to popular protest (N. Y. *Times* dispatch) but none from Roosevelt who had declared this forbidden, even on receipt of the snippy insulting reply. Simultaneously the American liner "Manhattan" was held up at Gibraltar and mail seized, as is the mail from neutral Italian ships.

Following the gentle protest of our State Department at the seizure of all German exports to the U. S. (cf Bul #25), Cordell Hull submitted a questionnaire. A British reply Dec. 25 was "abrupt", brief. Only under "very exceptional circumstances" will Britain "allow shipments of German goods to the United States from German or neutral ports" (*Herald Tribune* Bureau, Wash., Jan. 4). As to how long would be the delay, Britain replied, "not necessary" to say how long it would take to make up its mind. The applicant would have to be content.

So subservient are our State Department officials to the British that such insults are not resented. The Boston *Herald*, recognizing that even the gentlest of protests is too much for them, says it "could not have been a pleasant note for Mr. Hull to write the British. . . . At this late date it is no secret where American and Mr. Hull's sympathies lie in the present conflict."

Number 2 British propagandist, hard working, tired voiced Lord Lothian, at Chicago, in January, speaking of this war, "explained the real prize is sea power, the issue 'freedom or tyranny' " (*Time*, Jan. 15). He admitted the Allies had done badly with their last victory which we had fought to bring them, but promised they would be good next time, and assured his audience he was not "trying to drag you into this war"

"His speech was one of the most effective, skilful briefs yet delivered for the Allied cause. It was the sort of talk which earns Britain a reputation for fair dealing and open-minded thinking. To keep its sprawling Empire together Britain needs that reputation as much as she needs her powerful Navy. . . . The 'weakness' of Britain is that she can no longer survive without the moral approbation of the world. Today, in . . . widely separated capitals . . . other British envoys . . . are working just as hard to convince other nations that Britain's cause is their cause, that Britain's defeat would be their tragedy" (*Time*, Jan. 15).

"Lord Lothian's Chicago speech, whether deliberate propaganda for the British cause or not, was propaganda none the less. There are two sentiments that invariably incline the American people . . . to think . . . perhaps America should intervene . . . a constructive peace . . . and . . . Fear of . . . America's position . . . if . . . the British navy be swept from the seas. . . . The British ambassador's speech may have been as innocent of any intent to sway or arouse the American people as he said it was. But . . . if Lord Lothian ever does want to indulge in deliberate propaganda, he has hit upon the two cardinal points that would be of greatest use to him." (Editorial, Boston *Herald,* Jan. 8)

Fear, Lothian hopes, may bring America and Britain together, to pool their resources, or at least to tap ours. Fear, Mr. Roosevelt continually stimulates. The submarines he used to see on all our coasts brought many a laugh, but put across the fake 'Neutrality' Bill. He still wants others to fear the possibilities of attack upon us.

A year ago, preparing for the great armament appropriations, the President told Congress on its January assembly, "It has become necessary for every American to restudy present defense against the possibilities of present offense against us".

The hysterical situation that has been worked up plays right into the hands of the military and naval men. "It's a great day" for them. But there are honest men among them who regard this defense program as an impossible joke. As far as they can and still be listened to, men like Major Eliot and others try to make us see this. And as F V. Drake in the *Atlantic,* Jan. 1940, makes clear, the air force we are building is not adapted to our defense and will be obsolete before it can be used unless we send it over seas. [8]

There is nothing to defend against. Before any European offensive force can cross the ocean, other than the British fleet, they will be exhausted strangling each other. But the game is to organize a force that can be thrown in on the British side, if need be. That's what Lothian and Roosevelt want and what Americans are being prepared for

"The European war has so drenched Washington in uncertainty that immediate political problems seem to carry extraordinarily little weight," writes Henry Ehrlich, Boston *Herald,* Jan. 12, from Washington. The President has used it to thrust into the background Farley and McNutt He is using it to set up Hull, who will eventually be bowled over He uses his ambassadors as promotion men for his own game. He uses it as an excuse for covering up his domestic failures. Ehrlich says the Republicans don't know whether his latest move "was a sly effort to pull their legs, or a serious endeavor to place political unity above partisanship".

Elated at flattery from the Anglophiles (perhaps you remember that old fashioned American dislike Josh Billings had for Englishmen who hadn't lived in England), the President pulled a fast one in putting

over his budget.   By cutting down flood control and relief, with the
'sleightest of hand' he made a pass at economy, though we will probably spend more this year than ever before.   There are all kinds of tricks
that can be done with figures, and though his apple farmer neighbor
who has to stand for them sometimes makes a wry face, the President
smilingly puts it over.

What fun is made of "propaganda hunters".   Old fashioned Yankees
used to be shrewdly curious and sometimes suspicious of these shell-
game men   Some who remember how we have been burned in the past
believe we should not invest much more money in British imperial projects or Allied ventures.   These are dubbed "isolationists" to make them
feel insignificant, solitary, and alone.

Snubbery and snobbery, sometimes interpreted as prestige, are the
most effective ways of controlling little men, for whom vigilance alone
can not maintain liberty.   It is only for those who dare to speak up
And soon, as in France, they will all be in prison.

The President and his political family are convinced that they are
crusaders for "right", that Hitler and Mussolini are incarnations of
"evil" who must be annihilated by any means (cf Bul #20).   Hull, who
would probably stop short of the President's extremes, feels strongly.
"Neutrality" can hardly be expected from those who are enlisted against
"evil" and to bring about "orderly processes everywhere".   The Administration desires to do everything possible to assist the Allies, and that
means bring evil and detriment to their opponents.

So we are financing European armament and war.   In addition to the
drainage through gold purchases (read Graham and Whittlesey, "The
Golden Avalanche", Princeton University Press), there are other pipelines that act as a constant drain upon our financial resources.   One,
very effective in the last war, is the granting of special privileges, remission of taxes, and allowances for expansion of American plants necessary to meet foreign munition contracts   As twenty-two years ago, this
is being so arranged as to constitute subsidy from our taxpayers of hundreds of millions to England and France   There is plenty of detailed
evidence in the books as to just how this was accomplished.

Edison, political innocent, was wisely chosen to attempt to put across
the atrocious fascist Navy Bill, which Borah mildly said was "perfectly
startling".   It completes our totalitarian organization and makes Roose-

velt dictator whenever he should declare an emergency. Edison has so 'faithfully polished up the handle of the big front door that now he is the ruler' of Mr Roosevelt's big navy. However the President will continue to be his own Secretary. With sick men, incompetents, and dummies, he holds more portfolios in his cabinet than Mussolini ever did.

Maintaining our "neutrality" costs the taxpayer a good deal of money. The German tanker "Pauline Frederick", which had lain in Boston harbor for three months with a million dollar cargo of lubricating oil, was recently seized on a lien of $48 and an expensive guard put in control.

The shipwrecked sailors from the Columbus have been held at Ellis Island at government expense. The crews of the Queen Mary and Normandie have not been restrained. Now the Columbus sailors are to be shipped off to some remote place where they can be watched, and eventually they hope to cross the Pacific by Japanese steamer The British will be informed as to where they are. Just watch and see if they are not taken off by a British warship.[4] Remember how the Columbus was trailed and advertised? Remember the Bremen?

There are contact men who may now be met on the clippers and the planes to Canada, from whom you may confidentially gather that in March, the unified command anticipates and hopes that Hitler will bomb London and Paris and push his troops through Holland to obtain better airplane bases. All munitioneers selling to Holland insist on full payment before March.[5] They will tell that Russia is road building and fortifying the region about Odessa, which great Russian seaport is only a day's thrust from the border of Bessarabia, where Rumania is again massing troops previously withdrawn. In the mandate of Syria an army of a million is being assembled. On the border of Afghanistan the Soviets are reported to have massed 800,000.

The strongest statement our President has made has led us to believe that it is not his "intent" that "mother's sons" shall fight on "European soil". Does he know of the possibility of war in Asia?

January 12, 1940

NOTES

[1] "Surfeited with tales of military miracles, newspaper readers probably were not startled when the St. Louis *Globe-Democrat* reported on February 9, '250,000 Reds Routed by Thomas F. Hawkins, Associated Press Staff Writer'." Lavine and Wechsler, who discovered this choice headline ("War Propaganda and the United States"), go on to say, "Possibly the most sustained, dramatic, and ulti-

mately unconfirmed story of Finnish achievement—fostered by the Associated Press, the United Press, and individual correspondents—was the widely publicized, black-headlined report that the Finns had penetrated Russian soil and cut the Murmansk railway   After the story had appeared and reappeared for several weeks, George Seldes asserted that a prominent newspaper editor had probed the story and found it utterly lacking in confirmation "

(2) Lloyd George, who served Great Britain in the last war, is from time to time a source of terror to the conservatives   He comes too close to blurting out the truth.   May 9, 1940, he said, "We gave, not merely in the treaty itself but in a document signed by M. Clemenceau (then Premier of France), on our behalf a solemn promise that if Germany disarmed we would immediately follow her example   That was not carried out and there is no government more responsible for that than the present national government which came to power in 1931. . . There was a certificate of the Ambassadors to say disarmament was complete and we did not carry out our bargain.   The same thing applies to minorities.   I repeatedly called them to the attention of Benes (former President Eduard Benes of Czechoslovakia) in the conference at Paris.   He gave a direct pledge to the conference that if Sudeten Germany became a part of Czechoslovakia—and the same thing applied to Hungarian Slovaks—the same autonomy would be given to them as in the Swiss Federation   That was not carried out. . . .   The creation of this terrible power in Germany and the spirit behind it which make it so formidable is due to the fact that we did not carry out our promises."

(3) What the British think of the airplanes we have sent over is shown in excerpts from various issues of The *Aeroplane* quoted by Beatrice Abbott in The *Patriot*, December, 1940.   "The big Boeings, proudly known as the 'Flying Fortresses' by the American Press, are not new or formidable except that they can carry a heavy load of bombs for a moderate range or a moderate load of bombs for a long range. . . .   By British standards the B-17s are most poorly armed, and, because of their size, should make easy targets in the air or on the ground.   Their maximum speed of 268 m.p.h. is too slow to offset their poor defense and the Boeing B-299Y (the Company's designation of the machine) has been on the export list of the Aeronautical Chamber of Commerce of America for some time.   Thus, according to the complicated manner in which Americans officially excuse the selling of munitions to Great Britain while maintaining an Ambassador in Berlin, the big Boeings are 'technically obsolete in the U.S.A.'   As fighting machines they are in fact obsolete in any country in the World   Apparently the American organization, which is called 'the Committee to Defend America by Aiding the Allies', started the campaign to press 30 of the big Boeings on Great Britain" (September 27, 1940).   "Although armament of the fighters can be increased the improving of that of the bombers such as the much vaunted B-17 is not so easy. . . .   In the B-17, for instance, no tail turret is possible because of the single fin and rudder and because the center of gravity would be thrown out.   We are still unpersuaded on the merits of the Airacobra. . . .   The fact that we have a batch is explained by our decision to take the French 'left overs'. . .   The policy we want to prevent is that of buying inadequately armed

and inadequately equipped aeroplanes, or cramming fine young men into them and of the sending them over enemy lines in circumstances in which they would not stand a fair chance" (November 8, 1940).

(4) At last reports most of these seamen were still held prisoners by the U S government on Angel Island in San Francisco Bay, perhaps to protect them from seizure by the English as had happened to the few who sailed on a Japanese steamer. (cf Bul #25)

(5) This is evidence that those on the inside know pretty well what is going to happen, though the public are given through the information bureau what is supposed to be good for them. Sometimes the public learns too much and interferes with plans. Popular revolt stimulated the Congressional fight over the Neutrality Bill, which postponed our anticipated entrance into the war, and popular protest has repeatedly postponed that step.

100 BRITISH PROPAGANDISTS IN AMERICA

More than a hundred British lecturers, speakers, writers are now in this country acting as propagandists, working subtly to bring us into the war. This number is in addition to the exchange professors.(1)

We have collected material and data on these, the significant part of which would run to more than ten pages of this size. If there is sufficient demand and some contribution toward expense, we will put it in shape and have it duplicated. (cf Bul #7 and Notes)

Forty-two British propagandists and lecturers in the U. S, with personal particulars, were listed in a special supplement to *Uncensored*, October 28. A score are mentioned in *Propaganda Analysis*, Dec. 5.(2)

The British Ministry of Information emphasizes it has no "intention" of sending lecturers or propagandists to America. If that's so, they are "bungling their job of not carrying on propaganda in the U. S. and bungling it badly. Despite their no doubt fervent efforts, lecturers and tourists are coming here anyway" (*Propaganda Analysis*, Dec. 5).(3)

But they are not bungling hard enough to satisfy. *Punch*, which Oct. 4, with tears in its linotype declared in its "humble opinion . . this country has sadly neglected the vital problem of providing Americans with opportunities for hearing the British point of view put over with authority; and at whatever cost in money, first-class speakers whose reputations are above suspicion, should now be sent across the Atlantic."(4)

Congress approved, June 8, 1938, "an Act to require the registration" of those who "disseminate propaganda",—which would have barred the greater number of foreign propagandists who are now flooding the country, skilfully, subtly working to bring us into the war.[5]

Quietly, without publicity, this was mysteriously made useless and innocuous by an amendment "Public—No. 319—76th Congress, Chapter 521—1st Session, H. R. 5988", which has made it possible to flood the country with British propagandists though paid for their services.

The mimeographed list of 363 propagandists that are registered, issued by the State Department last October includes advertising men, steamship lines,—almost no real propagandists. But late in December, Bookniga, the Russian bookstore in New York through which Russian literature has been disseminated, was closed and the managers given the maximum fine of $2500 for violation of this registration act. So it will be still harder to learn about Russia. Let us promote ignorance.

A Congressional Resolution to investigate this British propaganda in the U. S. is in order. A number of the hundred or more U. S. Senators and Representatives approached on this have replied with interest.

Sen. Clark of Missouri, Sept. 28, 1939, introduced a Resolution calling for a committee of senators "to make a full and complete study and investigation of the activities of any person, firm, or corporation acting for or on behalf of any foreign nation, by way of propaganda or otherwise, having as their ultimate goal or tending to cause, directly or indirectly, a change in the neutral position of the United States in the conflicts now being waged abroad."[6] Rep. Tinkham of Massachusetts is interested and may introduce such a Resolution in the House.[7]

Write these Congressmen and your own Senators and Representatives now, if you believe this is a matter that should be investigated.

January 13, 1940

NOTES

[1] In December, 1939, a cursory study of the bulletins of the Institute of International Education endowed by the Carnegie Corporation revealed some scores of exchange professors, and at that time there were in this country 6000 foreign students, 1586 of whom were British subjects

[2] Scores of lecturers from England were available for engagements, whose dossiers could be consulted in many offices including the International Institute and the British Library of Information. The latter was cautious in answering inquiries, tactfully suggesting that so and so was in this country and might consent to speak.

Propaganda in a less obvious form is spread by musicians, artists, and actors Some of them returned to their native lands at the beginning of the war to enroll in the armed forces,—among them Laurence Olivier, Robert Montgomery, Charles Boyer, Herbert Marshall. They stayed only a few weeks, i.e. long enough to receive instructions. The lull before the fall of France gave them an excuse to return here. Strangely enough they are here yet.   ˉˉ‒ ‒ ‒ ‒ .

(3) Sir George Paish, famed London economist, a dear, naive old soul of 77, anxious to do his bit, and observing what was being done by younger colleagues, came here last summer for a lecture tour. Once here, he looked about and observing the closeness of the fight on the conscription bill, decided that "now was the time, etc" During a round of calls on various senators he indulged in a typically septuagenarian boast about his share in the last war—how he personally won the United States over to the Allied cause Lord Lothian of course, disowned him and advised him to run along home A member of the embassy staff, in a less tolerant mood said, "We wish someone would drop Sir George Paish over Germany as a pamphlet" (*Time*, Sept. 9, 1940).

(4) The later invasion was admirably planned. Julian Huxley and other scientists appeared at our scientific meetings. But labor leaders appealed to labor. Titled people of society appeared at our cocktail parties Albert Duff Cooper and Lord Marley made protracted speaking campaigns. Sir William Wiseman, head of the British Intelligence, in this country during the last war and now a partner in Kuhn, Loeb & Co., "explained smilingly that he was here on private business", as was Sir John Reith, former head of the British Broadcasting Company. Authors, humorists, economists, humanitarians,—there were few in England that could speak or inveigle that did not find their way to America made easy. As the swarm increased, editors attracted attention to their propaganda but no action was taken

(5) The law required foreign agents to register but the State Department and the F B I. made "no organized efforts to uncover foreign agents who have failed to register" (Boston *Transcript*, Oct. 27, 1939). I wrote,—"Dear Mr. Dies· I am tremendously interested to see an announcement that your committee is going to dig into British propaganda now going on in this country.

"Publicists, journalists, Senators and Congressmen all assume that the propaganda is going on all about us, but that it is so subtle, so difficult to detect that they can't identify it.

"Since the last war scientists, sociologists, psychologists, archivists, researchers have made enormous investigations of the propaganda which brought us into that war. Lasswell and Casey's 1935 bibliography lists 4500 titles, nearly all on international propaganda published after 1932. "Propaganda For War", by H. C. Peterson, University of Oklahoma Press, 1939, explains vividly the British technique of twenty-five years ago.

"Ten years or so from now the survivors of this war will gather courage, energy to make an investigation of the propaganda that brought us into it. With difficulty, from the traces that have been left in documents, from the memoirs and confessions of survivors, they will piece together How much simpler it would be to bring the actors today before a Congressional committee."

(6) Senator Bennett Champ Clark in a radio address of May 5, 1939, inserted in the *Congressional Record* of May 8, 1939, at the request of Sen. Nye, after charging that the President, under guise of measures "short of war", was leading us to active participation said, "More than a year ago (1938) I charged in the Senate . . . that the Nation was to be subjected to a deliberate, amply financed, ably led propaganda participated in by high officials of the Government including high-ranking officers of the Army and Navy designed to make this country war minded and to prepare public opinion in the country for another costly adventure abroad. That prediction has literally come to pass and we have had in the public press, over the radio, and in the utterances and writings of high public officials the efforts to lash our people into the pre-war frenzy that will ultimately lead to our being called upon to offer up hundreds of thousands of lives and billions of dollars of our national wealth in quarrels with which we have no direct concern.

"The United States can stay out of the next war if it wants to and if it understands what is necessary. . . . Such a policy means the sacrifice of the transitory profits which come from warmongering. . . It will be far, far cheaper for us in the long run in blood and treasure and in the perpetuation of our most sacred institutions. . . . It will save us from footing the bills for other nations whose aims are not our aims and whose democracy is not our democracy."

(7) As bitterness increased and the determination to destroy Germany mounted, men like Priestley and Wells who had opposed war and ridiculed propaganda were again enlisted. Mr Wells who played so active a part in propaganda of the last war invited "more or less officially, to do propaganda in Europe or America" wrote, "I will be damned if I lend myself to any propaganda". But he came and did it though not satisfactorily to the Colonel Blimps who denounced him in Parliament.

June 12, 1940 (Chicago *Tribune*), Sen. Wheeler asked Sen. Holt what had happened to the Clark Resolution to investigate British propaganda Sen Holt replied, "I do not think it has the approval of Lord Lothian, the British ambassador". Nor had it of the Administration. Investigation would have changed the course of recent history, and not in the way that Lothian and Roosevelt desired.

AN INTIMATE LETTER TO READERS

What you don't know won't hurt you perhaps. But there is no question that knowing things that are not true does a tremendous amount of harm. The purpose of these Bulletins is to controvert much that is generally accepted, to uncover sinister propaganda, to expose bunk. That is not fashionable at present.

Our universities and the financial centers on which they are so dependent deprecate the importance of propaganda, maintain that we are propaganda proof, and cast aspersions on the propaganda hunters.

At the propaganda conference at Harvard (cf Bul #16), the tendency was to ignore or deny British propaganda. It's as though nothing should be said that would be displeasing or not wholly agreeable to Thomas Lamont, President Roosevelt or Lord Lothian   Sidney Fay, Professor of History, who was once a courageous exposer of bunk and now plays extremely safe, according to the Boston *Herald,* Dec 16, "said" this country was suffering from 'an overdose of propaganda against propaganda' and warned against trying to ferret out propaganda".

Some like him write that I am "wrong-headed" because my attitude does not coincide with theirs. Some claim that I am wrong on my facts, by which they mean the facts presented are unfamiliar to them, and anything that is unfamiliar is wrong.

No periodical will print the material put forth in these Bulletins. Editors following financial and administrative leaders accept attitudes and beliefs without too close scrutiny as to who promotes them. There are two great centers in our western civilization for the propagation of ideas on national affairs. Propaganda originally applied to religion and the Vatican is still effective in propaganda. But the British Foreign Office, too, maintains a permanent organization, constantly improving its technique.

In the U. S. it is still possible to criticize our foreign policy. In Canada that time has passed. In England, a brave exhibitionist show of freedom is made on "complaint days" in Parliament and at Hyde Park Corner. In France, the places of "enforced residence" are more to be feared than those of Germany. For a vivid and horrible personal account, see *Direction,* Darien, Conn., Jan. 1940, pp 20-28.

When such disclosures or interpretations as I am putting forth become illegal, I shall scrupulously keep within the law. How long they can be continued depends upon the support received.

Both the British and our Administration through their chief spokesmen have admitted with bitter regret that the popular protest which stimulated and prolonged the debate in Congress last October on the embargo postponed America's direct participation in the war for many months. The Finnish situation has been used to the utmost to change that. But it can be postponed some more.

The making of these Bulletins has taken practically my whole time for months so that I have neglected my personal and business affairs though I still have to run a busy office to make my living. It requires the full time assistance of two secretaries and part time of five or six others. Personally I take, read, mark and clip with assistance more than a hundred periodicals,—see, read, annotate hundreds of the new books each year.

There is no secret stuff here. It is all to be found if you have the eye to see it, if you know where to look for it. Much of it is on the inside page of the N. Y. *Times* and *Tribune,* more comes from obscure periodicals and news letters.

News fragments must be fitted together to make a picture of any significance. Usually that is done for a purpose by someone who is paid to accomplish it, who can afford to pay for it.

The interpretations in these Bulletins are not paid for except by voluntary contributions. My interpretations of human behavior are influenced by my training as a biologist, and of international affairs by many years of traveling in Europe and five trips in as many years around the world. Sometimes a forecast is ventured when I believe I see clearly the forces acting behind and can make some estimate as to their relative strength. When you know who holds the power, what they are capable of doing, what they want, then you can come pretty close as to what they are going to do, and what is going to happen.

Most historians working from papers and documents which have been prepared in the past to deceive, as is present propaganda, sometimes forget that it is only men that act, individuals who create attitudes in groups, mobs, peoples, nations. It is important then to know the men behind the scenes, if possible. Few Americans as yet know that their opinions, views and present emotions are those that were planned for them by Sir Robert Vansittart.

The emergency is great, the time is short. Most who receive these Bulletins on request must necessarily lie low and play safe. Some are enthusiastically appreciative as is this wise, knowing and shrewd lawyer who writes me,— "As you suggest, the rank and file of the English are admirable human beings, the same is true of the French and the Germans. Furthermore I believe Chamberlain, Daladier, and Hitler are patriotic, unselfish leaders, but I further believe that back of Chamberlain and Daladier are a group of racial minority friends who would willingly see every Englishman and Frenchman killed, if only their lust for power and material things could be satisfied. The same goes for our own Administration.

"To me it is apparent that Chamberlain and Daladier were forced into it. Hitler responded because he knew that supremacy might as well be determined now as later. With an Administration clearly friendly to war, I do not see how the U.S.A. can avoid entry into the conflict. Thereupon the slaughter will be speeded up, a million good Englishmen will die, a multitude of French, and Americans.

"Isn't it a tragedy that the blinded American people must sit idly by, and be led into the awful carnage of war, solely because they cannot see that the very group which brought on the European conflict are also bringing us in. This summer I saw what Civil War had done to Spain.

"But, we are headed again for a World War. Our Administration at Washington insists upon such a course. You cannot stop it, but you are doing your bit towards delaying the holocaust, and I admire you for it. I do hope that you can keep up the good work."
January 15, 1940

NOTES

(1) Bulletin #29 accompanying this on the same date, stated these Bulletins "to keep us out of war" are published as emergency, time and energy permit. The editions have varied from 10,000 to 500 depending upon money and help available. Originally sent to friends and educators, they go now to those whom it has been suggested would welcome them and those who cooperate by writing or sending stamps or checks to aid in the expense of distribution.

The number distributed and the time this can be continued will depend upon the support received. As the list lengthens, it becomes necessary to cut off those who have not been heard from for some months.

No charge is made for these Bulletins. Don't hesitate to send the names of your friends who would appreciate them. Clippings, suggestions, letters, stamps, checks—any encouragement will tend to continue and broaden the distribution

This Bulletin brought such overwhelming response, so encouraging and stimulating, that although we were anxious to turn to other things, we felt obliged to continue, and produced the next one with some assistance from Canadian correspondents to be followed for the first time by a contribution in verse.

WHAT WAR HAS BROUGHT TO CANADA

Business, yes,—sacrifice of civil liberties, hysteria, recrimination, unconscionable greed and profiteering, are Canada's "share in the Empire war effort".[1] Political squabbles are intense. The French-Canadian element, temporarily buffaloed, constitute a larger and more dissident faction than the Mohammedan element in India which Britain claims as an excuse for continued control.

Hepburn attacks Mackenzie King for selling to Russia, a 'potential enemy', a million bushels of wheat, for inefficiency in war management and failure to properly equip the few thousand Canadian troops already raised, 75% recruited from the unemployed. A Canadian, quoted by *Life,* says "We are at war with Germany, yet we could not win a war with the state of Michigan".

News from Canada is strictly censored,—outgoing letters opened, incoming letters stopped, but with the political pot boiling some news comes across. Parliament, (Jan 25) four hours after opening is dissolved and a general election called. The greed for profits brings evidence of greed.

"The idea that every 20 years this country . . . should be called upon to save a continent that cannot run itself . . . seems to many a nightmare and sheer madness," Prime Minister Mackenzie King declared last March. Recently over the radio he said, "Canada is engaged in a war which is a crusade to save the liberty of mankind".

What bribes, pecuniary and propagandist, brought about this change will provide an interesting study for the future historian.[2] Tweedsmuir, trained in Milner's Kindergarten and head of Propaganda at Chatham House during the last war, the King and Queen's propaganda visit, and anticipation of profits contributed to this change.

"Sugared bait" Hugh S. Johnson, Oct 27, called the British plan to spend $3,500,000,000 in Canada, with consequent expansion of their industrial plant. The American government has added sugar to the bait, he reports,—$400,000,000 to be put into the St. Lawrence-Great Lakes Seaway. This is being sold to Canada as power development, to the Middle West as the Great Lakes Seaway, which Johnson calls "a nice custard-coated sucker-lure", as it is "primarily a power project".

What the actual figures are, which are quoted so wildly, it is difficult to ascertain. In September, it was reported that Britain would make a $700,000,000 investment in industrial establishments in Canada Then in December, the great industrial expansion plan was off The first plane could not be turned out for two years, it was found. Canadian war orders have not mounted as anticipated.

"Canada so far is actually spending more in Britain for aircraft than Britain is spending in Canada", states *Business Week.* A N. Y *Times* dispatch, Ottawa, Nov. 7, reports Canada "would be called on to make a preliminary expenditure of $700,000,000 . . . to train 25,000 empire aviators every year. . . . Canada might eventually collect costs from Australia, and New Zealand . . . might find herself 'holding the bag' ".

Canada is already $231,000,000 in debt (AP, Jan. 8).—Transport Minister Howe said the war was now costing Canada $4,000,000 weekly. Nov. 24, Finance Minister Ralston estimated that the first year of the war would cost Canada $315,000,000, twice what was spent in the first twenty months of the last war (*Life*, Dec. 18).[3]

In an effort to cover up what is behind the scenes, censorship in Canada is tighter than in Britain (*Time*, Nov. 20). The Mounties are now raiding houses for books and other forbidden printed matter (*New Republic*, Jan. 8, 1940, *Common Sense*, Dec. 1939).[4]

The clause in the Censorship Act on "Prohibited Matter" is practically identical in the laws of France, Great Britain, Canada, and the Smith Bill that passed our House last May. The penalties differ, but can of course be changed,—France, the guillotine, England ten years. Under this law, one Stewart, an "educated journalist", was on Jan. 18 (N. Y. *Herald Tribune*) sentenced to 2 years imprisonment for being business manager of a newspaper that "denounced the war".

Within two weeks after Canada entered the war, Frank Watson had been convicted for "making statements like to prejudice recruiting", and sentenced Sept. 28 to one year in prison. Watson's words were, "The Canadian Government could find a hundred million dollars to employ men at $1.30 a day to go over and stop bullets but it had not found any money to help the single unemployed before the war." 75% of the recruits are reported to be unemployed.

A member of the Vancouver Legislature, Mrs. Dorothy Steeves, in a speech Nov. 3 was threatened with prosecution by the Premier for saying, "What a farce it is to accuse Germany of breaking solemn promises when Great Britain, France, and all governments broke as many as Germany." "A member of parliament may safely attack the decision of the government to prosecute the war, but for a newspaper to quote such a speech . . . may result in arrest of the editors and printers", writes E. P. Park in *Common Sense*, Dec. 1939.

A Vancouver correspondent writes, "If you people across the line think you are subject to British propaganda, you should live over here for a while, and you would learn what British propaganda is really like: we are immersed in it twenty-four hours a day." Reporting that these

Bulletins sent him were confiscated, he adds, "The latest official action on censorship is an order in council which makes it possible for the government to declare any organization illegal if a single member thereof makes a statement contrary to the provisions of the regulations made under the War Measures Act!"

A Montreal man writes, "The War Measures Act in force here, is growing more oppressive daily. 'The Progress of the War' is thereby assured, and 'free speech' becomes a historical reference." Apropos of the recent Quebec election, he adds, "Duplessis, with the Reds in view, —Begged Ottawa to Padlock too;—so Mr. King with gracious tact— Adopted the War Measures Act—And then Duplessis found—worse luck,—He was more subversive than Tim Buck" (A Canadian radical).

Another writes, "The following jingle, composed at a party, is spreading rapidly by private circulation. If published here, the educator would get six months." "The British troops on the Dardanelles—Were shot to bits by British shells—Sold to the Turks by Vickers —And many a good Canadian youth—(Cheering Democracy, Freedom, Truth)—Will shed his blood on foreign shores,—With his body filled with British ores,—Canada's nickel, and Canada's scrap,—Sold to the German, sold to the Jap,—While Wall Street Watches the tickers."

"Despite the neutrality law, the U S. has actually taken sides . . . As far as the war in the west is concerned, the allies do not need men But they do need to supplement their own manufacturing facilities, newly geared to the requirements of war, with the highly developed and greatly specialized heavy industries of the U. S. This has been accomplished through the repeal of the arms embargo" (The *Financial News Commentary* of Ring and Co., Toronto, Jan. 5).

"Canada has been brought under the Monroe Doctrine", writes Allen Dulles, N. Y. *Herald Tribune*, Dec. 13. President Roosevelt has guaranteed the defense of Canada. We are generous not only with our money but with our promises, and still not all Canadians are grateful. One hysterical patriot from Toronto, reading about these Bulletins, writes a vituperative letter about "guttersniping". This war hysteria is crossing the border. It's on its way in this direction.

That Ottawa would soon be the capital of the British Empire was prophesied by Wythe Williams (*Time,* Nov. 28, 1938), and by R. Buckminster Fuller in "Nine Chains to the Moon", 1938. A mining engineer writes me recently, "For several years I had to visit Canada two or three times each year and with the visit of the King and Queen along with the shipment, for safe keeping of 600 million in gold to Ottawa, 'they' are jubilant over the expectancy of a removal of British Government to Canada. What a field the U. S A. will be for a distribution of 'honors' (?) to amiable Americans? (tho 'honors' are much cheaper now) But what a situation. Royalty on American soil."

"The pomp and circumstance of a royal court so close at hand would exercise a subversive influence upon our own upper classes. . . . Each year would see more title-seeking, intermarriage, and acceptance of aristocratic thought by our wealthy socialites, until finally one could say truly, as now tempted, that 'Britain's frontier is on the Potomac'," writes D. H. Briggs in the Boston *Herald*, Jan. 9.

In attracting attention in these Bulletins to "current idiocies", international events are considered from the standpoint of America. It is pitiful to see the English people intellectually and physically starved. But it is more pitiful to see one's fellow citizens gulled, fooled, robbed, and liking it. I love England as my forebears have since Norman times, but I love America more. I hate no peoples. What hates I have left go for the deceit that covers greed. If sympathy bends me from the path of reason, it goes toward those who are getting the dirty end of the stick. I want to see the British Empire preserved but continue to progress, to see it rescued from the gang that has been running it since 1931.

But if England cannot find better men to run their government than the present gang, that is something for us to weep about, not to interfere with. But when the same gang attempts to run us, as they are now doing, that is something for us to rise up and rebel against. And the time to rebel is now, for they are ganging up on us and soon there will be laws we will have to obey that will prevent even the mildest protest. *January 26, 1940*

NOTES

(1) "It was Canada's idea, when the war began, to make her contribution to England not so much with soldiers as with money, munitions and foodstuffs. . . . German success has changed all this," *PM*'s special correspondent writes from Ottawa, July 8, 1940. That was the idea that the British sold to Wilson in World War I We were to send only a token force to show good will.

Eve Curie, arriving in New York to make thirty lectures last January, 1940, told her public "France does not need more men in this war . .   5,000,000 men are enrolled. . . . We do not want another nation to send military help . . . we do need your sympathy and moral support". That is what England has been singing lately but Roosevelt knows better, so that when Wheeler suggested plowing under every fourth American boy, he got hot under the collar.

(2) Canada did not get all the business she had been promised. A correspondent from Montreal, Dec. 9, 1939, wrote the New York *Times*,—"The real issues behind Canada's participation in this war are distinctly economic and cultural, not of distant ideological import but of immediate Canadian implication"

A Chicago correspondent writes June 30, 1940, "Today a lady (a Canadian) returned to this city after a short stay in Canada. She stated that the people were much incensed towards Britain for the apparent bungling of the affair abroad and particularly the Norwegian campaign. One Canadian outfit sent had not been heard from since sailing to Norway. One item particularly irked the Canadians —their factories have been set up to manufacture war equipment especially airplanes and accessories, and now for nine months they haven't received any orders. Britain has given them all to the U. S."

(4) March 13, 1940, the *Chr Sci Monitor* correspondent from Ottawa wrote "curbs on civil liberties arouse many Canadians . . . bitter political controversy in the year of the federal election campaign". Papers have been banned, radio broadcasts censored, mail houses raided, homes raided, "so-called Padlock Law".

(3) "Premiers of Canada's five poor provinces" of the nine, in conference called for reform, opposed government plans. "But crafty old MacKenzie King" had a dictator's answer To pay for the war he announced the Dominion Government would raise the income tax, levy inheritance tax, cut off its contribution to provincial unemployment, ration gasolene. ("Farewell to Reform", *Time*, Jan 27, 1941)

A CANADIAN VIEW

Rigorous repression of opinion in Canada turns the intelligentsia to sprightly or spiteful verse which they mail out anonymously to us.[1]

IF HITLER'D GONE TO ETON

(Inspired by His Majesty's Broadcast on Christmas Day)
The Playing Fields of Eton,—so beautiful and green!
From them have come a Race of Men, the Finest ever seen!
And we'll back up those Gentlemen, who rule us with a Rod,
For His Majesty exhorts us to take "the hand of God"!

We are really very clever, and we know what we're about,
And although they haven't bombed us, we have our own "black-out".
It makes us rather nervous, but it's a clever stunt,—
We bump off our own civilians, and leave Germans at the Front

Can we take it? Do we take it? We rather do, I'll say!
So give three cheers for those who made us what we are today.
They've taken all our money, our tea is getting thin,
But we still have our 'Old School Ties' and Mister Chamberlain.

If Hitler'd gone to Eton, I think you will agree,
The world would be a better place for our Morality.
The Nazis are not Gentlemen, they haven't any Heart.
We bear the White Man's Burden and try to do our part.

And those disgusting Bolsheviks,—they, too, have let us down,
Although we stooped to meet them,—with a condescending frown,
We sold out the Spanish people, the Czechs and Slovaks, too;
They didn't give us any thanks,—but still we muddle through.

We like poor little Finland,—perhaps it's not too late
To use this nice Red Herring in lieu of better bait,
For Uncle Shylock's nibbling, and if he isn't clever,
We yet may hook the poor old fish,—it's better late than never.

We thought old Uncle Shylock was just a silly dunce
And that he was so gullible he'd come across at once.
We've fed him Propaganda of the very nicest kind,
But he just calls for more and more and won't make up his mind.

Sir Robert's sent the best he has to teach them over there,
His Majesty perspired in his heavy underwear.
Lord Lothian has worked so hard, and so has Mr. Streit,
But the stupid silly beggars just refuse to see the Light.

If they won't pay our war bills, who will, I'd like to know?
Our Gang has taken all our cash to run their bloody Show.
We can't exploit Australia or Canada,—too much,
But we do hope our Wall Street friends will stand another 'touch'.

They'll know as 'moral gentlemen' they're acting for the Best,
That they will surely get their 'cut', and we'll default the rest.

Religion and Morality we simply just adore
And as we've taken half the world we don't want any more.

From the Public Schools of England, where they rule 'em with a cane,
Have come our noblest statesmen, and Mister Chamberlain.
But when they tax us more and more and tax until it hurts,
I sometimes wish those 'Old School Ties' weren't worn on just stuffed
　　shirts.

January 24, 1940

NOTES

(1) Those already in the war seem to fall into verse more readily than we Americans who linger on the brink. Sagittarius in the (London) *New Statesman and Nation* presents this cogitation:

> The public we know is an ass,
> Fit only for general suppression,
> Its conduct incredibly crass,
> Its chatter one huge indiscretion.
> It has just enough wit to perceive
> A rather acute contradiction
> Between facts it is bound to believe
> And the newspapers' rose-colored fiction.
>
> On Monday our forces advance,
> On Tuesday, the foe has retreated,
> On Wednesday, prepared for this chance,
> Our fortunate feats are repeated,
> On Thursday we strike a hard blow,
> Our moves are completely effective,
> On Friday, however, the foe
> Has somehow attained his objective.
>
> The news for our good is controlled,
> Though our views are, of course, not requested
> We know that all may not be told
> Before it is well predigested,
> But the experts have never found out
> That nothing so daunts and depresses
> As the news of an actual rout
> After series of rumored successes.

A Scot correspondent has sent me the following poem by a "Welsh-born American", "neither of us would sacrifice the life of one American boy to save either of our countries of birth　Why should America be goaded into a war to protect the interests of those controlling the gold and diamond mines of Kimberley and the Witwatersand. . . . The rape of the two Boer Republics is something no Scottish-American can forget, even if the Jews of Lombard St and Wall St. would like everybody to forget. In this I insist I am not indulging in any anti-Jewish feeling, but merely to refresh the memories of Americans of my age of the most damnable outrage ever perpetrated by any power on another in the whole history of the world. . . . Not for me!"

PLOW UNDER

(Dedicated with affection and esteem to Burton K. Wheeler, U S. Senator from Montana)

> Plow under the cotton, Plow under the corn,
> Plow under little pigs, All squealing forlorn,
> And with them plow under, O far over sea,
> The Boys of America, Born to be free!
>
> Plow under! Plow under, With old martial thunder,
> The Youth of the Nation In some foreign loam!
> Plow under! Plow under! And tear them asunder
> From Father and Mother, and Sweetheart and Home!
>
> Plow under Propaganda's Tom-toms on our door,
> Hysterical Ballyhoo's Wild dancing to War!
> Plow under harangues—Of the War-Crier's plea,
> Enslaving America, The Land of the Free!
>
> Plow under! Plow under! With God's own great thunder,
> The wars of all Nations, Their greed and their slime!
> Plow under! Plow under! From Man tear asunder
> The War-monger's passion, The Munitioner's crime!
> But never plow under, Even o'er the blue sea,
> Boys not born to be butchered, Boy's born to be free!

EMBROILING THE NEUTRALS

The war goes on with increasing bitterness. Those who do not hate with sufficient intensity are not 'ethical' and lack 'moral responsibility'. The only proper attitude in respectable circles is emotional. Soon it will be hysterical, as twenty-two years ago.

Already the Germans are "executing children". Soon they will be "raping women". It is such "events" that are used to stir emotions. This cruder propaganda is more effective after Vansittart's finer art has prepared the way. But Sir Robert's marvelous organization, which has been working on us for three years, as pointed out in these Bulletins from the first, remains wholly ignored by Americans. And the British are too clever to deny it.

News is confused and contradictory. Situations are not clear. The public, badly informed, is unable to understand or interpret. For example, the Superintendent of Schools in a small Illinois town writes me, "Much of the information given in your bulletins has seemed so incredible that it is hard to believe it is authentic. I have taken the trouble to write to a person of national reputation. He stated that he was sure your purpose was one of true enlightenment."

Confused and alarmed, they naturally revert to 'moral' attitudes. It brings satisfaction to feel that you are 'right', the other is 'wrong', that you fight for 'righteousness', others for 'evil'. Then you may vent your hate with a clear conscience and a feeling of moral exaltation. That's what the propagandist organizations, set up and controlled for their immediate ends by those who rule us, have accomplished.

These Bulletins endeavor to make the confusion more intelligible, to select and arrange so as to reveal pattern. No pretense is made of complete knowledge or to present all sides, and opinion is discounted They are welcomed by those who don't want to be fooled, are not satisfied by wallowing in their emotions, but wish to understand. Those who have already passed judgment and condemned the women and children of peoples they dislike to starvation and death, are enraged. The brief notice in *Time,* Dec. 25, brought a flood of encouraging, commending, inquiring letters, but also vilification and threats of vengeance. We continue to elucidate while we can,—as best we can.

Churchill's demand that the neutral nations join England and France, "facing . . . the dull brutish force of overwhelming numbers", in the fight against "aggression and wrong" lest they "be devoured", carried, too, "a message for Americans who . . . seem willing to sanction the full use of the blockade weapon by the British", Stoneman cables from London, Jan. 22. To the neutrals this "is foreseen as a forewarning of a showdown". Churchill warned against "comforting themselves with the thought that the British . . . will strictly observe all laws and conventions".

Churchill's portrait accompanying this release does not show the "cherubic" countenance the press describes, but portentous bulk The

Churchill who utters words of defiance is the same who in his message last August flattered Hitler on what he had accomplished for the German people. It is the Churchill responsible for the tragedy that piled up the dead Anzacs on the beaches and in the gulleys of Gallipoli, and for the attempt to force the Dardanelles, where more British war- ships were sunk than had ever been in any one place and time [1]

To embroil the little neutrals, to enlist their manpower and again make these buffer states the battlegrounds, Churchill stressed, as have the London cables, the recent destruction of neutral ships, contrasting the neutrals' hard lot with an optimistic contemporary picture of Britain and France. He taunts the neutrals, "Finland shows what free men can do", and he praises the "resolute Turk".

Sour was the response of the neutrals to this demand and ominous threat. Berlin sees in "the whinings of Churchill" an effort to "spread the war". So unfavorable was the response that the Foreign Office apologized that this was not a statement of Government policy.

The threat in Churchill's urge that the neutrals "join the Allies against the forces of darkness has aroused outspoken indignation in those countries which are seriously determined to keep out of the war as long as they can." "Mr. Churchill's discussion of moral aims and purposes will not figure to any great extent in the final course of the neutrals . . . He proposed what many neutrals will regard as immediate national suicide . . . The failure of Britain and France to halt as much as one German tank in Poland will undoubtedly prove a primary source of skepticism." (Boston *Transcript*, Jan. 22, Jan. 23).

'Poor little Belgium' learned her lesson in the last war and wants to preserve her neutrality this time, as did the others in the last war with consequent prosperity. Her newspapers headlined the speech, "Strange Reprimand to Neutrals by Churchill", and added that her king and government were "better placed and qualified to judge the interests of our country". In the Netherlands they called it a "sharp attack on neutrals", and held for "strict neutrality". In Denmark they asserted, "The small neutral states will feel no gratitude to Mr. Churchill because he is again dragging them in. What they fear most . . is . . . the propaganda war carried on around them", and add, "Peace was not given to Finland. To stop this brutal and unjust attack is a greater and nobler task for the big powers than to try to whirl the remaining neutrals into savagery." The Italian press showed that Italy's "dignity" was "affronted" and that the British Lord of the Admiralty had " 'spilled the beans' by frankly revealing the policy that is considered here to be nothing less than open coercion of neutrals". (N.Y. *Times,* Jan. 22)

Foreign Office planned, as are all statements on foreign policy, Churchill's speech, though addressed to the little neutrals, was intended to have its great effect on the great neutral, the United States, whose credits, money, and munitions are essential to winning the war.

With superior political sense, with hidden propaganda, denied or unsuspected, Britain puts it over on us. With the aid of the President and Britain's financial agents, our universities and intellectuals have been brought to a highly 'moral' state of indignation, ready to sacrifice blood and money for the 'right' as they see it, just as in 1917. Shrewd horsetrading Yankees, as we are, sharp poker players, we are easily taken in, like our forebears in the shell game at the county fair. Unblinkingly we are still paying taxes on 40 billions war cost and interest of over a billion on our debt. Since 1933 we have spent nine billions on new armament, and through gold purchases contributed ten billions to rearming Europe, including Russia.[2]

Lord Riverdale has been over and told the President that the war is to be decided in the air and he must have 10,000 planes. So Secretary Morgenthau is now visiting American airplane plants and arranging to finance extensions by remission of taxes and subsidies, so that Britain may have her planes at no increased cost.

Such plant extensions for the benefit of the Allies in the last war cost the taxpayer some hundreds of millions. The need this time is greater. The cost will be more. It will be paid for largely in indirect taxes, which yield 60% of our revenue and can be made to yield more. Interest payments, too, which come from taxes, will increase with the raising of the debt to $50,000,000,000, as Morgenthau, acting for the President, advocates.[3]

Morgenthau "indicated" that "he was coordinating allied and American army and navy airplane purchasing in this country. Because he is acting for the President rather than in his capacity as Secretary of the Treasury, Morgenthau said he was not free to talk." (AP, Jan. 22)

Describing Morgenthau's efforts to meet the British needs through expansion of factories, Frank L. Kluckhohn in the N.Y. *Times*, Jan. 22, cautiously adds, "Some fear exists in official quarters here that if the British finance a vast expansion of airplane plants in this country a situation might easily arise wherein the United States might be left 'holding the bag' ". The Federal Reserve Bank under Morgenthau's direction is aiding in financing Allied purchases. The President has been able, through RFC and Export-Import Bank, to route money to the allies and their buffer states, sometimes in opposition to the wishes of their directors, and perhaps illegally. (cf Bul #22)

The President, intent on aiding the Allies in every possible way "short of war", believes he is fighting for 'civilization' and 'religion and morality' and against 'the forces of evil'. But the Administration is divided, confused, and fearful on many of these financial matters, and most of all on their greatest mistake, gold buying, as Graham and Whittlesey make clear in "The Golden Avalanche".

"Administration leaders, including the President", are reported to be "worried about the exchange situation" (N.Y. *Times*, Jan. 22). We are not skilful enough to sit in with the international gamblers. We have again become a debtor, not a creditor nation.[4] The denials of this situation by Goldenweiser in the Federal Reserve Bulletin and Cox in his *Gold Barometer* (January issues) are rather feeble.

Our fake 'Neutrality' Law established no credit restrictions that are effective between those who wish to evade them. France and England have no difficulty in getting credits if the transshipment method is used, and of course there is no restriction whatever on credits between private companies (cf Bul #18)

Even this does not satisfy the British, who are now promoting a clever scheme for the repeal of the Johnson Act and further modification of the 'Neutrality' Law, which imposes some restrictions on their credit, and which interferes they complain with British shipping.

Much publicity has been given to the possibility of Britain buying a billion dollars worth of airplanes, and more recently to taking a billion dollars worth of farm products. "Britain had agreed to take 40,000,000 pounds of government-held tobacco in addition to open market purchases" (Kluckhohn, N.Y. *Times*, Jan. 22). But to bring Turkey to their side, enormous bribe was necessary. Now they are taking Turkish in place of Virginia tobacco and gradually changing the taste of the English people (London wireless, N.Y. *Times*, Jan. 22).

This will create another pressure group among the tobacco holders in this country. Soon Southern Senators will be arguing for British credits that they may save the ruined tobacco farmers. Soon Western Senators will be urging credits that the packers and hog raisers may sell their products. The apple and the orange growers of the East and the West will be crying for credits to Britain that she may have our fruit, which she claims she can't afford to buy.

The War Fever has already crossed the Appalachians and has begun to spread like a prairie fire. With all these pressure groups endeavoring to relieve the bankruptcy of their constituents, the walls of the Johnson Act will go down under the blasts of American Congressional trumpets as did the walls of Jericho.

Hogs, tobacco, and oranges may help to win the war for the Allies.

Credits for the 'poor little' buffer states are easier. As Rockefeller used to hand out dimes, our President hands out ten millions to Finland, Poland, Norway. The others are lining up. "Sources close to the British government" (London, Jan. 17, CP) assert that the "Finnish front is essentially an Allied front". American journals and Congressmen are becoming aware that the Finnish propaganda news of valor and victories was to promote a loan.

And there is boring from within. American holders of surplus products are taking an interest in Finland's troubles. New England hurricane lumber, surplus Southern pine, have been cornered (Boston *Herald*, Jan. 11). The clever suggestion has been made that, though we can't get arms to Finland direct, the credits might be established and lumber shipped to England and France which need them. Then they could take care of getting arms to Finland (cf Bul #26). Thus far Britain's help has been in anticipation. The cables announce Britain "will increase" shipments of arms to Finland "in the next few weeks". So our New England hurricane may help Britain, and possibly Finland and our surplus hogs and tobacco may change defeat to victory. "All things work together for good to them that love God"—and Mammon—with sufficient continuity.

"Reinforcements now are coming, victory is nigh." In the phalanxes following the statesmen, recruited in the interest of 'saving civilization' (by destroying the source of our songs and our music), come serried ranks of ethicists and religionists, "marching as to war", while the Primate and the Archbishop of York softly intone, "Religion and morality we simply just adore, and as we've taken half the world we don't want any more".

The "holy war" proclaimed by Chamberlain still awaits the decision or compulsion of the neutrals, and the enlistment of the Greatest of all Recruits, whom both sides claimed in the last war. For there are those who believe "God is on the side of the strongest battalions".

And if God be with us, who can be against us, even though with odds of ten to one we "Strangle Our Enemy and Starve Their Children" (cf Bul #33).

January 26, 1940

NOTES

(1) Already forgotten is the build up for the shelved Generals Ironside and Gort, the heroes of the early stages of this war The build up for Churchill has obscured his other triumphs at Narvik, Dunkirk, Dakar. For a decade he was derided by the liberals of two continents as the most Tory of the Tories, and by the Tories as impetuous and irresponsible. Forgotten and denied, too, is his reported expression in 1936 of the prevalent opinion of that time that "America should have minded her own business and stayed out of the world war. If she had done so, the allies would have made peace with Germany in the spring of 1917, thus saving over a million British, French, American and other lives, and preventing the subsequent rise of facism and nazism". Griffin gives a full account of Churchill's interview with him, of the subsequent distortions, denials and resulting law suit in the February 1941 issue of *Scribner's Commentator.*

However, as Beatrice Abbott points out in a letter to the Boston *Transcript,* "If Churchill did not say some such thing, in the years 1919-1936, he would probably be the only British writer who did not It was what they all believed, when they became sane before, and what any who are left will believe when this is over Here is one such English statement on page 433 of 'A Richer Dust', by Storm Jameson, 1931- 'It would have been better if America had never come into the war, then no one could have won it and they would have made a decent peace.' " Dennis Sandys, son-in-law of Churchill, expressed the same view as late as 1939 (*Unity,* Jan. 20, 1941).

At the New England Forum early in February, 1941, Oswald Garrison Villard repeated Churchill's statement which brought a statement February 12 from Washington, "The British embassy wishes to state on the authority of the prime minister that it is totally untrue that he ever made any statement to the above or similar effect". That is what embassies are for,—to make such denials when necessary. But Churchill, whose 'build up' now presents him as a master of words, has through his long career been noted for his impulsive statements. When in 1926, as Chancellor of the Exchequer, he was using his oratorical gifts to denounce

Uncle Shylock for attempting to collect its war loans from Great Britain, he described Uncle Sam as "bloated with fabulous wealth yet squeezing vast sums out of war-stricken Europe"

"It was a slight slip of the pen in Churchill's statement a few weeks ago wherein he foreclosed the possibility of American troops coming to Europe in 1941 that raised a quibbling inquiry here to the effect that he had not eliminated 1942 or 1943." (David Lawrence, February 11, 1941)   John Chamberlain reviewing Quincy Howe's "The News and How to Understand It", 1940, remarks, "Mr Howe finds it a perennial mystery that correspondents who have been wrong about everything from Winston Churchill (remember when he was being drubbed as the world's worst Tory?) to Russo-German relations should still continue to get high fees for their services as haruspices and sages".

It isn't till a man is down and out that we can discover what he is. Until then we have the 'build up'. It's only by "hindsight" of which MacLeish is so contemptuous, that we can learn what he really is   *Time*, October 14, 1940, announcing the replacement of Sir Cyril Louis Norton Newall as Chief of Air Staff by Sir Charles Frederick Algernon Portal, noted that "Sir Cyril's removal, now that 'Tiny' Ironside and 'Tiger' Gort were in limbo, cleaned out the three leaders who were roundly acclaimed three months ago for the victorious retreat from Flanders. Only unbeaten generals are bear cats."

Churchill's former contemptuous attitude toward the Yanks persists today in England   Rustem Vambery reviewing G Garratt's "What Has Happened to Europe", *Nation*, April 13, 1940 says "The author seems to share, although in a more polite form, A P. Herbert's yearning: 'God protect us against a German victory and an American peace' . .   Mr. Garratt   believes that 'the European tragedy lies in our own minds'   Unfortunately it is easier to kill men than to change their misdirected mental energies"   More recently, C. G. Gray of the English *Airplane Magazine*, said, "I have a rooted objection to having obsolete or inconceivably dud American stuff planted on this country by American bluff and guff and blah and baloney   Some of us are so afraid that the U S A. will insist on coming over here and winning the war for us, as they did the last time   And another 20 years of being told that America won the war would be so hard to bear".   (*Life*, March 3, 1941)

But Thomas W. Lamont as a friend of Britain has to present things somewhat differently.   In Dallas, April 24, he said, " 'The more that we can help these allies obtain here their absolutely vital supplies of American agriculture and industrial products, the more will the war be kept away from our own borders and the sooner will the conflict end.   In other words cooperation along economic and financial lines is for America the road not to war but to peace ' " ("War Prop. and the U S"—Lavine—p 343)

(2) Now nine Billions is small change. Our Administration has almost forgotten to use mere Millions. Gold purchases in 1940, $4,749,467,000, also set a new high record

(3) How quickly all these anticipations have been fully achieved! All these

figures seem trivial. Two billions of contracts was the pourboire given the recalcitrant and independent Ford For further figures on plant extensions, etc , cf Buls #81 and #88. The dollar sign, our President has decreed, is no longer to apply to England's debt to us It will take a little longer to do away with dollar signs on our national debt. It can be done,—it has been in Russia, Germany.

(4) We went into the last war a debtor nation, with all debts paid and everyone owing us. "What terms we might have made in the way of possessions and privileges had we been as practical and realistic as some of the imperialists with whom we were dealing," exclaimed the late Eugene J Young, then cable editor of the New York *Times* in his "Looking Behind the Censorships".

"At the close of 1929 the world owed us around 25 billions, only ten billions of which are called war debts," as Raymond Gram Swing pointed out in *Ken*, May 19, 1938, commiserating with Uncle Sam, "the working fool". "We had a potential 20 billions of capital ready to work for us abroad . . When confronted with this unique privilege this country passed the Smoot-Hawley tariff, which made it difficult for foreigners to export to us their labor and goods . . . In 1930, at the height of our creditor position, we were being paid in dividends from abroad $616,000,000 more than we paid to foreigners. In 1936 we received only a net of $330,000,000. . . . To meet our deficit we went into debt to foreigners that year about $200,000,000." With all other nations reduced to penury, we held the leadership of the world, and with our vast credit resources we might have remade the world on democratic lines, to our heart's desire. Unfortunately we had no heart's desire We lacked political sense, financial intelligence So we threw away our opportunity, and the European political leaders, looking upon us as an easy mark, continued to bleed poor old Uncle Sam.

"It will be a shock to many to discover", Graham and Whittlesey in an article in *Foreign Affairs*, April 19, 1939, had made it clear, that "instead of being a lender nation . as had been the situation . . . we have in recent years, been a net borrower of billions . incurred in the purchase of gold on which we laid out, net, $1,134,000,000 in 1934, $1,739,000,000 in 1935; $1,117,000,000 in 1936, $1,586,000,000 in 1937, and $1,974,000,000 in 1938 " The cost continues to go on and we dare not stop it.

STRANGLING, STARVING, FALSIFYING,—FOR POWER

" 'Starving Germany out' is a phrase frowned on by London officialdom and always deleted by the censor—in deference to the sensibilities of humanitarian neutrals. But that is the Ministry's job."[1] (*Life*, Jan 15, 1940, "Contraband Control")

"We look forward to the day when we shall have strangled Germany's economic life so that she can no longer sustain her war effort", Minister of Economic Warfare Ronald H. Cross informed the Commons, Jan. 17, asserting that already Germany was undergoing economic strain as great as after two years in the previous war. Simultaneously in the House of Lords, Lord Hankey made a similar assertion [2]

Cross, "wealthy merchant-banker, young, attractive, an old Etonian and a diplomat" was selected as "a good front for a Ministry many of whose activities would be distinctly questionable to professional moralists. . . . All this was done with the greatest secrecy." (*Life*, Jan. 15)

The creator and organizer of this ministry, and the shrewd, hard force behind the scenes, is Sir Frederick Leith-Ross, since 1932 Chief Economic Adviser to the Government. He with "a score of Britain's shrewdest bankers and economists, and their 400 assistants, are fighting the real war against Germany—without benefit of publicity . . . attempting to choke the life out of the Third Reich.[3]

"Little has been allowed to leak out for fear of upsetting Anglo-American relations. And the British Foreign office, knowing the touchiness of the American public, has tried to instill caution into the heart of the Ministry of Economic Warfare. But 62 American ships were detained by the Allies up to Nov. 25. Some of them were held as long as three weeks." *Life*, Jan. 15)

How many ships have been detained since, it is difficult to ascertain, as the State Department is reluctant to alarm the American public and "has merely protested the length of time our shipping has been held". In "justification" for halting our ships, "the best case that Britain could make was to point to some $50,000 of money and valuables and a considerable number of food packages that have been apprehended". (Editorial, Boston *Transcript*)

Hull protested gently. He suggested that the Clipper give up its Bermuda call. Senator Lundeen impertinently interjected that England give up Bermuda. In quiet, secret conversations Lothian has brought Hull around, and it is announced that no more packages to belligerents will be accepted by the U. S. Post Office.

Reported in our papers as a sinister plot was the plan whereby one depositing $6.70 with the German steamship line could have that exchange transmitted by radio to Holland, whence a package of butter and cheese might be sent to grandmother in Germany (N. Y. *Times*, Jan. 22). This heinous practice has been stopped, it is understood.

"This weapon of starvation falls mainly upon the women and children, upon the old and the weak and the poor, after all the fighting has stopped", Winston Churchill declared in 1919, after the Armistice while the Allies were blockading Germany, resulting in 800,000 deaths.[4]

This war to 'save humanity' involved inhumanity, to 'save civilization' the abandonment of civilized processes. "A starving nation and a nation at bay, of what barbarity is it incapable? And how can such a nation lead a civilized life?" asks E. I. Watkin in The *Commonweal*, Jan. 5.[5]

"If thine enemy hunger, feed him", quoted the Bishop of Birmingham, protesting the "horrible" practice of exerting pressure on the men in the fighting line by starving the children and old folks at home. The Archbishop of Canterbury sternly rebuffed him, asserting that Germany, too, was depriving Britain of food (*Chr Sci Monitor*, Jan. 18). "Dumpy, round-faced" Archbishop of York piped up, "We are fighting for Christian civilization . . . a righteous war" (*Time*, Jan. 29).

Thirty-three prominent American Protestant clergymen and laymen have made the headlines lining up with York and Canterbury (cf Bul #57 Notes). In a manifesto condemning those who "from ignorance or moral confusion" are "guilty of moral irresponsibility" in not promoting hate and war, and declaring, "The churches in the United States are under obligation to lead" in fanning the flames.

Repudiating Anne Lindbergh's view that "no good can come out of this war" and Benjamin Franklin's that "no war is good", and ignoring the experience of the last war, these leaders believe they have found something 'evil' which all should hate. But alas, they can never work us up to the intensity of conviction of the days of the Inquisition, and they can never restore the old warfare where the hated conquered were put to the sword or sold into slavery.

"Bloodthirsty Preachers. How They Fanned War Fever in 1914-18" is the heading under which *Newsweek*, Jan. 15, recalls "Preachers Present Arms", 1932, by Ray H. Abrams. "With the possible exception of Mohammedanism" no religion "has been more devoted to Mars than has Christianity". Then Bishop Manning called peace "thinly disguised treason" and Rabbi Wise demanded the "slaughter of the Boche",— which culminated in Liberty Loan posters demanding, "Kill the Hun— Kill his Hope. Bayonet and bond—both kill!"

The more articulate obscenities on the Kaiser and his Huns of the learned professors at Harvard, whose temperature is again rising (cf Bul #16), were perpetuated in a similar book, published about the same time. Of the blood-lust that overtook the erudite Harvard faculty, G. R Stange reminds us in The Harvard *Progressive*, Nov., 1939.

Confusion of view, both in England and here, in regard to this so-called phoney war has been due to change in plans. In September when England went into the war it was anticipated Poland would hold for months, Hitler would bomb London, and that would bring America in immediately Then the push on Leningrad from the Mannerheim Line was to come in the spring. Disappointment brought confusion.

The Ministry of Economic Warfare has become increasingly important as economic warfare has been accented Money, credits have become all important. And America, old Uncle Shylock, is the ultimate source

The letter signed by Lord Beaverbrook, formerly Max Aitken, Nova Scotian pulp magnate, cabled to the N. Y. *Times* and published in all our newspapers Jan 6, was skilfully constructed for a purpose. It charged that the U. S. in 1931 had taken from England two billions of gold and forced England off the gold standard.

Britons, it whined, had never expected to pay their war debt. Americans had said it was a gift "The first American request for a funding of the debt was not made until 1922, and Mr. Andrew Mellon was responsible for the decision to press for a settlement."

The plausible falsification of incidents, events, and issues is not apparent to the ordinary reader, and no economist or money expert has been bold enough either to explain its deceitfulness or to risk his professional reputation by coming to Beaverbrook's support The late Eugene J Young, long cable editor of the N Y. *Times*, makes all this simple enough in his chapter, "Simplicities of the Great Money War" in his book "Looking Behind the Censorships" (Lippincott, 1938).

Following the Beaverbrook letter came the Churchill (cf Bul #32) and Halifax speeches of Jan 19 "The *Times*, London, which frequently reflects official views, will point out editorially tomorrow that yesterday's speeches of both Mr Churchill and Viscount Halifax, the Foreign Secretary, were complementary in their statements of the British case." (London, cable to N. Y. *Times*, Jan. 21)

England's foreign policy is traditionally planned by the permanent staff of the Foreign Office The pattern of the rearranged plan is becoming apparent. The sequence in recent pronouncements gives evidence of the planning of a master mind

Sir Robert Vansittart, former Foreign Office head, who for three years has disappeared from the news and is listed merely as "Adviser to the Foreign Office", typifies and symbolizes and perhaps is that master mind. The organization he has built since 1936 has been kept even more secret than was the Masterman organization in Wellington House twenty-five years ago. But as a consequence, unsuspected, its effect on American opinion has been even greater. His organization has so used events and news as to give us our present attitudes and emotions.

Chamberlain, Jan. 31, preparing the way for further credits from the U. S., "expressed regret that the concentration of dollar resources in America for munitions and other war supplies has forced curtailment of purchases of other products there" (AP, London, Jan. 31), intimating that credits would permit the purchase. (cf Bul #32)

Fortune, February, 1940, guardedly accepting Graham and Whittlesey's explanation that our gold purchases are financing the European war, says, "Since 1934 the U S. has received about $10,500,000,000 of gold from abroad. Of that amount some $2,800,000,000 has been in settlement of a favorable trade balance on the part of the U. S. Most of the rest of the gold flow has been accompanied by a vast, unwelcome entrance of foreign capital . . giving Europeans credit in the U. S. and narrowing the American creditor position with the rest of the world",—which means we have been transforming ourselves from a creditor to a debtor nation, as Graham and Whittlesey have explained. ("Golden Avalanche", Princeton University Press, 1939)

"Those credits, plus the fact that we shall go on accepting gold, are proving a godsend to the Allies . . The British Empire has an estimated gold reserve of about $2,000,000,000, and its yearly output of gold is $700,000,000. . . It can use its credits, its reserve, and its gold production to purchase supplies from the U. S. The U. S., in short, has for some time been helping Europe's rearmament and is now implicated in Europe's war. The method is not the same as the Morgan loans of 1914-16, but the effect is not much different." (*Fortune*)

In the last war they paid us with gold bonds, which we still have, now with metallic gold, dug by indentured black labor and sold to us at a huge profit. We will still have it twenty years from now.

The strategic military plan is also becoming apparent. There is only one thing to fight for,—power. Oil, today is the source of power, the spoils of war, as once were slaves, gold, coal. 70% of the world's oil is on the American continent, part of it controlled in Venezuela, as in California and Texas, by the British, through Royal Dutch Shell, the late Deterding's organization.

Only other great oil basin is the Caspian-Black Sea region. Persian and Mesopotamian oil are already British controlled. If Britain can control the Baku oil and Rumanian oil, the nations of Central Europe and Asia are powerless,—to raise a plane, roll a tank, move a boat.

Dutch Sir Henri Deterding, once "The Most Powerful Man in the World" (Covici Friede, 1938), through a deal with the decadent Russian government, thought he owned Baku oil. The Bolsheviks interfered. As a result, Great Britain spent four billions after the Armistice, Deterding hundreds of millions of his own money, and forced Churchill to force Wilson to send American forces to carry the American flag into Murmansk, the White Sea, Siberia, and the Caspian Sea. But they failed to get oil. (cf pp 23, 189)

Now Britain with a bribe variously stated at from 750 millions down has secured Turkey with its army of 500,000 and is massing in Syria an army of Indian and Negro and colonial troops.

President Roosevelt has assured us that it is not his "intent" that any "sons of American mothers" shall fight on "the soil of Europe". With a war in Asia ahead, that assurance becomes ominous.

To enlist manpower to fight we must create hatreds. Organization and skill and improved technique has made that possible by slight distortion and partial suppression of the news. Spiritual leaders, university authorities, and intellectuals must be won first.

For those who preach against 'Force' in the name of 'morality' and 'democracy', there may be a sadistic satisfaction in strangling,—the thugs of India made a religion of it. In 'starving' there is perhaps vicarious ascetic compensation. Blessed are they that hunger and thirst for righteousness' sake.

You are paying taxes to carry on all these idiocies, to support some hundreds of the legislators and administrative officials in Washington. Many of them know very little, nor what to do, as their acts and speeches prove. But they want your vote. Tell them how to get it. They want to know that. They will listen.

One mother has written to "all Congressmen and Senators and

received over a hundred answers. All acknowledge the seriousness of the situation, but are afraid. The old case of Nero fiddling. At least we can call 'Fire'. I feel with you the urgency. You are my mental mentor".
February 2, 1940

NOTES

(1) "The Incomparable Atrocity" is what the *Christian Century*, Dec. 11, 1940, calls "The starvation of 18,000,000 non-belligerent men, women and children in Europe, innocent victims of a war in which they are not involved". We have the food, the plan and the organizations to carry on, but a little group of merciless British Tories and their stooges prevent our doing so. American charity has given this past year $51,700,000 from the personal pockets of the American people for the English, French, Finns, but now refuses to do anything with Britain's blockade for starving and strangling the peoples of Europe. The American Friends Committee, 20 South 12th Street, Philadelphia, will supply you with facts and figures, conservative but horrifying.

Herbert Hoover continues to repeat by radio and print and in a pamphlet "When Winter Comes to Europe" his appeals for food for the starving millions by selling surplus American farm products for which their cash is already on deposit in this country. But this "is receiving a cool reception here from officials who look upon hunger as a potential weapon". (London cable to *Chr Sci Monitor*, Aug. 12, 1940)

Herbert Hoover, *Chr Sci Monitor*, Nov 23, 1940, writes of the 37,000,000 people of all faiths in Europe who face famine this winter but who have ample financial resources in this country to pay for food. In view of the form in which the Gallup Poll question was phrased, he was surprised that "38% approved it".

Sec Wallace attempted to salve the Administration's conscience by reminding us that in our own country we have hungry people to feed. *PM*, June 25, 1940, "Federal Surplus Commodities Corporation estimate that there are today 20,000,000 of our own people who do not have adequate diets, and 9,000,000 hungry school children. . . . One top-flight Agriculture Department official sums up: 'If you feed the people of Europe—that's Christian charity. If you feed the people at home—that's socialism.'"

But pro-British zealots and university presidents who act as stooges, including President Conant of Harvard, signed a protest assailing Hoover's plan. These wise men told us Hitler cannot be trusted, that he would seize the food, but Hoover who has had as much experience tells us "It is well known from experience with similar conditions in the last war that 10,000,000 lives in Belgium and northern France were saved without any sacrifice of military advantage. Precisely the same objections were raised at that time. That service was repeatedly praised by British and French prime ministers. We believe it can be done again." (*Living Church*, Jan. 8, 1941)

Lord Lothian on his return from England, acting for the British Tory regime, rejected Hoover's plan and stated "the British government . . . feel the deepest sympathy . . the risk of starvation has been greatly exaggerated . . . any shortage of food . . . is solely due to German action" (AP, Dec 10, 1940). It is a normal supply of foodstuffs from the Americas for which cash is already here that the British blockade cuts off, and Britain tells us it is their duty to punish these Europeans this way because they are bad And Mr. Roosevelt and our Administration is all agin' sin.

(2) "Even if the war should end tomorrow, millions will die of starvation. Regardless of what comes, more than 1,000,000 will die in Poland alone this year", declared H. T. Lewis, professor of economics at Harvard and authority on distribution of food (Boston *Herald,* June 16, 1940) "It is a fair estimate to say there are 10,000,000 under arms. For every man . . there must be two in the background to maintain him." These 30,000,000 must be fed first What is left over goes to the others "As the British retreated from Belgium they destroyed everything." Belgium imported "8 per cent of the fodder for its livestock. This importation now has been shut off" as in Holland When people are "deprived of the right kind of food, resistance becomes lowered and disease sets in After that comes pestilence . . Hunger, disease and pestilence come in that order A man may die of pneumonia" because of "lack of nutrition to resist the disease".

"In the wars of the last century such widespread suffering did not threaten There was some vestige left of freedom of the seas—for which, in part, we fought the world war. Except for an actual blockade of a definite area of coastline, trade in supplies which were not contraband of war was permitted." This blockade for starvation "is a terrible heart-sickening problem . . an inescapable part of modern war which destroys everything, not merely armies and ships and cities but . all that is left of 'the little mercy of man'." (Hugh Johnson, Nov. 29, 1940)

(3) The ultra religious Halifax and the bluff, cherubic Churchill use the British navy to prevent the usual supply of food reaching Belgian, French, Dutch and Norwegian children. They hope Hitler will have to feed them and if they do die, the British rely on other more skilful propaganda and control of communications to place the onus on the Germans

The indentured labor system on which the British Empire rests is largely dependent upon keeping large areas near starvation. This is true in India. In Central Africa, the wife, hut and poll tax is necessary to force labor into the gold and diamond mines A helpless people can protest against this starvation policy only by hunger strike. Gandhi by fasting has shaken the foundations of the British Empire. Woman Suffrage won the vote by the hunger strike. The Irish won their independence through the courage of Mayor Sweeney of Cork who died of hunger in jail. His record has recently been broken, April 16, 1940, AP, by "Anthony Darcy, 32-year-old prisoner" suspected of membership in the Irish Republican army, sentenced to three months' imprisonment, who "died after a 52-day hunger strike".

George Bernard Shaw in "What I Really Wrote About the War" states Britain's case honestly. "Not bombardment, but starvation and civil ruin, have brought England's rivals to their knees; and this starvation and ruin have fallen heavily not only on neutral countries, but on England's own Allies, who have escaped the fate of Russia and Germany only by being rationed from England. From the Ural Mountains to the shores of the North Sea there was starvation everywhere, and from Warsaw eastward there were whole countries of which it was affirmed without improbability that there was no child seven years of age left alive. We have by our blockade caused 763,000 persons to die in Germany of 'malnutrition', a polite name for starvation. By 1917 we had increased the civilian mortality by 32 per cent above the figure for 1913. Next year we got that appalling figure up to 37 per cent This does not include influenza cases More than 50,000 children under fifteen died in 1917, and 15,000 girls and women under thirty. These are only the deaths the condition of the survivors may be imagined

"The real difficulty is that she can, and does, ruin half the world to save herself in time of war, and is, indeed, unable to obtain a decision by any other means; for it is evident that had all the ports been open and all the seas free throughout the war the armies might have fought for ever without having to surrender to famine . . . the command of the sea means a power of life and death over Europe, and this constitutes a hegemony against which the world will rebel as surely as it rebelled against the mere threat of Pan-German hegemony.

"The lethal command of the sea is not a Right: it has only to be nakedly stated to show that it is a Might and nothing else.

"The next war, if permitted to occur, will be no 'sport of kings', no game of chance played with live soldiers and won by changing them into dead ones, but a scientific attempt to destroy cities and kill civilians Not the soldiers alone, but all of us, will have to live miserably in holes in the ground, afraid to look at the sky lest our white faces should betray us to a hostile aeroplane; for our houses will be heaps of charred bricks " (Shaw)

(4) Pleading for the "Quakers" who "are asking for help to send food to France, to the Low Countries, to Norway", Dr. Alice Hamilton, long connected with the Harvard Medical School health courses, tells of what she saw in the summer of 1919 in Germany as the result of the blockade after the Armistice. "The slow destruction of people of flesh and blood . . . hospital wards full of children with multiple bone tuberculosis, with great masses of tuberculous glands . . . tuberculosis of the lungs, and the form called lupus, 'the wolf', because it eats into the skin, forming deep ulcers . . . and outdoor hospital . . naked boys lay in the sunshine, the only thing that the blockade could not shut out, their ribs and shoulder blades showing through their skin, their arms and legs like sticks (there are millions in India continually like that) . . . their midday lunch, a bowl of soup made of coarse meal—12 per cent bran—and green leaves with a few drops of vegetable margarine . . . the terrible 'turnip winter' of 1917 . . . children of three years who had never been able to learn to walk, boys of thirteen

and fourteen who were little old men, shrunken and weazened." Freda Kirchwey, the editor, publishing this in the *Nation*, Dec 14, 1940, apologizes for so doing and insists that this starvation blockade must be carried out more widely and effectively this time. To such degradation has a liberal journal in a Christian land come to endeavoring to maintain morality and civilization.

"The starvation period of Central Europe due to the blockade and its criminal extension during the period of wrangling over the spoils of war shows the effect of insufficient nutrition upon the development of the body. Apprentices in Vienna, measured in 1919 and 1921" showed a difference in height of up to 3 centimeters and weight up to 3 kilograms, says Franz Boaz, in his "The Mind of Primitive Man". (cf 1938 Handbook of Private Schools by Porter Sargent)

(5) "Will Europe Hunger This Winter?" asks Peter Drucker in the *Sat Eve Post*, Nov. 30, 1940. "Goering, Goebbels and Himmler seem to think that hunger will mobilize public sentiment in the defeated countries against the British blockade, so that French, Norwegian, Belgian, Dutch and Danish people will come to regard Germany's fight against Britain as their own fight against the threat of hunger and starvation."

THE THREAT TO OUR 'CIVIL LIBERTIES'

Coming events cast their shadow before. "A group of representative citizens", college presidents, trustees, lawyers, industrialists, and the like, "discusses the vital question of U. S. international relations", in the Fifth Round Table, on which Raymond Leslie Buell, as editor, reports in the January *Fortune*.[1] To old fashioned Americans who believe in democracy and free speech, their conclusions are startling. (Our own questionings are interpolated in parentheses)

"Although democracy's most vital tenet has been freedom of speech,[2] democracy has always presupposed agreement on certain moral values . . .[3] such as the existence of certain individual rights that the majority could not overturn (How can this be interpreted but as referring to the right to do with "what is one's own" regardless of the welfare of the majority?) as well as on intellectual and moral standards that gradually work in the direction of truth. (How can a standard work toward truth? How can one work in the direction of truth without uncovering untruth?)

"During the past twenty years many intellectuals have contributed to the undermining of these values by their debunking of nearly every aspect of American life[4] (Does this refer to the so called "muckraking" which brought to light political and other abuses, graft and privilege?

Should similar abuses be kept hidden and secret?) and by creating an attitude of mind (Does this mean an inquiring, investigating attitude of mind?) that may play into the hands of totalitarian ideas.[5] Some Americans are so eager to keep out of war that they do not hesitate to distort the issues involved (Does this mean challenging the idea that the war is for religion, morality and civilization, rather than for power?)

"In the opinion of the Round Table this mental atmosphere—this propaganda of disbelief . . . may bit by bit undermine the assumptions of democracy (By democracy do we here mean "representative government" as it is?) unless it is changed   The often expressed uncertainty as to the validity of our past institutions (Slavery?   Protective tariffs?) as well as the existence of any ideological issue (?) in the present world crisis creates a spirit of disillusionment that may finally lead many to grasp at the false dogmas offered by the totalitarian religions.

"To obtain unity against a foreign danger a democracy must inevitably curtail discussion;[6] a sense of peril demands sacrifice, particularly in respect to civil liberties, in order that the nation may survive." (*Fortune*, Round Table, Jan. 1940)[7]

Such unity as Great Britain achieved by resort to a 'National Government' in 1931 is justified only when there is "a real imminent threat to the safety of the nation", the Boston *Transcript* comments editorially, Jan. 5. Such unity is a threat to the people. In Great Britain since 1931 there has been "a weakening of English democracy". France is today a dictatorship ruled by decree.[8]

We, too, are failing to face and solve our problems and threatened with the failure of our democracy. We may become fascist by fighting fascism, as Huey Long prophesied. It was this failure of the socialistic republic in Germany that brought disaster and that resulted in unity under a dictatorship which we so dislike and hate.[9]

Now if ever is the time for open discussion,[10] for the questioning and challenging of every view and statement that comes to us, lest we soon find put over on us, as planned by numerous bills now before Congress, a "national unity". As the *Transcript* commands, "Let us crab every act we do not approve". (cf Bul #26)

President Roosevelt, in his address to Congress, January 3, reiterated his call for "national unity", and he warns of those "seeking to muddy the stream of our national thinking, weakening us in the face of danger.

We must combat them as we would the plague. We cannot afford to face the future as a disunited people Some in our midst have sought to instill a feeling of fear and defeatism in the minds of the American people". Roosevelt has scared us with enemy submarines on our coast and in the same speech pictures us "in the face of danger".[11]

Hull, Dec. 31, N. Y. *Times,* spoke of "the remarkable degree of unity shown by the American people . . the absolutely necessary basis for keeping the nation strong within . . . providing the conditions under which this country can make its appropriate contribution".[12]

Lothian, at Chicago a few days later, emphasized "Matters of Common Interest". British-American unity is evidently what both aim at.

In France, the penalty for free speech is the guillotine William H. Chamberlin in the *Chr Sci Monitor,* from Paris, Jan 31, tells of a still sterner decree to penalize rumors, what the French call 'bobards' The Japanese have a better way of suppressing "dangerous thought",— thousands of articulate thinkers have been immured incommunicado for the duration. In China they lop off their heads,—which prevents their further use.

Our administrative and industrial heads, crudely emulating Hitler, apparently would be better satisfied with a million heads with but a single thought, all pulses that beat as one, all hates that blaze as one.

When the Senate acts favorably on the Smith Bill which passed the House last May, these Bulletins previously planned "To Keep America Out of War" will become unlawful, subversive. But their purpose is not pacifist. It goes far beyond Hating no peoples and admiring most, it seems to me desirable to stop waste and abate hate, to enlarge understanding through better descriptions of events, and to begin at home. So these Bulletins will be continued "To Save America First".[13]

Borah was girded for the fight.[14] A few days before his death he wrote expressing interest in these Bulletins and desire to help toward the expense. Now we must carry on with his colleague Johnson, his disciple Nye, and other brave and free men [15]

Write American Civil Liberties Union, 31 Union Sq West, N. Y. C for information on: The Omnibus Gag Bill (Smith Bill, H.R. 5138), The Military Disaffection Bill, The Sedition Bill. Send for: "How To Keep America Out of War", by Kirby Page, Box 247, La Habra, Calif , 96 pp , 15c, 12 for $1.00 "Memo on the Movies, 1914-1939", by Wini-

fred Johnston, Cooperative Books, Norman, Okla., 68 pp., 50c, 6 for
$2 00. (Startling in its revelation of propaganda, and the forces and
money behind.) [16]

February 3, 1940

NOTES

[1] *Fortune's* trial balloon seems to have achieved its purpose. In the succeed-
ing year, the suppression first in our universities and later in our everyday life of
long accepted American doctrines of individual freedom of thought and speech
has gone far. And the courts have ruled that freedom of speech is a "qualified
and not an absolute right" (N.L R B , Ford Motor Co. case).

[2] "Never in history has liberalism been in such peril of total eclipse as at
the present time" remarks William Henry Chamberlin in *American Mercury*,
Dec. 1940. "J. Edgar Hoover of the FBI" claims "the time is rapidly approaching when as a nation we must choose between the welfare of the great masses of
Americans and a few interlopers who hide behind the Bill of Rights while they
undermine the nation."

Our Administration is rapidly coming to assume that those who are not with
them are against them Fines and imprisonment are in prospect for those who
"decrease confidence in the government". That is necessary for Germany perhaps. In the system toward which we are trending which Harold D Lasswell
designates as "The Garrison State" (*American Journal of Sociology*, Jan , 1941),
"problems of morale are destined to weigh heavily on the mind of management
It is easy to throw sand in the gears of the modern assembly line, hence, there
must be a deep and general sense of participation in the total enterprise of the
state if collective effort is to be sustained. . . . The use of coercion can have an
important effect upon many more people than it reaches directly; this is the propaganda component of any 'propaganda of the deed'. . . . The duty to obey, to
serve the state, to work—these are cardinal virtues in the garrison state."

[3] "Democracy was a reflex and result of the Industrial Revolution, of the
rise of businessmen to wealth and influence. Some civil rights—like those of
Magna Charta—had been born with expanding commerce, and had antedated
machine industry, but those rights had been confined within a narrow class and
range Freedom of competition brought on . . . a hectic rivalry. Liberty and
equality, once allies, became enemies, when one rose, the other fell; the strong
called for liberty, the weak for equality, and the strong won." (Will Durant,
"Self-Discipline or Slavery", *Sat Eve Post*, Jan. 18, 1941)

[4] The keynote here sounded was taken up by MacLeish, the President's
appointee as Librarian of Congress, who led the chorus of those singing for the
favor of the President and the pro-British. "The Poet of Capitol Hill" is shown
to be an ideological turncoat by Morton Zabel in *Partisan Review*, in the first two
issues of 1941. (cf Bul #92)

[5] "Totalitarian ideas" so labeled are feared, but totalitarian practices are
rapidly being adopted by our Administration. (cf Buls #38, 92, 93, 97) We

preach democracy and practice totalitarianism as was prophesied long ago by Long. We have quarantined Americans against German and Russian ideas, scientific and technological as well as political. European scientific publications no longer reach this country Our libraries and scientific institutions are having them held in storage in Europe. This quarantining of our scientists and thinkers against foreign ideas would seem to show great lack of confidence in our democracy and the ability of our learned men to withstand any other influence. It might indicate to a psychiatrist that unconfessed to ourselves we have doubts. We don't defend gravitation, we believe in it because we are satisfied it works.

The fear of 'ideas' is a revival of the medieval fear of the Church which has survived in Japan where the government organizes police efforts and private societies to suppress dangerous thoughts The Tokugawa shoguns for more than two hundred years succeeded by forbidding communication with the outer world. But since Commodore Perry broke through the ban, western ideas have brought change rapidly.

This obsessive fear of 'ideas' comes out in William Allen White's recent editorial in the Emporia *Weekly Gazette.* Approving the "lease-lend" and "all aid", he writes, "Don't answer back that Hitler can't cross the ocean He can't cross the ocean with tanks and guns but he can cross with ideas, with an economic set-up, with governments gone Socialist or Nazi, filled with hatred of our democracy, forcing us to economic isolation. In that way wars are generated "

(6) In the current diplomatic game of bluff and counter bluff, "any true and realistic comment", says Hugh Johnson, Sept 30, 1940, "on actual military conditions not designed to bolster any American bluff is branded as appeasement. If matters get much hotter, it will soon be branded as treason"

And in a similar strain, laments H. L. Mencken (Baltimore *Sun,* Sept 29, 1940), "Once the war that the Hon Mr Roosevelt is now carrying on de facto becomes war de jure, all that remains of free speech will vanish as certainly as it vanished under Wilson, and the rights of the citizen in that department will be reduced to the right of the howling 'Ja'."

(7) The most straightforward presentation of civil liberties today is given by Wendell Willkie in "Fair Trial" in the *New Republic,* March 18, 1940. He was making a case for the public utilities, and so he could tell what otherwise would have been labeled 'red'. "You may hate Nazism as much as I do. But even a Nazi is still entitled—in America—to fair treatment under the law. If a member of a chamber of commerce, for example, had misappropriated $500, there would have been no such exposure of the victim and no such punishment" as was applied in the case of Fritz Kuhn. "The charges finally came down to a matter of $500 of Bund funds which he had unlawfully taken—although the Bund gave him unrestricted power over expenditures and apparently did not care about the $500. Kuhn was sentenced to from two and one-half to five years in Sing Sing. The most notorious defaulter of recent years received only five to ten years in the same penitentiary for stealing several million dollars."

Earl Browder "was arrested and indicted for swearing falsely on a 1937-38 passport application that he had never had a passport before. He was found guilty of this false swearing and sentenced to two years on each count and a $2,000 fine. Judge Manton received only two years and a $10,000 fine for selling justice. . . . If you truly believe in protection of civil liberties you will wonder whether Browder was sentenced to four years in jail and a $2,000 fine because he made a false statement on a passport application or because he was a Communist Party member."

(8) Unity of thought through suppression of unpleasant truths was perhaps more successfully carried out in France than in any other country. "Censorship and traditional military reticence combine to blur the picture, good or bad In France, only a week before Paris fell, a wave of desperate optimism swept the country, electrifying even the indifferent French workers" (*Time*, Sept 9, 1940). The former Paris correspondent of the Manchester *Guardian* in an issue in July, 1940, designated the censorship as contributing greatly to the French collapse. "The censorship did not merely suppress unpleasant truths but it encouraged pleasant falsehoods. . . . The result of it was eight months of perfect complacency followed by a fearful shock."

(9) Jonathan Daniels, in the *Nation*, Jan 18, 1941, tells of an AP dispatch from Hattiesburg, Miss , reporting the finding of "the body of Private Alton Beans" in an unoccupied tent. "It was sent by train today to Ravenna, Ohio. Camp Shelby sources refused further information " Comments Daniels, "There are enough such cases to indicate that a good many military and naval men—by no means all—regard the free press of a democracy as undesirable. . . . Some military men are using their power to suppress news in a manner which suggests that some of them have learned more from Germany than methods of mechanized warfare."

(10) Says Senator Holt, "If one delivers a speech against war, I doubt if he could even get the story into the classified advertising section of certain newspapers But if one says that we should go to the aid of the Allies or that we should go to war, immediately he gets front-page headlines. I ask my fellow Senators to check the financial background and tie-up of the newspapers which are so actively interested." And Sen. Wheeler adds, "Not only would one get headlines in the newspapers but his picture would be taken and circulated all over the United States through the motion picture theaters of the country."

(11) Mr. Roosevelt over eight years has "seriously undermined the foundations of popular rule in America. But the forms of democracy still exist," the N. Y. *Herald Tribune* remarks editorially, and calls for vigilance in testing the President's intentions.

"The Pattern for War Is Repeated" Villard tells in The *Christian Century*, Jan 22, 1941. "When war comes there will be the same mobbing of all who dare to stand out against the President's policy, but it will be worse this time because President Roosevelt is now setting the example. These words he used in his message to Congress 'The best way of dealing with a few slackers or troublemakers in our midst is, first, to shame them by patriotic example, and, if that fails, to use the sovereignty of government to save government'. Such words are unprecedented in our history It was the first time that a President of the United States has threatened to use the power of the government in peace-time to suppress criticism and dissent—this in a democracy!"

The prophecies of Mark Twain in his "The Mysterious Stranger" a generation ago have now been twice repeated,—"I can see the loud little handful—as usual —will shout for the war The pulpit will—warily object—at first; the great, big, dull bulk of the nation will rub its sleepy eyes and try to make out why there should be a war, and will say, earnestly and indignantly, 'It is unjust and dishonorable, and there is no necessity for it!' Then the handful will shout louder.

"A few fair men on the other side will argue and reason against the war with speech and pen, and at first will have a hearing and be applauded, but it will not last long; those others will outshout them, and presently the anti-war audiences will thin out and lose popularity.

"Before long you will see this curious thing; the speakers stoned from the platform, and free speech strangled by hordes of furious men who in their secret hearts are still at one with those stoned speakers—as earlier—but do not dare to say so. And now the whole nation—pulpit and all—will take up the war cry, and shout itself hoarse, and mob any honest man who ventures to open his mouth; and presently such mouths will cease to open.

"Next the statesmen will invent cheap lies, putting the blame upon the nation that is attacked, and every man will be glad of those conscience-soothing falsities, and will diligently study them, and refuse to examine any refutations of them, and thus he will by and by convince himself that the war is just, and will thank God for the better sleep he enjoys after this process of grotesque self-deception "

"The Coming of War" as familiarly pictured two generations ago by Leo Tolstoi, author of the great epic "War and Peace" has since been many times repeated,—"The editors of the daily press will begin virulently to stir men up to hatred and manslaughter in the name of patriotism, happy in the receipt of an increased income. Manufacturers, merchants, contractors for military stores will hurry joyously about their business, in the hope of double receipts.

"All sorts of Government officials will buzz about, foreseeing a possibility of purloining something more than usual

"The military authorities will hurry hither and thither, drawing double pay and rations, and with the expectation of receiving for the slaughter of other men various silly little ornaments which they so highly prize, as ribbons, crosses, orders and stars.

"Idle ladies and gentlemen will make a great fuss, entering their names in advance for the Red Cross Society, and ready to bind up the wounds of those whom their husbands and brothers will mutilate, and they will imagine that in so doing they are performing a most Christian work.

"And when the number of sick, wounded and killed become so great that there are not hands enough left to pick them up, and when the air is so infected with the putrefying scent of the "food for powder" (that even the authorities find is disagreeable), a truce will be made, (the wounded will be picked up anyhow, the sick will be brought in and huddled together in heaps, the killed will be covered with earth and lime, and) once more all the crowd of deluded men will be led on and on till those who have devised the project; weary of it, or till those who thought to find it profitable receive their spoil." (Tolstoi)

(12) "The unity idea is a pro-war idea and its wet nurse is the Creel-like Council of Democracy" *In Fact*, Dec. 2, 1940, is informed, and quotes a report of the Council,—"The Research Department should be responsible for investigating reports of subversive activities made either by affiliated groups or directly through the mail, and for proper presentation of this data to the FBI or other governmental agency".

In Fact, quotes also Committee's executive vice president, Douglas Auchincloss, "If the American people are to maintain their right to make the United States into a better political, social and economic society, the tremendous slumbering spirit of American democracy must again be re-awakened, strengthened and mobilized   by a non-governmental, non-political organization analogous to those 'Ministries of Public Information' or 'Enlightenment' in the totalitarian regimes."

Following close on the heels of Paul Mallon's near debarment from White House press conferences, comes information (*Chr Sci Monitor,* Nov. 12, 1940) that cancellation of one of President's regular bi-weekly conferences "on the ground that 'he had no news to offer' " caused some degree of consternation. "The function of the White House press conference, in the view of Washington correspondents who have seen many presidents come and go, is not merely for the President to 'offer news', but for the correspondents to question the President on matters of public interest". News handouts, take it and like it, are not yet wholly acceptable to the ace reporters in Washington.

(13) The task is to save us from fascism here   Mencken sets the stage (Baltimore *Sun,* Sept 29), "Thus we move toward totalitarianism in fact if not in name.   The United States becomes indistinguishable from Roosevelt, just as Germany is indistinguishable from Hitler, Italy from Mussolini, Russia from Stalin, France from Petain, and the Latin-American 'republics' from their xanthous despots.   Such is 'social progress'   Such is the doom of democracies "

(14) "I have got strength 'enough for one more good fight", said Senator Borah, lying on his couch under a blanket in his Senate office a few days before his untimely "death blocked plans   to wage a new national campaign for a foreign policy .   . safer than President Roosevelt's".   "It may take another bath in blood to teach this country", he said, but "he hoped to write into the Republican platform this year a plank . . . for a hands-off policy toward the present European war".   (AP, Jan. 21)

(15) Walter Davenport in *Colliers,* February 15, 1941, on "You Can't Say That —America's Imminent Censorship and How It Will Work", says, "The present plan is to sell the war to the masses.   The sales campaign will glorify ship launchings, military parades, camp festivities, naval displays.   But revelations of strikes, sabotage, and laggard production will be discouraged—at best minimized".   The

President in a conference a few days later lectured the reporters on ethics, morals and patriotism, for the publication of news in regard to U. S airplanes having been sent to Singapore. February 26, 1941, AP, Lowell Mellett, his aide, in charge of these matters, appeared at a House hearing to advocate an appropriation of $1,500,000 to put his bureau on a permanent basis.

(16) See also these two items—Roscoe Pound on the "Twilight of Liberty" in the *Nation's Business*, August, 1940, reviewing how our civil liberties were won and where they had been lost, L B Milner, "Freedom of Speech in Wartime", *New Republic*, November 25, 1940, recalling the hysterical, irrational and savage legal actions in the last war.

THE COMING RED DRIVE

A red drive is preparing, events plainly show. We are headed for a great round up. The last great red drive followed the last war. Our Quaker Federal Attorney General Palmer had been worked up by the Creel propaganda to a high state of hysteria.[1]

In Boston in 1920 hundreds of deputies between midnight and four A.M. routed from their beds over 1500 suspects and huddled them into the corridors of the court house and other public buildings. It took days to sort out those who were to be deported or indicted, and to permit the innocent to return to their homes.

The new red drive which is to bring the hysteria that will put us into the war gathers momentum. The Dies Committee prepares the way,—pillorying and persecuting unorthodox groups. An enormous number of investigators have been added to the Government secret service payrolls Headlines and sensational newspaper items stimulate volunteer spy hunters.[2]

Attorney General Murphy has declared the government will fight "the purveyors of hatred, the provokers of division and strife". This echoes the President's "We must combat them as we would the plague".[3]

With this growing hysterical hatred, it is no longer necessary to be fair or just. The flimsiness of the charge on which Browder was convicted has been revealed only in *The Nation* and *Newsweek*. The latter, Jan. 29, says, "He had written 'none' after the words: 'My last passport was obtained from.' On that charge, America's No. 1 Communist was indicted last fall for fraud. . . ."

Time reported, Jan. 22, "Last week . . . the chief of the G-Men, John Edgar Hoover . . . an author of no mean capacity . . . had a whiz of a plot . . . terrific . . . a scheme to sweep aside New York City's 18,000 police, bomb a Jewish newspaper office and the Communist *Daily Worker*, wipe out all the Jews, seize U. S. Government gold in Manhattan, sabotage and then commandeer public utilities, set up a U. S. dictatorship. . . . The props included twelve Springfield rifles . . . a collection of soup and beer cans with accessories for turning them into bombs." Hoover "rounded up . . . 18 . . . charged them with conspiracy against the U. S. Government".[4]

Laughed at by the newspapers, Hoover changed the charge to intended sabotage, "hinted that the charge might have been used principally as a means of holding the men". (*Chr Sci Monitor*, Jan 17)

Yankee Governor Aiken of Vermont, no red or red baiter, declared, "The war . . . was a Godsend to the group now controlling the Government. They have used it as a smokescreen. . . . Washington added fuel to this smoke fire in all kinds of ways. The White House saw submarines off Cape Cod. Only yesterday we saw the front pages covered with scareheads about the arrests of 17 men who plotted to overthrow the Government. . . . We have an Atlantic Ocean between us and the war in Europe, but we haven't 3000 miles of water between us and Washington "

Aiken charges the government by such measures is attempting to increase the war fever and "to teach a lesson to other citizens who feel like criticizing the Government. . . . There are indications that some people are becoming afraid to speak out for fear of reprisals. You see what happened by dropping of partisanship in Germany and Russia. Now above all times men and women must speak out freely what they think about the way the Government is conducted in this country "

The President's desire to quarantine us from aggressor nations is proving effective. Only propaganda reaches us. The Russian bookshop is closed, the 'Friends of the Soviet' disbanded, such meager information as we have been getting, shut off. Ignorance is the ground out of which hate grows.

Scientific periodicals now, as during the last war, are cut off from us. The Smithsonian Institution, Washington, which customarily acts as a clearing house for foreign exchanges, has forwarded no periodicals since August, 1939. The War Documentation Service, Philadelphia, R H Heindel, Director, tells us that a Joint Committee on Foreign

Relations, N Y. Public Library, has arranged for foreign agents to hold in storage scientific and scholarly periodicals that cannot be forwarded because of the embargo.

The Harvard Phi Beta Kappa, usually heard from only at Commencement, through Paul Olum, first marshall, pointing to recent actions limiting academic freedom at Harvard and other universities, is undertaking a national drive for an "intellectual defense fund" (Boston *Herald,* Dec. 10). "The Harvard chapter 'is communistic', the Rev Francis E. Low, S J., of Boston College said yesterday afternoon in an address before the Boston College Club of Cambridge He urged those present to use their influence in asking new appropriations for the Dies committee" (Boston *Herald,* Dec. 11).

N Y. *Times,* Dec. 24 (UP), reports that Martin Dies said continuance of his "investigation ultimately would result in the 'deportation of no less than 7,000,000 aliens employed in American industries.' "[5]

Anti-alien bills are flooding Congress. Four have already passed one branch and are awaiting action in the other (house). The Hobbs Bill, H.R. 5643, would imprison indefinitely aliens who cannot be deported. "The guns of reaction are booming", announces the Civil Liberties Union, 31 Union Sq West, N.Y.C.

"The first and greatest sacrifice which a nation in arms requires of its citizens is the sacrifice of reason itself", remarks John Kelly in the *Commonweal,* Dec. 29, 1939, in a "Reply to Jacques Maritain"

This was exemplified by the case in 1917 of a man who "was sentenced to a long term of imprisonment for stating his belief that the Supreme Court would declare the Draft Act unconstitutional". ("Wartime Censorship in the United States", *Harpers,* Jan., 1940) [6]

Watch the acceleration of the red drive. There are few 'reds' The idea is to scare the 'pinkos' and the 'fellow travelers', to put the fear of God into the unorthodox.[7]

Beware the release of dramatized stunts, atrocities, already prepared in the propaganda factories as in the last war, to further arouse our emotions and enlist those who stand for 'right' and 'justice' [8]

February 9, 1940

NOTES

(1) "In 1918, D. T. Blodgett of Iowa was sentenced to 20 years for circulating a pamphlet calling on the voters of the state not to reelect a congressman who voted for conscription . The producer of a movie, 'The Spirit of

1876', which portrayed scenes in the Revolutionary War, got 10 years because some of the scenes were unflattering to the British army . .   Herbert S Bigelow, a pro-war liberal, was kidnapped and horse-whipped 'in the name of the women and children of Belgium.' "   These are a few examples of the war hysteria cited by H. R Fraser in The *Townsend Weekly,* reprinted in The *Progressive,* Jan. 4, 1941. He goes on to say "the present Attorney General of United States, Robert H. Jackson, was in 1917-18 a citizen of Jamestown, N Y , vice-president and general counsel of the Jamestown Street Railway Co." and "director and general counsel for the Jamestown Telephone Corp.   Jackson opposed sending our boys to Europe. . .   felt the sting of insinuations .   . slights and rebuffs.   But he stood his ground."

(2) June 6, 1940, AP, "President Roosevelt requested $6,558,800 to reinforce the Federal Bureau of Investigation and other Justice Department units responsible for dealing with subversive activities".   The President "said he concurred in the department's expectation 'that there will be a great number of prisoners to be handled' ".   Attorney General Robert H Jackson, denying that the Justice Department contemplated "a mass drive or wholesale arrests" requested 500 additional agents, "$500,000 additional for salaries and expenses of United States marshals".

Prisons are for the trouble makers, the unadjusted, those who are behind their times and those who are ahead of their times,—men like Gandhi, Kagawa, Niemoeller, Eugene V Debs, John Brown, Thoreau, Thomas Paine, William Penn, John Bunyon, George Fox, Cervantes, Socrates, Peter, Paul, Jesus. All these were punished for heterodoxy, for non-conformity   How those who punished them must cringe today as the imps of hell drive the red hot irons deeper into their livers. H. G. Wells answered Thomas Lamont's question "What will you be doing ten years from now",—"I will probably be in an asylum for the sane". Thoreau, in the Concord jail for refusing to pay taxes to a government that spent the money to return slaves, visited by Emerson who asked "Why are you here, Henry?" shaking the bars of his cell shouted, "Waldo, why aren't you?"   And in his cell he wrote his essay, "Civil Disobedience" which has since shaken the British raj to its foundations   Gandhi learned of it through Tolstoi and arriving for the round table in London, stepped off the boat with a copy in his hand.

Churchill, in his farewell to Lord Halifax, referred to him as one "in whose heart there burns the fire of resistance to aggression and oppression, and whose sympathies and nature make him the sincere and undoubted champion of justice and freedom".   This was the same man who put Gandhi and 47,000 Indian patriots in prison when he was viceroy

September 10, 1940, AP, J. Edgar Hoover of the FBI told Rev Owen Knox, president of the Civil Rights Federation, who had written that action of his agents "makes it dangerous to individuals to express ideas" that "it is time to draw a line of demarcation between liberty and license".

(3) " 'Potentially Disloyal Persons' Kept Under FBI Surveillance" headlines the *Chr Sci Monitor* in a dispatch from Washington, Jan 25, 1941   The FBI now has a personnel of 15,000 and Atty. Gen. Jackson says is working with other

divisions of the Justice Department, field offices of the Immigration and Naturalization Service and United States Marshals and Attorneys in every judicial district and with the Naval and Military Intelligence, maintaining surveillance of fifth column elements, spies, saboteurs or other "potentially disloyal persons",—to whom? to what? "The FBI can cryptically announce: 'We know them.' "

(4) A three-page story of J. Edgar Hoover's activities in the past twenty years, was given in *Uncensored,* Feb. 17, 1940. "Hoover was head of the General Intelligence Division from 1919 to 1924, when . . it compiled biographies, according to the Attorney General's report in 1920, 'of all authors, publishers, editors, etc , showing any connection with an ultra-radical body or movement", including Justice Stone, Senators Wheeler and Borah, Dean Roscoe Pound, Felix Frankfurter, John L. Lewis. "The FBI has now been granted $10,000,000 for the next fiscal year " In September, 1939, the FBI organized a 'General Intelligence Division', the activities of which were described by Hoover in November before the House Appropriations Committee He told how there had been "compiled extensive indices of individuals, groups, and organizations engaged in these subversive activities . . . or any activities that are possibly detrimental to the internal security of the United States". (*The Nation,* March 2, 1940, "Our Lawless G-Men")

Hoover's methods of operation were dramatically demonstrated the other day in Detroit when he chose five o'clock in the morning as the hour to rouse twelve reputable citizens of Detroit from their beds and bring them into court in chains on charges the Attorney General several days later dismissed " (Photographs of this were published only in 'radical' papers)

Senator Norris, *Congressional Record,* Feb. 26, 1940, attacked our "American Ogpu", and *New Republic,* March 11, 1940, had an article "Investigate the American Ogpu" telling the story of our FBI and its illegal acts. In the same issue, John T. Flynn answers the question, "Who's Behind Hoover". "When J. Edgar Hoover runs a Gestapo . . . the blame is so clearly traceable to the President that there can be no equivocation about it."

(5) Congressman Dies, out for a $1,000,000 appropriation for his committee, January 25, 1941, made an alarming appeal in the eloquent Huey Long style for suppression of the terrifying dangers that threaten us internally.

Solicitor General Francis Biddle, in charge of registering three and a half million aliens, told them that they will "be required to tell what organizations they are affiliated with" and "what is their general attitude toward democracy". If they were native-born free-thinking, free-speaking, free-swearing, old-fashioned Americans, they would let out a string of expletives in reply. Or if they were philosophically inclined they might reply that their "general attitude toward democracy" was that there wasn't near enough of it

(6) An essential step toward totalitarian dictatorship is the elimination of those who might warn against it America is filled with refugee writers from Germany but a similar process is going on here Among the columnists who have been eliminated because they were not singing in the dominant key have been Dorothy Dunbar Bromley and Ernest Meyers of the N Y. *Post* and Harry

Elmer Barnes from the Scripps-Howard chain   Oswald Garrison Villard, former owner and editor of the *Nation* was obliged to withdraw his contributed page, and John T. Flynn, brilliant economist and author, similarly found his position on the *New Republic* impossible.   Lawrence Dennis in his *Weekly Foreign Letter*, Jan, 1941, explains the situation on the latter in the *New Republic*. And so the dissident voices are gradually stilled   *Unity*, Jan. 6, 1941, remarks, "Our newspapers and magazines are competing with our colleges and universities for leadership in the campaign for war."   H. L. Mencken's Sunday editorials disappear from the Baltimore *Sun* after February, 1941.

(7) Commonwealth College at Mena, Arkansas, for 17 years sought to bring education to the ignorant share croppers of the neighborhood and aroused the enmity of the landowners and employers. Charged with Communism, anarchy, it was frequently attacked, raided   August 30, 1940, the college closed and transferred its assets to the New Theatre League   In September the director of the college was arrested, charged with "anarchism", the property confiscated and sold at auction   "They drove off our dairy herd (24 head), two teams of mules, and hauled away our office fixtures, our dishes and cooking utensils, and other goods   Yesterday afternoon, during a downpour of rain, they snatched books by the thousand from the library, threw them into an open-top truck, the floor of which was covered with what would have been coaldust if the rain had not made lava of it . . ."

Highlander Folk School at Monteagle, Tenn is another school that according to the *New Republic* "prepares efficient spokesmen for labor" which are not desired by "the vigilant leaders" of Tennessee   It, too, is under fire though one of the sponsors is Eleanor Roosevelt.

(8) Bulletin #36, February 9, 1940, gave a list of the Bulletins issued to that date and immediately projected, adding "No charge is made for these Bulletins   Originally sent to personal friends and educators, as the list lengthens it becomes necessary to cut off those who have not responded or cooperated. We are in the war now   Last year we gave billions for European armaments, including Russian, chiefly through gold buying. To 'defense', which helps the Allies, we gave more billions. We are getting in deeper   These Bulletins are not to express opinions or to present all sides, but to reveal what is generally unknown or unrecognized. By uncovering untruths, it is hoped to slow down the growing hysteria and to do something to save America first."

INTERNATIONAL INANITIES

A Washington internationalist writes appreciatively of "your gay attacks on current idiocies". The show goes on,—a continuous performance (1)

Just as the 'red drive' is gaining momentum, Sen Lodge is unkind enough to charge the Administration with aiding and arming the Soviets against the Finns by exports of copper, rubber, tin, and oil, increased from 3 millions in July to 10 millions in December. The

N.Y. *World-Telegram,* Feb. 9, carried a two-column article with photographs, maps, and a list of steamships engaged in this trade.

With all our sympathy for the Finns, the loan has lagged. Congress was inclined to let the bankers raise the money, but the bankers knew it was not a good risk,—not even to sell to the public. Now as the weather permits the Russian steam roller to get under way, Roosevelt insists on more money. He "scraped the bottom" of the Export-Import Bank to give them ten millions, though only a few have been used.

"The Administration knows that this loan is essentially futile. . . . The people may fancy that we are about to provide tangible help to the Finns; the Administration knows better . . . Is it wanted because it might operate to break down public resistance to the extension of credits? . . . It should be the duty of House members to smoke out satisfactory answers before the Finnish loan is approved" (Boston *Transcript,* Feb. 15)

England has long promised help while waiting for American money, now lets it be known confidentially (Pearson and Allen, Feb 15) that three divisions of "Allied troops" are preparing to bolster the Finns,— one Canadian (cf Bul #30), one Polish (cf Bul #24), and one French

Meantime Uncle Sam may turn an honest? penny selling old World War rifles to the Swedes to re-sell to the Finns An AP dispatch reports, Feb. 8, that President Roosevelt so proposed to Swedish Crown Prince's son Bertil, here to make purchases. The Johnson Act may stand a little longer (cf Bul #32), for the British have arranged (Paul Mallon, Feb. 16) for 170 million pounds of American tobacco on credit.

Scolding the Youth Congress "like a grandfatherly Tory", the President said, "The most absurd thought that I have ever heard advanced in the 58 years of my life" was that the U S S.R. might go to war with us, and that we should go to war with them was "an equally silly thought". (cf p 23)

Perhaps he hadn't consulted with Mr. Chamberlain or Lord Lothian of late, nor had he listened to Sen. Vandenburg who in September had said, "I frankly question whether we can become an arsenal for one belligerent without being the target for the other. I doubt if it is possible to be half in and half out of this war." (*Time,* Sept. 18)

The silliest thing recently heard was that Under-Sec. Welles, appointed by the President to plan the coming peace, was being sent to visit European countries to "learn" something His Groton-Harvard-State Department conditioning should render him immune. Sen. Clark promptly expressed opposition to sending "roving ambassadors" abroad. Perhaps he remembered the damage done by House and Davis

Under the title of "Pax Britannica", *Newsweek,* Feb. 12, discusses the 'Federation' plan that Great Britain is selling to British labor, and to America through Streit. 'Dismemberment' plans are more popular in France. Maps in *Newsweek* show the present German territories divided into twelve parcels for hungry and vengeful neighbors. 'Atomization', London armchair strategists call it.

The 'imperial tone' and 'highhanded' attitude with which Britain puts it over on the statesmen of "what a World-War, British envoy called the 'sheeplike American People' " led to Hull's 'peppery protests'—for home consumption. "The wave of resentment and anger" died when Hull "expressed hope" (Jan. 30, UP) after talking with Lothian. From London, Feb. 6, we learned all these matters had been "cleared up", while from Rome, (Feb. 7, UP) we heard that mail by American Export steamers and Clipper plane via Bermuda has been twice opened and delayed three or four weeks [2]

"Angry denunciation" of Great Britain's interference with our mail and ships broke out in the Senate again Feb. 15 (AP). In the House, Rep. Maas proposed that warships carry the mail to prevent the British from examining it to get cost data and business information so that they could underbid us in the world's markets, as they did in 1914. He recalled that the first American ships sunk in the last war "were sunk by the British—not by Germany".

To placate our susceptible Washington officials, Great Britain offers to convoy American ships, which they divert to their contraband control bases, as forbidden by our President's proclamation (N.Y. *Times* dispatch, Feb. 15) Pearson and Allen, turned humorists in their column (Feb. 8) told us State Department officials were peeved "Don't be surprised if the searching of American ships by the British brings on searching of British ships by the Americans."

Try as they may, neither Roosevelt nor his State Department can completely please their British imperial masters, who are contemptuously indignant at our American shortcomings Not only is it our fault that Britain had to go off the gold standard as Beaverbrook complains (cf Bul #33), but it's also due to us that Britain's war is not coming on as it should. We don't properly cooperate in enforcing her blockade, and our 'Neutrality' Law isn't fair to British shipping.

But her "most unkindest cut" to Welles and Roosevelt was a jab below the 'Neutrality Belt', while the twenty-one American "republics" were in session at Rio de Janeiro devising new "keep off" signs. Bluntly, Britain informed the Americans that the zone was a myth, illegal from the standpoint of international law, and could have no influence on Britain's conduct of the war. "Britain must be certain the zone would not be used to deprive the Allies of their fruits of superiority at sea", the British note declared.

But the 'Neutrality Belt' has been a source of entertainment for the President, who "follows the movements of all the destroyers, Coast Guard vessels and plane carriers that make up the patrol . . . Sometimes he plots patrol movements himself and suggests an order to . . . Edison or . . . Stark" (Alsop and Kintner, Jan. 13). And now, Feb 15, he is mysteriously off into the thick of it, as he says to the "Cheruble Islands", perhaps as rumor again says, to meet Mussolini at the Azores.

The Japs never 'declared' their 'independence', but they show spunk It was not merely the government but the people who protested at the British destroyer's removing the 29 German sailors under the shadow of sacred Fuji. Britain was obliged to surrender in part,—and the protest goes on,—though America does her part for Britain. Our Adm. Yarnell, urging embargo, said Feb. 10, "It is a question of principle, and what the effect of our action may be is immaterial."

The Athenia has become of legal interest. It's a matter of damages. The lawyers want to know who's to pay. Harried State Department officials are studying the affidavits of more than 100 Americans, no one of whom claims to have seen submarine or torpedo. If sunk by a "Nazi undersea craft", it would be possible "for the State Department to ask damages of the German government" for Americans on the Athenia. If due to "an internal explosion or a floating British mine", then action would lie against the British Donaldson Atlantic line or the British government. (N. Y. *Times* dispatch, Jan. 27) [8]

Britain's up in the air, but not very effectively. 2350 captive balloons, costing $5000 each, require twenty men and a lorry,—a total of about $12,000,000 and 47,000 men. The Germans refuse to get entangled. So far this barrage has interfered with only one civilian plane, which crashed into it killing both occupants. (*Newsweek*, Jan. 15)

Sir John Gilmour's appointment as Minister of Shipping, derided in an English journal as the most astonishing since Emperor Caligula made his horse a member of the Roman Senate, roused resentment in English shipowners when this man with no knowledge of shipping announced that on Feb. 1 all deep water ships would be requisitioned. (*News-week*, Jan. 15)

The Germans may eat crow. But the French will eat horse. Arrangements have been made for shipping from Boston "at least 2000 horses a month . . . total . . . probably . . . 70,000 . . . for war purposes" (Boston *Herald*). This is to be supervised by the Animal Rescue League. This recalls Remarque's description in "All Quiet" of a horse, torn by a shell, starting to run and getting tangled and thrown by his trailing intestines.

Borah's death was greeted by the *L'Ordre* (AP, Paris, Jan. 20) with the statement that the loss of the Senator, whom they said had denounced France as a "constant menace to peace", "does not diminish in any way our position in the United States. All to the contrary".

Bon mot of the week comes from *Chr Sci Monitor* editorial, "Titles of nobility become symbols of democracy",—speaking of Lord Tweedsmuir. Let college presidents and D T.s who wish to make this a "holy war" read the Koran. Mohammed had the secret. Up to four captives could be retained as wives, and warriors who fell in battle against the 'forces of evil' were guaranteed four houris in a perfumed garden.

The most extravagant contemporary attempt to attain the ne plus ultra in chauvinistic glorification is perhaps that of the veteran editorialist J. L. Garvin in the London *Observer*, Jan. 21, 1940, "This war in the moral sense is the greatest of wars. The Allied cause is true and glorious in the Miltonic sense. It is a war for European freedom and for the rights and hopes of man in all the world." He may have felt the challenge of the late British poet H. Wolfe:

> "You cannot bribe or buy or twist,
> "Thank God! The British journalist;
> "But when you see what he will do
> "Unbribed, there's no occasion to!"

February 16, 1940

NOTES

(1) Jan 21, AP, "Moscow broadcast the threat that Russia would declare war on the Finns unless they returned weapons 'stolen' from Red army troops guns and tanks captured by the Finns".

(2) Secretary Lansing tells in his "Memoirs" how "seized American business letters were copied by the London Board of Trade and passed around to British business men who thus learned U. S trade secrets and got an edge on their U S. competitors". Today the gentle protests of Mr. Hull are for home consumption, as were Mr. Lansing's in the last war, for as he later explained, " 'there was always in my mind the conviction that we would ultimately become an ally of Great Britain' and that then 'we would presumably wish to adopt some of the policies and practices which the British had adopted.' " (*Life,* Feb 5, 1940) Mr. Polk, of the State Department, in 1917 remarked to the British Foreign Minister, "Mr. Balfour, it took Great Britain three years to reach a point where it was prepared to violate all the laws of blockade. You will find that it will take us only two months to become as great criminals as you are."

(3) The Athenia claims seem to be pigeon-holed at the State Department and further information suppressed. An AP cable, Sept. 1, 1940, from Berlin, referring to the sinking of a British ship carrying 320 British refugee children to Canada, suggesting a mine and denying the possibility of a submarine, brought this editorial comment in the Boston *Herald,* Sept. 2, 1940, "When the Athenia was sunk by undetermined means at the outbreak of the war a year ago, Germany contended the British sank it with the idea of ascribing the guilt to Germany " In the "Encyclopaedia of World History" (Houghton Mifflin Company, 1940), the revision of Ploetz's famed "Epitome", compiled and edited chiefly by Harvard professors, most of whom show an hysterical provincial pro-British trend, we read, "Sept. 4. Sinking of the British ship Athenia with considerable loss of life. The origin of the attack was never determined "

The State Department was equally secretive in regard to the route of the Army Transport, "American Legion", bringing refugees and royalty from Petsamo Reporters were told "It's a military secret". The British and German governments both knew. It was a secret only from the American people (*Uncensored,* Aug 31) The transport, under Captain Torning, reached Petsamo "via the short and normally safe route near Iceland" and Captain Torning expected to "head home by the same course", *Newsweek* reported Sept 9, and *Time* claimed the President, who has in the past seen submarines where they were not, had knowledge that if they took the northern route a German submarine was to hold them up and kidnap the crown princess. The "American Legion" was directed by the President through the State Department to take a course through the Scottish isles, which the Germans warned was mined.

ON TO DICTATORSHIP

A "modern, stream-lined totalitarian dictatorship" is what we are coming to, Sen. Taft warned a Lincoln Day North Carolina audience.

President Roosevelt, telling the Youth Congress how prosperous the U.S had become under his rule, spoke of the 'absolute dictatorship' of

Russia with a note of jealous bitterness. To these spirited youths without jobs he offered not bread but circuses. He put on his juggling act with figures, his balancing act with the budget. He needs greater dictatorial powers for himself, and puts it up to the naive son of Edison to put this over on Congress, and advances him for trying.[1] A list of over a hundred Acts which delegated to the President powers "not specified by the Constitution", was inserted in the *Congressional Record* at the request of Sen. Wiley of Wisconsin, July 5.[2]

Sen. Vandenburg in September introduced a resolution calling on Attorney General Murphy to report on special legislation which bestowed on the President extraordinary or emergency powers. The Attorney General, according to *Time*, Sept. 18, was "under the strictest White House orders not to talk publicly about the extent of these powers". But after ten days he reported that his staff had not completed the task but had found upward of 100 Acts, some of them dating back to the 18th century, which bestowed emergency powers on the President.[3]

"There is almost unlimited legal authority and precedent for any steps the Chief Executive might wish to take in confiscation of property,[4] suppression of liberties, and commandeering of public opinion As far as the letter of the law goes, he could even send a 'Punitive Expedition' to Europe so long as no formal declaration of war—which must be made by Congress—was involved." (*Time*, Sept. 25)[5]

A leading Washington journalist is now writing an article on the President's powers. These "Emergency Powers" are analyzed in a special 3-page supplement to *Uncensored*, Dec. 23. A list of such Acts, with extended analysis running to several pages, has been published as "Blank Check Powers of Presidency" by the National Committee to Uphold Constitutional Government, 18 E. 48th St., N.Y.C. In preparation for the use of these powers, minorities are being suppressed, organizations disbanded, freedom of thought limited, fear instilled in the people, the 'red' hysteria promoted.

Meantime to whet the appetite of industrialists for M-Day, 'educational orders' to the amount of $43,000,000 have been placed in thousands of plants, and 'sealed orders' for untold amounts in 10,000 plants throughout the country, thus stimulating the newspapers and the people of the small towns to look forward to the M-Day opening of these orders, and prosperity. The old war time boom has come back to Bridgeport and similar centers We are taking the "fool's gold" the President warned us against. But the gold will prove to be more truly 'fool's' than even he then anticipated.

A New York mother writes, "My son in prep school was told in class by the military instructor that executions will be used to enforce conscription in the next war. I think it significant that civil courts relinquished Grover Cleveland Bergdoll to General Court Martial for trial on charge of draft evasion this last year. This firmly established the precedent that a man is subject to military trial and possible death penalty from the moment that his draft card is issued. You will remember that it was never alleged that Bergdoll received a draft card. During the last war seventeen men were sentenced to death by court-martial for refusal to serve in the army. Did you hear about that at the time? I didn't. The sentences were commuted to long imprisonment, but the military power-precedent was established and last.year accepted by civil courts in the Bergdoll trial."

With the closing down on freedom of thought, with the elimination and driving underground of a political party, come the pathological hates characteristic of war psychology, preparing us for totalitarian control and dictatorship.[6]

Feb. 6 (UP), Detroit,—"Federal agents moved again today in the government's campaign to crush subversive activities, arresting twelve reputed Communists and fellow-travelers who are accused of recruiting soldiers for the Spanish Republican Army." Bonds were placed at from $2500 to $20,000 and prisoners held in default. "The indictment was based on an 1818 law prohibiting the recruiting on American soil of soldiers for foreign wars " The Penalty is one or two years imprisonment and $10,000 fine. N Y. *World Telegram,* Feb. 10, reported on the prosecution of the friends and veterans of the Abraham Lincoln Brigade in N.Y.

Brave men sacrificed life, liberty, and the pursuit of happiness for what they believed was democracy, to fight against fascism in Spain. Now their friends are hunted and persecuted At the same time Mr. Roosevelt said it would be all right for American volunteers to join the Finnish war and no obstacle is raised to volunteers going to Canada, France, or England.[7] This is in accordance with the President's sympathies for the British and their imperialistic attitude and is part of the 'red drive' against those who would "muddy the stream of our national thinking" and in the interest of "national unity" of thought.

Feb 16 we learn by AP dispatch, after the above was written, that the previous day, the President having sailed on his mystery mission, Atty. Gen. Jackson halted proceedings initiated by Murphy and ordered dismissal of "indictments at Detroit". He announced that the alleged offenses had occurred in 1937 and 1938, that the FBI investigation had been completed last March, but that no action had been taken till December when one of Murphy's last official acts, just before Roosevelt had advanced him to the Supreme Court bench, was to order a proceeding before the Grand Jury, which returned indictments Feb 6.

The Civil Liberties Union had protested this as "an attempt essentially to punish a political minority for its view under cover of technical violation of the law". Jackson privately had declared, according to *Newsweek* Periscope, Feb. 12, that he would not permit the Department of Justice to persecute minority groups because of political opinions. But it remains to be seen how much one man may be able to do to impede the momentum of the 'red drive' now on.

Vigilance today may yet preserve for a time some of our liberties.
February 16, 1940

NOTES

(1) "America needs strong government; it needs strong leadership to attain strong government; only the president can provide it with the leadership it requires" writes Harold J Laski, the brilliant British economist Mr. Laski spent the academic year, 1939-40, touring and lecturing in this country, authorized by the Foreign Office for, of course, his trip was conducive to enlisting the more radical elements in America to sympathy and aid for the British. Mr. Laski in his book borrowed too freely from W E. Binkley's "Powers of the President" published in 1937 by Doubleday, Doran. To their protest, Laski feebly replies in the *New Republic*, Nov 18. As Walter Millis writes (N.Y. *Herald Tribune*, Aug 4, 1940) : "Professor Laski's formula for the successful working of democracy under modern conditions is to insist upon large powers accompanied by clear and direct responsibility."

(2) Burton Rascoe, in *Uncensored*, Oct. 12, 1940, facing the election, wrote· "The President nowadays enjoys powers that are not conferred upon him by the Constitution and that are a direct violation of the system of checks-and-balances upon which our government was founded Under our Constitution, in Congress alone is the right and function of declaring war invested But there is a lamentable loophole . . . taken advantage of by every president—William McKinley, Theodore Roosevelt, Woodrow Wilson and Franklin D. Roosevelt—who has chosen to do so.

"The loophole is this: The State Department of the United States is the most autocratic body of any democratic or semi-democratic nation in the world, more autocratic than the Foreign Office of Great Britain . . . responsible only to the President and it is administered by the Secretary of State, who is a cabinet appointee of the President. No public or Congressional check can be instituted to invalidate or halt whatever commitments of the United States the State Department has made or is about to make to foreign powers.

"Not until a method has been found to obliterate this loophole and restrict the powers of the State Department will our government function as the Constitution dictates and as the Founding Fathers wished it to function As it is, even aside from the 'emergency powers' which were granted to President Roosevelt when no palpable emergency existed, the President of the United States now has dictatorial powers which are not exceeded by the powers enjoyed by Stalin, Hitler or Mussolini and are infinitely greater than the powers of the Mikado or the Prime Minister of England"

(3) Editorial Research Reports (1013 Thirteenth St. N W , Washington, D C.) issued Sept 12, 1940, a 19-page report on "The War Powers of the President" ($1 00) which deals with "Roosevelt's Defense Moves and War Powers", "Sources of Chief Executive's War Powers", "President's Powers as Commander-in-Chief", "Statutory Powers Delegated by Congress".

"In the conduct of foreign affairs" writes Hubert Herring in "And So To War" (Yale University Press, 1938) "the President of the United States is the most powerful constitutional ruler of our times. For all of the constitutional checks upon him, he exerts an almost absolute power in the area of the greatest national danger. He can, on his sole responsibility, take steps which make war inevitable for 130 millions."

(4) The Detroit *Free Press*, July 30, 1940, editorializes that the bill sponsored by Senator Josh Lee of Oklahoma "is not a wealth conscription but a property confiscation bill. Under it, a citizen who might not have a dollar of cash or income to his name would be subject to confiscatory assessment against whatever property he might possess—his home, his insurance, all his tangible or intangible possessions, regardless of their value and with utter inconsideration for his probable impoverishment."

(5) Hubert Herring, in "And So To War", makes clear again the power that rests in the hands of the President of the United States, who, "by his uncontrolled right to send notes of any tenor, by his right to make speeches which are inevitably interpreted as the expression of the official view of the nation, by his right to grant or to withhold recognition from any new government, by his major hand in treaty-making, by his appointment of diplomatic officers, by his dominance over the State Department, and by his powers as Commander in Chief of the armed forces, can bring about international situations that make war likely, and invite those "incidents" which make war inevitable These rights, added together, give the President of the United States the power to make war "

(6) Senator Henry Cabot Lodge, Jr., broadcasting Sept 25, 1940, calls atten-

tion to the "stories that another deal is contemplated, whereby our navy is to be given the use of foreign naval bases in the extreme far east", and throws out the question "when matters of this kind—any one of which would be a major congressional issue in ordinary times—are settled secretly by the Executive, it is small wonder that American citizens ask themselves; 'if the Executive can do these things without action by Congress, can he not also declare war without Congress?' "

Regarding the trend to war and dictatorship, Hugh Johnson says in broadcast Sept. 5, 1940, "The further it goes the more we shall have to give up every attribute of American freedom and democracy, and the closer we shall approach a war dictatorship which will be as drastic as any known in Germany or Italy", and General Robert E Wood clinches the thought in his statement, broadcast Oct 4, 1940, "The course we are pursuing is bound to involve us in the war "

(7) Editorializing under the title, "Hell Bent For War", the New York *World Telegram,* Oct 18, 1940, says, "the whole world is talking about America fighting .   everybody talks about us getting in .   War today would be murder, suicide, insanity   It would cost us our democracy and destroy the last citadel of that freedom which may some day save the world when this madness is ended."

THE GOLD MENACE

In five years we have bought more gold than existed in the world before 1900. Gold from the African Rand and the Siberian tundra, dug on our standing order, we bury in Kentucky.[1]   Gold we take today, bonds twenty years ago. We have the bonds. We will have the gold

Messrs Roosevelt and Morgenthau may yet be in a worse fix than Midas   How they wish they had never looked upon the glittering stuff

When the U S S R 'Kim' dumped 5 million dollars worth of Russian gold bars at San Francisco February 6, it set off pyrotechnics. The Secretary of the Treasury was forced to admit we had bought Russian stamped gold bars to the amount of 247 millions, direct or through other countries   Considering Lord Lothian's large interest in 'Kaffirs', and Britain's needs, it seems hardly fair to patronize Soviet competitors, even though Morgenthau admitted we had taken 4916 millions in gold bars from the United Kingdom in the same time. (AP, Feb 8)[2]

In the Senate Vandenburg and Townsend had charged the U.S A with financing the U S S R in its war on Finland   They figured a clear profit to the U S S R. of $34 89 an ounce, the 11c difference going for imported materials and advice

J. D. Littlepage, a hardboiled American Alaskan mining engineer, in "In Search of Soviet Gold" (Harcourt, Brace, 1938) tells how Stalin conceived the idea of stimulating production of gold, which has no value in the U.S.S.R , to sell to the capitalistic nations.

The gold problem is being forced upon the attention of the public, and has come into the headlines in the past month, though the book review mediums have studiously ignored the one book on the subject, Graham and Whittlesey's "The Golden Avalanche".

Up to December 1, it had sold 600 copies. Bul #19 on that date and subsequent Bulletins emphasized its important message. Copies were sent to Congressmen and Senators. Mrs. Margaret Stuart Ogilvie of Asheville, N.C., a Bulletin reader, wrote every Congressman and Senator advocating a $15 duty on gold and received a hundred replies. "The Cross of Gold" in February *Events* paraphrases the "Avalanche".

Graham and Whittlesey show that this gold buying policy was adopted as a temporary expedient by the President to raise prices Originally the gold purchased was 'sterilized'. Due to the pressure of the banking fraternity, the gold now passes through the banks, who take their cut, and so constitute a vested interest to continue gold buying.

"The cost of the United States of maintaining our gold policy has thus far been more or less concealed   Our purchases have the doubtful virtue of indirect taxes in that people are largely ignorant of the burden that is being laid upon them." (p 222) Graham and Whittlesey had made it clear in their earlier article in *Foreign Affairs*, April, 1939, that our gold purchases had changed us from a creditor to a debtor nation.

The British Empire and our banks have an interest in perpetuating this gold buying. Authorities agree that the practice is not self-corrective. Roosevelt and Morgenthau dare not face the situation, but console themselves with the knowledge that it helps "the Allies".[3] That it helps Stalin, too, is a bitter pill. And they ignore the fact that the half billion of Korean gold from Japan, with silk, has provided the means to destroy China.[4]

And so more Kulaks are sent to Siberia to dredge more gold with bigger American dredges, and more Negroes are indentured in Africa, forced by higher hut tax, poll tax, wife tax, to dig more gold, a mile and a half underground, in drifts cooled by American refrigerating machines.[5] For the 'dirt' on African gold promotion, Lothian's 'Kaffir' interest, see "Qui Veut La Guerre?" in *La Revue Hebdomadaire*, November 16 and 24, 1935,—astounding revelations of methods of British imperialism.

"Gold Manipulation and Depressions", an economist's-study, with charts and statistical data, published by James True Associates, Washington, D. C., shows how "depressions in the United States have been created and the stock market controlled through gold manipulations".

Winthrop Aldrich of the Chase Bank suggests that we put the gold into circulation. This brought a ray of sunshine to the Treasury, but it was quickly shown that you couldn't put seventeen thousand tons of gold into circulation. The *Sphere,* Feb., 1940, (Whaley-Eaton, Wash., D C.) has a long article on this modern Midas story.

A. A. Berle, for the President, suggests as a way out that the gold be given away. The idea is to bribe neutral nations to be less neutral. In 1923 British economists suggested giving the U.S. all their gold in payment of their debt and then going off gold. Since then we have given them our resources for gold and now we are to give the gold,— which is better perhaps than to continue the expense of guarding it [6]

"To date the Federal Reserve Bank has not taken any position with respect to the various proposals which are being advanced for treatment of the gold problem", H. L. Sanford, Mgr. of the Research Dept., writes in response to my inquiry. In the *Federal Reserve Bulletin* for January, E. A. Goldenweiser, Dir of Research and Statistics, dolefully analyzes the predicament of "the $17.6 billions of gold which is of little or no use to us now". He sees "no simple solution to the problem", but claims, "An abrupt cessation of American gold purchases would create chaotic conditions in the exchange market".

George Clarke Cox in his *Gold Barometer,* Jan. 15, mentions with something of irritation and resentment, as no longer to be ignored, "The Golden Avalanche". His comment is limited to Chapter III, "Why Gold Comes to the United States". Admitting that the policy followed since 1933 "is unsound and dangerous", he makes heavy going in attempting to refute Graham and Whittlesey. Bogging down in a discussion of the effect on exchange, he confesses that his "far from expert knowledge" has been supplemented by that of "real experts".[7]

Professor Graham writes, "Where Goldenweiser's 'Opinions' conflict with ours we, not unnaturally, think that he is wrong. The same statement holds still more strongly about Mr. George Cox's effort which

gives evidence of having been written under the stress of deep emotion.
I am enclosing herewith a copy of my reply to Mr. Cox in which I
hit merely the high spots of the answer I would make to him if I felt
that his statement were worthy of any serious attention."

Last year our payments for gold were over three billions. This
coming year we will buy more. All this will be paid for eventually
by the taxpayer out of American labor and resources. A duty of $15
an ounce would stop it. But it will not be stopped. Many forces have
been enlisted to continue this once little understood 'Subsidy for War' [8]
February 20, 1940

NOTES

[1] The Bank of France storage vaults for gold, eighty feet below the surface
of the rock foundation, were even better protected with steel and concrete than
the Maginot Line and moreover could be instantly flooded   May 31, 1940,
the Bank reported a gold reserve of a value of about 1693 million dollars, most
of which has come into possession of the Reich

Eliot Janeway optimistically prophesied, "Britain has unlimited gold supplies
in Africa, whence gold is mined, shipped over here, buried again in Kentucky,
and regarded as payment for the goods we send her. As long as Britain's gold
supplies are limitless, and our willingness to accept the metal continues, she will
need no credits such as were given her in the World War."

[2] The U S Commerce Department, Jan. 13, AP, reported that gold imports
set a new record for 1940 amounting to 4,749 millions. The peak was reached
in July with more than 500 millions. The flow of Russian gold may be increased
by the lifting of the "moral embargo" by the State Department in January,
1941, in an attempt to cousen Stalin. "That this 'friendly gesture' to Moscow
will accomplish its purpose may be doubted", editorially remarks the Detroit
Free Press.

[3] "This rebellion rolling around the world is also a fight against the rule
of the gold bloc, the last citadel of which is in the Kentucky hills. Gold was
the heavy blood of the empire. But the deep irony of the present conflict is
that most of the heavy blood had been siphoned out before the battle even began
The old-time economy of England was weakened and half-broken before assault
started   Even token payments on the debts, the last salve of honorable conscience, had been abandoned. Curiously enough, the United States, trying to
bolster up the empire, trying to save the gold bloc and traditional financial and
trading methods, helped destroy the system that gold represented quite some
time before the Nazi onslaught. We drained away the blood of France and
the empire   Now it lies congealed in gold bars in our vaults

"Do we imagine, as France foolishly sought to do in the Balkans, that because
of our gold we can buy up Latin America like so many pounds of coffee? That
we can sell goods unless we buy? The fact is, our old weapons of finance capital,

of dollar diplomacy, of the gold standard, of loans and investments have been grounded   Today we are blocked off from most of Europe and the Near East and from much of the Orient, and the uncomfortable feeling is growing that we ourselves may be well boycotted long before we have a chance to boycott anybody else " (Beals, 'Pan America", Houghton Mifflin Co., 1940)

(4) Then shrewdly schemed our Franklin: 'Do not gold and hate abide

'At the heart of my Magic, yea, and senseless fear beside?

'With gold and fear and hate I have harnessed state to state,

'And with hate and fear and gold their hates are tied.' (Apologies to R K)

Our purchases of gold have financed rearmament, not only of England, France and Russia, but of other countries that had gold to sell. Morgenthau admitted to the Senate Sub-committee of the Committee on Banking, March 2, 1939, that he had the power to buy $2,000,000,000 worth of gold at any time. That was supposed to be profit on mark up but there is only one way money can come to our Treasury. That is through taxes.

"The *Daily News* said tonight that the U S. cruiser Louisville brought $250,-000,000 in foreign gold into port .   . last Thursday", AP reported January 25, 1941 "The Louisville 'accidentally met' the King George V .   . outside the 300-mile neutrality zone and proceeded with her to the Virginia capes." This isn't the first time that the American navy has been used to cart in the loot of the British Empire to sell to us.

(5) The 22,000 millions or more of gold that we have in storage is largely an investment in the British Empire   If the British Empire goes under, its value will be greatly decreased   The British made more than the profit on the gold in selling it to us   Purchased for the most part at $35 an ounce, it cost perhaps $11 on the Rand, yielding a large profit to the owners, to the South African government keeping it loyal, to the steamship lines, the insurance companies, the British government in taxes all along the line   It has resulted in maintaining the empire system of indentured labor and continuing the depopulation of central Africa through recruitment, impressment and indenture of black labor kept in barbed wire compounds on long contracts prolonged by fines. Diamonds, produced in the same way for a similar group, pay even larger profits because of the monopoly maintained and the myth promoted that an engagement or a marriage in America is hardly respectable unless the $30 a week clerk pays $100 for a half carat diamond that cost a few dollars to produce   It is notable that the Beit diamond interests of Kimberley have recently increased their American appropriation for advertising

(6) "When you play marbles and the other fellow wins all the marbles, the game ends   You must then think of some new game   When all the gold is in the United States and it doesn't come out again, the world must think of some other medium of exchange " (Dr. Walther Funk, quoted in *Newsweek,* August 5, 1940) (cf Bul #97)

(7) Acres of tripe have been printed by moneyed experts and journalists on this gold subject during the past year. We suggest only a few from a thick

folder: "Gold Marbles", Editorial, *Sat Eve Post*, Nov. 16, 1940; 'Fantasy in Gold" by Rep. A. H. Andersen, *Scribner's Commentator,* and *Congressional Record,* May 9, 1940, "Gold and Its Power" by Rep. J. Thorkelson, *Congressional Record,* Feb. 26, 1940, "A Program for Gold" by B. Graham, *Dynamic America,* April, 1940. Harry Scherman, president of the Book of the Month Club, amateur economist, author of "Promises Men Live By" in "The Real Danger in Our Gold" (Simon and Schuster, 1940), is sure of the value of gold but fears the power of the government.

Much of the literature is in academic language, revealing enormous research, expressed in equivocations, evasions, and straddling, so that it is difficult to dig the nuggets out of the verbiage and to translate it into intelligible English Notable among such books is "The Treasury and Monetary Policy, 1933-1938", by G Griffith Johnson, Jr, (Harvard University Press, 1939). It deals with "Gold Policy", "Stabilization Fund", "Sterilization Policy", "Silver Policy", etc.

"The problem has been to achieve recovery, and to that end monetary policy and monetary instruments alone—such as might be exercised by an independent central bank—have proved ineffective, they could create the money but not the borrowers. . . . The policy now appears to be predominantly opportunist, with implementation in the form of manipulations of the sterilization program, changes in reserve requirements, and Presidential pronunciamentos . . One may, it is true, be skeptical of the wisdom with which the monetary instruments will be used, but the possibility of abuse extends throughout the whole sphere of governmental activity and is a risk which must be assumed under a democratic or any other form of government Contrary to general belief, the risk appears to be no greater in the monetary sphere than in others, and to the degree that the influence of pressure groups is less "

(8) Jonathan Daniels, in his Raleigh, North Carolina *News Observer* in an editorial "All That Glitters", says in part, "Last time, writes Porter Sargent of Boston, the purchasing Europeans paid us with gold bonds. We marked them down We reduced the interest We still have the bonds, not one cent of principal paid. This time they are paying us with gold We now have most of the world's gold, and it is piling up on us. We will soon have practically all. And we will keep it, Mr. Sargent thinks. Nobody will want it. He may be right."

"The Real Danger in Our Gold", Harry Scherman, Simon and Schuster, 1940, is reviewed in the Harvard *Crimson,* February 4, 1941, in part as follows "Uncle Sam is now sitting on top of the highest pile of gold the world has ever seen— nearly 21 billion dollars worth of the precious metal, nearly three-quarters of all the gold in the world. Further, the President by executive decree can fix the weight of the gold in a dollar pretty much as he pleases By raising the value of its gold hoard, the government can make another tremendous paper profit to fill the hole in the budget left by deficit financing. Thus in 1933 F. D. R. made $2,800,000,000, by reducing the gold in the dollar to fifty-nine cents This modern Midas touch, though, would also bring its difficulties Such an increase in government expenditures would multiply the money supply, raise prices, and bring on inflation. Mr. Scherman, who makes no bones about distrusting our 'entrenched bad government,' thinks that the only protection for the common man against these dire consequences is to repeal the Gold Prohibition Act. However, Mr. Scherman has found only one of the numerous Ethiopian tribesmen in our gold pile. The New Dealer's inflation which he fears would at least come by wilful choice; but the tremendous excess reserves now in the banking system could just as easily finance a major boom which both Treasury and Reserve Board would find hard to combat."

OUR FRIENDS REPLY

From the hundreds of letters received, impossible to acknowledge personally, five pages of brief quotes were printed in this Bulletin. Only a small part are here reproduced.

University Presidents Hutchins, Brewer, Kent, Dykstra have commented previously. Others continue to. "If you cut off the bulletins, I shall cut you off in my will!" Isaiah Bowman, Johns Hopkins Univ, Md., Dec. 13, 1939. "Keep my name on your list," James P. Baxter, 3rd, Williams Col., Mass., Jan. 4, 1940. "Read with interest," Alan Valentine, U. of Rochester, Jan. 22, 1940. "Will be useful in my senior seminar in propaganda. Thank you for the fresh, vigorous way in which you state the case. I wish we could get your colorful language more frequently in academic circles," Wm. Alfred Eddy, Hobart Col., N. Y., Mar. 1, 1940.

College people write in appreciation. "Very fine piece of work in trying to make our people conscious of propaganda today," J Duane Squires, Colby Jr. Col., N. H., Dec. 29, 1939. "I feel the need of it as a balance against much that I hear in a contrary sense, and I hope it lasts as long as the war does," Harold J. Tobin, Dartmouth Col., Dec. 23, 1939. "My understanding of current events would be incomplete without them," J. Garton Needham, Simmons College, Mass., Jan. 8, 1940. "Stimulating, provocative and put together in a very pithy manner," Esther Isabel Seaver, Wheaton College, Mass, Jan. 18, 1940. "Valuable contribution to our knowledge of the international situation and methods employed," A. B. Faust, Cornell U., Dec. 30, 1939. "#22 is a 'hum-dinger'," Philip W. L. Cox, N. Y. Univ., Jan. 3, 1940. "Your bulletins are of tremendous importance," Goodwin Watson, Teachers Col., N. Y., Jan. 30, 1940. "You are performing a most important and significant service," O. W. Reigel, Washington and Lee Univ., Dec. 6, 1939. "I am strong for the competent work you are doing," Prof. Harl R. Douglass, Univ. of N. C., Jan. 20, 1940.

College Libraries keep complete files. "I find that the Bulletins are being read here," Bernhard Knollenberg, Yale Univ. Libr., Conn , Jan. 17, 1940. "Hope that we can obtain a complete file, and be placed on your mailing list," K. D. Metcalf, Harvard Univ. Libr., Feb 1, 1940. "Would appreciate having them regularly as they are published," Robert K. Johnson, Pacific Univ. Libr., Ore., Dec. 18, 1939. "Deeply appreciate the bulletins and assure you that they will be of use to our students," Henry T. Buechel, Univ. of Wisconsin Libr , Wis. "Some of your bulletins have been received in the Library from the President's office. For fear that we may not count on receiving them regularly in that way we shall be grateful if you will place us on your mailing list," Lawrence Heyl, Princeton Univ. Libr , N. J "The bulletins have reached this Library through one of our teaching members. If you wish to send them to me direct for the Library, I should be glad to cooperate," R W. Noyes, Syracuse Univ Libr , N. Y. "This type of news-bulletin is much in demand among students," Robert Lang, Oberlin Coll Libr., Ohio.

Private school people, principals and teachers, have expressed appreciation. A proportionate few are quoted. "I shall be very glad to receive these Sargent Bulletins. With a great deal I do not agree but I am always glad to read the other side," Lewis Perry, Phillips Exeter Acad., N. H., Nov 23, 1939. "Keep going and shoot the works," F. Dean McClusky, Director, Scarborough School, N Y., Nov. 30, 1939. "The most lively reading that crosses my desk," Allan V. Heely, Head Master, The Lawrenceville School, N. J., Dec. 1, 1939 "Fascinating, trenchant, and informative," Edwin C. Zavitz, Headmaster, Friends School, Md , Dec. 8, 1939. "Deeply indebted for your provocative bulletins. You are doing a very great public service and one that is especially necessary at this time," George S. Hamilton, St. Paul's Sch., Md., Feb. 5, 1940. "Continue to keep firing away with both barrels, not even troubling about the 'whites of their eyes'," Joel B Hayden, Western Reserve Acad , Ohio, Jan. 5, 1940.

Public school superintendents, principals, and teachers have written for these Bulletins, many explaining that they are displayed and read in the library or used in schools. "By all means continue to send your admirable material. The more you can reach the better," Joy Elmer Morgan, N.E A., Washington, D. C., Nov. 28, 1939.

"Much of the information seemed so incredible that it was hard to believe it authentic. I have taken the trouble to write a person of national reputation. He stated he was sure your purpose was one of true American enlightenment," E. B. Burroughs, Ill., Jan. 22, 1940.

Journalists and publicists of leading weeklies and newspapers have editorially mentioned or reprinted these Bulletins. " 'You are throwing light where it needs to be thrown'," Mrs. Dorothy Dunbar Bromley, *N. Y. Post,* Jan 6, 1940 "Most interesting and stimulating. I am pleased to be on your mailing list," Joseph J. Thorndike, Jr., *Life,* Jan. 10, 1940. "They· are provocative, informative," Edward L. Bernays, N. Y., Feb. 17, 1940. "I enclose my check . . . to help get out your very valuable bulletins. I have a boy at stake, as well as some sense of decency," Benjamin C. Marsh, D. C., Jan. 23, 1940. "Tremendously interesting and provocative," Jonathan Daniels, The *News and Observer,* Jan 12, 1940.[*]

Authors and professional men were quoted extensively previously. "By all means continue the bulletins. I enclose a small cheque to keep hold the fort of intellectual honesty and Yankee common sense," Henry Beston, Mass., Feb. 2, 1940. "Again and again impressed by the value of your bulletins. If we can have more like it there is a chance we can keep America out of war," Jerome Davis, Conn., Dec. 16, 1939. "You are doing a swell job," Norman Thomas, N. Y, Dec 23, 1939. "A magnificent example of Yankee independence and courage. Keep it up as an inspiration to all of us to be honest and fearless," Will Durant, Fla., Dec. 29, 1939.

Army and Navy Officers, active as well as retired, express appreciation "Your bulletins have put new hope into my heart. I believe every word you have written because I know what you write squares up with the facts," D. E. D. Dismukes, Rear Admiral, U.S.N. Ret, N. H., Jan. 21, 1940. "Could distribute some to advantage. I enclose check to be used to further effort to prevent our involvement in this war," Claude Bailey, Lt. Comm., N. Y., Feb. 7, 1940.

Senators and Congressmen, more than 100, have received these bulletins. Many have responded approvingly. "Glad to hear your opinion on various pertinent questions which confront us and I feel that I gain considerable from studying your views," Sen. Arthur Capper, Jan. 9, 1940. "Interesting and provocative," Rep. Bruce Barton, Jan. 3, 1940. "Send me a complete file," Sen. Rush D Holt, Jan. 18, 1940. "Read with interest," Sen. Charles W. Tobey, Jan. 5, 1940. "Certainly value your bulletins. Your point of view seems to be exactly the same as mine," Rep. George H. Tinkham, Nov. 21, 1939. "Enjoyed your bulletins," Rep. James E. Van Zandt, Jan. 6, 1940. "Impossible to wade through all material which comes but your bulletins are brief and extremely interesting on subjects that interest me," Rep John M. Vorys, Jan. 12, 1940. "Saw in *Time* an account of your 'Bulletin'. Should like to have," Late Sen. William E Borah, Dec. 26, 1939.

From East to West people write in appreciation. "From time to time, I would like to send you a small contribution for the great American cause you are so finely and ably defending," The Misses Faxon, Mass., Jan. 9, 1940. "More people like you are needed to spread information to correct stupid prejudices of the public and to combat the evil warwork of the administration," Mrs. Paul R. Pope, N. Y., Dec. 30, 1939. "Of the publications interested in the current international situation, yours seems to have progressed furthest in its desire to seek truth," William W. Remington, N. Y., Jan. 15, 1940. "Keep blowing away the smoke screen so we can see the boys in action," Paul E. Richter, Pa., Jan. 3, 1940. "I admire what you are doing in a country where intelligent patriotism is so rare," Margaret Stuart Ogilvie, N. C., Jan. 3, 1940. "It's like going without some essential, like a cup of coffee in the morning, when I don't have your peppery messages to read," Steve Bradley, Idaho, Feb. 13, 1940. "I hope they will grow into a publication," Myles Connolly, Calif., Feb. 13, 1940 "Invaluable in clarifying statements and events. Keep your mid-Atlantic periscope facing Eastward!" Lloyd Morain, Calif., Dec. 28, 1939.
February 21, 1940

NOTES

Bulletin #46 included excerpts from letters from members of Congress and Judiciary and acknowledged interest from Senators Borah, Capper, Holt, Lodge, Nye, Reynolds, Shipstead, Tobey, Wheeler, Walsh, Bridges, Clark, Danaher, Frazier, Lundeen, Downey, Vandenberg, Barbour, LaFollette, Overton, Townsend; Representatives Tinkham, Luce, Schafer, Treadway, Van Zandt, Vorys, Barton, Fish, Ludlow, McCormack, Shanley, Casey, Dies, Martin, Lemke, Whittington, Gilchrist, Brewster, Holmes, Wigglesworth, Austin, Clason, Voorhis. Only a few are here reproduced. "Thanks for your exceedingly interesting and illuminating enclosure," Sen. Arthur H Vandenberg, Jan. 2, 1940. "Glad to have your views and to give them my serious consideration," Sen. Burton K. Wheeler, Jan. 3, 1940. "Read with much interest some of your bulletins and I shall be glad to have them continue   I am particularly concerned over the gold problem," Rep. Ralph O. Brewster, Mar. 22, 1940

These Bulletins appeal to the judicial mind accustomed to weighing evidence. Many members of the bar and bench have written. "I have been receiving and read with interest the Bulletins on the conflict between the Allied and Totalitarian Powers," Judge George A. Eberly, Nebraska, Mar 11, 1940. "I have appreciated receiving Bulletins," Judge Bayard H. Paine, Neb, Mar 23, 1940.

Bulletin #47, "Voice of the People" quoted from more intimate letters from our readers. A few showing keen appreciation are here reproduced.

"Read your 'Bulletins' with great interest and gratitude. . . . You pinch balloons, but you always put something of substance in their place. You do reveal what is 'generally unknown' and 'unrecognized'," Mrs E. D. Johnson, Conn, Mar. 19, 1940. "Dynamic, timely, invaluable describe your bulletins. I had dug similar information out of our few honest and courageous sources Americans need at their disposal. Please know that we will be telling our audiences over the radio at public meetings, and in our newspaper, of your great work and spreading the truth just as hot as you dish it up," Frank Marquette, Calif, Mar. 15, 1940. "Very instructive and enlightening," Miss Fredrika M. Parks, Me, Mar. 3, 1940.

Bulletin #48 warned readers to "Beware of 'Every Effort Short of War' " and increased spending, suggested pertinent things to read and do at that time, and quoted Congressman Tinkham who in a release April 29 brought out, "startling new evidence . . . convincing proof that continuance . . ." of Roosevelt and Hull "means war for the United States". Tinkham claims the Administration's assertions as to their "intent" to keep us out of war are "mendacious and intended to deceive the American people"

OUR SECRET ALLIANCE WITH GREAT BRITAIN

"Evidence that President Roosevelt and Secretary of State Hull have been guilty of collusive action" in entering into a fifty year secret alliance with Great Britain in the Pacific was presented in a statement Feb. 19, 1940 by Rep. Tinkham, for twenty-five years Congressman from Massachusetts. The N. Y. *Post* and Ehrlich in the Boston *Herald* reported this, though apparently AP and UP failed to do so.

An agreement for "joint activity" in the Orient, the late Eugene J. Young, long cable editor of the N. Y. *Times,* pointed out in his "Looking Behind the Censorships" (Lippincott, 1938) has been in existence since the London Naval Conference of 1935-6. "On all important

questions London and Washington should consult each other . . . but
in all cases Britain must take the initiative. . . . Because of the secrecy
with which all proceedings there (the Orient) have been surrounded,
particularly American secrecy, the realities have perhaps not been appreciated." [1]

Why should such knowledge be suppressed in this country while in
England it is boasted about? [2]   Such alliance is referred to with confidence in Lord Lothian's scholarly quarterly, the *Round Table*, Sept.
1939 (cf Bul #7). From this same anonymous article, perhaps supervised by Lothian just before he came over, we quote further:

"In the event of a threat of war, President Roosevelt . . . will ex-
haust every possible effort to tell the dictators that the power of the
United States will be to some degree opposed to them. If war is actually precipitated, President Roosevelt will call a special session of
Congress . . . and will seek the practically guaranteed repeal of the
arms embargo clause. The full . . . resources of the United States
would then be at the disposal of Great Britain and France. The probabilities . . . are that the history of 1914-17 would be foreshortened
and repeated. The United States would be watching Asia. The fleet
continues to be concentrated in the Pacific . . . plenty of reasons for
anxiety at Tokyo. Thus is the United States doing her bit, taking care
of her assignment, in the informal and unofficial alliance of the democracies." (cf Bul #95)

"Anglo-American Collaboration" in "Anglo-Japanese Relations" is
treated in an accompanying article recognizing "the traditional objection of the United States to any commitments in the nature of an alliance". But there is a "parallel action . . already . . a substantial
measure of agreement". "It is true that we are more concerned than
is America with the protection of specific commercial interests." [3]

Some years before, the U. S , surveying a route for the Trans-Pacific
Clipper, had under consideration for stations Canton and Enderbury
Islands. Then followed a chain of incidents, the significance of which
has never been fully revealed. Quoting from Tinkham's statement.

"In March of 1937 the British Government took formal and legal
possession of these islands. A year later, after our State Department
had had secret correspondence with Great Britain, the United States,
according to the press, seized the islands . . . which act in itself was

an act of war, without some previous understanding with Great Britain." This dramatic act for the American people concealed the "secret negotiation with Great Britain", and in August, 1938, a "joint communique . . . announced that the two governments had agreed to set up a regime for the use in common of these islands". And the same month President Roosevelt at Kingston, Ontario, guaranteed the defense of Canada.

In April, 1939, "an agreement respecting the joint control of the two governments over these two islands" was revealed. Ostensibly this was "for civil aviation", with "the provision whereby the two governments may secretly agree to use the islands for any other purpose".

This joint control involved joint defense in case of attack. "Such an arrangement constitutes not only a political alliance, but what is more, a military alliance." "No such arrangement with any other nation" exists, and it has never been submitted to Congress, although it is to run for fifty years and is equivalent to a treaty with a foreign power.

"This alliance was closely followed by our notice to Japan of termination" of the 1911 trade treaty. This action on the part of the President was to head off a similar move on the part of the Republicans. There was no consultation with England, at which they complained (cf Bul #7). The *Round Table* writer whines, "They did not even let Downing Street know ahead of time. News cables .   . carried . . . British disappointment at not having been forewarned. .   . It is important to record that President Roosevelt and Secretary Hull were not trying to startle the British   They were trying to be helpful   It is definitely hoped (American) action will take some of the pressure off Great Britain in China . . . and thus be indirectly helpful in Europe " (*Round Table*, Sept.)

The *Round Table* writer, in the December issue, goes on to say that American "Far Eastern Policy may serve to prevent a Russo-Japanese deal which would be catastrophic to British interests in the Orient". But if Russia wins Japan, it is hoped "the United States will accept Far Eastern responsibilities a bit more fully, and thereby ease pressure on Britain". And Lord Lothian's *Round Table* prays for a third term and the continuance of Roosevelt's foreign policy as the salvation of British interests in the Far East.

Coincident were the increased appropriations for American fortifications in the Pacific, joint war maneuvers of British and U. S. vessels at Singapore, withdrawal by Britain and France of the majority of their China garrisons, leaving Japan "fulminating against the U. S. in its role of watchdog". (*Time*, Dec. 11, 1939) [4]

"The United States is being deliberately entangled in Asia for British political purposes. British economic interests in Asia are ten times greater than those of the United States", Rep. Tinkham declared, and with his statement he released a letter dated July 25, 1939, from Legal Adviser Hackworth of the State Department, in which he said: "Without the consent of the British Government . . the exchange of communications with Great Britain with respect to Canton and Enderbury Islands could not be made available for your inspection"

Tinkham, one of the few old fashioned free-thinking, free-speaking Americans left,[5] replied: "Prior to 1913 . . . we published everything, and . . . we were in a position to do this freely because we had no secret commitments. A country in which secret engagements are made, which are not to be disclosed to the legislature or the people without the consent of the other party, is necessarily living under a dictatorial regime. The acceptance of such a situation . . . demonstrates that the legislature has abdicated its functions. It seems to me that there should be an independent and thorough examination of the transaction in question by the Congress."

Tinkham concludes, "The making of secret commitments which cannot be disclosed to the people or to the officials of the Government is the policy of dictators. Pres. Roosevelt and Sec Hull make a fateful mistake if they believe that when loyal Americans . . . obtain control of this Government there will not be an investigation of this political alliance and of other political commitments made in the interest of Great Britain."

Has there been a secret alliance in a hundred years that eventually redounded to other than the disgrace of those who were involved? The memoirs of Wilson, House, Lansing, Page, the Americans who were responsible in 1918, reflect no credit upon them. The memoirs of the British propagandists like Masterman, Parker, Earl Grey, Arnold Bennett, H. G. Wells, who put it over on us, give no evidence of respect for their American confreres.

Little wonder that Lloyd George impatiently declared that "if the people knew how they were ruled they would rise in rebellion", and that Voltaire is said to have remarked that "people will continue to commit atrocities as long as they continue to believe absurdities". The truth of the latter was proved. The former is yet to be.

What a field for investigation centers about the unknown events of 1937-38, when Vansittart was building his new secret propaganda organization, and Roosevelt turning to the "fool's gold" which he had spat upon. But will the history departments of our universities or our endowed peace societies be interested? No, they will not touch it, if you can depend upon their record in the past. They fail us in time of need. As H. G. Wells tells us of a previous crisis,—

"There were the universities, great schools, galaxies of authorities, learned men, experts, teachers gowned, adorned, and splendid. This higher brain, this cerebrum, this gray matter of America was so entirely uncoordinated that it had nothing really comprehensive, searching, thoughtout, and trustworthy . ., . to go upon. Organized information and guidance . . . wasn't there. And it isn't there now."

The academic chair holders, the bureaucrats of the foundations, will not take a chance nor take a risk. Their curiosity is killed. They are cautious and wary For the security of the subservient they have sacrificed their liberty, as Mark A May, Director of the Yale Institute of Human Relations, recently remarked. Again they will gather round the carcass at the next peace conference, if there is any, with "uncoordinated bits of quite good knowledge, some about this period and some about that, but", as Wells remarks of the last peace conference, "they had no common understanding whatever".

"I suppose Mr. Maynard Keynes was one of the first to open our eyes to this worldwide intellectual insufficiency", remarks Wells (*Harper's*, April, 1937). "What his book, 'The Economic Consequences of Peace' practically said to the world was this,—These people don't know anything about the business they have in hand. Nobody knows very much, but the important thing to realize is that they do not even know what is to be known. They arrange so and so, and so and so must ensue, and they cannot or will not see that so and so must ensue. They are so unaccustomed to competent thought, so ignorant that there is knowledge and of what knowledge is, that they do not understand that it matters."

And so Americans today are kept blinded, ignorant, because of syco-
phants in our universities, who talk about 'morality and religion' and
'saving civilization', while they destroy freedom of thinking in their
own faculties and kill curiosity in their undergraduates,—and because
of hypocrites of our national Administration, lapping at the boots of
the British Tories, fooled by the skilled, politically trained, hard bitten
Vansittarts and Lothians, who cannot but hold us in contempt [6]

If this be an "expression of opinion", something we usually avoid,
then let us add to it this article of our faith, that—if the American
people were informed, not deceived, they could be depended upon to
act more wisely than their rulers and foolers.

March 6, 1940

NOTES

[1] An editorial, "War Before Preparedness?", Boston *Transcript,* Aug. 22,
1940, referring to John T. Flynn's remarkable little book, "The Country Squire
in the White House", says "Mr. Flynn is authority for the statement that in the
latter half of 1937 Mr Roosevelt secretly proposed to London a joint Anglo-
American blockade of Japan, not merely a blockade by propaganda, but a
blockade by naval force; that he wanted Britain, France and Soviet Russia to
join him in the use of armed strength for the economic strangulation of Germany and Japan; that it was Britain which balked, and that this is the explanation of Mr Roosevelt's 'Quarantine Speech'."

[2] Anthony Eden told Parliament on Sept. 21, 1937, "We are constantly and
daily in close consultation with the Government of the United States. Over
and over again, we have taken either parallel or similar action and that in itself
is an indication of the closeness of such collaboration." A little later, Feb 12,
1938, Lord Plymouth told the House of Lords, "The British Government has
been in constant consultation with the Government of the United States in connection with events in the Far East. Action has been taken independently, but
it has almost invariably been along parallel lines."

Gilbert Murray, chairman of the League of Nations Union, the same month
in an address to the National Liberal Club, said, "We have given the American
Government assurance that we are ready to support them in any action which
they may take facing any risk The trouble is that it was a confidential communication of the government that most people here do not know of and the
great American public does not know it or believe it for a moment." Winston
Churchill reported in a speech, March 7, on the close cooperation of the American and British navies (cf also Raymond Moley, "After Seven Years")

"Ambassador William C Bullitt caused a sensation at a city hall banquet
here tonight by declaring France and the United States were 'indefectively united
in war as in peace' " Bonnet praised this speech and two days later in a public
address declared, "I have been moved but not surprised recently to hear your

countrymen declare that if France were again attacked they would come again to her defense." (N. Y. *Times*)

(3) The March 1938 issue of the *Round Table*, more than a year and a half before the outbreak of the war, said, "The President and his foreign policy advisers   . are promoting a strong and positive policy . .   of political collaboration with the democratic nations   As to the Far East   some of them are talking freely of a possible Anglo-American naval blockade—a step that is miles beyond what public opinion would support in anything like its present mood   There is a great deal of other movement which would be more disquieting if it were known to isolationist opinion.   The President's discussions with his naval officers have definitely dealt with the possibility of a long-range blockade of Japan.   Through representatives, he has been in closest touch with the British Government   Capt. R. E. Ingersoll, Chief of the War Plans Division of the Navy Department, spent late December and early January in London, conferring with the Admiralty.   His outward mission was to find out what is happening technically in British naval construction.   But a mission of even more importance to both Governments, it may safely be assumed, was to discuss the possibility and ways and means of naval cooperation in the Far East   Captain Ingersoll's unheralded visit . . . has no .   precedent in Anglo-American relations.   When the general public comes to know of these goings-on, opinion may well take fright, reasonably or not   A certain mistrust of President Roosevelt's foreign policies has long been brewing, particularly among some of the more ardent New Dealers who believe that overseas adventuring gets in the way of domestic reforms"

(4) "The new Axis-Japanese mutual defense pact . .   is a kick-back from secret covenants being negotiated between the Roosevelt administration and Great Britain with regard to Oriental policy and proposals for the use by the United States of British Far-Eastern bases, such as Singapore   Just as England had hoped to salvage her own Far-Eastern interests as a result of an exhausting conflict between Russia and Japan, she now turns to the United States to accomplish the same end " (Carleton Beals, "Pan America", Houghton Mifflin Co , 1940)

(5) George Holden Tinkham, affectionately known as the "Tink", has for 25 uninterrupted years been Representative from the same Boston district   Usually he spends electioneering time big game hunting but has been returned with increasingly large majorities.   He is an old fashioned, red blooded American, who fights before the drop of the hat for the rights of the individual, his own or any other.   He was the only Representative in Massachusetts to vote against conscription and "was to last year's final tax bill, a lone dissenter, 358 to 1" (cf illustrated sketch in *Life*, Dec. 16, 1940).   The Congressman figures that his ancestors came to this country to get away from the English kings and sees no sense in the U. S 's backing up onto the same old flypaper again.   In 1933 he accused Nicholas Murray Butler of being 'seditious' because of his activities as head of the Carnegie Endowment for International Peace.   'There will be no peace on the American continent', cried Mr. Tinkham, 'unless he retires to England or fights the second battle of Bunker Hill.'

In 1937 Tinkham cabled Hull from Geneva "that Congress should upon re-assembling 'seriously consider the impeachment of the President and yourself for high crime and misdemeanor'." In 1938 he again took Roosevelt to task for approving the Italo-British agreement and accused the President of follow-ing the lead of Great Britain in foreign affairs. 'The course which he (the President) followed in this instance', said Mr. Tinkham, 'is what would be expected of a high commissioner of a British-mandated territory, the governor of a British crown colony or the governor general of a British dominion'. (That was three days before Roosevelt went out to sea to meet Halifax, a member of the British Cabinet and who a newspaper correspondent described as 'not too high powered mentally'. And ten days later, Halifax was actively calling, lobby-ing, with Chairman Bloom and Chairman George of the House Foreign Affairs Committee for the speedy passage of the 'lend-lease' bill. Patriotic American organizations protested and demanded that Halifax be thrown out of the country and Feb 3 Representatives on the floor of the House rose in rebellion and denunciation of Bloom's obsequiousness in the face of Halifax's vilipendency)

January 16, 1941 (AP), Tinkham was still leading the attack declaring that Roosevelt and Hull had "betrayed the American people" through four "overt acts" in "committing the country to war". They "have plotted against the peace and safety of the United States by knowingly and designedly committing the United States in advance to active participation in the present wars of Europe and Asia". Tinkham declared that his mouth "is one that shall not cease to open as long as breath remains in my body".

George Bernard Shaw expressed himself equally bravely twenty years before "The secret treaties which followed were not even announced. In short, for purposes of foreign policy the British Empire is governed by the Foreign Office and not by Parliament. Parliament is supposed to be able to refuse to vote supplies, and thereby have the last word in the matter.

"What is more, the Americans and English, being relatives, have a power of hating one another that no strangers could attain. Throughout the whole nine-teenth century there was no bad blood between the Germans and the English. they were allies and friends. During the same period there was continual bad blood between the Americans and the English: the closely related blood feud between England and Ireland was hardly less cordial." (Shaw, "What I Really Wrote About the War")

(6) "The diplomacy of the Roosevelt administration had brought the United States to a position in which it did not have a single point of support among the great powers of the world, save Great Britain, in her dire distress This was 'isolation' with a vengeance and in the circumstances amounted to an alliance with Great Britain, real if only tacit, which was likely to be brought into play at any moment by events in Europe or Asia or both. This was the position prophesied by the London *Saturday Review* in 1898, when the commissioners of the United States at the close of the war with Spain were sealing the im-perialist adventure in the Philippines: 'The American commissioners at Paris are making their bargains, whether they realize it or not, under the protecting

naval strength of England, and we shall expect a material quid pro quo for this assistance [to the United States]. . . . Above all we expect her assistance on the day which is quickly approaching, when the future of China comes up for settlement.' . . . The assistance thus publicly mentioned in 1898, had been forthcoming in 1917 and the prospects of 1940 were clear in tendencies, if not yet in outcome." (Beard and Smith, "The Old Deal and the New", Macmillan, 1940)

FINLAND'S DEBTS AND CREDITS

"Finland always pays her debts",—this is so constantly reiterated that it impresses some as propaganda to improve credit standing in furtherance of additional loans.[1] Now that Finland faces Poland's fate, our sympathy goes out to the people being sacrificed.

$139,035.96 appears to be the total amount that Finland's debt to the U. S. has been reduced since it was originally contracted in 1919. A. D. Peterson, Assistant Commissioner of Accounts and Deposits, Treasury Department, Washington, D. C., responding to my inquiry, writes Feb. 27, "The original indebtedness of Finland was $8,281,926.17. . . . As of December 15, 1939, Finland has" made payments on the interest and principal "leaving the total amount of its indebtedness $8,142,890.21". The difference, a decrease, is $139,035.96.

In 1923 "the indebtedness as funded was $9,000,000 including the original principal amount of $8,281,926.17 and accrued interest of $718,073.83," Mr. Peterson writes. "The statement that advances to Finland after the World War amounted to $18,000,000 is not correct".[2] The 18 millions (Bul #22) some writers mention would approximate the amount of the balance due compounded at 5%.[3]

The Finnish Information Center, Fifth Avenue, N. Y. emphasizes in a release that Finland is one of the least debt burdened countries in Europe, and Finland's handsome Minister emphasized at the N. Y. *Herald Tribune* Forum the low debt, making Finland appear a good risk New York bankers recently appealed to did not consider Finland a sufficiently good risk to float a private bond issue to sell even to the gullible American people and Finland's 5% and 6% bonds have been quoted recently on the N. Y. Exchange at from $22 to $40.

England and America have a large stake in Finland, as brought out in *Economic Notes*, Jan., 1940, of the Labor Research Association, which I understand from Benjamin Marsh who reprinted some of it in *People's Lobby Bulletin* ($1 yearly) is written or supervised by Robert W. Dunn, a Yale graduate, who published, about 1926, a book on American Foreign Investments. Quoting from the *Notes*:

"Finland borrowed from other countries, including the United States, Great Britain and Sweden, during the years 1920-38, a total of over ten billion finmarks or about $204,082,000. These loans to the Finnish government did not include short-term government borrowing corporate loans or direct investments in Finnish corporations.

"In 1939 there has been a further increase in Finland's foreign indebtedness 'due to the necessity of financing the cost of armaments as well as other capital expenditure.' (N. Y. *Herald Tribune,* Sept. 3, 1939). Sweden extended to its neighbor another loan for defense.

"Finland's . . . government loans from this country totaled $32,-100,000 (net face value) at the beginning of 1936. These long-term portfolio loans (paying interest of 6% to 7% or more) include new loans extended in 1930 ($8 million) and 1934 ($5 million). These are the publicly-offered Finnish government, state and municipal loans, represented by bonds in the hands of American bondholders, and sold here through the National City Co. They do not include short-term private loans made by American bankers." England floated a $5,-000,000 loan at 6% in 1923 and a smaller one in 1920 and at the end of 1937 held Finland's bonds to the amount of over $55,000,000

Americans have invested $12,000,000 and Britain $5,000,000 in the Industrial Mortgage Bank of Finland The International T & T (Morgan) owns and operates Finland's telephone system, the International Nickel Co. of Canada its nickel mines. Thirteen American corporations have branches in Finland with investments of $1,643,000 (U. S. Dept. of Commerce). The Ford Motor Company of Finland, est. 1926, reported net profits of $130,000 in 1938. Thirteen American investment bankers seek relief for the Mannerheim-Ryti government N Y. *Times,* Dec. 9, describes them as having " 'close business dealings with Finland and its Prime Minister, Risto Ryti', a British knight, governor of the Bank of Finland which dominates the financial affairs of Finland." (*Economic Notes,* Jan., 1940) (Bul #22)

It is on the President's insistence that the Export-Import Bank, which was established to stimulate trade, has granted $30,000,000 to the

Finns, $15,000,000 to Sweden, $10,000,000 to Norway, and perhaps $10,000,000 to Denmark.[4]

Jesse Jones, apparently disgusted, said that not all of the first $10,000,000 to Finland had yet been allotted. "He insisted, in effect, that it was not his business what Finland did with the automobiles, lard, peas, oil, cotton, soap and other commodities purchased with the money advanced by the bank. He had heard nothing of a report that the Finns were swapping lard bought in this country with Export-Import Bank funds for British arms. 'We've lent them the money and we can't follow it across the ocean.' " (Boston *Herald,* March 1, 1940)

These credits go through London, but how far we will learn later Submerged in propaganda, we know little. Any old fashioned American whose curiosity remains alive can easily find subjects worthy of investigation Who is this Michigan lumber merchant, Hober (?) who is reported to have bought up all New England hurricane lumber (except Rhode Island, holding out for higher price)? How is it that Sen. Brown of Michigan was so active in promoting the Export-Import hundred millions for Finland? How is the deal getting on (cf Bul #26) by which we are to sell this hurricane lumber to the Finns (whose chief industry is lumber) who will sell it to England and France in return for their promise of munitions.[5]

Referring to British failure to help Finland, the Boston *Transcript,* Feb 29, editorially comments, "Britain in her conversations with Russia before the war, paved the way for this attack by refusing to urge Finland to make any concessions". At this late date, the American "assurance to help is meaningless. . . It amounts substantially to giving a man a cookie while his door is being battered down".

London's White Paper on the Anglo-Russian-Finnish situation promised weeks ago is still held up "The document as originally prepared failed to make out as good a case against the Soviet government as the compilators planned" (R. Daniell, dispatch from London, N. Y. *Times,* Feb 7). "One suspects that neither party to these negotiations is anxious to publish the documents involved because both were dickering behind the scenes with Berlin at the same time" (*Nation,* March 2).

"The Russians believe, honestly I think, that they are not fighting the Finnish people but for the Finnish people against Anglo-French capitalists and their Finnish hirelings,—not a question of breaking the

Mannerheim line but of breaking Mannerheim and his dark forces of reaction. They believe they are liberators in Finland." (Walter Duranty in a cable to the N. Y. *Times,* Feb 27) Hugh Johnson in his column says "It is clear now that the aid Finland needs is never going to be given to her. This example of what European nations who are able to help are willing to do . . . is their business—not ours. But, by the same token, keeping out of Europe is our business—not theirs."

Could some of this money raised for the Finns, which will probably never reach them, be used advantageously in the U. S.? Milo Perkins, U. S. Department of Agriculture, told the Associated Grocery Manufacturers in N. Y. C. recently that using the stamp plan to distribute surplus foods shows that, even with prunes, if the underfed one-third could buy them, there would be demand for 38% more prunes than have been produced. So the surplus would become a shortage even with prunes if the hungry were fed. But feeding hungry Americans would destroy morale.

Through the early part of 1915, Secretary of State Bryan stood firm against loans to the Allies. When Lansing succeeded, he argued, "We have more money than we can use. We ought to allow the loans to be made for our own good." Sept. 11, 1915, John Brisben Walker, noting a proposed loan of a billion dollars, wrote Lansing, "These millions are badly needed in America. The money which Mr. Morgan proposes to lend can only be obtained by making use of the U. S. Treasury reserve . . . or else deceiving the small investor into accepting a war loan". Of this letter, Wilson wrote to Lansing, "This is a most extraordinary letter. I am sure you know how to handle it." Queer fellow, Walker! Lansing did! In less than 18 months the Yanks were on their way.[6]

March 6, 1940

NOTES

(1) While the build up for Finland's credit was underway, the American press constantly reiterated that Finland always paid. December 15, 1940, Finland finally defaulted on her payments seeking an extension of time. Later it was discovered that "with the exception of Liberia", Finland was the only one to pay. The Boston *Herald,* Nov. 21, 1939, commenting editorially exclaimed, "This is astonishing news for us ignorant Americans. We have all been under the impression that Finland alone has met her honest obligations honorably Is it possible that the zeal of the BBC propagandists outruns their information, or that they are so anxious to make a good cause better that they are not confining themselves to the facts?"

(2) "Under the funding agreement with Finland, provision was made for paying its indebtedness in annual installments running over a period of 62 years" (A. D. Peterson, Treasury Department, letter, March 27, 1940).

(3) February 13, 1940, I wrote to the Boston *Transcript,* "In the 'Newscope' last Friday (or Thursday), I noted 'Finland, as is well known, is the only country that repaid the United States on debts following the last war. Now it is suggested she be lent again the $5,891,000 she repaid'.

"Isn't this a propaganda myth which has been promoted in 'the build up' for additional loans? My understanding is that the original loan of the U S to the Mannerheim White Government was 18 millions, that this was later scaled down to 9 millions, that on this amount only token payments were made until recently With the last payment ($243,693) $866,803 had been paid. With the remission of this last payment by the President and the granting of the additional 10 million from the R F.C , total advances to Finland amount to $27,376,-890 on which the total credits in 20 years amount to $623,110 This is irrespective of what Mr. Hoover and Gen Ryan have raised, and the additional loans pending.

"The point I wish to make for correction is that on a debt of 18 millions that has stood for 20 years, Finland's total payments credited to date are only some $623,110. Isn't this correct? Where am I wrong?"

The Managing Editor, Alden B. Hoag, replied February 19, "The acting Newscope editor passed along your letter to me, with the private and impertinent explanation that I am enclosing I think what you say is rather illuminating, especially in the light of the current disposition to place Finland at the head of the class in financial integrity, with England and France far at the foot."

The enclosed note was, "All these figures doubtless are true—it's well known that Finland's debt wasn't a war debt per se. Which is why I so carefully said Finland was the 'only country that repaid U. S on debts following the war'. You can't go into all the details every time unless Mr. Sargent wants to contribute another $100 to hire some more help."

To the editors of the World Almanac I wrote February 12, "On page 275 of the 1939 edition of the Almanac I find that Finland's total debt is now $8,-233,157, while total payments are listed as $5,656,599 The total debt, scaled down 50% from eighteen millions, was nine millions, so the total payments must have been $857,110, including the last payment which was remitted. Can you elucidate or explain your figures?"

E. Eastman Irvine, Editor of the World Almanac, replied, "The figures on the war debts owed to the United States, as given on page 275 of the 1940 World Almanac, are as furnished to us by the United States Treasury Department, and are accepted by us as accurate and official. If you are in doubt about them I would suggest you communicate with the Treasury Department."

To Secretary of the Treasury Morgenthau February 12, I wrote, "Can you have sent to me a list of the payments made by Finland on her indebtedness? In a N. Y. *Times* dispatch, December 15, on the occasion of Finland's last payment of $234,693 the dispatch ended, 'The balance of the Finnish debt was said by the treasury to be $8,142,890'. That would mean that on the nine millions less than one million had been paid in the approximately twenty years the debt has been running Am I correct in understanding that the advance to the Finnish Government after the war was eighteen millions, which was later scaled down to nine millions? I find the most confusing statements made in the newspapers, in the World Almanac, and elsewhere about this matter."

February 27, A D Peterson, Assistant Commissioner of Accounts and Deposits of the Treasury Department, replied, "Receipt is acknowledged of your letter of February 12, 1940, requesting certain information in regard to the indebtedness of the Government of Finland to the United States. There is enclosed a statement [detailed, tabulated, confusing] showing the payments made by Finland on its indebtedness to date which covers all amounts that have become due and payable.

"The statement that the advances to Finland after the World War amounted to $18,000,000, which amount was scaled down to $9,000,000, is not correct The original indebtedness of Finland was $8,281,926 17. Interest accrued prior to funding amounted to $1,027,389.10, of which $309,315 27 was paid The indebtedness as funded was $9,000,000 including the original principal amount of $8,281,926.17 and accrued interest of $718,073 83.

"Finland has paid a total of $5,891,291 77 on account of its indebtedness to the United States, of which $957,533 23 was for principal and $4,933,758 54 for interest, leaving the total amount of its indebtedness $8,142,890 21." (The total reduction in the original indebtedness amounted to $139,035.96).

March 2, I wrote Mr. Peterson, "You state 'the original indebtedness of Finland was $8,281,926.17'. That was in 1919? and at 5%? which would now have amounted approximately with interest to the 18 millions some writers mention if there had not been cancellation and reduction of interest at the time of refunding $139,035.96 then is the total amount of the reduction of the Finnish debt since originally contracted, as you state, 'leaving the total amount of its indebtedness $8,142,890 21'.

"In the meantime I have heard from Congressman Tinkham I have also before me *Economic Notes,* Jan 1940 In this issue, pages 4 and 5 (as recently quoted in *People's Lobby Bulletin*), he gives the figures you have given but tells also of Finnish government additional loans in this country at the beginning of 1936 amounting to $32,100,000, and a total of long term government loans from the United States, England and Sweden to Finland between 1920 and 1938 of $204,082,000.

"In addition to this, he details eleven Finnish government loans sold in England since 1938 totaling $50,000,000 and of American investments in Finland including $12,000,000 in the Industrial Bank of Finland, from all of which I gather that the U. S government and its citizens now have loans or investments or have made contributions to Finland to the amount of between one and three hundred millions Would the Treasury Department have knowledge of these loans or should I make inquiry of the State Department?"

March 29, Amos E. Taylor, Chief of the Finance Division of the Department of Commerce, wrote, "Your letter of March 2, addressed to the Treasury Department, has been referred to this Division for reply to your questions relating to loans to Finland. "From 1923 to 1939 the nominal amount of Finnish loans publicly offered in the United States was $82,000,000. (Source· Trade Promotion Series No 104, 'American Underwriting of Foreign Securities') Of that total, one loan in 1934 of $5,000,000 was for the purpose of refunding a loan issued earlier and therefore did not involve any new capital

"During the years since these loans were issued, Finland has reduced the outstanding amounts annually, in conformity with the provisions of the bond contracts and occasionally, by extraordinary redemptions, have retired entire issues In addition, Finnish investors have bought up these bonds in the open market The net result has been that the par value (nominal) of United States holdings of such bonds at the end of 1939 was estimated at about $9,000,000."

(4) While Dr. Frederick L Schuman was advocating a "conservative defense loan" of 500 million dollars for Finland, and Congress was debating a loan of considerably smaller proportions, Dorothy Thompson (N. Y *Herald Tribune*, Jan 19, 1940) said that a refusal to make such a loan "would be equivalent to standing for international anarchy and serving notice on the world that we are scared". In the *Congressional Record*, January 24, 1940, Rep Case of South Dakota stated that the hearings on "the independent offices appropriation bill showed that the Finnish loan is a loan to the Finnish Trading Corporation and not directly to the Finnish Government".

(5) October 22, 1940 (AP), disclosing that a Senate Interstate Commerce subcommittee was about to institute investigation of "price chiseling", Chairman Wheeler mentioned possible investigation of recent increase in lumber prices. "The lumber people claim that the Government ordered a tremendous amount of lumber at one time, taxing their capacity to get it out We want to find out if their increased costs justify the increases they have made in prices."

Land graft was also returning big dividends to speculators as it had in the last war when Col Deeds went to town and made millions buying up lands to resell to the government for airports. (He now has a billion dollar yacht and hasn't given it to the government.) *Economic Notes*, November 1940, reported, "An Associated Press dispatch from Washington, October 10, tells us that War Department estimated that land speculators 'had cost it nearly $500,000 in two months'." Pearson and Allen, January 27, 1941, tell of Indiana land deals by army officials, uncovered by the investigation of the Inspector General.

"The American faith . . . is essentially faith in a perpetual land boom", Lawrence Dennis makes clear in his letter to Schuman in the *Nation*, Jan. 11, 1941. "The American people will not be made aware of their true interest . . until they have suffered far more than they have ever suffered up to now." It was this profiteering from speculation in the public lands that gave John Quincy Adams so many headaches. The American dream has been the hope of making profits through rising land values

(6) Bulletin #43 began "Let's Save America First—Let God Save the King. This war last year cost us billions. It will cost more this coming year We

have attempted in these Bulletins to disclose how and reveal something of the forces that promote our participation. The purpose is not to present all sides, to express opinions nor to assume a judicial attitude, but to disclose what has been concealed, to slow down the war hysteria, to do a little toward saving America first." There followed a list of Bulletins to date with the titles of some projected and the statement that they were sent without charge to those who requested or are recommended.

A TIME TO BE ON GUARD

The democratic process in action has in the past few months, through aroused public opinion, thrice stopped the President and the forces behind him. And we hear less from university presidents that youth must fight for religion, morality, and civilization.

It is the result of thousands of groups and individuals that all over the country have sprung into action. Newspapers and Congressmen have at crises been deluged with letters and resolutions of protest. News letters, hundreds of them, have been circulated to the hundreds of thousands hungry for information which the periodical press dare not publish. Pamphleteering has been revived.

In defiance of the President and press propaganda, popular protest led to the long embargo fight in Congress. The President had called Congress only after he had enough votes pledged to do what Great Britain wanted. The *Round Table* (founded and long edited by Lord Lothian) voiced the British disappointment at the "furious war of propaganda which was waged against repeal" and which postponed America's early participation. (cf Bul #22)

The Finnish flare-up, which may have been planned in Britain's Foreign Office as the last straw to bring us in (cf Bul #21), through no fault of the President and much to the disappointment of his friends, failed to bring us in. March issue of the *Round Table*, just arrived, in an anonymous article "America in Suspense", written Jan 26, says.

"All the big drums of publicity are thumping for Finland. It is the story of Belgium all over again. . . . Americans . . . indulged in an emotional orgy over the Baltic sideshow. The day of greater American participation in the struggle . . . has become a great deal nearer. The Soviet attack on Finland may be called one of the greatest historical 'accidents' of our time. By virtue of the emotional drive here on behalf of Finland . . . the practical difficulty of remaining emotionally partisan and physically uninvolved increases in intensity. More realistic counsels would . . . give Finland every possible aid—and the same might be true of Britain and France as well, although we have not reached that point yet"

The third rebuff followed the Administration's use of Cromwell at Toronto to gauge public opinion. His speech seemed a trial balloon to see how far the Administration might go (Paul Mallon, Mar. 22). Cromwell said no more than Hull and Roosevelt had already put forth (cf Bul #26). Cromwell remained at his home in New Jersey for some days, apparently was not summoned to Washington, was not reprimanded, nor should he have been. "Hull found that the address contravened standing instructions" regarding statements "likely to disturb the relations between this and other governments", correspondents were told, and that Cromwell was admonished not to repeat.[1]

Welles' 'secret' mission was well publicized by Mussolini and Hitler. British resentment at the threat of peace led the Administration to thrice deny that Welles was a 'peace salesman',—simultaneously through Mr. Roosevelt in press conference, Sec. Early in Washington, Welles in Rome.[2]

This is an economic war. In America our contributions are concealed. Look for credits surreptitiously granted, holes in the Neutrality Law, allowances for plant expansion After the last war all such costs and credits were unloaded on the taxpayer,—manufacturer to banker to government to taxpayer. An improved technique may be anticipated. It is already arranged that the taxpayer shall pay for the billion dollars of airplanes and munitions built for our defense which the president is turning over to Britain and France.

"The duration and character of the war depend on the American elections", it is generally believed in London and Washington (Whaley-Eaton, Feb. 27). It cannot continue without American resources.

The war is now costing England, Sir John Simon tells us, 9½ billion dollars a year, 40% of the national earning (*Chr Sci Monitor*, Mar. 16).[3] The London *Economist* estimates the cost for 1940 at $12,800,-000,000, and 1941 at $16,000,000,000. In France the Deputies were told in 1940 the costs would be $7,400,000,000, more than 40% of the national income.

The war will be in part paid for by indentured labor in the Union of South Africa and the Federated Malay States, and by concealed contributions from this country which would be promoted by 'Union Now' and 'Federation' with France and England.

The Keynes plan, called "deferred spending", would take part of each working man's wage and give him in return the government's promise to pay after the war (cf Bul #97). England's promises to the U. S. in the last war may well warn the English working man to beware. When it is all over they may say, "You hired our protection, we hired your money". Keynes has hope of repayment by a capital levy, if any capital is left.

The mendicant mother country is already levying on her daughter Commonwealths. Australia's 'defense' budget has been multiplied six times, New Zealand's five times. Rebellious South Africa is being kept fat on gold dug from the depths with indentured black labor and sold to gullible Uncle Samuel Shylock at many times its cost to the profit of Lothian and other holders of 'Kaffirs'. (cf Bul #39)

The menace of our gold purchases is coming into the consciousness of Americans. Since the first stirring created by Graham and Whittlesey's article in April, 1939, *Foreign Affairs,* their book published the middle of November, our Bulletin early in December,—several score of articles have appeared and recently the newspapers have taken it up.

This threatening thunderhead to Roosevelt and Morgenthau may become a cyclone when it's known that this gold unloaded on us to support rearmament and the war may be as worthless as the gold bonds of the last war.

Congressmen have been rather chary to stir up this subject. But recently they have opened up on the silver bloc, a similar but lesser mess.[4] There is hope of getting publicity for the way our resources are being drained to the profit of the owners of South African gold mines. More vigorous protest against American participation in and contributions to the war may come with April hearings on bills that have been introduced in Congress on gold purchasing. Though banking and imperialist interests will oppose and suppress, it may become known that a duty of $15 an ounce on gold would slow up and might stop the war.

Protests against mail seizures at Bermuda have subsided since the N. Y. *Times* editorially reminded, Feb. 24, that this is only what the British had long been doing at Gibraltar and on the British coasts, and the State Department announced that with the end of the Bermuda season the Clipper would omit Bermuda and stop at the Azores.[5]

At the Azores the British will have no difficulty examining the mails. They have long acted as though they owned Portugal Portugal, it is understood, entered into an agreement in 1938 to prevent German U-Boats from using the Azores Three British ships, 126 guns, with a loss of 120 British killed, three times attacked an American privateer Armstrong, at Fayal, September 26, 1814. The Americans abandoned, the British burned the ship. Portugal received indemnity. All the U. S. received was an old 44-pounder salvaged from the Armstrong.

The stakes at issue in this war are so great, the forces so enormous, the expenditure so colossal, that a temporary lull should be a forewarning,—a time to hold one's fire, to be alert, to prepare for the coming offensive. The democratic process must win a fourth time. The propagandists are at work. *Friday,* 114 East 32nd St., N. Y. C., March 15, 1940, discloses the work of British propagandists more fully than has yet appeared in print.

Getting out these Bulletins interferes with other important work. But with so many stupidities to be exposed, with our periodicals detailing facts without relation to their background, with our intelligentsia misinformed and deceived by Sir Robert Vansittart's very efficient propaganda in America these past three years, I must carry on. I can "do no other".

In *Harpers,* April 1940, Lundberg in his article on "Newsletters" makes a well meaning reference to these Bulletins as "anti-war, anti-British". I have explained repeatedly that I and my ancestors have been 'pro-British' since William the Bastard and 'pro-American' since the time of John Harvard If we were being deceived by the Germans or Russians into pouring out our treasure and our blood for them, I should be suspicious of their propaganda and selfish forces and endeavor to expose it. As for this war being in the interest of religion, morality, civilization, that is in the same class as the last war being in the interest of democracy. This must be apparent to those who have not been propaganda poisoned.[6]

March 27, 1940

NOTES

[1] A copy of the Toronto speech of Cromwell, for which he was reproved, advocating our more complete participation in the war, and evidently sent up

as a trial balloon to test American opinion, was reported to have been on the President's desk at the time the speech was made

(2) Mr Roosevelt, highly sensitive to changing conditions, in his talk on peace, condemned the Versailles Treaty and praised those who "sought to promote an international order based on human justice", still ignoring the economic, and re-emphasizing the "moral basis", covertly inflaming us with the declaration that "It cannot be a righteous peace if the worship of God is denied". With his eye on the Pope and the Catholic vote, he referred to those who "denied the equality of souls before the throne of God". He knows, of course, that Germany subsidizes the Roman Catholic Church and pays from taxation millions of dollars annually to support her priests. Someone in the Foreign Office, London, had the quick sense to cable that Roosevelt's ideals coincided with those of the Allies. Quite a change from angry Chamberlain's and frustrated Churchill's earlier threatening tones!

A letter in the *Chr Sci Monitor* at that time asked, "Do the governments of Europe dare to stop the present war? . . Is there any Government in Europe that dares face the problem that would follow peace, the return of these millions of workers to an industrial field where there would be no possibility of their being reemployed?"

(3) These figures seem trivial compared with recent reports. In addition they are borrowing heavily of their own people where they can, floating loans, using capital, etc. So the 40% was only the beginning. In the final year of the last war the British expense was $10,700,000,000, about half the national income at that time.

(4) The "Silly Silver Subsidy" by the United States of Mexico, Canada and Japan, was the subject of a tirade in a Boston *Transcript* editorial. "Since the passage of the Silver Purchase Act in 1934, the Government has bought more than 2,200,000,000 ounces of silver at a cost of more than $1,000,000,000 This unwelcome stream of silver has come chiefly from foreign sources Last year, for example, the amount of foreign silver purchased was almost five times greater than that bought from domestic producers Because of a parliamentary technicality, the United States Treasury must unfortunately continue the costly folly of purchasing foreign silver at an excessive price. The Senate . . . passed the Townsend bill to repeal this fantastic legislation, but senators from the silver-producing States who had fought the measure still had an ace in the hole . . . that under the Constitution all tax measures must originate in the House. The provision which requires the Treasury to buy the total output of American silver mines at the exorbitant price of 71 cents an ounce, when the price in the open market is only half that sum, should also be repealed."

Representative Schafer of Wisconsin, June 30, 1939, commenting in the House on Roosevelt's insistence on continued power to devalue the dollar, stated that the President was "an ex-international banker of wide experience and a former attorney for international bankers. Under his gold and silver policies the international bankers, foreign owners of, and speculators in gold, waxed fat when

Mr Roosevelt forced Americans to turn in their gold for $20 67 an ounce or go to jail for 5 years and then imported more than $10,000,000,000 worth of foreign gold at $35 an ounce "

(5) The change of stops to the Azores was not made. It would probably have proved ineffective. Within the Neutrality Zone the British continued to hold up steamers and take off goods or passengers at will,—probably the first time since because of it we fought the War of 1812. If there were American protests they were so feeble as to receive little attention

Time, Oct. 28, 1940, reported that when the American liner Exeter arrived at Bermuda west bound, they took from Captain Brousse "two sealed 'paquets de courrier' from Foreign Minister Paul Baudouin to Ambassador Henry-Haye". This "seizing" of "diplomatic correspondence" was "even more bizarre".

December 7, 1940 (AP), the Brazilian liner Buarque arriving at New York from Rio de Janeiro, reported that the British at Trinidad had seized 70 cases of cloth and alcohol consigned to firms at La Guayra, Venezuela, because those firms "were on its blacklist for having traded with Germany". The Brazilian coastal steamer Itape about the same time was stopped in the Neutrality Zone by a British armed auxiliary who removed some 20 Germans aboard. The Brazilian protest was more vigorous than ours and the Inter-American Neutrality Committee threatened to recommend the closing of American ports to British war ships Later when Japanese citizens were removed at Bermuda and their money seized, Japan entered vigorous protests as she had when Britain removed from a Japanese steamer in the Pacific, German seamen from the S.S Columbus. (cf Bul #37)

The French freighter Mendoza, laden with food from Uruguay for France after being several times forced by British cruisers to return, was finally seized a few miles off the Brazilian coast by a British cruiser because it had held no 'navicert' Four other steamers with food cargoes for France are being held. London cable, January 15, (AP) says Britain has no intention of permitting them to carry freight or food to France. Uruguay protests and has interned temporarily a British seaplane crew that came to a forced landing in Uruguayan waters. Argentina is reported to be exerting pressure on Uruguay to stand firm, and threatens to take over control of Uruguay if they do not. All this meets with no protest from the U. S. State Department, while the officials of the British Foreign Office, which has contemptuously defied President Roosevelt's neutrality belt, thumb their collective British noses.

(6) The civilization and morality we are to spend and fight to preserve: Royal Commission, headed by Anthropologist Guinness, studying our near neighbor the British West Indies (which Sen Lundeen proposed we take in payment for what Britain owes us), reports Jamaica population, 98% black (descendants of West African slaves), "a dungheap of physical abomination", 70% of Jamaica's 1,138,558 tubercular, 75% bastards In the Leeward and Windward Islands, ruled by professional colonial administrators, "the investigators found squalor, economic decay, unrest" (*Time,* March 4). Parliament, on receipt of the report

of the Commission, proposed to spend 20 millions a year for ten years on all British colonies, four million a year on the West Indies, that is 2/5 of a penny a week per head. Brailsford asks why spend so much on the Indies and not on the others? Window dressing to impress us close at hand? and to justify a price raise when we buy from there?

OBJECTIONS RAISED BY CORRESPONDENTS

The flood of letters received requesting or acknowledging these Bulletins generally express appreciation. Some raise objections. Impossible to reply individually to all, I take this means of replying.

George V. Denny, Town Hall, "May I express the hope that your zeal for facts on the liberal side will not lead your bulletin to neglect facts on the other side. You are doing a good job. Keep it up!"

C. Judson Herrick, world known neurologist, "I always read your bulletins. I find them interesting, perhaps chiefly because I disagree with almost everything you say. The man who can see only one side of a question makes an efficient propagandist, but it ill becomes him to be too caustic about propaganda that he does not like. But this seems to be the democratic way to juggle the truth out of situations which are too complicated for most of us to understand. So keep going "

The 'other side' means little to one who sees many sides. Anything that has only the 'other side' is pretty thin. Personally I like to get the light from many facets. It is the neglected side or sides, the unfamiliar, the hidden, that I attempt to present. As others discover and take up a phase, I cooperate but leave it to them. But I cannot stand by idly and see my fellow countrymen, through deception, led to such disastrous idealism as in the last war.

'Judicial',—there is no attempt to be. Who am I to 'judge'? The evidence that has been suppressed or falsified or that others have failed to discover, I must present.

Otto F. Kraushaar, Smith Col., "It is important that such facts as you give be generally known so that we can attain clearness about what is at issue in the war now in progress. At the same time, I wonder if it serves a good purpose in the present crisis to breed hatred and contempt for a people and a government that, while not coming into this with clean hands, has over the years stood for those human values to which we also subscribe."

Hatred of the British I have no desire to breed or foster. I don't feel it. There is too much of that sort of thing. If what I put forth is twisted or untrue, I hope to be corrected. If it is merely unfamiliar, then the unthinking will consider it untrue. The English are articulate, have well organized methods of publicity. They made a good case for themselves in the last war. They are doing well at it this time, at the expense of my fellow countrymen, whom I cannot see swallowing untruths without attempting to present something that will save them from this propaganda poisoning and unnecessary hate.

George W. Lloyd, Mt. Vernon Seminary, "I do not concur with you in your apparent fear of propaganda. My faith in the intelligence of the average man is such that I do not believe he can be swung—certainly not as easily as he was at the time of the last World War."

A New England newspaper publisher, "If I did not know you to be very fair minded I'd have been amazed at your fulmination against British (present) propaganda My only reaction is that in this as in everything the British are a little late. For over seven years this paper has received books, pamphlets, radio programs and photographs of every conceivable description from 'Friends of Germany', 'Friends of Italy', 'Friends of Japan'. If the millions wasted on this drivel had been put into food there'd have been a different story."

German propaganda was on his desk, British propaganda, more subtle, perhaps in his blood, I wrote him. Later he wrote, "British propaganda, we all know, is very subtle, very clever. We seem to be constitutionally susceptible to it Your bulletin is the best example of propaganda analysis in action we have ever seen I am reprinting it."

A university professor whose anonymity we preserve, "Please stop sending your bulletins. You seem to be pro-German."

Anti-British or pro-German I am not. I have lived much in other countries in five journeys around the world and pride myself on being able to get into other people's skins, black, yellow, and brown, and to look out at their world through their eyeholes. My ancestors have been American and English for hundreds of years. I always return to England feeling it is my ancestral home. The English gentleman at his best is unsurpassed, just as, at his worst, is the English 'tripper' But I am against the present Tory crew now ruining England. I am against Roosevelt's foreign policy, but that does not make me anti-American.

The only label I will wear is that of an old fashioned, free thinking, free speaking American. I don't believe that democracy was advanced by the last war, nor that this war will advance religion or morality. Nor do I believe that we can save civilization by destroying the civilization that gave us our music, our research methods. My loyalty is to my fellow Americans to save them from the gullibility of twenty years ago, when we squandered our wealth and resources. But again, due to those emotionally aroused by British propaganda, we are wasting our resources on war, when we might be building a better America.
March 29, 1940

WHAT THE LAST WAR COST

War is waste, of lives, of labor, of wealth, and of the earth's resources, soil, oil, metals, that can never be replaced.

When Coolidge in the 'twenties said the cost to us would be 100 billions, that seemed extravagant.[1] Our loans to the Allies, cut down, still remain 12 billions. Our national debt of 44 billions is largely the result of war.[2] And pensions now seem inevitable for the two million surviving participants, if votes continue to count [3]

What did the last war cost? No one has yet dared to estimate. Costs have been arrived at by adding amounts appropriated.[4] 370 billions, the Encyclopedia Americana gives for the World War, more than the total property value of the U S. But that's only a small part of the cost, which did not end with the close of the war. Add the cost of eighteen or more wars since, the cost of armaments since, the cost of the present war which grew out of it. And that's not the whole cost.

"More soil probably was lost from the World War, between 1914 and 1934 than in the whole previous human history", Jacks and Whyte tell us in "The Rape of the Earth" (Faber & Faber, 1939). "Today, destruction of the earth's thin, living covering is proceeding at a rate unparalleled in history . . . fertile regions will become uninhabitable deserts Already a million square miles of desert has been formed."

John Durant, who has brought the figures up to 417 billions, writes, "Strip six inches of topsoil from the face of the earth and the world becomes a desert without life, without human beings. The rich Persian fields, where Darius ruled, are now deserts. North African plains where Hannibal defended the rich lands of Carthage are now but burning sand."[5]   Add cost of dictators, loss of opportunity, freedom, democracy, to the estimate. "Volcanoes grow dim and the stars reel and swim" when the mind attempts to estimate,—figures no longer mean anything.[6]

So let's go back to our own country, America, and see if we can estimate the cost, not in dollars merely, nor in property destroyed, nor in the lives ended, nor in the expectancy value of the future labor of the dead or incapacitated. The lives that still go on,[7] frustrated, the decreased efficiency of those who survive, are the big loss. Idle labor, idle plants, due to economic dislocation consequent on the war, have cost us about 300 billions, the Monopoly Commission was shown.[8]

Some will denounce anyone who asks "How much?" as amoral, without soul. "What shall it profit a man if he gain the whole world and lose his soul?" But who is it now telling us how to save our souls, and what do they hope to gain? To save our souls, then, shall we destroy the lives of others and leave the world a desert for our survivors?

There has never been a good war nor a bad peace, Benjamin Franklin and other wise men have told us. If this is a good war,—and there are those who say it is, for religion, morality, what you please,—it must be the first one But they told us in 1918 that that was the last war, to put down militarism, to spread democracy.

Were they right? How much shall we stake on their being right this time? Let those fight who wish, but shall we let them take by force our sons for cannon fodder? Will the world be better for it if they do? *May 15, 1940*

NOTES.

[1] 44 billions is the unpaid cost of the war, which was 63 billions, made up as follows· direct cost (1917-21) 25, continuing costs (1921-38) 26, unpaid debt of foreign countries 12 These are minimum figures, adding only full billions. Not shown in the dollar columns is the larger cost, previously paid for, of navy ships lost (71), merchant ships lost (171), a total of 527,000 tons, and other property previously paid for amounting to some additional billions, lives lost, killed or died of wounds, 140,000, wounded 243,000. A hundred thousand veterans have received hospitalization. The cost of producing an adult in our economy is $12,000. We used to produce a negro slave in the '50's for $1200. Figuring the wounded as depreciated 50 per cent and the dead at 100%, the loss in value of manpower will be about 3 billions, a total thus far of about 70 billions in actual reduction of national assets The rest of the 100 billions is in the soil and resources.

(2) "The last war cost the U. S.   . $32 billion .   10 per cent was paid
for by increasing production . .   60 per cent was paid for by letting the
capital plant of the country deteriorate by postponing the normal new construction of homes, churches, hospitals, power plants, highways, and so forth. And
about 30 per cent was paid for by producing fewer consumption goods and
reducing the standard of living of certain classes of the people." ("U S Defense:
The Dollars", *Fortune,* Nov. 1940) (cf Buls #99 and #50 and Notes)

(3) "Wealthy people who think that a national army will defend the interests
of the wealthy are simply naive. The demands of the American veteran for
the bonus and for pensions should enlighten them   Already the United States
Government has paid out $8 billion in pensions and bonuses on account of
the last war, which is about the same amount the Civil War cost us in pensions,
but the pension bill of the last war is just beginning to grow." (*Weekly Foreign
Letter,* Sept. 12, 1940)

"The Civil War cost $3,328,000,000 in direct costs, and mounted to approx-
imately $8,000,000,000 because of debt interest and pensions. The war with
Spain cost $528,000,000 to which was added $1,452,000,000 in pensions and
debt interest   The American share of the war of 1914-18 was $24,135,000,000
directly, and has reached $57,000,000,000 by now in pensions and interest, not
mentioning the economic dislocations resulting from the war", according to a
survey made by National Economy League (*Chr Sci Monitor,* Nov. 13, 1939).

The Department of Commerce, March 16, 1940, gave figures to the effect
that 4 3% of the 1939 national income went to meet the cost of past wars. But
this included only direct costs, not the large incidental and continuing costs.
A broader view would make the cost of the last war to us the total decrease
in our income over what it would have been had we stayed neutral as did the
Scandinavian countries and Holland, with consequent prosperity. The economic
dislocation due to the war, as the President has pointed out, in high price for
wheat, plowing our grasslands, our dust bowl, our floods, permanent loss of
topsoil, the one source of our food, and exhaustion of natural resources, oil
and metals, irrecoverable loss, capitalized modestly at 300 millions.

(4) "Coin is the sinews of war", the monk told Grangousier   That was true
in Rabelais' time.   It was true in the time of Chamberlain, true until, deprived
of gold and trade and exchange, the European central powers showed that it
was labor, work, that coin was only a bankers' device for measuring human
effort, human accomplishment. (cf Dreher, *Harpers,* Oct , 1940; Buls #53, 97)

The Carnegie Endowment for International Peace is engaged in putting
forth an ambitious series of post mortem studies on the late War   One of
these is "The Costs of The World War to the American People" (Yale University Press, 1931) by John Maurice Clark, Columbia University   He gives
the actual expenditures of the government on war to the end of 1921 as
$40,000,000,000. ("Private Schools", Sargent, 1932, pp 88-9)

(5) "More of the earth's essential resources have been used up this century
than in all of man's previous existence on this planet. The United States con-

sumes more non-reproducible materials than any other country on earth, and of most goods as much as all the other four great western Powers of Europe combined " (Carleton Beals, "Pan America")

(6) "The defense of democracy, as I understand it from reading the newspapers, means the abolition of democracy here so it can be restored abroad", said Bertrand Russell in a lecture in New York shortly after his arrival in America "When one comes from England to America one finds America much more monarchial than England."

(7) "Two years after the Armistice the plight of war's human debris was pitiable. Over 300,000 wounded and disabled were the partial price of our adventure. Of these the most desperate cases were 71,000 mental patients and 38,000 tuberculosis victims. F. W. Galbraith, Jr., National Commander of the American Legion, estimated, on the basis of an investigation, that there were 10,000 of the disabled in cellars, poorhouses, insane asylums T W. Salmon, a disinterested and competent investigator, thus reported (*Literary Digest*, Jan. 22, 1921) 'Veterans with nervous or mental troubles were without provision for care and were quartered in institutions for the criminal insane, addicts, and vicious degenerates, without Federal supervision' ", Samuel Hopkins Adams tells us in "The Incredible Era. The Life and Times of Warren Gamaliel Harding" (Houghton Mifflin, 1939).

(8) Eddie Rickenbacker, American Ace, now head of Eastern Airlines, who was injured in a crash in March, 1941, on the eve of another war, in 1940, recalling that America had borne approximately one-fifth of the cost of the first World War, said, "The close of the World War and subsequent events have brought about the disillusionment and realization that the winner and loser of such a conflict must suffer the consequences alike. There are millions still unemployed, billions of dollars are being paid in additional taxes, hospitals are still filled with thousands of veterans, wrecked mentally and physically, all of them once the flower of American manhood.

"The cost to the world approximated $250,000,000,000. With this staggering sum we could have built homes costing $2,500 each on 5-acre lots costing $100 an acre. We could have equipped each of those homes with a thousand dollars' worth of furniture and given such a home to every family in Russia, Italy, France, Belgium, Germany, Wales, Scotland, Ireland, England, Australia, Holland and the U.S A

"In those lands we could have given to every community of 40,000 people or more a $2,000,000 library, a $3,000,000 hospital, and a $10,000,000 university And if we could have invested the balance that would have been left in a way that would have brought a rate of 5% annually, there would have been sufficient to pay an annual salary of $1,000 each to 125,000 school teachers and 125,000 nurses. Had we stayed clear of it, as few deny now that we should have done, we could have paid for one-fifth of the above program with the money it cost us. We could have had all those furnished homes and libraries and hospitals and universities in our own country, and there would still have been a few billions over for reconstruction aid in Europe."

HOW MUCH SHALL WE WASTE ON THIS WAR?

"Meet force with force", Mr. Roosevelt recommended, April 14, to the South American politicos. To the scientists, May 10, in a second appeal to representatives of the South American dictatorships to unite with him in support of "individual liberty, civil liberty, democracy", etc.,—but speaking also as the President to the voters of this country,— he used familiar phrases meaninglessly, sought to stir fear.

"At Lima . . . we feared . . . that the Americas might have to become the guardian of western culture, the protector of Christian civilization. Today the fear has become a fact. You and I . . . will act together to protect and defend by every means our science, our culture, our freedom and our civilization." (No morality or religion this time.)

"Force without stint", Mr. Wilson called for twenty-three years ago Lasswell in his "Propaganda Technique in the World War" speaks of him as "the great generalissimo on the propaganda front . . . his monumental rhetoric, epitomizing the aspirations of all humanity. Such matchless skill as Wilson showed in propaganda has never been equalled."

Roosevelt may snatch his laurels. The build-up is continuous. Cromwell's Toronto trial balloon is followed by definite explanation of what the President would like to do, put forth so that all connection can be denied, in the "American White Paper" (Simon & Schuster, 1940).[1] Alsop and Kintner, the authors, recognize that the President, while not advocating sending an army to Europe, might advocate using our Navy and Air Force to help the Allies win the war, and has every intention of extending loans, credits,—even gifts when Allied cash is exhausted [2]

"If we go that far we might as well count ourselves all the way in. Some of us remember the early April of 1917, when it was said, and widely believed, that our entry into the World War meant only that we would lend money, send our Navy, and dispatch, at most, a 'token' army", Ernest Lindley, the President's biographer, reminds us. (*Washington Information Letter*, May 1, 1940)

Frederic William Wile, Washington *Star*, April 24, says, "It is the plainest speaking to emanate from an authoritative quarter—authoritative because one of the authors, Joseph Alsop, is a cousin of the President, enjoys his confidence and manifestly is writing, if not on White House inspiration or at its instigation, at least on˜the basis of information available only in that exalted region."

"Alsop and Kintner write for the fifty largest papers in the country, —the N.A.N.A. They are two former N.Y. *Herald Tribune* lads. Joe Alsop is a Harvard man, formerly on the Crimson. His father is a banker in (I think) Hartford, Conn. He writes like a Morgan partner and is very, very pro-British. Kintner comes from an old line family in Philadelphia—has an in with the *Sat. Eve. Post*—that is where they got their start", a Washington correspondent writes me. "Joe Alsop and Robert Kintner certainly write an editorial worthy of the 'House of Morgan', every day. You might think that Lamont was writing it." Alsop has just been nominated for the Board of Overseers at Harvard.

On armaments Mr. Roosevelt has spent 9 billion up to January 1. Then Congress gave him another half billion. He has been calling for a half billion more. (Now overnight this has risen to two-and-a-half billion, which will make 12 billion he has spent for armament.) [3]

Incidentally in ten months the total expenditure has been eight billions, three billions of which have to be borrowed. We are paying more than a billion in interest. The President and Morgenthau have shown their skill in juggling figures, and as prestidigitators in taking our attention off the expenditures they are intent on. But now they are so emotionally aroused to 'fight for the right' that costs are not to be considered. Raise the debt limit, borrow, repeal the Johnson Act.

Manufacturers and bankers will be paid, of course. The cost will eventually come on the taxpayer, as before. Profiteers are not suffering under the New Deal. Million dollar incomes are plentiful, as in 1929. Banking deposits and profits are rising. March Bulletin, National City Bank, reports profits of 960 manufacturing companies, after depreciation, taxes, reserves, showed a rise of 98.1%, workers' hourly wage earnings advanced 1% (*Economic Notes,* April and May, 1940). Standard Statistics, April 4, forecasts a substantial increase in 1940. (cf Buls #66, 81, 88)

The crew that is running England, whose lead we are following, are doing even better. For example, Handley Page, English aviation company, has declared dividends in the past four years of 30, 50, 20, 30 per cent. But stock dividends make the 30% this year the equivalent of 365% on 1935 holdings. (cf *Uncensored,* May 11 and April 27.)

We have been getting into the war gradually,—slipping, sliding in. We are so far in now that it is only a question of how much deeper.

It is time for the people who will have to pay in sweat and blood to decide how much more to spend in view of results we may achieve A banker, asked for credit, sets a limit They will call us "Uncle Shylock" anyway. Let us, who have to pay the piper eventually, decide on the limit. Public opinion, manifested by votes, will be the restraining force upon our expenditure.

Don't be fooled by the reiteration of the slogan that we are "the best informed people in the world" We are most fully informed with misinformation. Call it 'explanation' or 'propaganda', much of it is misleading or untrue. The situation is misrepresented to us.

Challenge those who are so overcome with hysteria that they don't count the cost. Don't let the snobs snub you Write your legislative representatives. They are interested in keeping your vote. Write them, "Let's save America first, let God-save the King!"[4]

May 15, 1940

NOTES

[1] The development of our so-called foreign policy since Munich as formulated by Hull, Welles, Berle, with contributions from Bullitt and at first Kennedy, is traced in the "American White Paper". The President's message on the abrogation of the Arms Embargo, embodying Hull's views, was drafted by Berle, Messersmith, Moffat, with the advice of Norman Davis After the seizure of Prague the policy took more definite form, summarized under five points. (1) "Only by disarmament and an opening of trade can the world return to common sense" (the President's aphorism), (2) "Neutrals are parties at interest in a modern war, and particularly in the post-war settlement" (Welles speaking after Prague), (3) No political commitments outside the Western Hemisphere but economic commitments, (4) Since victorious dictatorships would not conceivably join in disarmament and an opening of trade, the democracies are to be aided by "methods short of war", (5) "Whatever happens, we won't send troops abroad" (the President to the War Department after the outbreak of war). Are Singapore, Brazil abroad? Are we building heavy tanks, to be completed in four or five years, for home defense or for use against the Siegfried Line?

Brigadier General G. M Barnes of the United States Army was the presiding officer of the Tank Committee, made up of executives of the War Department plus U. S manufacturers of tanks, and representatives of the British Purchasing Commission The Committee is coordinating and pooling the facilities of these companies: Baldwin Locomotive, Bethlehem Steel, Pullman Standard, Pressed Steel Car, in the building of tanks first to fill the two hundred million dollar British order and "what is most significant—these are tanks to carry the war to the Continent—tanks by which Britain will take the offensive"   (Pearson and Allen, Feb 14)

(2) Though the Allied cash is not exhausted and gold and other assets in this country of Great Britain and frozen assets here held of France still exceed $11 billions, Sen. King introduced a bill and Sen. Pepper followed up October 1 calling for more help for England. He urged that we "give till it hurts in augmenting the material resources of England so that they may be assured of superiority in the air". Pain eventually produces numbness.

(3) By October 1, 1940, recess of Congress, the appropriations amounted to approximately 15 billions for the year, a total of 24 billions given Mr. Roosevelt for "defense" But these appropriations were merely a start. The debt limit was raised from 45 billions last summer of 49 billions, and in February to 65 billions. "What sum it will reach if the English succeed in unloading the whole cost of the war on us, God alone knows, but if anyone suggests $100,000,000,000 I shall certainly not holler for psychiatrists", bellyached H. L. Mencken, October 6, 1940. "The late Woodrow Wilson, though his heart beat for humanity quite as wildly as Roosevelt's, yet remained a Scotch Presbyterian, and in that character he kept a sharp eye on the cash drawer."

Number, quantity, value are so taught or mistaught in our schools that most English speaking adults have no idea, no basis of comparison, no conceptions on these subjects Number, quantity and value could be taught to children so that they would be of assistance to them in living. Give them basis for comparisons Government agencies use columns of figures to befuddle A bunch of figures gives the average man the jitters We refrain from any jokes about women and check books

(4) Bulletin #51, "The Comeback", ran to four pages of excerpts from appreciative letters received from educators, librarians, pastors, forum speakers, etc of which we quote but a few

"Last night I read all the bulletins. Amazed at how much you condense in each page In the more than 40 folders the research work must have been very extensive. I thank God that you are here on earth at this time to do this particular work "—Brown Landone, Fla "You are rendering a public service in calling attention to certain facts, and in emphasizing a point of view that does not seem to find adequate expression in the usual channels."—W. Brooks Graves, Temple Univ , Pa "Keep up your great work   .   The importance of what you are doing increases every day, as the persistent forces of the war psychology make their impress upon the minds of Americans "—Avery Dulles, Mass

"Excellent reviews and interpretations of present problems"—Earl Saxe, The Southard School, Kans   "Must admit to being usually in the opposition with regard to the bulletins, but I always find them interesting and very provocative, and should be sorry to have them stopped"—J. D. Allen, Polytechnic Prep

Country Day Sch., N. Y "We have been enjoying your bulletin and appreciating it"—Edna Elliott, The Desert Sun Sch., Calif "Have enjoyed them very much, preserved them. Trust that you will continue this service"—Floyd C Fretz, Supt. Bradford City Schs., Pa

"These are hysterical times and sober men are likely to be sent to prison!"— Charles Beard "You are doing a swell job, and don't forget to send me everything "—Hubert Herring, Committee on Cultural Relations with Latin America. "I've just finished reading with much interest and profit your latest bulletins." —Walter B Cannon, Harvard University Medical School. "I have enjoyed reading your bulletins and apologize for not having expressed earlier my appreciation for receiving them."—Mark A. May, Yale University Institute of Human Relations. "Interested in the bulletins you sent."—Wendell L. Willkie. "Have been receiving your bulletins and reading them with interest "—Frank D Graham, Princeton University, co-author "Golden Avalanche".

Bulletin #52 was of contemporary interest in response to questions of correspondents. "What To Do Now" suggested, that the socially minded join or organize a group, the politically minded vote, individuals, writers challenge speakers, send letters to newspapers making known their attitude and protesting what they consider abuses.

"One feels hopelessly ineffectual when one lists once more the few ways of making public opinion felt—letters to the President, senators, congressmen and the newspapers; mass meetings, the forwarding of resolutions, talks on the radio (when there is no money available for such talks)—that is all that one can say I have long wondered whether this is not the fundamental weakness of democracy, this inability of the masses to do what rich, powerful pressure groups can achieve The dissenting peace-lovers or anti-conscriptionists or opponents of large armaments simply cannot make their wishes known and controlling even where they are in the vast majority. Here is a rock upon which the ship of state may be foundering and democracy being riven asunder. Here is something to my mind far more ominous than the presence among us of spies and agents of dictators and fifth columnists generally. For we can deal with the latter if we wish; there is no immediate remedy for that lack of majority rule which theoretically is supreme in the United States." (Villard, *Christian Century,* Jan 22, 1941)

WHAT THIS WAR WILL COST US

U. S. Federal peacetime spending at the rate of 25 millions a day (Whaley-Eaton, Apr 2) equals Britain's spending in its war effort. Since Jan 1 appropriations by Congress for Army and Navy have mounted to over 4 billions. But we can't put all the blame on the present administration. 'Peace-loving', we are war mongers. Our 1920-33 expenditures for armaments ($11,839,327,866) exceeded any other nation's.[1]

Newsweek, June 3, reports Mr. Roosevelt "refused to divulge the

defunct War Resources Board's suppressed report of Nov. 11, 1939"
which "criticized Army and Navy procurement methods, recommended
formation of a group similar to the War Industries Board". --- — __

The War Department reports that, since 1930, 4 billions have been
spent on the mere maintenance of our skeleton army and national guard.
As a result, "just 68,000—the five divisions that have been conducting
maneuvers in Louisiana and Texas—are organized and equipped as
they would be upon taking the field". (*New Republic,* June 3)

In September, before the war began, Hitler announced that he had
spent 90 billion marks, 36 billion dollars, on rearmament. How that
was possible, Hitler explained to the English writer G. Ward Price
("Year of Reckoning", Cassell, Ltd., 1939)—"The fundamental difference between your economic policy and ours is that in England you
work on a basis of capital, whereas the basis of the German system
is productive labour. After inflation and the world slump, practically
no capital existed in Germany. So I had to devise new machinery. The
effectiveness of that machinery can be judged by the results. As for
your expectation of our collapse, I may say that the greatest economists
in Germany have been foretelling it for the past six years, but they
have given that up now because even experts cannot afford to go on
being wrong for ever." (cf Bul #97)

Gen. George C. Marshall, chief of staff, has testified that it costs
us 21 times as much to maintain our army as any European country. At
this ratio, the cost to this country of an army equivalent to the German
would be 750 billion dollars. "Department spokesmen point out that
the average monthly pay in the U. S. Army is $39 a month; in Italy
it is 65 cents" (*New Republic,* June 3)—a ratio of sixty to one   And
soldiers pensions in this country are in an even higher ratio. So it is
well in planning an army like Hitler's to allow not 21 times more but
50 times more, which would be 1800 billion dollars. That would buy
all property in the U. S. several times over.[2]

Money is what the Administration asks, but more is necessary. *Life,*
June 3, says, "Most amazing of all is the spirit that built and drives
this engine of conquest. For the Germans are not supermen. Seven
short years ago they were the bitterest, most frustrated people in Europe
Then out of the very dregs of German life rose a man with an Idea that
galvanized a desperate nation. It was he who put a whole nation on

short rations that the Army might have guns and tanks and airplanes
It was he who bred the generation of young fanatics in love with the
art of war.   It was he who seemed last week to be closing the covers
on four centuries of European history."

Lives, too, will be necessary.   P. J. Philip cables from Paris, " 'There
will be 20,000,000 dead and destruction everywhere before this business
is finished', one commentator said today".   (N.Y. *Times*, June 2)
June 7, 1940

NOTES

(1) "The cost of the United States of entry into another World War would very
likely be double the cost of the last World War, and would result in a 'lowered
standard of living for generations to come', it is estimated in a somber study of
modern war costs by the National Economy League   The League, which is identified with very conservative political opinion here, suggests that the annual
expenditure for direct war costs alone probably would amount to $30,000,000,000
as compared with $15,000,000,000 for the war in 1917-18; and that the public
debt, now near the legal limit of $45,000,000,000 might well reach $70,000,-
000,000 to $75,000,000,000 in the first year and pass $100,000,000,000 in the
second." (*Chr Sci Monitor,* Nov. 13, 1939)

London cable to N Y. *Times,* Feb 4, 1941, "Cost of war to Britain $16,000,-
000,000 for year", is about the same as the U. S. is planning to spend   We are
good spenders.   World War I cost America almost as much as it did Britain.
Britain may be able to unload a larger part of the cost on us.   They notify us
that for the 60 days ending March 31, they will need 600,000 pounds or about
something short of $3,000,000.

The New England Letter of the First National Bank of Boston, early in 1941,
said, "The present war is the costliest conflict in history   British expenditures are
placed at nearly 15 billion dollars a year   On a population basis, this would be
the equivalent of about 45 billion dollars annually for the United States"   Paul
Mallon, Oct. 25, 1940, reported, "Defense commission publicity . . . disclosed
expenditures are now running at a rate of $200,000,000 a month   Last year, long
before the defense commission was established, the rate of expenditure was
$100,000,000 a month.   Current plans contemplate a hopeful outlay of $1,000,-
000,000 a month, from 13 to 18 months hence"

(2) British Major L. L. B. Angas in his digest #70, Jan 4, 1941, tells us,
"Invasion of Germany would however require an army and air force at least
double the size of Germany's.   Say 8 to 14 million men   The British Empire
might provide half (the Empire has only 75 million whites), so U.S A (and or
Russia) would have to provide the other half, say 4 to 7 million men.   This being
so, if the Washington plan (eventually) is to smash Hitler completely, America
will have to build an army of 50,000 tanks and say 7 million men (half to be kept
in America), and not just rely on the hope or sporting chance that an air force of

say 150,000 planes, could alone bring the German Government down. Looking at all these different alternatives together it seems rather ridiculous for America to take any part in this noble war (to Root out Evil), unless she is going to go whole-hog and try to root out Hitlerism altogether"

In February, 1941, the daily expenditure for the war was estimated roughly in millions of dollars as follows· Great Britain, 53; Germany, 28; United States, 20, Italy, 10; Japan, 3, Canada, 3. (*Economic Notes,* March, 1941)

A FOUR BILLION DOLLAR ELECTION FUND

Political opponents strong for national defense openly charge Mr. Roosevelt with using the world situation to insure a third term His defense of expense leads some to question if this expense is not for defense of the New Deal The Boston *Herald,* May 27, editorially says,—"If he will only realize that a President must be elected this year and that some criticism of his methods is inevitable, and if he will extend to other citizens the same respect for unselfish and patriotic motives which he expects them to extend him, all will be well "

"The President's speech to Congress was undoubtedly the most brilliant piece of political strategy and the most adroit use of a given situation that have ever been seen in this country", says Villard in *The Nation,* June 1 "Roosevelt has a veritable genius for timing, for seizing upon an event and exploiting it to the full for his administrative or political purposes. His speech was in many ways a typical Rooseveltian performance—embarking the country on a huge economic program before the proposal had been thought through. I have reason to know he is worried greatly by the fear of foreign invasion."

The above explains perhaps why Roosevelt announces, "I am a pacifist", why he speaks with emotionally aroused sincerity in terms of large abstractions, 'morality', 'religion', 'saving civilization', and would down 'evil' at any cost, as would Cromwell or a Torquemada.

Republican opponents were elated at the announcement of increased taxation necessary to meet the administration's huge appropriations "If anything can defeat Roosevelt next November this will do it", one House leader was heard to say. (Paul Mallon, May 29) [1] [2]

Willkie, as early as May 20, predicted the President's defense funds would run to 5 billions, and asked, "Why was it that Mr. Roosevelt . . . failed to get his money's worth for the $7,000,000,000 already spent on defense?" Taft charges, he has "failed to develop an Army and

Navy with essential modern weapons". Vandenburg proclaims, "It takes more than appropriations to make a national defense". Dewey (not John) attacks, "It is not enough to appropriate more billions of dollars. Our problem now, more than ever before, is not to be solved by the mere spending of money." Gannett even more drastically assails the incompetence. "Ernest T. Weir, head of the American Iron and Steel Institute, angrily reechoed Congressional charges of money 'poured down a rathole', demanded an accounting." (*Newsweek,* June 3)

"The seethers for a third term have alarmed Congress into giving them $3,282,011,352 for their campaign fund,"[2] H L. Mencken writes (Baltimore *Sun,* May 26), "but what good the money will yield for the rest of us remains to be seen. A number of stock jobbers disguised as airship builders will grow rich, another huge horde of bogus experts of all sorts will snuggle up to the public trough, and the air will be blistered and fermented by fresh waves of crooning from the White House, but there is no evidence whatever that all the waste and uproar will stop the war, or even influence its course. This is no argument against arming. On the contrary, I am strongly in favor of arming, and have been in favor of it ever since my conversion to Christianity, now many years ago Roosevelt and his goons began trying to barge into the war even before there was a war. Anyone who objects is denounced as a traitor to the flag, and accused of taking bribes from Hitler. If England wins, we will pay the bills; if Hitler wins, we will pay the damages."[3]

June 5, 1940

NOTES

[1] The cost of presidential elections in the past is dealt with in an article in *Fortune,* July, 1940 Trustworthy records go back only to 1912. In the 1860 campaign the National Committee expenses were only $150,000. The first million dollar campaign was 1880 In 1896 Mark Hanna brought the big money, 3½ millions to put McKinley in In 1920 Gen Woods spent $1,700,000 In 1928, Mike Benedum (cf *Fortune,* Dec., 1940), "one of the richest unknown men in the U.S ", who made his money in oil, contributed half a million to support Hoover and spike Mellon, his rival and enemy.

The 1936 national, state, and local campaign expenditure, according to the Congressional Lonergan Committee, cost 50 million. The National Committees spent only a third of that,—5½ million Democratic, and 8 something for the Republicans. In 1940 Garner spent $400,000, McNutt $200,000, Taft $150,000, Dewey $200,000. *Fortune* does not tell how much Willkie spent but published estimates have run as high as $8,000,000.

The rising cost of electing the President is in part due to the increase in the number of voters to be reached. William Harrison was the first president to poll over one million, and two million was not reached until Lincoln's second election. Benjamin Harrison was the first to poll over five million. McKinley, Theodore Roosevelt and Taft each polled something over seven million William Harding jumped to sixteen million. And Roosevelt in his three elections polled 22,821,857, 27,752,309 and 26,361,762.

(2) January 24, AP, reported that "Senator Guy M. Gillette of Iowa, Chairman of the Special Senate Committee investigating campaign expenditures" made a " 'rough guess' that between $50,000,000 and $60,000,000 was spent on political campaigns leading up to the recent elections". Actual contributions had been reported "aggregating $24,174,223" The Republicans had received $16,476,040, the Democrats $6,284,463.

(3) Bulletin #55, "No More Millionaires", was held at the time as inexpedient to publish, but was later issued with some additions as #66 under the same title.

Bulletin #56 printed comment from correspondents, an increasing number of them presented anonymously because of the change in the national situation We quote only a few:

"There is something slightly satanic in your ability to force your readers to face irritating problems which they have gone to great pains to ignore."—I. S. Mattingly, Conn.

"You have, so far, been righter than anybody (unless I include myself). I am afraid that in spite of all you can do, we'll pay for the farce. But keep up the fight ! We are going to strip ourselves to the bone, when we could use the money to develop our resources and give our people a better way of life But we've got too many who don't want a better way of life "—Burton Rascoe, N. Y

"You are doing America a splendid service exposing the propaganda and trickeries being used to get us into war, especially the subtle connivings and under-cover work of Great Britain, which for some reason is being overlooked. But how much longer will honest Americans be allowed to speak out, defend American interests? Not much longer, if we are to judge from ominous signs coming from Mr. Roosevelt and other leaders Already pressure is being exerted via speeches, radio talks, editorials, statements to the press (a la Breckenridge's recent shot at Lindbergh) making it a disgrace and a crime to be for America or Americans—while it is an honor for Americans to forget about America and think only of Great Britain. After all this condemnation of totalitarianism it looks as though Roosevelt and the pro-British crowd now plan to put full totalitarian measures in effect in the U.S.A. It's mighty serious and all good and free Americans should rally together, before that right has been taken from us."—Thomas Burke Benton, Calif.

"You are doing a splendid work It would be nice to talk to you and find out your views on the possibility of stemming the flood tide of propaganda and pro-British bias, fairly bewildering in its lack of clear thinking or intelligence."—Mrs C. R. Thayer, Mass.

"I always have respect for the man who has the courage and initiative to expose the fraud and propaganda that is deluging us. It is impossible to estimate the moral damage that can be done by selfish nations and people alike. I think you are doing a grand job "—Major Al. J Williams, Pittsburgh, Pa.

"As the days drag on I disagree with you less and less, perhaps I grow sicker and sicker of the British ruling gang. We seem determined out here not to get killed if we can help it; and I think that it will take a good deal of cheering to get us into line   They'll get us into line of course; but it will be a job.   And there's hope before the job's done the Kilkenny cats will be clawed away clear down to their tails "—S A. Nock, Kansas State College.

"We have here, in this community, some people who have suffered a good deal at the hands of the Nazis. They seem greatly distressed at some of your revelations, but they have no reason to trust the British ruling group any more than the Germans   Your statements are very fair and illuminating "—Paul B Sears, Oberlin Coll , Ohio

FOR WHOSE RELIGION?

To God the embattled nations sing and shout,
"Gott strafe England" and "God Save the King".
"God this", "God that", and "God the other thing".
"Good God!" said God, "I've got my work cut out".

This poem was written by Sir John Squires at the beginning of the last war. It might have been written today. Hector Bolitho tells a story of a religious writer who sent a book to be copyrighted. Feeling that the book had been divinely inspired, in the space for the author she wrote "God". A formal letter from the Department informed her that "No book may be copyrighted unless it is written by a citizen of some specified country". God only knows what country he is a citizen of. Everybody's claiming him.

"Gott mit Uns" was the note sounded by the Kaiser in the last war. But when have a people gone forth to slaughter without claiming that God was with them?[1] They still play football "For God, for Country, and for Yale". A Christian people must claim they are fighting for their God, just as a Mohammedan people must claim they are fighting for Allah. War cries issue from the churches as war impends. That religion will be increased or morality improved by the killing, rape and rapine they advocate to some does not seem likely [2]

The universities and their beneficiaries are first brought into line.

Financial control through trustees and foundations make that easy. But they, too, claim divine sanction.

With the opening of the academic year, the presidents of our great universities, inspired by their trustees and prospective donors, sounded off for religion and morality They were following the lead of our great President who was preaching from the text given out from Whitehall with responsive readings from Wall Street. (cf Bul #16)

Whose religion is this for? Not for the Pope's. He still speaks of peace as something desirable Myron Taylor, a personal representative of our President, has gone to the Vatican to lead him to worship the British war god. But the former legate to Germany well knows that the German government still, in war time, out of taxes pays the salaries of her Roman Catholic priests,[3]—that 26 new churches were built and 370 remodeled in Germany in 1938.

Cardinal O'Connell of Boston proclaims, "We want no part in this muddle of a row in Europe We are sorry for any horror that comes to any race or flag, but we cannot make the same mistake we made in the other war". [4] Cardinal Dougherty at Philadelphia, June 1 (AP), declared that "we should mind our own business and not become cat's-paws" in international rivalries. The World War taught Americans "not to intermeddle with the rival struggles of greed and vengeance of European countries".

The *Living Church,* leading high church periodical, denounces its English-born, British bigot, Bishop Manning, and the more recent statement of the clergymen and laymen who lined up to promote hate (cf Bul #33). "The 27 Christian leaders, however great their sincerity, are definitely exercising their leadership along the well-trodden road to war. It saddens us to see the clergy, including our own Presiding Bishop, in the forefront of those who are urging our nation along that road It looks too much like the preaching of the dangerous dogma of the holy war".

Mr. Roosevelt's "gabble" for "what he so humorously calls 'religion and morality' may give the judicious pause", H. L. Mencken remarks. Is his the god of the British far flung battle line, "beneath whose awful hand we hold dominion"?[5]

With some of the old threadbare slogans and some new hypocritical insincerities, we are being worked up more rapidly to the same state

of hysteria, as twenty-two years ago.[6] We seem just as gullible as our
forbears of whom Samuel Butler (1612-1680) wrote in "Hudibras":

"For as we make war for the king
"Against Himself, the self-same Thing.
"Some will not stick to swear we do
"For God, and for Religion too".[7]

June 7, 1940

Notes

[1] At the time Hore-Belisha was thrown out of the cabinet, a Boston *Herald*
commentator remarked, "There is more than just a feeling about bounders, they
say, in the Hore-Belisha row, and the win-the-war slogan isn't really God and
the right-er-people."

[2] "The religion may be the worship of Mammon, and the philosophy that of
a pirate, but they are all effectively agreed on it, and will cut throats for its sake;
and so they will triumph until their opponents learn the lesson and find unity in
a common religion and philosophy of their own " (G Bernard Shaw in "What
I Really Wrote About the War", 1934)

[3] Hitler, in his speech to the Reichstag, Jan. 30, 1939, stated, "The National
Socialist state had closed no church and had influenced no church service. On
the contrary, he emphasized, the National Socialist state had paid church taxes,
which rose from 130,000,000 marks in 1933 to 500,000,000 in 1938, besides
92,000,000 marks in state and communal subsidies How much, he asked ironically, had France, Great Britain and America paid the churches in the same time?
But if the German churches should really regard this situation as unbearable, the
National Socialist state is ready at any time to make clear the separation between
church and state."

"These 'voluntary grants' are in lieu of property taken away from the Church
in former times and they are independent of Church taxes. By the process of
Gleichschaltung the Church had already by 1936 lost 5,185,000 marks that the
Bavarian Government had been accustomed to pay. These things were clearly
set forth in "The Struggle for Religious Freedom in Germany" by Arthur S.
Duncan-Jones (Victor Gollancz, London, 1938) which deals with the Protestant
and Catholic effort to maintain their freedom to criticize political forces and
political and social measures from the standpoint of their position and the
Church, and to influence or control the education of youth.

"Though the Nazis have jailed over 10,000 pastors, priests and monks for long
or short periods, an unknown number have been beaten to death, the churches
stand far higher in German esteem today than they did in the easy-going '20s
Church congregations have grown remarkably. Sales of the Bible have shot up
from 830,000 copies in 1933 to 1,225,000 in 1939, topping Mein Kampf by
about 200,000." Each bishop has been required to "promise to honor the constitutional government and to cause the clergy of my diocese to honor it" (*Time*,

Dec. 23, 1940)   Those who have not, like Cardinal Faulhaber in Munich who used his pulpit to make political speeches, have had a hard time.

Persecution in America of religious sects is not unknown. The American Civil Liberties reports,—"Documents filed with the Department of Justice by attorneys for Jehovah's Witnesses and the American Civil Liberties Union showed over 355 instances of mob violence in 44 states during 1940, involving 1488 men, women, and children", and cites many individual cases of savage atrocity. This religious sect takes the bible literally, refusing to worship or bow down before idols or symbols in which they include the flag. They put loyalty to God before loyalty to state.

In 1918 in Cincinnati, Herbert S Bigelow, was taken miles away from his home at midnight by men in an auto, stripped, flogged and tarred, as were other pastors, negro, white, American and German   The persecutions during our excitement from 1918-20 and of our mass arrests of Reds under Quaker Atty. Gen. Palmer make just as good material for hate propaganda in Germany.

(4) On his eighty-first birthday, Dec 7, 1940, Cardinal O'Connell, in denouncing the "exalted hysteria" of people about him, declared "the vast majority of the American people are for peace, and notwithstanding too prevalent propaganda from all sides   They have taken it for granted that the authorities in Washington said what they meant and meant what they said when they promised to keep us out of the war   There are certain expatriates . . who are raising their voices in very loud accents with a preposterous proposition that America sink her individuality and become sort of a tail end of a foreign empire" (Boston *Transcript*). And again a month later he dramatically appealed for neutrality and cautioned his hearers "to resist the Machiavellian influence of foreign propagandists".

(5) While the Archbishop of Canterbury leads the Hate Hitler forces, the Dean of Canterbury is an ardent supporter of the Soviets. The Archbishop of York who is second only to Canterbury whom he automatically succeeds, called a conference that met January 7 to 10, 1941, at Malvern College attended by 500 church leaders including 23 Bishops, 14 deans. The Archbishop called for "a new order of society". Dorothy Sayers, the novelist, attacked the church for its trivial views of morality accenting sex, and asserted that "to upset legalized cheating, the Church must tackle the government . . the politician, the press." Sir Richard Acland, the fifteenth baronet in his family, declared, "The whole structure of society   is, from the Christian point of view, rotten"   The conference resolution passed unanimously, "The war is not to be regarded as an isolated evil. It is one symptom of widespread disease and maladjustment." (*The Witness,* Jan. 23, 1941)

Time, January 20, gave three pages to the report of this conference, and declared that the church "stole a march on the Government with a program of post-war aims" calling for the abolition of the profit system   *Time,* February 3, reported, "U S. clergymen are moving steadily away from their pre-war pacifism".

(6) In June when this Bulletin on religion was written, the hysteria was mount-

ing so that it seemed inadvisable to publish these statements of the vicars of the prince of peace, the great Cardinals of the American Catholic Church. While for a time the appeasers were denounced as traitors, the exponents of morality and religion in Washington and in our great universities no longer held as valid the teaching of Christ, "Blessed are the peacemakers for they shall see God".

(7) Bulletin #58 was a single sheet to accompany reprints from the *Congressional Record*, some 40,000 of which have been mailed out without enclosures under Congressional frank, or with enclosures at my expense. Included in these reprints were Lindbergh's radio address Belonging to no organizations and sponsoring none, I nevertheless occasionally have brought and continue to bring to the attention of my readers organization activities which seem of interest and immediate importance

WITCH HUNT AHEAD

So ran the headline in the Boston *Evening Transcript*, June 4, over an AP dispatch from Chicago, quoting the psychologist Dr. Robert N. McMurry on the national hysteria.[1] "I venture the prediction that before this hysteria runs its course you are likely to see the worst witch hunt in American history—and possibly the establishment of concentration camps. It is not a matter of intelligence. It is a matter of people letting their emotions get so much control they can't do anything about it. In an hysteria the veneer of civilization is stripped off and all of the public's sadistic tendencies come to the fore Reason is stopped. Logic goes down the rat hole The danger will be that for every bona fide fifth columnist caught there will be a lot of people finding themselves in a terrible jam. There are many people who are looking for justification for attacks on other people they don't like "[2]

On the same date a Boston *American* editorial says, "America is confronted by two great dangers", first that the willingness of the people to "support any measure of preparedness" may result in our becoming involved in foreign war. "Much more immediate, and far less heeded, is the danger that our system of free government and free enterprise may be subverted—subverted not by the known enemies of our institutions, but by professed friends and guardians of these institutions through the enactment in Congress of destructive legislation in the guise of 'emergency' measures."

Newsweek, June 3, commenting on Roosevelt's national defense fireside talk, said, "In the President's strong denunciation of saboteurs and Fifth Columnists there was an implication of growing sensitiveness to opposition, of a tendency to lump all critics of his new program as hirelings of foreign ax-grinders."[3]

"Why don't you run a bulletin on the British Fifth Column in this country? They are just as treasonable as the Germans, since they want in effect to turn over the sovereignty of this country to London "—A Harvard undergraduate editor. (cf Bul #27)

"If the British Lords who are in this country doing all in their power to draw this country into the war are not expelled or put into prison along side of Fritz Kuhn and others like him, we will be over there fighting England's war like the Frenchmen are doing, while the British sit by and laugh, and call us nit-wits and suckers, as they have been doing for so long".—A Portland, Ore., attorney.

"We need someone like you to bring to us in no uncertain tones the danger to our people of the 5th column formed in England and spreading here, aided by English funds and propaganda. The effect of this 5th column's activities on our president is alarming. He seems obsessed by his duty to England, forgetting he may lead our country to destruction and under British domination again".—A San Francisco author.

"And we urge the passage of a law for the immediate expulsion from the U S. of any man who advocates war without accepting the full responsibility of his advocacy. Those who think we ought to go to war can prove their faith by enlisting in the army".—Three N.Y.C. authors.

As early as February, in Bulletins #34, 35 we warned of "The Threat to Our 'Civil Liberties' " and "The Coming Red Drive".[4] [5]

June 8, 1940

NOTES

[1] Syndicate columnist, Frederic Sondern, Jr., (Burlington, Vt, *Free Press*, Nov. 30, 1940), offers a suggestion as to one of the lines along which this hysteria and witch hunt will run: "The big push is starting. Everyone who doesn't agree with the White committee is going to be labeled and blasted as a Nazi or un-American in some way. And the America First committee, as other similar organizations—opposed to aid to Britain is going to blast back. The witch-hunts are going to be terrific and the truth harder and harder to find "

Time comments June 10, 1940 "George Norris rose in the Senate to recall World War I raids, when 'hundreds of persons entirely innocent were arrested, shackled and handcuffed just because their enemies made false charges against them.' Many could recall when anti-German feeling ran so high that it was hazardous to say "Auf Wiedersehen" on the street, when German opera singers were howled down, the Boston Symphony's German Conductor Dr. Karl Muck was interned, and the father of Senator La Follette was burned in effigy." Hysteria reached its height in this country after the war was over, in the Palmer red raids of 1920 Here in Boston before daybreak one morning in March, as I remember, thousands of homes were broken into, some 1700 people were pulled out of bed and carried off, crowded into the jails and the corridors of the court-house. It was three days before they could be sorted out and the great majority sent home as innocents.

(2) Bainbridge Colby tells us, "in Europe the Fifth Column is in disguise; with us it is in office". Carleton Beals in "Pan America" (Houghton Mifflin) states, "our own worst Fifth Column is not that of disguised enemy aliens, but political incompetence and selfishness".

William Henry Chamberlin in *American Mercury*, Dec. 1940, speaks of the Fifth Columnist as a term "thrown about as a general epithet of abuse Repression and intolerance are a source of strength to a totalitarian state They are a source of weakness, of internal poisoning, to a democracy The danger to American democracy of permitting homegrown communists and fascists to express their views freely, subject only to the restrictions of the ordinary laws against libel and incitement to disorder, is very much less than the danger that would be implicit in launching a campaign of arbitrary repression. Such a campaign, by its very nature, knows no limit What might begin as a process of cracking down on fascists and communists would soon become a witch hunt against all isolationists and pacifists, would certainly end in the establishment of the totalitarian theory that the administration can do no wrong."

Edmund Taylor, author of "Strategy of Terror" in *America* for Sept 14, 1940, tells how to identify Fifth Columnists It is almost as startlingly hair-raising as "How to Tell the Wild Flowers", a book popular generations ago in what were then pink parlors. Perhaps unintentionally it is extremely funny. Based on his terrorizing experiences in France, he tells us that a Fifth Columnist is the person sitting next to you at dinner.—More recently at Ford Hall Forum (Boston *Herald,* Nov 25, 1940), Mr Taylor, 'while advocating that Fifth Columnists be shot as traitors . . characterized Colonel Lindbergh as a 'three and one-half per cent American' . . . a 'softee', influenced by Nazi propaganda" and advocated an organization "to suppress un-American activities".

(3) By November, 1940, educational publications were filled with such government propaganda as "Fighting the Fifth Column· How Schoolmen Can Aid the FBI" by John Edgar Hoover, Director of the Federal Bureau of Investigation, appears in *Nation's Schools*

Martin Dies presents his report to the country in the form of his book "The Trojan Horse in America" (Dodd, Mead) giving 300 pages to the Red menace, 20 to Nazi activities, 15 to Italian Fascists, and 8 to native brands of authoritarianism, and levels his guns at such notable figures as Mrs. Roosevelt, Ickes, Jackson, Frank Murphy and Archibald MacLeish. Then, according to *Time*, Dec

2, 1940, "Dies produced a bigger show than ever". Raiding German and Italian organizations in Chicago and with "similar raids in eight other cities under way, Dies brought up his heavy artillery, released his 413 page, thickly documented white paper" which "had passages as juicy as any E. Phillips Oppenheim tale".

In England John Anderson, former Governor of Bengal, where he ruthlessly repressed rebellion, caused so much resentment that he was transferred to another post. Protest rose so high in the Commons that he agreed to release 10,000 suspects whom he had imprisoned. (*Time*, Aug. 12, 1940)

(4) "Witch Hunt The Technique and Profits of Redbaiting" (Modern Age Books, 1940) by George Seldes, author of "Lords of the Press" and editor of *In Fact*, brings together much interesting material culled and clipped and quoted from newspapers and other periodicals

(5) Bulletin #60 gave a list of all Bulletins and again explained that they were "sent without charge on request and to those proposed".

WILL BRITAIN WIN OUR ELECTION?

We are being rapidly and efficiently "sold" participation in Europe's war, by much the same methods the oil burner salesman uses on us boobs The "Committee to 'Defend' America by Aiding the Allies" is putting on high pressure. Naturally the President approves. Some believe it better to swap horses crossing the stream than the ocean.

"Our Election and Europe's War", *Sat Eve Post*, May 11, is by Demaree Bess, who writes, "The stage seems to be set for a final struggle between those Americans who want to bring us into the Allied-German war and those who want to keep us out. That struggle coincides with our presidential election and seems likely to dominate it.(1)

"It is almost three years since President Roosevelt began to pull and push the American people back into the thick of world politics. An Englishman .   . said to me: 'It would be wonderful for us if Mr. Roosevelt received a third term'." "British and French governments" refused "to negotiate a peace . . . so long as they could see that vast untapped reservoir of . . . the most powerful neutral, the United States.(2) "Mr Roosevelt was confident he was running no danger of involving the United States in war", that he could "outbluff" Hitler and Mussolini "in the European poker game". (Alsop and Kintner confirm this.)

"Too Many Germans?" asks Wallace R. Deuel, *Sat Eve Post*, May 25. "British propaganda is more effective than the others . . . and therefore more important . . . plausible and popular to most Americans . . . who take Hitler at his word. Many believe that the destruction of Hitlerism is really their war aim" It would do "virtually nothing whatever toward solving Europe's fundamental problem Hitler represents and personifies the reaction of the German people", who "are entirely too numerous, too able, too advanced economically, too strategically located, too energetic"[3] to suit those who "find the distribution of the world's goods fairly satisfactory[4] as it is" and "have withdrawn from the processes of accumulating empires and hung up a sign which reads, 'Quiet is requested for the benefit of those who have retired'."[5]

The "Year of Reckoning", G. Ward Price, the English writer, entitles his latest book (Cassell Ltd., 1939), in which he tells us, "The present crisis in Europe is not due to the German government being made up entirely of fiends, or the British Government of hypocrites. It arises from . a fundamental divergence of view The subject of this difference is the German belief . . . in their mission of reorganizing the relatively backward and undeveloped regions lying between Central Europe and the borders of Asia". He quotes Ribbentrop·

"It is a quite natural and unavoidable process. Whether you approve of it or not, you cannot prevent it. If you are unable to agree to the steps which Germany is taking, the best thing for Britain to do is to stick to your path and leave us to follow ours Fate has called Britain to be the centre of a great world-Empire. We do not interfere in the internal affairs of the Empire, and we do not recognize your right to interfere with Germany's natural evolution"

"The French and British are really shocked and outraged by the Nazis' treatment of smaller and weaker peoples. But nations do not enter major wars because they are shocked and outraged by what happens to somebody else". Americans have to be scared. In 1898, Hearst newspapers so scared the wealthy of Boston of bombardment by the Spanish fleet that they moved their valuables to Worcester safe deposit vaults.

June 14, 1940

NOTES

[1] Commenting on the "amazing impertinence of the press of foreign countries in butting into the American election", David Lawrence writes, Nov. 6, 1940, "The British press was most offensive The editorials there said clearly

that there was no difference in foreign policy between the two candidates, but asked Americans to realize that the British wanted Roosevelt re-elected " That Britain believes she won our election is evident from their practical annexation—sending two months later a member of the British government, Lord Halifax, on a British battleship to be greeted at sea (foreign territory) by our 'Furor'. Ten days later Halifax was conferring with the chairmen of the Committee on Foreign Relations and both House and Senate on the time table of the 'lend-lease' Bill (cf p 312)

(2) Complimenting Willkie, Churchill "in the name of the government and people of London congratulated President Roosevelt on his re-election, declaring that the American President had never failed to extend them a helping hand We shall now receive the support of the products of the gigantic munitions productions and the matchless workshops, furnaces and foundries of the American union" (Raymond Daniell, N Y *Times* cable from London, Nov 9, 1940)

(3) "That is the trouble with the Germans,—they work when others loaf. In ten years travel around the world before War I, I saw lit up until near midnight the German offices in Hong Kong, Bankok or Bombay The British, already then largely Scotch, closed their offices at two or three for the races, later to sit around their clubs cursing the swine who were stealing their markets. Worse still, those damn Germans adapted the stuff they tried to sell to the needs and desires of the people Such betrayal of European standards was just too much for the British merchants So the Germans had to be knocked out and now we have got to do it again." (From a letter published in *Time,* Dec 2, 1940)

(4) In "The Rise of New York Port", Robert G Albion tells how the patroons (Roosevelts) and their Tory friends grew so rich they couldn't get their sons to go to work and were forced to put the management of their affairs in the hands of impecunious Yankees. (The Irish grandfather of William and Henry James built the family fortune on this patroon decline) Later immigrants in time succeeded,—in New York the Jews, in Boston the Irish.

There is a predictable rhythm in these changes of control Once the British Empire was run for the ruling classes, the landed aristocracy of England But fox hunting and port did not equip their descendants to take over Abler lieutenants were recruited from Scotch underlings, more acute in finding opportunities for exploitation, expropriation, export, and the other extraordinary measures needed to live on the labor of others But the Scotch enriched, softened, gave way to the facile, acquisitive Jew. Old residents used to say, "India is a country conquered by the Irish, administered by the English for the benefit of the Scotch" But today the Scotch don't get all the dividends Parsees and Armenians take their share. "Blessed are the meek;" they have always inherited the earth

With oil the source of power, the Dutchman, Deterding, with the aid of the British Empire and in alliance with Teagle of Standard Oil, became "The Most Powerful Man in the World" His ablest lieutenants, surviving competition and elimination in the exploiting of oil resources, were three Armenians—Gulben-

kian, Hacobian, and Essayan.   But it was to their control, Royal Shell, that
Chamberlain in the spring of 1939 turned over all the oil resources of the Empire.
Now though oil conscious, they have become uxorious, soft, ripe for the plucking
by the formerly down-trodden, rickety, starved survivors of the 1919-20 British
blockade.   (cf Bul #13 and Notes)

"The way of salvation of humanity,—" Mencken said in his Sunday sermon
Dec. 1, 1940, "first the underprivileged are liberated from the law of natural
selection by one gang of bogus messiahs, and then another gang of bogus messiahs
falls upon the liberators, to the loud applause, and usually with the hearty aid,
of the underprivileged".

(5) Bernard Shaw early made a suggestion that would have shortened the last
war.   He wrote Nov. 14, 1914, "We must kill the German women if we mean
business when we talk of destroying Germany.   Men are comparatively of no
account.   Kill 90 per cent of their German men, and the remaining 10 per cent
can repeople her.   But kill the women, and *delenda est Carthago*".   Shaw, who
dislikes "the moral babble (Milton's phrase) of his sanctimonius colleagues" is
humane and realistic in his suggestions but he does not tell how to accomplish the
result he wishes   Bacteriologists might discover a disease that, propagated and
spread over Germany by airplane, would destroy the reproductive power   Or
physicists may discover a ray, they have in fact, which could even be directed from
a distance for that purpose.   To some, such measures would seem more humane,
even more Christian, than the slow killing of the children, the old and the weak,
by deprivation, malnutrition, starvation   But that is justified by the practices of
the British blockade of the past and the present, and upheld by American moralists, college presidents and bishops.

100% (ANGLO-) AMERICAN (IMPERIALIST)

Under the title "Sworn to Secrecy" the May 20 issue of *In Fact* said,—
"Eighteen prominent figures met secretly on April 29th.   America, they
resolved, must be in a position to give whatever aid—even armies—
required by the Allies.   Apparently called by Frederic R Coudert,
legal advisor to the British Embassy in 1915-1920", attending were [1]
Thomas W. Lamont, Nicholas Murray Butler, Henry L. Stimson, Wendell Willkie, Lewis Douglas, Frank Polk, and Philip M. Brown, who
"submitted a memorandum . . . expressing the outlook of those present.   Neutrality legislation must go.   Nothing must stand in the way
of America giving full help to Great Britain and France, even if that
means armed aid." [2]

In the Harvard *Alumni Bulletin* April 16, was published a letter from
Thomas Lamont, influential alumnus, tactfully rebuking the undergraduates reluctance to accept "the moral issues" of this war.[3]

The *Bulletin* in its issue of April 2 had resurrected, published, and editorially endorsed with 'absolute accord', a speech of the previous January by J. L. O'Brian, '96, Buffalo and former Federal attorney, in which he announced that "the constantly reiterated warnings against propaganda are actually producing a new type of intellectual coward- ice". (cf "Universities Promote War", in "What Makes Lives")

The implication of this type of threat has resulted in many who were formerly aware of propaganda now denying that they can smell any- thing, and the dismissal of columnists whose olfactory sense functioned.

Presidents Conant of Harvard and Seymour of Yale early in the year had come out for undergraduates moral responsibility for the mess in Europe. This led the Harvard *Crimson* to denounce them as members of "the road gang that is trying to build for the U. S. a super-highway straight to Armageddon" (cf Bul #16). In the spring hundreds of Harvard undergraduates had signed a petition voicing "determination never, under any circumstances, to follow in the footsteps of the stu- dents of 1917".

At the meeting of the Associated Harvard Clubs in New York, May 17-19, presided over by Mr Lamont, the signatures of 34 members of the war class of 1917 were secured to a letter, skilfully drafted, which again rebuked Harvard undergraduates for lack of moral responsibility.

This letter was printed in the Harvard *Crimson* May 21, with an ac- companying editorial reaffirming "the reasoned conviction that the way in which America drifted toward war in those years was unintelligent and unworthy of our nation". Both of these were reprinted in the Harvard *Alumni Bulletin* of May 21, together with Librarian of Con- gress Archibald MacLeish's lament that "the young generation is dis- trustful of all words and distrustful of all moral judgments".

Simultaneously with the meeting of the Associated Harvard Clubs, Grenville Clark, New York attorney and member of the Harvard Cor- poration, published a letter in the N. Y. *Times*, May 18, in which he advocated a program similar to that formulated at 'the secret meeting' of April 29. This plan was reiterated in Mr. Clark's later speeches in which he called for an army of three million men, and toward the end of the month in speeches by Mr. Coudert, Senator Austin, and President Conant and President Seymour, and many others thereafter.

The Committee to Defend America by Aiding the Allies "emerged into plain view" a little before this. Something of the methods of its promoters were explained in the issues of May 25 and June 15 of *Uncensored* (112 E. 19th St., N.Y.C.)

William Allen White of Kansas was made the nominal head, perhaps because of his geographical position and because he had previously been used to head the National Committee which fought the arms embargo. This new organization has been referred to in the press as Mr. White's committee. He issued an idealistic and innocuous statement of principles, and said, "We are doing nothing with mirrors There is no trick in this. We are trying to crystallize the overwhelming sentiment." [4]

A Kansas banker writes me confidentially, "William Allen White has been one of the biggest curses in Kansas politics since I was a boy. He means to be liberal but only succeeds in being a fool He is a man cursed with a clever pen, a kind heart and no critical faculties. He has been on the side of every silly reform that has been proposed in Kansas during his time. He has no sense of sportsmanship whatsoever. He dabbles in politics constantly and has substantial influence which is most unfortunate. He uses his heart to do his thinking with, can make the cruelest remarks of any newspaperman in these parts, and he shrivels up into a little ball of nothing at the slightest criticism of himself. About the time Harvard gave him an honorary Doctor's degree he made the widely published statement that although age was creeping upon him 'he had no fear of death but only of senility' which made me snort aloud for he was probably the only known member of the human race who was senile before he was adolescent." [5]

Clark M. Eichelberger, the active director of the organization, is right hand man for President Butler, active in all pro-British propaganda and the National Director of the League of Nations Association. Mr. Eichelberger, referring to Mr White as chairman, announced (N.Y. *Tribune,* June 9) that the committee had "chapters in more than 125 towns and cities, and hundreds more are being formed".

The busy New York headquarters, described in *Time,* June 17, is now rapidly organizing state, city, town, and ward committees all over the country, with mass meetings promoting a 'lynching bee' type of hate hysteria, as on Boston Common, June 16, when Col. Breckinridge announced, "The blood drenched Hitler is at our gates".

. Committee members have been strategically selected,—attorneys, Anglophiles, Nazi-haters, and liberals who might do damage if not made captive. The publicity has been marvelously managed (P. and A , June 7). Tremendous sums have been spent on page and quarter page advertisements in metropolitan Sunday newspapers with the "Stop Hitler Now" slogan, and on huge posters in subways. Guile has been used, not too successfully.[6]

The strategy and organization has followed something of the English method, learned from the Oriental,—fear and flattery, snub and snobbery, prestige or ostracism. Prominent men have been chosen to lead. In Massachusetts, Conant is at the head, Ex-Governor Fuller is chairman, and dynamic young Harvard attorneys who may be rewarded with receiverships or reorganization fees have been put in charge [7]

"Harvard faculty members and students fear being disciplined for peace pleas", *PM*, June 18, reports on Boston, in surveying the war fever in cities throughout the country.

At the Harvard Class Day, June 18, violating a general agreement to keep war out of the Class Day celebration, a Boston bond broker, rebuking the class orator, boasted his own courage and denounced the cowardice of the undergraduates.

At the Harvard Commencement, June 20, Conant, who in his baccalaureate sermon had spoken of "creeping paralysis of our loyalties",— (in 1776 the Loyalists were unceremoniously driven out of Boston),— cautiously appealed against hysteria but lauded loyalty of alumni. (cf "How Universities Are Controlled", in "What Makes Lives", p 202).

Ward MacL. Hussey, '40, in his commencement address declared, "Let us fight in this country for what we want" and "decried gross inequalities of income, mob hysteria, and acquisitiveness" (Boston *Herald*) [8] "Alumni angry over the 'pacificist' attitude of some members of the senior class expressed themselves only by tearing anti-war posters" (Boston *Herald*, June 21), and passed resolutions favoring conscription. The liberal opposition, suppressed, met later to protest "alumni slanderers of youth as cowards". Outspoken Kirtley Mather, professor of geology, appealed, "Above all, men of 1940, don't be misled by hysteria and propaganda".

Backed by Senators Wheeler, Clark, Lundeen, and Nye, Senator Holt on the floor of the Senate explained who was behind,—"It's our war",

PM in its first issue, June 14, reports that to Holt "it is all as simple as a nursery rhyme". The senate Munitions Investigating Committee, headed by Nye, established that the Morgan bank was a partisan of the Allies from 1914 on and did what it could, which was a great deal, to get the United States into the first World War. As purchasing agent for the Allies, its commissions amounted to more than $20,000,000; as banker, millions more. Lord Northcliffe is supposed to have said that the British spent $150,000,000 on propaganda between 1914 and 1917

"The British 'Fifth column', as it parades across the pages of the *Congressional Record,* is more impressive than the Buckingham Palace guard. Thomas W. Lamont, the Morgan partner, leads the procession in busby and kilts. Behind him, prodding him with a pike, comes Lord Lothian, the British Ambassador. Then follow the Wall Street bankers; Henry L Stimson, former Secretary of State; Lewis Douglas, former Budget Director; President James Conant of Harvard and assorted newspaper publishers The device on their shields of British gold is William Allen White, rampant against the format of the Emporia *Gazette.* The British Fifth Column is 100 per cent American. The money behind White's advertisements is surely American money contributed by wealthy Anglophiles . . . sincere in their belief, shared by leaders of the Roosevelt administration, that the British Navy is this country's first line of defense and its destruction would imperil the Western world." [9]

Senator Holt, reacting to the appointment of Stimson, who advocates throwing our navy yards open to the British fleet, recalled that there had long been pressure from London to get Woodring out. " 'It has succeeded', Holt shouted. 'Did Lord Lothian, the British ambassador, tell the President?' Holt said Woodring tried to do everything within the law to aid the allies, but to look out for the United States first, while his successor's policy was 'to do anything for the allies that is necessary and America be damned'." (Boston *Herald,* June 21)

The ruling Tory crew has wrecked England and the British Empire. [10] It's rule or ruin with them. Shall we let them drag America down? [11] *June 21, 1940*

NOTES

[1] Of the seven mentioned, Willkie was invited but not present as he told Boake Carter (July 8) "An invitation came in for me to attend a meeting like that As a matter of fact I had another engagement I am not attending meet-

ings like that." William Allen White was reported present (cf Bul #67). The others of the eighteen, Seldes writes me, included "a number of leaders from church and peace organizations. I have been trying my best to get you the complete list of names of the 18 original members of the WAWhite pro-Britain committee, but this is now impossible. The person who got me the list took me to see the preacher who gave it to him and this is the answer: there were several preachers present, 3 well-known men among them, and they were all under the illusion it was a peace meeting, and they signed. But they have now withdrawn; and for this reason my informant will not divulge the names of any persons except those who still support the movement." Charles G. Ross, associate editor of the St. Louis *Post-Dispatch*, after full investigation published a 3-page, 13,000-word account of the organization of the White Committee, but tells almost nothing about this initial meeting and avoids probing into those who were actually behind the movement.

(2) Brown Landone writing in the Winter Park (Fla.) *Herald* says (July 5, 1940), "On May 2nd last, I was in Boston. On that day I was told by definite statement, that a Boston banker who had just returned from New York City the day before, had confidentially told his close business associate that a group of important bankers had held a closed meeting, arranged to finance our entry into the war in Europe, and had determined that war should be declared about September 1st, 1940—if leaders of both major political parties could be brought into line."

As early as March 14, 1938, Hubert Herring in "And So To War" (Yale University Press) wrote: "A host of editors, business leaders, and professional men in Boston, New York, and Philadelphia are convinced that the United States would do well to cast its lot with the British Empire. Their conviction is profound, their argument convincing." British and Americans speak the same language, think alike, have interests in common, even to the point of mutual prosperity and safety. There is a natural and inevitable bond between the two peoples. (p 95)

Speaking of the April 29 secret meeting, Senator D. Worth Clark in an article entitled "The Men Behind Our War Scare", wrote in *Scribner's Commentator*, August, 1940, "It has been stated on the floor of the Senate that the man who called that meeting was Frederic Coudert, who helped generate the propaganda that took American youths to their deaths in 1917, when he was legal adviser to the British Embassy. Who else was there? Thomas W. Lamont, a partner of J. P. Morgan and Company, whose banking interests throughout the British Empire are more important to them than their interests in the United States. Then there was Lewis Douglas, who recently resigned as president of a Canadian university, and Frank Polk, an active propagandist in the first World War. And who else was there? None other than Henry L. Stimson, who has since been nominated as Secretary of War by President Roosevelt."

(3) "The more articulate alumni who think they run the show have again fallen into the same militant hysteria as in 1917. Some of them are sincere,

some are stooges, and some are scared   The Harvard *Alumni Bulletin* which
conservatively keeps the small proportion of graduates to whom it goes uninformed as to what is going on, not unnaturally promotes the views of Lamont
and Lothian." ("What Makes Lives", p 191)

(4) "Lead, Kindly White" is the title of an editorial in the Harvard *Crimson,*
Oct 25, 1940, which deals with the faculty promoted American Defense, Harvard Group, then a "lusty infant" of four months, "an informal adjunct of William Allen White's Committee" nourished by "Minturn Sedgwick, Vice-Chairman of the White outfit" who speaking at Harvard "said in describing a hypothetical transfer of American bombers to Great Britain, 'The President is all
for the plan, but only if public opinion gets behind it   That's where the William
Allen White committee swings into action, and pretty soon, Bang! and the
deal is done '   This was not sheer boasting, for the White Committee is probably the most powerful propaganda agency America has ever seen   Later in
his speech Sedgwick said that 'unless a miracle happens, it looks as if Uncle
Sam will be in the war' by next summer.   If Sedgwick has his way, this is how
it will happen: When White and his satellites, among them President Conant,
decide that American resistance has been sufficiently weakened, the knockout
blow will be delivered, and the United States will be blasted into war by a
barrage of skilful propaganda shaming Hearst's puny jingoism of 1898."

"A propaganda organization . . . built up carefully as such . . . a campaign to sneak America into the war" are the characterizations given by the
Milwaukee *Journal* in an editorial.   "This committee has worked skilfully.   It
has proceeded from the known fact that American public opinion would not
now support sending American troops to Europe   But who can doubt what its
final hope is?   Our quarrel with the Aid the Allies Committee is that its objective is not out in the open   Everything points to the conclusion that its real
purpose is to take the United States into the war.   Then why does it not say so?"

(5) William Allen White, whom *Time* describes as 'apple faced', is a kindly
soul interested in helping others   He writes me graciously:—"Thank you very
much for your note and your kind words   I was interested in the bulletins you
sent.   Sometime if you have anything of particular interest, remember me "

His desire to be popular and loved by all has sometimes brought him into bad
company, as in the Kansas bonds scandal, letter explaining his resignation from
the 'White Committee' (cf Bul #67)   At times he has lent himself to the
powers that be, as in his editorial "What's the Matter with Kansas" in which
his advice to the Kansas Populists to "stop raising hell and raise more corn",
which met with as cordial reception by the then "economic royalists" as did
Hubbard's "Message to Garcia", and was as wide spread in millions of copies

More recently, along the same pollyanna line, he wrote attributing the rise in
the living level in Lawrence County, Kansas, during two generations, to the un-
earned increment of the land   If we understand correctly, this is due to keeping
people off the land who might use it, which has resulted in "Grapes of Wrath"
migrants.   Meantime, the natural resources of Kansas soil and oil reservoirs

have been drained off to foreign countries on national credit to the profit of the few. Governor Ratner of Kansas (AP, Dec. 2), raising a howl because we were to let Venezuelan oil in under a lessened tax, "contended-that the con-cession on Venezuelan oils would be detrimental to the domestic petroleum industry, especially in Kansas". That suggests that their standard of living is in part due to the high price charged American people for oil.

(6) "The William Allen White Committee . . . is getting . . everything it has plugged for. Government propaganda backs up White Committee propa-ganda to propagandize the government to do what the government wants to do. ('Government-Roosevelt-Lothian ') It got American Legion to reverse past anti-intervention policy, provoking a protest rally of anti-war veterans here next week " (*Kiplinger Washington Letter*, Oct 19, 1940) A letter from a Chicago correspondent told how at a Legion meeting an attempt was made to pass a resolution to "Aid the Allies in every way". It was discovered just in time that the proposer was an agent of the White Committee.

(7) Thurman W Arnold in his "Folklore of Capitalism" deals with "The Ritual of Corporate Reorganization",—"the doctrine of vicarious atonement through which the debts of an industrial organization are forgiven". "A corporate re-organization is a combination of a municipal election, a historical pageant, an anti-vice crusade, a graduate-school seminar, a judicial proceeding, and a series of horse trades, all rolled into one—thoroughly buttered with learning and frosted with distinguished names. It was like a Chinese play. The techniques used were the same as those of any political organization." (pp 230, 237, 239) (cf "Strategy and Techniques of Protective and Reorganization Committees" in "Report on the Study and Investigation of the Work, Activities, Personnel and Functions of Protective and Reorganization Committees", Part VI, "Trustees under Indentures")

In the reorganization of Paramount Publix (*New Yorker*, Aug 3, 1935), learned counsel entered bills to the amount of $3,650,000. Grenville Clark's firm put in bills for $957,000.

(8) James R. Conant, Jr, son of the President of Harvard, in his class oration at Exeter, June 19, 1940, took "a point of view totally different from that of our parents", without "the same horror that our elders have displayed. We have not groaned about the rights of neutrals or about German barbarism. Rather, we have been awed by the cold-blooded efficiency and daring of the Germans, Hitler, as a man who can strike quickly and accurately, has won our admiration." (Phillips Exeter *Bulletin*, July, 1940, *Private School News*, Sept, 1940)

(9) The official list of contributors were put in the Congressional records of the Senate in mid December by Senator Holt. It included high ranking officials of J. P Morgan & Co., Lehman Brothers and a number of partners, Kuhn-Loeb & Co and members of families affiliated, and such well known families of wealth as Guggenheim, Harkness, Harriman

(10) In 1936, reviewing Romains' "Men of Good Will", which explained the

last war and forecast the fall of France, we referred to "the sinister crew who represent the heavy industries and manipulate the puppets of the British ministry . . . ready to wreck the League and deliver Abyssinia to Mussolini." In the 1938 edition of the Handbook of Private Schools, dealing with "The Fear Psychosis" we were led to write of "Nations Gone Mad", of "Britain's Policy" and the part played by "British Propaganda" in making "America The Cat's Paw" English public schools were identified as the "Breeding Ground of Imperialism". In dealing with those in control of England, "The Wreckers", we quoted Englishmen who denounced the Tory crew for wrecking the Empire

(11) This supplement to Bulletin #62, was sent confidentially to thirty or forty senators, representatives, public men and candidates for office who had manifested great interest in these Bulletins. Only a little of it is here reprinted

Of this April 29 meeting attended by Lamont and Willkie nothing appeared in the newspapers until it was made known in the Senate by Senator Holt, who told the story as we had written it to him. In the newspapers it appeared only in the American *Guardian*, June 21 *In Fact*, July 1 issue, under the title "Pro-British Fifth Column", said—"In the midst of the war hysteria which employs the term 'Fifth Column' to smash the Wagner Act and other social gains by labor, Senators Rush D. Holt, Burton K. Wheeler, Ernest Lundeen and Gerald P. Nye, isolationists, have named as the British Fifth Column in America: Thomas W. Lamont, Lord Lothian, Henry L. Stimson, Lewis Douglas, Conant of Harvard and William Allen White Senators used the same list published in *In Fact* in its first issue, headed 'Sworn to Secrecy'. The 18 pro-war men we named later became the leaders of the Committee to Defend America by Aiding the Allies. They inserted the 'Stop Hitler Now' advertisement in the press. *In Fact* had White's name, did not use it awaiting confirmation, loathe to believe he would ever be found in Big Money Company preaching war."

The Kansas Banker referred to in #62 is J R. Burrow, President of Central National Bank, Topeka, who writes June 18; "Mr White has a thin voice that can scarcely be heard across a dinner table, and for a man whose notoriety has drawn him into innumerable gatherings over forty or fifty years, he has acquired the least in the way of good manners of any prairie state notable I can think of. He has written a number of books, only one of which, 'The Court of Boyville', has any merit whatever, but his newspaper pen catches the public fancy to an extraordinary degree as you well know." Again on the 29th Mr. Burrow wrote, "It was quite all right to quote me in your last bulletin or any other time when you think it is constructive. As far as my comment about William Allen White is concerned, I would be delighted to send Mr. White a copy and have it published under my signature anywhere although I would not seek that because I certainly bear the man no malice. I don't suppose anybody ever lived who had better intentions, and I must always remember (whenever possible) that my estimate of him might be entirely wrong.

"Feel free to copy our advertisement any way you wish. I get great joy out of hearing businessmen talk about what bad business it is for a bank to publish that kind of an advertisement. We're not a big bank, and we don't make a lot of money, but since 1929 we have earned a good deal more than our net worth in 1929; we've doubled our volume, returned to our stockholders about 80% of the investment they had in the business when the stock market broke, and have probably increased our net worth retained in the business by 30% or 40%. While such advertisements as this are not designed to secure business, they incidentally prove to be a thousand times better advertising than the same space would be if it were devoted to extolling the virtues of our little institution "

The advertisement referred to was a paid full page in the Topeka *Daily State Journal*, which began, "Don't Declare War! Prepare Rapidly for Defense! Stop Playing Politics with National Safety! Congress Refuse to Adjourn! To declare war when to all practical purposes we have no army and no weapons and no air force, and when Hitler is at the highest point of his military strength, would be an act of fools. It would be a complete surrender to Allied propaganda. It must not happen! The pressure the Allies put on Washington is terrific. It is abundantly clear that Roosevelt wants war. He has all but promised it. The pressure he can put on Congress is tremendous. The pressure the people can put on Congress is greater " This is over Burrow's own name

An editorial in Col Knox's Manchester, N H, *Union* called William Allen White "a great American and a sterling patriot" and referred to him as "the wise, kindly, peace-loving sage of Emporia". On July 3 Senator Holt brought out in the Senate committee investigation that "Knox through his financial obligation resulting from the purchase of the Chicago *Daily News*, is beholden to International Bankers with interventionist designs".

40 MILLION CONSCRIPTS

June 7 in a leading editorial the N Y. *Times* came out for immediate conscription. The President approved, his followers chorused. Senator Norris said, "I'm not for it".[1] June 8 the House Military Committee favored the use of our National Guard anywhere in the Western hemisphere.

June 20 a bill was introduced in the Senate. It provides for the drafting of all men from 18 to 65, nearly 40 million. After all eliminations, at least 7 million would be left, and we have officers and physical facilities for training only 50,000 new men a month (*Time*, June 24). The measure is sponsored by the National Emergency Committee of the Military Training Camps Association, actively promoted by university men and self styled as representing "the thought and opinions . . . of many prominent persons in various walks of life" (N.Y. *Times*).

Secretary Hull, responding to his honorary degree at the Harvard Commencement, where conscription and war were being preached by alumni and faculty [2] and opposed by undergraduates who saw no reason for the slaughter, "pleads for American way", rebukes "brute force combined with fraud and guile" (a psychoanalyst might have thought the phrase was subconsciously determined by the President's announcement the preceding day).

The President in his press conference, June 18, had confided his plans for a new way of life for Americans,—more armaments, taxes, conscription, and "an attempt to discipline the nation's thinking [3] as well as its physical functioning, to restrain the most violent of its dissident elements without abrogating the basic (sic!) civil liberties of free speech, press and worship" [4] (*PM*, June 19).

Landon came back, "It is typical that such an important subject would come up not in a message to Congress but at a press conference." Glen Saxon, of the resolution committee, "It's just short of socialism" Henry P. Fletcher, former GOP chairman, "I don't think I'll comment on the President. It might hurt his feelings."

"The totalitarian threat to the 'American way of life' which we are supposedly fighting could be the very thing we might thus accept", Gen. Hugh Johnson snorted. [5] We are fighting "European revolution toward National Socialism" and adopting socialism "not so 'national' ". "Another 1936 'overwhelming mandate' would project us into war, give us a war dictatorship no milder than Hitler's and probably perpetuate it." "Part of the War Department effort . . . is a whoop-la recruiting drive. An hysterical ballyhoo campaign to drum up a war fever is exactly what we don't want now—especially during an election on the third term. [6]

"Every boy who preferred scientific training rather than drilling in columns of fours", he said, "would be called a heel and every impulsive youngster who was fifed and orated into signing up would be a hero". We would "not get the best material". [7]

Rep. Ross A. Collins (Miss.) appealed June 10 for the spending of our 5 billion "along lines of worth-while military preparedness". He recalled that during the four years he was chairman of the Military Appropriations Committee, "I urged motorization, mechanization, and aviation . . . more fire power rather than additional man power. Let us not . . . assemble multitudes of young men trained in 'fours right'. Instead let us train these young men to be scientists, chemists, mechanics and skilled workers. More men for parade-ground training?_ No! It is . . . the devices of the ingenious and the scientific that we need." [8] *June 21, 1940*

NOTES

[1] Two months later Senator Norris added, "It seems to me that the recruiting stations not only have discouraged enlistments but the effect of their action has been to prohibit them". Senator Walsh added to the chorus of the opposition (Aug. 20), "Until voluntary enlistments on a fair basis have been tried and there is evidence of a real need, I am not disposed to embrace, in peacetime, the power of the government to conscript" And on Aug 27, Senator Johnson charged, "the Burke-Wadsworth peacetime conscription proposal became a menace to our liberties"

Suppressed for nearly 100 years was Daniel Webster's charge, "unconstituitional", of the Conscription Bill then under debate. The principles "are not warranted by any provision of the Constitution . . . not connected with any power which the Constitution has conferred on Congress The Constitution is libelled, foully libelled. Where is it written in the Constitution, in what article or section is it contained that you may take children from their parents and parents from their children to fight the battles of any war in which the folly or the wickedness of Government may engage it? An attempt to maintain this doctrine upon the provisions of the Constitution is an exercise of perverse ingenuity to extract slavery from the substance of a free government." (Charles Beard, "Rise of American Civilization, Vol 1)

Judge William Bondy, in Federal Court, heard counsel state that the situation now "is not parallel to that which arose through litigation concerning other draft acts". Counsel charged that any peace time conscription act "obliterated" the Bill of Rights "We are not now at war. Our challenge relates to the assumption that Congress when the nation is at peace can enforce conscription as provided by the act of 1940" (AP, December 3, 1940) Moreover "a worker is deprived of his job and earnings if he is conscripted and the penalty for failure to comply with the law is 5 years in prison and $10,000 fine. A manufacturer who fails to comply is liable to 3 years and $50,000 fine and while his factory is taken over by the government he receives complete compensation for its use!"

"Suppression of dangerous thoughts" is a well recognized function of the Japanese Imperial Government. But private societies are also organized in Japan for a similar purpose.

[2] President Conant of Harvard appeared before the Senate Military Affairs Committee, July 3, 1940, to support the Conscription bill. This may have been at the suggestion of its co-author, Grenville Clark, most influential member of the Harvard Corporation, who seems to be taking over the toga of Thomas Lamont, the most influential of Harvard alumni

Dr. Conant advocated "compulsory selective service" in a "free democracy" (Compulsory for some, selective for those who are free. There is magic in those words.) He said, "The passage of this bill would . . . prove to any doubters in this country the extent of the dangers with which we were faced". (The danger seemed to some doubters one of internal totalitarianism and dictatorship) Conant added, "It would be a clear signal to those powers from whom danger comes . in this new world of force" (That is, it will scare and implies that the use of force is new) "In so much it might serve as a preventative of war". (Shaking your fist to scare the other fellow and prevent his attacking,—is this a fair interpretation of this seemingly muddy thought?)

(3) "The United States must mobilize as quickly as possible", Vermont's Senator Warren R. Austin warned the Burlington Rotarians (Burlington *Free Press*, July 23, 1940) because all those opposed to conscription, "those pacifists", those who believe this is a step toward war, "those isolationists, those long on relief, I say, they need discipline"

(4) As the spiritual mobilizers caught the President's cue, President Frank Kingdon of Newark University declared "Perhaps now is the time when we must check freedom for certain groups by democratic methods in order to continue our own freedom". (*Christian Century*, September 4, 1940)

(5) "Hanson Baldwin, military expert of the N. Y. *Times* . . . opposes peacetime conscription . . . because he thinks 'its adoption would create a profound, lasting and inescapable change in the economic, social and political life of our country and might well retard the growth of our civilization' ". *Uncensored*, July 27, 1940)

(6) "Something smelly in the War Department", chirped Hugh Johnson (Sept 27, 1940), "too many Harrys". Wrong-horse Harry Stimson came along to head the Department "apparently because he had just made an all-out interventionist speech proposing something perilously close to a war alliance with England".

(7) Conscription advocates were swinging a double-edged axe. General Johnson feared "we would not get the best material", in volunteer enlistments, but Senator Glass protested "We ought not to take the cream of the young men with spirit and courage enough to volunteer and leave the rest in bombproof shelter". (cf Buls 72, 77, 79, 80, 85)

(8) Bul #64 "Against Roosevelt's War" quoted contemporary statements.

Willkie—"In a democracy only the people have a right to decide upon war. The duty of a President is to be the restraining and the calming influence in all periods of crisis."

Hoover—"There is no ground for defeatist fear " "There must be an end to provocative speech by our officials. We have been following the suicide road . . . that led to disaster in Europe."

Landon—"The President offered to the Allies 'the material resources of the nation' . . . as if the material resources of the nation were his to dispose of . . . interpreted by the British as . . . meaning that America is about to enter the war. Only Congress has the authority . . . and Congress has not the slightest notion of declaring war." ."The United States cannot keep out of war if Roosevelt 'continues to say and do every damn thing he pleases '." _

Republican Platform—"The Republican party is opposed to involving this nation in foreign war. We are still suffering from the ill effects of the last world war."

Gannett—The Republican Party "must be the anti-war party . . the firm and uncompromising opponent of Roosevelt's war-inviting policies".

Aiken—"Our administration has deliberately herded us along the path to war You don't believe that the present government of the United States, if given totalitarian powers, would ever return them to the people—and I don't either."

C. F. Adams—"The President of the United States with no authorizing vote of Congress, has committed an act of war thinly veiled by a technical device which may rob the act of its legal significance".

Gen Johnson—"Our government not only did little to prepare itself, but encouraged the equally helpless allied nations to declare the war that has already ravaged or destroyed eight trusting nations. So—"They are fighting our war'." (June 14)—"Mr. Roosevelt has at last 'reluctantly decided' to attempt to hurdle the third term barrier . . . impossible without war hysteria. Therefore, we have war hysteria It is shooting craps with the country's destiny and the lives and fortunes of our people for the pride of a single man."

Col Robt. R. McCormick (Chicago *Tribune*)—"Insanity and nothing less"

Col. MacNider—"I am fearful that the role of the great war lord appeals to Mr. Roosevelt This situation well may prove too much for one so anxious for the pages of history It would be a kind and generous move on our part to remove the temptation from him."

Senators:—Holt—"I shall raise my voice to object to creating incidents when this country is ripe for somebody to set off the dynamite in order to cover up the failures of the past " Wheeler—"Any man who advocates our entrance into this war and who does not enlist now in the cause of the Allies is a cowardly traitor to his country". Danaher—"It is not our responsibility to 'preserve freedom' . . . any more than it was Great Britain's responsibility to preserve Czecho-Slovakia and Poland Obviously her course was dictated by her national interest. So should ours be " McCarran—The United States faces "an emergency which was created, I am sorry to say, by some expressions which were uttered by the head of this government not very long ago, which aroused the hatred of foreign countries at war." Nye—"One thing seems certain: The President promised military support to France", which he was "unable to deliver" when the "terrible moment" came. Reynaud's appeal "indicated clearly that France . . . felt entitled to ask for it". Johnson (Colo)—"It would cost the United States the lives of 5,000,000 men and $100,000,000,000 of borrowed money for this Republic to defeat Germany in Europe, and our economic system would be thrown so completely out of gear by such an ill-advised adventure that it could never be righted under our present form of government "

Representatives:—Plumley—"This alleged defense bill . . . is an unconscionable fraud on the public and on those people who must pay the piper as the New Deal fiddles along . . . Rank deception." Martin—"Every ideal of Americanism has been imperiled by those who would make our Government and our nation tools to be manipulated by one man at the head of a great and unelected political bureaucracy."

Boston *Transcript,* June 21—"He cannot dissociate his own selfish political success from the welfare of our nation. The people can have no faith in a President who makes national defense a game of political football " Detroit *Free Press,* June 11—"The people have consented without protest to the spending of many billions in the belief that they are investing their money in an insurance policy They have not agreed that it shall be tossed into a gigantic gamble on the turn of the dice in Europe. There is a growing belief that . . there has been more politics than there has been patriotism " *Time,* June 24— " 'Whoa, Mr President', cried the Detroit *News,* sensing in Franklin Roosevelt's non-belligerent intervention a pull toward war Hundreds of letters approved (8-to-1) the St Louis *Post-Dispatch's* bitter declaration that the President, unless checked, would take the U S. over the brink of war " Wall Street *Journal*—"This is no time to speak loudly while armed with a couple of feather dusters, one 'in hand' and one 'on order'."

THE BUILD-UP FOR WILLKIE

Bunkum is what presidential campaigns are built on. In the democratic process votes must be won, bait used. To rule 'em, fool 'em

The purpose of these Bulletins is to expose bunk, to provide data for sound interpretations, not to give opinions, our own or others, not to be partisan or political. But as Bulletin #62 dealt with the Administration, we are here dealing with its opponents.

The 'build-up' for Willkie is like that of Landon in 1936, Charles Michelson, of the Democratic National Committee, tells us in his weekly release "Dispelling the Fog" "The Kansas Governor did carry Vermont and Maine, so somebody must have believed in the picture painted to make him palatable to the voters. Fortunately for the Republicans Senator McNary is a thinking, rather than a talking individual, which will save him from embarrassing heckling." (N Y. *Times,* July 6)

How Landon had long cannily built his local political fences, how Hoover in 1934 chose him as a stalking horse for his own intended comeback, and how "Big Business climbed on the Landon band-wagon

in ever increasing numbers—all the way up to the family of the House
of Morgan" is interestingly and entertainingly explained by W. G.
Clugston in "Rascals in Democracy" (Richard R. Smith, New York,
1940). The Landon myth was blown up to presidential size. "If they
could elect Landon they would be able to discredit and discard most of
the New Deal innovations; big-business buccaneers would again have a
free hand to continue their monopolizing of the wealth of the country;
the old process could be resumed with renewed vim and vigor." Millions were poured into the campaign not so much in the hope of winning
as in preparation for a win in 1940. Hoover was given his opportunity
to make his great speech before the convention, "and his clackers and
applauders did one of the best jobs of putting him over that was ever
seen in a public assemblage".

The 1940 Philadelphia convention sprang right "from the grass roots
of the country clubs of America", sideswiped politically-minded Mrs.
Nicholas Longworth, the Alice blue Roosevelt. "Just how . . . the Republican Party got its baby giant panda, the overstuffed, furry man with
the owlish eyes," Jonathan Mitchell explains in the *New Republic,*
July 8, 1940. "His sponsorship was little less than august—Mr
Thomas Lamont, hiding in a hotel bedroom at Philadelphia until im-
plored to leave town, and the head of the National Manufacturers
Association, Mr. H. W. Prentis, Jr."

"The headquarters staff was dismayed, while Willkie was greeting a
swarm of delegates, to see Thomas W. Lamont of J. P. Morgan & Co.
walk in, greet 'Wendell', and wish him good luck. Willkie's assistants
advised that Commonwealth & Southern officials stay away from his
headquarters" (*Newsweek,* July 8). Paul Mallon writes June 28, "Persons waiting outside Willkie's hotel door . . . noticed emerging at
1:30 AM a group from the Lehman Brothers Wall Street house."
Patterson's *Daily News* and *PM* have dared tell much about Willkie
that other papers suppress. Seldes' July 15 issue of *In Fact* shows Willkie to be Lamont's man aspiring to the fascism Huey Long predicted

"Political writers are still trying to analyse the change of sentiment
upon the part of some 893 delegates", says *Editorial Research Reports,*
a Washington service to newspapers. (*PM,* July 4) "The Western
Union . . . delivered over 40,000 telegrams to delegates on . . . the
night of the nomination." Delegate Bleakley "received 22,500 tele-

grams and letters urging him to vote for Mr. Willkie." (*PM*, July 4)

"Mr. Dewey told his sympathizers, bankers isolated non-Willkie delegates and saw to it that telling messages were dispatched from hometown bankers and others whose advice might carry at least an implied threat of possible economic sanctions" (*PM*, July 3). "Many of these wires . . . bore signatures of prominent industrial and financial men, including Stock Exchange members, officers of Wall Street and out-of-town banks, railroads, factories, publishing houses . . . and socialites. Some of the telegrams carried terse orders . . . others threatened."

"Several Democratic Senators . . . are considering . . . investigation . . . to find out whether the telegraphic storm was inspired and, if so, by whom. The Senate Campaign Expenditures Committee has full authority to investigate influence used on the Republican convention." (*PM*, July 4)

"The assertion . . . that the enthusiasm of the petition signers for Mr. Willkie was purely spontaneous, that it sprang up like crocuses on the lawn, is nonsense" (Mitchell, *New Republic*, July 8). High pressure salesmanship of solicitors of great advertising agencies and law offices aided by socialites and debutantes brought the number of signers of petitions to 4½ million, while Old Dr. Townsend got twice as many.

"About a year ago, a group of business acquaintances started to see 'if something couldn't be done for Wendell'. The leader, most enthusiastic member and hardest worker, was Mr. Willkie himself." (Mitchell) Stimson before the Senate Committee admitted he had attended the 'secret meeting' at Coudert's office, April 29, to meet White, but denied it was secret. (N Y. *Times,* July 3) [1] Mr. Willkie told Boake Carter (July 8) he was invited but did not go (cf Bul #62).

Organization began to appear after that meeting (cf Bul #62). Great legal firms lent their lawyers, great public utilities their publicity men, advertising and public relations firms their professional talents. Russell Davenport, managing editor of *Fortune*, Bruce Barton and Robert Johnson, advertising aces, a host of publicity geniuses within telephone distance of 40 Wall Street, as detailed in *Time* July 8, sprang into action. [2] Most of these had been enthusiastic for the "wonder boy" Dewey until he was put in the shade by "miracle man" Willkie.

Mr. Oren Root, asked by a UP reporter as to his own plans for the future if Mr. Willkie was elected, replied that his own political ambitions would be ended with Willkie's election. "Why? Because when he is elected the opportunities in this country will be so great one will not need to aspire to public office." (cf *Commonweal,* July 12).

"The question is what set of forces, economic and social, are to conduct our government—the historic American processes or some new and somewhat foreign methods of concentrated control",—Farley, (*Life,* Jy 8) "A vital struggle for power . . . has begun", a 'Financial Service', Washington, D.C., writes, "a struggle that will affect, for the next four years, the relations between business and government. Within each party, which blocs, what opinions, will prevail?" [3]
July 9, 1940

NOTES

[1] Stimson "said he had nothing whatever to do with organization of the committee aside from attending two luncheon meetings". He gave his age as 73, asserted his appointment had "no relation to politics whatever" He maintained that British warships should be permitted to use Atlantic ports and navy yards He realized that he had been called a "war monger". Asked if he were a member of the law firm of Putnam and Roberts, counsel for Wendell Willkie's Commonwealth and Southern, he admitted he had "offices with them".

[2] Willkie "had the formidable research ability of Raymond Leslie Buell, an able scholar of international affairs and a pre-quarantine advocate of collective security. Mr. Buell was research director of the Foreign Policy Association which is part of the Carnegie Endowment network of collective security organizations whose logical offspring is the Committee to Defend America by Aiding the Allies. To join Willkie's staff he resigned as Round Table editor of *Fortune.* Willkie's closest adviser is Russell W. Davenport, former chairman of the board of editors of *Fortune,* whose particular interventionist enthusiasm is Clarence Streit's 'Union Now' ". (*Uncensored,* Sept 28, 1940)

[3] A 6-page Supplement to Bulletin #65, sent confidentially to Senators, Representatives and publicists, gave much additional information in regard to Willkie. Only a little is here reprinted.

"The president of this company (Consumers Power Company) is Mr. Wendell L. Willkie, who with a small group of associates owning a few million dollars worth of the common stock of Commonwealth & Southern, controls this billion dollar utility empire covering eleven states and uses this method of political control as a matter of company policy", said Paul H. Todd, formerly chairman of the Michigan Public Utilities Commission, in an address at Washington April 29, 1939.

"This $13,000,000,000 industry has the best-organized political machine in the United States today, down to precincts and townships, and is one of the

chief political agencies of the plunder bund and fascists to deliver the 1940
election into the hands of reaction," wrote Judson King, director of the National
Popular Government League, in a personal letter October 6, 1939. *Bulletin* of
the League Jan. 25, 1939, states: "The utility combine is the strongest, best
organized political machine in the United States today, and has been since the
election of Herbert Hoover in 1928. Power put Hoover in the White House
Power is attempting to put another Hoover there in the pretense of saving this
Nation for democracy."

"Willkie attended a dinner in New York given in his honor by Thomas W
Lamont representing J. P. Morgan & Co., and attended by Morgan partners
and leading business men, bankers and politicians. This was the time the Big
Money Okayed Willkie. At this dinner Willkie not only advocated all aid to
the Allies, but declared for an American Expeditionary Force to fight on foreign
soil." George Seldes tells us in *In Fact,* July 15, giving at length the dope on
Willkie, "a complete reactionary" Pearson and Allen, June 28, 1940, tell us,
"Wendell Willkie and John L Lewis had a secret dinner". Morris Ernst, their
host, "later went to see Russell Leffingwell, a J. P Morgan partner, and related
what had happened". They report in the same article that "the day the Convention opened Thomas Lamont, principal J P. Morgan stockholder, and Frank
Altschul, of Lazard Freres, secretly conferred with influential delegates in behalf
of Willkie".

In his address to the Press Club in Washington, Willkie shocked the cynical
journalists with his fascist plans. Ninety per cent of the press and more is
under the thumb of Wall Street. Only *PM*, Patterson's *Daily News* (N Y.),
the Ameringer *American Guardian*, print other than laudatory dope on Willkie.

W. G. Clugston of Topeka, Kansas, (author of "Rascals in Democracy",
1940) writes, "I would say that he is a composite of Doherty, the late Huey
Long, a shrewd country lawyer and the most high-powered insurance salesman
you ever saw Such a man, with the kind of backing he has, is bound to be
dangerous." Senator Wheeler on Willkie,—"The Republicans have . . nominated a man who has said our first line of defense is in Europe I do not subscribe
to that. Our first line of defense is preserving democracy,—seeing that the aged
are protected,—seeing that the 10,000 unemployed get work,—and seeing that
civil liberties are preserved."

Who discovered Willkie? General Hugh Johnson has consistently promoted Willkie and now vociferously claims that he was first. Walter Lippmann,
'loudspeaker' for Thomas Lamont, for months has consistently promoted Willkie. Dorothy Thompson has long been singing his praises. Senator Bridges
also claims discovery rights.

Russell W. Davenport, managing editor of *Fortune,* who resigned in April
to give his whole time as Willkie campaign manager, was probably the author
of the unsigned two-page article in the April issue, which must have been prepared in February The *Sat Eve Post,* June 22, featured an article by Willkie
which must have been prepared not later than May.

Willkie's career as a magazine writer, which began as a defender of the utilities, and was carred on in the *Atlantic,* gradually became political with his eloquent espousal in the *New Republic* of civil liberties,—for the communists, fascists, and the utilities. The Browder, Kuhn, and Commonwealth and Southern case was never put better   (cf Bul #34)

Oren Root, Jr., in April, 1940, began his letter writing campaign. A young New York lawyer, Princeton '33, member of a firm of corporation lawyers, his father, Oren Root, was a nephew of Elihu Root. This family of lawyers has been closely associated with utility companies, as their own personal biographies in Who's Who disclose. Young Mr. Root lives with his mother and her second husband, Col. Henry S. Breckinridge. His mother, Aida de Acosta, Spanish and Catholic, was active in the Liberty Loan campaign and the Anne Morgan organization in the last war

Col. Breckinridge, from Kentucky, was Assistant Secretary of War, 1913-16, served in France, has been president of the Navy League, is violently active in promoting the Committee to Defend America, and on Boston Common, June 16, announced, "The blood drenched Hitler is at our gates" (cf Bul #62) Who's Who and the Social Register tell much about the members of the pro-British "Fifth Column" that is so active in promoting our 'participation'

The Philadelphia Convention opened June 24 with Wendell Willkie "the most colorful candidate". June 26, "Employing every known technique of propaganda Mr. Willkie and his friends have convinced a great many delegates
there is a demand at the 'grass roots' for the late-starting candidate" (*PM*) "Bruce Barton, Robert Johnson and the rest of his handlers are convincing when they tell you the Willkie campaign made no sense politically. They just didn't have anyone who knew the racket. They did know inside out what was publicity and what kind was most effective "   (*PM*)

Among the propaganda technicians engineering the 'spontaneous' Willkie movement are, (*PM,* June 27, states) "Bruce Barton, author, advertising executive and Congressman, who tells us he has been a Willkieite so short a time Originally he was for Tom Dewey . . Charlton McVeagh .   . joined the Landon forces four years ago, volunteered to handle publicity for Willkie; Russell Davenport, who quit a good job as managing editor of *Fortune* to become a king-maker; Oren Root, who started forming Willkie clubs before he had talked with Willkie about it; Robert Johnson (former Managing editor of *Time*), who wasn't very busy with his publications, Fred Smith, one of Barton's publicity firm .   . Blythe Emmons, a young man who just wanted Willkie to be President   . if there was a coordinator, Davenport was it, but he says he wasn't very successful at it. The telegrams to delegates are mostly the work of Root. The top-flight radio and magazine publicity has been mostly the work of Davenport and Johnson." How this telegram campaign was promoted and paid for as revealed through some blunders was reported in *PM,* June 26.

Willkie's foreign policy, a subject new to him, like FDR's since 1937, was 'made in England'. Mr. Willkie participated with Van Zeeland, former Prime Minister of Belgium, Owen D. Young, whose "Plan" hastened the coming of Hitler, Winthrop Aldrich, at the meeting of the Economic Club of New York, December 12, 1938, when Thomas Lamont praised The Pax Britannica and expressed anxiety that there would be no peace unless we support Great Britain. Lamont's most recent restatement of 'our moral responsibility' to preserve the privileges of the British Tories has been put forth in an address, reprinted in the Phillips Exeter *Bulletin* and in a letter to the Harvard Alumni *Bulletin*, April 16, 1940, in which he rebukes the undergraduates for their indifference to "The Moral Issue". (For Mr. Lamont's views on their moral issues, see the SEC report on his friend and fellow alumnus, Richard Whitney, briefly reviewed in the Handbook of Private Schools, 1940, p 188-9)

Helen Kirkpatrick cabled the Chicago *Daily News* from London, June 29, that "the nomination of Wendell L Willkie is hailed by the entire British press as 'the end of isolationism' in the United States The British people have never heard of Willkie and were slightly bewildered yesterday".

But evidently they accepted him because of his endorsers and backers. The London *Daily Express* said, "We do know that Mr Wendell Willkie hates the Nazis. We also know that he has been louder than his rivals in demanding aid for the Allies, the Allies being at this moment us British, with the dominions, and no one else besides So that aid for us ceases to be an issue in American politics. Both sides are for it " The London *Times* in a column and a half editorial wrote, "Willkie . . . has left no doubt whatever of the sympathy which he shares with President Roosevelt for the Allied cause and with the same desire to forward it in every practicable way."

NO MORE MILLIONAIRES

The present struggle for power between political groups is measured in part by profits. Making provision for war has increased profits. The greater the urgency, the higher prices rise, the wider the profit margins and the more intense the struggle for political control.[1]

"If we face the choice of profits or peace, the nation will answer— must answer—'We choose peace'. It is the duty of all of us to encourage such a body of public opinion in this country that the answer will be clear" (Roosevelt, Chautauqua, 1936). This Bulletin is to that end.[2]

Newspapers only in their financial pages reflect this increase in profits. Exceptions are the LaFollettes' weekly, the *Progressive*, (Madison, Wis) and the *American Guardian* (Oklahoma City, Okla.) edited by the 70-year Oscar Ameringer, whose recently published autobiography, "If You Don't Weaken", has been so favorably reviewed.

The financial news letters of Whaley-Eaton and Kiplinger prognosticate 'earnings' trends. *Economic Notes* (80 E. 11th St , N.Y.C) occasionally presents startling figures, *Uncensored* items on war. profits. Financial journals and bank letters report enormous 'earnings'.[3]

The National City Bank (April *Bulletin*) reported an increase of profits in the year 1939 over 1938 of 63 6%. This was for 2480 major companies, after taxes and less deficits. But in the first quarter of 1940, 240 leading corporations showed a rise of 74% in their profits over the first quarter of 1939. (N.C.B. May *Bulletin*) [4]

"The sharpest gains were registered in such lines as metals, machinery and equipment, paper and petroleum. A number of representative companies in certain lines, however, had the largest first quarter earnings in their history" (N C.B. May *Bulletin,* and *Economic Notes,* June). The per cent increase in the first quarters of these two years was for U. S. Steel 2500%, Youngstown and Republic 480% each, Bethlehem 350%, Studebaker 800%, Fairchild Aircraft 274%, Martin Aircraft 218%. (*Economic Outlook*).

"Betterment in profits was naturally more pronounced, as a rule, in those industries benefiting directly or indirectly from the European conflict", the Wall Street *Journal,* May 3, reported. Profits for the first quarter of 1940 were up, over the same period for 1939, for 16 of companies 145.6%, 9 railway equipment companies 425.1%, 12 machine and tool companies 490.7%. In *Sat Eve Post,* May 18, Ray Millholland describes the machine tool industry as "Biggest War Baby".

The huge defense program of the government "is the basic factor creating business optimism." Advertising agencies report increased appropriations by clients. One stated, "Our volume is ahead of any year in our 17 years in business". (*"Editor and Publisher"*, AP, July 5)

"Patriotism is not enough to produce the goods under a system whose vitalizing principle is profit." "We must look largely to private enterprise, and we must expect to pay through the nose." (K. Hutchison, *Nation,* June 8) [5]

Profits will be made long before finished products are produced. The Administration advances 30% with the placing of the contracts. The goods will be delivered perhaps 18 months later. The profits accrue during Roosevelt's second term. His successor will wait for deliveries (cf Paul Mallon, July 5).

"Who Betrayed France?" (*Nation,* July 6),—Heinz Pol tells of ore shipments to Germany between 1932 and 1938 of more than 30 million tons. And this continued right up to the war, according to Frank Hanighen. The Comite des Forges, with the connivance of French Cabinet members, arranged this. Daladier and Bonnet, Gens. Weygand, Gouraud, Petain were "Cagoulards", opposed to fighting Germany "The French offensive along the Moselle River last September had to be stopped short because" Gen Michelin, of the famous tire family, was responsible for holding "dozens of cars loaded with heavy artillery" and "did even worse with the tanks". "When the Germans occupied the region . . . early in June, they . . . used . . . against the retreating French" these 70-ton, fast, maneuverable, heavy armored tanks.

Pol tells of dallying in airplane construction. Air Minister Cot "did not do much". His successor La Chambre was "infinitely worse". He insisted "that it was unnecessary to place large orders in America

"Under Air Minister Pierre Cot, fabulous sums were spent for planes that never saw the light of day" (Fodor, Chicago *Daily News,* June 25). "Hundreds of American planes which for months before the totalitarian war had waited at Casablanca (French Morocco and elsewhere) were never assembled because French plane manufacturers sought more advantageous business arrangements with their Government." (cf Bul #96 and Notes)

U. S. Engineering experts, from Spain (AP, July 5) described French factories as "some of the world's best equipped", which under the Germans might turn out as many as 1350 airplane engines a month.

France "was defeated by probably less than 100,000 German air, tank, infantry and artillery specialists. The proper spending by the French of $500,000,000 on modern airplanes, tanks and anti-aircraft guns, from 1937 to 1939, might have changed the entire outcome. French generals told me during the Flanders battle that with 1000 more planes, 1000 more tanks, and 3000 more guns, they could have won " Edgar Ansel Mowrer, who hates the Nazis, so reports July 2, from Lisbon.

"Germany will obtain . . .1570 American-made airplanes . de-livered to France in the last 18 months" (AP, June 24). Recent cables tell of seizure by the Germans of 100 new tanks imported but never used

Daladier and Mandel, who enforced the savage censorship with thousands in concentration camps and hundreds before firing squads, fled on the S. S. Massilia, were refused landing at the French colonies. AP cable, July 8, suggests they may be prisoners at Marseilles or Gibraltar "Reynaud's fate is still not known." A legitimate inference is that intensive censorship has much to conceal. They 'destroyed confidence in government' and have met with their fate.

"The collapse of all French resistance . . . simply can't be explained except by soft spots" (Gen. Hugh Johnson, June 25). Censorship has concealed graft and greed for war profits. "If there was ever a country ripe for revolution, it is France today. (*Life*, July 8).

England was assured by Stanley Baldwin, Nov., 1934, "that in a year's time we will be twice as strong as Germany in the air" (cf D. Reed). Baldwins Ltd. preference shares (steel), from 1932 to 1936 increased in value more than 800% (Hanighen, *American Spectator*, July, 1936).

Most of the members of the British Government had investments in munitions companies, the testimony before the Royal Commission showed. This investigation had been inspired by the popular outcry following Sen. Nye's munitions inquiry in the United States.

"The people who live on the manufacture of armaments . . . since the war . . . have been insisting that their profits have been highly modest and have produced as proof their balance sheets, which at first glance confirm the allegation. They indicate, by their very obscurity, that they have been doing better than they want the world to know The companies, under this system, can declare exactly what figure they like, safe in the knowledge that it is not possible to accuse them of making high profits out of war. They don't dare to show them in fear of arousing public opinion" (William H. Stoneman, London cable, May 31). To promote rearmament industry, manufacturers may postpone payment of taxes under certain conditions until after the war (when they may be bankrupt).[6]

The 100% excess profits tax announced by Attlee, head of the Labour Party, (AP, June 4) fooled the English people and the Americans. The N.Y. *Sun* commented: "It will be difficult for many Americans to understand how Britain can expect anyone to make the tremendous extra productive effort required by war without some stimulus other than the vague one that it is necessary to save the country. The first

thing that capital will require to work harder in war time is some assurance of a larger return."

The joker is that the 100% excess tax is to be assessed on profits
over and above the average for the preceding four years   Handley-
Page Aircraft in those four years declared cash and stock dividends
totaling 365%. (cf Bul #50) So for the current year the 100% tax
will apply only after stockholders have taken profits of 91%.

"Censorship is being clamped on the news at the present time, but
there are some awful scandals which are below the surface in Europe
today and which are just waiting for peace to blow the lid off the tea-
kettle. There is one horrible munitions scandal that is being mentioned
in diplomatic circles in whispered tones, but this is all that we can say
for the present. It involves some of the highest personalities." (Washington *Diplomatic Letter,* July 6)

The scandal in England may break as in France before there is peace.
Then there may be no peace. If Daladier and Reynaud hadn't sat on the
safety valve so long and hard, it would have been better for them.   .

Good reporting, sound interpretation, understanding, should increase
our 'confidence in government', help us to avoid what France's leaders
brought that country and what impends in England   Isn't that defense?

President Roosevelt's July 1 "special message recommending a steeply
graduated excess profits tax took Congress by surprise. Only 10 days
ago the Administration helped block an excess profits tax that was on
the verge of passing" on the ground "that Treasury experts would require two or three months to properly prepare a program. Many members of Congress thought politics was involved." (*PM,* July 2)

"The White House explained Mr. Roosevelt's recommendation for
an excess profits tax was timed for the reconvening of Congress and the
opening of the fiscal year. It may have been coincidental with the
rising of the sun at 4:37 A. M. that day or the imminence of fourth of
July, but it also coincided with the nomination of a forceful Republican
presidential candidate a few days earlier. Premature talk about stop-
ping new millionaires is good politics." (Mallon, July 3)

The Nye Committee, though impeded and stopped by Roosevelt (cf
Q. Howe, "England Expects", pp 36-7), led to popular demand, promoted by *Fortune,* to nationalize the munitions industries.

"President Roosevelt produced the famous red herring of 'taking the profits out of war', a far better and more practicable scheme—it was suggested—than buying out munitions plants. This diverted public opinion" (Hanighen, *Am. Spectator,* July, 1936). The American Legion for years offered specific proposals to "take the profits out of war".

Consequently Mr. Roosevelt, drafting the Democratic Platform of 1936 (cf Beard, Midpassage"), declared, "We shall continue to observe a true neutrality . . . to work for peace and to take the profits out of war".

For those who are foolishly preaching that statesmen should keep their promises, it may be interesting to observe that Mr. Roosevelt's record does not show that he has lived up to this clear and solemn promise to the American people on which he was elected.

Speaking of the President's emphasis on material armament, ships, light and heavy artillery (he likes to play with gadgets), H. S. Ford, secretary of the American Military Institute, Washington, D. C, in *Nation,* July 6, points out that it is easier "for a rich man to buy his way into heaven" than "for a rich nation to buy its way to victory".

"Industrial mobilization isn't just madly appropriating billions. Ballyhoo about billions . . . tends to pacify the demand of the people for drive and effectiveness Appropriations should be no greater for any period than can reasonably be spent in that period", remarks Gen. Johnson, July 4, remembering that Congress was just adding another 4 billions, bringing total appropriated since Jan. 1 to around 15 billions.

There will be some sort of excess profits tax. (cf Kiplinger, June 22), probably on the English 'fool the people' system, 'excess' over average earnings of several preceding years. But "to make war unattractive to business interests" would be unwise.

"No new group of millionaires", President Roosevelt has promised. No more millionaires, he has accented. But under his present policies, there will be plenty more for the old millionaires.

July 10, 1940

NOTES

[1] "Not all the defense money is going for defenses," writes Paul Mallon, Sept. 22, 1940. "The appropriations apparently are being stretched to cover just about every phase of government activity under the sun, not the least of which is re-election of Mr. Roosevelt for a third term. National defense is only the new neon sign of the New Deal. Inside nothing is changed. Business is proceeding as usual, but expanding, everything from social welfare, federal concern with those who are ill, crowded and unsanitary, PWA, TVA, housing,

right down to the sweetest and most expensive publicity ever conceived in the mind of man".

(2) Senator Hiram Johnson stated (AP, Sept. 17, 1939), "I take my stand with the Roosevelt of 1936, not with the Roosevelt of 1939. We are marching in the shadow now—down the road to war. All the ills so eloquently pictured in the President's Chautauqua address of 1936 would soon be upon us, and the making of money would be predominant—'fools' gold', the President called it then. 'Fools' gold' it would be now. "The blood letting", said Johnson, "which would inevitably follow, if we heed those who cry aloud for repeal, and great war profits would bring all the horrors and anguish of war, just as it did 20 years ago."

(3) Wall Street *Journal*, October 7, 1940, reports "the ten largest banks" of New York City increased their assets to 16 billions from 14 billions in one year from September 1939. "Three fourths of the approximately $2,000,000,000 gain was made by the five bigger banks", whose deposits totaled 10 billions While for August 1, 1940, *PM* reported a jump of 50% in industry profits, the November 1940 issue of *Fortune* reports. "For the first six months of 1940, the National City Bank Letter for August showed enormous increases in corporate profits. Profits on textiles were up 51 per cent above 1939, chemicals 39 per cent, steels (excluding U. S Steel) 250 per cent, electrical equipment 66 per cent, metal and mining 41 per cent.

(4) "According to the Standard Statistics Company, 400 large industrial corporations are making 34 per cent more in 1940 than in 1939 " Comparative earnings of some war-babies for the first nine months of 1940 and 1939, after allowing for normal income tax but not for excess-profits tax, are as follows in millions: U. S. Steel 69 to 12, Republic Steel 12 to 3, Bethlehem Steel 34 to 11, Anaconda 22 to 11, Curtiss-Wright 8 to 4. (*New Republic,* Feb 3, 1941)

"National City Bank" in its December 1940 Bulletin "for the first nine months of 1940" and 1939, shows for 284 companies "directly affected by war and defense program" a rise of 79 2% Excluded were those companies dealing in wood, paper, iron and steel in which the percentage had risen to more than 100%.

Profits in Britain of 1769 companies in the first nine months of 1940 came to 344 as compared with 380 million pounds in 1939 (*Economic Notes,* Jan 1941) Vickers while building great reserve declared 10% dividends for four years Chairman Sir Herbert Lawrence, asked to explain this, uttered that armament kings' classic: 'The question of the manufacture of arms by the State or by private firms has been obscured by a certain amount of prejudice. The prejudice is the expression of an honorable but mistaken ideal respecting the sanctity of life and the iniquity of war ' "

(5) Last year the gross business of the Newport News Shipbuilding and Drydock Company was . . . $36 million. This year they will do a business of more than $500 million, chiefly with the Navy. They will sell common stock to the public to yield them a profit of $6 million on their investment less than three months ago of $18 million (*PM,* August 5, 1940)

(6) "There is certain evidence of profiteering on every bit as large a scale as in 1914-18 The true size of profits is obscured in a variety of ways", such as amounts set aside to pay bondholders, or for taxes, or in the form of excessive depreciation reserves, in addition to extra reserves for "contingencies". (*Economic Notes*, Sept 1940)   (For other data on profits cf Buls #24, 38, 48, 50, 88)

IS WILLKIE'S WHITE BLACK, AS PAINTED?

"Give me ten billion dollars and I could make a Chinaman president". This cynicism is attributed to William Allen White by a letter-writer to *PM*, July 2 *PM* has not replied to inquiry for confirmation.

To "Ol' Bill White", "this lovable, pseudo-progressive Kansan", "I devote considerable space in my book", writes W. G. Clugston, well-known Kansas attorney of vouched integrity, in his "Rascals in Democracy". "No living journalist has done more to uphold the existing order of society by preying upon the emotions of the people and patting the Main Street Overlords upon the back. No one presents such a perfect picture of the Pseudo-Progressive who succumbs to the temptation to parboil his ideals in the fleshpots." White's "appetite for power and prestige" led him "to dominate the public affairs of his state" and "drove him into acts and alliances" with some connected with "the Kansas million dollar forgery" of state bonds. "White led the fight to . . . exert undue and unjust influence on the Senate Court of Impeachment" to save "the attorney general".

"What the People Said", by W. L. White, son of William Allen White, tells in fiction what Clugston calls "this amazing corruption of the government. Young White made it plain . . . that his able, talented father was of that weighed-and-found-wanting leadership."

"I liked your comment that Seldes had 'reverence for White'. That is what everybody has who doesn't know the man. All of us reverence little children. Putting a pen in White's hand is like putting a loaded shotgun in the hands of a two year old", writes J R. Burrow, president of the Central National Bank, Topeka.

George Seldes had written me that he had so much "reverence for White that when we got the list of names of the people at this 'secret meeting', I spotted William Allen White and could not believe that the great editor, my friend, and the endorser of all my books would be in that conspiratorial company. I cut his name out, not to suppress, but to confirm, and went to press without hearing from him Imagine my shock on learning that he was actually heading the committee."[1]

"The Truth About Wendell Willkie" and the Committee is printed in July 15 and May 20 issues of Seldes' *In Fact*, "For the Millions Who Want a Free Press". (cf Buls #62, 65)

White's Get Us Into War Now Committee has changed its name, since the beloved ally, France, the acme of 'civilization' for which we were to fight, became the most hated enemy of Britain, whose hates we adopt. Now "The Committee to Defend America", it publishes full page ads. "Stop Hitler Now", financed by a "list of sponsors" (*PM*, July 5), probably from the same class as those who financed full pages for "Union Now", N. Y. *Times*, July 15, Boston *Transcript*, July 18.[2]

"Union Now", flourishing in the spring under Lothian's fostering care (cf Bul #11), under the brilliant Willkie sun wilted To revive it, before France collapsed, Mr. Streit wrote the President to "take the American people and the world by storm with a declaration of In-ter-dependence", because "All us Americans know in our hearts that we do depend now on the French and British for our freedom and peace".[3]

Appropriately on July 4 the N Y. *Times* reported Streit's new "decla-ration of independence" to "reunite the English-speaking world" But this independence of Britain and her colonies wholly ignores the other (if such there are) "peace-loving and liberty-loving peoples wantonly attacked by ruthless aggressors" that were still referred to in the Demo-cratic Platform, published July 17 (on which the best Democratic minds of the nation had been bent for days), and to whom the Platform promised "all the material aid at our command, consistent with law and not inconsistent with the interests of our own national defense".

This 'Unite with Britain' propaganda is now sounded with all stops open Publicity to 'promote and save democracy' is spread through the nation's press. Editorials in parallel columns plead "For Union of the Free" and incongruously expound "The Democracy of Conscription".

A British mission is now in Washington to induce us to enter into partnership to pool our economic resources, our Navy, our arms, as France pooled hers with Britain. The outcome,—the carcass that the profiteers left, now being picked by the two vultures Churchill and Hitler,—should warn us what such 'union' may come to (cf Bul #11)

"America can be saved only as she lends herself to foreign-devised schemes for world salvation," we Americans have been led to believe.

Against this foreign importation of propaganda George H. Cless, Jr., warned us three years ago in his "11th Commandment" (Scribner's, 1938), "a vigorous, timely appeal to Americans to quit the disastrous game of saving the world and turn their thought and energies to saving America". He has continued to build "backfires to the international propaganda of Streit and his kind". (cf Bul #15)

The enclosed letter to his home town 'Willkie-White Committee' shows that this forum speaker and Chamber of Commerce executive has had an eye for "International Political Humbuggery" and an olfactory sense for stenches that arise from Whitehall, Washington or Wall Street. His bombardment he reports brought a "feeble and puerile" comeback.[4]

The White connection has led some charmed by Willkie's personality to look a bit more deeply, like W. G. Clugston of Topeka, who writes, "Some of the powerful interests behind the Willkie candidacy are starting a drive towards totalitarianism; that is the only way they know to keep the masses of the people from continuing to demand social security objectives. The powerful interests that promoted Willkie at Philadelphia want us to get into the war.

"Willkie's primary interest is in the established institutions, especially those of big business Always his major energies have gone into the service of the predatory special privilege groups that have sought to run the government from behind the scenes. And now when these groups feel that they must come out into the open and take over the government directly, and in their own name, he is the man to put forward to lead the movement. The propaganda that will be put out in his behalf during the next four months will make pale by comparison every other propaganda campaign And I think the people are liable to be taken in by it. I hope I shall have to be thoroughly ashamed of myself for having so misjudged a man and a movement."

These Bulletins are sent without charge only to those who request or are recommended. No intent here to attack or espouse, rather to expose the hidden.

July 19, 1940

NOTES

[1] When there is no urge or pressure to prevent, Mr. White is a liberal minded humanitarian. His caustic treatment of the ethics of advertising and on his biography of Calvin Coolidge, is more nearly honest than any other that has been

reproduced. In his "Freedom of the Press" (1935), George Seldes quoted White, "Unless democracy is indignant at the encroachments of plutocracy, democracy cannot fight When plutocracy destroys the sources of information which should make indignation, plutocracy has paralyzed democracy." (cf Handbook of Private Schools, 1935-36, p 83)

The differences between Mr. White and the Committee were brought into the open in December, 1940, when he published an editorial in the Emporia *Gazette* headed "Not Our War". "This is not our war. The United States would be foolish to get into it because if we got into it we would be weakening . the cause of world democracy. This is not our war. We should do everything possible to keep out of it. Until we are actually attacked by the totalitarian powers, this is not our war "

After the N. Y. *Times* called White down for boasting before a group of publicists of his publicity tricks, it must have been gratifying to him to have had Herbert Hoover come forward and say that the Americans were not treating either William Allen White or Charles A. Lindbergh fairly This, along with an inquiry from Roy Howard, led Mr White to declare publicly through the Scripps-Howard papers that he was never interested in war and that his only reason for being a member of the Committee was "to keep this country out of war". Whereupon Lindbergh threw him a Christmas bouquet, congratulating him on coming out for the slogan "The Yanks Are Not Coming". "Mr White has rendered a great service to this country by clarifying his position and the position of his committee. Many of us have felt in the past that Mr White's committee was intentionally leading us to war Mr. White has now clarified this situation He offers us as a slogan the motto, 'The Yanks Are Not Coming' "

Explaining his resignation from the Committee in January, 1941, Mr. White wrote to John Temple Graves, II, Birmingham, Alabama, newspaper columnist, "In two of our chapters, New York and Washington, we have a bunch of warmongers and under our organization we have no way to oust them and I just can't remain at the head of an organization which is being used by those chapters to ghost dance for war."

So the White Committee was no longer White,—till "President Roosevelt intervened personally to keep his old friend, William Allen White of Emporia, Kansas, as head of the Committee" (P. and A , Jan. 7, 1941)

President Henry Noble MacCracken of Vassar, one of the original supporters of the Committee, had earlier gotten out Early in December, 1940, in a letter to the N Y *Times* he had expressed grave concern that the policies of the Committee "are calculated to bring us into the war at the earliest possible moment" and expressed the belief that the steps outlined by the Committee as necessary would "commit us to a definite war policy for which our country is not prepared and which she is not willing to undertake Those who believe that the United States should not enter the war at this time should record their opposition to the policy declared by the Committee. I must express my preference for the American way of defense "

(2) Robert Sherwood who wrote these "Stop Hitler Now" advertisements is also the author of "Idiots' Delight", but now one of the most violent of the "war mongers."

(3) "Support for General de Gaulle, crystallized by an agency called 'France Forever', has thus far been inspirational rather than monetary. Writers and journalists have orated in behalf of Free France. U. S. ambulance drivers have volunteered for service in Africa. Cooperating in the cause for Britain are realists and sentimentalists, people who love England for Shakespeare and Shelley, people who realize America's safety depends on Britain's elegant aristocracy. Best publicized are New York's cafe Anglophiles. Meat for them was the Star Spangled Ball staged by the White committee at New York's Astor Hotel where Gypsy Rose Lee dispensed her pentacled costume, star by star, for England's sake. War relief has become a big business. But little by little it has assumed also the characteristics of show business, seeking support from those who care less for the quality of mercy than for self-indulgence and personal fame. By last fortnight many a sympathetic contributor was fed up with the outer forms which a great cause had assumed." (*Life*, Jan. 6, 1941)

Mrs. Roosevelt "is advocating appointment of a co-ordinator of American relief to Britain". There are "approximately 120 agencies registered with the State Department" collecting relief for Great Britain (*Chr Sci Monitor*, Jan. 4, 1941). In view of the activities of the American Red Cross which has collected for Britain $9,000,000 up to January, 1941 not all these seem necessary. Even the best of these, like the Red Cross, have frequently in the past been under attack for their high overhead.

(4) The distribution of this letter of George H. Cless, Jr. of Glens Falls, N. Y. brought him many replies and great praise. Thousands of copies were later distributed in pamphlet form. J. B. Priestley in his broadcasts made extended comment which is reprinted in his latest book. Cless poured scorn upon the dupes of those who were using White as a puppet to head their propaganda machine. At its "verbal cannonading, Voltaire turned over in his grave and repeated again: 'People will continue to commit atrocities as long as they continue to believe absurdities,' and the Shades of Elihu Root return to remind us that 'when foreign affairs are ruled by democracies the danger of war will be in mistaken beliefs'. All of us are just being fooled." And he brought Hilaire Belloc to testify from "The Contrast", " 'We of Europe shall solve our own problems; . . it is our own affair; we alone understand it. And let me add this: every public man from Europe, especially every professional politician, who approaches the people of the United States, begging them to interfere in our affairs, is a liar, and knows that he is a liar . . . the inducements offered, the flattering phrases chosen, are lies . . . and the fine phrases about peace and justice and humanity and civilization and the rest of it, are hypocrisy and a poison.' "

(5) From Bulletin #68, "Newsletters", we quote briefly: "The private newsletter has become an important source of information, publishing what the newspapers suppress or neglect. Some of these are printed. More are mimeo, multi,

or planographed.   There are said to be 500.   We have in our files copies of
perhaps 100, and receive a score regularly."
  There followed a list of the more useful, of which the following are still published   *In Fact,* Chatham-Phenix Bldg., L.I. City, N.Y , George Seldes, editor,
fortnightly, 10 months 25¢; *People's Lobby Bulletin,* 817 Fourteenth St. N.W ,
Washington, D.C., Benjamin C. Marsh, editor, monthly, $1 a year; *Uncensored,*
112 East 19th St , N.Y., Cushman Reynolds, editor, weekly, 6 months $2.50,
(published by Writers Anti-War Bureau) ; *Week by Week,* 3034 P St N.W.,
Washington, D.C., Franklin Roudybush, editor, weekly, $5 a year; *Al Williams
Daily Column,* reprints on request, c/o Pittsburgh Press, Pittsburgh, Pa.; *Economic Notes,* 80 East 11th St , N Y., published by Labor Research Association,
monthly, 65¢ a year; *The Weekly Foreign Letter,* 205 East 42nd St , N.Y.,
Lawrence Dennis, editor, weekly, $24 a year.
  Of those listed, some have been discontinued, like the *Washington Informa-
tion Letter. The Week,* the English communist newsletter, formerly mailed or
cabled, is now suppressed, as are James True's *Industrial Control Reports.*
  Of the financial letters, the oldest is the *Whaley-Eaton Service,* Munsey Building, Washington, D C., weekly, American Letters $25 a year, Foreign Letters $30
a year.   There is also the *Kiplinger Washington Letter,* National Press Bldg.,
Washington, D C., weekly, $18 a year
  An extensive list of newsletters and periodicals dealing with war has been
published as Bulletin #3 of the War Documentation Service, 1300 Locust Street,
Philadelphia, Pa , Richard H. Heindel, Director, 15¢.   Similar collections of war
material are now being made by O W Riegel of Washington and Lee Univ.,
and by the Hoover War Library.
  The justified lack of confidence in the press has revived the newsletter of the
censored press of a century or more ago.   Just as pamphleteering played a part
in the great revolution of the 17th century and the revolution of the 18th century, so the private newsletter has of late been essential in distributing information.   The ubiquitous and omniscient Dorothy Thompson, in her column, Feb.
9, 1940, expanding on the private newsletter, explained that they are needless.
One can get the whole truth in the newspapers and especially in her column.
  The newsletters have died, hundreds of them,— withered like the summer
flowers before the blast of Administration and British measures.   Albert Horlings,
in the *New Republic,* Jan. 27, 1941, reporting under the title of "Appeasers",
on the organizations that would keep us out of war, the great majority of which
"are not either quiescent or are actively supporting aid to Britain", lists only
America First Committee, 1806 Board of Trade Bldg , Chicago; American
Peace Mobilization, 1116 Vermont Ave , N W , Washington, D.C.; Keep America Out of War Congress, 22 E. 17th St., N.Y ; No Foreign War Committee, 100
E. 42d St., N Y ; World Peaceways, Inc , 103 Park Ave , N Y., Writers' Anti-
War Bureau, 122 E 19th St , N Y.
  "Countering Propaganda" ("What Makes Lives", pp 175-80) deals with
the means and measures taken by private organizations to meet the emergency

of the flood of propaganda from the government and from abroad. The Institute of Propaganda Analysis, founded by Clyde Miller with money from E. A Filene, publishes monthly bulletins. The private newsletter is dealt with more at length, and some books that expose propaganda are mentioned.

Ferdinand Lundberg's "News-Letters: A Revolution in Journalism", *Harpers*, April, 1940, shows the need of them to supplement the newspapers. "Outsiders believe they will be secretly brought under the wing of the government, their prestige among key people capitalized for war purposes, their reports doctored under the threat of being refused the mails." Incorrectly he refers to the Sargent bulletins as "anti-war, anti-British", whereas their purpose is only to correct the falsities put forth by British propaganda Personally, I am all for perpetual, biological warfare such as has existed on this earth for millions of years, and continuous revolution. Why put a spoke in the wheel when it is revolving smoothly. I have been pro-British since William the Bastard and pro-American since the time of John Harvard, but I don't like the foreign policy of the desperate crew that is ruining England and the Empire to save their own fortunes. But that is England's business What I am howling about is the way we Americans are swallowing bunk, poison, just as we did twenty-three years ago What I object to is the growing totalitarianism in this country which means dictatorship, the ending of freedom of speech and the things that we value under the fuzzy designation "democracy". (cf "What Makes Lives", pp 178, 9)

In "The News and How to Understand It", (Simon and Schuster, 1940) Quincy Howe mentions the newsletter. "The caution of the daily papers and the refusal of the liberals to quit their ivory towers have opened up a new field of journalism In the April, 1940, issue of *Harper's*, Ferdinand Lundberg had an article about the growing importance of the news letter—weekly, fortnightly, and monthly. Porter Sargent, who issues an informal multigraphed bulletin of his own, estimates that there are now as many as five hundred of these news letters in the United States and says that he has a hundred different ones in his files.

"But Mr. Lundberg is probably correct when he estimates that three of the news letters have ninety per cent of the circulation — the Whaley-Eaton Service, the *Kiplinger Washington Letter*, and the *Business and Legislative Report* of the Research Institute of America. The various Whaley-Eaton Services, of which there are several, pioneered in the field. They go to six or seven thousand people a week, sell for $25 to $30 a year, and cover Washington news, foreign news, and the Far East. The *Kiplinger Letter* costs $18 a year and reaches 40,000 people a week Kiplinger himself used to cover the United States Treasury for the Associated Press. He started his letter in 1921. Whaley and Eaton are two lawyers who went into the newspaper business and then started their own information service in 1918. Kiplinger brings inside Washington stuff to businessmen; Whaley-Eaton specializes in facts and little-known background material.

"The commercial services flourish because they really deliver the goods, and they deliver the goods because they know what their readers want and then go out and get it. The Kiplinger and Whaley-Eaton people, for instance, never attend press conferences   They get all their information and impressions from talking to government officials   Frequently, too, people come to them with information that they want made known.   None of these services depend on advertisers; the commercial ones do not even tell their readers what the readers want to hear.   They can speak quite frankly but cannot afford to make too many mistakes.   Franklin Roudybush publishes a diplomatic letter from Washington, *Week by Week*.   It is staffed by diplomatic, army, and naval experts and has a good record of forecasting events abroad   The International Statistical Bureau of New York also has a fortnightly foreign letter, with the emphasis on economics.   Neither of these two has any axe to grind and both have done a better job of analysis and prophecy than the newspapers, magazines, or radio

"Then there are a host of propaganda news letters.   In reading any propaganda news service it is therefore just as well to make the same allowances you would make in reading any other publication." (pp 142-146)

(6) Bulletin #71 "What Every American Should Read" attracted attention to newspapers that publish the usually suppressed,— Ameringer's *American Guardian*, Oklahoma City, Okla, $1 a year, LaFollettes' *Progressive*, Madison, Wis., $2 a year.   It mentions additional books that do not conform to generally accepted attitudes on international and national affairs (cf Buls #13, #15) "Dynamics of War and Revolution", by Lawrence Dennis, incorruptible realist who frankly recognizes totalitarian tendencies, was published in June by the author, 205 E. 42nd St., N Y.C.   Lothrop Stoddard's "Into the Darkness" reports with discretion on Germany as he found it last fall.

"The printed word has, except for brief periods, always been under control. The Vatican still maintains its 'index expurgatorius'.   In America we have more subtle methods   Newspapers, magazines, publishing houses, have been bought or bought into, their policies changed   Writers of books, once bold and free, are now cautious and avoid interference.   Such writers find a ready market for their wares   Those who do not conform seldom find publishers   No man in this country has been more influential in determining editorial and publishing and educational policies these past twenty years than Thomas Lamont " ("What Makes Lives")

DOCTORING THE MONROE DOCTRINE

Declaring that the record proves the statements of both President Roosevelt and Secretary Hull "are deliberate falsehoods", Representative Tinkham, July 12, in the House unloosed a slashing attack against the administration's foreign policy and asserted that "their disclaimers of United States participation and involvement in territorial and political affairs of Europe and Asia are utterly false".

Tinkham was referring to Hull's July 5 reply to von Ribbentrop's reminder that the second part of the Monroe Doctrine implied that the

U. S. was to keep out of Europe. Hull had asserted that the U.S. "pursues a policy of non-participation and of non-involvement in the purely political affairs of Europe". No wonder Tinkham called that a "deliberate falsehood", and went on to say that Hull "did not meet squarely the German challenge that the policy has been one of interference".

The President the next day, graciously attempting to ease the situation, through Secretary Early informed the newspapermen that the Monroe Doctrine (like Gaul) is divided into three parts, one for America, one for Asia,[1] and one for Europe. "There should be an application of the Monroe Doctrine[2] in Europe and in Asia similar to its interpretation and application for this hemisphere." (N. Y. *Times,* July 9)[3]

Arthur Krock, having slept on it and still in amazement, wrote July 8 in the N. Y. *Times,* "Well folks, this is the story of the great, new and confused interpretation of U. S. foreign policy at Hyde Park Saturday . . in which views of the President were circulated which upset the State Department, left expert and lay readers guessing, and spread the surmise in the Far East that Japan was being given a hint how to snatch the Netherlands Indies and French Indo-China without any objection."

"The Roosevelt-Hull remarks, coupled with the show of naval strength,[4] may have been designed to impress Latin-Americans on the eve of the Havana conference of the 21 American republics, which opens July 20. Prospects of the United States getting adequate cooperation . . . are less and less favorable . . and few Latin American nations are manifesting any genuine enthusiasm for Washington's militant policies." (*Newsweek,* July 15)

Fact is our 'good neighbors' in South America don't return our love. They are still suspicious, though we poured out hundreds of millions for political graft, banker's loans and bonds, in part repudiated or unpaid. Brazil, with loans in the '20's of nearly a hundred millions, and another 120 millions recently in cash and credits, still through its dictator, Vargas, has expressed greater admiration for Hitler's fascism than for Hull's democracy.[5]

The State Department has failed to remind us that South Americans are Europeans,—Spanish and Portuguese,—that, nearer to Europe, they go to Paris rather than to New York,—that up to the '90's when South America was made an excursion point for our new 'white fleet', we knew little and cared less about them, and they returned the compliment,[6]—that our war with Mexico and annexation of half of its territory, followed by our war with Spain and the annexation of its territory in the New and Old Worlds, were followed by a period of 'dollar diplomacy' which gave South Americans a well founded suspicion of 'yanqui imperialismo'.[7]

State Department and newspaper propaganda has misled the American public in regard to South American trade. Before 1900 our trade with Latin America amounted to little. Europe practically monopolized it. Great Britain, which had invested billions to build up Argentina,[8] had about a quarter of South America's trade, Germany, which had a large population in Brazil, had about 15%. During the World War the U. S. trade increased to more than half the total, as Germany's was totally wiped out and Britain's decreased. Since the war Germany has slowly gained back her Latin American trade, which in 1939 reached about the level of 1914. The U. S. trade has diminished to about 35%, but is well above the 1914 figure. Britain's trade, slowly falling off, was in 1939 less than 15% of the total, while the trade of U. S. and Germany proportionately was making about an equal increase.

Startling figures are sometimes given in the American press in regard to the S. A. trade of the aggressive Germans.[9] A reported 400% increase in their trade in Peru may on analysis be found to have been an increase from 1% to 4%, while U S. holds a much larger percentage.[10]

Most writing on South America is adapted to the North American taste and is often by journalists who have been extended courtesies by steamship or aviation companies Katherine Carr's "South American Primer" (Reynal & Hitchcock, 1939) is sound, shrewd, alert. It should be prescribed reading for our President and Secretary of State

After the South American countries had won their independence from Spain, Canning, Britain's Foreign Minister in 1823, busy in the Far East, to guard England's American possessions persuaded the U. S. to warn other European countries to keep out. The "Doctrine", enunciated in a message to Congress, has preserved Monroe's name and kept British possessions free from aggressors. The idea had already been expressed by the Nipmuck Indians, who named the largest pond in Massachusetts Lake Chaugogagog-manchaugagog-chaubunagungamaug. Translated it means, "You fish on your side, I fish on my side, nobody fish in the middle.[11]

The Monroe Doctrine for a century has been "more honour'd in the breach than in th' observance". It did not prevent Great Britain from taking in 1833 the Falkland Islands which Argentina had settled in 1820 and the British occupation of which she periodically protests,—nor the seizure in 1859 of Guatemala territory to add to British Honduras, which Guatemala continues to protest,—nor France from taking over the island of San Bartholomew from Sweden in 1877 or from beginning the Panama Canal, the wreckage of which was unloaded on us through a piece of financial skulduggery,—nor the 1940 seizure by the French and British of the Dutch islands of Aruba and Curacao.[12]

The present Administration in its endeavor to "maintain orderly processes everywhere" has stretched, strained, and doctored the Doctrine. Hull, from acting as traffic cop on the Burma-China road where the British were trying to gain some strategic advantage as the rainy season landslides close it, has had to hurry off to Havana for further doctoring of the Doctrine and to explain his international comedy of errors to the second string diplomats of the second class South American powers which have accepted invitations to the party.

Well, there is no limit to what we will do for our 'good neighbors'. Now we propose to buy all their products, to establish a cartel with billions of American capital and to take, at a net expense to the American taxpayer estimated at one billion a year, (cf Bul # 74) everything they produce so they won't have to bother to send it to Europe.[13]   But as our farmers object to our marketing South American wheat and meat, we have intimated that we will dump it in the sea rather than let it go to Hitler's Europe

To their inquiry as to how long this arrangement would last, the South American countries have received no reply. They seem a bit suspicious that after we have starved their best customers in Europe and cultural and blood relatives, we might stop buying their products and then they themselves would have to starve.[14]   They seem to lack understanding that the U. S. is carrying out the humanitarian methods of the British, who endeavor to avoid bloodshed in battle by strategic retreats to prepared positions, and to frustrate and render impotent the enemy's fighting forces by first starving their women and children.

Our Latin American neighbors have difficulty in understanding Anglo-Saxon humanitarian impulses and morality. To them the North

Americans seem hypocritical, just as they to us seem callous. With Christian charity we attempt to explain their shortcomings as due to the machinations of the wicked Nazis. So it becomes our duty to do something for our little Latin brothers, whether they like it or not. And this the more because our hypertrophied consciences make us perhaps subconsciously aware that we have done nothing for South America except to loot it of its resources through the Grace-Morgans and the Rockefeller-Guggenheims and to finance revolutions to put in power dictators more receptive of our bankers' propositions. Ford's attempt in the Amazon to bring back Brazilian rubber, which the British stole, is one saving . . . —no, one can't say 'Grace',—in South America.

Our good intentions of battling to save civilization have bogged down now that the great exemplar of all that was finest in civilization, France, has revealed its inner workings. Now that Britain is at war with France and so bitterly hated by the French, it is difficult to work up enthusiasm for Lothian's war for morality. And now that Cardinals Daugherty and O'Connell have so emphatically repudiated Mr. Roosevelt's plans and the Pope has bestowed his blessing upon the new government in France, the war for religion seems to have been deflated.

But our industrialists have been educated with war orders, and their mouths are watering for war profits. They can't be let down. We must rush through conscription before the present hysterical fear subsides. Uniforms, munitions, accessories for two to four million men will stimulate industry, pacify the unemployed, and yield a good margin of profit. As there are to be 'no new millionaires', it behooves those there are, to cough up for full-page advertisements, campaign funds, anything that will prevent interference with this noble plan.

But enthusiasm may collapse unless we have some martial stirring.[15] "When, where and how the United States will give military expression to Mr. Roosevelt's bellicose utterances" is the "important uncertainty". "Latin America may be the interventionists' ace in the hole or last card. It is a swell field in which to cook up incidents to give the interventionists a lever with which to work. . . . If anti-Hitler hysteria cannot find a battle-field in Europe, it will have to manufacture one in Latin America, where the victims will not be Nazis but Americans of both hemispheres." (Dennis, *Weekly Foreign Letter*, July 13, July 3)[16]

Some 'incident' may require a military demonstration against Nazi 'aggressors' somewhere in S A   Victorious military heroes may return, drums beating, banners flying, as did Teddy Roosevelt from "Cubia".

I hope I am wrong.   But like the President, in all conscience I must warn my fellows of what I see, and bring such support as possible to Tinkham and the "little group of wilful Senators".

July 20, 1940

NOTES

(1) "Thus the 'new order in Asia' is to Japan what the Monroe Doctrine is to the United States" writes Carleton Beals in "Pan America" (Houghton Mifflin, 1940), adding, "We would be equally upset if Japan were constantly to send us presumptuous notes concerning our relations with Panama and Brazil and the new world order".   And Beals directs our attention to the thought that "we opposed Japan's 'new Asiatic order' while upholding our own Monroe Doctrine which has cloaked previous aggression, and we hold onto the spoils it gave us."

(2) "The Monroe Doctrine (political) is strong as the navy for which Mr Hull has 'cleared the decks'   The Monroe Doctrine (economic) can be long as our purse — and foresight   For a hundred years assailed by Latin-American statesmen and politicians as a unilateral declaration drafted in the self-interest of U. S imperialism, becomes for all immediate and practical purposes the prime instrument of common hemisphere policy — the moral and the political bulwark against totalitarian imperialism." (*Fortune,* Sept , 1940, "Twenty Nations and One", p. 74)

(3) 'Hemisphere Defense' is a recent slogan, a catch word that replaces 'Dollar Diplomacy'.   In Argentina, Brazil, Chile, newspaper editors and government officials recognize it as a new device for the United States Control of Latin American business,—loans, oil, copper.

"Edwin C Hill disclosed that a Hemisphere Empire group is forming in the U S A , that 'Empire Imperialism' is proposed, and that it is 'all to the good'. Columnist Clapper admits the blunt fact 'we may have to be using American troops in the Western Hemisphere for protective occupation'   Washington warmongers, in other words, are willing to follow Hitler's plan of 'protective' occupation of Norway, Denmark and Holland, for the Western Hemisphere'.

"The same forces .   . who have succeeded in having the United States intervene in Mexico on many occasions, are clamoring for an invasion as the first step in Hemisphere Defense   Mexican Government officials inform us that every uprising in Mexico since 1910 has been financed and inspired by: 1 American business interests; 2. the State Department , 3 the reactionary press   There can be no revolution in Mexico after the July elections unless the State Department approves it !" (*In Fact,* June 17, 1940)

(4) What fun the President must have had shifting the pins on his hemispheric map in preparation for this "show of naval strength".   "In the Pacific, the gunboat Erie anchored off Guayaquil, Ecuador, while the cruiser Phoenix, bound for

Valparaiso, Chile, passed the Panama Canal . . In the South Atlantic, the cruisers Wichita and Quincy left Montevideo, Uruguay, and the destroyer O'Brien patrolled the Brazilian coast   In the Caribbean, five destroyers were reported speeding from the Virgin Islands to the French island of Martinique." (*Newsweek*, July 15, 1940)

(5) The Brazilian government announced today that all printed or written matter adjudged to be propaganda for or against any of the belligerent Powers would be barred from the mails " (AP, Jan 31, 1941)

(6) "Concerning Latin-American Culture", (Columbia Univ Press) is edited by Charles C. Griffin and published for the National Committee of the United States of America on International Intellectual Cooperation, which is sponsored by the Division of Cultural Relations of the State Department. This is a series of lectures by specialists on the, to us, little known culture of our neighbors to the south   Notable are Freyer's "Some Aspects of the Social Development of Portuguese America" and Smith's "Brazilian Art". Rios' analysis of the Spanish state of the sixteenth century reveals a setup like that of today's totalitarian states, with the whole art of dictatorship at a high state of development.

"The problem of what to do about Latin America is not so much a lack of opportunity as a question of defining our immediate and long-range objectives; the methods by which we shall attempt to attain them; the guarantees on which we shall insist. Yet whatever we do, if we approach the problem merely from a dollars-and-cents point of view we shall not succeed at all, for more than any other single factor, the differences in cultural and historical backgrounds have made a nightmare of the century-old dream of Pan-Americanism   The Germans and the Italians have been subtle. Besides their military missions, they also sent their best scholars and lecturers to Latin America; they invited to their countries influential Latin-American professors, whom they received with great ceremony. Nothing delights a Latin American more than when another nation shows respect for his culture and brains." (*Fortune*, Sept. 1940, p 155)

"The problem in the round," as *Fortune* sees it,—"At the high of 1937 our trade with Latin America was nearly $1,300,000,—1/6 of our exports, 1/5 of our imports   Their total trade that same year exceeded $4 billion, 1/3 with us. They are not so important to us as we are to them   With our own vast internal market, the Latin-American trade is not economically decisive. The entire U S export trade represents between 5 and 10% of the national production "

In Peru and Chile, U. S. capital dominates through copper and nitrate. In Argentina and Uruguay, British capital dominates through beef and wheat The external debt of the national governments of South America is $3 billions, one third owed the U.S., the rest chiefly to England. The total debt is much greater Between 1929 and 1932 their export trade declined from $2,900,000,000 to $1,-600,000,000. So they were obliged to default on bond payments. Seventy-seven per cent of the dollar bonds are not in default. "From 1932 to 1938 Germany pushed up its share of Latin-American imports from 9 4 to 16.2 per cent—chiefly at the expense of the British." (*Fortune*, Sept. pp 142, 146)

The Latin American Economic Institute was organized in the late summer of
1940 "to undertake the search for a sound economic basis of inter-American
relations", long neglected by this country. William P. Everts, Boston attorney,
is temporary chairman. Other sponsors include Stuart Chase, economist; David
Cushman Coyle; Dean Robert G. Caldwell, of M.I.T., Prof. Herbert Ingram
Priestley of the University of California; Dr John F. Normano, economist;
Prof. Kirtley F. Mather; and Felix Knauth, formerly assistant to the president at
Middlebury College, as executive director (*Chr Sci Monitor*, Dec. 7, 1940)

(7) How archaic were once President Roosevelt's imperialistic ideas. In
January, 1934, he declared, "The definite policy of the United States from now
on is one opposed to armed intervention The maintenance of constitutional
government in other nations is not, after all, a sacred obligation devolving upon
the United States alone. The maintenance of law and the orderly processes of
government in this hemisphere is the concern of each individual nation within
its borders first of all." (Langsam, "The World Since 1914", Macmillan, 1940)

How our secret imperialistic policies are developing is evidenced from a cable
by John W. White to the N. Y. *Times* from Montevideo, Nov. 9, in which he
announces "Uruguay and the United States have reached an agreement . . on
the basis of a proposal made by Uruguay last June that the bases be Pan-American
rather than United States bases and . . . open to occupation by forces of any and
all American vessels engaged in continental defense "

Last June before the Havana conference "the United States sent Capt. W. O.
Speers of the U S. navy and Col. Ralph Wooten of the United States army air
corps to Montevideo as secret agents to sound out the Uruguayan government on
the question of ceding bases to the United States for purposes of continental
defense. A Uruguayan congressional investigation had just uncovered a Nazi
military plot The United States agents asked Uruguay what assistance it would
need . . and what facilities it was prepared to extend They inquired further if
United States armed forces would be guaranteed free use of all air field and port
facilities and means of communication.

Mysterious are the intrigues whereby the British maintain "dominion over
pine and palm". For years, more particularly for months in 1940, Americans,
and others through our State Department, have sought to utilize Bolivian tin,
to establish smelters in the U.S by endless negotiations, intrigue, lobbying Jesse
Jones has the money and any number of companies are willing to enter upon it
The tin ore is piled up and awaiting shipment but nothing happens All is
blocked. The British know how to do it. And we still pay tribute to them
for our tin and rubber produced by their indentured labor. (Pearson & Allen,
Feb 11, 1941)

(8) "Dollars for Argentina", an editorial in the Harvard *Crimson* Dec 14,
1940, reminds us "that the British have been virtually in control of the economic
life of the Argentine . . . the land of the tango", that "they are the largest single
customer".

Our loan of 100 millions to Argentina is an attempt to solace her for the loss of her European markets, but *La Prensa,* the famous Buenos Aires newspaper, throws it back at us. "Nothing profitable nor durable can result for the economy of our country from these agreements" These and other woes of President Pierson of the Export Import Bank in bribing our proud Spanish neighbors, in attempting to make little brothers of them, are dwelt upon in *Time,* Feb. 10, 1941.

(9) Dr. Leopold Melo, Hull's most formidable opponent among the representatives of the great South American democracies, understands the Nazi's trade methods and enjoys a joke Pressed for an answer to an inconvenient question as to the trade possibilities of the South American democracies, he replied· Mira, Señor, once in Peru during colonial times an enterprising merchant imported a large number of eyeglasses The Indians had no need for them, and they did not sell So the merchant prevailed on the Viceroy to pass a law requiring the Indians to wear eyeglasses in order to have certain privileges " (R H Sharp, *Chr Sci Monitor,* Aug 3) It caused a little spluttering in the Balkans when the Nazis worked off their surplus aspirin and harmonicas Such could be worked off more easily in South America.

(10) "Germans may be based, in menacing numbers, on the coast of Peru, German submarines may be sneaking in and out of Peruvian inlets and harbors Emissaries of Japan, teeming with sinister thoughts, may be encamped all along the west coast of South America.

"But if so, these Germans and Japanese are the most marvelous camouflagists in all history. They must be impersonating trees or rocks or Peruvian guano birds. Some day, when I have time, I mean to sneak up on suspicious-looking trees in Peru and suddenly yell 'Heil Hitler!'" If they convulsively stretch out a branch in the Nazi salute, I shall then chop them down with an axe (brought along by me for that express purpose) disguised as a fountain pen The position of the Japanese, to be sure, in Peru's trade, is not what it was. There, as elsewhere in South America, they are in retreat. 'Recession' is a mild word for describing what has happened to them in the Peruvian market during the past few years." (Ybarra, America Faces South, pp 243-4)

(11) As originally conceived by Canning in England, and by John Quincy Adams and President Monroe in this country, the Monroe Doctrine was an example of pacific initiative which forestalled and prevented possible war. It did not contemplate any control by the United States over the new states of Central and South America, nor did it interfere with any existing sovereignty It merely gave notice that any future European attempt at dominion in that region would be regarded by us as an unfriendly act. Backed by the parallel statement from England—then wholly master of the high seas—it proved effective in preventing any such attempt from being made. Moreover, it announced our intention to resist hostile attacks in Central and South America from overseas This claim was not, indeed, admitted by European nations; but it was respected." ("The Frontiers of the United States", A Lawrence Lowell, *Foreign Affairs,* July, 1939—p 663)

(12) Secretary of the Navy Knox, at the 'lend lease' bill hearing, brought forth this bon mot, "British control of the seas has enabled the U.S. to maintain

the Monroe Doctrine for 118 years, to build a strong and peaceful land" (*Time,* Jan. 27, 1941)   Britain just before had burned our capital, bombed our cities, invaded our soil.   And during the Civil War, ships built in Britain retarded our commerce and Canadian forces threatened to invade us from the north.   Since then Britain seized Guatamela, threatened Venezuela, France invaded Mexico. Has any other country ever landed one uniformed soldier in North America?

(13) The cartel plan reminded Hugh Johnson, July 12, of how "Joseph could successfully buy and store the surplus of Egypt for seven fat years and then sell it at hold-up prices during seven lean years until he owned all of Egypt.   He could do it because he had a dream-book and a direct wire to the pearly gates."

"What the cartel presupposed was a super-hemisphere trading bloc or clearing-house   Its author is a young man named Dudley P. K. Wood, until recently one of Harry Hopkins' assistants in the Department of Commerce   Mr. Wood, who had spent some years in Nazi Germany as the representative of a U.S. business firm, had been pondering the likely consequences of a German victory in this hemisphere.   He got in touch with Mr. A. A. Berle, Jr, in the State Department (cf Bul #98).   Between them they evolved the cartel.   Nothing was done about it until the day France got her terms—much sooner than Mr Roosevelt had expected   Sensing the shock this would be to Latin America, the President reached out for a white rabbit   The delegates at Havana shied away from the cartel   The President, after the first enthusiastic pronouncement, let it drop; no other statesman in this election year rose to sponsor it   Losses at best might run from $150 million to $300 million a year—no one knows " (*Fortune,* September, 1940, p 149-50)

In "America Faces South", T. R Ybarra writes, "Between 1931 and the summer of 1939, the colossal total of 67,000,000 bags of coffee, it is reliably esti-mated, each containing 132 pounds, went up in smoke—nearly nine billion pounds of coffee!"   From the AAA we learned that "whenever you try to buy a farm surplus it magically mushrooms in size"

The Administration plan had been to dazzle our little neighbors with a display of billions and to dismay the Nazis   "If the Havana Conference", Whaley-Eaton remarked July 23, "decides to pool Inter-American raw materials, it will greatly reinforce the British effort to control commodities at their source.   This would, in effect, be an extension of the British blockade system to the Western Hemi-sphere, in the London view, and would be greatly helpful to the British cause." "Perhaps the greatest danger of all is an imperialist war, likely an undeclared war in Mexico or some more distant South American land which we shall be told is a defensive operation—much as the German occupation of Belgium or the Russian war on Finland was 'defensive' "—Norman Thomas, Sept 21, radio address, "War or Democracy".

General Smuts, who helped think up the League of Nations, said the cartel would provide a basis for exchange between "these two groups of free peoples: North and Latin Americans on the one hand and the countries associated with the British Commonwealth of Nations in the war against Hitlerism on the other" F. B. Holt, *Chr Sci Monitor*, July 23, 1940)   Hull's charge against the Germans in his Havana address that "these forces shrink from no means of attacking their ends" might have seemed to his Spanish speaking auditors equally well-directed against the English speaking people who seem to have gotten ahead a bit. To a Peruvian it might seem even more aggressive.

(14) The Latin American is more of a realist than North Americans generally realize. "Living precariously off raw-material exports, the Latin has always had —and for years to come must continue to have—a poor man's stake in the freedom of the seas. Whoever rules the trade routes can overnight become his economic overlord." (*Fortune,* Sept. 1940, p 75)

"It will be remembered that Germany made numerous contracts for delivery of goods in South America this Fall   British exporters are reported as somewhat amused over the German failure to fill orders. Germany has made deliveries . . with American goods. Germans have for years been the distributing agents for a number of American producers   They simply made their American orders large enough to cover the German contracts   Additionally, it appears that the penalties incurred were largely in name only   The damages are paid in marks, and in marks that are only good for purchases inside Germany. So, they are merely book credits the value of which is extremely problematic " (*Whaley-Eaton Service,* Oct. 29, 1940)

Lionel Portman in "Three Asses in Bolivia" (Houghton Mifflin, 1922) tells of a trip with two English mining engineers to Bolivia, of the wealth of metals, tin, silver, gold, lead, wolfram, antimony and bismuth. Since the days of the Incas, fabulous wealth has come from these veins and is still coming. "The huge mines now existing are but a fraction of what might exist. Only capital and spirit are needed to multiply them   The pity is that this capital and this spirit come as a rule from America and Chile rather than from England. Very little has ever been done by our people to acquire and develop Bolivian mining property, and still less in proportion is being done today. Ignorance of the country and lack of confidence in it are the rule rather than the exception with us; and by degrees all the wealth that might be ours is slipping away to people of other races."

(15) Others have seen the possibility of a South American 'incident'. "If you fight Hitler at all it will be in Latin America", Dr Enrique de Lozada, former secretary of the Bolivian delegation at Washington, was reported as saying, Boston *Transcript,* July 23, 1940.

(16) Father Divine, "Peace, it's Wonderful", buys adjoining real estate and cuddles up to good neighbors   His plan works   Why not in South America? He suggests "that the United States purchase Central and South America and make all the Americas one democracy." (AP, Dec. 11, 1940)

CONSCRIPTION IS OPPOSED

Newspaper headlines have promoted the belief that it was all over, that the conscription bill had "passed" (Boston *Herald*), perhaps meaning 'reported' by the committee. Three days later, July 28, Dorris, N. Y. *Times* dispatch, reported the bill, "perfected", would be "voted on formally" on July 30. The vote "is regarded as perfunctory"; — It's "non-partisan", we are told, because Rep. Wadsworth, reactionary Republican, and Sen Burke, lame duck Democrat, jointly introduced it.[1]

Debate opens in the Senate on July 31. It will be bitterly opposed by Sen. Taft, Vandenberg, Wheeler, Norris, and "numerous others who have publicly criticized the bill" (Dorris). Then it goes to the House.

Introduced as "a bill to protect the integrity and institutions of the United States", it "declares" that they "are gravely threatened and that to insure the independence and freedom of the people . . . it is imperative that immediate measures be taken".[2]   Senator Wheeler said, June 25, "I don't believe we're in any emergency. The only emergency is that conjured up in the minds of a few people who want to see us go to war and send our youths to Asia and Europe."

The British Navy burned our undefended shore towns in 1776-'83, 1812-'14, tacitly assisted the rebellion against the U. S., 1860-'64, "gave Napoleon III the green light to transport a large French army and his puppet Maximilian across the Atlantic to Mexico. Britain took advantage of the situation to turn the self-governing community of British Honduras into an Empire colony", threatened Venezuela in '87 and again in '95-'99. "Can we be any more sure about England than England was about France? Politicians and admirals are being arrested in England, too." Upton Close in "Common Sense for Americans", *Living Age,* August, 1940, thus challenges clichés and dispels hysteria.

The "few people" who met secretly in Coudert's office, April 29, including Lamont, Stimson, and Grenville Clark (cf Buls #62, 65), have with the President and through committees been active in promoting the present fear that we would be in great danger without the protection of the British Navy.

Grenville Clark, leading member of the Harvard Corporation and Wall Street lawyer who presented a bill of $957,000 (reduced by the court to $870,000) in the Paramount Picture reorganization (Thurman Arnold, "Folklore of Capitalism", pp 256-8), soon after the 'secret' meeting began to promote conscription through the N. Y. *Times* and the Military Training Camps Association, made up of Wall Street alumni of the great universities (cf Bul #63). At the Senate committee hearing Mr. Clark and Julius Ochs Adler of the N. Y. *Times* were the leading proponents [3]

The bill provides for the registration of men from 18 to 64, with a penalty of not more than 5 years or a fine of not more than $10,000, or both, or on court martial "such punishment as a court martial may direct".[4] As originally drafted, it was proposed to pay those drafted $5 a month. This has been raised to $21 to quiet the popular outcry.

"The army plans for the induction into service Oct. 1 of 400,000 men for training, with an additional 400,000 to be called next April. Then, in October, 1941, an additional 600,000 would be inducted into service to give the United States a trained army of at least 2,000,000."[5] The National Guard "will train the conscripts in the art of modern military science" (Dorris, N. Y. *Times*, July 28).

The 'conscript', the victim of cruel and militaristic Czars and Kaisers was regarded with pity and contempt by free Americans a generation ago. The National Guard, who are to act as instructors, have had little opportunity to learn "modern military science". Originally for local home defense, they have been limited to a weekly drill and a few weeks summer encampment Except for a few 'crack' regiments they are of material inferior to the university R.O.T.C.

Our Army officers should be learning more of modern military science instead of drilling raw recruits Few of our generals even have yet commanded a division In "Generals Without Ideas", H. S. Ford, in the *Nation*, July 6, portrays our Army officers realistically and without pity, as General Crozier in "Brass Hats" and "The Men I Killed" presented British generals in all their stupidity.

Conscription will temporarily weaken our defense. Registering and classifying 42 million citizens will take the time of important men

Conscription is not needed.[6] Volunteers will respond to the call to defend their country or this continent.[7] In the first five months of the last war, 563,000 volunteers enlisted, and 1,300,000 up to August, 1918, when the draft went into effect Only 2,000,000 were sent overseas

One volunteer should be worth two conscripts A rebellious conscientious objector is an expensive recruit 1300 conscientious objectors in the last war were condemned to prison, some to torture. There will be more this time Hope that they may be treated more gently is hardly justified by the present persecution of Jehovah's Witnesses because they make such a nuisance of themselves (Editorial, Boston *Transcript,* July 26). To one brought up to believe, as I was, that Jehovah was the only God and a jealous one, it would seem Jehovah's Witnesses are nearer the original Christians than Bishop Manning or Archbishop Lang.[8]

In "Mobilizing Civilian America", just published by the Council on Foreign Relations, Tobin and Bidwell of the Dartmouth faculty make no attempt to justify the dictatorial process realistically described. The first sentence of the book tells the story,—"For a nation at war today there is really no business except making war".[9] Maj.-Gen. McCoy, U.S.A. retired, in the foreword tells us, "75 per cent of our national effort in a new war would be civilian". Reviewed are the mistakes made in the last war, many of which "are being repeated today". "All the planning of the General Staff for the past twenty years has been ignored."

Our defense need is trained mechanicians E. A. Mowrer reports July 2 that France "was defeated by probably less than 100,000 German air, tank, infantry and artillery specialists" (cf Buls #66, 96) Sen. Downey declared he knows "no better way to create saboteurs and disloyal people than to conscript mechanics to service your planes". (AP, July 5)

Those of draft age are properly skeptical and incredulous at the false alarms of imminent danger and pumped up hysteria. "They do not want to be sold as French people were." (Jane Sargent, N. Y. *World-Telegram*) To create a sound morale we must establish "confidence" in those who control the "government", who command the Army, and, if we are to fight and sacrifice to the limit, in the final ends that are to be won.

"Winning a war depends not only on the success of military operations; it depends also on the conclusion of an advantageous and enduring peace. The danger to democracy from war lies . . . in the loss thereafter either of the popular will to restore democratic controls or of the means of expressing that will." (Tobin and Bidwell)
July 29, 1940

NOTES

(1) "Senator Burke praises Hitler and Nazi rule as he returns", was the heading in N. Y. *Herald Tribune,* Aug 30, 1938, to which Norman Thomas called attention when he testified "it is symbolically appropriate" that Senator Burke should be author and sponsor of the peace time conscription bill

(2) The army's conception of its duty in "protecting the independence and free-

dom of the people" is revealed in its definition of democracy, Manual No. 2000-25 (now recently revised) "Democracy: A government of the masses. Authority derived through mass meetings or any other form of direct expression, results in mobocracy. Attitude toward property is communistic—negating property rights. Attitude toward law is that the will of the majority shall regulate, whether it be based upon deliberation, or governed by passion, prejudice, and impulse, without restraint or regard to consequence " General Shedd, revealing the armies' view of democracy before the Senate Military Affairs Committee (July 12) said,—" .
the principles of selective service are so fair, so just and so democratic, they produce the men we need at the time we need them".

(3) "How is it that what seems to be an administration-approved bill happened to turn up under the sponsorship of a lame duck anti-New Deal senator and a Republican representative of no official position in the House? Why all the supporting propaganda activity from the Military Training Camps Association?"
. The administration wanted such a measure The War Department firmly and unanimously believed it necessary It has kept a similar bill in its safe all along But as this is a presidential campaign year and war is not yet imminent, the government officials, especially those in the White House, deemed it strategic to let the measure originate and progress along non-political lines, which would relieve the New Deal from sole responsibility for it The original bill actually was drawn by the Military Training Camps Association of New York City, a group of business men, attorneys and reserve officers, many of whom are Republicans,—Henry Stimson, the man now installed as his assistant secretary, Judge Robert P. Patterson. Such men as President James B Conant of Harvard, Julius Ochs Adler, general manager of the New York *Times*, Col 'Wild Bill' Donovan, who was in the Hoover cabinet, and the eminent New York attorneys, Elihu Root, Jr., and Grenville Clark, had a hand in it" (Paul Mallon, Aug. 7, 1940).

(4) In a long-winded, confused sentence of over 200 words, the bill provides for the prosecution of anyone "who in any manner shall knowingly fail or neglect to perform any duty required of him under or in the execution of this act, etc etc " It then gives the president power to "prescribe the necessary rules and regulations to carry this act into effect". What an imaginative president can not do with this power, would be hard to guess.

(5) Responding to pressure from both sides, army mobilization plans proved to be extraordinarily elastic. Only 300,000 men were requested of Congress in May 1940, but by July the number had increased to 2,000,000. Then it developed that they could not all be taken in at once, but in batches of 400,000. Two days debate in the Senate caused army leaders to say Senatorial delay had forced them to postpone their plans to January 1941 Subsequently plans were announced to call for 50,000 men November 1 and later groups of 75,000 up to April 1941 Inasmuch as the army was already receiving nearly 30,000 volunteers a month, it would not seem that the supply of manpower was one of their greatest worries

Voluntary enlistments have come along at an unprecedented rate By October 16, 1940, the *Christian Century* was able to say "The army announces that, because of the strain on its facilities caused by mobilization of the national guard and reserves, and because volunteering is larger than at any previous time in its history (there were 5,000 more recruits in September than in May 1917, the previous record month), it will probably be able to take less than 100,000 of the 16,500,000 young men to be registered this week! In other words, it now develops that what the army wanted was not men but to fasten the system of conscription on American life. It was the effect on America, not on the dictators, that was primarily at stake when the hysterical campaign was whipped up which finally succeeded in stampeding Congress."

By December 9, 1940, *Life* reported "Only 18,700 men, most of whom had volunteered after registering for the draft, were summoned in the first draft call. As fast as the Army can build tents and barracks, this first trickle of rookies will become a flood By the end of next June the Army expects to have 789,000 conscripts under arms." "Further induction of draftees will be postponed until next month" (AP, Dec. 3, 1940). Voluntary enlistments exceeding expectations and lack of facilities played a part in the decision.

(6) One C.C.C director who took the trouble to survey his men reported that more than half of them would choose the army in preference to the C.C.C if the pay were equalized Two-thirds of them would join the army if the C C C were abolished (and pay was the same). Ninety per cent thought they should receive some sort of military training. Here was a reservoir of some 500,000 men Army heads looked the other way. (David Lawrence, Aug. 14)

(7) "England in the last war, under a threat of more imminent danger recruited in 14 months two million men from a population about two-fifths as large as ours " (Tobin and Bidwell, p 111)

(8) "Faithfully bringing up the rear, as he has on every reactionary public policy in a generation, came the Right Reverend William T. Manning, Episcopal bishop of New York. . . King James I of England once put his foot down and said, 'No bishops, no king!' Ever since the Anglican bishops have been gratefully loyal But our Protestant Episcopal Church no longer owes its primary allegiance to the British crown. Some gentle person should whisper this fact to Bishop Manning Now, as in 1917, the Anglophiles lead the drive for the draft." (*Christian Century*, September 4, 1940)

(9) "With some severity, the President refused to make public the industrial mobilization plan that has been drafted since the world war . . . in answer to a question about the plan, the President asked why he should make it public any more than publishing the plan of the Civil War " "But", said General Hugh Johnson, "it is in no sense an old plan It is not only a fire-new plan, but it is the only plan there is. The mistakes of 1917 are being repeated with nauseating regularity—and consequent hopeless delay . . . because the President and his administrative family were so fascinated with their habit of 'brilliant experimentation' that they didn't want anything to interfere with it Above all they didn't want to have any other influences in government" (September 3, 1940). "In both the press and Congress . . . the larger question of the direction and control

of war by a democracy has not been adequately considered—except to make invidious comparisons with the systems and supposed efficiency of the totalitarian states" (Tobin and Bidwell)

FROM OUR CORRESPONDENTS

To share one's ideas with others is a normal urge, but opportunities are limited. Five thousand letters a week are sent to Boston newspapers but few are printed (Boston *Transcript,* July 20). Hundreds of thousands of letters on legislation in prospect are sent Congressmen,—but few reach the public eye (cf recent survey by St. Louis *Post-Dispatch*).

From Bulletin readers throughout the country hundreds of letters come to me, some confused, some argumentative, as to "the lesser of the two evils for president". It would be unkind to attach the names to their positive views at that time on the burning topics of the hour even though they were used in the Bulletin Briefly we summarize:—"Well, which is it,—welch with Willkie or ruin with Roosevelt?"—"He's a better anti-war bet than Willkie with the International Bankers backing him"—"Any attempt to prove that Wendell Willkie was put over by the House of Morgan is just pure nonsense"—"Absolutely no tradition against a fourth or fifth term"—"Roosevelt will stop at nothing to destroy those who disagree with him. It is the attitude of a natural born dictator"—"Retaining this outfit in Washington for a third term would certainly be far more dangerous and would result in national calamity".

The press is commented on by many because of its domination and unreliability "With the incredible inaccuracies and omissions of even our 'respectable' press, the work that you are doing is invaluable."

Dwight L. Bolinger, Washburn College, Topeka, Kansas, writes thoughtfully:—"Skepticism toward the press is more widespread than it has ever been before, but I cannot be so optimistic about our having immunized ourselves against its falsehoods and half-truths. For I have observed repeatedly that those who cry 'damned lies' at the newspapers, in the same breath utter some absurdity, with unsuspecting credence, that they have picked up from those very papers. The pressure of the 'news' is so unremitting and so insidious that we cannot be on our guard against it all the time, with the result that at critical moments we are too liable to act upon the persuasions and suggestions which the agencies of the news have managed to get past our vigilance. The newspapers

have given to us the unthinking acceptance of mere facts, of superficiali-
ties which are no better information about the human race than that
which a man on Mars, if he had a sufficiently powerful telescope, could
get by observing its antics In other words, with no sympathy nor psychological understanding presupposed. Of course, the papers do permit themselves the luxury of analysis once in a while, if the terms may
be kept at the level of generalities so that no one may be offended, or
if the events are sufficiently remote, as with a foreign war, so that not
many people here are closely affected. But on the significant and vital
matters they are silent I even sometimes suspect them of having deliberately provided themselves with a kind of innocuous news in the world
of sports so that attention could be drawn there and away from the
fundamentals that might offend someone—for it is undeniable that
American interest in sports owes more to the newspapers than to anything else."

"The War Monger would lead some human beings into a premature
and absorbing fear of other human beings,"—M A. G , Sparta, Ill.
"We are distressed by the unscrupulous attempts of the war-makers to
misrepresent the country's opinion as being overwhelmingly behind the
President's motives. Nothing is more important than to keep artificially-
produced war fever down,"—E. V., Stanford University, Calif. "We
are as anxious as any intelligent Americans to see America stay as far
removed as possible from this holocaust of hatred and wholesale murder,"—W. E., Ojai, Calif.

"Isaiah once said 'the fruits of righteousness shall be peace',—which
puts the two in proper order I think. And when his nation went into a
war hysteria, he said 'in quietness and confidence shall be your strength',
not an arms race! I certainly appreciate your bulletins, and think Isaiah
would too!"—Rev. J. R. B , Philadelphia, Pa.[1]
July 31, 1940

Notes

[1] Bulletin #83, "Another Symposium From Our Correspondents Letters",
was made up of quotations from letters stimulated by the preceding Here space
prevents only the briefest recountal Independence of thought, and freedom to
express it, is the essence of democracy. This is lost under dictatorship, is not
permitted in an autocracy. We are losing it,—and not too gradually.

Again the democratic process has worked. Writing Congressmen, voicing
protest, has halted autocratic executives (cf Bul #44). It is a noble little band

of fighters that has opposed the plan of Roosevelt allied with his formerly scorned "economic royalists" to put 42 million men under draft.

Senators,—more appreciative letters have been received recently from the following (cf Buls #40, 46)—Maloney, Hiram Johnson, Norris, Shipstead, Tydings, Capper, Holt, Tobey, Lodge, Nye, Reynolds, Wheeler, Walsh, Bridges, Clark, Danaher, Frazier, Downey, Vandenberg, Barbour, LaFollette, Overton, Townsend, Bone. We quote a few:—

"These succinct summaries are indeed worth while. You deserve commendation for your efforts in awakening America to the folly of involvement in Europe's age-old quarrels,"—Sen Burton K. Wheeler. "I am sorry that more people of your frame of mind are not active in trying to stem the tide now setting in so strongly toward war. I am going to read 'What Makes Lives', and a hurried examination indicates that it is more than interesting. I hope that other members of the Senate will secure your releases,"—Sen. Homer T. Bone. "An occasional message of this nature is a source of real stimulation and encouragement. I like your bulletin,"—Sen Arthur H. Vandenberg

Representatives,—appreciative letters have come from Luce, Elliott, Rogers, Treadway, Schafer, Vorys, Fish, Ludlow, McCormack, Shanley, Casey, Dies, Martin, Lemke, Whittington, Gilchrist, Holmes. Wigglesworth, Austin, Clason, Voorhis, Sandager, Brewster, Tinkham

"Your bulletins are most enlightening and I enjoy reading them immensely. Appreciate your keeping my name on your mailing list."—Rep. James E Van Zandt. "I certainly do read your bulletins You and I feel the same way about foreign policy,"—Rep. Bruce Barton

Writers and publicists continue to send encouragement among them Burton Rascoe, H. L. Mencken, Al Williams, Henry Beston, I. S. Mattingly, Brown Landone, Charles Beard, Jonathan Daniels, Carleton Beals, Will Durant, W. G. Clugston. While most editorial and column writers on political and international subjects have had to yield to hysterical pressure of prevailing fashions, a few have preserved their integrity.

"Thank you for one of the most stimulating, intellectual evenings I have ever enjoyed I am reading your bulletins with great interest,"—Paul L Cornell, Conn. "I am particularly impressed by the apparent fact, evidenced by the correspondents whom you quote, that you reach people who are apparently far from even liberal in their outlook. What your bulletins contain, enforced by your own prestige, may have some effect on minds long unaccustomed to doing any thinking,"—Rockwell Kent, N. Y "With Roosevelt, it only means waste, inefficiency and low-grade, stupid militarism,"—Oswald Garrison Villard, Conn "The interventionists are growing less and less sure of themselves, and I fear their 'principals' aren't making their job easy for them The picture of each side starving the other, plus innocents in Europe, is going to give this country a double wrench, isn't it? I am very interested in your bulletins,"—Upton Close, N. Y. "Democracy once scared hell out of the tories Now totalitarianism is scaring hell out of the democracy worshippers. Whichever side wins, people will adjust. Life will go on,"- Tom Dreier, N. H.

School and college people,—most educators have been obliged to take to cover or adopt the protective coloration of their trustees and the foundations and donors that support them. Some still continue to cerebrate and remain articulate. Some have indicated their interest in the Bulletins such as Presidents Bowman, Kent, Hutchins, Valentine, Professors Squires, Douglass, Cannon, May, Reiser, Headmasters Perry, Heely, Hamilton, Allen.

"They will make an interesting file to which reference can be made after this hysteria is over," Walter H Mohr, George School, Pa. "My purpose in submitting this check was to make a very humble contribution toward expense of the inimitable Sargent Bulletins. These bulletins are worthy of wide circulation," J. Garton Needham, Simmons Col. "We need an army of men like you to stem the tide of making an army out of the entire population,"—Walter H. Beck, Concordia Teachers Col., Neb.

Bitter and hysterical times ahead—it is a frightful reflection on the Administration, State Department, government officials, the press and our intellectual leaders, that Czaristic persecution should be anticipated by those who attempt to get at the truth and tell it. All that was anticipated last winter in Buls #34 and #35 has now come to pass But worse is ahead. Recall the Palmer red drives of 1920. To Thomas Lamont's query as to the future, H. G. Wells hoped to be "in an asylum for the sane". But even in this panic and hysteria you can't keep a good man down. Here are some.

"Keep up the good work just as long as the F.B.I. allows you to,"—E. H. Warner, Univ. of Arizona, Tucson "Go on giving this vital information· when we are in the war they'll shut you up,"—Canon Bernard Iddings Bell, R. I. "In this respect you are doing magnificent and unique work which, for the good of us all, I consider important and courageous,"—E. H Pope, Ontario, Can.

Fan mail—hundreds of letters from all parts of the country bring appreciation and encouragement. We quote, as in the past, from but a few. "Your information is vital and in a form that can easily be understood and passed on," Frank King Marquette, Hollywood "I was particularly interested in knowing the sources of some of your facts as I have long been aware of the unreliability of magazine and newspaper comments on activities of today,"—John A Wickham, N. Y. C. "There are few places to turn any more for sanity in national affairs, and yours is one of them,"—J C. Fuller, Oregon. "Your bulletins continue excellent, instructive and much to the point in this propaganda ridden land,"—Hawthorne Winner, Phila.

QUICKSTEP TO WAR
By H. L. Mencken

"Enthusiasm for the draft seems to be oozing away, even among the New Dealers. It is a pity, for no alternative scheme for the national defense is so equitable or so effective. But it is certainly not surprising, for even the most innocent radio fan must have begun to wonder of late whether the Roosevelt hullabaloo over the national defense rally has the national defense for its object. .. The line-up seems to be Roosevelt first, England second, and the United States only third. . . . Nine-tenths of the current blather about grave perils to the United States is blather only. There is not the slightest evidence that the Totalitarian Powers, whether European or Asiatic, have been planning any attack on this country. On the contrary, they have been at great pains since the beginning of the war, often at serious cost to their interest, to treat it with politeness. All the major invasions of American rights have been made by England, not by Germany, Italy or Japan. In so far as the United States is now, or has been, at odds with any of the totalitarians, it is simply and solely because the Roosevelt Administration has constantly and deliberately given aid and comfort to their enemies, in violation not only of international law and the statutes of Congress, but also of common honesty and common decency.

"The Journalistic and other Anglomaniacs who have been trying to cover up that plain fact have failed altogether   It is known to everyone of any sense, and it cannot be disposed of by banal nonsense about the preservation of American ideals and the defense of religion and morality. There is nothing in American idealism that commands stabbing a neighbor in the back, and there is no article of either religion or morality that makes a virtue of false pretenses.

"The Hon. Mr. Roosevelt has been howling for England since long before the war began; indeed, it is perfectly reasonable to argue that the English would have hesitated to plunge in if they had not been sure of his support in advance   The moment the first shot was fired, that howling translated itself into overt assistance, and such assistance still continues, day in and day out. It colors every detail of American foreign policy. No item of that policy is unrelated to the dominant purpose of helping the British Empire out of the mess confronting it, and setting it once more upon its legs

"If it were true, as the Hon. Mr. Roosevelt and his associated fire-alarms allege, that the Totalitarian Powers are planning to attack the Americas, then it would certainly be only elemental prudence to hang on to such defensive materials as we have in hand. But that is precisely what has *not* been done   On the contrary, hundreds of airplanes that are sorely needed here have been shipped abroad, and at this minute the Anglomaniacs around the Throne are trying to devise some means to send American destroyers after them, though it is specifically forbidden by law.

"What this folly may come to in the end is already indicated by a painful example. In the days before the French plunged down to disaster by serving as the goons of England, American airplanes were sent to France in large number. When the French took to their heels, leaving the English to fight it out alone, many of these planes were captured by the Germans, and are now being used to bomb England. If, now, England also blows up, and the Totalitarian Powers ask the United States for an accounting, thousands of American planes will be available to help them in the negotiation.

"The plan to send destroyers after the planes is based upon the theory that the English navy is a philanthropic organization consecrated to saving us from Hitler and the Japs.

"When the United States went to their rescue in the war of 1914-18 they were on their last legs, and without American help they would have succumbed in short order, navy or no navy. As one of their own generals put it, their backs were to the wall. We not only sent them our own navy and reinforced them with a large army; we also lent them immense sums of money.

"But there was never a cent for the American taxpayer He was not only bilked out of his money; he was also sneered at as a low and swinish fellow, and Uncle Sam became Uncle Shylock.

"Such are the altruists that the Hon. MM Roosevelt, Hull, Welles, Stimson and company now ask us to trust again. Such are the racketeers of religion and morality that we are to supply with planes needed badly at home, and destroyers needed even more badly, and more and more billions of money that we'll never see again, and a million conscript replacements for their own tattered and thrice-beaten army, now once more with its back to the wall."

The above comments of Mr. Mencken of Aug. 4, abbreviated from Bulletin #74 was supplemented by comments of July 28 of which we quote one paragraph. "The real objection to Roosevelt is not that he is running for a third term, but that he is an infernally bad President, and a generally suspicious and dangerous character. The more piously he howls against the bad faith of the dictators, the more the fact is rubbed in that his own solemn word is worth precisely nothing. Even his stooges at Chicago belched sadly when he told them that he didn't want a third term, and was taking it only as a matter of conscience and public duty. In the course of nearly forty years' attendance upon political orgies I have heard many whoppers, but that one was surely the champion of them all."

Though political and journalistic exigencies distracted his attention, he constantly reverts in his sermons to the great American preoccupation 'morality', and we find him commenting on "The Progress of the Great Crusade", "Counter-Reformation", "The Gospel of Hatred". From "Advances in Moral Science" we quote, "Nearly all the accepted publicists of the country, whether official or journalistic, appear to view the titanic struggle now going on as if it were a simple conflict between good and bad, right and wrong. On the one side there is a band of innocent Sunday-school scholars, engaged in holding a peaceful picnic in a sort of cosmic Druid Hill Park, and on the other side there is a gang of wicked ruffians from across the railroad tracks, bent upon chasing the little angels home and stealing their ice cream. . . .

"The English, for long months, wooed Mussolini with every device known to international seduction, seeking to induce him to rat on his sworn allies and stab them in the back. Can anyone doubt that if he had been base enough to yield he would have been hailed as a virtuoso of virtue comparable to the brave generals and honest politicians who made off with the Polish gold reserve? Yet when he refused he was transformed instantly into an ogre with nine horns and seventeen tails, and the President of the United States denounced him piously as a disgrace to humanity, to the almost unanimous applause of the corps of American editorial writers"

August 4, 1940

$500,000,000 FOR SOUTH AMERICA

The publicity given the President's proposal of July 22 for another half billion for South America served as bait to bring the politicos to Havana. By greasing the ways and the palms it helped Hull's 'Triumph'.[1] As Under-Secretary Welles said, it "would constitute a most effective and important part of the program of inter-American economic cooperation and hemispheric solidarity". (AP, July 21,—or, as

PM put it, July 25, " a demand for chips with which to play the Pan-American diplomatic game seriously".)

This half billion was modestly offered as a temporary substitute after ridicule had killed the Administration's cartel plan. (cf Bul #69) It served to bait the trap for the great South American 'democracies' who are looking to a winning Germany as their future best customer.

"It is fairly safe to guess that half a billion will be but a beginning; that a single year will send us three times that into the red and that this sum will be multiplied for each year we keep up this folly,"[2] remarks John T Flynn in the *New Republic*, Aug. 5.

Interpreting the $500,000,000 "as a bribe" Ralph Robey, in *Newsweek* Aug. 5, writes, "If this is a part of a broad defense program it's time to stop the soft-hearted nonsense about simply being a good neighbor and get down to the hard-boiled business of just how and to what extent we propose to regard South America as our frontier." Jesse Jones, through whose hands as director of the American Export-Import Bank the money must pass, "has indicated quite clearly that he doesn't know what the proposal is all about—that apparently it is a scheme for getting $500,000,000 with which to play around in South America in any way that the Administration decides".[3] (Robey, *Newsweek*)

Our government and our people have put five billions and more into South America since the last war. From this were paid bankers' commissions and politicos' bribes. Some of this is represented by bonds which today can be bought up for some cents on the dollar. Little of it will ever be repaid.[4] Nor need one expect this half billion to be repaid [5] The purpose, as realists know, is to help Britain enforce the starvation blockade, to prevent South American food and resources from reaching Europe,—at the expense of the American taxpayer.

The bill to make the half billion available through the Export-Import Bank and the Inter-American Bank was finally reported to the Senate early this month after stiff opposition in the Appropriations Committee. The minority report, signed by seven Senators, declared it "unconstitutional", "futile", "harmful", "wasteful".[6] (AP, Aug 6, 7)

Senator Adams questioned the "authority to take money out of the taxpayers' pockets to help the citizens of Brazil" (N. Y. *Times*, July 30). Sen. Taft declared the loan 'ridiculous', 'foolish', and added, (AP, July 31,) "We have spent a billion and a half dollars in holding our surpluses off the market. If we are going to hold South American surpluses off the market, there is practically no limit, it seems to me, to what we can spend, all with complete futility."

Isn't it worth while to 'Save A Billion When We Can'?

August 9, 1940

NOTES

(1) "Buying friendship" is the term used by Beals, who writes "The new five hundred million dollar commodity purchase loan bonds bill, on the eve of the Havana conference, was a thinly disguised effort to buy off the Latin American delegates so they would goose step with the American political program."

(2) "The handing over of American tax moneys on a silver platter to governments in default, to dictators without scruples, without proper strings attached, has merely meant the creation of credits which, in certain instances (like the reciprocal agreements), benefitted Germany or England more than ourselves The transfer of such lending from private to governmental agencies now compounds many previous mistakes. We are likely to throw away the money of American taxpayers on countries, already in default on private loans, with no commensurate benefits to ourselves or the peoples of the countries concerned If private loan conditions were sound the government would not have to risk the taxpayer's money " (Beals, "Pan America")

(3) These loans, explains Beals, "are first of all political loans more subordinate to State Department power politics than to trade objectives" "Our new government loan policy is the same old game of dollar diplomacy, or keeping dictators in power against the wishes of the people."

(4) The State Department motive was, not trade, but repayment of private debts. As much as for trade purposes, loans have been made to help liquidate previous private loans, British and American, and to salvage American investments, or help secure domestic legislation favorable to American business. This too is dollar diplomacy dressed up in a new deal costume "Money lending is an old and indispensable device of orthodox diplomacy," said the Boston *Transcript*

(5) The *Congressional Record* of Feb 28, 1940, tabulates outstanding loans of South American countries and the amount in default in millions: Bolivia $60, Brazil $356; Chile $182, Costa Rica $8, Ecuador $12; El Salvador $12, Haiti $8; Mexico $273; Panama $17, Peru $85; Uruguay $56. Columbia has paid $3 on $146 millions outstanding, Guatemala $2 on $5, Argentina $213 on $233. "Our public opinion never sanctioned former interventions in Mexico and the Caribbean," wrote *PM*, July 22 "It always suspected that taxpayers' money and mariners' lives were being spent to protect the dividends of oil companies and insure the repayment of loans to New York banks."

(6) The minority report signed by one third of the committee asserted that "the new policy has a distinctly anti-German flavor" and said that "the policy of international surplus control is not only futile, but positively harmful to the pro-

ducers of South America and North America alike" (AP, Aug. 6). The appropriation was finally made.

The Inter-American Bank, which grew out of Welles' post-Panama Economic Advisory Committee, "was to be capitalized at $100 million and cooperatively owned, but the republics have been chary about putting up capital. So the Inter-American Bank, for the present, is dormant, and the Export-Import Bank remains the only institution geared to fill the gap. Altogether the Export-Import Bank has advanced about $207 million in Latin America. For Brazil the bank advanced $2,275,000 for purchase of Moore-McCormack ships" (doubtless at a good profit to the transferring company). The Export-Import Bank lent Chile $12 million for hydro-electric plants. (The General Electric lobby should have been helpful in this). "Perhaps the most tantalizing single commercial possibility in Latin America is the famous iron-ore deposits of Brazil, ranked qualitatively and quantitavely with the best in the world Jesse Jones of the RFC has let it be known that he is 'ready to go into this thing fifty-fifty with any experienced U. S. steel company'." (*Fortune,* September 1940, pp 152, 154)

HULL'S HAVANA 'TRIUMPH'

The 'Triumph' of the Hull[1] Havana Program filled Americans with pride that we were saving our "good neighbors"[2] from Nazi machinations. It was a "marked success" in "the moral if not material" sense. (AP, July 28) [3][4]

"At Havana these last few days orators have extolled the democratic way of life and the liberty-loving peoples of the Western Hemisphere. Dictator Vargas of Brazil, and President Baldomir of Uruguay, to mention only two American heads friendly to Herr Hitler and Signor Mussolini, must have laughed up their sleeves."[5] (*PM,* July 26)

The 'unanimity' announced was in the headlines. The Boston *Herald,* July 29, explained "Two of the four points agreed on at Havana are important only as declarations of opinion The other two points . . . will obviously require considerably more study and collaboration by the interested states." And the Boston *Transcript,* July 29, apologized, "The Act of Havana was so phrased" as to give "Argentina a means of appearing to support American unity while reserving the privilege of doing nothing at all".[6]

Of Argentina's reiterated demand for the Falklands,—of Guatemala's claims to British Honduras, both seized by the British since Monroe's time,—of the recent seizure by the French and British of the Dutch possessions, Aruba and Curacao,—on these the cables were silent.

The *Transcript* explained July 29 that Argentina "thinks Germany may win the war and she does not want to jeopardize her commercial future by any present hostile acts towards the Germans. Also, she mistrusts the United States on the basis of past performances."[7]

Further, Argentina was conscious that the loss of her profitable trade with Germany had been compensated for recently by an equal increase with Germany's immediate neighbors. (cf Paul Mallon, Aug. 2)[8]

The chief article of the agenda was to establish a cartel, to aid the British in their blockade of Europe (cf Bul #69) "Now, of course it is perfectly reasonable to argue that we should do this in order to cripple Germany and help England. But we ought not to pretend that we are doing it to help South America," writes John Flynn, *New Republic.*

"Prime tactical accomplishment of the Havana Conference is one that is never mentioned officially The agreement to seize and segregate as independent any American colony suffering a change in administration in its homeland, will open the way for this government to expand and to fortify the Monroe Doctrine by applying the new principle to Martinique. Don't think the administration will hesitate when the time is ripe." (Mallon, Aug. 2)[9]

Two days after the Conference Roosevelt was taking steps[10] which might lead to the seizure of Martinique by American forces should an emergency develop. Censorship shuts off all news.

August 9, 1940

NOTES

[1] "If a piece of paper would keep the Americas free, he [Hull] had the paper," jibed *Time,* Aug. 12, 1940.

[2] Carleton Beals quotes the Omega Nueva, "At last the Yankee military heel is planted on the soil of South America The 'good neighbor' policy has been so much smoothing syrup The eagle flies southward. South America now must unite or die. Nazism is a remote and passing menace Yankeeism is an immediate and permanent menace now and for all time."

[3] It fell "short of what Mr. Hull and his capable assistant, Mr Lawrence Duggan, in charge of the Division of American Republics, undertook to obtain at Havana The U. S wanted to set up at once a 'collective trusteeship', with itself a senior partner, over those foreign dependencies already adrift—notably Martinique, Aruba, Curacao, French Guiana, and Surinam This proposal Senor Leopoldo Melo, head of the Argentine mission, finally beat down." But the newspapers of September 6, 7, 8 reported that Melo declared Roosevelt a liar and Roosevelt returned the compliment.

Ten years ago, to keep foot-and-mouth disease out of this country, a clause in the Smoot-Hawley tariff imposed a total embargo on meats from Argentina Roosevelt "negotiated the Sanitary Convention, which would have rectified what the President himself described as an 'obvious inequity'. But the Senate has never ratified it." (p 150, *Fortune*, Sept. '40)

A cable, Sept. 6, 1940 (N. Y. *Times*) from Buenos Aires quoted Dr. Melo as saying in an address that when he visited at Hyde Park after the Havana Conference, Mr. Roosevelt repeated to him the assurances which he gave when he visited Buenos Aires in 1936. Putting aside the text of his speech, Melo said extemporaneously, "Mr. Roosevelt told me that the present hour is one of political and electoral struggle and, therefore, not propitious to push this issue, because there are some Western senators who are more inclined to listen to the aspirations of their voters than the indications of their President. I replied, 'Oh, well, between good friends there is no need to rush matters such as this. We can wait until after the elections.'" This "stirred up a political storm' in Washington, AP, Sept. 7. "The White House issued a denial. Rep. Horton said in a statement, that 'once again Mr. Roosevelt has to deny that he has made a secret agreement. . .' that Col Fulgencio Batista, President-elect of Cuba, told the Cuban Legislature recently that a treaty was in preparation with the United States to cut tariffs on Cuban sugar. 'That, too, was promptly denied by Mr. Roosevelt.'" Sen Thomas reminded that last March 28 he had predicted, if the Hull trade agreement program was endorsed, just such lowering of tariffs on "Practically every agricultural commodity we produce. I might well have added that we could expect this after the November election"

Another N. Y. *Times* cable, Buenos Aires, Sept. 7, says Melo "tonight denied" having quoted Roosevelt "as saying that after the November elections the Senate would ratify the sanitary convention", but merely "that the senators logically would listen to their voters, since the present hour was a political one and not propitious for considering this matter, for which a solution would be found later". (Melo's words) (*Fortune*, Sept. 1940, "Twenty Nations and One")

(4) With all the publicity on the bases acquired, nothing came out at the Havana Conference, almost nothing has been heard in regard to the Dutch possessions of the West Indies seized by the French and British simultaneously, and almost nothing has been permitted to appear about the French possession, Martinique, besieged by the British But it is apparent to anyone who thinks twice that all these years the access to the Panama Canal was directly controlled by Great Britain, threatened by France, or by any power that possessed the Dutch islands The necessity of America's obtaining the key points in the Caribbean, held by Great Britain, has been repeatedly emphasized, more particularly by W. Adolphe Roberts in "The Caribbean: The Story of Our Sea of Destiny" (Bobbs-Merrill, 1940). (cf p 461)

(5) "If we support such dictators we have no kick coming if at the first propitious moment they return to the roost of the Nazi coop, where they more logic-

ally belong, or if the people, on throwing them out, repudiate debts for money squandered by non-representative rulers". (Carleton Beals, "Pan America")

(6) C H. Haring, Professor of Latin-American History and Economics at Harvard, wrote in the *Chr Sci Monitor* a fortnight after the Conference, "The Latin American countries may even be skeptical of our ability to protect the entire hemisphere against European aggression. They have before them the fate of the smaller nations of Western Europe which were unable to depend upon the defense promises of England and France, however sincere these promises may have been. Meantime from Germany they receive alternatively threats of reprisal and promises of a lucrative post-war trade In no case can the United States hope to occupy the place of Europe in the Latin-American economy."

(7) "Once more the Latin-American press is beginning to bristle with accusations of Yankee imperialism," reported Beals. "One Argentina daily has shouted 'The wolf has sloughed off his sheepskin and is again about ready to pounce' Quiet word was passed to Washington by Argentina that too many good will battle ships were nosing about "

(8) "An official publication of the Argentine ministry of finance reports her trade with Hitler fell off from 56,000,000 pesos to 3000 in the comparative five months' period of last year and this. But deeper back in the official statement is an accounting of the increased business which Argentina did with four neutrals surrounding Germany at the same time Her exports to Italy jumped from 5,000,000 to 42,000,000 pesos, to Switzerland from 2,000,000 to 5,000,000, to Sweden from 11,000,000 to 14,000,000 and to Denmark from 7,000,000 to 9,000,000 " (Paul Mallon, August 2, 1940)

The blockade of Europe has destroyed South America's trade and brought economic distress which both Great Britain and the United States endeavor to alleviate. In December, 1940, the Administration let it be known that they were about to loan 100 millions to Argentina "Great Britain has lately advanced $80,000,000 to Argentina, $40,000,000 of it in cash, to get a little of the Argentine trade. But who pays it? Great Britain has no money. So, New York bankers advance the money to Great Britain And where do the New York bankers get the money? The United States government increases its debt It issues United States Bank Notes. They loan the money to Great Britain. Then we tax ourselves to pay the interest on our bonds and our money Yet we know we will never be paid." And by whatever devious methods, eventually Uncle Sam's children pay. (Brown Landone, "Voice of the World")

(9) When the proposal was made at the Havana Conference that the fate of the orphaned European possessions be determined by plebescite, the U. S was in "a particularly sensitive position due to the continued refusal to grant statehood to Puerto Rico and Hawaii" (*Chr Sci Mon.*, July 23, 1940). In an emergency the agreement provides that one nation may act alone. That leaves us free. "The United States, because of its military strength, will have the major role in determining when there is an aggression in the Hemisphere." (*PM*, July 30)

(10) Roosevelt was indeed taking steps toward an emergency. "The Navy has

begun organization of a trouble shooting expeditionary force composed of U S Marines for any hemisphere emergency, and four destroyers are now being fitted out for use in the rapid transportation of this Inter-American 'police' force. High speed transports and cargo-passenger ships acquired from private lines are ready for immediate action and the Fleet Marine Force remains prepared to leave its Quantico, Virginia, base on eight hours' notice." (*Week by Week*, Aug 10)

(11) "The program of a Western Hemisphere economic front need not postulate an exclusivist system. The other nations of the globe, regardless of the nature of their governments, should have free access to the Latin-American market." (Beals, "Pan America", p 514)

WILL THE DRAFT BE HONORED?

We are being drawn on for 12,000,000. The President says he was drawn on, but it is charged that he drew the draft himself. Are the voters so fooled that they will honor that draft in November? Allied with the British Tories, their financial agents, and those whom he formerly derided as "economic royalists", Roosevelt, with their combined control of newspapers and all the means of forming public opinion, presents conscription as democratic and popular.

"If the proponents of conscription feel that it is necessary to have the draft to save democracy . . . they ought to be willing to submit the question to the people," challenged Wheeler in the Senate, Aug. 10 (AP).[1] That was perhaps a joke. But it was greeted with alarm by the 'proponents'. Editorials, "No Referendum Wanted" (cf Boston *Herald*, Aug. 12) see "great practical difficulties in the way" and delay, too.[2] Such difficulties and delay can not be tolerated, when there are such 'technical' difficulties and necessary delay in the profits tax.

We might have had Ludlow's referendum on war had it not been for Roosevelt's valiant stand against it. He wisely remarked it would "cripple any President in the conduct of our foreign relations". To win votes Roosevelt has been obliged to declare, "I am a pacifist", "I hate war". John T. Flynn in his candid biography, "Country Squire in the White House" (Doubleday, 1940) quotes earlier deliberate statements showing that Roosevelt has long advocated conscription

When he was Assistant Secretary of the Navy in 1918 he declared,— "Our national defense must extend all over the Western hemisphere, must go a thousand miles out to sea, must embrace the Philippines and over the seas wherever our commerce may be." "We must create a navy not only to protect our shores and our possessions but our merchant ships no matter where they may go in time of war."—"The people of the United States should adopt definitively the principle of national government service by every man and woman at some time in their lives." After the war was over, in 1919, Roosevelt said, "I hope that there will still be some kind of training or universal military service." Now on the verge of achieving this lifelong ambition as the result of the hysteria he has stimulated, Roosevelt must be guiltily happy."

The popular rebellion against conscription is a contest between the common horse sense of our citizens and this drive of the President hiding behind the little group of British actuated bankers and their acolytes who so completely control public opinion.[3]

The press is seemingly unanimous for conscription. A double column editorial, "The Foes of Conscription", Boston *Herald,* Aug 6, claims 70% to 80% of all papers are for it. But the James S. Twohey Associates, publishers of a weekly *Analysis of Newspaper Opinion* in their August survey showed that only 52% of the national press approved

In an editorial Aug. 3, the Boston *Herald* proclaims that 90% of the people favor conscription. Letters to Congress opposing conscription it was intimated Aug. 6 were actuated by propaganda organizations But a *PM* letter writer tells how scared he found people, not daring to sign a petition against conscription.

Newspaper headlines have led people to believe that conscription was inevitable, and that the bill had already 'passed' (cf Bul #72). The leading part in this deception, played by Col. Julius Ochs Adler's N. Y. *Times,* is detailed in *Uncensored,* Aug. 3. Speeches, broadcasts favorable to conscription were featured, news of opposition relegated to inside pages. The Plattsburg training, since repudiated by the War Department, was promoted, with a picture of Col. Adler in uniform.[4]

The much advertised results of the *Fortune* and Gallup polls have shown progressively an increasing number favoring conscription.[5] "If the issue had been differently phrased, there might not have been such a heavy affirmative vote", as Frederick Lewis Allen remarks of another poll regarding our helping England and France ("Since Yesterday")

"We advertising men know of course beforehand what the reaction of the public will be. That's why we started the Gallup polls", remarked a leader in the advertising world, now in politics.

Late in July the Senate Committee was all set to report the bill. "Then the storm broke" (*PM*, Aug. 2). Thousands of citizens took up their pens and wrote Congressmen and newspapers. Protest meetings were held everywhere and groups organized to march on Washington.

Vandenberg "got 10,000 letters over the weekend opposing the bill. Senator Wheeler says he got 2000" (*PM*, July 30). The press endeavored to ignore this uprising. But the legislators paused, "waiting for further word from home" (*PM*, Aug. 2).

"To keep the bill alive the Senate Committee . . . allowed it to be whittled down . . . to draft only those of military age—between 21 and 31" (*Chr Sci Monitor*, Aug. 2), thus reducing the number from 42 million to 12 million. To make it still more deceptive the title of the bill omitted "reference to compulsory military training".

The Commander-in-Chief drafted Army and Navy officers to appear before the Committee to make headlines to deprecate voluntary enlistment and clamor for conscription. Some were thus obliged to reverse positions previously taken. The Chief of Staff, Gen. Marshall, had testified (unreported) July 12, "I think we secured 18,000 men in June Our quota . . . about 15,000 . . . we reached . . . ten days before. In other words, recruiting went ahead in good shape." (The rate of enlistment in July increased greatly, making conscription even less necessary, but the figures are not generally publicized.) [6] Asst. Chief of Staff, Brig.-Gen. Shedd, admitted, "We are getting them faster than we thought we would". Maj. Gen. Reckord, Adj. Gen Maryland National Guard, testified, "My thought is that the proponents of this bill have taken a much larger bite than was necessary at this time" (*Uncensored*).

"How any fair-minded member of Congress could say that we have given the voluntary system of enlistment for the U. S. Army a fair trial and that it has broken down, and therefore we need the compulsory service, is beyond my understanding", Woodring wrote Sen. Vandenberg, Aug. 3 (AP).

Wheeler commented, "Woodring, through his long experience as head of the War Department, should be in better position to know the facts than a lot of frightened bankers and Wall Street lawyers who are backing this draft bill". [7]

Stimson, who replaced Woodring, agitatedly told at the hearings of the "very great danger" of direct attack by Hitler and "the possibility that in another 30 days Great Britain herself may be conquered". Conscripting "the whole manpower of the United States from 18 to 64 will have a tremendous moral effect both inside and outside", he clamored.

"Wrong Horse Harry" was the sobriquet he had earned as Secretary of State Though England then snubbed him, he is still subservient and advocates sending part of our Navy over there and opening our navy yards and ports to the British fleet.[8] Discounting Stimson's hysteria, the Committee cut conscription from 12 million to 900,000, in line with the recommendations of Sen. Lodge and Rep. Fish for a limited highly trained army of 750,000.

The president, facing a vigorous and uncommitted opponent, and knowing that conscription was political dynamite, had avoided a public statement, but was now forced to come out with a mild endorsement of "selective training" as "essential to national defense" (N. Y. *Times*, Aug. 3). At this the Senate Committee again somersaulted and in the seventh draft of the bill returned to 12 million. And so the bill was reported Aug. 5, two weeks after the newspapers had led the public to believe it was all over.

Conscription, then, is Roosevelt's measure, his ambition. All the king's horses and all the king's men failed to put it across without him. Conscription and perhaps war may be necessary for his election

"Evidence continues to pile up . . . that President Roosevelt's defense program has more to do with his campaign for a Third Term than national defense President Roosevelt's strategy is to . . . set up before the election a war dictatorship. In this way he hopes to cinch his re-election " (*Weekly Foreign Letter*, Aug. 1)

His 1936 "fools' gold" of war profits is the bait with which he wins the support of the "economic royalists", in his attempt to break the third term tradition and make for himself 'a place in history'.

Willkie has cannily evaded the traps set to commit him on conscription. But he has maneuvered Roosevelt into declaring for it.[9] Willkie waits to see the whites of their eyes before firing So the intelligent "independent voter" waits on Willkie, hoping to know on August 17 what he stands and fights for. For all know,—"If you draft Roosevelt, he will draft you!"

August 12, 1940

NOTES

[1] President Hutchins of Chicago like MacCracken of Vassar and Valentine of Rochester has preserved something of his independence and sanity Most

universities are presided over by mad, whirling dervishes who, when they pray, prostrate themselves toward Wall Street In endorsing conscription he warned that, "It should be understood—that—all this military business is justifiable for national defense, not on the ground that it has any educational, moral or spiritual value The greatest discipline of all is to have to do a job on your own, go through with it and deliver The life of an army private is the opposite of that "

(2) "Volunteering is obviously the quickest method of providing men for the army," comment Tobin and Bidwell And Hugh Johnson commenting on Representative Fish's amendment providing that the conscription be delayed for 60 days in order to permit volunteer enrollments, acidly remarks that conscription machinery could not be set up to "provide even 100,000 men in less than 60 days," a prognostication which has been amply proved in the ensuing 60 days

(3) It was such a little group who instigated the change in our neutrality laws, started the Willkie campaign, promoted conscription, set up the two White Committees Working quietly and secretly at first, basing their action on high moral grounds, they have been marvelously successful because of their command of the means of communication and cooperation with the Administration.

(4) The Plattsburg Camps "were designed from the start to be (as their successors still are today) not as practical schools of war but seminaries whence propagandists for preparedness might be distributed throughout the population" (Walter Millis of the N Y *Herald Tribune,* as quoted in the Congressional *Record,* August 22, 1940).

(5) George Gallup and Saul Forbes Rae in "The Pulse of Democracy—The Public Opinion Poll and How It Works" (Simon and Schuster, N.Y., 1940) say, "The object of this book . . is to describe and defend" this instrument for "reporting public opinion". The Gallup Poll attempts "to provide a continuous chart of the 'opinions' of the man in the street" Public opinion "is not the product of an omniscient group mind, but rather a dynamic process resulting from the communication and interaction of individuals in an ever-moving society. Whether his ultimate goal is to encourage the clear and honest expression of public opinion, or merely to create an 'enlightened' majority, no ruler can stay in power without having some measure of the mind of the mass of the people."

Gallup from March, 1939, conducted "surveys on the question of sending arms, war supplies, or troops to the Allies The mood of the people, the precise strength of isolationist sentiment, on the one hand, and interventionist sentiment on the other, were charted. . . . The leaders of the country could know, in advance, what politics the people were likely to accept or reject, and how much 'selling' or coaxing was necessary to put any policy across. Barely twenty years after the armistice, a decisive majority of voters (70 per cent) were saying that American participation in the last war had been a mistake. The really significant news of 1938-39 was a marked shift in sentiment toward giving all aid 'short of war'."

Senator Lundeen told the Senate (Aug 12), "The Gallup Poll states that Minnesota is 57 per cent for the conscription bill and 43 per cent against it. That is one of the most fraudulent polls I have ever heard of. Our correspondence from Minnesota shows 50 to 1, some of it 100 to 1, against this proposal." Pro-conscription senators were noticeably more hesitant about proclaiming their convictions than were the antis.

The Gallup Poll reported "64% of Montana's voters favor conscription". Montana's Senator Wheeler, strongest opponent, was renominated 3 to 1 over his antagonist. A Gallup recount showed 62% favoring Burke-Wadsworth bill. Wheeler in a letter to *Time,* Sept. 2, declared the Gallup questions were "weighted". "I know Montanans . . . and I can assure you that Dr Gallup is . woefully wrong." *Time,* strong for conscription, made a weak reply. Wheeler was re-elected by an overwhelming margin In Idaho, the Gallup Poll showed 73% of its voters wanted peacetime conscription, in California 66%. But the opponents of conscription won the election by large majorities.

(6) June enlistment figures were 16,177; July, 23,234 according to Senator Burke (August enlistments were expected to pass 40,000—Yankee Network News Report, September 4). "Marshall acknowledged that a page containing a favorable report had been removed from the August issue of *Army Recruiting News*" in answer to a charge by Senator Wheeler, but denied that he or Stimson knew about it. "It is just incredible to me—the judgment that was displayed there," he added

(7) July 10, AP, Woodring in his first public address since leaving the Cabinet said "I am a strong advocate of keeping this country out of recurring European wars". "Harry Woodring is perhaps not a big man but is certainly an honorable, decent one possessed of a reasonable degree of horse sense", a prominent Kansas businessman wrote me in the summer of 1940

Sen Clark served notice that he would call upon the President to make public Woodring's letter of resignation, "to personal" to publish. In the House, Rep Carlson asked an inquiry into Woodring's "dismissal". Woodring's own pro-phesy of what would happen to him was quoted in the Topeka Capital (June 20). After his arrival to receive a degree from Washburn College three weeks before (June 1), he had said: "There is a comparatively small clique of international financiers who want the United States to declare war and get into the European mess with everything we have, including our man power. They don't like me because I'm against stripping our own defenses for the sake of trying to stop Hitler 3000 miles away   Eventually they'll force me to resign "

Demanding that the President resign, Sen. Nye urged that Woodring be called to testify before the committee who are protesting the appointment of Stimson to the War Department. Woodring's testimony, he believed, would show he had been ousted because he refused to transfer "national defense secret No. 1", a bomber sight, to Great Britain.

(8) "The day the United States of America selected the Honorable Henry L Stimson to be Secretary of War the Burke-Wadsworth peacetime conscription proposal became a menace to our liberties, Senator Johnson charged (August 27). The former Secretary of War . . . bitterly opposed peacetime conscription, and he

was, therefore, at the instigation of the Plattsburg crowd, removed and supplanted by a reactionary interventionist from Wall Street, who has been on record for 23 years as favoring conscription in the United States " (*Patriot*, November 1940)

(9) "Watch Wendell Willkie", advised lugubrious General Johnson, August 7. "If his progress continues toward the November victory now apparently in sight, we will be in it (the war) before the end of September." But the Willkie vision was a summer mirage. After a stumbling acceptance speech on August 19, Willkie was content to spend the following month passing out wise-cracks.

WAITING FOR WILLKIE

Weary of fireside platitudes, fed up on 'charm' after eight years of it, intelligent independent voters look to Willkie hopefully for a positive fighting program. It is "the independent vote" Willkie has declared, that will decide the election. Will Willkie win? The Gallup and *Fortune* polls say he is ahead. But in July, 1936, they told us Landon then had 276 electoral votes and would win. Roosevelt forged ahead because he had the best 'line'. [1]

Now both candidates are holding their fire. One pretends indifference, the other skilfully sidesteps. But Willkie forced Roosevelt to come out for conscription which he had avoided as political dynamite. The three-point program Willkie announced immediately after his nomination is practically the same as Roosevelt's: "Defense"—O K., but stop hysterical squandering—"Economic Rehabilitation"—O.K., but make it for all—"A United People"—O K., but not by suppression.

Willkie's working backers fall into two groups,—the older banker group, and the younger experts in publicity and advertising [2] If Willkie listens to the latter, he will seize the public imagination and win votes by vigorous attack on Roosevelt's vulnerable foreign policies and hysterical spending.

Let Willkie come out strong against Roosevelt's "Military Expedition to South America" and his "Naval Exhibition on Asiatic Coasts". Let Willkie show that he will act for himself, not merely for the financial group that made him president of Commonwealth and Southern. Let him lead, not be led. Let him show there is no ring in his nose [3]

Let him appeal to the American heart (purse strings) by coming out with some simple statement like, "I have been in the utility business There have been abuses. But I have lowered rates. If I am elected president, you will get more electricity and cheaper."

Let him come out strong for saving a few billion whenever possible. "What is a billion?" It's what Roosevelt bawls for every Monday. It's his paregoric,—expensive, but the only thing that keeps him quiet.

Let Willkie make it clear that prosperity can come only after the destruction of war has ceased. "Save a Billion When You Can."[4]

August 9, 1940

NOTES

[1] "Are public opinion polls in themselves propaganda instruments? Consciously or unconsciously, they may well be, for the selection and wording of the questions which they put to their sample cross sections fall into one or more of four categories· (1) Omission (2) Commission (3) Suggestion (4) Objectivism " "The directors of the three best known opinion polls, George Gallup of the American Institute of Public Opinion, Elmo Roper of *Fortune,* and Archibald Crossley of the Crossley Polls, were all schooled in commercial polling. Dr. Gallup still is research director of the Young and Rubican advertising agency with which he was associated before organizing his Institute in 1935 Mr Roper and Mr. Crossley have been associated with market research for many years " ("Polls, Propaganda, and Democracy", *Propaganda Analysis,* Nov. 11, 1940)

Opinions result from repetition of what has been heard and accepted,—slogans and abstractions. Hitler in "Mein Kämpf" knew this too "Our ordinary conception of public opinion depends only in very small measure on our personal experience or knowledge, but mainly on the other hand, on what we are told; and this is presented to us in the form of so-called 'enlightenment', persistent and emphatic "

Bryce in the eighties recognized, "The art of propaganda has been much studied in our time, and it has attained a development which enables its practitioners by skilfully and sedulously applying false or one-sided statements of fact to beguile and mislead those who have not the means or the time to ascertain the facts for themselves."

"The question whether the plain people really itch to save democracy all over again is not to be decided by Gallup polls, for, no matter how adroitly their questions on the subject are framed, they put reluctance at a disadvantage. When a poor boob is approached by a brisk stranger on the street, or at his house door, and asked whether he is willing to fight for his country, he is almost certain to answer yes, and when he is asked if he prefers Churchill to Hitler, he is certain to answer yes again, for he has heard about the FBI's heroic pursuit of fifth columnists, and he is well aware that anyone is a fifth columnist, by the official definition, who is not willing to serve in the English fifth column My guess is that the majority of plain Americans . . . are a great deal less eager to sacrifice their legs or lives for England than the editorial writers of the newspapers appear to think The issue, to such poor folk, is not one between embracing Hitler on the one hand and fighting for 'religion and morality' on the other, but simply one ·

between barging into a bloody quarrel and staying out   They are all ready enough to defend this great Republic if it is ever actually attacked, but they are very far from convinced that pulling England's chestnuts out of a very hot fire is the same thing as defending the Republic." (H. L Mencken, Oct. 20, 1940)

(2) In the Willkie camp, the younger men in closer touch with the people wanted Willkie to come out more strongly against participation in the war, but that was not what he was being financed for   He could not do it.   It was not Willkie but others who were responsible for reducing the number to be conscripted from 42 million to 12 million   Right there Willkie lost 30 million votes, as I pointed out early in July to a Willkie worker, explaining how already he had missed the bus on the conscription issue   Roosevelt had 216 electoral votes nailed down.   Willkie could not prevail with no popular issue and only millions in his campaign fund where Roosevelt had billions.   "Willkie was on cordial terms with few Republican leaders, as exemplified by the remark of Representative Clare Hoffman, another Michigan Republican   'When Willkie was nominated,' said Hoffman, 'I wired Ernie Weir and Tom Girdler: You nominated him, now you elect him.' " (Pearson & Allen)

(3) Many were fooled and disappointed by Willkie. Col. Robert McCormick of the Chicago *Tribune*, one of his ardent supporters, headed a post election editorial "The Barefoot Boy a Barefaced Fraud", in which he remarked of the "Republican Quisling", "Mr. Willkie may be unable and he may be unwilling to make explanation of his thoroly dishonorable conduct, but an explanation is due the country and if he will not make it, his co-supporters should be forced to make it."   "Who paid for the telegrams which swept in upon the Republican delegates and made them think that the rank and file of the Republican Party was arising en masse to demand the nomination of the New Deal Democrat?"   "Who organized the network of conspiracy which packed the galleries of the Convention hall and caused the delegates to take leave of their senses and go into a trance?"   "This fraud, which will become historic as the strangest party betrayal on record, requires investigation."

Philip F. LaFollette in a radio address referred to the " 'fixed fight' of the past campaign where the President and Wendell Willkie vied with one another in professing their love of peace, only to team up on the road to war once the ballots were counted"

(4) Millions voted for Willkie in order to vote against Roosevelt.   Millions more would have done so had he had a policy of his own, shown that he was not a mere hired man.   Hundreds since the election have expressed in print their disgust with themselves that they voted for him, that they were fooled.   Both he and Mr Roosevelt are doing what the pro-British of lower New York and the British Foreign Office would have wanted them to do.   It has led one editor to write, "You can even hear it said in the Indiana grocery stores and filling stations that 'Willkie practically put Roosevelt in office'   'What's the use of having two rival political parties if the titular head of one not only fraternizes with the titular head of the other but actually aids him in carrying out his policies?' "

Well, it helps in the game, "Heads I win, tales you lose".   The great families and their industrial interests by subscribing to the campaign funds of two parties have long played this game successfully.   But there is always the game of striving for personal power   It was rumored that Roosevelt might make Willkie chief administrator of the 'lease lend' program but with billions to spend that might enable Willkie to outsmart Roosevelt who is too smart to be outsmarted.

"Charging that the ex-candidate (a J P. Morgan man, incidentally) had completely deserted his pre-election position in making the trip to England, Senator Capper of Kansas apologized to the voters of Kansas for his support of Wendell Willkie last fall, declaring that Willkie is giving his supporters of last fall a 'pretty raw deal'."

UNITY THROUGH CONSCRIPTION

National Unity may result from conscription but it may prove to be not the kind Roosevelt has been howling for, not the 'unity' by suppression hoped for by the group of 'down-towner' pro-Britishers who surreptitiously conspired to put conscription across for what there was in it.[1] It seems incongruous that these bitter Roosevelt haters should be working to achieve the totalitarian control toward which Roosevelt is moving so rapidly. Auto-intoxicated with the hate they have generated against both Roosevelt and Hitler, they are no less dangerous because they are intensely sincere.

Once we become conscious of this confused situation, there may result an intelligent uprising that will unite the nation against those responsible. Already formerly discordant elements, warring labor factions, opposed religious sects, have united in opposition.

For the first time A.F.L. Green and C.I O. Lewis have come to agreement to oppose conscription   The railroad brotherhoods are with them   Here is a solid bloc of 8 million votes in opposition. (*PM*, Aug. 11) Catholics, numbering over 20 million, and 8 million Methodists are united against conscription.   Add those represented by the Federal Council of Churches, the Farmers' Unions, and you have 40 million united in opposition to the draft.

The Press has deceived the public as to its own unanimity (only 52%, Aug. 1-Twohey), and, in its headlines, the inevitability of conscription. Editorials have promoted the idea that the draft is 'fair' and 'democratic',—an easy view for those who can influence draft boards.

Gallup and *Fortune* polls report results their backers desire.   The questions could be so shaped. Army and Navy officers have been whipped into testifying contrary to formerly expressed views. (cf Buls #77)

The French, after generations of conscription, had 6 million long trained conscripts under arms. A few hundred thousand skilled, trained mechanics and aviators turned these brave men, badly directed, without faith in their leaders, into a fleeing, despondent mob.

Our present aims,—conscription before trained specialists, mobs before mechanization, profits before defense, win the election at any cost, increase hysteria, suppress the same and the thinking,—may lead us to the desperate conclusion the French have come to: "The French army was perfectly prepared in 1914 for the war of 1870. The French army in 1939 was perfectly prepared for the war of 1914."

In England, Churchill is beginning to conscript industry (Whaley-Eaton, Aug. 6). And labor is demanding that wealth, too, be conscripted by capital tax as has been done in Germany and Italy.[2]

Only an intelligent elite may quiet the spreading hysterical hate, the growing totalitarian ambitions of our President, the short-sighted greed of our industrialists Only returning sanity of our citizens can save those now in the saddle from the fate of the former rulers of France. Unity through suppression and compulsion promises later dissolution.
August 19, 1940

NOTES

[1] In line with the prophets of unity through conscription, the Boston *Herald*, Oct. 16, 1940, the day of registration, editorializes: "All over the country today there will be manifest a pronounced spirit of unity and devotion to the national welfare — and that is something in a nation of 130 million people of diverse origin. What a triumph of deliberate democratic procedure it will be. The far-sighted Grenville Clark of New York who wrote conscription law, and his associates have been advocating such a system for years. They argued that compulsory service in the army or navy for a limited period would unify the people, level class barriers and give the nation additional vigor and character." Endorsing compulsory military service and declaring it of benefit to youth, General Pershing wrote the Senate Military Affairs Committee, "Such a measure in my opinion would promote democracy by bringing into intimate contact and on an equal footing young men in all walks of life." (Washington Correspondent, *Chr Sci Mon.* July 3, 1940)

[2] "You can't ask democracy to fight for 1932 or 1937 or 1938," write the editors of *New Statesmen & Nation* as quoted by *Time*, Dec. 2, 1940 "You can't point to three million unemployed, to . . holocausts and to dismantled ship yards

and call that the democratic way of life. Their function should be to use this situation in which employers themselves realize the need of far-reaching change for the benefit of the common man They have in this war a unique opportunity Where do our leaders stand?"

British Minister of Labor Ernest Bevin stated where he stood in a speech before the London Rotary Club:— "After the last war there was a failure to recognize that it was largely, as indeed this one is, a great civil war which must determine whether we are to be ruled from the top or must have government responsible to the people I want to give you the new motive for industry and for life I suggest that at the end of this war, and indeed during the war, we accept social security as the main motive of all our national life" (*Time*, Dec. 2, 1940).

THE TIDE TURNS AGAINST CONSCRIPTION

Two strong men stand face to face, fearful lest any word or act may alienate votes so much needed in the approaching election. Willkie's acceptance matched Roosevelt's weaseling, both endorsing conscription, in principle, but tossing back this political dynamite into the lap of the Senate, which had waited first on one, then the other.

From Willkie to Washington, even after his acceptance speech had gone to press, pressure "sped by wire, phone and messenger . . . to save the draft bill". Urging the opposite course, 30 Republican Congressmen telegraphed, and Willkie's friends, Barton and Halleck, were "importuned privately". (Paul Mallon, Aug. 16)

The popular protest that broke early in the month increased the second week of August to hurricane violence in the Senate, and gathered intensity before the House Committee. About to report the bill Aug. 9, they were forced to prolong the hearing to call additional witnesses

On the 14th, Senators were reported "about evenly divided for and against. Ten senators today held the balance of power" (Boston *Transcript*). "Whether or not the draft is voted, there seemed slight doubt about the summoning of the National Guard for a year of training", remarked the *Transcript*, which had been strong for conscription.

On the 15th, when the Senate recessed, *PM* announced four Senators, Norris, LaFollette, Lundeen, Shipstead, would determine the issue And Kluckhohn (N. Y. *Times*) forecast that they would accept the Maloney amendment postponing conscription till January 1,—after election. August 17 (UP) members of the Senate claimed an 8-vote margin in their drive to modify the Burke-Wadsworth bill.

Again the democratic process of protest against pressure had worked to defeat the Administration, for the fifth or sixth time.

It was in May that the campaign for conscription was launched-by Clark and Adler. By late July the newspapers had through deception and misrepresentation convinced many that it was all over (cf Bul #72) Few had the boldness to speak up But so potent were those sane voices heard above the mob roar that in a week the draft was defeated. The bill, rewritten, called for only 900,000.

That forced Roosevelt into the open, and all conscription's reserves were called up.[1] Pressure brought even the *Transcript* and *PM* over to the attitude of hysterical hate on which the campaign is based.

The drafted war horses were again trotted before the Committees to trumpet hysterical warnings,—Knox to explain, "We'll be left without a friend in the world"[2] and why he had flopped on his attitude of some weeks before that an army of 300,000 would be sufficient (AP, Aug. 14),—Stimson to prophesy Great Britain may fall in "another 30 days", implying Hitler's invasion was imminent (cf Bul #77). General Johnson, Aug. 14, emboldened, declared both the Rooseveltian and Willkian forces were playing "politics with this war".

But wars are politics carried further. Wars result when diplomats are at the end of their resources. The French called this war "diplomacy under arms", reminiscent of Clausewitz' classic "War is politics continued by other (i.e forcible) means". (Grattan, *Harper's*, Feb 1940) Hate must be created by propaganda before explosives can be used on a large scale. The purpose in politics, diplomacy, or war is the same,—through force, threat of force, or bluff, to seize control.

Conscription, seizing command of manpower, is an important step in gaining control. If the people are sufficiently scared and filled with hate, they more readily yield their liberties to those whom they are led to believe may save them Senator Wheeler in his three-hour speech to the Senate, August 13, made this apparent.

Roosevelt as President, with extraordinary emergency powers granted in more than a hundred legislative acts, with billions to spend, hundreds of millions at his whim, has on his payroll over one million civil servants. Other millions on relief receive largess through him.

As Commander-in-Chief he has today more than 700,000 armed men, soon to be 900,000 under laws already passed. He wishes to conscript

42 million men additional. Just the threat, the fear of it, will give him control of votes. If he gets 12 million conscripted, 2 million of them under arms, on his payroll, his control of votes may continue his power.[3] "Laws of 29 States deny to all men in the armed service the right to vote" (Boston *Transcript,* Aug. 20).

A permanent standing army preliminary to a totalitarian dictatorship is the purpose of the promoters, John T. Flynn charged over the radio, Aug. 16, adding, "I have just come from a terrorizing movie calculated to prepare me for this". Newspapers and radio were doing the same.

Senator Wheeler, following, declared that we are on the road to war, that Stimson as early as 1916 had advocated conscription, that in 1920 a bill had been introduced into Congress providing for it. He charged that the Army, ignoring the law which provides for one year enlistments, refuses to accept recruits for less than three years.

The annual cost of the conscript army will be from one to two billions, not provided for in the 18 billions appropriated for defense. The annual individual cost of an enlisted soldier is about the same as for a boy in one of the better private schools, about $1200. The maintenance of 25 recruits for one year may result in killing one enemy. The cost of killing in the last war was about $25,000 per head. So we may be bankrupted before the Germans are exterminated.[4]

If conscription is the 'democratic' way, then, Senator Wheeler emphasized, Russia and Germany have been the great exemplars of democracy. So Roosevelt follows in the footsteps of Hitler in inspecting his armed forces, talking of 'my government', by which he means himself.

The 'selective draft' may work with a democracy against an inferior enemy. But it is not compulsory universal service, necessary for a total war against a totalitarian enemy For total war, manpower, industry, and capital must all be drafted . England has learned this, and is following Germany's example. France did not. We Americans are contemplating total war against all the totalitarian countries of Eurasia by methods less adequate than France used against Germany alone

To maintain morale of the total forces of a total war, industry and capital must be conscripted. The selective draft will prove 'unfair'. Writes Lawrence Dennis, Aug. 15 (*Weekly Foreign Letter*): "If F.D.R. gets selective compulsion, the New Deal politicians will be able to wangle the selection so as to coerce voters and suppress his oppon-

ents and critics. Selective drafting for compulsory military service is a
process for practical politicians to conjure with. If the British go under
before election, it will improve Willkie's chances of election and pre-
cipitate a bad market break and business slump. The only plan at
Washington is still that of Mr. Roosevelt's third term campaign."

Conscription of all youth under wise direction would have value. The
National Educational Policies Commission in its latest release assures
us that our democracy has "failed to present" to youth "a great and en-
nobling goal. The apparent enthusiasm and loyalty of youth in totalitarian states are not simply the products of regimentation and propaganda. Their deeper source is found in the fact that these systems have
given youth work to do." (*Time,* Aug. 19)

This is true of the CCC, which Roosevelt adopted and adapted from
Germany, where the system was inaugurated in the '20's by Rosenstock-
Huessy, now professor at Dartmouth. And now that the pay has been
equalized, army volunteers from the CCC will increase, especially if
the term of enlistment is shortened. (cf David Lawrence, Aug 14)

If we are to make soldiers for defense, "the time to train them is while
they are really young and impressionable,[5] and can be converted into
soldiers without breaking their backs, punishing their wives and children, dissipating their savings, and wrecking their work in the world",
remarks The Sage of Baltimore, Aug. 11.

Senator Gillette, however, sees no emergency and lacks confidence
that the training will be valuable until they can be equipped. He says,
"This idea of letting the boys sit around for a year playing stud poker
and blackjack is poppycock" (*Time,* Aug. 12). He has evidently been
around army posts and seen the kind of joints that gather about. He
doesn't want boys taken from their homes to learn about life,—of a
kind that isn't nice to put in print. Perhaps he has heard Legionnaires
sing obscene versions of "Hinkey, dinkey, parley voo". Maxwell Stewart, one who has been through it, in "Conscripting America" (*Nation,*
Aug. 3) tells of how "the average soldier idles" at cards and dice, "in
bars or brothels", largely because "he can literally find nothing else to
do". Good books, magazines, are rarely provided.

About equipment, the Army hopes by Jan. 1 to have its present forces
fully equipped for war as of 1914. Our First Army of 90,000, now
maneuvering in northern New York, is using gas pipes for guns, trucks,

so labeled, for "tanks" (AP, Aug. 15). In two years we may have modern equipment (not all yet 'on order'), for the 900,000 at present authorized. And by October, 1943, Knudson tells us, we could have equipment for two million conscripts (AP, Aug 15).

Enlistments meantime, though limited to three years and stringent in rejections, are higher than ever before and far above the Army quota. The Navy has a waiting list of 7000. (cf *Uncensored*, July 27).

This conscription is not for defense That's an absurd pretense. It is for totalitarian dictatorship, to unify the nation, regiment the people, suppress dissident thought, restrain labor, and of course to encourage industry with newer and better plants and increased profits.[6] Hysteria based on 'false fears unscrupulously promoted by the President', as Willkie charged, is the flood on which they hope to put it across

That the President is looking for an "incident" to put us into the war and will find it if Willkie's chances grow, has been charged [7] Sending the "American Legion", after warning, through the mine-infested Scottish Isles seems to justify this charge commonly made. To prepare for this he authorizes Bullitt's recent alarmist Philadelphia speech, which was promptly denounced as "treason" on the floor of the Senate.

Within Roosevelt's grasp is even greater power than he now holds, greater than was ever held by any human on this earth. It can only be achieved through the cultivation of hysteria and hate, and conscription And this has been his ambition since 1918 (cf Bul #77)

When later our now muzzled cloistered scholars analyze the forces that have brought about this conscription, they may find that through Washington and New York they have emanated from the British Raj, fighting for life and fortune. Such analysis may reveal back of these personal agents, historic trends and world wide tendencies toward collective economy.

The old men of the tribe, symbolized by Lamont and Stimson, behind the more obvious spearhead of such as Clark and Adler, influence the press, radio, and other mediums of communication, in the hope of continuing a 'way of life' that has proved profitable to their cronies.

In the President a long latent underlying predilection in favor of a standing army, and a passion for dictatorial control,[8] has been given impetus by the appearance of a powerful opponent in the coming elec-

tion. Conscription is a factor in the struggle for votes, power, profits.[9]
August 20, 1940

NOTES

(1) Senatorial opponents of the draft had hardly opened their mouths when the press and administration-inspired commentators started to berate them for delaying action On the third day of debate Sen. Taft protested against the savage pressure for haste. Next evening Gen. Marshall, Army chief-of-staff, on a national radio hook-up said, "Further delays might seriously jeopardize the effectiveness of preparations to provide the nation with adequate military defense". (*PM*, Aug. 5)

(2) That there is nothing new in our friendless condition is explained by Samuel Crowther ("America Self-Contained", Doubleday, Doran), "We in the United States have today no friends among the nations of the earth . . . this, and only this, have we accomplished by dint of nearly two decades of insistent meddling into the affairs of other nations". And Demaree Bess, the European correspondent for the *Sat Eve Post*, writes from the Bristol Hotel, Paris, July 25, 1940, "As seen from this angle, American foreign policy looks more screwy than ever. We seem to be determined to make enemies of every strong or potentially strong country in the world. If, after doing that, we go to war with them all, the sorry picture will be complete. Whatever happens, we have succeeded in making every other country hates us, with excellent reason. If that is what our so-called statesmen were aiming at, they have been past masters in getting what they wanted."

(3) Section 8H of the Burke-Wadsworth Bill provided that, "Any person inducted into the land or naval forces for training and service . . . be permitted to vote in any election occurring in the State of which he is resident, if under the laws of such State he is entitled to vote in such election " But anyone familiar with the red tape of applying for and delivering an absentee ballot — plus the need for signing it — will be dubious of the effectiveness of this provision.

(4) Col Robert R McCormick broadcasts (Oct 6, 1940) that in only a short 400 day war against Germany alone "we would be sure of a cost of 400 billion dollars, and several million ruined lives"

(5) "The Draft ought to be made as popular as possible, and it ought to be aimed at raising contingents of born brutes and young brutes. For our total war forces, we've got to have men who are strong, smart, young and brutal." (N. Y. *Daily News*, Washington *Times Herald*, Sept. 12)

The value of conscription for democracy and for individual discipline is accented Major General John F. O'Ryan, an advocate, has said, "The first thing that must be done is to destroy all initiative, and that with the training fits men to be soldiers. We have to have our men trained so that the influence of fear is overpowered by the peril of an uncompromising military system often backed up by a pistol in the hands of an officer. The recruits have got to put their heads into the military noose. They have got to be jacked up. They have got to be bawled out."

(6) "Senator Ashurst recalled that the World War had made 23,000 millionaires and Senator Walsh declared industrialists had told him they would not manufacture for the government at 8 or 10 per cent profit because they were getting
18 per cent or more on foreign contracts. All this embarrassed many senators,
who left their seats" (*PM*, Aug 22). "A high ranking naval officer complained
that the navy was having difficulty in obtaining materials that went into fighting
ships" (AP, Aug. 20). Admiral W R Furlong, chief of the naval bureau of
ordnance explained to the Senate Appropriations Committee that "the difficulty
was due to tax requirements and limitations on profits, together with the fact
that American manufacturers could do business more profitably with the British".

(7) General Johnson, recalling how in 1917 he had written a memo suggesting
a draft of 1,000,000 men says it came back "ink-spattered by an angry pen-point
that had punctured the paper and spurted indignation. It was initialed 'W.W.'
and said in effect that the American people would never stand for a draft of a
million men, that our contribution was to be largely in money and supplies, that
it was absurd to think of an offensive in any such terms!'"

(8) Whether consciously or unconsciously, Roosevelt follows with machine-like
precision the road to dictatorship. For "there is only one certain, fool-proof way
of setting up a Fascist dictatorship, and that is by proceeding under the pretext of
'saving' something or other. 'Saving' the country from the Reds appears to be
the most popular with American Fascists, but 'saving' the 'old pioneer spirit' or
democracy, or 'Christian' civilization are also popular," remarks Lt Commander
Charles S. Seely, U.S.N , Ret (*American Guardian*)

(9) Bulletin #84 was an emergency release after the conscription bill had
passed the Senate and before the final action by the House. It included a letter
which had been sent "to all Liberal Members of the House of Representatives".

'AMORTIZATION AMELIORATION'

This delectable phrase conceals the "invisible but unshakable" purpose of Mr. Roosevelt to ameliorate his relations with those he formerly
scorned as "economic royalists", while fooling the voters that the war
profiteers are being taxed.(1)

Congressional leaders "were eager to inspire speed in the national defense program by granting reasonable depreciation allowances at once"
(Paul Mallon, Aug. 6) Responsive to 'Industry' and its lobbyists, they
were willing to deceive the taxpayers with the idea that there were enormous "technical difficulties" to be surmounted in planning taxation on
excess war profits.(2)

The finance capitalists who control these war industries wanted amortization, what the government had to give, promptly. They were more
than willing to postpone the tax on war profits, what they had to pay (3)

The battle was won by the President, but 'Industry' got the spoils. The plunder promises to make the billions of war profits of twenty years ago look picayune. And "no aspect of the war effort of 1917-18 has brought more shame . . . than the egregious profits". With the "cost-plus-percentage contracts . . . profits rose in proportion to every extravagance". (Frederick Lewis Allen, *Harper's,* September, 1940)

What is amortization? "It is bluntly, the policy of building new factories at the public expense, and giving them to industry as a present from the people. The public builds the plant, and the public then pays for it gradually in the added cost of defense supplies. The industry owns it in the end."[4] This is the result of "dickering, secret so far as the public is concerned" (E. J. Hopkins, *PM*, Aug. 9), which makes possible unusual generosity toward the favored.

Curtiss-Wright, to enlarge its plant, receives a loan of $92 million at 4%. "Offered as a non-recourse loan . . . the government would have no claim against the Wright company if it failed to repay the loan. All the government could do in that case would be to take the factory Since the plant would be financed entirely by the government, the government would really be taking back its own property if the Wright company for some reason wanted to drop it.

"The *Wall Street Journal* reported on August 2 that while the loan was for $92,000,000, 'the cost of the proposed plant and its equipment is understood to be only $37,000,000 or $38,000,000'. When asked by the Journal correspondent about 'this apparent discrepancy', Jesse Jones said, 'We don't believe it would be in the public interest to break down that total at this time'.

"As this is being written, the Wright contract has yet to be signed. The company is now asking for five-year amortization instead of eight. Incidentally, a vice-president of this finicky company, T. P. Wright, was assigned to the Defense Commission on June 8 to help speed up production" (I. F. Stone, *Nation*, Aug. 17). This is the commission that determines the loans and their terms.

"For an $18,000,000 plant to command a $92,000,000 credit from any bank, including a federal one, may make financiers blink, but that is what has been arranged". The Curtiss-Wright loan is only a little over five times the value of the plant. But Boeing Aircraft, with a plant worth $3,000,000 has been awarded a loan of $32,000,000, more than ten times. And Boeing will own it in five years. (*PM*, Aug. 9)

Other aviation companies, of course, could not be permitted to be jealous or sulky. Moreover the companies that supply materials like steel, for aviation, must be kept happy.

Grace of Bethlehem demanded that the government put up the money or permit "sufficient profits to compensate them for creating these facilities" (*PM*, July 28). He "had no right to invest stockholders' money to fill government contracts for arms" (*PM*, Aug. 2).

Olds of U. S. Steel, which under Baruch's price fixing for the government in 1916 earned $48 per share, in 1917 $39 (Allen, *Harper's*, Sept., 1940), announced that his company would not manufacture "armor plate until Congress passed a law permitting amortization of construction costs in five years, with exemption from profits taxes " (*PM*) [5]

Knudsen, who is protecting the Government's interests today, finds himself in the embarrassing position of bargaining with the duPonts, who control General Motors, which employs him. Simultaneously he has to bargain with General Motors for a loan of $25,000,000 and with duPont "for $20,000,000 of new powder plants which the public will pay for and duPont will operate .. . without risking a cent". (*PM*)

DuPont common stock from 1915 to 1918 paid dividends of 458% (Allen, *Harper's*, Sept., 1940). Pierre duPont at that time wrote, "We cannot assent to allowing our own patriotism to interfere with our duties as trustees for the stockholders".

How did these great corporations extract such enormous gifts and profits from the New Deal? "They went on strike " The Packard Co., which was offered the contract for planes that Ford had turned down when he learned that 60% of them were going to England, "demanded $30,000,000 for a new plant, and guaranteed profits" (*PM*, Aug 9)

The strike was effective Stimson complainingly revealed before a Senate Committee that while 400 millions had been appropriated in June for 4000 airplanes, contracts for only 33 had been signed by Aug. 9. To speed the program, he urged quicker amortization and larger profits. [6]

All this "buck-passing" [7] on the part of Government officials as to why the delay in getting defense under way "is the sort of thing that has put half a French Cabinet on trial at Riom", editorialized the Boston *Transcript*, Aug. 12. And David Lawrence asked, "Are the American people getting the truth about their defense program or are they being misled and lulled into false security as were the people of France ?" [8]

In England the steel industry had created a scandal so that the London *Economist* demanded an investigation. "Sir William Firth . . . managing director of the $100,000,000 Richard Thomas Steel Company . . . charged that the company had obtained a contract to supply steel shells at a price yielding the company the fantastic profit of $45 a ton." *Nation,* Aug 17, editorial "Profits Above Patriotism" remarks, "The empire may founder, but British big business holds its profit margin" [9]

In America 'Industry' demanded the repeal of the Vinson Act limiting profits to 8% on aircraft and naval vessels, though affording assistance in enlarging plants. This Act had been passed in June when it was found that the maximum limitation of 10% had been interpreted as the minimum [10]

To meet this demand, "the White House released a plan . . . that would . . . abolish the existing profit limitation and . . allow for the amortization over five years of plant expansion". (*PM,* July 11)

The financial group in New York who control 'Industry', and who have spent money in promoting this war, claim that they "are not free agents. They are trustees responsible to the stockholders for the proper management of the business. This responsibility is moral, legal and unequivocal. it is to make profits for their stockholders. It would be morally, legally and unequivocally wrong" to sign any contracts "except for profit and without risk", wrote Ralph Ingersoll in *PM,* Aug. 12.

"How persuasive these arguments have been, even to our vindictive and foggy-minded President, is witnessed by the fact that when the showdown came last week it was the President and his renegade royalist advisors, not the industrialists, who gave way. They arranged to insure the industrialists both profits and freedom from risk.

"The trustees of the stockholders of the corporation of America, who have been asked to cooperate in arming this country against invasion by a foreign power, are showing themselves selfish and greedy", "under indictment by the public for not cooperating with the government in its armament program". "It's about time the people of the United States got on to it and got mad about it." [11]   Workers on naval craft in Southern shipyards, striking for an advance of 10 cents an hour, had been denounced by Congressmen as traitors   Army conscripts, who are not guaranteed against loss of life, limb, or normal profits, if they attempted a sit-down strike, would be courtmartialled and perhaps shot.

The President, however, surrendered completely to this hold-up of the sit-down strikers who control 'Industry',— the men whom he had

denounced as "economic royalists". As E. J. Hopkins wrote in *PM*,
Aug 18:

"The National Defense Advisory Commission has at last apparently
persuaded the 'striking' industries to go ahead", by permitting them to
do as they please,— that is, to strike later if, insured against loss, they
are not satisfied with their profits. Moreover, those who control industry hold a club over future legislation, for 'Industry' has "permission to
quit work midway if it doesn't like what Congress does".

· "Infinitely 'More Liberal' Excess Profits Tax Than During World
War Now Assuming Shape" was the headline of an article by Henry
Ehrlich in the Boston *Herald*, July 30.

"Sugar coating to get the people to swallow amortization", Senator
Bennett C. Clark, Aug. 10, called the proposed bill for tax on war profits,
— whittled down to yield a paltry 190 millions the first year,— only
about twice the amount of the single loan to the Curtiss-Wright Co.

Rear Admiral W. R. Furlong, chief of the Navy's Bureau of Ordnance, testified Aug. 20 (AP), " 'Progress has stopped on the procurement of materials that go into ships'. . . because industry has found business with the British more profitable". The condition had not much
improved on August 21 when Pearson and Allen wrote, "A sit-down
strike far worse than anything pulled by the C.I.O in the automobile
plants of Michigan is now being staged by some American industrial
leaders. It is a sit-down strike against the production of war and navy
orders until industry sees what kind of a tax bill will be written by
Congress."

"Billions for Defense — But Not 1% Less for Profit."
August 23, 1940

NOTES

(1) "Accelerated depreciation" was the term preferred by John D. Biggers,
president of Libby-Owens-Ford Glass Corporation, and now a dollar a year man
on Knudsen's Defense Advisory Commission, who has proved a skillful and aggressive defender of rights of manufacturers to make profits and avoid taxation

(2) In the long battle over "technical difficulties", all through the hot summer,
"while the committee continued its liberalizing and simplifying in redrafting the
bill, treasury officials renewed their demand" that at the end of the five years, the
government still have some say as to what was to be done with the plants they
had presented. But Biggers told them that this "would frighten private capital"
and 'impede the whole rearmament effort" (N. Y. *Times*, Sept. 8, 1940) Biggers was able to marshall any number of assistants, secretaries, Senators, lobbyists

and lawyers to assure the committee how much they would be frightened and how much defense impeded. In spite of the valiant fight of John L. Sullivan, Assistant Secretary of the Treasury, Biggers won and all "strings" were "removed" (Boston *Transcript*, Sept. 20, 1940)

The government wished to preserve the privilege of acquiring the property, which it had paid for at the end of the five year period, at the original cost less tax deductions. But "Biggers explained that the sole purpose" of giving the plants to the companies "was to induce private capital to go into the manufacture of defense commodities". (N.Y. *Times*, Sept 5, 1940)

(3) "In the interest of speed . . . industry has urged that the amortization proposal be separated from the excess profits tax measure. The administration . . . has consistently opposed this separation for reasons which seem obscure" to "The Investor" (Boston *Herald* financial columnist, Aug. 3). "The President suggested adding to the bill provisions lifting the profits limitation and easing the amortization of new plant costs." The excess-profits tax represents "a roundabout method of preventing profiteering . . . to let the manufacturers make any profits they can get away with and then try to get it back in taxes" (*PM*, Aug 4). "Business men won't sign contracts calling for plant expansion until this bill is passed. In the words of Phil Murray of the CIO, they are waiting for the gravy boat" (T R B , *New Republic*, Sept. 2). Oct. 25 (AP) "Officials said that the treasury had given the broadest possible interpretation to the law, and that once a company had qualified expansion for the amortization provisions it could not lose the advantage of such accelerated depreciation "

(4) The banks are bursting with cash. National City alone has deposits of $2,740 millions, nearly half of it in cash. John T Flynn tells us in the *New Republic*, Oct. 14, 1940, "The risks involved in these investments are such that in all likelihood no one but the government will undertake to finance them."

(5) "Here we have the spectacle of industry refusing to go ahead on an 8 per cent profit", commented Sen Wheeler (Aug 4). "If a soldier should take the same attitude — he would be court-martialed", declared Sen Joseph Lee (Aug. 17).

(6) "It turned out — Secretary Stimson told the country so — that having successfully arranged to make their profits without risk, they are still refusing to play ball until they know what taxes their profits are to be subject to" (Ingersoll, *P.M.*, Aug 12). Stimson's attitude reflected that of the National City Bank, which in its July Bulletin urged private financing of plant expansion for defense on the ground that "this will mean less burden on the Government, less deficit, less government bonds to be sold—and will tend to preserve and strengthen the system of private enterprise, which our defense is meant to protect".

Pearson and Allen, middle of September, reported, "News of recent contracts was released only to offset the impression that the work was not getting ahead. Secretary of War Stimson had stated on Aug. 9 that contracts had been let for only 33 planes of the 4000 authorized in June. Just a month later, Sept. 10, the War Department released figures that . . . the number of planes contracted for was 2797. These figures were put out to reassure the public   But from now on . . . the War Department is following the lead of General Marshall, who says: 'You can't play poker with everybody looking at your hand'."

"Agreement by all major plane manufacturers to go ahead on the defense production program without waiting for Congressional action on amortization of plant breaks up a blockade so tight that in seven weeks contracts had been let for only 33 airplanes" (Washington dispatch in *Business Week*, Aug. 17, 1940) And even this agreement "is understood to cover only that part of the program which can be undertaken without new plant expansion.   Admiral W. R. Furlong told committee that U. S. Steel Corp., after completing plans for $4 million plant expansion for armor plates, had refused to go ahead until 'it had received concrete guarantees concerning depreciation rates'." (*Wall Street Journal*, Aug. 21)

"Even *United States News*, business spokesman, admitted (Aug. 23) that 'at some key points in some industries where plant expansion is required, the companies involved refused to turn a hand until they could see their profit without any element of risk involved.'" (*Economic Notes*, Sept, 1940) - -

(7) Sen Nye, speaking on the New England Town Meeting, Aug. 14, "said the defense program was being delayed because of the uncertainty of its need; doubt of the causes that allegedly challenge the world today; lack of knowledge by our military establishments concerning the types of machines and tools necessary for a new method of warfare; failure of some industries to respond to the needs of the program for want of assurances of larger profits, lack of foreign policy knowledge by Congress and the public; and fear of the aftermath of this large upset of our economic order".   The largest factor, however, he charged, was "lack of confidence" in the President, "in the purpose of his declared emergency, in his ability to properly spend the billions marked for defense".   (Boston *Herald*, Aug. 15)

(8) Our patriotic financial authorities through their spokesmen, Willkie and others, warn us against interfering with business and tell us that the Popular Front in France through its concessions to labor brought about the debacle Melvin M. Fagen, in two articles in the *New Republic*, Sept. 2 and Sept. 9, refutes this with figures showing that the "index of general industrial and metallurgical production" and the index of "metal manufacturing" increased under the Popular Front and diminished after it had passed.

(9) *Economic Notes*, Sept., 1940, reports enormous profits on the manufacture of steel helmets   These are for protection against the shower of steel fragments. The anti-aircraft barrage has thrown into the air to fall on Londoners, a mass of metal probably a hundred times as great as the Germans have been able to transport by airplane.   The cost of this defense which is destroying London is largely due to the rapid deterioration of the expensive high powered anti-aircraft guns which after only a limited number of shots must be reconstructed.

(10) "In Germany . . . profit making has ceased to be the primary concern of a business.   Increased economic output . .   industrial plants working to fullest capacity, no unemployment and a phenomenal rise in national income have fa-

vored the investor. But on the other hand . . . gains have gone to swell the State's income rather than profits. Since 1934 6 per cent has been the 'interest rate ceiling'." (London dispatch to *Chr Sci Mon*, 1940) (about July) (cf Bul #97)

(11) In an editorial "Business and Blackmail", Sept 2, 1940, the *New Republic* tells of the suits Thurman Arnold is about to bring against the oil companies. August 12, it was reported "The National Defense Advisory Commission has asked Mr. Arnold to postpone the anti-trust suits against twenty-two of the major oil companies on the ground that the government needs their loyal cooperation in carrying out national defense." They "have to be bribed to participate in the defense of their country". Through the ownership of pipelines which pay them dividends of 36% they cripple competition of the independents and gouge the American people out of 300 millions a year.

THE PRESIDENT'S PREDICAMENT

It was on the occasion of the dedication of the building at Hyde Park that is to house the President's papers, that the press reported his fatherly, benevolent address to the some score of assembled employes of the estate. It was like a feudal lord addressing his serfs.[1]

This side of the man is emphasized in the portrait drawn by John T. Flynn, "Country Squire in the White House" ($1.00, Doubleday, 1940).[2] The picture of the President as a strong man is due to "the unconscious propaganda" of "newspapers, radio, movies and people" more than to "the five hundred newspaper publicity men carried on the pay rolls of various New Deal bureaus".[3]

"The office of the president is the most powerful on earth. The people generally pay homage to the great office." The president suffers from an "excess of adulation and dramatization. His supporters rhapsodize about him. Presidents get blamed for not solving problems that no man can solve. That is what has happened to Mr. Roosevelt."

Flynn believes "that the capitalist system may well be doomed through the unwillingness of its own defenders to do the things necessary to save it, but that its collapse in this country now would be the worst of all calamities". Toward this Roosevelt is heading us.[4]

Flynn analyzes the Roosevelt myth by explaining his background,—the 3% Dutch, 90% English blood, the dominance of his imperious mother who held the purse strings, the English influence at Groton and Harvard, his failure as a student, his inefficiency as a businessman, the relatively meagre family income to maintain position in the top millionaire class of the Hudson Valley families, the value of his name to promoters, law firms and politicians, his draft into politics, and Wilson's seizure upon the 'maverick' Roosevelt for Asst. Secretary of the Navy.

"Roosevelt was looked upon in the department as God's gift to the admirals." He believed "that military training educates young Americans to be better citizens", and under the influence of Lord Reading, the English ambassador, saw "England standing between us and the Kaiser, while we played the craven's role". In the orgy of naval spending, billions passed under the hand of this young man. And this went on after the war. In 1920 he advocated "$1,000,000,000 a year for maintaining the Navy". After the war, ten cruisers costing a billion, and ninety-seven destroyers costing 181 million, were laid down. Rusting since then, recently reconditioned, these 'obsolete' destroyers are the ones he is to give to England. And all these after the war were built on the extravagent cost-plus profiteering system   (p 21). He boasted that "he had broken enough laws to be put in jail for 999 years".[5]

The President's predicament is due to this "shaping of his public career", at a time of profiteering and reckless spending for war. His salary as Assistant Secretary was the highest he had ever had, $10,000 a year. "The total earnings of the whole family during the (past) eight years will amount to something over $2,500,000. This is certainly an excellent showing for a period of pronounced depression."

"Politics, vacillation . . . preoccupation with war problems and the affairs of Europe, and only a dim perception of the profound problems of economics and finance that dominate our scene, good intentions mixed with confused ethical concepts — these have brought the President to the tragic point where the only thing that can save his regime is to take the country off into a war hysteria."

"At the end of seven years there are still eleven million people idle, and the revival of private investment is as distant as it was in 1933. Suspension, even contraction, of government spending would be followed by an immediate economic disaster while Roosevelt is president.

"But national spending becomes increasingly difficult. Useful peacetime projects . . . roads, parkways, playgrounds, schools, hospitals, clinics, housing, etc.", which "the Federal government may build . . . have to be maintained by the local governments   Today the local governments refuse these kinds of projects. Most of them are in grave financial difficulties, cannot meet their school budgets, their welfare and highway budgets. Governments that spend soon arrive at a point where resistance to spending becomes imperious. When this point is reached in spending programs, there is always one kind of project left . . . which particularly breaks down resistance among the very conservative groups who are most vocal against government spending. That is national defense.

"The Congress and the nation . . . was howling for economy only six months ago." Now "the President of the United States can say without a whimper of protest that the manner of raising money for a seven-billion-dollar airplane program is a mere 'minor detail'.

"However, it is not possible to get the people to consent to vast outlays for national defense unless you frighten them, make them fear that enemies are about to assail them, and this is what has now happened.

"He, his state Department, his military subordinates are continuously doing and saying things of a provocative character. Then came the spy scares . . . not given out by subordinates but by the President himself in order to give them the greatest explosive propaganda effect.

"The Democratic platform of 1932 declared 'For a navy and an army adequate for national defense, based on a survey of all facts affecting the existing establishments, that the people in time of peace may not be burdened by an expenditure fast approaching $1,000,000,000 annually'." He was to "put an end to government spending and above all to government deficits, particularly government borrowing from the banks".

"The President has now thrown off all pretense of neutrality. But he is still trying to make people believe that the Germans can invade the United States by airplane — a proposition so preposterous that he cannot get a single military man to support it.

"The President's love of military and naval might and display, his truculence about the command of the seas, his well-known sympathies both by blood and sentiment with England, his belief in the doctrine of collective security, his dilemma in . . . spending, the rising tide of political antagonism" are "the conditions that set his mind off in the direction of military adventure."

August 26, 1940

NOTES

(1) "My ambassador", referring to Kennedy in his Boston speech, Oct. 29, 1940, may be technically correct, if the President is the 'sovereign' of the state, —though Americans have usually pronounced that 'servant',— but those who heard the intonation of "my" heard a proud, arrogant, assertive possessiveness. This can't be due to his weekend guests. Royalty today is not arrogant.

(2) In his preface Mr Flynn warns that this little book is not to be taken as a campaign document, or as a biography, or a comprehensive analysis of the New Deal. His purpose is to make us familiar with how the President came to be as he is and what leads him to act as he does. It is a study in human behavior which violates tabus that should be violated in the case of all public men. The myths built about them by the publicity agents should be dissipated if the people are not to be continually fooled (cf "What Makes Lives", pp 7-104). But it is natural that book reviewers in partisan publications should have interpreted this as an "attack". There have been, it is true, scurrilous and slanderous attacks promoted by the Roosevelt haters, such books as "New Deal Goose Step", "Fugitives From a Brain Gang", etc.

(3) Writing of the public's picture of a President, but referring specifically to Coolidge, Flynn says, "A president is a party leader. His own party is forever busy displaying him in a favorable light. The figure in the public mind was created by advertising, publicity, twice-told tales . . . as completely a fiction as Lydia Pinkham, Father John, Dr. Munyon or any of the other characters of advertising fiction."

(4) The following further bits from Flynn illustrate Mr Roosevelt's financial prescience, economic grasp, and responsible statesmanship: "Just before the crash he saw everything 'in a very healthy and prosperous condition'. After the crash he spoke of it as a mere passing event that affected only those who had tried to gamble" Flynn tells us. When Roosevelt became governor of New York there was "a surplus of $15,000,000 in cash", but he left "a deficit of $90,000,000". He "was never in the slightest degree interested in economic problems, had no understanding of them" When Borah pressed him to do something about silver, he exclaimed, 'Well, why not? I experimented with gold and that was a flop. Why shouldn't I experiment a little with silver?" In the presidential campaign of 1931 he asked the voters "simply to assign to me the task of reducing the annual operating expenses of your national government". He denounced the Republicans for "fostering regimentation" and for "the tendency to concentrate power at the top".

(5) Representative Joseph Martin, of the famous firm of "Mah-ton, Bah-ton & Fish", August 24, 1940 (AP), stated that the President "had made and broken 57 major promises in eight years" and had declared "67 or 68 crises and emergencies". No wonder Mr. Roosevelt jealously accuses European dictators of breaking promises

(6) Bulletin #83 briefly summarized as a note following #73 was a symposium of comments.

CONSCRIPTS OR VOLUNTEERS

Postcards, letters, telegrams, to your Representatives now will be effective as never before Elections are coming. Votes will be needed.

By only two votes the Senate last week defeated the Maloney amendment to postpone the draft and encourage volunteers. The Fish amendment to the same purpose in the House won by thirty votes, Sept. 5.

The success of the Fish amendment would be a bitter defeat for the Administration, discourage his allied 'economic royalists', and encourage Willkie to take a more definite stand for some other form of the 'selective service' which he endorses.

This Burke-Wadsworth conscription bill embodies ideas advocated by both Stimson and Roosevelt in articles and speeches since 1917.[1]

For "Defense" it is useless. Blindly, its promoters are planning some such expeditionary force as that of 1918.[2] (cf Bul #77).

"The Burke-Wadsworth bill is an excellent device for procuring the 'cannon fodder' ",[3] declared Sen. Edwin C. Johnson, August 27, on the floor of the Senate, — but, "To assist Britain with manpower, we had better get 10,000 pilots and 30,000 ground men ready at once. A large conscript army will avail her nothing She, too, needs skilled men and not 'cannon fodder'. In the battle of Britain, which has been raging for weeks, fewer than 50,000 men are engaged on both sides."

Over 4 million men are already under arms on English soil, including contingents from Canada, Australia, New Zealand, Poland, France.

"It was the spearhead of 50,000 men that beat France", reported Col. W J Donovan to Secretary Knox on his recent return as observer

This conscription bill is not for defense It is for regimentation,[4] dictatorship, totalitarianism.[5] Remember Huey Long's prognostication that fascism will come to America in the guise of anti-fascism.

Fear and hysteria must be promoted to breed fascism. An American patriot, quoted by Sen E. C. Johnson, said, "I am not afraid that Hitler will come to America. I am afraid that he will not come, because I know that when he does come he will be destroyed."

Willkie in his acceptance speech shows no fear He said, "I promise to outdistance Hitler in any contest he chooses in 1940 or after. We shall beat him on our own terms, in our American way."

Amend the Burke-Wadsworth bill, postpone it, defeat it, and Roosevelt and Stimson will have to abate their hysterical devotion to the British Tories and pay a little more attention to the wishes of their erstwhile countrymen, the American people. Willkie then might be encouraged to come out for some other form of 'selective service'.[6]

Roosevelt is following in Hitler's footsteps[7] along the road to dictatorship. Let's stop this drift to totalitarianism.

"Short of war",[8] says 'short-of-dictatorship' Roosevelt "Men do not jump halfway down Niagara Falls", remarks Sen. Ashurst.

September 6, 1940

NOTES

[1] "The Armed Horde 1793-1939,—A Study of the Rise, Survival and Decline of the Mass Army" (Putnam's, 1940) by Hoffman Nickerson, carries on the title page " 'Universal, conscript, military service . . . with its twin brother universal suffrage . . . has mastered all continental Europe, . . . with what promises of massacre and bankruptcy for the Twentieth Century'—Taine: 'Origines De La France Contemporaine,' 1891 " The book is dedicated to Major-General J. F. C. Fuller, "British Army Ret., Master-Analyst of War", whose forecasts and prophecies and warnings have proved true to the embarrassment of those higher-ups who formerly derided him. The proclamation of the French Assembly in 1792 announced "The young men shall fight; the married men shall forge the weapons . . . the women will make tents and clothes . . the children will make up old linen into lint; the old men will . . . preach hatred."

Nickerson's thesis is that conscription and the mass army originated with the French Revolution and is a feature of democracy and will always favor revolution. "The all-devouring totalitarian state was invented not by the dictators of today but by the democrats of the first French Republic." All this was pointed out by Lawrence Dennis in his letter of August 24, 1940 in which he said, "Many, for example most of the members and supporters of the Civilian Military Training Camps Association, favor conscription because they believe it will be a force for conservatism and an antidote for the subversive isms and for revolution In this belief they are 100% wrong. Conscription was born in the French Revolution and forced on Europe by the revolutionary Napoleon . . ."

[2] Speculation on the line of march of that expeditionary force is made by Paul Mallon (Nov. 6, 1940) : "Next big struggle of the war will be made for Africa—the whole of it—and that is where the British will want us to come in " Assuming that "in the end the British might roll right back up to Berlin by any path the Germans could cut to Africa, across the Dardanelles and Gibraltar", Mallon brings out that for such a back door invasion of Europe, "the British would need every ounce of military might they can muster. They must keep large forces at home to meet the threat of invasion which will be kept constantly before them. Up to now they have not been able to use more American help than they have been getting. But they will be able to use it then. Pressure for American participation should be expected to grow accordingly."

[3] "Of all the familiar 'bunk' perpetrated in the name of war, none is quite

so disgusting as the 'bunk' in connection with the Conscription Act. On registration day (October 16) the newspapers united in one great chorus of acclaim of the millions of young men who began the glad march in support of Uncle Sam This was the answer of America to Hitler—'the response of free men,' said the New York *Times,* 'to a sense of common peril'! President Roosevelt himself led the vanguard of pretense when he spoke of 'more than sixteen million young Americans reviving the 300-year-old American custom of the muster'. But what we seem to remember is that 'the muster' was a purely voluntary enrollment for armed service of the state—the free action of 'free men'. But this conscription measure is compulsory. A penalty of five years in prison, or $10,000 fine, or both, was laid down as applying to any and all who disobeyed the nation's summons" (*Unity,* Nov 4, 1940)

(4) The plan is to give 800,000 one year of training each year so that at the end of five years we will have 4,000,000 trained men. Up to Jan 1, 1941, only 25,000 registered conscripts had been inducted. Meantime there was, under the surface, rebellion against this useless, arbitrary act in the name of 'defense' which had disrupted army organization, taken the time of army officers, prevented progress in actual defense measures, the building of a technically equipped army Already millions of homes for months have been distraught, wives and mothers on tenter hooks. Draftees, who have given up their jobs have been rejected by the thousands of doctors taken from their normal occupation of healing, returning dejected to their homes branded as unfit because of lack of teeth or perhaps because they didn't pass the Wasserman Test.

"More or less under arms, when the Army last totted up (Nov 21), were 106,833 mobilized National Guardsmen, 387,811 three-year Regulars only 18,000 of an expected 90,000 one-year draftees and volunteers. Call of 96,000 additional Guardsmen must be delayed (anywhere from one week to two and a half months) ; so must further drafts. . . . Of 40 camps for National Guardsmen, only 15 were on construction schedule. Two were two and a half months behind, one was 60 days behind.

"In New England, where an abundance of lumber could be salvaged from hurricane-felled trees, camp constructions waited for lumber from the Pacific Coast. . . . Contractors working for cost-plus-fixed-fees could afford to snatch labor from near-by rivals who had lump-sum contracts, thus delaying construction at other camps and highlighting the lack of a planned labor supply. . . .

"Mr. Stimson's explanation that the Army, having in the first place overestimated its ability to absorb recruits, could be accused of nothing more than undue optimism." (*Time,* Dec 23, 1940)

"Educators, sociologists and physicians met in Chicago and learnedly discussed The Family in Wartime. The delegates were not prepared to bet a plugged nickel on the family's immediate prospects. Already, declared Professor Willard Waller of Columbia University, although the U S. was not at war, the national-defense program had begun to raise hell with U. S families. He ticked off wartime dangers: Disruption of relations between parents and children; Increased prostitution, Increased delinquency; Spread of venereal disease, Undermining of the morals of young men who leave home to work in defense plants; Disillusionment of youth, post-war. . ." To the learned sociologists' warnings, Somerset Maugham irritably retorted that the family had nothing to do with it. When you run for an air shelter, you don't look around for the rest of your family, that France failed because family ties were too close (*Time,* Jan 6, 1940)

(5) And Senator Ashurst bemoaned the fact that "when once we put this continental system upon our people, we shall have done it forever. . . If you impose this continental European system you will walk out of this chamber having taken from your people more liberty than you ever gave them. . . "

(6) A congressional "proposal to limit conscription to 21-year-old men was premature by at least three years" military authorities said (AP, Dec. 26, 1940). Yale's President Seymour recorded in his annual report "a system of university military training for university students during four-month periods of intensive summer drill" This brought enthusiastic reactions at Yale (Harvard *Crimson,* Nov 9, 1940)

(7) "Is the Draft Only A Beginning?" asks the *Christian Century,* Jan 8, 1941. "Propaganda by government" promotes "changes in public opinion . . 'voluntary' associations, well provided with necessary funds, spring mysteriously into prominence, take the brunt of 'softening' public opinion, then subside when their object has been accomplished" The "American Defenders of Freedom, Inc." proposes "universal registration" and military drill for all. "It duplicates at almost every point the network of 'voluntary' regimentation with which the nazis have enslaved Germany "

(8) John Haynes Holmes, in *Unity,* Sept. 2, 1940, points out there are two tenable positions as regards America and the European war, stay out or get in. "What we cannot understand, and find hard to respect, is the attitude of those who want us to stay out of the war, and yet want us to go in at least to the extent of aiding England by every means in our power 'short of war'. We must maintain our neutrality—and yet send planes and ammunition to England, sell destroyers to her for her fleet, provide goods and food and money, and yet ourselves remain at peace. This straddling of the issue is of course ridiculous There is only one way really to explain so inconsistent a policy. The advocates of 'everything short of war' really want to take America into the war and propose to do so. But they see the people overwhelmingly opposed to this idea! Therefore they set themselves to the task of cajoling the people, frightening them, persuading them, and little by little committing them, until they are at last aroused to war, unknowingly involved in war, and thus brought to the point where they are in and cannot draw back. These 'short of war' people, headed by the President, are now engaged, step by step, in betraying the nation into war It is dishonest business, and we despise it as much as we fear it."

"There is no doubt that the United States will go to war. Those in command are perfectly mad to be 'in the game' ", stated Senator Hiram Johnson to the AP, Dec 4, 1940

THE VOTER'S DILEMMA

"The President's Predicament" produces "The Voter's Dilemma". The resulting confusion is well expressed by a forward-looking publisher, Richard R. Smith, New York City, who writes August 28, 1940: "Your bulletins leave me in a state of doubt. . . . You state that you are trying to expose and not to advocate, but one who is as active as you must have his own convictions.[1] You obviously are anti-Roosevelt, but I am wondering what your real attitude toward Willkie is. If one accepts your bulletins, one might as well conclude that we had better jump in the river or at least stay away from the polls on election day."

Let's have more light before we are convicted. Convictions of the past still leave me penitent Fooled by Theodore's "Square Deal", Woodrow's "New Freedom", and Franklin's "New Deal", I would willingly wend with Willkie were I not suspicious of a "raw deal" [2][3]

The popular myth 'Willkie" has been beautifully built by the country's most talented artists in advertising and public relations. Russell Davenport, who discovered Willkie a year ago in a week-end at his Norfolk home, is himself poet, painter, philosopher, with "a passion for astrology". Before the Republican National Convention, he secured the date and hour of birth of his associates "His own chart . . . showed that he had a 'good year ahead', he was willing to admit, but he never would tell what Willkie's showed . . . He has an idea that he has discovered the 'perfect control problem', the scientific approach by which he can test the validity of his astrological forecasts" (Ehrlich, Sept. 1).

Willkie's horoscope is also cast by the editors of the *New Republic* in their twenty-page Special Section of Sept. 2 on "This Man Willkie", who "has accepted a fearful responsibility, as President Roosevelt has". They give an unpleasing picture of how he "fought the TVA with injunctions, spite lines, paid propaganda and whiskey at elections", how "his Michigan company tried to suppress a labor union".

"It is astonishing in how many ways he resembles President Roosevelt. Like That Man, he is an actor born to the stage " At the National Press Club in Washington, his "hearers found his advocacy of a business government almost indistinguishable from fascist doctrine". Like Roosevelt he looks forward to concentrated authority, willing to prove Huey Long's thesis that American fascism is coming in the guise of anti-fascism.

"Willkie . . . is not a business man as that phrase is commonly understood. He is not a capitalist. . . . He is not an industrialist." As a public utility man, he is "not a production man or a salesman", but "a fixer and front man". "He never had to meet a payroll."

"Since he was front man for the entire Commonwealth and Southern system, it is fair to hold him responsible for the misdeeds of his subordinates. Accepting just such responsibility is what he was paid for."

"The apocryphal story of Mr. Willkie, as told by Russell Davenport in *Fortune,* has it that Mr. Willkie had no responsibility for this fraud" by which the C. & S. stockholders took a loss of three-quarters of a billion. But Mr. Willkie was the general counsel for the corporation, "a responsible, if not ranking, part of its management".[4]

The *New Republic* editors make it clear that "the record shows that Willkie, far from having had absolutely nothing to do with 'that phase of American life' was one of those responsible for the speculative orgy. . . ." [5]

"While Yet There is Time to Think" is the foreboding title of the editorial in the *Sat Eve Post,* Sept. 7, from which we quote:

"In a kind of hypnosis,—produced partly by propaganda designed for people who believed themselves to be cynical and immune, partly by a sincere crusading evangel carried on by those whose emotions, as we think, have overcome their reason, but mainly by a Government whose foreign policy, to call it such, has been compounded of a spirit of moral grandeur, international heroics, delusions of a military power not in being, false premises and panic,—this country now goes where it does not look and looks where it does not go. . . .

"Our enemies, the Administration keeps telling the people, are Germany, Italy and Japan, naming them. Not one of them has made a gesture of war toward us. . . .

"In June, the American Government entered the war against Hitler by acts of physical intervention all the worse because they were futile. In July that same Government is telling the people they are in grave danger of being attacked by Hitler . . and the National Guardsmen in New York training with gas-pipe guns! What a triumph for state-craft! What strategy!

"These are the conditions under which there has been created in the country a war psychosis, misled by cries of 'Stop Hitler Now!' and 'Defend America by Aiding the Allies'. We had nothing to stop Hitler with. We do not believe that an invasion of the United States by Hitler is among the imminent possibilities. . . . Nor do we believe that fifty or sixty destroyers from the U. S. Navy would save the British Empire. . . . Let us jealously mind our own defense in the great manner of a great people, resolved to be let alone. . . .

"Who is going to put the German thing back? The British? They are not able. Shall we do it? Unless we are willing to go to Europe and destroy it there, we may as well make up our minds now that we shall have to live in the same world with it, maybe for a long time, whether we like it or not.[6]

"None the less, for that reason, only all the more, we should, we must create on this continent the incomparable power of defense. After that we shall see For after that we shall be again as we once were, safe and free and dangerous."

The president is not a god, an autocrat, nor a dictator. He is the servant of our republic, the creature of every democratic voter.

We voters have made him president. We have given him power. Our elected representatives have delegated to him some of their powers Let's not worship a myth. Let's strip away the fake and see our public servants and candidates as they are.

While yet there is time to think, let's be men and vote for men.

September 6, 1940

NOTES

(1) A conviction, in the police court or in my own mind, indicates the case is closed The man with a conviction is no longer interested to hear anything new on the subject. You cannot change his mind or his attitude. I hope to be always free to consider all new evidence that comes to me and I want to be always looking for it. That is the way of modern science.

(2) Boston *Herald,* Sunday, Nov. 3, on the eve of election, carried on its front page a picture of 49th Street near Madison Square Garden packed from wall to wall with young men and women attentively listening to loud speakers carrying Willkie's voice. Why? Humanity still hoping for a messiah, still waiting for the answer to "What shall I do to be saved?" All he could offer them was the

time-worn abstraction for which Charlotte Corday sacrificed her life and on the guillotine discovered what crimes could be committed in its name. In a column adjacent to this picture, Robert Choate, in an editorial commenting on how Willkie has crept up in the campaign, remarked, "It can be done".

(3) But "Willkie takes his responsibilities with high seriousness It is altogether possible that if elected President he would serve one hundred and thirty million Americans even more faithfully than he served two hundred thousand C & S. stockholders" (Dorothy Dunbar Bromley, "The Education of Wendell Willkie", *Harper's*, October, 1940).

(4) Secretary Ickes, responding to Willkie's assault on the corrupt "city machines" that supported Roosevelt, came back, "I can tell you whose baby the corrupt political machine is, or at least I can name its paternal ancestors for two generations back. Its grandfather is the railroads of America. Its father is the public utilities" (Oct. 18, AP)

(5) Both parties had plenty of reserve ammunition which was never used in the campaign But Edward J. Flynn, Democratic National Chairman, as things warmed up did say, Sept 28, "Willkie's nomination was demanded by Wall Street financial interests, fronted by Mr. Lamont of J P. Morgan & Co   . he has successfully represented the large moneyed interests of this country against the plain citizens   ". He had been discovered by Mr. Lamont in 1935 and put to straightening out the rather desperate Morgan promotion, Commonwealth & Southern (cf *New Republic*).

Flynn further asserted that Willkie "has been a machine politician all his adult life . . . He was a Tammany County committeeman in New York, he was associated with the State Central Committee in Ohio, he was affiliated with the Summit County organization in that same state. He was a spellbinder for the organization in Elwood and he was a lobbyist in Washington as well as in various States in which he lived." Again he charged "the Nation's press was 'under a dictatorship of financial interests of advertisers' " When the Democratic *Times* flopped to Willkie, Flynn quoted from a speech of Sulzberger in 1937, "The New York *Times* this year has lost a large amount of advertising . . . because of its support of President Roosevelt during the (1936) campaign".

(6) The heavy tanks we are designing (and building ?) which cannot be completed for three or four years, could have only one conceivable use and that is against the Maginot or Siegfried Line. The force of two million or more that we are planning to equip could only be used as an expeditionary force in Europe. But isn't the chief desire of the Administration to destroy Hitler? And how can it be done without going after him?

THE PRESIDENT'S SECRETS

Wilson's "open covenants openly arrived at" are regarded as more 'obsolete' by our President than our planes, destroyers, tanks.[1]

Secrecy marks all the President's dealings with his British friends. This is our 'foreign policy'. Lack of faith in the American people, arrogant contempt for all except votes,—that is our 'domestic policy'.

The secret alliance with Britain to protect her Pacific possessions, exposed by Representative Tinkham (cf Bul #41), contemptuously denied by the State Department, later disclosed by the Japanese (July 3, 1940, by radio, not in American papers), again denied by the State Department, finally confirmed by the British Foreign Office,—the more recent secret alliance to defend and finance Canada,—commitments unfulfilled to France,—all these secret treaties unconfirmed by the Senate we know of only through leaks or foreign sources. [2]

Reynaud went down appealing to the President to send his promised help. What will he say under oath at Riom? Churchill, after the Democratic Convention in Chicago, put in continuous pleas for these same destroyers (Roudybush, Sept 14). Senator Pepper explained "Britain would get the destroyers 'as soon as Congress and the public become accustomed to the idea' " (*Newsweek, Sept.* 16).

"Only the blind can fail to see that the United States is moving rapidly toward participation in the world struggle. Measures 'short of war' have been expanded to measures at the point of war. . . . The U. S has moved to the point where it is committed to assist the British Empire in the war with Germany", ruefully mourned the *Army and Navy Journal*, Aug. 24. "We are preparing to reinforce the British navy with over-age destroyers, a preliminary to the dispatch of more powerful vessels." [3]

When on his train the President arrogantly announced to the correspondents that Congress was then being told "as a matter of information" of the 'fait accompli', he quipped on the 'coincidence' that Churchill had promised that the British fleet would never be surrendered. [4] Three weeks before, while this was in preparation, questioned by correspondents "about the possibility of trading the destroyers for bases . . . Franklin Roosevelt had flatly denied any connection—but reporters knew better than to believe him". (*Time,* Sept. 16) [5]

When the destroyers arrived at Halifax, they found there assembled "crack Royal Navy men", which Churchill explained as due to "the long arm of coincidence" (*Time,* Sept 16, p 17). It was all an "act of almost boyish spontaneity", piped the London *New Statesman.*

First Lord of the Admiralty A. V. Alexander expressed "utmost pleasure and satisfaction". Rear Admiral Stewart Bonham-Carter, chief of British naval operations in the North Atlantic, said, when he took them over in Canada, "They are magnificent ships. They are in perfect condition. They are the equal of our VNW's and the equal of any ships we are getting." How many weeks of careful planning had it taken to bring about this condition and the many coincidences?[6]

During these long and secret preparations the President quietly deceived the people, but "permitted private groups and individuals, most vocal of which was William Allen White's Committee to Defend America by Aiding the Allies,[7] to keep the matter in the public eye. On Aug. 4 the committee induced Gen. Pershing in a worldwide broadcast to advocate transfer of the destroyers." (*Newsweek*, Sept. 16)

From the White Committee's Washington observer, John L. Balderston,[8] we learn that "negotiations were proceeding in London and Washington regarding urgent British war needs in addition to the 50 destroyers" and the "500,000 rifles, 80,000 machine guns and 750 cannon" sent to England "in June and July". Britain needs also "a score of motor torpedo boats . . . long-range flying boats . . . long-range bombers . . . the entire output of tanks in this country . . . the use of American airfields in Texas and southern California to train pilots for the Royal Air Force . . . another 250,000 Lee-Enfield rifles". (Boston *Herald*, Sept. 6)[9]

The following ten days showed great progress in making these transfers. Trial balloons were sent up in the press as to proposals, and then the actual transfers proceeded secretly.

Up to Sept. 7 announcements came from Washington and Ottawa of plans to deliver 229 World War tanks to the Dominion for training purposes. There was protest and outcry and questioning as to why the First Army at Ogdensburg had been obliged to use trucks and milk wagons in their maneuvers in place of tanks.[10]

Actual transfer of the tanks to Canada has consequently been soft pedaled. But indignant editorials (Boston *Transcript*, Sept. 16) denounce "This strange transaction . . . still kept secret . . . so devoid of sense".

Now our Boeing bombers, flying fortresses, are being sent across. William Allen White had urged wiring the President "to send 25 flying

fortresses, as many combat planes as possible and 20 torpedo boats".
The N. Y. *Times* reporting this (Sept. 13), adds the U. S. "has approximately 53" of these flying fortresses.

Our first line fighting planes had already been sent secretly. Four
out of five of the new planes manufactured now go direct to the British
(Paul Mallon, Sept. 12). While deceptive figures of planes on order
were being announced, we have less than 300 fighting planes, according to Army figures published Sept. 4, and less than 1500 more planes
have been ordered for delivery in 1940 and 1941. "The White House
did not dispute these figures" (Kluckhohn, Boston *Herald,* Sept. 6).

Leases that will be void if the islands are taken over by another
are all we got But Britain has more than 10 billions of quick assets
in this country and has a standing debt of 4 billions with us.

What we are to give for these leases, in the words of Lord Lothian,
is "naval and military equipment and material which the United States
Government will transfer to His Majesty's Government". No limits
are stated. (*Uncensored,* Sept. 7)

But the conjecture is that the price we paid for the leases which may
easily be abrogated is, in addition, the war debt. "If the Roosevelt-
Churchill agreement contains secret clauses, one of their chief subjects
is the war-debt settlement. . . . Cancellation of the war debt would
have permitted" further "credits in Wall Street now forbidden under
the Johnson Act", writes T.R B. in the *New Republic,* Sept. 16.

Marquis W Childs wrote recently in the St. Louis *Post-Dispatch* that
while England's credits here are far from exhausted and there is no immediate need to repeal the Johnson Act, "officials will be careful to
avoid the subject until it is felt that public opinion has been prepared
for the first official intimation of such a move".

Senator Lundeen had long demanded that the British, French, and
Dutch islands fringing our coast and the Caribbean, threatening our
cities and controlling the approaches to the Panama Canal, be seized
for our own safety and their value credited to the old war debt of
10 billions, declaring, "America will never be paid in any other
way". A Gallup poll showed that 66% of the people approved his
plan.[11]

He bitterly opposed the President's involving us in the present war,
"a continuation of the war which was started on that fateful August

morning in 1914", as the N. Y. *Herald-Tribune* reminded us on the approach of its anniversary, 1940. Churchill more recently, on Aug. 20, told the House of Commons that "this war is, in fact, only a continuation of the last".

Lundeen was national chairman of the "Make Europe Pay War Debts Committee", Bond Building, Washington, D C. He was "one of the three remaining Members of Congress who, over 20 years ago, voted against American participation in the first World War", which he looked upon as "a tragic mistake".[12]

The sudden death of Senator Lundeen, the second senator to die in a plane crash, shocked the nation. It is reported the Senate is to investigate the matter. Pearson and Allen in their column, Sept. 13, say, "A G-man, a Department of Justice attorney, and an FBI secretary were on the plane with him . . . the Department of Justice probably will deny that they were shadowing the Minnesota senator, but the fact is that at least one of them definitely was. . . . Whether certain foreign agents figured that they were about to be exposed, whether G-men on the plane tangled with Lundeen in flight, or whether it was an act of God and the weather may never be known."

The British in their desperate need look to our resources as a means of saving their Empire. "Most officials" look on the destroyer deal "as a preliminary step . . toward a final alliance between Britain and the United States. . . . In the final analysis most people here still regard the United States as some sort of colony" (Robert P Post, wireless from London, N. Y. *Times,* Sept. 8). The *New Statesman* announces, "We are even brothers in war, indeed a miracle of improvisation".

That the President has lost faith in the American people, Willkie has discovered. Columnists and cartoonists for months have made it apparent that his interest was in the 'Battle of Britain'. Willkie brings him back to the 'Battle of America'. 'Obsolete' is the President and his pro-British-Groton-Harvard coterie.[13]

When from the *Army Recruiting News,* pages on the success of volunteer recruiting were removed, sentries posted to prevent these pages from being circulated, as discovered by Senator Wheeler,—Stimson testified that neither he nor his Chief of Staff knew of it. It must have been some subordinate whom he could not discover or court martial. Obsolete "Wrong Horse Harry" should be transferred to the British.

Our President moves in most mysterious ways his wonders to perform. He plants his bases far at sea,—and rides upon the storm,—of hysterics that he has stirred up toward a third term.

September 18, 1940

NOTES

(1) After Munich the President, with Hull, Welles and Berle, formulated a four point foreign policy Feb. 9, 1939, Mr Roosevelt told his press conference, "The foreign policy has not changed and it is not going to change", and gave its four principles, "No. 1—We are against any entangling alliances, obviously",—this last word thrown in perhaps saves the President's conscience. Later he emphasized, "Your Government has no information which it has any thought of withholding from you" (*Congressional Record,* June 10, 1940).

"This administration is already under suspicion", declared Gen Johnson, August 23, 1940 Mr. Willkie, early in October, asked the President "Are there any international understandings about America's entrance into the war that we, the citizens of the United States, do not know about?"

Just before election in his Philadelphia speech, Mr Roosevelt assured us,— "There is no secret treaty, no secret obligation, no secret commitment, no secret understanding in any shape or form, direct or indirect, with any other government, or any other nation in any part of the world, to involve this nation in any war or for any other purpose "

There has been "a whole series of secret deals, of surprise announcements, of undiscussed commitments and of unratified international agreements", said Anti-War News Service, Nov 1, 1940, pointing out that the President had kept secret the Canadian agreement for joint military and naval defense, the destroyer deal, the transfer to Great Britain in June, 1940, of 15 or 17 shiploads of tanks, planes, guns which we learned of months later from Churchill These things "may not have been secret to the British—but they certainly were to the American people".

(2) London, Aug 21, 1940 (AP) "British Office sources today confirmed reports the United States had leased the islands of Canton and Enderbury in the southern Pacific from Great Britain as air bases. The lease, these sources said, is for 50 years, with a provision that it can be extended indefinitely Canton and Enderbury Islands, mere dots on the map of the Pacific, came under the joint control of the United States and Great Britain April 6, 1939, by virtue of a 50-year agreement, reached after a year's negotiations as to their ownership . . . Britain and the United States took the new Hebrides Islands as the example for their joint control The New Hebrides, on the south Pacific, were placed under a condomium in 1906, being jointly administered by commissioners appointed by Britain and France "

(3) The Congressional interpretation was that the President had in mind "an offset against the British debt as the quid pro quo in the contemplated transac-

tion". Senator Wheeler, Aug. 17 (AP) advocated "cancellation of a portion of Great Britain's war debt in exchange for leases on naval base sites in Britain's western hemisphere possessions. . . He told reporters, however, that he was 'glad to see that the President is not considering trading American destroyers for these naval bases and thereby weakening our own defenses.' "

"In June, by accident, the Congress discovered that the Government by executive will had released to Great Britain a number of small fast torpedo boats, called the mosquito fleet, then building for the U. S. Navy. The Congress was about to accept this as a 'fait accompli' when it found on the statute books a law . . . passed in 1917. . . : 'During a war in which the United States is a neutral nation, it shall be unlawful to send out of the jurisdiction of the United States any vessel built, armed or equipped as a vessel of war, or converted from a private vessel into a vessel of war, with any intent or under any agreement or contract, written or oral, that such vessel shall be delivered to a belligerent nation', under pain of fine and imprisonment." (Editorial, *Sat Eve Post,* Oct. 19, 1940)

Chairman Walsh of the Senate Naval Committee, Aug. 13 (AP), over the radio said that transfer of destroyers would be "an act of war". "Either we should enter the war and give our all, or we should stay out of the war and retain our fleet intact for the defense of our own country. . . Our present need is to train . . men and young officers on every ship we have so that as the new ships are commissioned . . the sailors . ᵣ . will be ready to man the new ships . . . Some of these over-age and heretofore decommissioned destroyers are being converted into fast mine layers, aircraft tenders and anti-aircraft vessels, types urgently needed in our own navy. . . . There is only one group who can honestly favor the transfer of our destroyers. This group has advocated our entrance into the European war from the beginning." If, as Pershing said, "We shall be failing in our duty to America" if we do not do everything possible to save the British fleet, then, Walsh said, "why should we not send at once our best ships, our fastest planes, and our trained men to handle them?"

(4) "What this transaction really means, in plain English, is that the United States has taken over the defense of two thirds of England's colonial possessions, now and forevermore . . . And for that lofty privilege, judging by the precedent just set, we'll have to pay her in airships and warships . . I confess to a dense ignorance of naval strategy, a science in which the Hon. Mr Roosevelt is said to be 'facile princeps', as he is in public finance, constitutional law and radio crooning. But I can't help wondering why, if a base at Bermuda will be valuable to us, a base at Gibraltar, or even at Portsmouth, would not be even more valuable. Perhaps the former will be acquired anon, along with the Singapore base. . . . As everyone knows, it is one of the ancient bulwarks of religion and morality, i e., of English control over the seas, and no doubt the Hon Mr Roosevelt will welcome the chance to save it from the Spanish infidels, whose claim to it is as plainly immoral and against God as Mussolini's claim to security in the Mediterranean, or Hitler's in the Bad Lands east of him, or the Japs' along the Asiastic coast." (H. L. Mencken, Oct. 6, 1940)

(5) The President's 'whopper' deceived few. The secret preparations could not be wholly concealed. The stage setting had taken time. The preceding day the President in his speech at the dedication of the Smoky Mountains National Park had forecast the possibility, his crisp notice to Congress already written. Churchill had been brought to agree not to sink his Navy. Admiral Stark had prepared his statement on the obsolescence. (cf *Uncensored*, Sept. 7, 1940)

(6) In the award of $15,000,000 which England paid us in settlement of the "Alabama claims" for damage to our commerce, for ships outfitted in England during the Civil War, this principle was announced, "As a neutral government, she (Britain) was bound to use diligence to prevent the fitting out, arming, or equipping within its jurisdiction, of any vessel which it had reasonable ground to believe was intended to cruise or to carry on war against a power with which England was at peace".

(7) The ardent White Committee advocates claimed that the fifty destroyers might save the British Empire. They have not as yet, as is evident from the demand for additional destroyers and almost everything else. Paul Mallon saw the situation sanely, August 19, 1940, "Fifty destroyers would do the British some minor good although not in their present predicament." August 24, 1940, David I. Walsh, warning against stripping our navy, asked, "If 50 destroyers failed to save the world—what next? . . ❧ To help the Allies this embargo was lifted by act of Congress, and all private industries, except shipbuilders, have been since October last at the disposal of the Allies. Next Government contracts were cancelled in order to deliver to the Allies the airplanes of the Army and Navy we had 'on order' for ourselves." January 1, 1941 (AP), the Foreign Policy Association, asserting that only America was able to furnish assistance to Britain on "the scale required", did "not attempt to pass judgment on the fundamental question of whether the United States should or should not resort to measures which might be regarded as acts of war".

(8) John L Balderston of Beverly Hills, movie script writer, former long-time correspondent of American newspapers in London, one of the thirty signers of the June statement to demand immediate declaration of war, instigated by "the Miller group" (cf Bul #62), undertook to produce a series "of 'wire letters' for distribution to a selected list of about 50 newspapers. These letters, which have been put out from Washington at the rate of about two a week, contain 'background' information for editors on the needs of Great Britain and the progress of the White Movement." Telegraphed under the aegis of the White Committee as the William Allen White News Service, Miller had these letters "mimeographed and distributed by mail among the members of his group and perhaps 100 others throughout the country". This information is from Charles G Ross' "Inside Story of White's Propaganda Engine" in the St. Louis *Post-Dispatch*, Sept 22. In condensed form, this article appeared in the *Christian Century*, Nov. 6, 1940.

(9) Clark M Eichelberger, executive director of the White Committee, Sept 5, 1940 (AP), said, "One man in every four now under arms in Great Britain is

equipped with weapons from this country . . . half million rifles, 80,000 machine guns, 700 field guns and 'mountains of ammunition' have reached England from the U. S.".

We have confusing reports and rumors as to the number of first class combat planes possessed by the army and the navy, and the number that have been sent abroad. Aug. 20, 1940 (AP), "Churchill gave the first official word today of the safe arrival in England of surplus American army munitions valued at $37,000,-000 which the administration released nearly three months ago. . .   Munitions included 600,000 Lee-Enfield rifles . . . 500 world war 75 millimeter field guns."

Not being permitted to know, we can only assume that no price was paid for these but that they were gratis, included in the "naval and military equipment and material which the United States Government will transfer to His Majesty's Government", as Lord Lothian put it, in payment, with the destroyers, for the leases   Nor was it known until mid-September that all this material made up fifteen (some reports have seventeen) shiploads and that the total value was probably many times that of the '50 destroyers'. Mention that "the American Government next, out of its own, arsenals supplied Great Britain with fifteen shiploads of arms and munitions" was made in the *Sat Eve Post* editorial of Oct. 19, 1940. The President forgot to tell us this, though he has recently assured us that there are no secret alliances, no agreements, no information to give out   And still the ardent 'all aid to Britain' advocates claim we have done nothing but take the 'cash' and let Great Britain 'carry'.

The White Committee also demanded for England the American secret bomb sight. This U. S. army bomb sight has become almost a myth. Without definite knowledge, the American people are led to believe that it is enormously superior. That the American people are fooled in regard to the superiority of their aircraft is evident from the English reaction to them (cf Bul #26). We are led to believe also that knowledge of the sight has not leaked to the Germans nor the British. The British of course already have it. The airplanes flown over must have been equipped with it. The Germans probably have it too now. Most of the publicity given about the secrecy of our marvelous bomb sight is suspected to have been hind sight after it had already been released and captured by the enemy for what it was worth

About this Balderston wrote, "At this point this dispatch hastens to censor itself.   . . If we give a secret weapon to a friend, that weapon sooner or later may be captured by the enemy and used against us " This issue of the "William Allen White News Service" telegram also urged public pressure on the army and navy chiefs

"Upon publication of the Balderston statement of British needs, Chairman White immediately disavowed it as the program of the committee. . . . He said that neither he nor the committee favored sending the British any war materials which army and navy authorities might consider necessary for American defense . . that the Balderston program was an inventory of British needs rather than an immediate objective of the committee." (Charles G. Ross, St. Louis *Post-Dispatch*, Sept. 22, 1940) In November Mr. White announced that Balderston was no longer connected with the Committee. And in December Mr. White was no longer connected

(10) Canadians are asking what economic arrangement is to be made between Canada and the U.S. There is none, as there was no military arrangement between them before the Ogdensburg conference, August 18 The Dominion is spending half a billion a year on arms, allotting 120 million for new plants, and has already incurred a war debt of over a billion. "In plain terms Canadians are asking whether the United States is prepared to defend and support this business structure, as well as the Dominion's coastline . . . That the United States will be ready to pay the lion's share of joint defense works, such as the proposed base in Newfoundland, is accepted here as certain. But a much wider co-operation in economics and finance is foreseen by many Canadians and would be welcomed by all" (Bruce Hutchison, *Chr Sci Monitor*, Sept. 7). Expectations in Canada are that 50 million will shortly be lent her from the U. S. Government-owned Export-Import Bank (Hutchison, *Chr Sci Monitor*, Sept. 9) American troops in their August maneuvers in northern New York were using gas pipes for guns while the President obviously there to inspect them was arranging for the delivery of our 'obsolete' tanks to Canada for training purposes. The *Sat Eve Post* listed for the Pennsylvania National Guard, one division, the requirements and materials on hand, and a very small percentage,—but 15 shiploads had been sent to Britain in June as additional payment for leases

(11) "To build and fortify an advanced fleet base would cost at least $200,-000,000 (the rock-bottom estimate for doing as much as Guam)." (*Time*, Sept. 16, 1940) Before the end of November a preliminary 75 million had been allotted to them.

The President "knows that there is in this country, a well-developed sentiment in favor of the acquisition by the United States of air and naval bases in the possessions still held by European powers in the waters adjacent to the Americas He assumes, and perhaps correctly, that the American people will overlook the fact that we have already handed England enough money on a silver platter to more than pay for all the territory she holds on this side of the Atlantic—excepting Canada, of course. In exchange for our destroyers, what do we actually get? Merely the privilege of defending British possessions in this hemisphere against an Axis assault." (Chicago *Leader*, Sept. 6, 1940)

Lothian said "bases granted 'in exchange for naval and military equipment and material'. All the leases were for ninety-nine years and 'free from all rent or charges'. Robert Jackson's opinion was a masterpiece of legal casuistry, interpreting statutes to mean things never intended by them and finding the transaction consonant with international law by the simple expedient of ignoring the distinction between private and governmental transfers of arms from neutrals to belligerents." Roosevelt on Sept 3, 1940 sent a communication to Congress: "The right to bases in Newfoundland and Bermuda are gifts—generously given and gladly received. The other bases mentioned have been acquired in exchange for fifty of our over-age destroyers." (quoted in Schuman, "Night Over Europe.')

Like the cantonments, the cost of the bases continues to increase. In June we not only gave the destroyers but seventeen shiploads of munitions. Great Britain gave us permission only to lease for ninety-nine years acreage. Pearson and Allen tells us February 28, 1941, "The 125 acres purchased in Bermuda will cost $1,500,000, or $12,000 per acre. In comparison, residential property five miles from the District of Columbia costs only $1200 an acre." In Trinidad, after long jockeying, the cost of the land was settled for $3,000,000 on which to build an army base costing $51,000,000. In Newfoundland, the Army and Navy will spend about $33,000,000. "At one time during the Navy's negotiations over island bases, Admiral Stark got so exasperated that he said in effect: 'Do you want our munitions or don't you? If so, cut out the haggling ' "

"The Carribbean: the Story of Our Sea of Destiny" by W. Adolphe Roberts (Bobbs-Merrill, 1940) is written from the standpoint of present international issues. The Civil War demonstrated the need of Caribbean naval bases. President Johnson stated the doctrine that "the West Indies naturally gravitate to, and may be expected ultimately to be absorbed by the Continental states, including our own". Following the war with Spain we 'acquired' a naval base at Guantanamo, Cuba, and at San Juan, Porto Rico. In the first World War, fearing German acquisition, we bought for $20,000,000 the Danish West Indies which Hoover, visiting, referred to as "the poor house of the Western hemisphere". Mr. Roberts emphasizes "the necessity of our acquiring from Great Britain key points of the Caribbean—-at least Port Royal, Jamaica and Nassau, Port-of-Spain and the islands of Barbados as well". He observes that "it would be eminently wise for Great Britain .   . to yield these . . ."

(12) Lundeen, who in 1917-18 in the House voted against entry into the war, has always been a consistent fighter against meddling in Europe. Boake Carter in "Why Meddle in Europe", (McBride, 1939) tells of the World War experience of Lundeen, "one of the few men who was able to withstand the hysteria and propaganda of 1917': "Because of his conscientious vote against American participation in a futile crusade to make the world safe for democracy, he was reviled throughout the land as a traitor. He was not only barraged with rotten eggs and overripe tomatoes, but with stones and bricks. Worse, however, was to befall him. Some true American 'patriots' locked him up in a refrigerator car and left him there to die an icy death, a fate which his aggressors (!) felt was even too good for such a scoundrel and traitor. By sheer good luck, a trainman passed by and rescued him, at the last moment, from freezing to death."

(13) "The word 'obsolete' has been dinned into the consciousness of the American people for months now. The purpose has been deliberate and artful in its application. In a generation of Americans inured to the machine age and its common shop talk, 'obsolete' has a meaning all its own. . . . 'Obsolete' destroyers . . . were pictured as rotting away in the navy yards, of no value to

anybody. General Pershing was handed a carefully written speech to read over the radio to that effect" (Editorial, Detroit *Free Press*).

> "He takes a portion of our fleet
> Before we ever use it
> And says, 'For us it's obsolete,
> But maybe George can use it'

> "He dubs our Boeing bombing planes
> Outmoded and passé,
> But for Brittania's domains
> He hopes they'll save the day.

> " 'Twould make the young in heart feel sad,
> Depressed and sorely smitten,
> To hear, 'You're obsolete, my lad
> So go and fight for Britain.' "

(Ruth Kremen)

"Send 50 over-age professors to England" was a slogan on one of the placards carried in the Yard when a hundred Harvard students picketed a rally held by the undergraduate Militant Aid to Britain Committee, Dec 6, 1940.

William Yandell Elliott, Harvard Professor of Government, 'yandells' anarchistically for war, cravenly yodels, "Even if England goes down, we are not licked We can defend ourselves and the western hemisphere; but at what cost!" At the meeting of Harvard alumni held in the Yard Dec. 7, Elliott, declared that the "simple test for right action" is to spite Hitler, "It does not mean all aid to Britain short of war. It means that this country must make the decision on all aid to Britain at the risk of war."

PROTECTING WAR PROFITS

The patriotic cooperation of industry must be enlisted in this defense program. So we were early cautioned not to hurt feelings by speaking of "merchants of death", nor to insist on management risking stockholders' capital Our Congress and Administration have been most patient as the sit-down strike of capital was prolonged.[1]

The "excess profits tax bill" as passed by the Senate 46 to 22, Sept. 19 (AP), raised the normal corporation income tax to a maximum of 24%. It made a gesture of taxing war profits "defined as excess", to a maximum of 25 to 50%. That will fool some, and win some votes.[2]

The yield will be relatively insignificant, possibly only 160 millions the first year, on a war expenditure of 5700 millions. But two-thirds of this will come from the normal income tax [3]

"It is supposed to be an excess profits bill, but I find that less than one-third will come from war profits. This bill doesn't tax war profits, and I want the record to show that I don't want any part of it", indignantly declared John Sullivan, Assistant Secretary of the Treasury, with the backing of Morgenthau. (Pearson and Allen, Sept. 18) [4]

In the last war, on an expenditure of 7000 millions, 1917-21, the excess tax raised 2500 millions (*Economic Notes,* Sept 1940). In Canada today the excess tax is 75% (Boston *Herald,* Sept. 14), in England 100%.

Seldom has there been seen in Washington "such a concerted and successful tax lobby" (Pearson and Allen, Sept 18). The result of their cooperation with industry and our legislators in working out the "technical difficulties" is a lawyer's triumph.

Chairman Doughton of the House Ways and Means Committee usually writes the first draft of a tax bill. His North Carolina neighbor, Clay Williams, Reynolds Tobacco Co., once an appointee of the Administration, a pillar of the U. S. Chamber of Commerce and the National Association of Manufacturers, spent the summer in Washington helping Doughton, Pearson and Allen tell us. "Despite this, the tax bill, as it came out of the House was a far more nearly genuine excess profits bill than when it came out of the Finance Committee of the Senate." [5]

"The most complicated bill enacted in Congress in my twenty years" declared one of its House authors (Paul Mallon, Aug. 30). "Highly complicated", "impossible of comprehension", "an imponderable mess", others remarked. "The worst hodge-podge that ever was drafted Nobody knows what's in it", said Missouri's Senator Clark.

At continued hearings, Chambers of Commerce of the U S, of Boston and other leading cities, through attorneys protested "terms disturbing and disastrous" to industry. The Senate as the result of the flood of protest and pressure from lobbyists softened the blow to industry in five particulars, removed existing restrictions on profits, and permitted the five-year amortization (cf Bul #81). Moreover the Senate protected and preserved the multimillionaires' tax exempt bonds. [6]

Each corporation may determine the amount it is to be taxed, by the bill's formula. There is a choice of two ways of juggling figures,—(a) excess over average earnings of the previous four years, with additional $10,000 exemption, or (b) excess over 8% on invested capital, with exemption of $8000. (AP Sept 19) [7]

Industry is pictured by our press as a shy maiden, retiring and sensitive. Capital is nervous. Management is conscientious, unwilling to risk their stockholders' resources unless insured safety and profits But private enterprise, properly wooed, and fattened on profits, is of course more efficient than the slave labor of totalitarian states.

Our President is in the difficult position of being a candidate for office, somewhat disturbed by puncturing attacks of his opponent, and hoping to win votes on his war program while holding his erstwhile 'economic royalists' in precarious alliance with prospect of profits.

Industry, whose strategic brains operate from lower New York, has made an enormous investment in lobbyists, public relations, advertising men, and the press, as a means of influencing public opinion so that private enterprise may be stimulated to provide jobs and patriotically protect our country

Industry recalls the many lean years and reasonably hopes now to get something back on its investment, which is to make possible a great revival of industrial prosperity.[8]

With all the readaptation of their plants, retooling, peace looms as the great risk, which would mean enormous loss. It is foolish to expect these financial manipulators to exhibit any great length of vision.

One cannot blame the manufacturer who typically remarked the other day, "Hell, you can't make a profit out of this war! If you do make something, labor will get it, and what they don't the government will take. You get a fat contract, make a big investment, and then your contract may be abrogated or peace may come The only thing to do is grab what you can while the grabbing is good, sure that the opportunity won't last long. If you figure on 20% you will be lucky if you make 5 So I'm not interested in 20%. If it looks like a sure 40, I'll go into it But let's get more while we can."

Academic inquiry into the motives, patriotic and otherwise, of those who are investing time and money in promoting the present war, will doubtless be undertaken, after the mass hysteria—which has yet to reach its peak—has passed.

Such an autopsy, scientifically performed, will reveal much more than any present vivisection. The centers of infection and the pus pockets uncovered will be shocking even to those familiar with the less heinous revelations that followed the last war.

But America's present task is to bring industry to higher production in providing for our defense. Under our economic system there must be the incentive of profits.[9]

Let us hope the excesses and abuses may not exceed those of the last war and may not bring more disastrous results.[10]

September 20, 1940

NOTES

[1] Facing a similar situation in the summer of 1918, Edmonds, editor of the *Manufacturers Record*, wrote Secretary of the Treasury McAdoo, calling to his attention "the danger to the very life of the nation which will come through the creation of the impression that the business men of the country are engaged in profiteering".

[2] LaFollette's *Progressive* called it "a pious fraud". *New Republic* editorial refers to the "Excess-Profits Sham" "The bill had been ordered by the President two months ago to prevent war millionaires Far from doing that, shouted Massachusetts' Allen Treadway, 'this bill set up a new class of war millionaires—namely, so-called tax experts. Anyone who can explain this can become a millionaire overnight' " (*Time,* Oct. 14, 1940).

This bill, "whisked through the House in less than four hours" (AP, Aug. 30, 1940), repealed the provision of the Vinson Bill limiting armament profits, against which the armament manufacturers had been on strike. Originally the Vinson Bill had been regarded as generous. The *Nation,* Nov 18, 1939, remarked, "The current war will certainly make the world safe for armorplate manufacturers and shipbuilders. . . . The terms of the Vinson Bill are made to order for the armament profiteer The Secretary of the Navy may waive competitive bidding. He may also lend up to 30 per cent of the value of the contract at low interest rates to the shipbuilder".

Senator LaFollette, whom Vandenberg, Sept. 20, assured the Senate had more detailed knowledge of tax legislation than any other member, told the Senate that "the excess profits portion of this bill violates every principle of sound tax theory. 1 It raises no appreciable amount of revenue; 2. It is inequitable in that the small amount of revenue which it raises will be paid in the main by those corporations least able to pay while those corporations most able to pay are left untaxed; 3. It confirms and entrenches those corporations which possess a monopoly and quasi-monopoly position in our economy. If there was ever a tax measure which promises to perpetuate monopolistic corporations in their monopolies, it is this one "

LaFollette's weekly, The *Progressive,* Sept 21, commented, "Monopolists and prosperous corporations will pay practically no increased taxes because of two 'jokers' in the bill. One joker is the provision allowing corporations optional methods in computing tax liability. The Treasury loses every time with this provision. The other joker is the so-called 'earnings method' of computing excess profits. Under this method, a corporation that has earned substantial profits in the past may continue to earn those profits without additional taxes. . . . Here is the way it works out in a specific case. Corporation A is well established and has been making big profits for years, perhaps by a monopolistic control of the industry. Corporation B is a new corporation just beginning to compete seriously with A For simplicity's sake say both of them invested capital of $5,000,000 Corporation A has been making an average of $1,000,000 a year for several years. Corporation B has been having a tough battle competing with A and has averaged only $200,000 a year during the last four years. This year, at last, it gets upon even footing with A and makes $1,000,000. Under the Senate bill corporation A will pay no excess profits tax but B will pay $249,000."

(3) As the bill finally passed, its "yield was estimated at $525,000,000 on 1940 income and between $900,000,000 and $1,000,000,000 in subsequent years . . . a mere drop in the bucket when compared with $15,000,000,000 in defense outlays".

(4) "The Senate junked most of the Treasury's excess profit formulas—presumably in the interest of the little business man. But a study of the axed measure discloses that besides the 'little fellow', certain big fellows also will benefit —in fact, very handsomely.

"One of these happens to be Coca-Cola Company, Georgia's richest concern It will benefit to the tune of something like $10,000,000. Coca-Cola made a net profit of $29,000,000 last year and on the basis of its 1940 first quarterly report should make a net of $33,000,000 this year. Under the Treasury's tax plan the company's excess profits tax would have amounted to $13,000,000 But Senator George, a member of the powerful Finance Committee, fought these proposals so vehemently that . Coca-Cola would be taxed only around $4,000,000—or approximately $10,000,000 less than the Treasury proposed" (Pearson and Allen, Sept. 30, 1940)

(5) Senator Connolly introduced an amendment of over a hundred pages on income tax, to be effective in case the U S "declares war". In the last stages, Senator Pittman "got blanket exemption for his friends who are engaged in mining various 'strategic' war materials", and someone else for airlines. (*Time*, Sept. 30, 1940)

(6) Tax exemption securities in 1937 totaled $50,522,000,000 of which the banks held $20,916,000,000 (*Time*, Oct 3, 1940). In 1940, these totals had increased to $65,000,000,000 and $31,000,000,000. In 1937 the interest amounted to $1,554,000,000. To the man with a $500,000 net income, a 3% tax-exempt security offers the same return after Federal income taxes as a taxable security yielding 10 71%. The opposition in the Senate was based on the effect it would have on the large holdings of the banks But Wendell Willkie in June, 1939, wrote, "If we are going to tax any investments, it would seem more reasonable to tax the safe ones and exempt those that are ventured for the sake of industry".

(7) "By choosing the invested capital procedure of determining tax-free earnings, United States Steel, to illustrate, can earn about $10 per share before any

excess profits taxes would become effective. Steel's current rate of earnings, therefore, is estimated at approximately $11 a share, after all taxes, or nearly $4 more than would be the case if only the average earnings basis had been allowed in tax calculations." (Edson B. Smith in "The Investor", Boston *Herald,* Oct. 5)

"Philip Morris, on the other hand, earns far more than 8% on its capital, would normally choose the base-period option. But because it has forced its way into the big money in the last five years, its average net income in 1936-39 is much less than it will be this year. Philip Morris . . . will therefore get it in the neck." (*Time,* Oct. 14, 1940)

Railroads, utilities, oil, department stores, airlines, will escape the tax, while aircraft, rayon, paper, electrical equipment, will be hard hit (*Time,* Oct 14) Companies that "get it in the neck" will doubtless spend more money on lawyers and lobbyists in the future.

U. S Steel seems to have been as favorably treated in the long struggle over solving the "technical difficulties" as it could have been had it employed skilled attorneys and lobbyists, as would seem to have been necessary to maintain iron and steel exports to Japan in opposition to public opinion (cf I F Stone, The *Nation,* Oct. 5)

U. S. Steel seems to know its way about Washington In the summer of 1917, the financial editor of the N. Y *Herald Tribune* wrote, "It is considered unlikely, however, that steel profits will be cut down to anything like a normal basis as long as the war lasts If 1917 steel earnings could be only half as much as estimated they would still be 3½ times as large as the last full year of peace. The buyer of steel stocks finds much comfort in such reflections as that "

[8] "Corporate profits in 1940 may be from $1,500,000,000 to $2,000,000,000 higher than they were in 1939. But the excess-profits-tax bill was so badly [skilfully] drawn that very little of this money will go to the United States Treasury.

"Consider Tom Girdler's Republic Steel Corporation. This company should make about $17,000,000 in 1940. It averaged only a little more than $7,000,000 a year for the 1936-39 period Its excess-profits tax ought to be half the difference between these figures, or about $5,000,000 But by basing the tax on capital investment, Republic will pay no excess-profits tax. Its capital, plus surplus, plus one-half its debt, add up to $300,000,000. As eight per cent of this amount is $24,000,000, Republic will have to make more than $24,000,000 before any excess-profits tax can be collected.

"Bethlehem Steel average just under $19,000,000 profit per year from 1936 through 1939 This year it should make about $48,000,000 and pay an excess-profits tax of $14,500,000. But "due to the attention of its attorneys and lobbyists to 'technical' details with Congress last summer, it will have only "about a $1,000,000 excess-profits tax to pay" (*New Republic,* Jan 6, 1941)

Wall Street Journal, Feb. 3, 1941, "showed that a list of the first 78 industrial companies to report full-year profits showed net income, after all reserves for taxes, of $410,614,470, compared with $279,814,744 in 1939—a gain of 49%" (*Economic Notes,* March, 1941)

(9) "To succeed in the war we must keep business, big and little, on a profitable scale of prices There is no other hope or prospect for the country" (N. Y. *Sun*, 1917). "Of the thirty billion dollars spent" in the last war under-such men as Baruch and Willard, "fifteen billions constituted 'reasonable profits to stimulate the patriotism of the business interests." 2 5 billions were recovered in excess- and war-profits taxes in 1918, and 1.4 billions in 1919. This time we are not attempting anything like that (Carl Dreher, *Harper's*, Oct. 1940)

"Conscript wealth and what have you got to defend?" asked Westbrook Pegler in his column, Sept. 1940 Said Wendell Willkie, "Wealth in the hands of the few is the only thing democracy has that is worth fighting for".

(10) Senator Holt speaking on politics in national defense, *Congressional Record*, Sept. 23, 1940, pointing to numerous cases of profiteering, warns that those who charge extravagance and waste are smeared as being against defense In the making of contracts, he tells us " . . this so-called speed is only an excuse . . They are not negotiated to increase speed. Time will prove that the war profiteering coming out . . of 1917 look small in comparison "

THE 'WEALTH CONSCRIPTION' HOAX

The confusion in Washington has spread over the country It results from attempts to fool the people, to work them into a lather of hysteria That's the means of winning their votes. They call that 'politics'.

Votes must be won to perpetuate or gain power That is what the big fight is about There are but two ways to make a donkey or an elephant go,—threat or bait Threat of imminent peril is promoted by movies, radio, press Hysteria stampedes voters. As compensation for the multitude, the bait is 'conscript industry', 'conscript wealth'.

The 'conscription of wealth' sections in the Burke-Wadsworth bill are mere political expediencies to get through the draft of manpower, and will then be "eased off", *Business Week* points out September 7.[1]

"So far as this conscription of industry rider, which the Senate tacked on to the military draft bill . . . it was one of those politically inspired measures passed for the obvious purpose of making it easier for some senators to defend their vote for the conscription of young men", remarks "The Investor" columnist in the Boston *Herald*, Sept. 4.

The 'draft industry' measure, reports a leading financial advisory letter, was "apparently not contemplated by the New York group which originated the draft bill, thinking of it as a form of discipline for the irresponsible masses, a 'conservative' measure".

Of the senators who voted 69 to 16 to 'conscript industry', "paying a just price for rentals and materials", Senator Byrnes pointed out it would reassure the constituents of those coming up for reelection that, if the poor voter were conscripted, the rich, too, would be soaked.

The bill, which passed the House 330 to 83, was denounced by some senators as a mere political gesture without teeth. Some false teeth were inserted,—one, a single sentence of some 600 words, had enough holes in it to afford ample professional opportunity for dental lawyers.

Willkie, exploding with indignation, shot off his mouth at this assault on business. Democrats jibed that he had fallen into the trap set for him, losing votes. His politically wise associates claimed that his outburst was responsible for the new false teeth put in to win votes.

The President, in his speech to the Teamsters, which he thought might be 'political', won their votes by pretending he needed power to 'draft industry'. But he had this power already twice over. A rider to an appropriations bill in June provided for it. Moreover, the National Defense Act of 1916, still in effect, provides that "without Congressional action he may forward the Army's munitions procurement program by commandeering industrial plants". (Tobin and Bidwell, "Mobilizing Civilian America", Council on Foreign Relations, 1940. cf Bul #3) [2]

"Even Secretary Wallace, who hitherto has not been lacking in candor, has gone on the stump to repeat the fiction about the need for 'conscripting industry'." (David Lawrence, Sept. 6)

"The way New Deal pitch-men are talking up the subject of drafting capital has inspired some popular suspicions that they may have a plan. They have—and several", hinted at by Mrs. Roosevelt in her column, by Jerome Frank in a speech, by Adolf Berle, and by Leon Henderson.

"The idea of conscripting capital makes an excellent official off-set" to the draft of young men. (Paul Mallon, Aug. 12)

September 20, 1940

NOTES

[1] *Business Week*, Oct. 5, 1940, declared, "Defense Commission officials insist that industry need have no fears regarding conscription of plant". Political commentators and tipsters "inside Washington" assured employers there was nothing dangerous in this "wealth conscription". Once the draft was passed the slogan would be forgotten

[2] "The power to seize plants in time of war is conceded as constitutional, but it is not conceded in times of peace The President's open avowal of the right to commandeer plants in time of peace means that he alone is to be the judge

of what is 'national defense'. Under the vague terms used and under the sort of opinions recently enunciated by the politically-minded attorney general, any man and any business now can be commandeered at any time for any reason. This is dictatorship." (David Lawrence, Sept. 13, 1940)

MORE AND MORE MYSTERIES

"Attorney General Jackson denied categorically that the department of justice was investigating Lundeen", Boake Carter states, September 20 The office of the FBI told him "the 'G man' on the plane was en route to his first assignment. . . . He had no more to do with Lundeen than the cow that jumped over the moon. The 'FBI secretary' was not a secretary, but a typist, setting out on her annual leave. . . . The 'department of justice attorney' was a lawyer from the tax division, without connection whatsoever with the FBI. . . . 'Sen. Lundeen was not under investigation. . . . We are not engaged in spying on senators or congressmen, and we don't intend to. We are doing more right now, as a matter of fact, to prove the Americanism of many unjustly maligned people in these days of hysteria, than to prove their un-Americanism.' "

Pearson and Allen's story (cf Bul #87) is thus refuted. In their column, Sept. 26, they report that Clay Williams refutes their story that he spent the summer lobbying for the tax bill. (cf Bul #88)

The National Federation for Constitutional Liberties has filed suit in the name of Rev. Owen Knox of Detroit and others against the commissioners of the District of Columbia, the Metropolitan Police Department of Washington, the Capitol Police, the National Park Service, and individual police officers.[1] The police are accused of having "beaten, bruised and severely injured several" in dispersing a meeting to protest the conscription bill attended by over 2500 News of this was suppressed, except by LaFollette's *Progressive* Sept. 21, *American Guardian* Sept. 20, *In Fact* Sept. 23.[2]

Agitation for better sanitary facilities in barracks so the boys won't die like flies as they did in the Spanish war will receive more attention. In the last war, though the proportions were reduced, more died from disease, ca 66,000, than from battle injuries, ca 55,000

"An inner exposé of the greatest private propaganda organization ever perfected in this country, the 'Committee on Defend America' (cf

Bul #87) . . . is a painstaking analysis of the men and motives . . . by the skilled newsman Charles G. Ross of the St. Louis *Post Dispatch.*" (*Congressional Record,* Sept. 21, — Paul Mallon, Sept 26)

Senators Clark and Lodge, Sept 26 (AP), were still battling on the floor of the Senate to save our bombers, though the British aviators had already had arrived from overseas to seize them.

"Has America Duped Britain?" subtitled "Will the New Deal's war-like promises, that lulled Great Britain into a false state of security, be a cause for the downfall of Europe?", — "Col. Lindberg's Mail", tens of thousands of letters evidencing popular support, — the sadistic treatment of conscientious objectors by our judiciary and military — all these and more appear in October *Scribner's Commentator.*

"Guilty Men", the publishing sensation of England, which puts the present mess on Baldwin, Chamberlain, Simon, Halifax, et al., is now published in America by Stokes, $1.50. The author, "Cato", is conjectured variously to be Wells, Beaverbrook, Hore-Belisha, et al.

"Seven Mysteries of Europe" are explained by Jules Romains from personal knowledge of men who let France down, — *Sat Eve Post,* Sept 21, ff.

"Why Hitler Wins: A Lesson in Technological Politics", much needed by Americans, suppressed by the press, smothered by Whitehall and Washington propaganda, is by Carl Dreher in October *Harpers* September 27, 1940

NOTES

[1] Justice Wheat granted "an injunction to restrain the Metropolitan Police and the District Commissioners who were charged with arresting leaflet distributors and violently breaking up peaceful meetings and public prayers recently held in Washington by the anti-conscription lobby in opposition to the Burke-Wadsworth Bill" (*American Guardian,* Sept. 27)   The Rev Mr Knox declared, "The effect of this victory is not a local matter . . .   The National Federation for Constitutional Liberties is proud to be able to make so substantial a contribution to the defense of democracy and the real traditions of America."

[2] *Friday,* Oct 4, 1940, gave the matter six pages, with dramatic photographs of police brutality. "The press, almost without exception, suppressed or dismissed with scanty mention news of protest movements, police disruption of an all-night prayer vigil, and violation of elementary civil rights. . . Draft foes, entering the Capitol, were forced to take off insignia and buttons "

HELL BENT FOR ELECTION

Anything for votes, for votes are power. That's the American way. Roosevelt offers a stick of candy, while Willkie promises Churchill's "Sweat, tears, and blood". People prefer taffy.[1]

The foreign policy of each is essentially the same because both serve the same masters. One must go to Lord Lothian's British quarterly, The *Round Table,* to find in advance a forecast of what American policy and opinion is to be. (cf Buls #7, 22, 41, 44)

In the September issue, just arrived, the supposititious American writes, "Roosevelt or Willkie . . . will go just as far in the direction of aid to Britain as public opinion will permit him . . . The larger mass of national opinion is still . . . strong enough to block really forthright and speedy action in aid of Britain. The sale or transfer of the destroyers . . . would be a bold step, only slightly behind actual belligerency . . . American policy flows along and responds primarily to events in Europe, secondarily only to domestic politics. The same will be true after election day. . . '' Suppose we decide to transport and convoy refugee ships; suppose one is sunk "

Sinkings, after all our scares, have failed to bring us in. But when the flag is fired on, that's another thing Political considerations may determine whether this will be before or after election It is within the President's power to put the flag where such an incident is sure to occur Roosevelt croons, "I hate war now more than ever",[2] Willkie chants, "I'll never lead the U. S. into war".[3] Wilson entered upon war expecting to offer moral and economic aid, but prepared to send a million men. "It was not necessary to desire the war in order to bring it to a head, if only care was taken to make the preparations so complete as to make war unavoidable", Veblen sapiently observed.[4]

Promoting this war with Roosevelt are his once hated 'economic royalists'. Their press is all for war, and ominously is more completely for Willkie, 90%, than it was for Landon, 80%. Working for war, paradoxically, they prevent Willkie's election, insure Roosevelt's.

Newspaper and radio commentators have been given the same slant In a symposium of Washington correspondents, only one, Kenneth Crawford, declared the election would go as in 1936. The others wrinkled their brows, dodged the issue, or plumped for Willkie.

Scribner's Commentator almost alone is countering Washington and

Whitehall propaganda, making a brave stand "against the insidious wiles of foreign influence" as George Washington put it.

"The Bum's-Rush to War" is General Hugh Johnson's theme in the September issue. Like "Cato", he "points the accusing finger at the 'honorable men' who are trying to involve our democracy in an international crap game played with loaded dice". "Mr. Roosevelt is committed to the hilt to this course of 'War Now'. . . . Let's stay out until we are ready to get in. Let this be America's watchword: 'Complete Defense and 'No War' now'."

Senator LaFollette and Johnson were first to address the new organization sponsored by such outstanding and diversely interested citizens as Henry Ford, John T. Flynn, Jay C. Hormel, Mrs. Alice Roosevelt Longworth, Hanford MacNider, Eddie Rickenbacker, Gen. Robert E. Wood. Write 1806 Board of Trade Bldg., Chicago, for program, buttons, stickers of the "America First Committee".[6]

The "Defend America by Defending Britain" committee's meeting in Chicago, (General Johnson, Sept. 23) was "harrangued by several eminent breast-beating war criers. Our perennial breast beating Boadicea, Dorothy Thompson, was put on to do her well-known war dance."

"This administration is headed straight for war", Johnson says, and urged Willkie to take "squarely to the American people . . . the stark issue of war or peace".[6] But Willkie can't. He is hog-tied by the people he is working for, as Mencken explains in his *Sun* editorial, Sept. 25, under the title "Heil Roosevelt".[7]

"The collapse of the Willkie campaign, though it may wring many a tender heart, is certain not to be put down as unexpected. . . . It is not, however, his failure to grapple effectively with such riddles that has ruined the hon. gentleman, but rather Roosevelt's bold and adept working of the war scare. That scare, in fact, is largely his own handiwork. . . . If it is the first function of a demagogue to raise up a bugaboo, and the second to convince the boobs that he can save them from it, then he has demonstrated his virtuosity. . . .

"Unhappily for Willkie . . . nearly all his partisans among the economic royalists were just as enthusiastic for the same crusade, and full of preparations to make even more out of it than they made out of the last one. . . . Thus poor Willkie had to go along, and in his speech of acceptance he not only did not challenge Roosevelt's warmongering, but actually tried to go it one better. . . . So the poor lad took to the stump with his withers already wrung."[8]

The President believes that he was drafted for a third term because his fellow citizens believed him to be the one and indispensable. Such self-deception may be excusable. But now he wants to appoint his successor,[9] and Wallace, he tells us, is the only one qualified. How long would it take Willkie to arrive at such self-confidence?

"Most Democrats here are relying on the President's handling of the foreign situation to keep them in power another four years" (Ehrlich).

"Mr. Roosevelt seeks to perpetuate himself in power by frightening us", charged Representative Hoffman (*Congressional Record,* April 23). Roosevelt knows the potency of fear In 1933 he said, "The only thing we have to fear is fear".[10]

Roosevelt's "war adventure has cost 14 billions, and we are hardly at the beginning of it", Mencken, Sept. 8, reminds us. And it may run to 100 billions in the next four years. Would Willkie save a few billions?

Let none believe that we would unduly influence any free American to vote for one candidate or another. Such guilt shall not rest upon our conscience. Still in doubt and seeking enlightenment, we grasp at straws, one day at Willkie, another at Roosevelt.

Fervently we hope the result may be so close that there may be inaugurated in 1940 one touched with some humility, with some faith in his own people, some skepticism toward foreign power politics, some hesitancy about shedding American blood in Asiatic waters or on African or Brazilian soil, with desire to "Save America First".[11]
September 28, 1940

NOTES

[1] "The Hon Wendell Willkie's grisly warning . . . that there are splitting headaches ahead for the American people got no applause from his immediate hearers, and there seems to be little disposition to ponder it in the country at large. The intellectually underprivileged have been fed on stick-candy so long that their systems reject all other ailment" (H. L. Mencken, Aug. 25, 1940). "Roosevelt's way you get sick later on. Willkie's way you gag immediately. For the life of us, we can't see why American business men want to have a Wall Street tycoon try his hand administering to the American people a stiff dose of defense castor oil unflavored by funny money. For ten years the American people haven't been able to stand peace without funny money. How

can they take conscription without it and under a business president who can't even croon?" (Dennis, *Weekly Foreign Letter*, Sept. 19, 1940)

(2) Norman Thomas, the third and perennial candidate for president, warned that the American people "will be exceedingly ill-advised" if they let the declarations of the two major candidates "lull them into false security". "That the candidates have thought it necessary to make such declarations is a tribute to popular opposition to war. . . . To make these pledges meaningful, these candidates for the vast and increasing powers of the Presidency must commit themselves to a program consistent with their pledges to keep our peace — as their programs are not. War is not a sudden or accidental phenomenon; it is not something to be accepted or rejected at the last moment It is the logical consequence of the acts that have gone before."

The war spirit in Washington grows, though labeled 'defense'. Involvement begins to mean a "shooting war", we are told by a Washington financial advisory service in their private letter to clients They tell us that Roosevelt assumes reelection, but until after election will be reticent about plans for defense collaboration with Britain After election things will move much faster. The generals, of course, glad to sound the note of imminent danger, which increases their importance and the money they get, are now acting with the Administration's assent.

(3) "When I say that I mean it", added Willkie. "I believe that the United States should give all possible help to Great Britain, short of war", he continued, "and when I say short of war I mean short of war".

The tone is reminiscent of the Bellman in Lewis Carroll's "The Hunting of the Snark", — "Just the place for a Snark! I have said it thrice, what I tell you three times is true." — " 'Tis the song of the Jubjub! The proof is complete, if only I've stated it thrice "

Said Willkie further, "And when I am President, you will never hear of any great event after it has happened". He's going to keep it a secret, before and after?

(4) Meantime, while the candidates wrangled about who would best keep us out of war while extending all aid to Britain, the war was taking its toll in America, — army and navy airplane crashes weekly, three explosions of powder mills in New Jersey within a few weeks.

(5) Charles G. Ross in the St Louis *Post-Dispatch*, Oct 27, 1940, summarizes his investigation of the "America First Committee" in September. General Robert E. Wood, Chairman of the Board of Sears Roebuck, is perhaps the leading spirit. To counter the efforts to get us into war of the White Committee, it has raised money for newspaper advertising, radio and meetings But it lacks the organization and the skilled publicists that have been enlisted for the White Committee by its Wall Street sponsors Sidney Hertzberg, who has been editor of *Uncensored* has recently assumed charge of its publicity.

"No Foreign War Committee", New York City or Cedar Rapids, Iowa, organized late in December, started off even more vigorously under the chairmanship of Verne Marshall of the Cedar Rapids *Gazette* which put up the money for full page advertisements in 50 newspapers throughout the country appealing for Christmas gifts to keep us out of war.

(6) "Not war for democracy, but war or democracy is the choice before the American people", said Norman Thomas over the radio, Sept. 21. "It is time to face facts and to use words correctly. If all we want is a 'good' dictatorship, or an American dictatorship, rather than a 'bad' or foreign dictatorship, let us be men enough to say so. If we want war, let us say so But let us not dare to talk about the possibility of throwing 130 million Americans into the incalculable suffering and loss of distant war and of still saving democracy. There would be no half-way war. . . . So great is modern war's destruction, so essential is virtual dictatorship to waging it, and probably to the task of rebuilding when at last the guns are stilled, that it may be doubted how soon any nation, caught in it, can establish democracy. . . The choice is war or democracy " There is little to choose between the policies of the two major candidates, as Thomas points out. Of Willkie he says, "He likes the song but not the way his rival sings it!"

(7) "The fundamental difficulty of the honorable gentleman, of course, lies in the fact that he has no real issue, and appears incapable of framing one", says Mencken, Sept. 8. "When he swallowed the Roosevelt foreign policy all the rest of the New Deal rumble-bumble went down with it, and he has since presented the spectacle of a man choking on his own false teeth. So choking, he is estopped from hollering, which, in a candidate for office under democracy, is a burden almost as demoralizing as a sense of honor. . . . I am not arguing here that his position on the war is wrong . I am merely arguing that it hamstrings him in his campaign, and leaves him sawing the air."

(8) "To those who hoped . . . that the Republican campaign might be based on opposition to Roosevelt's foreign policy, Willkie has been a bitter disappointment. . To those voters who do not see U. S interests primarily in terms of the defense of Britain, the campaign is no contest. . . . That the American electorate is being cheated of an opportunity to decide its foreign policy in this election is obvious and on the record. If it is also being denied proper consideration of specific steps through actual collusion between the two candidates, the U. S. has achieved a unique dictatorship, one in which two parties go through the motions of opposing each other." (*Uncensored*, Sept. 28, '40)

(9) "Observers . . ask whether any President should be permitted to succeed himself, either for a second or a third term, if he allows his nomination to be brought about by what Woodrow Wilson once termed 'illicit means', namely, the use of presidential power to influence delegates. "Certainly the President not only brought about his own nomination for a third term through the means of officeholders and others obligated to him, but he dictated the nomination of the vice-presidential candidate, Henry Wallace. Shall American Presidents be allowed by the electorate to use their offices to continue themselves or their own choices in power? This is more than the third-term issue It is a

question of truly democratic and representative government." (David Lawrence)

"We declare it to be an unwritten law of this republic that no man shall be eligible for a third term of the Presidential office." This from "the Democratic national platform of 1896" was the basis on which "Joseph Ferreira, a New Bedford attorney, petitioned the Supreme Judicial Court for a restraining order to bar the name of President Roosevelt from the ballot in Massachusetts". In his brief, he claimed that it would violate the "unwritten law", the established "usages and customs of the American people".

(10) This note from his First Inaugural Address contrasts with Mr Roosevelt's present attitude. As a contributor to *Unity*, July 1, 1940, says, "The President is crying 'fire' in a crowded theatre, with the fire still many blocks away".

(11) Events since February 26 have justified the article in the Chicago *Daily Tribune* of that date under the headline "President Sets Cap for Role of Peace Arbiter. Eyes Third Term as Means to End", which began, "President Roosevelt, it was learned today, has bared to several Democratic officials the ambition to become the pacificator of Europe and Asia either as President of the United States or as the appointee of his successor to represent America in the peace conference that will end the war . . Unless the United States enters the war, Mr. Roosevelt cannot be assured of a hand in the peace . . . Mr. Roosevelt can look forward to a place at the peace conference, provided he or a President of his choice occupies the White House at the time."

DICTATORSHIP TODAY

The President, a great humanitarian, desirous of bringing about 'orderly processes everywhere', is unconsciously preparing the way for a dictator. He doesn't know he wants to be a dictator, nor do most of us know he is. It is a question if Mussolini meant to be. But that is unimportant. The way of the transgressor is hard The road to hell is paved with good intentions, Dr. Johnson told us. My Presbyterian forbears taught me the pavement was skulls of innocents

And Webster reminds us, "Good intentions do really sometimes exist when constitutional restraints are disregarded. There are men in all ages who mean to exercise power usefully; but who mean to exercise it. They mean to govern well; but they mean to govern They promise to be kind masters; but they mean to be masters. They think there need be little restraint upon themselves. Their notion of the public interest is apt to be quite closely connected with their own exercise of authority. They may not always understand their own motives."(1)

What with shifting our frontier from The Channel to Dong Dang and points west and east, what with 'dedicating' the long finished, 'inspecting' the yet to be begun, our President has been too occupied to give much attention to domestic affairs or make 'political' speeches. But he has taken a leaf from the royal ladies of England and the dictators of the totalitarian states on how to increase his popularity and dramatize his good intentions. [2]

Roosevelt's "phenomenal blind spots", on 'political' speeches and unpleasant news, amazed Paul Mallon (Oct. 6). "With an almost straight face, he excused himself from comment on" the Japanese foreign minister's promise to declare war on the U. S. if we attempted to preserve the status quo in the Pacific, "by saying he had never heard of it. But a few seconds later . . . asked if it were true that Germany and Italy are trying to defeat him in the election, he pulled from his pocket . . . and read . . . to the conference in detail" Matthews' dispatch. Rome immediately denied interest in the election. Matthews, ordered to leave Italy, explained it was "because Roosevelt made a political issue of my story and the Axis feels it must answer". (AP, Oct. 7)

Gen. Hugh Johnson burst out, Oct. 6, "This is the third term party's most treasured bunk — that Hitler wants Willkie and therefore that the latter's candidacy is fifth column stuff. Haven't we got real issues?"

Roosevelt's bid for the support of Hitler-haters boomeranged, as Harold Brayman explained, Oct. 8 (Boston *Transcript*). "The President apparently did not expect the public to be agile enough mentally to see that if Hitler and Mussolini do want him defeated they must certainly know that the way to bring that about would not be to announce it."

The politician uses issues only to get votes. But there are other ways. 'Defense' prompted by hysterical fear involves haste and waste. [3] On defense projects carpenters are getting $16 a day, plumbers $30, double for overtime. Their votes are won. [4]

Industrialists, bankers, erstwhile 'economic royalists', are bribed with enormous profits They are getting what they want without the help of their hired man Willkie. Democratic billions prevail over Republican millions. With 60% of the popular vote last time, Roosevelt won all but four of the electoral college. But he had only the WPA then. [5] For a fourth term he may achieve better than 90% of the votes, — for less than which Hitler or Mussolini would hardly permit an election. [6]

Dictators at first have a hard time winning a majority. But as they can implement promises and threats, their percentage of the popular vote increases. Last June, Mencken prophesied, "No Republican candidate will be able to stand up to Roosevelt. . . . He will have the boobs in a frenzy of fear, and . . . the choice before us will be reduced to the solemn privilege of voting 'Ja'."[7]

Roosevelt and Hitler came into office at about the same time through a popular revolt against the stupid blundering of their predecessors Like Mussolini, the pioneer in their art, they have strengthened their control through golden radio promises.[8]

The dramatic, supplemented by pageantry, enters into the art of fooling the people, and national unity is finally achieved through regimentation of the beguiled Gangsters stand in with those who can win popular support. The big city bosses know their way. They preserve the City Council as Hitler his Reichstag and Mussolini his Senate. The old forms of government must be preserved, elections and legislatures, to confirm or confer extraordinary powers, because of emergency.

"Human beings", Daniel Webster foresaw, "will generally exercise power when they can get it; and they will exercise it most undoubtedly, in popular governments, under pretense of public safety."

Thomas Jefferson, refusing to be drafted for a third term on grounds of emergency in 1809, said, "If the principle of rotation is a sound one, as I conscientiously believe it to be, with respect to this office, no pretext should ever be permitted to dispense with it, because there never will be a time when real difficulties will not exist, and furnish a plausible pretext for dispensation."[9]

Franklin Roosevelt near the close of his first term said, "In 34 months we have built up new instruments of public power. In the hands of a people's government, this power is wholesome and proper. But in the hands of political puppets of an economic autocracy such power would provide shackles for the liberties of the people."

Now Roosevelt is even more convinced that these great powers should not pass from the one indispensable to another except of his choosing

A hundred legislative acts have conferred upon the President powers not specified in the Constitution (cf "On to Dictatorship", Bul #38), and many of Wilson's wartime powers have not been repealed. Twice in the past year the President has declared emergencies bringing into effect war powers.[10] David Lawrence, Oct. 15, wrote: "Mr. Roosevelt has created a deep distrust among . . . citizens, who believe he has emphasized crises in our foreign relations" to promote his third term "Every Gallup Poll has shown that sensational speeches and dramatic actions by the President in foreign policy have sent upward the curve of Mr. Roosevelt's political strength."

"This is the pattern of dictatorship", declared Willkie at Syracuse, October 15, "the usurpation of power by manufactured emergencies, the circumvention of the Legislature, the capture of the courts. . . These are the last steps on the road to absolute power "

Most of our Federal legislators for nearly eight years have ridden into office on the wave of Roosevelt's ability to win votes. Consequently they are responsive to his behests.

Legislation is initiated for this subservient Congress by the executive. Bills are drawn up by the President's assistants, on order.[11]

A tax bill ordered by the President must constitutionally originate in the House. "Technical difficulties" brought out in public hearings result in its being worked over secretly in committee with lobbyists and lawyers representing those who will be most affected by it. The so-called excess profits tax bill (cf Bul #88) ran to five hundred pages. At the last moment amendments were introduced running to several hundred pages.

The House and Senate will have passed quite different bills, which must then go to a conference committee supposed to harmonize the intent of the two legislative bodies. The choice of appointees by the presiding officers of each house, the secrecy of their procedure, their accessibility to lobbyists and lawyers and representatives of the Administration, afford opportunity for the legislative function to be usurped by those who have the ear.

How the Administration may secretly legislate itself additional powers was brought out in a colloquy in connection with the Overton-Russell amendment for conscripting industry. (cf Bul #90)

Senator Downey protested he couldn't understand the amendment. Senator Russell, the author, called his attention to a similar provision already incorporated in one of the defense acts. (cf Bul #25) Senator Wheeler informed them that this later provision "was written into the bill in conference and nobody in the Senate or House knew it was in the bill". This Russell and Downey admitted,[12] and Senator Maloney added that they were not the only senators who didn't know what was put into bills in conference after they had left the floor.

"If the Congress that makes the law finds strange writing on the statute books, how much more liable is the citizen to be astonished", editorially remarks the *Sat Eve Post*, Oct. 5, commenting on this "The power of Executive Government increases. Running ahead of it, with the ecstasy of a revelationist, is a senator named Pepper. Why think any more? Let the Government think. Let the people desist and be governed. . . . And . . . he says: 'If that be dictatorship, make the most of it.' "[13]

A Huey Long dictator would see in the 'conference' method great opportunities to put across decrees with a semblance of legality. Have a henchman introduce a discordant amendment so the bill has to go to conference. See that the proper men are on the committee. Write into the bill the desired clause and rush it through. It's all legal. But neither the legislative body nor the people need know of or approve it.

The executive today brings about situations, stage events, cultivates an emotional moral atmosphere in which hate, the motive power, can be directed or diverted.[14] "The means of communication . . . are loaded with propaganda . . . appeals to emotion . . . what to think, what to believe, whom to love and whom to hate, all with intent not to inform the public mind, but to manipulate and possess public opinion" (*Sat Eve Post*, Oct. 5). The fear of imminent peril established, an emergency is declared so that extraordinary executive powers, granted for a time of actual danger, become effective.[15]

Popular attention is diverted from the enormous power to control economic resources and expenditure, greater than ever held by any other man in the history of the world. Other sources of danger are kept before the people, — enemy submarines on our coasts, communists or fifth columnists within our walls, the danger of some other 'form of government' and the 'overthrow' of ours.[16] 'Emergency' makes it possible or imperative for the executive to act unconstitutionally, to change the 'form of government' while the people patriotically applaud their savior.[17]

Wilson to protect us against the bandit Villa put the country into war in Mexico, to protect us against the communists put American troops into Siberia and Russia without consulting Congress. McKinley was forced by Hearst and Hanna to acts that led to war with Spain which Congress had to support. False news, suppressed news, deceived the people. And it has happened since. It is happening now.

"This now power-happy intelligence representing itself to be your Government has the daring to present to the American Congress what in Europe is called the 'fait accompli' ", editorializes the *Sat Eve Post*, Oct. 12. "There is a disaster worse than war. We are concerned only with . . . how your Government, instead of telling the people what it meant to do or what it was doing until it was done, by indirection, by subterfuge, by cleverness, by beating the law, uncontrollably pursuing its own will, did involve this country in the European war it was resolved to stay out of."

"America's present peril lies in no lack of strength, or of resources, or of courage. Its real danger lies in the chance that, to meet the totalitarian challenge, it may be forced to adopt totalitarian disciplines. Its great and unique good fortune is that Americans can still choose whether it will or not." (*Life*, June 10, 1940)

Our present representatives and senators are either oblivious of or complacent to this creeping dictatorship. Most of them are intent on getting their share of war appropriations for their clients or districts.[18] Local newspapers everywhere reflect that their representatives have won for their districts war contracts, some of the ten or fifteen billions that is to be spent. And that is what the voters seem to appreciate.

Learn how your senators and representatives voted on the acts that you objected to Support those that voted in accordance with your wishes. That is the least an intelligent voter can do.

There is a little group in the House and in the Senate who deserve encouragement and support. They have stood boldly against this drift to dictatorship and imperialism, against meddling in foreign affairs. They believe that we should give every attention to building our defensive forces without hysteria and waste, and meantime attend to our own business and avoid stirring up trouble in distant countries

Re-elect them to show that there are still some free men who stand for honesty and sanity. A larger vote, even if they do not win, will mean a little more caution on the part of those who do.

You still have a vote. The secret ballot offers opportunity to exert some choice, though 'safe' men on both sides have probably been nominated. We are hell bent for war, for dictatorship and totalitarianism, because of hysterical fear promoted by our government and our press. We are scared because we are dumb driven cattle.[19]

Let us stand against Hysteria and Waste and for a Sound Defense. *October 16, 1940*

NOTES

[1] Speaking of Mr. and Mrs. Roosevelt, H G. Wells in his "The Fate of Homo Sapiens" doubts "if these two fine, active minds have ever enquired how it is they know what they know and think as they do. . . They have the disposition of all politicians the world over to deal only with made opinion They have never enquired how it is that opinion is made . . A mere fraction of our knowledge is self-taught. What we know is nine-tenths hearsay. We have heard, we have read. The stuff in our heads was mainly put there by society."

[2] "So far in his campaign only two speeches have touched at all on any domestic, political or economic problem. Those were the addresses before the teamsters' union at Washington in which he promised lavishly to aid labor and the one at Chickamauga Dam in which he discussed the TVA and the power question During the 80-day period since the Democratic National Convention" "the President has made 12 trips out of Washington which have kept him, Harold Brayman tells us, away from the White House for 43 days against his presence there 37 days." (Boston *Transcript*, Oct. 8)

The President's twenty minutes in a steel mill may do something to stimulate our defense because of his intimate knowledge of metallurgical processes. But Mr. Willkie has challenged this On the President's trip to Norfolk, "A newspaper correspondent accompanying the President asked a foreman in one of the plants how they were getting on with national defense and to his astonishment heard the foreman reply: 'We were getting along fine until they pulled this inspection on us and then we had to stop work for 10 days to get everything shipshape to be inspected' " (Brayman, Oct. 8).

[3] Camp Edwards was originally estimated to cost about 7 millions. In November, incomplete, the estimate was raised to 17 millions. On Jan 16, 1941, Rep. Albert J. Engel of Michigan charged on the floor of the House "waste and extravagance in the construction of army housing at Camp Edwards . . On the basis of expenditures to date . . . army housing . . . would cost 70 per cent more than last summer's $466,371,000" or a total of $766,000,000. The final cost of Camp Edwards he put at $29,000,000. The contract had been awarded to T. J Walsh of Idaho who had in June, 1940, "contributed $2500 to the Democratic national campaign fund . . and . . . $2500 more to a Roosevelt organization in New York state " The pathetic waste of time, lumber and nails was related by a worker at the camp, A De Lorenzo, M I T.,

'33, in a letter to the Boston *Herald*, December 11, 1940. The lumber had been hauled from Alabama and Oregon. Meantime vast quantities of New England white pine hurricane lumber near at hand remained unused. In January, Governor Saltonstall was appealing to the Federal Government for its use February 26, 1941, AP, the army admitted the cost of Camp Edwards and Fort Devens, Mass. would be 31 millions above the original estimate but blamed the weather as well as their own change of plans The cost for construction at Edwards had risen to $900, at Devens for additions and improvements to $1000 per man That means that probably more than 40 or 50 millions of dollars will have been poured into Fort Devens since 1914. If that were figured in, the cost per man would be several thousand. But the lavish expenditure in the south for filling in swamp sites for cantonments, exalted prices for previously worthless real estate for new airports and factories, makes these things in the north seem like Yankee thrift.

Sept 21, 1940 a leading Washington financial letter predicted, "Direct negotiation of cantonment-building contracts, not public bidding, will be used largely, for sake of speed . . . and at the risk of scandals." Representative Holmes of Massachusetts, Sept. 28 (AP), criticizing the new Washington airport, charged that it was "a conspicuous monument to the waste and inefficiency by which the New Deal has saddled a 50 billion-dollar debt on the country" Holmes said it would cost $16,000,000 when complete and that "competent engineers" had estimated it could be built for $4,746,000.

This extravagance is inevitable on the negotiated contract on the cost plus basis The more waste, the higher the cost, the greater percentage profit to the contractor. After the last war, extensive investigations brought out scandalous waste and profits.

At Nitro in 1917-18, building on the cost plus 10% plan, contractors, to make more money on materials sold the government, hauled good lumber from the boxcars direct to gigantic fires which were kept burning three weeks at a time Carpenters testified more lumber was burned than was used in construction. Carloads of linen, hay and bread were dumped in the fires Carloads of steel and copper wire were dumped to grade and fill in ravines, and when investigation threatened, the records were burned.

But while it is going on, any attempt to attract attention is hushed up as unpatriotic. An editorial in the Boston *Herald*, Jan 20, 1941, entitled "Waste? 'Hell-an'-Maria' ", quiets the hysterical saying it is going on all over the country and tells how in the investigation after the war, Charles Dawes just back from France, where as purchasing agent he knew all about it, silenced and ended the investigation by his ejaculation "Hell an' Maria   . We had a war on hand". Such explanations seem entirely satisfactory to the American people who are to sweat to pay for it. They are easily bluffed.

Oscar Ameringer in his autobiography recalls how this labor racket was worked twenty years ago "Sam Gompers' partnership between capital and labor . . had worked marvelously during the War because the 'ten-per-cent-plus' clause in government contracts did not worry about cost — in fact, the higher the cost, the greater the plus. As to how ten-per-cent-plus had harmoniously united the interests of capital and labor, these two examples will suffice. I called on a friend employed by a plumbing firm doing work at Fort Sill. When I located him, he and another plumber were painting a small radiator. One held the small tin can of paint, the other held a half-inch brush. Both moved with the deliberation of the slow-motion movie. When I said, 'Why don't you fellows use at least a two-inch brush on the job?' the answer was, 'Oh, yeah? And get bounced by the boss?' On the same occasion I saw a carpenter acquaintance cut out two feet from the middle of a twelve-foot board and throw the two ends on the handy scrap pile. When I asked him why he hadn't sawed the two feet from the end of the board, his reply was, 'Say, where have you been living? Don't you know that the more we waste the bigger the profit for the boss? Do you think I'm going to be bounced for being stingy with Uncle Sam's dough?' " (Oscar Ameringer — "If You Don't Weaken", Holt, 1940, p 360)

(4) Quarter page ads in Boston papers early in October, 1940, sought thousands of additional carpenters at $1.17 per hour, time-and-a-half on Saturdays, double time for overtime and Sundays. Shortly thereafter Boston taxicab companies advertised for women drivers, so many men had departed to earn carpenters' wages at Camp Edwards on Cape Cod The local carpenters' union affiliated with the A F.L. raised its initiation fee to $75, two or three times the normal fee elsewhere and about all a man could net in two or three weeks work The Administration, encouraging such rackets and destroying the power of less corruptible leaders, is following the practice, with labor unions, of totalitarian countries.

A month later, just after election, the general manager for the Walsh Construction Company, which has the contract for Camp Edwards, was reported to have said, "We've been letting out some men. . . . It's a weeding-out process. From a peak of nearly 20,000 workmen the job is now down to about 15,000." The day before, Maj -Gen. James A Woodruff, commanding officer of the 1st corps army area, Boston, in a speech complained "that there were still no barracks at Camp Edwards . . . 3000 . . . workmen were laid off with the announcement that the peak of the construction job . . . had passed". (Boston *Herald*, Nov. 14, 1940)

(5) Herbert Hoover, Nov. 1, 1940 (AP), in a nation wide broadcast "noted that the Department of Labor has said there are about 4,500,000 persons on the federal payroll throughout all its agencies and asked 'Do you think that, in another four years, you have a chance to defeat such a presidential power for himself or his successor?' "

(6) "Powers ten times as great as any executive ever previously wielded in this country have been lodged in the White House by recent laws· powers over all classes of people, powers to drive them out of business by taxation or tariff interpretations, powers to destroy their savings through alteration of the

value of money, powers over their wages and hours and old age benefits, powers over their livelihoods through benefits, patronage and relief, powers to make profitable the friendly industries, construction companies, etc, and thus destroy their competitors, powers over their private lives through the vast espionage systems of the income tax bureau and the FBI — but above all the powers over credit, money and the economic lifeblood of the nation. No citizen is immune from the grasp or threat of government today.

"An unscrupulous politician — say one no more unscrupulous in regard to conscientious restraints than the late Huey Long — could perpetuate himself in office indefinitely [Frank Roosevelt's friend, Frank Hague, would know how] by the mere threat of aggressive use of these powers He could drive newspapers out of business by his political enforcement of the wage and hour laws and other pinching He could prevent radio from talking about him by using the power to deny licenses through his appointees on the federal communications commission. He could destroy congressmen who oppose him by the same artifices he uses on business opposition, doubly strengthened as far as politicians are concerned because they cannot face the scourge of devastating propaganda, tax scandals and organized slur campaigns. He could subdue any opposition not in the lunatic class by pressure never discernible to the public

"These things are obviously not evident to the two-thirds of the people who voted in the *Fortune* poll, but they explain tersely why many fair-minded authorities suspect democracy itself can fall by this single popular attitude toward a 'silly and outworn tradition'. Don't forget they still hold elections in Germany and Russia " (Paul Mallon, Sept. 26, 1940)

(7) "Four years more of Roosevelt will see the United States converted into a military despotism hard to distinguish from an Asiatic empire, and no one will have any right that the idealists at Washington are bound to respect Of all the virtues that used to enter into the make-up of a good citizen there will be none left: the places of all will be taken by a new one, to wit, the virtues of voting right Those who do it will be rewarded from the public treasury; those who fail will be mulcted. Consider what happened at the Democratic National Convention at Chicago. It was, in form and substance, precisely like the Reichstag sessions that Hitler calls at long intervals There was only one choice before the so-called delegates they could vote 'Ja' or they could be damned. The step from ostensible representatives of the people voting 'Ja' to the people themselves voting 'Ja' is a very short one . . If Roosevelt gets his war, it will already be firm official dogma that questioning anything that he and his associated charlatans do is a sin against the Holy Ghost." (H. L. Mencken, Aug. 25, 1940)

(8) "Power is given to rulers for promised returns in equivalent satisfactions." It cannot be "assumed that a Hitler, a Huey Long, a Mayor Hague, maintain their power contrary to the wishes of their people. . . Machiavelli was quite clear that the ruler is doomed who does tread on the toes of his people . Satisfaction is vital to the retention of power " The besieger of a city

used to recruit with promise of loot. Today the political leader, and it is especially true in a democracy, must reward his followers with jobs to hold them. ("What Makes Lives", p 115)

"The President would never have made his speech [Charlottesville] if he didn't think the people of America were ready to follow him into war to back up the assertion of the principles of freedom. . . . Unquestionably the President feels he is keeping abreast of public opinion and that America is about ready to take up arms in defense of human liberty. . . . Mr. Roosevelt recalls how President Wilson mobilized the opinion of the whole world behind the American entry into the war." (David Lawrence, June 12, 1940)

(9) The British had been treating us like recalcitrant colonials Perhaps Jefferson sensed a war coming. Perhaps he stepped aside to let his successor lick them Jefferson realized that, "For us to attempt to reform all Europe and bring them back to principles of morality, and a respect for the equal rights of nations, would show us to be only maniacs of another character."

(10) "President Roosevelt has signed new law legislation giving him authority to take over war materials and supplies which have been sold, but not delivered, to a foreign power" (AP, Oct 11). With this he can seize the 100 airplanes sold to Sweden, the machine tools for Russia held up in San Francisco.

(11) Ramsay Muir in his third edition of "How Britain Is Governed" enlarges on the growth of bureaucratic power and the effectiveness with which it is controlled, the dictatorship of the Cabinet and how badly it is used, the vices of electoral systems, the powerlessness of the House of Commons.

"Dictatorship in America begins next weekend", wrote David Lawrence, September 24, 1940, on the eve of Congress' adjournment "It may be benevolently intended, but technically it will be as complete as in any totalitarian state in the world. For when Congress adjourns there is no constitutional way by which it can be called back into session of its own initiative. Only the President, under our Constitution, can call an extra session. . . It has been said again and again that vast powers can be delegated to a President without fear of dictatorship because at any time Congress can be called back and these powers revoked. But if public sentiment were critical of a President, and even if there were a unanimous desire on the part of members of Congress themselves to come back into session, the Chief Executive, fearing a revocation of his powers, could actually keep Congress from coming into session until the date of opening of the next regular session . .   The truth is Mr. Roosevelt regards Congress as superfluous and unnecessary "

(12) "Senator Russell replied: 'I do not know where it went in. . . . It is in the law at the present time.' Then Senator Downey said. 'I have a total sense of inadequacy in dealing with the multifarious problems which now flow before us. I do not pretend to know more than a small part of what is happening in Washington, or even in the Senate.' Senator Maloney gave him comfort, saying 'I ask the senator from California not to chide himself too much, because he is in pretty much the same position as a number of other

senators. . . . So that he may be sure there is no need to censure himself, I wish to say that members of the Senate and members of the House have not been able, at least for the most part, to find out how this language got into the naval bill ' " (*Sat Eve Post,* Oct. 5, 1940)

(13) The Senate was discussing adjournment in October, 1940. Senator Clark suggested they might better go home, for after every weekend the President "comes back with a recommendation for another four-or-five-billion-dollar appropriation. . . . By staying in session we have cost the American people some $15,000,000,000 . . we have not been able to prevent the President from diverting one-seventh of our Navy . . in the absence of the Congress. . . . We might as well adjourn and go home, because the President will do what he pleases anyway "

(14) Americans are being "terrorized into believing that this is our war and that we will be attacked if we remain neutral", Senator Walsh said in a radio address, Oct. 18, 1940. "No public man has dared to advocate openly and directly our entrance into the European war because they know the American people would resent it . . Their method is more subtle, better conceived, but they have an eye always on the ultimate goal. Many European nations have no choice between war and peace We are not presented with any such alternatives We are protected not by 20 miles of channel but by 3000 miles of sea We have no problem of over-population We need no colonies We seek none We retain no longings to avenge ancient wrongs "

No opportunity to instill hate is missed by the President. Every speech he makes, even dedicating a school, permits gentle persuasion "In these schools and other American schools, the children of today and of future generations will be taught without censorship or restriction, the facts of current history or current knowledge. Their text books will not be burned by a dictator who disagrees with them; their teachers will not be banished by a ruler whom they have offended", Roosevelt said, October 5, 1940, dedicating three Dutchess County schools October 8, congratulating the Boston *Herald* on its Book Fair, he repeated this idea "I like the idea of a Book Fair. It emphasizes that while in some countries books are being burned and free speech is being suppressed, in our own land we still have complete freedom to write our opinions, to have them published and to have them read And also we have complete freedom to read the opinions of others " We cannot, of course, comment that this burning of books in Germany was a historic event, symbolic, while the burning of negroes in America is not, — hysteric, perhaps, but not historic.

(15) William Henry Chamberlin in "War — Shortcut to Fascism", *American Mercury*, Dec., 1940, asks, "Is it possible to resist the totalitarian onslaught without going totalitarian in the process? When did America most resemble a fascist state? . when we were engaged in our great crusade to make the world safe for democracy. Nazi judges and Nazi guards in concentration camps would certainly voice gutteral approval of some of the twenty-year sentences meted out to war critics."

(16) "The passage of the conscription bill, bringing an American Hitlerism nearer, tragically illustrates the fact that it is easier to teach people to_fear the hypothetical and imaginary, rather than the obvious danger. Doubly is this true if the hypothetical danger is foreign. To escape a comparatively small danger of attack by Hitler, we swallow the certainty of our own brand of Hitlerism" (Norman Thomas, Sept. 14, 1940).

(17) "The Constitution of the United States paves the way for democracy and good government, but leaves the final result to the people themselves. Democracy does not guarantee good government. It is merely the gateway to good government — the only one which can lead to it. Democracy rests on freedom and order, neither an end in itself" (Florida *Times Union*)

"Democracy involves equality before the law — equality of opportunity so far as may be, but no more Legislation may provide for education and normal living, but primal differences arising from heredity cannot be erased by any kind of statute. 'All men are born equal, but get over it before they die.' " (David Starr Jordan)

"If our rulers did a good job they would be secure. But they blunder There is resentment. And someone comes forward and offers hope and gets votes He is given power. He retains power by creating fear and continuing to offer hope, complying with traditional forms insofar as possible while he increases his power to perpetuate it And he, continues to ride high until some awful series of blunders brings tremendous suffering and revolt. The 'he' may be a man, an autocrat, a group, an oligarchy, a parliament, a legislature But there is always the tendency in desperation to put your faith in one man, to revert to dictatorship" ("What Makes Lives", pp 114-119)

Voltaire cynically suggested that "the art of government consists in taking the most money possible from some citizens and giving it to others," and "it is hard to free fools from the chains they revere. . . . As a final result, matters are so adjusted that under a show of popular suffrage the people, nevertheless, have legally no power to accomplish anything against the will of the king; that is, every movement not originating with the ruling class is checked somewhere by veto."

(18) "I have been about the country a little", writes John T Flynn in the *New Republic*, Oct. 14, 1940. "And I have been greatly edified at the splendid activity among civic groups wherever I have been, to offer their communities to the government as sites for defense factories and locations for government war expenditures. The most commendable spirit infects all industrial and community groups to have their share in the great work — and of course their share of it."

"National Defense and the Birmingham District" (Alabama) is the title of a pamphlet done in three national colors, each page with the flag superprinted, which announces that the district and Alabama "Hum with Direct and Indirect Defense Orders — Millions of Dollars and Thousands of Men At Work Indicate a Record-Breaking Year". Shell forging, loading, — destroyers, ships, air school, aluminium plant, ammonia plant, add up to over a hundred millions, high wages and profits, and big votes for the Administration. And so it is all over the country.

(19) The voters, whipped up to hysteria through fear of perils that impend, are oblivious to the real peril But even though it be too late to stop a movement so well launched, so admirably and skilfully directed, in which all the forces of the world's greatest empire and our so-called democratic machinery are enlisted, it is not too late to slow and check it, though to do so is to be denounced by newspaper editorials and radio voices, as 'obstructing defense'

IN HITLER'S FOOTSTEPS

Two stone axe heads were better than one, for trading. The early bird to accumulate a stock became the first capitalist But it is the 19th century economic set-up for which we reserve the term capitalism, which in the 20th century became finance capitalism.

Inevitable change is inevitably resisted by those who have benefited from the established order. Feudalism for centuries resisted the advance of capitalism, but received fatal blows in Napoleon's time. In their death struggle those who are about to die may bring about war.[1]

Pessimists, Spenglers and Sorokins, see in all this only the turn of the wheel, no movement of the axle. Others see ground covered, a drift toward something vaguely comprehended as collectivism. National varieties, known as Fascism, Nazism, Stalinism, have grown out of specific local conditions, though they may owe something to theoretical writings.

The seizure of power over people is a wholly different matter which has developed locally in all periods of history, with castled feudal barons as with American city bosses, whose achievements Willkie is now so earnestly exploiting.

"Our own drift toward collectivism in America" was recognized by James Mooney, vice-president of General Motors, at the annual meeting of the Associated Industries of Massachusetts, in Boston, October 17 "Over the past fifteen years, real democracy in the original American sense has been tried less and less as a remedy for our troubles And that goes for England and France, our 'sister democracies', just as much as it does for America."[2]

"The Rooseveltian system, though it maintains the outward forms of democracy, is plainly totalitarian in tendency." (H. L. Mencken, Oct. 27, 1940; cf also Buls #97 and 98)

Collectivism has no necessary connection with dictatorship. A city boss isn't interested in the social system. But most Americans confuse this drift to collectivism with the seizure of personal power by would-be dictators who would have it believed that their assumption of power in emergencies is essential to the public good.

Jim Farley, who was concerned solely with putting a man in power through building up increasing majorities, described himself as a "vote broker". John Chamberlain in "The American Stakes" (Carrick and Evans, 1940) sees all government as the broker between competing pressure groups, and regards democracy as a 'limited racket'. It all comes down to crafty old Louis XI's "To reign is to dissimulate". The art of ruling is as always the art of fooling. If the people's purses and bellies be empty, fill them with idealism, call on them to uphold religion, morality, and democracy.[3]

Politicians must still make their appeal through the old abstractions, 'liberty', 'democracy'. Roosevelt, demands "a free government for a government of free men".[4] He is the government (L'etat c'est moi), the one indispensable man, whose 'faits accomplis" a tamed Congress accepts like a present-day Reichstag or an Italian Senate, and votes billions not knowing how it will be used, and hundreds of millions for pin money for which no accounting is expected. He assumes that his fellow citizens have "Freedom of information, knowledge and press.—Freedom of religion.—Freedom of expression.—Freedom from want; greatest possible cultural and commercial intercourse among nations "

How the Administration may encroach on such freedom is brought out by Paul Mallon, September 15, commenting on the "Overton-Russell provision allowing the government to take ownership of any plant or 'facility' if the owner did not accept a government contract. The word 'facility' was so broad it seemed to cover everything including the implements of free speech—press and radio."

"A people may prefer a free government, but if", warned John Stuart Mill, "by momentary discouragement or temporary panic, or a fit of enthusiasm for an individual, they can be induced to lay their liberties at the feet of even a great man, or trust him with powers to subvert their institutions, in all these cases they are unfit for liberty."

"In the last 20 years representative government has been abandoned or destroyed in two-thirds of the world by the rise of personal power", proclaimed Herbert Hoover, October 24, at Columbus. "I do not suggest that Mr Roosevelt aspires to be a dictator", but "he has builded personal power to a dangerous point. . . . Those who play with power the world over contend they are working for the public good. This grasping for power is universally based on manipulating the public mind with emotional appeals to fear, to greed, and to hate."

The academic mind is the first to be so manipulated, now as twenty-two years ago Our university faculties, intimidated or bribed, our canny MacLeishes, aware of the immediate main chance, our emotional Mumfords, their gland valves wide open, give the pitch for hymns of hate on morality and religion, the words by our university presidents [6]

And those to whom all this is tinkling brass and sounding 'symbols' are today denounced with the zeal of a Torquemada as 'subversive' and destructive of 'national unity' The high priest of the Library of Congress, as of old the priests of Baal, cries out against the iconoclasts who would destroy his idols, overthrow his gods

Abstractions, which so largely control human behavior, may be mere scare words, bugaboos, like fascism and communism. Symbols may be translated into granite or into bronze. Critically studied, their history known, their interest increases.

A manufacturer is spending $40,000 to chisel off a facade the ornaments innocently placed by his architect long before Hitler adopted the swastika, that ancient Central Asian symbol perpetuated by our Southwestern Indians. Should Mussolini take Suez, become more formidable and more hated, we may have to remove the fasces from our Federal buildings [6]

The roots of fascism like its symbols reach far back into authoritarian times. Isn't the Old Testament fascist and the New Testament democratic? Isn't it natural enough, then, that there should be authoritarian and communal elements in our social system? Nor is it strange that much of American origin has been adopted by the dictators.[7]

To the anthropologist with scientific eye all ways of doing things, all modes of human behavior, are elements of the culture of the people who use them. Such cultural traits are communicable, transferable, and usually the diffusion or exchange works both ways.

So there has been much give and take, exchange of cultural traits between Germany and the United States There was a time when we boasted of exchange professors and students. And our university teaching was dominated by German trained Ph D.'s.

The Youth Movement of Germany was influenced directly by the American rediscovery of the outdoors[8] and our summer camps[9]. Both Mussolini and Hitler took much from the Boy Scout movement which, as developed under Beard and Baden-Powell and a score of others, borrowed from the North American Indian and the South African Zulu.

But the dictators have adapted other American practices of which we are not so proud   To the Gestapo have been suggestive our sadistic methods of intimidating and suppressing Negro and Communist, the rubber truncheon, the third degree inquisitorial methods developed in American police stations, and the refinements of the water cure and other cruelties we practiced to 'pacify' the conquered Filipinos.[10]

In return it was natural enough that at the time of our economic collapse and the changes that followed, that we should look for measures that had proved successful elsewhere. While chanting our 100% American hatred of everything foreign, we have without recognition and with denial adopted and adapted these to our use.

Most of the 'social gains' of the New Deal, employment insurance, old age pensions, and the like, are a belated effort to catch up with European practices, which originated mostly in Germany and were adopted long ago in England

Of the New Deal innovations, perhaps the most successful and generally applauded is the CCC, adapted from German predecessors. Instigated by Rosenstock-Huessy, now a professor at Dartmouth, these voluntary work camps developed in Republican Germany.[11]

With the general tightening of belts, a state of siege and the necessary economy of human effort and resources, Hitler conscripted both sexes. Just that plan, under the promptings of Harry Hopkins, was announced last spring by the President.[12]   The camps for boys and girls were to be 25 miles apart with a rocky road between". But the little group that seized the opportunity to write the conscription bill reverted to the ideas of the Kaiser.[13]

"The most amazing of all New Deal adventures in propaganda",

Paul Mallon tells us, is "the Goebbels system . . . the original work of the President's new adviser, Lowell Mellett . . a former Scripps-Howard editor", who appointed one Robert Horton. All releases, press and radio, passed through "the Horton bottleneck". No others were permitted to give out any information. (September 9) [14]

Secret alliances secretly arrived at, without the knowledge of the legislators and against the wishes of the people, are characteristic of totalitarian countries whose dictators must plan secretly and act arbitrarily. Deception is essential in fooling and ruling the people. [15]

It was easy for our experienced chief executive to give the "most solemn assurance", in response to Willkie's challenge, that there is "no secret understanding with any other government to involve this nation in any war". But inadvisedly he added, "or for any other purpose". [16]

Tinkham's charge of the secret understanding with Great Britain concerning the Pacific Canton and Enderbury Island (cf Bul #41), evaded or denied by our Administration, has since been confirmed by Japan and the British Foreign Office (cf Bul #87).

Roosevelt was of course as innocent of this as Wilson of the secret treaties of his time. [17] It will be remembered that four days before the destroyers were released, the President denied knowledge, though Churchill chortled over the consummation of arrangements made long before. [18]

'Inspection trips' have long been used by both Hitler and Mussolini as opportunity to exhibit themselves and harangue their followers. Our President as commander-in-chief makes inspection tours, which Willkie promptly pronounces "fake", Tech students "fishing trips". And the President, in dilemma, expresses doubt as to whether they are 'political', but in a hard voice declares he is having "a good time".

As fascism is put over on us in the guise of anti-fascism, as Huey Long prophesied, old forms must still be adhered to [19] The President still has a Cabinet but, like Mussolini, has assumed at times many portfolios We have a Defense Council, which has no chairman. "The Boss", as Knudsen terms the President, calls meetings when he pleases.

We retain the forms[20] and boast of "free elections"[21], but with defense billions for election funds, Administration largesse to carpenters, contractors, industry, and "economic royalists" tempts them to vote for more, giving up their freedom. [22]

Stung by charges of 'dictatorship', the President, September 20, rebutted "No dictator in history has ever dared to run the gauntlet of a really free election". And Al Smith, quoting him, "As long as we have free elections we need have no fear for democracy", comes back, "That's what Hitler says. The only difference is he says it in German. Try and get rid of him "[23]

Our "free elections" are not so free in many states, for the unequal and the hated,—for Negroes, Communists, and those unable to pay taxes. Ten million Americans, poor whites and Negroes, won't vote at this election Threats, violence, or poll tax requirements are used to keep them from voting.[24]

"Not So Free Election" (*The New Republic,* October 21) describes the "vicious electoral witch-hunt . . . under way. . . . In more than twenty-five states, intimidation, violence and crushing legislation have been used to keep minority parties off the ballot."[25]

"Hitler was elected to three consecutive terms in authority before he became a dictator. Mussolini was also thrice elected to his job before he turned despot. This third term thing seems to be the turning point for entrenched tyranny!" Irvin Cobb declared, October 25.

Drafting themselves becomes chronic with dictators. As they are indispensable, they too must appoint their successor. Dynasties start that way. It's easy to follow in the footsteps

Hitler promised his people everything without war, and for a time delivered. But by every agency of communication and propaganda he prepared for war. Like Hitler, our President hates war. But the same control of propaganda and "measures short of war" have brought us unawares to acts of war [26]

"This country wants no war with any nation", declared the President at Dayton, October 19. But, "By word and deed, by threat and by insult, despite our present pitiable state of comparative defenselessness, we have further antagonized already potentially or actually hostile and envious nations" (Irvin Cobb, October 25.)

When Joe Chamberlain was building popular opinion in England to support the growing British imperialism, the popular song of the day declared, We want no war, "but by jingo if they do, we've got the ships, we've got the men, and we've got the money, too". Roosevelt has the money, and he promises to "pile up our defense and armaments", and deliver to his English Tory friends.

"Outrageously false" the President branded "a charge that offends every political and religious conviction that I hold dear. It is the charge that this administration wishes to lead this country into war."[27]

But despite what his cousin would have called 'weasel words', never to send "sons of American mothers" to fight on the "soil of Europe", contrary to his "wishes", the "duty" of "religious conviction" may drive him to send aviators to die in the air, gobs to crimson the Channel, and American regulars to occupy Martinique, Singapore, Dakar, and to use the 80-ton tanks now under construction to break the Siegfried Line.

"Your boys are not going to be sent into any Foreign war", he assured Boston, October 31. "The purpose of our defense is defense."[28]

But in case of attack the Democratic Platform pledges to send our army "to fight in foreign lands outside of the Americas". And May 16 Roosevelt had told Congress, "An effective defense by its very nature requires the equipment to attack an aggressor on his route". (David Lawrence, October 28) And he is on his route as soon as he leaves home.

Cagey, the President has become, in the face of proved violation of his pledges. "I reaffirmed . . . in plain English three times in my speeches . . . without qualification . . . and I have announced my un-qualified acceptance."[29] Willkie, October 30, quotes Roosevelt's 1932 pledge to maintain the gold standard, to guarantee which Senator Glass was dragged from a sick bed. Five months later, Roosevelt broke the pledge. Four years later, Glass again dragged himself from a sick bed to denounce Roosevelt.

And Willkie asks the President, "Are you kidding Joe Kennedy the same way you kidded Carter Glass?" And he adds, "On the basis of his past performance with pledges to the people, why shouldn't we expect to be at war by April, 1941, if he is elected?"

Kennedy's frank voice, October 29, concealed the patchwork of his speech, remodeled after his long four hour wrangle with Roosevelt. He diverted attention from 'making' war to 'declaration' of war, repeatedly assuring that there would be no 'declaration'. It is out of fashion.[30]

"Regardless of an 8 to 1 popular majority against our getting into foreign war, we are headed straight toward it by the shortest path. . . . A few selfish and ambitious men are permitted to threaten all our basic liberties. . . . They are seeking primarily to preserve themselves and their own ideas at the dread risk of war." (Gen. Hugh S. Johnson)

"The Power to Make War" has been usurped by the President, the Boston *Transcript* editorially assures us, October 24, calling attention to John L. Lewis' "charge of dictatorial ambitions . . . neglect of internal problems . . . mismanagement of foreign policy", and that Roosevelt is "deliberately leading his still unprepared country into the European war".

The editorial reviews historically from 1778 the efforts to restrict the President's war making powers. After the Panay incident, the Ludlow resolution for a constitutional amendment to refer war to the people met with the approval of a majority of the House, but after President Roosevelt's opposition was lost by a vote of 188 to 209.

"Overweening abnormal and selfish craving for increased power" were charged by Lewis in his national broadcast While protesting that "he hates war and will work for peace", the President has shown by his acts that war was "his motivation and his objective" from the time of his "quarantine speech" in Chicago.[31]

"War has always been the device of the politically despairing and intellectually sterile statesmen. It provides employment in the gun factories and begets enormous profits for those already rich. It kills off the vigorous males who, if permitted to live, might question the financial exploitation of the race Above all, war perpetuates in imperishable letters on the scroll of fame and history, the names of its political creators and managers." (Lewis)

"Beware of measures short of dictatorship, for they are like measures short of war. Beware of personal power in the worshipful image. Beware of this European doctrine of indispensability, and of the saying that to challenge it is treasonable." (*Sat Eve Post,* October 12, 1940) [32]

You can still use your ballot to challenge such usurpations You are still a free man. Reducing the popular vote will deflate the ego of the mere man who in all sincerity and with religious zeal assumes the function of 'bringing about orderly processes everywhere', of putting down evil in other men,—who while declaiming against force, boasts that he is preparing the greatest force the world has known

There are those who with a feeling that they are "democratically privileged" will "go to the polls to make a free choice between two frauds" in what they believe to be the "Last Days of America".

But as you "Kiss the Boys Goodbye", you need not say farewell to

the freedom your fathers won   If you are of their stuff and fibre, you will gird your loins to fight, and build "A New America".
October 31, 1940

Notes

(1) "Change is the only constant", remarked the scientific minded C. F. Kettering, General Motors researcher and inventor   He deplores the world's dearth of creative minds. Like Socrates, he appreciates the density of ignorance in high places. "We're so terribly ignorant. . .   We hate to admit we don't know it all, and we keep ourselves back by pretending to have knowledge we don't possess." (Boston *Herald*, April 24, 1940)   In an article in *Reader's Digest*, January, 1938, Kettering wrote "It is all ahead of us. At every period in time there is somebody to say, 'I don't see what there is new to be done'.   Go out and look.   If we can cast off the bugaboo of 'Your world is finished', and put in its place, 'The world is begun', we have a marvelous future ahead of us.   We ought to quit being afraid of the future   Change is the law of life. We should work *with* change instead of being forced into it.   All our education teaches *finality*. Business clamors for *stability*.   Our thinking is conventionalized."   And Kettering is reputed to have said, "This world is moving so fast, we have to run like hell to stay where we are".

(2) "You now see . . . one word on all the clashing banners; Republicans, Democrats, liberals, radicals, Communists and revolutionaries all acclaiming democracy, and all alike holding themselves out to be its only true and devoted defenders   Does this mean that we have such a curious thing as a total defense of democracy?   On the contrary, it means that the American significance of democracy, too, has been lost   The word itself has become a political hotel, under no management, offering a once-respectable address to any and all ideas, harlotry not forbidden." (Editorial, *Sat Eve Post*, October, 26, 1940)

(3) These realistic views of government are from "What Makes Lives", (pp 114-119) which is further quoted:

Our university teachers, dependent on legislatures, foundations, and financial advisers to donors, continue to ignore that government is a practice and an art, only recently a theory, and not yet a science.

John Chamberlain, staff writer of *Fortune*, book editor for *Harper's*, regards the state as having originated as a 'strict racket'.   "Philosophical idealists such as Dorothy Thompson and Walter Lippmann frequently write brilliantly useless columns on politics because they either ignore or have forgotten the origin of State power in brutally unashamed force."

Eric T. Bell, the mathematician, in his "Man and His Lifebelts" (cf Sargent Handbook of Private Schools, 1938-39, pp 129ff) sums up Machiavelli's theory of government and Pareto's scheme of the 'elite' with clarifying realism.   "All government boils down to this: a select minority exploits, for its own selfish advantage, an unselect majority.   The true 'art' of government appears when the unselect majority is swindled into believing that it is getting that kind of government which brings about the greatest good of the greatest number "

"Those who today control the destinies of the majority of countries . . . generally misnamed statesmen, are only too willing to play upon the ignorant emotions of the people", cautiously explains Sir Stafford Cripps in "Dare We Look Ahead?" And Jerome Frank in his philosophic compendium "Save America First" remarks, "Statesmanship involves a handling of the folkways A politician is a working anthropologist. The less he is aware of his function, the less adequate his performance." Leslie Pape writes, "Important . . today is the use of propaganda to persuade and beguile the people into acceptance of economic and other conditions which perhaps need not and should not be accepted . . Censorship, incidentally, can be used to conceal embarrassing information or ideas." (*Social Forces,* March, 1940).

(4) "These two words, 'free government', taking them literally . . . can mean that government shall be free, not people. We get this from the Attorney General In June, last, he addressed the Institute of Public Affairs at Charlottesville, Virginia, on how to make democracy efficient . . . Democracy could be made efficient only by more government—more power and more freedom of government to punish individual conduct wherein it interferes with the main objectives of democracy, more power to coerce minorities, more power to prevent 'some freedoms' . . .

" 'The National Government has won its long fight to free itself of unwarranted limitations   . We have restored the vitality of a free government on which a narrow legalism was inflicting a kind of rigor mortis . . We have won for peacetime programs powers that in 1917 were felt could be used only in war emergency. . . The lines of future liberal policy are clear. We must move at an accelerated pace . . Once a decision is democratically arrived at, I see no reason why it would not be consistent with democracy to provide means to execute that decision with as much expedition and efficiency as the decision of a dictator ' " (Editorial, *Sat Eve Post,* Oct 26, 1940)

(5) The canny Scot, Archibald MacLeish, used here as a symbol only, is one of "The Tough Muscle Boys of Literature" according to Burton Rascoe, *American Mercury,* November, 1940 Their emotional sympathy for the downtrodden, the unjustly treated, and a fuzzy kind of idealism led many of them into the quagmire of Soviet Communism until the realist Stalin drove them out in confusion. Since then a healthy metabolism has led many to surrender to the fleshpots and flattery of old fashioned capitalism Those in bondage to university trustees and their overlords or to publishing houses and their advertising agency and banker friends excite compassion. Some have succumbed to continuous pressure as did the witches of Salem. Others have learned to respond to the coaxing flicks of the whip. Still others once hungry now have both feet in the trough. But that MacLeish, who had so many publics that would yield him a modest living as litterateur, poetaster, rabble rouser, should have surrendered to Administration and British blandishments for a mere ten thousand,—or is it fifteen?—a year as

the nation's "high priest" of literature in the Library in which Congressmen are so rarely seen, may impress some as tragic.   Perhaps it is only a canny Scotch trick of coming back at the Britons who even up to and during Johnson's time treated his people with such supreme contempt

This apologetic explanation is offered because of the merciless excoriation to which he has been subjected by Burton Rascoe,—not so much that he chides the Librarian of Congress for adopting Hitler's attitude toward books and people, nor because the citations from MacLeish's poems make him seem ridiculous   But when Rascoe proceeds to flay him as Apollo did Marsyas, the while giving Mac-Leish a severe bellyache by reminding him of how recently he had swallowed all the Communist propaganda, that seems "cruel and unusual" punishment, forbidden in our Constitution   But when he reminds the limp lump left of how he has endeavored to cover his Bolshevik incarnation with totalitarian he-man hooey, that simply isn't done   The slaughter reminds one of Chevy Chase where all day long Scot and Briton met in bloody fight, where "Of fifteen hundred Englishmen, Went home but fifty-three, The rest were slaine in Chevy Chase, Under the greene wood tree "

(6) The symbolic fasces, a bundle of rods bound about an axe were mere symbols of office of the lictors in later Rome, but to the early Romans, the rods and the beheading axe carried by their Etruscan masters were dread instruments

(7) The private initiative of the frontier and the open prairie is not possible in densely settled communities   In our cities we have necessarily communized our water and sewage systems, our schools and our hospitals, our health services Local charities follow the same plan.   The annual late fall drive for Community Chests corresponds with the German 'Wintershilfe'.

(8) "Rediscovering the Outdoors" (Sargent "Handbook of Summer Camps", 1935, pp 41-46) tells how from 'Victorian Indoorness', through Thoreau, Adirondack Murray, 'Nessmuk', the Appalachian Mountain Club, the summer camp again opened American eyes to the outdoors.   The story of how out of this, following the Civil War, came the summer camp, and the development of summer camp activities under Balch in the early 80's, is traced in the "History of the Summer Camp" (pp 33-110)

In America Dan Beard had developed scout and camp craft, and Ernest Thompson-Seton had revived the Indian woodcraft.   Boy scout origins and the derivations of their practices are described (pp 103-105).   "Lord Robert S. Baden-Powell, a colonel in the British Army during the Boer War .   . had been impressed with the training of the Zulu boys who before they are accepted as warriors get a training in woodcraft and self-reliance.   At fifteen, every Zulu boy, stripped naked, is given a shield and spear and sent into the jungle to make good   Failure means death " (cf also "The Rediscovery of the Outdoors", by Porter Sargent, *Yankee Magazine,* January, 1938)

(9) "The summer camp originated in New England fifty to seventy years ago In 1937 the Soviets bravely announced they sent to summer camp over 25,000,000 children, ten times as many as in America where the idea originated   The idea

of a military school for boys got its start at Norwich, Vermont in 1819 and spread all over the country. There was nothing of this kind in Italy until a century later when Mussolini adopted our New England and American ideas."

(10) "Other American methods, not so admirable, were those used on conscientious objectors during the war, the barbed wire enclosure for even the Boston Symphony Orchestra conductor. Our current horrible and sadistic methods of suppressing unpopular racial or religious minorities have recently been illustrated in the picture magazines. The 'third degree' was developed by our politically dominated American police at a time when in stabilized Europe police methods were on a higher, professional, well disciplined basis. Many of these modes of torture and suppression have been adopted by Fascist dictators. They have not gone so far as to use the water cure which Americans use to pacify the Philippinos or the blow torch on negroes in the south   Their use of castor oil and the steel whip may seem to them more humane." (Sargent Handbook of Private Schools, 1937-38. Cf also "The American Roots of Fascism" by Porter Sargent, *Yankee Magazine*, February, 1938.)

(11) Eugen Rosenstock-Huessy "was Vice-Chairman of the World Association for Adult Education in London, founder of the German labor camp movement and first head of the Academy of Labor in Frankfort-am-Main   He worked for two years on the staff of the biggest automobile factory in Germany and, during the War, commanded the German railroad system in front of Verdun." He "has devoted his life to an effort to realign and integrate the various social sciences There is not one of them: Psychology, History, Economics, Theology, Law, Philology, Linguistics, Political Science, Education, Biography, to which he has not made original contributions and of which he has not been frequently asked to give an accounting before important academic groups. A former Lowell lecturer in Boston, he now holds a chair of Social Philosophy at Dartmouth College " (cf "Out of Revolution" Morrow)

On May 21 and 23, 1940, at the Annual Conference of CCC Educational Advisers, First Corps Area, Dartmouth College, Rosenstock-Huessy modestly referred to the origins of these work camps and pointed out the possibilities of extending the same opportunities to all American youth. "The CCC camps revolutionize . . the idea that citizenship is 'to be profitably employed'. . . . The true citizen is a man who can employ his profits in a civilized manner; this is the opposite from being profitably employed. . . . A product, if good, is a mass product. Therefore, we also produce unemployment in mass and we don't know what to do with it. . . . Our problem is not profitable employment but how to use the profit of unemployment . . .

"We have asked so long what is good for business, what is good for farmers, what is good for scholars, science, art, what is good for any class or profession The time has come to ask what is business good for, what are colleges good for, what is leisure good for? Shapeless youth forces this question upon us. . . . The farmer in 1830 A.D. . . . had his children . . These children worked daily Their work amounted to 2000 work hours per year. If you could furnish a Ver-

mont farmer today with two thousand work hours he would be a rich man. Instead, society pushes his children into its educational system and produces bell
boys'. . . . The farmer ceases to be the source of his own labor supply. We have
left our schools without a goal that goes beyond the school. . . .

"The Civilian Conservation Corps . . is an unusual opportunity for integration . . . We have massed production; and also, we have massed private life in
the so-called residential section, and we have massed vacations and leisure   This
breaks up the wholeness of life. It makes leisure and work and privacy, all
three, rather unreal. This division ought not to be. . . . The process of work
begetting thought, thought begetting fellowship and fellowship re-creating our
work, no longer is visible to the individual in our society. He is confused. . . .
The wholeness of man is imperilled in our modern society. . . .

"There is no other opportunity in our society where the modern mass man
could ever come to know the organic relations between the body, the soul, and
the mind. Now, a society in which this organic unity is lived nowhere, must
decay. . . . Somewhere and somehow, man himself must be reproduced to higher
standards not to higher standards of living gentlemen, but to higher standards
of life. . . . Perhaps, we need not call the standard that aims at the reproduction
of the whole man a 'higher' standard. It certainly is more comprehensive and
more wholesome. . . .

"In camp, they should not listen to the radio, but be made to sing. They
should not stare at one thousand pictures a week in the magazines, but embellish
their barracks with one excellent picture. I would try to make them create their
own activities."

(12) Trial balloons sent up from the White House attracted much editorial
comment during the last weeks of June. *PM*, June 20, 1940, reporting the President's statement "that training in the conscript camps will remove those elements
in the thinking of our youth which makes them 'critical of their elders' ", remarks, "We should hold little hope for the future of any nation whose young
people had ceased to be critical of their elders."

Soon after President Roosevelt's inauguration in March 1933, he announced
the establishment of the CCC camps to take the boys off the street corners and
out of the transient camps and to get money for their families. That was a year
after Hitler had coordinated all work camps under Nazi leadership. In 1934
the German university student organization voted that the work camps should
be compulsory before matriculation and in 1935, Hitler decreed that the work
camps be compulsory for both sexes. The German idea has been widely adopted
in other European centers. Kenneth Holland, Associate Director of the American Youth Commission, writes of work camps for youth in all these countries in
"American Youth" (Harvard U. Press, 1940). He makes recommendation as
to their future in the U. S, "As the camps and resident centers are established on
a permanent basis they should be carefully integrated with educational, vocational, employment, and adjustment activities of institutions already in existence.
It is to be hoped that established schools and other training institutions in the

United States will see in the labor camps a new technique for providing youth with practical experience better adapted to its needs and interests than the present academic school courses." (p 103)

(13) Dr. Walter M. Kotschnig of Smith College, in his "Unemployment in the Learned Professions" (Oxford, 1937) showed how a similar situation in Germany, youth dissatisfied, unemployed, made possible the overturn, brought about the present regime (cf "What Makes Lives," p 216). At the ninth annual New England Institute of International Relations, Wellesley College, July 2, 1940, he advocated establishment of hundreds of such work camps for every type of youth, pointing out that "The Germans suceeded because they gave youth new ideas and inspiration and will, and a strength which proved too strong for the West. It was not only their tremendous supply of tanks and planes which led to their success, but the spirit of their youth to give themselves wholeheartedly to the fight "

Rosenstock-Huessy with the support and backing of recent Vermonters, Dorothy Thompson, Dorothy Canfield Fisher, and recent Harvard graduates, Enno Hobbing, Frank Davidson, Richard Davis, has worked out a plan for enlisting the interest of the well to do in rehabilitating New England farms, a William James work camp idea which should provide "The Moral Equivalent for War" (cf Boston *Transcript* and *Herald,* November 23 and 24). Unfortunately the camp appealed to the government for, aid which was given and this aroused opposition on the part of Congressman Engel of Michigan, so that the direction of the camp was taken over by the government, after which a majority of the members seceded.

(14) "Government propaganda is under direction of Lowell Mellett, close aide to the President, center of a network of publicity agents extending throughout the entire gov't, coordinating all news policies   This system watches writers, radio commentators, networks and movies . . . often 'reminds' them of 'inaccuracies', points out the 'true truth'. Mostly the pressure is applied gently but effectively . . with few cases of real crack-down. Kid-glove method works well with radio especially, since radio operates by gov't license, and usually a hint is sufficient. Tightening up of propaganda techniques is now being planned, with view to major operations as essential part of war preparedness. It's regimentation of public thinking .   . creeping in, inching up " (From a confidential "Washington Letter", October 19, 1940) (cf also *Time,* Feb. 17, 1941)

"Two cabinet officers were actually requested by letter from the centralized office to have most of their publicity clear through Horton   A mimeographed appeal was made to all government departments. . . .   The effect was the creation of a single-headed dictatorial publicity arrangement somewhat like the Creel committee established during the world war, channelizing the most important news of the nation through a single fountainhead   It caused not only the mess on plane figures which has become public property, but innumerable inner squabbles, such as upon four occasions when Horton announced contract information which the army and navy considered secret data." Because of Horton's bungling, and conflicting information, this system of national defense commission publicity "is to be liquidated or at least resurfaced. . . . The commission itself is no longer to be hermetically sealed." (Paul Mallon, Sept 9, 1940)

At the dinner of the White House Correspondents Association, at which the President declared war through the correspondents rather than the Congress, the correspondents in their entertainment pictured Robert Horton, press chief of the Office of Production Management, "ordering his police guard to shoot reporters on sight". "A short film lampooned not a few public figures under the modest title of 'All We Know Is What They Let Us Write in the Papers' or 'It Ain't Necessarily So'. At one point the 'news' reel showed President Roosevelt and Mr Willkie in bed together in a scene titled 'Bundling for Britain'. On the President's side of the bed was a sign reading 'Tremendous Vast Assistance' and on Mr. Willkie's 'British Commonwealth (and Southern)'" (*Chr Sci Monitor*, March 17, 1941)

(15) "The President's transfer of fifty destroyers to Great Britain, without the consent of Congress . . . is the crowning act of supererogation on the part of a regime whose entire record smacks of arrogance" (Chicago *Leader*, September 6, 1940). The *Law Journal*, Aug 7, 1940, in an editorial spoke of the transfer of armed vessels to Britain as illegal.

The memorable blast on this act of the President came from the St Louis *Post-Dispatch* in two editorials, Sept. 3 and Sept 4, "Dictator Roosevelt Commits an Act of War" and "The Dictator Process in America":

"Mr. Roosevelt today committed an act of war. He also became America's first dictator . . . Although the President referred to his under-cover deal as ranking in importance with the Louisiana Purchase, he is not asking Congress—the elected representatives of the people—to ratify this deal. He is telling them it already has been ratified by him. . . .

"Under our Constitution, treaties with foreign Powers are not legal without the advice and consent of the Senate. This treaty, which history may define as the most momentous one ever made in our history, was put over without asking the Senate either for its advice or its consent. The authority which the President quotes for his fatal and secret deal is an opinion from the Attorney-General. Whatever legal trickery this yes-man may conjure up, the fact is that the transfer of the destroyers is not only in violation of American law, but is also in violation of The Hague Covenant of 1907, solemnly ratified by the United States Senate in 1908. It is an outright act of war. . . .

"Thomas Jefferson did not lease Louisiana from Napoleon Bonaparte He acquired it outright, to have and to hold forever Woodrow Wilson didn't lease the Virgin Islands from Denmark. With *the advice and consent of the United States Senate,* he bought them. In the case of Newfoundland and Bermuda, Mr. Roosevelt tells us that the right to bases 'are gifts—generously given and gladly received'. In other words, the great and rich United States is taking largesse from a nation that owes us some four billion dollars. We are accepting a tip, according to the President." (September 3)

"President Roosevelt's exchange of 50 American destroyers for leases on naval bases in British possessions in the Western Atlantic—a deal put through in violation of international law and Federal law and without consulting the will of Congress—is a perfect illustration of the dictator process at work. . . .

"This evident fact is in no way affected by the complaisant opinion of a subservient Attorney-General." An "exercise in legal sophistry—worked out by Dean Acheson, Thomas D. Thacher, George Rublee and Charles C Burlingham" published on the editorial page of the Sunday New York *Times* just a week after Pershing's plea and explaining how Roosevelt could disregard the previous opinion of the Attorney-General on the transfer of the mosquito fleet "was adopted by Attorney-General Jackson in the stultifying about-face which he executed in giving the President the legal go-signal on the deal. . . .

"There is every reason to believe that Great Britain would have been eager to give us the bases regardless of what was done as to the destroyers It now turns out that the acquisition of the destroyers may be a negligible item in Britain's total compensation. . . .

"President Roosevelt suggested yesterday afternoon that he may soon 'inform' Congress of other deals for naval bases to be acquired from Britain. At the same time, spokesmen for the Navy Department said that Winston Churchill's promise that the British navy will not be surrendered to Germany would remove the need for keeping any considerable portion of American navy in the Atlantic and leave it free to patrol the Pacific. Putting these two statements together, it would not be surprising if Britain confers upon us another supreme favor in the form of leases on naval bases in the Far East, from which we will be permitted to defend British possessions in that far quarter of the globe " (September 4)

"Your government has secretly collaborated with the British government by thought and act in a manner which, even if it had not been intended to involve the United States in the European war, could have had no other effect or meaning . . . For each act of intervention the public mind was prepared by propaganda. The first acts were a sampling, the adventure oblique . . .

"When the Congress had accepted these acts, your Government abandoned the legal subterfuge and went on to strip the American arsenals, until fifteen shiploads of arms and ammunition out of America's own inadequate defense equipment had been delivered to Great Britain. . . Your Government . . by act of executive will alone . . forms a military alliance with a country at war—namely, Canada—and proceeds to deliver American armaments there. . . . It is a momentous fact that the President of the United States, in time of peace, on his own responsibility, can meet the Premier of Canada in his private railway carriage and make offhand a military pact with a country that is at war with Hitler. It passes " (Editorial, *Sat Eve Post*, October 12, 1940)

Your government's Commander-in-Chief orders generals to reverse their testimony against their beliefs The President orders his attorney-general to reverse important labor decisions, to distortedly interpret the law on the "built or equipped with intent" which prohibited the export of the mosquito boats, to permit the export of destroyers.

The present Administration, through accumulation of power by legislative acts, by usurpation, has made the executive will the law of the land. The "executive will" magnifies the ego of a man frustrated in his domestic policies; by winning the favor of British royalty, whom he so loves to entertain. He scolds Chamberlain, bargains with Churchill, assumes the defense of British possessions in the Western hemisphere, supplies them with 15 shiploads of armaments (which leaks to a restricted public months afterward), with representatives of Australia and New Zealand plans their defense, enters into secret treaties to protect British interests in the Far East, makes unpayable promises to France, holds secret conversations with the Canadian premier and the governor-general, as a result of which he sends them our tanks, plans to finance their St. Lawrence water power development. (cf William H. Lewis, Boston *Transcript,* October 24, 1940)

(16) "An admission of a de facto Anglo-American alliance", Gayda, Mussolini's mouthpiece says, was proved by Morgenthau's statement of July 21 of the synchronization of war production for the U. S. and Britain Referring to the recent British supported attack on Dakar, "he said a Spanish diplomat, inquiring at a 'foreign office' (presumably London) was told that the expedition was made on American suggestion". (Boston *Herald,* November 2, 1940)

Uncensored, October 26, 1940, considering the exigencies of election, apologetically states, "it is perhaps ingenious to examine closely the President's 'solemn assurance', given during a campaign speech in Philadelphia, that 'there is no secret treaty, no secret obligation, no secret commitment, no secret understanding in any shape or form, direct or indirect, with any other government, or any other nation in any part of the world, to involve this nation in any war or for any other purpose.' . . . Were there not widespread fears that the President's specific acts were leading toward war, he might not have found it necessary to make so categorical and inclusive a disavowal . A President whose policies are trusted would be trusted to talk about more than the weather with a foreign diplomat."

An editorial article in the *New Statesman and Nation,* September 28, 1940, entitled "The Peace of the Pacific" is quoted: "Hardly was the auspicious arrangement completed by which the two English-speaking democracies pooled their defences in the Atlantic, when their Governments set to work to negotiate a parallel agreement for the Pacific. As Canada was included in the former, so was Australia in the latter negotiations. Provision may again be made to furnish the American fleet and air-arm with bases on British territory, and it is more than probable that Singapore will be placed at their disposal. . . .

"These two peoples share the instinct for improvisation and for the composition of Treaties-without-words. Henceforth it would be morally and even legally impossible for one of these two powers to engage in active hostilities with a third Power in either of these Oceans without involving the other. There is no time-limit to this tie, but fortunately it does not seem to Americans to be an 'entangling' alliance."

(17) Before a Senate investigating committee, President Wilson affirmed his

ignorance of the secret treaties. Colonel House, his mentor, averred,—"I was present at a meeting in the White House when Balfour discussed them with President Wilson " Franklin D Roosevelt, his Assistant Secretary of the Navy from 1913 to 1920, was an ardent admirer of President Wilson.

(18) Two days later, Winston Churchill makes a statement in the British House of Commons beginning· 'The memorable transactions between Britain and the United States which I foreshadowed when I last addressed the House have now been completed ' . . . And he adds that British crews are already there to receive them at the western side of the Atlantic—that is to say, at Canadian ports—by 'what one might call the long arm of coincidence'. (Laughter at this in the British House) . . .

"For the British we have only further admiration They wanted the destroyers very badly But they wanted much more. They wanted their possessions on this hemisphere to be defended, and here was Uncle Sam going to do it and give fifty destroyers to boot; and even more, they wanted the American Government to put forth its hand, as the Irish say, farther than it could draw it back, or, in the words of the British press, to 'take the plunge'

"In that same speech, announcing the memorable transaction to the House of Commons, Winston Churchill cheerfully said. 'No doubt Herr Hitler will not like this transference of destroyers. I have no doubt he will pay the United States out if ever he gets the chance ' ⸰ Thus it was reserved for the British government to announce to the world the fact that the United States had got into the war, so far into it that it could not back out." (Editorial, *Sat Eve Post,* October 12, 1940)

(19) Two men spoke out in Boston, Sunday, December 1st, 1940, so as to get the Boston *Herald* headlines on Monday morning "Watch Hitler conquer America!" cried John Haynes Holmes in the Community Church, Boston. "Watch him dictate to us vast expenditures for arms which, if he were here, we would call an indemnity, but since he is not here we call taxation¹ Watch him impose on us a war economy which is destined to wipe out every feature of our life which has happily distinguished us from Europe It is not the conquest of America by arms that we need to fear—but rather, we need to fear the fear of that conquest. . . . The armament program has but one purpose in the White House, on Capitol Hill, and in the offices of big business, and that is to prepare the nation to fight not for ourselves but for the British Empire, and not in America but in Europe."

At Ford Hall that same Sunday evening, Frederick L Schuman of Williams College, who had a bad time in 1933 when he was in Germany, and since has vied with the 'woman scorned' as a Hitler hater and a promoter of vengeful war, cried: "We need a dictatorship, but a dictatorship such as the Greeks and Romans had in times of trouble, not the type of dictatorship we ascribe to Germany. In this great struggle . . the fittest will survive and those who do will unify the world. . If we are too stupid and cowardly it will be done . . by those who have the greatest capacity of combining insight and foresight with blood,

tears, toil and sweat. If we do not do so we shall be stricken from the list of
nations and other masters will unify the world . . Even Italy and Germany may
not survive but the Jews will because they have been surviving such things for
5000 years and know how."

(20) "The hideous head of absolute government . . turns to the gaze of the
people only its benign aspect and . . . says to them: 'Your government is the
same as before. It is only conditions that have changed Everything, nevertheless, is within the form ' " (Editorial, *Sat Eve Post,* October 26, 1940)

"In Italy and in Germany the current dictators rose to power peacefully and
entirely within the form, if not the spirit, of the constitutions of their respective
countries After they had been elevated to power through the endeavors of their
party associates, all they had to do to make themselves supreme was to gather into
their own hands complete control over administration of the laws, using that
control to crush out all opposition", said Julius C. Smith of the American Bar
Association, addressing the Florida Law Institute last November. "Make no
mistake about it Even as Mussolini and Hitler rose to absolute power under the
forms of law . . . so may administrative absolutism be fastened upon this country
within the Constitution and within the forms of law." (Quoted in Editorial, *Sat
Eve Post,* Oct. 26, 1940)

(21) "Do you call it a free election when you sit in conference with the Boss
Hagues, the Boss Flynns and the Kelly-Nashes? Do you call it a free election
when the chairman of your committee—and he could not do it without your
knowledge—sends out lists of Government employees and seeks to collect campaign contributions from them? Do you count it a free election when you begin
to put pressure upon relief receivers and people upon WPA employment?" asked
Willkie at Milwaukee, October 21.

"The President endeavored also in his Philadelphia speech to meet the cry of
dictatorship by insisting that as long as there are 'free elections' no harm can
come to America. . . . Free elections no longer exist in the sense in which the
term has been used for generations in America . . . 10,000,000 families receive
checks nowadays or benefits of some kind direct from the Federal Government
WPA rolls have been increased each election year." (David Lawrence, Sept. 21)

Carter Glass on the floor of the Senate, June 24, 1937, declared, "The last election (1936) was carried by people who were getting favors from the Government,
people who were subsidized by the Government, people who were on relief "

(22) "Is the Roosevelt-Willkie campaign a hoax?" The Norman Thomas point
of view regarded the whole campaign as 'phoney'. The two party system had
actually become one party serving one set of interests Those interests had 'hired'
Willkie, and Roosevelt had 'bribed' them with prospects of huge war profits. A
vast majority of the people were against war, and within the Republican party
there was a large element which saw their opportunity of winning by coming out
on the popular side, against war That was successfully check-mated This
point of view smeared as 'socialist' now has surprising corroboration from Arthur
Krock, veteran Washington correspondent of the New York *Times,* who writes,

January 15, 1941, "During the Presidential campaign, both candidates . . . promised . . . limited 'aid to Britain' . . . 'short of war' . . . never to send American fighting men and units outside this hemisphere. But when the shadow-boxing of the campaign was over . . . the phrase 'short of war' did not again occur in the President's speeches . Mr Willkie told Republicans . . . that the defeat of the Axis is indispensable to American security " It was "therefore impossible . . to limit the military consequences. . . . The lease-lend bill which the President has proposed and Mr. Willkie has endorsed . . . runs counter to the promises of both platforms . . ."

(23) "What the dictators of Europe have criticized about America today is that despite its professions of freedom, it is really no different than totalitarianism except in degree or intensity. In Germany the one-party system prevails and the Government clique controls everything In America the New Deal clique is in power and controls everything from the courts to the legislative and nominating machinery so that laws and even nominations for senator and representative are made virtually by White House decree The Democratic National Convention at Chicago in July was a striking example of the type of thing in which the Nazis and the Fascists of Italy believe

"The forms are preserved—even the Reichstag and Nazi party are called together every now and then by Herr Hitler—but the control of such bodies is absolute through one-man domination Mr. Roosevelt's answer has been that dictatorship does not arise where 'free elections' occur and that the European dictators do not have to run the gauntlet of such free elections. But are America's elections free? The power of the purse which helped the New Deal win in 1936, is again in evidence in this campaign . . . employees are active despite the Hatch Law. The Department of Justice enforces neither the Federal Corrupt Practices Act nor the Hatch Law, and the Government employees know it. In other words, the party in power in Washington uses the whole Government propaganda machine to attack the opposing candidate and seeks by such propaganda to discredit the opposition nominee . .

"Until the people of the United States learn to repudiate every form of totalitarianism and intolerance no matter under what party label it rears its head and learn to do so in free elections which are uninfluenced by governmental funds and manipulated power, the dictators of Europe will only smile at the discomfiture of America. For, after all, why should a dictator in Europe be unhappy if his theory of government is ratified in another part of the world which has been outwardly professing scorn for the one-man government idea?" (David Lawrence, October 2, 1940)

(24) "Blunderbuss Americanism of Ku Klux Klan and vigilante society stamp is cropping out again—this time in the American Legion With pages of Hearst and Scripps-Howard publicity, the veterans have begun a campaign to keep Browder and Ford off the ballots in the coming election. Their most recent success was yesterday's decision of the New York Supreme Court barring the Communists from that State's election lists. Already ten other states have done this;

and in Pittsburgh forty-three Communist petition circulators, including a Harvard graduate, await trial on charges of fraud." (Harvard *Crimson,* October 31)

(25) Votes may be won or mortgaged also through legislation. The sugar Senators from Louisiana wanted legislation in the interest of their clients "Wallace would be so distasteful to Louisiana sugar growers that Willkie would carry the state" without this sweetening legislation. And Secretary Ickes and John L Lewis wanted mine inspection legislation. "Lewis is vitally needed on the stump" and CIO votes needed in the election (Mallon, September 13).

The President in June was anxious to have Congress go home But later when votes were in jeopardy he consented to their staying. They did stay, for two reasons,—they were reluctant to leave everything to the President, there were idealists, isolationists, what you wish to call them, who wanted to check the President,—but the great mass of congressmen, who were there to sell legislation, saw business ahead with the lobbyists. And they have been doing a big business all summer trading with them, trading legislation, concessions, laws, for something else It's a great market place.

(26) Senator Wheeler, July 2, 1940, at St. Louis, said. "All aid short of war—that is the catch-phrase of the day. Behind this smoke-screen lies the insidious propaganda of those who do not shrink from leading us down the road to war Every organ of propaganda is being employed. Full-page ads appear in many newspapers. The voices of speakers and commentators blare forth shrilly from the radio. Scare headlines stare at us from the press America is being bombarded by the interventionists. This is the same barrage that preceded our entry into the last war. . . . Roosevelt is doing his agonizing best to get us into the war. And he is doing so without the approval of public opinion. . . A few years ago the Senate Munitions Investigating Committee laid bare not only the sordid, behind-the-scenes story of the last war, but revealed plans already formulated for the conduct of the next one The committee found that 'the price of a war may be actual operating dictatorship' in this country." (St Louis *Post-Dispatch,* June 11, 1940)

(27) "Mr. Roosevelt explains his descent from his ivory tower and, in the convention-hall where he was nominated for his second term, begins his personal pleading for a third. He was witty last night. Was he wise?", asks the Boston *Transcript* in an editorial, October 24, 1940.

"The crux of the speech was an attempt to disprove the assertion that 'this Administration wishes to lead this country into war'. The attempt was not only unconvincing, in certain of its expressions, it very nearly assumed the tone most repellent to American voters. it approached a smug piety which, in turn, suggests hypocrisy" The editorial goes on to quote John T. Flynn, (cf Bul #82) on "The President's Dilemma", the necessity for continuing spending on war.

Next it quotes Amos Pinchot who "recalling how, as long as 17 months ago, the President expressed a belief that, should a European war occur, American involvement would be 'a virtual certainty' . . declared: 'Telling the aggressor nations that they are diseased and ought to be quarantined is certainly not peace talk. Charging their people with being unlettered, benighted and bestial" does not look like peace salesmanship. . . . Informing them that this country is ready to "match force with force" is silly and reckless talk calculated to inflame international hatred, provoke reprisals and set the stage for hostilities.' "

The President has adopted the Tory attitude, "that the only enemies of their country are certain wicked men called dictators . . . it is not to be denied that scotching the dictators . . . will give the English raj, or at all events its ruling class, a grateful breathing spell. But it is by no means certain that these benign effects, if they are ever achieved, will last. It is by no means certain that the democratic civilization we all venerate can survive the blows now raining upon it." (H. L. Mencken, October 27, 1940)

(28) "There is grave danger that the 1916 'He Kept Us Out of War' farce will be repeated", unless we have "a much franker and fairer statement than . . . that no American boy will be sent to fight in 'a foreign war'. . . . What is a foreign war? Wouldn't any conflict in which the United States found it necessary to engage become an American war?" (Editorial *Chr Sci Monitor,* October 31)

At Cleveland, November 2, 1940, the President again stated cagily: "There is nothing secret about our foreign policy . . . The first purpose of our foreign policy is to keep our country out of war." (There are those who see and believe that his meddling forced England into war inopportunely and has brought us to acts of war.)

"At the same time we seek to keep foreign conceptions of government out of the United States " (Conceptions, ideas, cannot be quarantined, have not been. We certainly owe much to England and France in our conception of national government and much to Germany for our ideas of municipal government.)

"The second purpose of this policy is to keep war as far away as possible from the shores of the entire western hemisphere " (Does that mean doing our fighting on other shores, in another hemisphere?)

"Americans are determined to retain for themselves the right of free speech, free religion, free assembly and the right which lies at the basis of all of them— the right to choose the officers of their own government in free elections. We intend to keep that freedom—to defend it against attacks from without and against corruption from within " (He has missed some opportunities in the past eight years in that defense.)

"Freedom of speech is of no use to a man who has nothing to say." (If the President believes you have nothing to say, from his point of view, he will shut you up) "Freedom of worship is of no use to a man who has lost his God." (Torquemada might have said this If you have "lost" the God of your childhood and found better gods to worship, you are to be persecuted.)

"The defense of our country requires national unity." (All must think as Roosevelt does)

And then he quoted a bastard version of holy writ. "And all the forces of evil shall not prevail against it For so it is written in the Book, and so it is written in the promise of a great era of world peace "

[29] "Roosevelt himself has promised categorically, on at least a dozen occasions, to keep out of the war, and with the most pious and eye-rolling solemnity, but . . . no one, in fact, believes Roosevelt any more, no matter how-hair-raising his oaths, save only when he promises to pour out more money. In that department he is still quite reliable . . His foreign policy, however it may be defended as Christian endeavor, has been unbrokenly devious, dishonest and dishonorable. Claiming all the immunities of a neutral, he has misled the country into countless acts of war, and there is scarcely an article of international law that he has not violated." (H. L. Mencken, October 20, 1940)

[30] Gen Hugh Johnson writes October 31, 1940, addressing "Dear Joe", "You quoted that great military expert, Walter Lippmann, that any fear we will send troops is absurd because the Atlantic is there . . You also say that, if Hitler can't cross 20 miles of English channel, he can't cross the Atlantic. Right. But also in your breath, you say that we must elect Mr Indispensable to keep Hitler from crossing the Atlantic. Why not get in step with yourself? . . Your air sponsor was the 'Kennedy Family'. Isn't that just another name for 'Somerset Importers, Limited', monopoly purveyors of Scotch whiskey and gin? With all that shipping shortage and British export quotas, is it good business to check out as ambassador to England just now? Goombye, Joe. Be good and you will be happy."

"There is no place in this fight for us . . . As you love America, don't let anything that comes out of any country in the world make you believe you can make a situation one whit better by getting into a war," declared Kennedy on his home coming, Christmas 1939 (cf Bul #22) Out from under the influence of the President, Kennedy has repeatedly expressed the same ideas To Louis M. Lyons, star reporter of the Boston *Globe*, director of the Nieman Fellows at Harvard, and syndicate writer for the North American Newspaper Alliance, Kennedy in the presence of others let himself out, and Lyons syndicated the interview in the Sunday papers, quoting Kennedy as saying that "democracy is finished in England . . . national Socialism is coming".

When Kennedy saw this in print and felt the repercussions from Whitehall and the White House, he protested that all was "off the record", but added, "Well, the fat's in the fire, but I guess that's where I want it". (Luther Conant, Jr., Boston *Transcript*, November 12, 1940) Later, in Los Angeles, he was even more emphatic in his declaration that democracy in England was dead, there was no place for us in this war. "And I will do everything I can, in every way possible, to keep the United States out of any war anywhere."

When the *Globe* reporter asked Kennedy, "Did you support Roosevelt with some misgiving?" Kennedy replied, "No. I supported Roosevelt because I felt he's the only man who can control the groups who have got to be brought along in what's ahead of us" "You mean the men who control industry?" the reporters asked "No" said Kennedy, "They have a stake that they've got to defend I mean the have-nots They haven't any stake or ownership. They've got to take it in whatever faces us."

In his "The History of the English People", John Richard Green, telling of how the King went back on his promises to Wat Tyler's 'sharecroppers', said, "At Waltham he (the King) was met by the display of his own recent charters . . . But they were to learn the worth of a King's word. 'Villeins you were,' answered Richard, 'and villeins you are   In bondage you shall abide, and that not your old bondage but a worse!' "

(31) Mrs. William H. Fain, Greenwich, Conn., wrote President Roosevelt that "she was in sympathy with his humanitarian and social objectives. 'But the tone of both addresses, seems to me calculated to build up a psychosis which may drive us into a war in which we could be of little help to Europe, but in which we might lose our own liberty as well as the lives of our youth". Bruce Barton, in a radio address, said that when Mrs. Fain requested the return of the letter to refresh her memory, she received from the Department of Justice a photostatic copy which bore a stamp "criminal division"   Barton objected that 'a courteously-worded criticism from a woman to her President would cause that citizen to be recorded in the files of the criminal division of the Department of Justice.' " (AP, October 30, 1940)

(32) "A shout of 'dictator' in a local theatre during the showing of President Roosevelt's picture in a news reel" brought 30 days or $50 to the shouter. (AP, October 23, 1940) The excuse was "disorderly conduct". He could as well have been taken on vagrancy. He was not working at the time.

A newspaper reporter, almost as outspoken, was not quite so drastically dealt with. "The other day a newsman even asked Roosevelt if he intended to become a dictator. Here is the actual colloquy, though without quotes on the President's word. (Boston *Transcript*)

"Question: 'Mr. President, in coming political speeches, do you intend to answer charges made by your political opposition that you are seeking to become a dictator, and that if you are elected there will be nothing to prevent you from doing so?' (Most questions are shorter and simpler than this one, which had been written out in advance.)

"The President replied, That is interesting   It has everything except the kitchen stove in it   Who wrote it?

"Questioner: I did

"The President Good boy My congratulations to you.

"Questioner: Is there an answer?

"The President· My congratulations to you. It is beautifully worded.

"And that, except for the laughter, ended the cross-examination "

BUILDING A LOYAL OPPOSITION

Our President has been re-elected for a third term by a majority[1] of 5 millions, but the 22 million votes cast for his opponent form the basis for the strongest opposition a President has ever faced.[2]

"The cry for national unity and good sportsmanship" was immediately raised, assuming that 22 million would abandon convictions merely because they were outvoted, though they recognize with Paul Mallon (Nov. 8) that "nothing that was true last Monday became untrue on Wednesday".[8]

Editorialists and publicists have been sounding variations on this cry for unity rather than dissension. "Unity" might mean "the negation of democracy, the decay of the two-party system. . . . 'Unity' of that kind is a synonym of eunuchy", editorialized the Boston *Herald*.[4] "Real unity American style, is not incompatible with sharp debate . . . critical examination of every proposal . . . an attitude of inquiry, obedience to personal convictions, attacks on the opposition".[5]

"Your function during the next four years is that of the loyal opposition", Willkie told his people in his nationwide radio address after his defeat So he disposed of the unsound suggestion that in order to present a united front to a threatening world, the opposition should now surrender its convictions and approve blindly of every act of the Administration. He rightly warned that this is a "totalitarian idea— a slave idea" and that it must be utterly rejected.

"Our American Unity cannot be made with words and gestures. It must be forged between the ideas of the opposition and the practices and policies of the Administration. Ours is a Government of principles and not one merely of men. Any member of the minority party, though willing to die for his country, still retains the right to criticize the policies of the Government This right is embedded in our constitutional system," editorialized the Boston *Transcript*, Nov. 12.[6]

"His Majesty's Constructive Opposition", an editorial in the Harvard *Crimson,* says of the "confused conservative", "With Mr. Willkie's demand that the opposition be strong, alert, and watchful, there will be general agreement. It would be well, however, if the opposition were also realistic. For, to paraphrase the Republican leader, 'only the realistic can be effective, and only the effective can be valuable'."

"We do not want unity in the sense of totalitarian government in which the voice of all opposition is silenced", Senator Vandenberg declared November 9 (AP). Senator McNary said, "I am wishing Mr. Roosevelt and Mr. Wallace grace, and their Administration prosperity. We shall try to furnish them a worthy and vigilant opposition."

"Americans have differed deeply with each other in this period over the economic and social policies of the government, over political trends in our government, and now, in recent months, over our relation to the war in Europe", writes Raymond Clapper (*Life*, Nov. 18, 1940).

"Mr. Willkie and his supporters were accused of secretly favoring appeasement. President Roosevelt was accused of secretly maneuvering to take this country into war. It is clear, even by the pledge that President Roosevelt himself felt it necessary to make in the campaign, that a considerable portion of our population is opposed to active participation in the war. . . . A feeling of anxiety, of mistrust . . . arises out of his personality, his public character, his seeming love of power, his poorly disguised eagerness to obtain a third term. There is a fear that Mr. Roosevelt will construe his re-election as a mandate."[7]

The defense program may serve "as a catalyst to draw us all together". "Even if Mr. Roosevelt has secret designs" and "powerful as the presidential office is", Mr. Clapper does "not believe that one man can use it to force the nation into war", and therefore we should "lay aside suspicions on that score".[8]

The President normally possesses great power. In Civil War times Secretary of State Seward could say, "We elect a king for four years, and give him absolute power within certain limits, which after all he can interpret for himself" Lord Acton, the English Catholic historian, had before his mind all the examples of history when he wrote, "Power corrupts—absolute power corrupts absolutely".[9]

Today our President, while having most of the special war powers given President Wilson, has enormously increased powers granted in more than one hundred legislative acts (cf Bul #38)

"The President: Office and Powers", N.Y. Univ. Press, 1940, by Edward S Corwin, a scholarly historical survey, fully documented, warns us that "the Presidential power is dangerously personalized".

Mr. Roosevelt's intent is to do everything short of war for our British friends. His carefully phrased assurances not to lead us into war leaves loopholes Mr. Wilson's pledges were quite as binding. Elected on the slogan "He kept us out of war", in five months he put us in.

When duty calls, Roosevelt will not fail to defend us against attack. He has told Congress that "an effective defense requires the equipment to attack an aggressor on his route" (cf Bul #93). Despite his wishes and intent it may seem to him his duty to send expeditionary forces to intercept the enemy on foreign shores.[10]

Col. Robt. McCormick told the nation by radio that Hitler could equip 10 millions to meet such an expeditionary force. We would have to have twice that number mobilized, our complete manpower. The cost he estimated at 400 billions, 1 million dead, 4 million wounded

Lord Lothian tactfully removed himself from the American scene before the election, and British propaganda took a new trend, skilfully adjusted to the occasion. Election over, British prospects became bright in the light of the might of the Greeks fighting for the right.

"Reporting . . . was weird. Whether for reasons of propaganda or because of over-anxious sympathy (*Time,* Nov. 18) Successive Greek "victories" when traced on the map, sometimes turned out to be steady Italian advances Italians were said to be deserting in droves, drowning themselves in flooded gorges, perishing in cold and hunger, suffering from the forays of wolves." (Poor Little Red Riding Hoods)

With the Japanese withdrawing from China, Italian warships destroyed by bombs harmless against British warships, it is made to seem we must get in quick to win any glory. "Come on in, the water's fine".

Stoneman, London correspondent for Knox's Chicago *News,* financed by Kuhn, Loeb, returns by Clipper to tell us we must put our industry on a 24-hour full war time basis, give all our resources, declare war, pay the bills. Lord Lothian is on the way back. 'The British are Coming'.[11]

'Eternal vigilance is the price of liberty'.[12]

November 19, 1940

NOTES

[1] "President Roosevelt's plurality was the smallest since Woodrow Wilson's 591,385 in 1916" The official count announced Dec. 13, AP, showed a record vote of 49,808,624, Roosevelt 27,241,939 (a plurality of 4,914,713 for President Roosevelt), Willkie 22,327,226, Thomas 116,796

Roosevelt received 54.7% of the popular vote,—but in the electoral college, he received 82%, 449 votes to Willkie's 82. A change of "less than 1%", "a shift of only 450,615 votes in ten states—ranging from 0 75% of the total vote in Wisconsin to 4.1% of the total in Delaware—would have given Wendell Willkie an electoral ticket to the White House". This has led to a lot of figuring on the part of amateur politicians A reshuffling of "180,000 votes would have given Roosevelt all 48 states In the 1896 campaign, a switch of 14,000 votes would have . . . put Bryan in the White House by two electoral votes   In Mississippi and South Carolina, only 11,000 popular votes are needed to win one electoral vote, whereas in Illinois it takes 144,000,—that is,—each voter in Mississippi exerts a political power in president choice equal to 13 voters in Illinois   A Tennessee voter exerts ten times the political power of an Iowa voter.   This burlesque of representative government justifies Senator Lodge's recent move for a constitutional amendment to do away with the electoral college.

Though Texas and California have almost equal populations, California casts nearly 3 million votes to a little over a million for Texas.   Georgia, nearly equal in population with Wisconsin, casts only some hundred thousand votes to Wisconsin's million and a quarter.   Alabama casts only a few thousand over 200 thousand votes to over a million for Minnesota, with about the same population. Iowa likewise casts over a million votes to between 3 and 4 hundred thousand for Virginia, where a disfranchising poll tax acts as in the above instances to deny the vote to many citizens.   Poll taxes and racial restrictions in the Southern states make it possible for only a small proportion of the people to vote,—Sen George, chairman of the Foreign Relations Committee was elected by 2 4% of the population of Georgia where only 10.3% may vote. Rep. Martin Dies was elected by 4 2% of the population of Texas where only 18% may vote. (cf Anna Louise Strong, "My Native Land", Viking)   Another estimate, perhaps for a later election, is "5.3 per cent of what should be the electorate in his district" (cf Dreiser, "America is Worth Saving", Modern Age Books, 1941)

All the candidates for Congress who came out strongly against the President's foreign policy, war and conscription were re-elected in spite of majorities for Roosevelt in their states,—Johnson of California, Shipstead of Minnesota, Thomas of Idaho, LaFollette of Wisconsin, Wheeler of Montana, Vandenberg of Michigan, Walsh of Massachusetts, and Maloney of Connecticut.   In Illinois, C. Wayland Brooks, non-interventionist, defeated Sen. Slattery   Representative Jeannette Rankin, veteran peace worker, was elected Congresswoman from Montana.   During the recent campaign, Vandenberg, vigorously disapproving of Willkie's foreign views "made several attempts to argue the matter with him. But Willkie dodged these attempts to convert him" (Pearson & Allen).

(2) The annual Gridiron Club banquet after the election was missed by Roosevelt for the first time,—a correspondent claimed because of his embarrassment at his "reduced majority"—another said he had gone "to inspect the West Indian fishing grounds" but he hurried back to lend Britain some more money.   Willkie was present, however, to hear the taunting song: "I'll never smile again, Because I bet on him   He'll never yacht again, Next time he can swim.   I'll climb no limb again And get it sawed in two, I'll never thrill again To somebody new." But the reply came back apparently from Willkie: "Out of the fight that smothered me, Blacker it was than Gallup's poll, I bring what's left of GOP, But some one else must dig the hole, Dewey and Taft, just get this straight, Vandenberg, Hoover and Old Guard corps, I still am master of your fate, I'll be the boss in forty-four."

(3) The press was even more overwhelmingly for Willkie than it had been for Landon four years before. Secretary Ickes at his news conference, in Fascist style addressed "a friendly inquiry . . to the newspaper publishers of this nation". "Last Tuesday we elected a President who was supported by less than 23% of our daily press This reveals a perilous situation requiring public consideration." Editor Herbert Agar of the pro-Roosevelt Louisville *Courier-Journal* in reply said, "There is a lot to say against the press, but the fact that it is against an individual does not prove it is not free " (*Time*, November 18, 1940)

(4) "Since election we have heard a lot about unity. I say it is the bunk. The election settled none of our problems—not one. It did not change wrong to right Merely because we voted is no reason why we should now . . . become mummies, kowtowing to the President and accepting his theories of government. No matter what may have been the vote, I am going to keep fighting for what I believe is right, whether Roosevelt approves or disapproves," declared publisher Frank Gannett (AP November 21) "The election result, thank God, was no mandate for us to go to war. We Republicans must fight every minute of the day in opposition to entry into the war, no matter how much they may talk about unity "

The James S Twohey Associates report, "After the election, 36% of the comment switches to the need for unity and most of this comment plugs strongly for a united front However, 8% stresses that it is up to the President to do his part and this group appears to imply that the President better play ball if he wants co-operation . . . the overwhelming majority of the press continued to pull for Willkie and to damn Roosevelt right up to poll time. . . . 4% charge Government checks and an army of jobholders influenced the result Overall acceptance of Mr Roosevelt's victory is by no means as complete and wholehearted as was the case in 1936 "

(5) Editor Jessup in Sinclair Lewis' "It Can't Happen Here" learned from his Fascist persecutors that all the worthwhile things in the life of man have come from the free play of the inquiring spirit, and that the preservation of that spirit is more important than any governmental system.

(6) Unity of opinion may be brought about by conviction (ask the judge or the warden), intimidation (ask the drill master or the gunman), or suppression (no need to ask Hitler or Mussolini), or all three. Paul Mallon intimates that the president has conferred with members of his staff on the matter of suppressing the opposition and at the same time putting the soft pedal on the war party. Those who are all for war are determined that in unifying opinion, their pattern shall be followed.

The Council for Democracy launched in the Fall of 1940 at well-publicized meetings in New York's Carnegie Hall and Fanueil Hall, Boston's "Cradle of Liberty", is for such unification The claim was made that they were reviving John Hancock's Committee of Correspondents This idea had been tossed about among the fascists' mind for a year, taken up by Henry Luce, he is said to have contributed $25,000 and lent members of his staff. C. D. Jackson, General

Manager of *Life,* is President. Chairman is the radio sob artist, Raymond Gram Swing. Chairman of the Executive Committee is Carl J. Friedrich, Professor of Government at Harvard, who in the early '20's came to this country as an exchange German student and now emphasizes his Americanism by his anti-Germanism. Secretary is Evans Clark, once of a Reddish tinge, whose wife, Freda Kirchwey, as editor, has made *The Nation* an organ of hate. "Let Freda ring", they whisper as she rants about the editorial offices Expensive advertising and literature announced its function was "to crystallize and instill in the minds of Americans" the ideas of the Council, "to engender the will to defend and promote" those ideas, "and to stimulate the *participation* of each individual in the activities necessary . . . to publicize and counteract the propaganda of all organizations and individuals whose" ideas are different. This language was a little too transparent so that it was immediately denounced in the public prints as another Creel Committee to promote witch-hunting. *In Fact* devoted its December 2, 1940, issue largely to explaining who was promoting it and to what ends The organization failed to arouse support and gain the blessing of the government, and fell flat.

(7) Just before the election, President Roosevelt, to allay the anxiety of the voters, expressed the hope that if elected for another four years he would settle the affairs of the world to his satisfaction and "there would be another President". But on March 4, 1937, after he had taken 'terrific punishment' as he confessed to Rex Tugwell on the Supreme Court 'putsch', he said, "My greatest ambition on January 20, 1941, is to turn over this desk and chair in the White House to my successor, whoever he may be, with the assurance that I am at the same time turning over to him as President a nation intact, a nation at peace, a nation prosperous " (Boston *Transcript,* Nov. 4, 1940) The nation was not at peace nor prosperous, but he had united his party for plunder, bribed the economic royalists with 'fool's gold' and given the labor racketeers their richest opportunity.

In his press conference, Nov. 8, 1940, after the election, the President, arrogantly gay, in response to a question, in mock humility told them he had erred on the conservative side by 109 electoral votes in his August sealed forecast of the results of the election When "asked if he cared to clarify campaign disclaimers of fourth-term ambitions", the President told the reporter to "go back to grade school and learn English" "When the correspondent said that he had read the President's statements, Mr. Roosevelt said that the reporter should read them again . . he could not undertake to teach the reporter English." (Chas W Hurd, N. Y. *Times* dispatch from Washington, Nov 8)

(8) Of democracy in England Harold Laski has said that the people pay the minority to oppose the government, to take maximum advantage of the government's mistakes, to insist that it is ruining the country and to flood the electorate with propaganda intended to show that the government is doing the worst possible things in the worst possible way. They put it frankly up to the government to justify its every act.

(9) "Leaving St. James, Hyde Park" (No, this is not London,—it's America),

is the caption for an illustration in *Time,* Oct. 28, 1940, under "National Affairs". Here are surpliced and cassocked prelates to whom the President's mother is addressing herself, while the President gives his attention to Princess Alice Shortly before he had entertained for the weekend the Duke and Duchess of Athlone. On Armistice Day, Nov. 11, AP, the President drove to Pook's Hill for a tea with the Crown Princess of Norway "He remained about an hour and a half." He called for "national unity" in his address earlier in the day, but told the nation we had a job of "unfinished business" The President referred to, of course, this second World War to crush Germany and protect and sustain the British Empire. To enlist America in that cause, the President was promoting the amazing myth that the British Empire and its fleet were necessary to protest our feeble country and democracy.

On December 19 an AP dispatch from Washington reported that "a brilliant dinner was given at the White House in honor of Crown Princess Juliana of The Netherlands, (while) . . . heading the guest list was Crown Princess Martha of Norway . . both royal refugees in the new world." Perhaps Congress would do well to provide for ermine, a crown and other necessary trappings in appropriating for the President's 'entertainments'

About that time we learned that Nehru, the great patriotic leader in India's long struggle for freedom, proposing to make a pacifist speech had been sentenced to four years at hard labor Simultaneously we were being told by Lord Lothian and other Englishmen that we must put our war economy on a twenty-four hour basis, give more of ships and money and devote all our resources to the preservation of Britain's imperial democracy.

(10) Our War Department is working on plans (or building?) 80-ton tanks The British are seeking to place an "order of $100,000,000 worth of heavy tanks —the big 40- to 70-ton monsters" (Paul Mallon, Nov 29) The only place where these tanks would be of value would be in breaking the Siegfried Line. The Harvard *Crimson,* in an editorial protesting Conant's radio plea for war, declared, "Millions of Americans have swallowed the yarn of invasion, while its originators talk cynically of defense, and prepare America for offense—for invasion of Europe by American arms, an invasion aimed at crushing Germany . . . Isn't there a tragic irony about going to war to save our markets, when within our own borders there are 40,000,000 people who are cold, hungry and without hope?"

(11) Stoneman, coming direct from London where Lord Lothian at the time was advising with the government as to the trend British propaganda should now take in America, explained that since "The British lost practically their entire supply of guns and automatic weapons and tanks in Flanders", all the resources of the U. S. and the Empire will be required to smash Germany and Great Britain alone cannot pay the bill. Emphasizing that an American expeditionary force was needed immediately, he made it seem like a lark,—we can satisfy our moral indignation without taking any risk.

"American bombers could be giving Berlin a shellacking . . . in broad daylight . . . without running even a sporting chance of being shot down." More-over, the American pilots are so well trained that they would be of tremendous assistance to the R A F in defending Britain. "A belligerent United States would eventually be able to make a stupendous and probably decisive contribu-tion of military, naval and air strength while a neutral United States, draft or no draft, is virtually marking time." An American declaration of war "would . . . turn the tide of morale . . . against Germany. In the United Kingdom it would give 46,000,000 people the definite assurance that victory was certain", and would make "the brave peoples of Norway, Czecho-Slovakia, Poland, France and Holland again begin to think of liberation as a certainty." Russia would begin to tremble, and the Japanese "might even find it possible to go into re-verse."

"If the Americans don't think that an American declaration of war would have any immediate effect, they are more modest than we have always thought. Just let them try it and see what happens." (Stoneman, Boston *Transcript*, Novem-ber 8, 1940)

"Last week Sir Walter Layton of the British Ministry of Supply, back from a visit to the U. S., told his own people that American arms production will not get rolling at full speed until the spring of 1942. This estimate is backed up by the best business judgment in the U. S and it is a sad truth for Britain." (*Life*, Jan. 6, 1941)

[12] Senator Guy M Gillette, Iowa Democrat and chairman of the Senate cam-paign expenditures committee, charged in a radio address early in December, "never before in American history have we seen a more patent, potent and po-tential attempt to influence the American electorate". The Gillette Committee revealed "three wealthy families contributed a total of $276,725 to campaign funds for Wendell L. Willkie.

"THE OPPOSITION SPEAKS UP"

To maintain the tradition of American freedom of thought and speech, a loyal opposition is needed. Through fear and intimidation, people everywhere are gradually yielding to the conditioning of the hate propaganda But since the last 8-page report in August heartening words have come from hundreds, whose encouragement we gladly share. A few, in part, are here reproduced. Educators were quoted in Septem-ber and November issues of *Private School News* to the number of some hundreds. They write telling how they value the Bulletins and use them in their classes, lectures and current events programs.

Writers —"Keep up the good work against the U S. getting into war", Harvey O'Connor. "You have a way of saying things which sticks in the mind", M. T. Harris. "Public spirit . . coupled with enlightenment such as yours . . . is water in the desert in this country just now", Edward Price Bell "Especially useful to become familiar with the problems of this country", Heinz Pol. "Continued admiration and gratitude for your great work for democracy", Myles Connolly. "I am always stimulated by the vigorous line that you take. You are a fresh breeze, not to say a tornado, in the dusty corridors of Academia", Harold D. Lasswell.

Editors—"Heartening to discover that there was one voice, at least, in New England which was advocating a policy for the United States other than to tie its fortunes with those of the declining British Empire", Paul Hutchinson, *Christian Century.* "As long as there is any way to get them out, may I be of those lucky enough to receive the Sargent Bulletins? Some day historians may find that . . these were as effective as the whole vast establishment of the established press. At least they have a freedom that is refreshing and wholesome", Alden B. Hoag, Boston *Transcript.* "Timely and stimulating. I'm doing my weak best to preach the same sort of gospel in this area", O. L Brownlee, Sioux City *Tribune, Iowa.* "We all read them around here and file them so we can reread them later. Sometimes they sound rather screwy; sometimes they are darn near brilliant, always informative, always interesting, and we'd hate to miss them", Harold Lavine, Inst. Propaganda Analysis "Your releases interest me. It seems to me that the more America becomes involved with Europe, the more we become like that unhappy continent, divided and quarreling," B. Bettinger, *Common Ground.*

People —"A brilliant ray of sanity on a quite dark horizon", George R. Faxon. "No man in America is doing a more valuable work than you", Bayard Boyesen. "You have done marvelous work", E O. Jones "Just what the country needs right now in large doses", Penn R. Watson. "Very sorry . . . it is uncertain how long you may be able to continue your valuable bulletins in this present crisis", Nina Almond. "Keep up your bulletins, even though you are 'a voice crying in the wilderness' ", L. A Otto, Jr. "By no means give up your work in analyzing propaganda", G. W. Sorenson. "While your efforts may at times seem futile, you have done more than anybody else to keep America a place where thinking can be done and difference tolerated", R. E. Romig.

"A fine, courageous, and helpful piece of work. . full of important news items and valuable opinions which demand expression", Richards Emerson. "I strongly commend you for this effort to enlighten the American people on vital economic, political and war issues", C. Walton Johnson. "Make hay while the sun shines that is, pull no punches and use your heaviest and most effective batteries before you are silenced,— which indeed you will be if the present trend toward dictatorship continues in this country", William T. Carpenter

"The publication of your bulletins in book form would be a valuable service to your contemporaries. Certainly it would be an aid, a compendium of condensed source material, for the future Gibbon who will write the history of 'The Decline and Fall of the Republic of the United States of North America'. The title should suggest that the events, trends and issues of the last few years, as covered by your bulletins, represent a stage (perhaps the final stage) of a movement which has been under way for a century or more. As I interpret American history, the United States has been moving 'on to dictatorship' ever since the Mexican War. . . . one of imperialistic aggression, suppression of minorities, conquest, oppression and exploitation of physically weaker peoples, and waste and destruction of natural resources," Dean Babcock.

Anonymous—"Do not cut me off your mailing list for those stirring and revealing Bulletins with which you are enlightening the American public to the danger which the present administration has brought upon this land. They are like a ray of sunshine through the fog Without your enterprise and the fire of H L Mencken and Senators Wheeler, Vandenberg, Holt and Lundeen, and the courageous Col. Lindbergh, I fear that America would long ago have given up hope, as the average man is now afraid to express his opinion " "I agree with those individuals who marvel at your ability and willingness, in the face of such discouragements, to continue the distribution of this helpful medium of enlightenment. Personally, I am quite discouraged with the outlook, and fear that the American people, utterly and hopelessly misguided by pernicious propaganda, will yet reach the point where they will welcome a war. I, with the many others whose endorsements have been inserted in your bulletins, regard your efforts as unselfishly patriotic . . . and I am hopeful that, through your efforts and the remaining few who actually see the true situation, this country may be saved." "Helpful indeed in these times of national and international crises Your editing

and publishing them at your own cost constitute an admirable example of spirited patriotic service."
November 19, 1940

NOTES

Of the hundreds of letters that poured in in response to the preceding, we quote briefly from a few public men, writers, educators and others, some of whom write so frankly that we quote them anonymously

"Listening to the President last night I was struck as always by the merciless-ness in his voice. It was a speech of defiance if you will, a defiance with one foot on a half-strength and the other on weakness, and there was not one humane or kindly thought, no compassion whatever for the tragedy which is so much of his making, nothing but catchwords, nothing but prejudices, and all afloat on a cur-rent of hate. After listening to it one could but wonder what spiritual discipline could best cleanse the mind of such eagerness of destruction Well, he has had his way with wretched Britain, which is now dying, the British orchard having been sacked, burned, hacked, and cut to cure a political problem which might be compared to a visitation of aphis. It seems useless to point out to them here that the life of the orchard is what counts No, it must mercilessly go on, abandon-ing all humanity and all common sense till the last poor English ploughman dies in his burning barn and the last poor mole catcher dies in his ditch. If we escape being tricked, bullied, or cajoled into this most wicked and foolish of wars, if the menacing cloud and oppression of coming poverty does not darken the entire life of the nation, every American will owe you a very great debt. The arrival of a bulletin means there is still hope, still intelligence, still light, still a human understanding of a problem which must be humanely solved before it is resolved politically " (A well known author)

"As a busy professor and part time lecturer on international and national affairs, I have learned to appreciate greatly your bulletins on current issues. They contain a startling and authentic array of 'behind-the-headlines' facts which are not only important, but are great time savers for any platform man " (A western professor)

"Things are getting tough for us now, but the fact that it is all the same as before makes it seem as comic to me as it is tragic I spent my indignation last time and have little left but resignation I think our trouble is that there is nothing to capture the imagination in being sensible and neutral Why can't you play the role of a new Peter the Hermit preaching a crusade not for, but against, England. There are enough people to get fighting mad on this and kindred issues to give these traitors pause. We are simply 'yellow', we sensible and loyal Americans." (A Harvard professor)

"Permit me to join with many others in telling you how much I have looked forward to receiving your bulletins We are repeating the events of 1917-18 in a form more intensified than most of us had even feared At least we have come to a point bordering on hysteria much more rapidly than we had expected." (A southern university professor)

"You are kind to realize that judges have no freedom of speech, and so I will content myself with thanking you for your kindness in sending me your sprightly writings " (A U. S. justice)

College Professors and Educators—"Your releases have been swell; done more good than you probably realize", George Hartmann, Columbia Univ. "A joy and an inspiration! Keep up the good work I use your bulletins regularly in my classes", C. H. Cramer, So Ill. Normal Univ "Your bulletins present little-known data in a refreshing manner," A. B. Hollinshead, Indiana Univ. "Greatly interested Keep up the good work just as long as the F B.I. allows you to", E H Warner, U of Ariz. "Much of what you cite I just can't accept, but I am glad to have information from any possible source", W. Carson Ryan, U. of N. C. "It looks to me as though the war-participation issue is now settled and we shall be inner and inner. The big question in my mind is now how to use the opportunities this world-shaking struggle will present, to advance progressive rather than reactionary adjustments. I gather the old-timers aren't so sure they can run England as they used to, and our chance should be much better", Goodwin Watson, Columbia Univ "Your interpretations of what is going on in the world are always of greatest interest to me", O. L. Reiser, Univ. of Pittsburgh "Your analyses of England and the war have been both intelligent and realistic I admire your courage in this prejudiced world", Francis M. Froelicher, Fountain Valley School.

"What tremendous energy, intellectual resource, moral fervor, and positive orientation you possess! I can not follow you all the way, but I am very glad that those who are critical of Britain have so vigorous a pen and so dynamic an organizer as you as their prophet", Philip W. L. Cox, Columbia Univ

"You're surely the Dynamite Kid of propaganda! Yes sir, you're the class of the weight of the fighters who are concerned with communication. For your guts and good sense I've frank admiration If only one fiftieth of those of us who are young, strong, and able, individually exercised half the energy you do, why perhaps you could put down your pen long enough to do a little Pacific Coasting," Lloyd Morain, Los Angeles, Calif.

Senators and Representatives—"There are still a few articulate voices speaking for sanity left in America and yours is one of them", Sen. Burton K Wheeler "You may be sure of my continued interest and efforts in behalf of American neutrality", Sen. Bennett Champ Clark "I look forward to reading them with great interest", Sen H. C. Lodge, Jr. "Read with interest", Rep. Thomas H Eliot. "As usual, I think your remarks have sense and shrewdness", Rep. G. H. Tinkham

More People—"Your bulletins were intensely interesting and decidedly challenging As you say, you and I are at one in believing that the great thing for our fellowcountrymen is to be for 'America First'. Our committee is keeping at it. There are those who feel that we are making a losing fight so far as the President's dictatorship bill goes. Occasionally I have my own fears but hope overcomes them I just cannot believe that this great Republic is going to join the 'Dictator Nations' with a shout of gladness", Bishop W. E. Hammaker.

"Thanks for all your splendid stuff which I read every word of," Lawrence

Dennis. "Please accept my heartiest congratulations on those of your Bulletins which I have seen, especially on their intellectual honesty and candor," Hoffman Nickerson "Accept my heartiest congratulations upon your bulletins, which so ably demonstrate, the manner in which asses can be prevailed upon to accept loco weed in the place of nourishing hay. Yours is a voice crying in the wilderness, but you'll always have the satisfaction of reminding yourself, 'I told the d—n fools to look out'," Frank L. McKinney. "Congratulations on your zeal and energy", Dr. Lyman E. Richards.

"It appears to me that Hitler is invaluable to Roosevelt, Bullitt, Ickes, Breckenridge and all others who continually quote him, because they make use of him going and coming They call him the world's greatest liar; they say 'you cannot trust Hitler', they remind you over and over again that Hitler has said this and that in 'Mein Kampf', especially that he has said the Germans intend to rule the world How can you denounce a man as a liar one minute, and the next minute quote him to prove some contention of your own? These loud-speaker artists want the listener to believe Hitler when Hitler's pronouncements can be construed as a threat to us—in other words, when our own politicians, for their own nefarious purposes, desire to scare the pants off their own people, they want us to believe Hitler is not a liar. They reserve the right to turn Hitler on or turn Hitler off, like a spigot, hot or cold, to serve their own purposes. Any attempt to hold Roosevelt to anything he said in a speech as recently as six, or even three, months ago would be regarded as absurd. Yet Roosevelt and his cohorts persist in quoting Hitler's speeches of several years ago, and everlastingly do they quote 'Mein Kampf' which, I believe, was written more than fifteen years ago. The president and his 'hatchet men' have time and again deliberately endeavored to scare the American people, whom they profess to love, by shouting at them the dangers which face us, and I cite particularly the well remembered radio talk by the president in which he told how few are the flying hours between Dakar and South America and, step by step, from Brazil to the United States It seems to me that evidence sufficient is at hand to prove we are occupying about the safest place in the world, namely. that practically every country in the world has sent its gold here for safe-keeping, also securities; royalty, ex-royalty, near royalty have flocked here; children have been shipped here for safe storage, ships are tied up here for safe keeping; and our swank summer and winter resorts are choked with rich refugees from the estates of England who instinctively head this way for safety. Yet our own president stands at the microphones and in dramatic tones assures us that we are not safe. I wonder if he was one of the two million, including a couple of college professors, who believed we had been invaded by the Martians " (Howard Cleaves, naturalist and lecturer, N Y., Feb 19, 1941)

PRODDING JAPAN INTO WAR

It was a profitable trade that an impoverished people built up with China after the American Revolution. Little wonder that old New

England families still treasure heirlooms, beautiful bits of porcelain which they call Lowestoft, brought back by enterprising youths who like Hasket Derby of Salem built their own boats, members of the family and community sharing the expense, and sailed around Cape Horn with no chart but a map torn out of a geography. It is not strange that New Englanders have long treasured a sentimental attitude toward the Chinese. And through the back stretches of our country returning missionaries from China have brought increased respect for a great people.

Today we are unwilling to face the fact that this China trade is not profitable to the nation as a whole. In recent years less than 3% of our foreign trade has been with China, including the British colony of Hongkong. This is less than half of our trade with Japan which before the abrogation of our 1911 trade treaty was our third best customer,—in 1938 taking 7 7% of our total exports (a falling off from 8.17% in 1935), while we were Japan's best customer, 6 5% of our imports coming thence (*Time*, Aug. 7, 1939).[1]

When Joe Chamberlain in 1894 began casting about for ways to protect Britain's interests in the East, she had a near monopoly, 65% of China's total foreign trade Since then Japan's trade has increased, encroaching upon Britain's so that today they are nearly equal

England and Englishmen are quite aware that their exports are 20% of their national income With 5% of our national income from exports, our foreign trade is relatively less important and we need not take our foreign relations so seriously. Even in the '20's when we were a peaceful people, when we were lending the money, never repaid, to buy the goods we exported, our foreign trade hardly got above 10% of our domestic trade. Consequently our foreign policy has never enlisted the interest of the whole country It has been characterized as "two steps backward" then "two steps forward". We have been inconsistent in first cancelling our armament program and then adopting a belligerent policy, or increasing our armament in retreat.

Why is it then that in our newspaper headlines, foreign trade looms so large? That is an interesting story generally distorted and suppressed which involves inside politics, intrigue, graft, and artificial promotions Kenneth Crawford in "The Pressure Boys" throws light on it and tells the story of Henry Herberman, "affable, go-getting New Yorker", a trucker in war-boom days. "The government subsidized the

Herberman companies to the extent of $45,000,000." Better known men got the money. [2]

A merchant marine must be protected by a navy which costs us more billions, which makes generous profits for the heavy industrialists, enabling them with this taxpayers' money to support an expensive staff of lobbyists and public relations men to promote 'defense', armament, and more profits. That's the house that Jack of 'foreign trade' built.[3]

The investments in China of Britain and Japan are likewise nearly equal. In 1931 of a total foreign investment in China, Britain's was 36.7% and Japan's 35%. American investments were relatively insignificant in comparison, 6%, less than two hundred millions. Either Japan or Britain had six times as great a stake. [4] "Our $750,000,000 stake in the entire Orient—of which a little more than one-fourth is invested in China proper—is less than the American people spend each year to witness college football and other sports events." (Walker Matheson, *North American Review*, Winter, 1938-39)

Our expenditure to protect American and British interests in the Pacific since John Hay's time has run to billions, totaling perhaps one hundred times the entire profit derived. For the few, of course, there have been big profits Our annual expenditure on military, naval and trade services approximates our whole investment in the Far East. [5] Frederick V Field in his "Far Eastern Survey· America's Stake in the Far East" quoted in the *North American Review*, Winter, 1938-39, gives the cost of our foreign service in Eastern Asia as $905,754 and adds to this detailed figures totaling approximately $300,000 for State and Commerce Departments, and a proportion of the cost of our Army and Navy running to hundreds of millions annually. To this might be added subsidies for our Pacific merchant marine.

This great relief to the British Treasury could not have been continued had it not been skilfully concealed from the American people. [6] Their hearts were made to swell with pride at our enterprise and prowess, and a protective attitude toward the Chinese was cultivated through missionaries and educational activities. The Burmese are perhaps a more delightful people, the civilizations of Hindustan equally great, but in neither was it necessary to enlist American sympathy to protect British interests.

How Joe Chamberlain, Britain's Foreign Minister and great empire builder, father of Austen and Neville, sold America the Open Door [7] policy in order to protect Britain's eastern interests, how the astute Alfred E. Hippisley of the Chinese Imperial Maritime Customs Service sold the idea to our Minister W. W. Rockhill, who sold it to John Hay, who sold it to the American people, is fully revealed in a heavily documented study by A. Whitney Griswold, assistant professor of government and international relations at Yale, in "The Far Eastern Policy of the United States" (Harcourt, Brace, 1938).

"The too-famous Open Door policy itself originated not in any seat of American government, but in the mind of an Englishman," writes Pearl Buck, reviewing Griswold in *Asia,* Jan., 1939, adding that it "has been a fiasco from its first dubious inception" and has kept our country "continually embroiled in all the intrigue and covetousness of the British Empire". "We entered boldly—via the back door of Eastern Asia— the arena of the world politics to which we denied ourselves access via the front door of Europe. It led Wilson and Lansing . . . into military intervention in Siberia. . . . The Philippines, taken on the assumption that they would be developed into an American Singapore, have become instead a British West Indies. Within ten years of their annexation Theodore Roosevelt, who more than any one man had planned and executed that stratagem, had regretted it, called the islands 'our heel of Achilles', and declared in favor of their independence. . . . And while thus extending our political interests over the face of the earth, we have officially condemned Japan, Italy, Germany, and Soviet Russia, the most formidable array of military power in history. . . . We have incited them all, simultaneously, to alliance and revenge." (A. Whitney Griswold, "Our Policy in the Far East", *Harper's,* August, 1940) [8]

In the fateful year of 1937 when Great Britain, anticipating a showdown with Germany, was looking for further support, secret arrangements were made between the United States and Great Britain to unload the policing of the Pacific on the United States Representative Tinkham as early as February 19, 1940, revealed this secret arrangement, which was finally confirmed by the British Foreign Office the following 21st of August [9] (cf Buls #41 and #87).

Lord Lothian's *Round Table,* in an article in the September 1939 issue, assumed that the United States would take care of British interests in the Pacific. In the December issue, it was announced that American

"Far-Eastern policy may serve to prevent a Russo-Japanese deal which would be catastrophic to British interests in the Orient." But if Russia wins Japan, it is hoped "the United States will accept Far Eastern responsibilities more fully, and thereby ease pressure on Britain." (cf Bul #22)

"America is now nominated for the position of watchdog to the British Empire. . . . Whilst the President sounds a continuous alarm against a maritime threat from the direction of Europe, he keeps the American fleet on the Pacific seaboard, where everyone not utterly bereft of his reason knows it is stationed for the purpose of protecting British interests in the Orient." (Chicago *Leader*, Sept. 6, 1940)

General Johnson, not so bereft, pictures "this strange diversion",— "Uncle Sam facing an aggressive approaching enemy, and strapping his shield of armor on his back instead of his belly, firing to the rear, and crying havoc about his own defenselessness in front". (*Sat Eve Post*, Oct. 5, 1940)

Meantime American oil, steel and munitions interests, behind the camouflage of 'embargoes' and 'licenses' have continued to take profits [10] In 1939 the U. S supplied Japan with 59% of all war materials which were paid for by our imports of 87% of Japan's export of silk. The havoc wrought by American bombs from American airplanes [11] has been exploited as Japanese atrocities, as Rogerson anticipated in his "Propaganda in the Next War" (cf Bul #1). "Japan's distinction is that she is unpopular. Her drastic underselling methods and her tactless dumping of shoddy articles at cheap prices have combined to create a widespread resentment against her. She is a commercial danger, and therefore the more easily, from the propaganda view-point, saddled with atrocities! That is a cynical observation, perhaps, but a truism nevertheless, for in war those nations with whom one is in sympathy can do no wrong: those from whom one has something to fear never do right."

Thomas Lamont is referred to by *Time*, November 25, 1940, as a specialist on Japan, "for the House of Morgan was once U. S banker for Japan". Some years ago Mr. Lamont visited Japan taking Walter Lippmann with him. This was at the time the 'Four Power loan' was proposed which Mr. Lamont turned down as a poor risk. The House of Morgan has served as an agent of the British government so Mr. Lamont is naturally interested in the protection of British interests even in the Far East. [12]

Societies, academies, leagues, of economic, political and social sciences are readily set up and supported as platforms from which to speak. At a recent session of the "Academy of Political Science" which Mr. Lamont annually addresses, he responded to the question "Should the U. S. tighten trade embargoes against Japan?" hedging,—"A private citizen not familiar with all the factors would not for a moment presume to suggest detailed measures to the Administration whose foreign policy along this line has been so carefully developed." "Nevertheless," says *Time*, "he pointed out inconsistencies and omissions in U. S. embargoes that still permitted Japan to get war supplies."

The popular outcry against supplying Japan with the essentials for her aggressive war against China has been met by announcement from the Administration of 'embargoes' on the export of scrap and oil. This profitable trade has not been materially reduced. The steel, oil and munitions interests have influence with the Administration inside the State Department so that these orders are so drafted as not to interfere with their business. Just how is fully explained by I. F. Stone in the *Nation*, Oct. 5.

Mr. Lamont should know, and probably does, better than Mr. Stone, just how to make friends and influence people in the Administration. His broad financial and public interests give him great influence too with foundations, universities, and all that is taught or published Subtle influences through the organizations of fund raising, public relations and communication by radio or print, make it possible to soft pedal the profit from arming Japan while promoting the use of armed force against her. [13]

Harvard's twenty million dollar alumni endowment fund was successfully raised immediately after the war, in no small part due to Mr. Lamont and his protegé John Price Jones, the champion Liberty Loan salesman. Harvard professors and officials have for twenty years been naturally if not necessarily responsive to the attitudes of so loyal and influential an alumnus. The former dean of the Law School is now the beneficiary of a roving professorship endowed by Mr. Lamont Sixteen of the Harvard Law Faculty in November, 1940, seized the headlines with a militant proposal that "we must deprive Japan of raw materials" for war. (Harvard *Alumni Bulletin*, Nov. 16, 1940)

James M. Landis, one of these professors, was long connected with the

Administration through the SEC, and must have some knowledge of why the State Department's embargoes have been so ineffective. The proposal reads just about as it would had it been drawn up in the British Foreign Office. It advocates that we "assume control of the Singapore Naval Base" though the Boston *Transcript* editorial, Oct. 22, tells us, "Washington's naval specialists consider Singapore too trouble-inviting and too far afield". The professors propose also "substantially unlimited credits" to China, to which we have already advanced 85 millions since 1933, of which 35 millions have been repaid, we are reminded in the above editorial. [14]

Late in November, this pro-British measure, for which the law professors acted as advance agents, has resulted in our advancing to China an additional hundred millions. The Detroit *Free Press* editorialized, "China is not a good risk. The $50,000,000 currency stabilization loan to the Chung-king Government was political." The currency stabilization fund is a hypothetical profit from the marking up of the price of gold It is an easy trick, manufacturing money this way. When the two billions are used up we can mark up the price of gold and have additional profit, on paper. But the loan to China will be paid by the taxpayer from the sweat of American labor.

The New England division of Mr. Lamont's second White Committee for America Second after defending the British raj, was given impetus through the drive of Mayo Shattuck, Boston attorney who may be in line for a receivership or a reorganization. Mr. Shattuck "advocated . . joint use of British, Dutch and American naval bases in the Far East to constitute a threat of instant action if Japan were to move against Hongkong, Singapore or the East Indies." (Boston *Herald*, Nov. 28)

Major Fielding Eliot, formerly of Australia where Japan's advances are feared, has been urging in his column that this is the time to smash Japan. "We have but to stir a finger, and they will sustain such a defeat as they will not recover from this side of utter ruin."[15]

Most timely in support of this thesis urging us to immediate war with Japan is the book of Robert Aura Smith, a cable editor of the New York *Times* and formerly a journalist in Manila. His book, "Our Future in Asia", Viking, published in October, is a hastily written but masterly presentation of Wall Street-Washington-Whitehall policy, a frank imperialistic plea that we smash Japan now and so protect Britain's interests not merely on the China coast but in Malaya. It has naturally received copious and favorable reviews.

Distracting our attention from our unprofitable ventures in the Philippines and China, he centers our attention on the wealth of the Indies, the richest portions of the French, Dutch, and British Empires where the tin and rubber come from. America's trade with the British and Dutch in Southeast Asia is, of course, vastly more important than the trade with China or even Japan Mr Smith at the "Town Meeting of the Air" in New York in December, 1940, dodged, refusing to answer or even consider a direct question as to the relative value of our trade with China and Japan. He was promoting the imperialistic view of trade and war of the N. Y. *Times* and of the British Raj and he stuck to his theme. He assumes that we would be deprived of our rubber and tin if the Japanese took control. But, insists *Fortune*, December, 1940 (p 153), "Even if Japan were to seize the British and Dutch East Indies, it would, if it were on friendly terms with us, certainly be as willing to sell us rubber, quinine, and tin as it is to sell us silk, of which it has a practical monopoly."[16]

Tin there is in Bolivia, it is true, but the British obstruct our use of it. [17] Rubber, ever more important, could be grown in Brazil, its native home. But Mr Smith objects that it takes seven years. Moreover, we could make our own rubber artificially but he questions if it is as good Experts say it is better. But it is not as cheap, he says. Of course it isn't Why pay an American wage for manufacturing artificial rubber even if it can be done with less labor when you can make bigger profits using native labor Starvation is an incentive for them to sign with a thumb print a contract which holds them in bondage seven years for a few cents a day. So Britain lives on indentured labor.

All this, of course, is promoted in the name of democracy, and in that name we must defeat those disturbing totalitarian countries in order that freedom for ourselves and the continuance of indentured labor may not quickly disappear from the earth. "The struggle for democracy has certainly gotten around into some strange back alleys. We began by proclaiming our adhesion to a war waged by England and France for democracy in England and France. But we are now over in the Pacific meditating a crusade to save the democracy of England, France and Holland in Java, British Malaya and Indo-China", John T. Flynn sardonically remarks in the *New Republic,* October 21.

The Whitehall-Washington-Wall Street plan to crush Japan before we have to invade Germany may be strategic. Now that we have made money out of Japan and now that she threatens the status quo of British, French, Dutch, and American interests, it is time to act. Between Pearl Harbor and Singapore we have no adequate naval base, while the Japanese with an almost equal navy have many intervening Asiatic bases,—Formosa, Hanoi . . . And if we do get to Singapore undamaged, Japan might sail for Honolulu and the Pacific coast and then what a panic there would be in America! Remember how the Spanish fleet terrorized the Bostonese in 1898, how they sent the contents of their safe deposit vaults to Worcester to be out of reach?

Japan has two 45,000-ton battleships coming off the ways very soon. So it is either smash Japan right away or wait five years for our new two ocean navy (cf Bul #25) [18] But that is about the time Col. Robert McCormick tells us that our expeditionary force will be invading Central Europe at a cost of 400 billions just for that alone.

Within the thousand mile circle that Smith draws with Japanese occupied Spratley Island as a center, there are 130 million Malays,— living under autocratic governments controlled from London, Paris, and The Hague which derive great profit from their indentured labor. The Japanese, of mixed Malay blood, might be quite as sympathetic to their customs and needs as their present rulers.

The people of Indo-China will have little to regret in the change. The surplus rice they produce is needed in Japan and Japan's products will suit them quite as well as those from Paris. A few thousand French officials and merchants and exploiters have administered the country, exporting millions annually without winning a reputation for humanitarian or democratic tendencies, and the condition of some of the mining concessions has been an international scandal for years. To repress dissatisfaction, labeled 'Communism', the guillotine has been kept working overtime, since the 1930 rebellion of the Annamese.

Recent dispatches indicate that the Cambodians are not loyally appreciative of their French protectors who are about to be driven out An AP cable from Manila, Dec. 11, 1940, tells us, "Within a radius of 100 miles of Saigon at least 20 major uprisings . . with as many as

10,000 natives participating in a single incident. . . . Planes left Saigon daily and . . . bombed the rebellious natives each time. . . . Two hundred natives were reported lined up and shot at the Saigon airport Nov 22." Dec. 14, 1940, a UP cable from Saigon reports, "Plans of native Communist rebels to attack French garrisons and seize arms and ammunition for a march on Saigon . . . have been frustrated. . . . More than 1,000 rebels were under arrest."

Sven Hedin, who knows more of Asia than perhaps any other European living, tells us in his life of "Chiang Kai-Shek" (John Day, 1940), that the present trouble between Japan and China is an episode. For more than a thousand years there have been similar incidents between them   Japan's present purpose is to take up what China failed to do and drive the Western exploiter and usurper out of the East where he doesn't belong. Penetrating into still unspoiled parts of the Far East in five trips over a period of ten years, I am prepared to testify that the East and these Easterners are more delightful where there are no Westerners. The very term 'treaty port' has long implied depths of degradation.   '

The "Retreat of the West" is on   No-Yong Park makes that clear with humor and liveliness in his book of that title (Hale, Cushman and Flint, 1937). "From the dawn of history the Asiatic overran Europe, bringing culture and religion. Rome conquered Asia Minor but was powerless before the Scythians of Asia Major. Asiatic hordes overran Europe and destroyed Rome and during the last thousand years they reached the plains of France through Spain and across Europe and later, long after New England was settled, thundered at the gates of Vienna " ("Human Affairs", 1938, by Porter Sargent, p 36)

As you look at the map of Eurasia on an 'azimuthal equidistant projection', you search over the vast expanse to finally find Europe jutting less conspicuously than Alaska from North America   There restless whites, once migrants from Asia, warring and persecuting each other, have in recent centuries rediscovered Asia. First the Norsemen raided south into France, England, the Mediterranean and Africa. Later the Portuguese learned from the Arab of the Chinese magnetic needle and with it ventured around Africa. From the Chinese ceremonial firecracker, the Europeans devised gunpowder for killing. Successively French, Dutch, English, perverting these to their uses, have with inflated ego imposed on the longer civilized Asiatics. Central Europeans, long deprived, now resentfully warring against the possessors, afford the Asiatic opportunity to hasten the departure from Asia of the whites, who culturally, politically, commercially and territorially are in retreat Asia, the great motherland of our European races, religions, culture, is now awakened to a new life. It's too late for us to successfully Westernize, vulgarize or destroy it.

But Britain has so long strutted over the earth and ruled the waves that she cannot retreat gracefully. Her acquired political skill, learned and adapted from the Eastern tycoons and maharajahs, still enables her to induce others to fight her battles, and to reinspire even her outcast and rebellious colonials to new loyalties to her old symbols.

In this policy of rule or ruin, it begins to look like ruin. Faded for the most part are the 26 puppet states set up at Versailles to separate Germany and Russia, to balkanize Southeastern Europe, to deprive or dominate Central Europe and preserve the British Empire. The maritime buffer states, enriched from tropic empires in the Indies or Africa, protected by the British Navy,—they, too, have fallen Now Britannia's hope of continuing to rule the waves lies in help from her distant colonies peopled by her former rebels and outcasts Kept in line by preachments on morality and religion, they too may go down in ruin in the attempt to preserve civilization and morality among the indentured blacks of African gold mines, the Tamials of the rubber plantations, and the millions of malnourished malcontents of India. [19]

But the subservient subjects of the British crown in London loyally declare, "We'll hold out as long as we can, then we'll let the two yellow races, America and Japan, fight it out." [20]

December 30, 1940

NOTES

[1] "Of our trade with the Far East, Japan's share has been double (at times nearly triple) China's for the past forty years. Of an estimated total of $12,630,000,000 foreign investments, . . $758,000,000 in the Far East. China's share of the latter is about $132,000,000 or a little over 1% of our total foreign investments", writes A. Whitney Griswold in "Our Policy in the Far East", *Harper's*, August, 1940

From 1931 to 1935, an annual average of 19% of the total foreign trade of the U. S. (24% of its imports, 15% of its exports) was with the Far East or approximately $724,500,000 out of a total foreign trade of $3,738,000,000. Of this sum, in 1935, 43% represented American trade with Japan, 24% with the Netherlands, India, British Malaya and French Indo-China, 18% with the Philippines, and 14% with China and Hongkong (3% of U S. total foreign trade). Thus approximately 8.17% of our total foreign trade, or about $312,000,000, was with Japan and 3.42%, or $130,410,000, constituted our trade with China and Hongkong. (Griswold, "The Far Eastern Policy of the U. S.", p 468)

(2) "From 1917 to 1937, Congress appropriated $3,624,000,000 to build the merchant marine and pay for its upkeep. . . . It paid private companies $175,911,000 above normal poundage rate to carry mail. It sold private operators 220 ships that cost $500,000,000 to build, at the bargain-basement price of $40,000,000. . . . The International Mercantile Marine could afford to pay a lawyer-lobbyist $370,000 in the five years following enactment of the Jones-White Law, even though it was defaulting in the same period on its obligations to the government. P. A. S. Franklin, its president, took $1,952,410 out of the company in thirteen years. Other officers received comparable salaries. Kermit Roosevelt, son of T. R., and Vincent Astor, intimate of the President, are connected with the I M.M., perhaps accounting for the kindness with which it has been treated in Washington regardless of the party in power." ("The Pressure Boys", Kenneth G Crawford, Messner, 1939)

(3) The imperialistic, commercial attitude of supplying other peoples with what our own workmen cannot afford to buy was well expressed at the Swampscott meeting of the American Institute of Banking, May 26, by William A. Irwin of New York, assistant education director. "We must build up markets in the South American countries, the Philippines, Mexico and China. In China alone, there are 400,000,000 potential customers. England found itself in the same position as the United States is today. That was 100 years ago, and she went imperialistic and prospered It would mean a bigger army and navy and a bigger merchant marine, that factories would have to be built, and that we would become the strongest empire in the world." (Boston *Herald*, May 27, 1939)

(4) In 1935 only 6% of our total foreign investments were in the Far East— $758,000,000. $387,000,000 of this was in Japan; $132,000,000 of it in China. Americans owned a mere 6% of the total foreign investments in China in 1931 as compared with Britain's 36% ($1,189,000,000) and Japan's 35% ($1,136,000,000). (Griswold, p 469)

(5) "If Japan closes us out of the China market our financial losses will be insignificant, our commercial losses potential rather than actual. . . . To drive Japan from her present conquests including Manchuria . . . would cost us more than we have gained from trade with China in the past or have any reasonable hope of gaining in the future." (Griswold, *Harper's*, Aug, 1940)

(6) Arthur Krock in the New York *Times*, addressing the President, "From the time of the 'quarantine' speech in 1937 you have done everything possible to antagonize Japan and force it into the Axis", coaches the G.O.P. on how "the foreign crisis might be turned to their campaign advantage. . . . If war with Japan were represented as the possible consequence of Mr. Hull's steady admoni-

tions to Tokyo, of the Chinese loans, and of the economic sanctions of embargo, it is improbable that many Americans would have any heart in the enterprise."

The danger that America will blunder into war as the result of "a stretching of the conception of American security to include such remote parts of the world as Singapore and the Dutch East Indies and Dakar", is what worries William Henry Chamberlin (*American Mercury,* Dec. 1940, p 395),—and well it may now that Britain has unloaded on us the defence of her West Indies as well as her East, while we are still impotent to help her either by invading Europe or by sending a navy to the Indies.

(7) The guarding of England's colonial empire necessitated command of the seas For two centuries up to the twentieth, only France had challenged it. After the defeat of Napoleon, up to 1880 the British navy was in a state of slothful lethargy Then in the 1880's sudden realization that France and Italy were more than a match in the Mediterranean resulted in an increased naval expansion program aimed against a possible French threat, for Germany as yet had not entered into the naval race. This forgotten period from 1880 to 1905 is reviewed in "The Anatomy of British Sea Power" by Arthur J Marder (Knopf, 1940).

Richard Heathcote Heindel, Fellow in History, The Library of Congress, on leave from U of Pa , where he has been Director of War Documentation Service, has published the result of years of study of contemporary journals and documents of England in "The American Impact on Great Britain, 1898-1914" (U. of Penn Press, 1940).

"The book shows that America's impact on Britain was far more considerable than has generally been supposed; that there was much talk about an Anglo-American alliance and Anglo-Saxon 'racialism', though surprisingly little about a brotherhood of democracies; and that, during the early years of this century, Britons were more troubled by the American than by the German economic peril", writes Gaudens Megaro, instructor of English and Italian History at Queen's College, New York City, and author of "Mussolini in the Making", reviewing Heindel's book in the *New Republic,* Dec. 30, 1940. The only thing threatening the American Monroe Doctrine in the 90's under Cleveland's administration was Great Britain in Venezuela. Our memories are so short.

The year 1898 Heindel refers to as the "Annus Mirabilis". Through our war with Spain we were launched on a sea of imperialism T Roosevelt took great credit to himself In following the gospel of A. T. Mahan on sea power, he was egged on by Cecil Spring-Rice, later British Ambassador to Washington during the World War. Joe Chamberlain acted as master of ceremonies. Heindel tells us, "The Continent suspected that Chamberlain had revealed the weakness of his country, disputed the identical interests, and called him a 'civilian Boulanger'."

With Britain's "temporary dissatisfaction with its Continental neighbors, a renewed analysis of its own imperialism, an alteration in the world outlook, a rediscovery of America, and the minor joys of an assumed, vicarious motherhood to an imperial youngster . . . the growth of the idea of imperialism in the U S was welcomed, if not its concrete manifestations The war acted as a cathartic for race sentiment. The weary Titan contemplated a new ally, and both nations emerged from isolation at the same time. . . . As Henry Adams had perceived, England had been brought into an 'America system'. . . .

"For England an alliance with the United States   would create an absolutely ideal situation. . . . It is thus almost hopeless to bring the English statesmen to any voluntary renunciation of this grand purpose England will only become available for other political combinations when her present hope of an Anglo-American alliance is shattered. .

"Evidently Hay had thought by the end of July that the British Government wished the U. S. to retain the Philippines or, failing that, to secure an option on them . . . By October 1899 affairs in the Philippines and South Africa had, as the *Times* suggested, 'a curious resemblance'. The press intimated, however, that Americans favorable to Aguinaldo were more influential than the pro-Boer British ! . . Many of the opponents of annexation agreed with Henry M. Stanley, the explorer, 'It seems to me this Imperialism is going to prove costly and disturbing to America, and her well-wishers are in doubt whether it be wise in her to take upon herself the task of regenerating the Philippines.' (Heindel, p 89)

"The *Westminster Gazette* (June 16, 1900) reflected, 'In our own controversies about Imperialism it is not amiss . . . to observe the corresponding debate which is in progress in the U S   r Even those who are Imperialists in this country may sympathize with a protest against Imperialism in a country of the nature and extent of the U. S. In spite of all that Little Englanders could find, and no matter what was the real meaning of McKinley's success in 1900, the American election was hailed in England as a "Victory in Imperialism".

"So that the details discussed here may not obscure historical perspective, may one not say that the upshot of Anglo-American relations between 1904 and 1914 was that both countries suspected that England could rely on us in event of any world crisis? This implies reciprocal influences. But the issue certainly meant more to Great Britain than to us", Heindel concludes

"Once the Panama Canal was acquired and on the way to completion, opinion held that our control over Central America was inevitable . . Suspicion of the Monroe Doctrine increased, papers recalled that they had predicted harsh treatment of the Hay-Pauncefote Treaty, and talked of 'unctuous rectitude and cynical treachery'."

The London *Economist*, March 8, 1851, declared, "The superiority of the United States to England is ultimately as certain as the next eclipse"   And Viscount Esher feared, "We may become a satrapy of the United States." "Sir Gilbert Parker declared in Parliament in 1905, 'In the Sandwich Islands, Samoa, and Mexico, the U S. had, to use an American expression, "chiselled" us out of our position ' " (Heindel)

William C. Johnstone's "The United States and Japan's New Order" (Oxford Univ. Press, New York, 1940) deals in the first two-thirds with "trade, protection of citizens, and observance of the Nine Power Treaty in China since the

Manchuria incident of 1931" and argues for the maintenance of the Open Door
policy.

(8) The alliance of Japan with the Axis powers was a bombshell to their
opponents Senator Nye declared, "Our policy has succeeded in driving Japan
into the arms of those who were the last ones we wanted her to associate with."
And Japan claimed it was due to the blundering of the U. S State Department.

To Hull who had been preaching morality to the heathen, it was a shock
which was hardly disguised by an attitude of tired sophistication. " 'We knew
it all the time' was the refrain of the statement the Secretary of State gave the
press, a statement which managed to achieve prolixity though but three sentences
long. . . . It is impossible to take these words at their face value without passing
a harsh verdict on our diplomats. . . . It is more charitable to assume that Secretary Hull's statement was a bold front on a diplomatic defeat", writes I F.
Stone in the *Nation*, October 5.

Time, Oct. 7, 1940, remarked on this "world coalition of totalitarian powers",
the first instance in 151 years of an open treaty of alliance aimed against the
United States.

It was little wonder then that Lothian rushed to Roosevelt, and that there
streamed through the White House in succession Hull, Stimson, Knox, Marshall,
Morgenthau and all the Defense Advisors, the representatives of big business
and Wall Street The Administration and the State Department were taken by
surprise, as was evidenced by the fact that a third of the fleet was due in Pacific
coast ports the next day

The Administration need not have been surprised had they not been so intent
on scolding others for evil ways Col House had foreseen just this situation.
In an entry in his diary in 1918 regarding the French demand for a Rhenish
Republic as a buffer state, he wrote, "We would run the danger of having everything from the Rhine to the Pacific, perhaps including Japan, against the Western
Powers. The Germans would at once begin to intrigue to bring such a combination against England, France and the United States "

Any number of informed people in Washington knew that this was inevitable.
In his Washington Diplomatic Letter, *Week by Week*, September 14, 1940,
Franklin Roudybush had announced:

"What is not clearly realized by most Americans is that the Madrid-Rome-
Berlin-Moscow-Tokyo diplomatic Axis is functioning with dreadful efficiency.
It isn't a very pleasant thought, but it is something that must be realized Furthermore, the Vichy Government is apparently trying to jump on the bandwagon. . . .
Never printed in the United States is the story of 'how the Nazi Ambassador in
Moscow arranged for the Russians to attack the Rumanians on the flank just
before the Vienna Conference, so that a harassed Rumania would quickly sign'
. on the question of the cession of Transylvania to the Hungarians What the
newspapers missed was the fact that the Nazis bagged both Hungary and Rumania by this agreement which allowed them to send in their soldiers to guarantee the frontiers of both countries .. "

Hitler's "next big diplomatic trick . . . was a Russo-Japanese Treaty". His "special envoy Wilhelm Keppler" flew from Tokyo to Moscow. The treaty, drawn up by von Ribbentrop, "fixes the zones of Russian and Japanese influence in the Far East It provides for an adjustment of the frontier which would put an end to the Manchukuo troubles, and finally envisages a 25-year non-aggression pact between Moscow and Tokyo. The Konoye Government had already agreed to the pact . . . before Keppler flew to Moscow. . . ." This would mean "the end of Russian assistance to China . . . pave the way for Moscow's intervention in Finland and Persia", for Japan "a free hand in Indo-China and the Dutch East Indies". (Roudybush, Sept. 14, 1940)

"Last spring, United States army officers seized a huge quantity of machine tools that the Russians had bought and paid for, declaring that they were needed for our own defense preparations The Russian ambassador, Mr. Oumansky, pleaded, cajoled, came close to tears in his anxiety to have the machine tools returned. Principally because the State Department felt that it ought not to be on bad terms with Russia and Japan simultaneously, about half the Russian purchases were grudgingly released Recently . . . the State Department decided on a rapprochement with the USSR . . Under-Secretary Welles sent for Mr. Oumansky for an affable little preliminary talk. According to report, Mr. Oumansky, sensing his sudden importance in the American scheme of things, brusquely demanded the remaining half of his machine tools." (*New Republic*)

"I see many indications that Roosevelt and our State Department (in foreign policy they are only office boys for Vansittart and the British Foreign Office) are preparing the groundwork for an effort toward a Soviet-American Alliance. The State Department recently gave out the news that they had been lying to beat all hell when they stirred up the Russian invasion scare about naval and air bases on big Diomede, and that there is nothing on the island and never has been except meteorological outfits Then came much publicized talks with Oumansky. And finally comes the issue of *Look* for September 10th, in which Drew Pearson and Robert Allen, unofficial mouthpieces for the President when he wants to put over some trick, publish an article suggesting U.S.-U.S.S.R. military alliances and ending up with the astounding words, 'Russia may yet be the salvation of the world's harassed democracies'. Come to think of it, the FBI and Gaypayoo ought to work very well together. I am amazed that Roosevelt hasn't worked out a plan to convert these new four million draftees into Storm Troopers Or perhaps he has " Burton Rascoe.

A Swiss manufacturer said to me the other night,—"I don't know what I'm going to do. Not much use going back to Europe if you Americans are determined on blockading it You won't let any food get to England or France once Hitler has taken them On the other hand, it won't be comfortable here either, when you have antagonized Hitler and Stalin and the rest of Europe and continue to prod Japan on the other side. Besides I like to say what I think, and that won't be possible here very long. Already in America it is like Germany in 1932. In the restaurants you don't dare speak above a whisper for fear of offending someone at the next table who thinks differently. That's the way it started in Germany No, I don't know what I'm going to do."

(9) England broke her alliance with Japan because of American objection. That left us with a responsibility of policing the Pacific. We failed to realize how formidable Russia and Germany might become. If England and America were now allied with Russia, it would be easy to dispose of Germany and then later to tame Russia, and when we had done that we could hold Japan to our ways and so make the world 'safe for democracy'. Now we are forcing Japan into an alliance with Russia. Now lest Japan and Russia come to an agreement, we are hoping that Russia will forgive and forget the insults we have heaped upon her, and lend us her aid though we have nothing to offer in return, neither promise nor threat that could be effective, while Japan and Germany have both.

(10) "When it first became known in San Francisco that scrap export licenses were being issued freely, a query was sent to Washington, D C. An answer came back from Colonel Russell Maxwell, army officer in charge of exports, that licenses were only intended to protect defense supplies and since there was no shortage the licenses were being issued upon request. . . .

"Why the President ever issued a licensing proclamation if no enforcement was actually intended is still an unanswered question. One belief is that Washington may have felt the attendant publicity of a proclamation would leave with the public an impression that some kind of an embargo was in effect

"Customs figures, incidentally, show gradual Japanese encroachment on the scrap market. In 1932, only 13,000 tons were taken from the Coast. In 1933, a year of increasing Japanese military activity, the total leaped to 142,133. In the first six months of this year, 232,943 tons were shipped." (*Friday*)

(11) UP reports from Hongkong that Japanese troops "have confiscated an estimated 1,000 American-owned motor trucks stored at Haiphong, Indo-China, awaiting transport to China " These manufactures were to be paid for out of the money American taxpayers loan to China. The Japanese have possession of the trucks, but we have no lien on the Japs for payment.

(12) "For the Department of State repeatedly to turn to American bankers for assistance in realizing the opportunities that lay behind the open door in China emphasized the theoretical nature of those opportunities. For the bankers to refuse this assistance showed that the American business community was not greatly interested in them." (Griswold, p 470)

"The so-called 'New Order' in Asia . . . in part looks toward the eventual complete elimination of Occidental imperialism from the continent of Asia. The United States . . at least for the moment, stands alone, except for a shattered China, in its opposition to Japanese aims. War with Japan at the present time would be a reckless and dangerous adventure. It might last for a decade. What are our interests in the Orient? . . . The cynical say we are protecting Standard Oil, but this is but one small part of the picture, . . . total American investments in the Orient all told do not equal in value the amount necessary to run a full-fledged war even six months. Our trade with China, even before the Japanese conquest, was a bagatelle compared to that with Japan . . . The chances are we shall not be able to impose our own criterion of international affairs upon the whole world The threat of a forthcoming oil embargo .   . helped to drive [Japan] southward into Indo-China and may drive her inevitably into seizing the Dutch East Indies—the very move we fear. England, hard-pressed for foreign exchange, has hastened to contract with Japan to make up for the deficiency The American policy wears the garb of folly It becomes merely diplomatic witchcraft—sticking pins into a supposed effigy of an imaginary Japan in the hope that the mailed fist will wither." (Beals' "Pan America")

Thomas Lamont, Nov 13, 1940 (AP), "sounded 'a friendly but urgent caution' to Japan to . 'abandon once and for all . . the idea of 'Asia's new order' . . . and declared that 'our only effective answer to the Far Eastern threat must be constantly increasing aid to England and continued and additional aid to China' ".

(18) "Watertight as a fish-net" is the United States embargo on scrap iron for Japan. That's the way it was characterized by Professor Owen Lattimore, editor of *Pacific Affairs* and director of the Walter Hines Page School of International Affairs at Johns Hopkins University, in an address in New York City, Nov. 9

"The Royal Dutch-Shell group and a subsidiary of the Standard-Vacuum Oil Company will supply 7,000,000 barrels of oil to Japan over six months," a New York *Times* dispatch of October 17 reported. "Arrangements have been virtually concluded for Japan to get 40 per cent of her oil requirements for the next six months in the Dutch Indies."

"Lofty moral discourses" and "threats which the other side knew were hollow" make it possible for Hull, like Stimson before him and like Roosevelt, to magnify his ego. "Within the department, over the objections of a more farsighted minority, the experts made a joke of the discourses by protecting the profits accruing to American business from the aggressions we were so nobly denouncing" Our trade "treaty expired in January of this year, but it was not until July that an 'embargo' on oil and scrap was announced. . . . The details were left to the State Department experts. When the regulations were promulgated it was found that the only scrap 'embargoed' " was one little used of the 75 varieties of iron and steel scrap, and "the only petroleum 'embargoed' was aviation gas" Moreover, "the 'embargo' itself was only a system of licensing. It is now revealed that few if any licenses were denied under these regulations . .

"The Japanese, with about a year's supply on hand, do not need our scrap as much as they did, and the scrap industry, with a defense boom in the offing, does not need Japanese orders. The big steel companies cannot oppose an embargo on scrap by claiming that we have an over-supply of steel and at the same time ask for a higher price for steel on the ground of a shortage   . Both big steel and the scrap industry have accepted the embargo with a curious equanimity. This may be the result of a new sense of patriotism or it may be something else." (Stone, *Nation*, Oct. 5)

Not yet embargoed are pig iron and steel, of which Japan took 126 tons the first seven months of this year. Not yet embargoed are oil, copper, and other raw materials. Meantime Canada is selling scrap to Japan, British Malaya is supplying pig iron. And they are getting their iron ore from the Philippines, which have no other market for it than Japan.

Since Stimson denounced Japanese invasion of Manchuria we have continued to supply them. But that's nothing. We are giving them our secrets of industry, building for them new steel plants, strip mills, just as Great Britain built their navy We are arming them against us.

"Since the start of the Sino-Japanese conflict in 1937, this government has bought $640,000,000 of Japanese gold and more than $15,000,000 of silver ($7,500,000 the first eight months of this year)—all at premium prices that no one else would offer. The sudden recent increases of these shipments lead authorities here to believe Japan is in a way preparing for war against us with our own money. By selling metals which she considers no longer useful for monetary purposes . . . she is enabled to build up credit in this country." (Paul Mallon, Oct. 2)

(14) Lest this convey the misapprehension that all Harvard's faculty has become hysterical and are "goosestepping in the British column behind General J. B. Conant and his classroom colonels" as one of them puts it, we suggest consulting the columns of the Harvard *Crimson,* one of the very few free speaking daily periodicals that still exist in the U. S. There occasionally, amid the vaporings and fumings of those gone mad, one may read "statements sober, sane, printable" from the few of the faculty and larger percentage of the undergraduates who have escaped the malady that swept over the university from 1917 to 1919 and now threatens even more dire results.

John K. Fairbank, instructor in history, specialist on the Far East, Quentin Roosevelt '41, who has recently returned from China and the borders of Tibet, in the Harvard *Crimson,* Feb. 25, 1941, make it clear that they understand that we are being used as a cat's paw for the British in the Far East while at the same time our oil and metal companies are making money continuing supplies to Japan

(15) General Hugh Johnson ridicules the "purely naval reasoning" shared by Mr. Roosevelt "that the Japanese navy is no good anyhow, that it is poorly designed and commanded; that it has only nine battleships against our fifteen, that it is a constant annoyance and that we can easily and might as well clean it out while the cleaning is good". Johnson asks "a purely materialistic question in dollars and cents What is this philosophy going to cost us, and is it worth that cost?" We will probably have to fight Hitler at the same time. Gen Marshall has testified that even to match Hitler's land equipment would cost us 100 billions. And to prepare for action in the East, that, Admiral Leahy says, would require tripling our Navy, would cost years of time and no less than 10 billions

(16) The writer of the article in *Fortune,* December, 1940, sees how we might be on friendly terms and how intercourse between the two peoples might easily be turned to mutual profit instead of the losses of war After analysis of the South Eastern Asiatic situation the conclusion is, "The case for an alliance with Britain and Australasia to hold the lines at Singapore . . must rest on other than

purely economic grounds. . . In 1943 or 1944, Japan will have eighteen capital ships to place in line of battle as against the U. S fourteen." (pp 154, 156)

Should hostilities break out, every naval man knows it is impossible for us to attack Japan directly. The accompanying force to support a naval attack would require the merchant marine of practically the whole world. The hope is a long range blockade to cut off necessary supplies, a blockade carried on at a distance of more than two thousand miles. That would still leave Japan access to the whole continent of Asia and she might survive. We might get tired after maintaining that blockade for some years and some of the blockade might be sunk by some nasty little boats or submarines. The Japanese have even more faith in their sun-goddess-descended emperor than we have in our Great White Father Roosevelt. One faith has lasted for more than a thousand years, the other a lesser time, and might fade

Fortune closes its survey of foreign policy with the sapient remark that if economically we are strong enough we may get "a respectful hearing from England" and if we are in armament strong enough it "should cause Germany to listen" "We must have a real plan for peace. Otherwise we may be committed to a choice between permanent isolation and active belligerent support of a bloody invasion of the continent of Europe. And neither of these alternatives can for long unite the U. S people." (*Fortune*, p 164)

(17) The U. S. must have raw materials that Britain and her buffer Holland monopolize,—rubber, tin, tungsten, chromite, jute—which they will sell us, while we "help the British Navy keep the lanes open . . . America is thus counted on to uphold Britain in a showdown. . . . She must always throw her weight on the side of freedom of the seas. In practice, freedom of the seas has always meant the continued hegemony of the British Navy", comments *Fortune*, Dec., 1938. The U. S must be kept "in a receptive mood to battle" for the 'freedom of the seize' We have long been anticipating interference with our supply of rubber from the East Indies. July 13, Stettinius, whose job it is to keep up our stock pile of raw materials, announced, "It is expected before the month is over a plan of synthetic rubber production will have been worked out which will eliminate our dependence on imports". Pearson and Allen, Feb. 12, 1941, tells us that the four companies at present engaged will produce only 10,000 tons of the 600,000 tons of rubber annually needed. But while Stettinius is "tearing his hair", Jesse Jones, valiant defender of British interests, delays RFC advances for synthetic rubber plants, maintaining the status quo for British sales and profits Knudsen tells the story of the priest who explained to his parishioners on inquiry, " 'Status quo' is Latin for 'the fix we're in now'!"

(18) When Roosevelt, about a year ago, first advocated building up our Navy, we heard a great deal about these 45,000-tonners. Some Congressman suggested 65,000-tonners, 80,000-tonners (cf Bul #25)

(19) Americans generally missed the humor of the thrust at Roosevelt and Hull's moral homilies, when December 19th Matsuoka at a luncheon in Tokyo came back at Ambassador Grew with the declaration that Japan was engaged in

a "moral crusade",—and Mr. Grew, inured to moral platitudes in which the State Department clothes its bellicose jingoism, discounted "the persuasive garb". (Boston *Transcript*, Dec. 19, 1940)

(20) America's leading woman electrical engineer, Vivian Kellems, was interviewed by the New York *World-Telegram*, July 9, 1940, which reported, "In London, where she went at the invitation of the British War Office to discuss orders for the new shell-lifter which her firm is manufacturing, she heard them say in The City, 'We'll hold out as long as we can, then we'll let the two yellow races, America and Japan, fight it out'."

Lord Northcliffe in 1919 returning to England after having brought the American press into line boasted on his return that he had left 130 millions in America to keep the press loyal. He implied that would do the job, for all Americans thought alike like sheep and were more gullible than any people he knew except the Chinese. This latter saying he repeated from Sir Gilbert Parker, who spent the early years of the war in America proving their gullibility

HOW COME FRANCE COLLAPSED

Correspondents and refugees have rushed into print with apologies and explanations trivial and tragic as to "why France fell". Some needed the pay, some had something to say The glib explanations of sophisticated journalists sound like the gossip of the cafe or the salon. Few get down to the grass roots,—'of even the country clubs'.

All this has brought little satisfaction to those who have known and loved France [1] And the number is legion, in North and South America, of those who claim France as a second motherland Why even the Californian of old, in the days of gold, who had struck it rich looked forward to going to Paris to die. The question "why" which implies plan, design, doesn't apply. To those who knew and loved her, the marvel has been that political France, the Third Republic, could last so long After the war France rode high. Her powerfully efficient army enabled her to impose her imperious will through her ruthless rulers, Poincaré, Clemenceau, and Barthou And she built a chain of armed states about her fallen enemy. From this pinnacle of power there was only one way to go.[2]

Most writers deal with the failure of the military. But the French journalist, Robert de Saint Jean, now in this country, believes that all was lost before Reynaud came in.[3] 'Wild Bill' Donovan, sent over by our Administration, in conjunction with E A. Mowrer reported (New York *Times*, Aug. 22, 1940), "The French infantry, repeatedly deserted by their officers, melted away. What happened to the French officers? For the most part they were hostile to the Third Republic " John Gunther after the event points out (*Look,* Aug. 27, 1940) the two important lessons gleaned from the French defeat,—"Infantry numbers bear an absurdly disproportionate relation to the outcome of battle.[4] Second lesson of the war is the importance of supply [which] can be assured only by complete co-ordination of national effort   The Germans possessed this co-ordination; the French did not."[5]

"Pertinax" (André Geraud), French political journalist, on arrival in this country, wrote, "The fear of radical social changes that war seemed likely to bring in its trail, has preyed tremendously upon the propertied classes ever since 1918. . . . It dawned upon them gradually that the Bolshevist regime was the logical outcome of a democratic regime run wild." Stubbornly they resisted adjustment to changed conditions. "No nation can attune itself to the exacting demands of totalitarian war, of a war to be waged against dictatorships, unless it succeeds in keeping clear from all social disturbances " (Boston *Herald,* Dec 8, 1940)[6]

Jules Romains, writing in deliberation from his chateau in the Loire his great epic "Men of Good Will", revealed himself as a great artist. Now a fugitive in New York, he looks dazedly back on the past seven years and writes for the *Saturday Evening Post* on the "Seven Mysteries of Europe" (Knopf, 1940). Here he reveals himself an amateur diplomat attempting, after surviving the last war, to live up to his resolve to prevent its recurrence. The mysteries are simple tragedies of greed, corruption, confusion, vacillation and incompetence. The book is valuable as a recital of Romains' own personal part in attempting to stem the flow of forces which apparently even now he does not comprehend. He adds nothing to his stature as a creative artist.

A liaison officer of the British Air Intelligence, Major Philip Gribble, kept a diary from May 10, 1940, when he was stationed on the Aisne until he finally took plane for England. Published with some discreet censoring in the *Saturday Evening Post,* Dec 7 and Dec. 14, 1940, this presents convincingly how inevitable was the failure. "The secret of successful (modern) warfare is very simple . . based on rapidity of action and lightning execution. . . . It is better to take wrong action than to take no action at all," Gribble remarks, reminding one of Nicolson's aphorism, "Better an ounce of brains at headquarters than a million men in the field."

Commenting editorially on these articles, the Boston *Transcript* points out that they confirm Romains' impression of Gamelin as a dreamer, the wrong peg in the hole, who had surrounded himself with advisers "equally uninformed concerning their own weakness and the enemy's strength. . . . Hadn't the British experts said it would cost the Germans months of effort and 1,500,000 lives to pierce the line at crucial Sedan? Yet, after two hours of bomb-diving . . . the Nazi mechanized infantry marched through a five-mile breach . . . lost barely 500 men. . . . Of the French 70-ton tanks . . . not . . . more than 20 . . . existed. . . . 500 fighting planes could have turned the tide at Sedan. Yet . . . the British Air Ministry" was at that time sending planes to bomb Essen "while the German front kept on advancing" to the Channel. "A single French sentry" guarded each end of the Maastricht Bridge. A German officer "in peasant clothes engaged the sentry in talk, shot him, held the bridge against his few uprushing comrades, while another 'peasant' " cut the wires to the mines. So obstacles that it had been estimated would take weeks and thousands of lives were overcome in a few minutes without loss of life. Initiative, drive, characterized these young Germans.

Gribble makes it perfectly clear how we English and Americans have been doped. A people in 'slavery' could not have created such an efficient army from scratch in the few years available. We have been assured that the Germans had no adequate staff of officers. They'd junked the Junkers. We were certain that France had the greatest army in the world, six million men under arms in September at the call of war. And the French love their soil and will defend it. And wasn't it a Republic, and the slogan 'Liberty, Equality and Fraternity'? But when the officers fell down or deserted, the poilus knew the words were hollow. The failure of the British left the French bitter, and the English and Americans were fooled. "The terrible tragedy at Dunkirk was transformed by skillful publicity into a heroic chapter in the history of the British people, and one of which they will always speak with pride." (*Saturday Evening Post*, Jan. 4, 1941)

Many of the books dealing with the 'fall', hastily prepared, are trivial. Maurois' "Tragedy in France" (Harper, 1940) is the sort of pabu-

lum he serves up to forums and women's clubs.[7] Clare Boothe in
"Europe in the Spring" (Knopf, 1940) expands the impressions and
prejudices of her letters and cocktail hour chit-chat. Hamilton Fish
Armstrong of the subsidized Foreign Policy Association comes out with
a lugubrious "Chronology of Failure" (Macmillan, 1940), covering
forty days from the German crossing of the Belgian frontier to the
signature of the Armistice,—the aftermath of what had been so fate-
fully sown long before.

"France Under the Republic" (Harper, 1940) with clarity and understanding, without acrimony, brings the story up to the outbreak of the
present war, revealing the deep-seated rot in the French body politic
which brought about the collapse. It throws more light on the later
events than the more trivially up-to-date books. The author, Dennis
W. Brogan, professor of political science at Cambridge University, who
had been much in America, brought his quizzical and critical Scotch-
Irish mind to bear on the American "Government of the People"
(1933) in a tolerant but disillusioning picture of political realities.
Just as this remains the best book on our American government,[9] so
his new book is the best that has been written on the French Republic.
In the study of these two so-called democracies, he sees corruption
without indignation, cuts through abstractions without becoming fren-
zied. As he admired America, so he loved France, though he saw the
common weaknesses carrying France a step nearer to the brink It is
human to admire the stronger and love the weaker. Etched with a fine
sense of historical proportion, with sensibility for comic realism, his
contemporary political characters march across the course of events.
And so we understand that those who survived till May fled in panic
and now malign or persecute one another.

"J' Accuse! The Men Who Betrayed France" (Dial Press, 1940), by
"André Simone", a pseudonym for one who knew the inside intimately,
is of "vital importance to every American", Carleton Beals emphasizes
in his introduction.[10] It reveals the internal rottenness of a decayed
oligarchy masquerading as a Republican government, which had been
imposed upon sturdy peasants, workers, shopkeepers, who love democracy, have zest for living.

The constitution of the Third Republic made the Senate elective by a
small number of electors who could be controlled. The Bank of France,

which is the government department of finance, was left in control of practically hereditary regents. Of the 31,000 shareholders, representatives of 200 families had the right to vote for its governor and fifteen regents,—a formality, because the seat was hereditary in families like the Rothschilds, now fugitive, the Mallets and Hottinguers, in control for over a hundred years and still holding on. The fifteen regents were on the boards of 250 companies, which controlled steel and heavy industries, armament trusts, Schneider, Skoda, Comité des Forges. The twenty-five-odd daily papers of Paris were for the most part owned or financially supported by this same group.[11] Others "begged in order to keep alive, as an editor of one of them told me . . . 'Secret funds' in the Government budget gave a constitutional blessing to corruption" and were used to make monthly payments to subservient journals.[12] "The censorship kept the French people uninformed or miserably misinformed", though the "kept" press hated the censorship because "ministers who can suppress attacks by means of the censorship will not pay."

"Corruption in Parliament was just as flagrant. . . . My informant estimated that of the 618 Deputies, at least 300 were on somebody's payroll. . . The Secret police, or Sureté National, was part of the political machine. . . .

"At the outbreak of hostilities, France was split, demoralized by the betrayals it had witnessed. It had no confidence in the leadership.   .
Laval had wrecked collective security. Blum's non-intervention policy had split the forces capable and willing to resist a Hitler aggression. Daladier and Bonnet had sold one ally, Czechoslovakia, down the river. They had demolished the mutual-assistance treaty with Soviet Russia At Munich the war was almost lost for France   . .

"France was not beaten by Hitler. It was destroyed from within by a Fifth Column with the most powerful connections in the Government, big business, the State administration and the Army."[13]

Dos Passos in the Boston *Transcript*, Sept. 25, 1940, points out, "The danger that threatens us most is not from across the Atlantic. it is the danger that comes from poor thinking and incomplete organization at home".

Heinz Pol, now in this country, is a German, liberal journalist long resident in France. In his "Suicide of a Democracy" (Reynal and Hitchcock, 1940), he gives us in broad perspective a picture of underlying conditions which made the collapse inevitable. A fugitive from the Nazis, he perhaps ascribes too great power to their machinations in France. Bonnet and Mandel, the weakness and corruption in the army, failure of tank and aircraft industry, made the collapse inevitable.

"I Saw France Fall: Will She Rise Again?" (Morrow, 1940), by René de Chambrun, gives the graphic straightforward account of an active participant. A direct descendant of Lafayette, and son-in-law of Laval, he does not conceal his admiration for the politics of his friends.

From 1935 to 1939 Lindbergh had unusual opportunities to see from the inside what the European countries were doing in aviation. Invitations poured in upon him because of his reputation, and unofficially, on his own, he visited the leading countries. But as a means of protection against false charges he was usually accompanied by a U. S. military attaché. His conclusions impressed Ambassador Kennedy, at whose request he wrote a report for the War Department. In his three visits to Russia he had had unusual opportunities to become acquainted with its air force, but his conclusions as to its relative weakness as compared with Germany's were unpopular in England. In America too he told the right people and they resented it. His conclusions hurt, and for his honest public service he has been and is still being persecuted and maligned, though his judgment of the superiority of the German air force has been amply proved. C. B. Allen, an expert in aeronautics, tells us about this in the *Sat Eve Post,* Dec. 28, 1940.

"France's military aviation" he found "appalling . . . hopeless, so far as the success of any conflict with Germany was concerned",—stagnation in the factories "paralyzed by politics", not one pursuit plane to equal Germany's best. Lindbergh brought back a feeling that "France was aware of her internal corruption, but resigned". The French people are fatalistic because their "lot was already predetermined by the politicians who were running the country".

"British military aircraft", somewhat better, "was outclassed" by the German, not only "inferior in numbers . . . in average performance, but their maintenance presented greater difficulty because of their variety. . . . The English scoffed at the information Lindbergh gave them about Germany." Like young Kennedy in his "While England Slept", Lindbergh "felt that England had been asleep to the perils threatening her very existence and was only beginning to awake—a victim of the lethargy that overtakes aging and self-satisfied nations".

The American airplanes that had been sent to aid France were still unassembled at Casablanca when France surrendered. And Hitler took them over, assembled and used them.

An American citizen who since the last war has been resident in France, Spain and Portugal, acting as agent for a New York bank, assured me it was useless to put the fault for the lack of airplanes on individuals It was due to the breakdown of the democratic industrial system of France. Neither Cot nor his successor, La Chambre, should carry exclusive blame. "Whoever the minister was, he could not have done anything. I don't think that the French ministers actually received any individual graft. But you need scapegoats. If you blame the French industrialist, you will be touching on the point.

"The orders for planes were placed with French contractors. They in turn placed the parts with different manufacturers, motors with one, chasses, another. When the French manufacturers could not deliver on time, orders were eventually and reluctantly placed in America. That cut down on their profit. Therefore such orders were delayed till the last moment The French contractor or manufacturer purchased of course through the Allied Purchasing Commission though the French Government guaranteed payment.

"The knocked down planes or parts were landed at Casablanca instead of Bordeaux, perhaps to avoid submarines French mechanics didn't know the American machines and at first were able to assemble only about one a week. Later they could assemble fifty a week. Then they had to be tested by the American pilots, so there was further delay after delivery in Morocco of some two to sixteen weeks. After the French debacle when the Germans took over, they had plenty of technicians already in Spanish Morocco and quickly assembled the planes."

Suspecting that Americans were misinformed by our authorities, I read to my friend a paragraph from "The United States in World Affairs 1939" (published for the Council on Foreign Relations by Harper, 1940) by Whitney H. Shepardson and Wm. O. Scroggs: "While the British government was introducing such an innovation as conscription, sweeping changes were also taking place in France. The despondency which has prevailed there in the days when Hitler was annexing Austria and stripping Czecho-Slovakia of the Sudetenland was now gone. In the space of a few months France had experienced political and economic regeneration. Factionalism had yielded to patriotism; the major industries were no longer bedeviled by 'stay-in' strikes.   . ."

"Absolutely untrue," was his quick response, "fairy tale. The Third Republic of France has been putrefying for at least the last thirty years, and it reached its point of culmination in the surrender of the Petain Government to the German generals."[14]

Consultant management engineer for the French Munitions Ministry during the World War, C. Bertrand Thompson for the last twenty years has lived in France and worked in French industry From the outbreak of the present war he was engaged by the French Air Ministry in training experts in industrial organization, especially in the manufacture of airplane motors and accessories. In the *New Republic,* Dec. 9, 1940, he tells us: "In the last ten years French politics has followed two main tendencies. On the one side, the radicals and Socialists with a Communist fringe, represented principally by Blum and Daladier. On the other side, the conservatives with a fascist fringe, represented by Laval and Flandin. Both groups wanted votes." How like the American scene! "In 1936, when M. Marcel Déat, journalist (cf Bul #22), became Air Minister . . . large-scale production of civilian planes was stopped and the policy of prototypes introduced. . . . to ensure constant improvement in design and preparation, without expenditure for actual production.

"When, six months later, M. Pierre Cot took over, this policy was continued through the critical years 1937 and 1938. M. Guy La Chambre, Cot's successor, stayed in the same rut, despite many urgent warnings." Cot and the government were putting reliance on Russia's four thousand planes and "accepted the judgment of General Gamelin, who had no faith in planes or tanks. . . .

"In 1936, the number of unemployed was exceptionally high for France The forty-hour week was imposed with the idea of spreading work. . . . There was . . . widespread class hostility. But it should not be charged to Blum . . . Corrupt politicians bred distrust of the governing classes. The pennywise capitalist policy killed respect for business leadership. . . . Prostitution of press and government completed the general disgust. . . . Apparent communism . . . was essentially a violent protest against the abuses of democracy, . . . a profound distrust of civil and military leaders."

The workman, a victim of sabotage, "saw private manufacturers fighting the state manufacturers by manipulation of priorities". Thompson gives an intimate view of three airplane companies and how they worked. He tells us one plane concern, not over-scrupulous, sought to cripple a competitor before absorbing it. The counsel for this company was "the Air Minister himself (now also under arrest at Vichy)".

So France lacked plans because of slowness in design, lack of planning and coordination, inadequacy of machine tools and motor production, low level of competence among manufacturers, lack of modern plants, the "horde of charlatans" acting as industrial consultants, and "internal politics". "All this was quite well known and led inevitably to collapse of discipline."

"In short, France fell a victim to all the political and industrial evils which can flourish in a democracy unless and until they are checked by a general patriotism based on confidence in a government of justice and fair play, equal opportunity, genuine interest in individual welfare, competence and honesty", writes Thompson. "French democracy was more like our own than any other. Some of its weaknesses revealed by the tests of war may find their counterpart among us under similar circumstances, as they have in England."[17]

January 3, 1941

Notes

[1] Why have we so loved France? A foolish question perhaps, for who ever really knew why he loved, or for what. In love or hate, reason flees as emotion surges and gives rise to poetic fantasies or calumnic Jeremiads. Sensuous impressions linger in the background,—the rare bouquet of a Montrachet, the aroma of an omelet aux fines herbes, the smile of a peasant girl, or the avaricious peasant whose clumsy cart wrecked our car, an encounter with red-tape officialdom, an outrageous hotel bill. Of such trivialities do we build our loves and hates Expatriates revelling in the cosmopolitan flavor of Paris, tourists intrigued by the catchalls on the periphery of France have never known that love.

Paris for many summers was my hideout, the place where one could be lost and forgotten, the riches and pleasures of the world within arms reach but I never loved Paris nor thought it beautiful though there were beautiful things to ferret out and things to love

The France her lovers knew was more difficult to find and more diverse,—rich or sparse, meager or gaunt, beautiful or terrifying,—the bleak Carse, the volcanic Auvergne, the wild gorges of the Tarne, the lush prodigality of Perigord, or the rocky gauntness of Brittany,—its people so varied, from the cider-soaked descendants of the Norsemen, the thrifty sea-faring Bretons, to those proud thread-bare Ligurian aristocrats who on the same soil these twenty thousand years have seen the Greeks come and the Romans pass.

They may hate or envy one another but they have in common the love of their French soil and respond to the same sentiment as they pass the simple village monument inscribed "to the children of France who gave their lives" that their daughters, widows, grandmothers may with horny hands hold the plow or stoop for the faggot or with eager finger glean the single heads of wheat.

Afoot, abicycle or in a little car, through summers over forty years talking with the peasants and vintners, waiters, I came to see the land through the eyes of the French people, to sense the fetid corruption, the growing lack of confidence, the smouldering discontent which compensating sops did not satisfy. And when you come to understand a people, you love them even more for the faults which you excuse than for their virtues which perhaps you still doubt.

Another lover of France, Henry Beston, writes in *The Patriot*, December 1940, "Almost every explanation has been given of the fall of France except the right one. France has been dead for some years. The killing and killing and killing of the last war was too much for her, and she simply died. You cannot kill a whole generation of our young and get away with it biologically or spiritually; out of such a hecatomb rises no 'élan vital'; no ideas, no forces; a nation becomes a kind of grave. In the beautiful country of l'isle de France, whose fields have been cultivated since the bronze age, I saw farms falling into ruin exactly as deserted farms are going to pieces here in the back country. 'Nous n'avons pas d'hommes. Mons fils est mort, mon frère est mort, et l'ainé de ses fils; le plus jeune est aveugle.' That was the sort of answer you got. It was this corpse of France which the French Foreign Office and the 'politicos' passively entered in this completely detestable and wicked war, giving the body a rifle and propping it up in a trench,—the expedient so often read of in old accounts. . . . The poor wretched cadaver died a hideous second death . . . leaving what was left of France to endure the insults of our vile and lying press.

"We do need a 'defense program'—the defense of our young, not only of their traditions, of their intellectual and spiritual heritage, but also of the very shirt tails and a roof over their heads. The young in the colleges are quite aware of what is going on, and understand the values involved, but they are indolent and helpless, and the faculties which guide them are all in favor of machine-gunning them to carry the slopes of cloud-cuckoo-land. . . . It seems to me that those of us who served France, futilely, in 1915, 1916 and later, must speak up to save America from the fate which has overtaken France."

Beston recommends E. H. Kerr's "The Twenty Years Crisis",—"a fair study of the crisis as a struggle between Political Utopianism and Political Realism. It is the only study I know of which considers recent history in terms of its philosophical bases",—and "Why France Lost the War" (Veritas Press), a translation of "a study published early in the war by a German scholar, giving in a few direct and honest pages the actual conditions in France"

(2) In "News of the French" (Faber and Faber, 1938) Montgomery Belgion, who has divided his life between France and England, reminds us that the Treaty of Versailles provided, "victors and vanquished would again be on an equality as regards how each would arm". But "for sixteen years France has exercised despotically the military hegemony of Europe".

Pertinax, the French journalist, writes, "Leadership of the politically rejuvenated continent devolved upon France" (*Newsweek*, Dec. 26, 1938) "France was in a position to give a new lease of life to the Europe of 1919. . . . Neither France nor Great Britain has shown herself morally and materially fit to keep alive the Europe they themselves had created at a gigantic expense of blood and treasure." (*Atlantic*, Jan. 1939)

"France was suffering from the effects of victory When, at Versailles, Germany was requested to deliver over or destroy all her armaments, General von Seeckt, who later devised a large share of the new methods which Germany has used in the present war, is reported to have said, 'This is a great boon for us, because it will force us to think out new war methods, to create new armaments, and that alone—if nothing else—will enable us to build a new army which will be really capable of winning the coming war.' France, on the other hand, had found the methods of 1914 successful in 1918 and was not prepared to abandon them." When Reynaud "in 1935 introduced a bill into Parliament" suggesting a mechanized army, "the answer . from the army commission of the Chamber of Deputies, delivered by M. Senac, was that the creation of such a special corps 'might contribute an undeniable element of power to the French Army', but that it was neither desirable nor possible because it was against 'logic and history' Meanwhile, Hitler was paying no attention to 'logic and history'." (*Living Age*, September 1940)

William Lytton Payne, in *Harper's*, January, 1941, taking issue with Roy Helton's contention in an earlier issue that America has softened and spoiled its young people, writes, "The fate of France, says Mr. Helton, was that of a country which behind a barrier of arms enjoyed a delicious respite. Not so, Mr. Helton: France was rotten to the core with disaffection nurtured on years of unemployment and hopelessness for its people, its youth, its soldiers, and its statesmen. Just there, Mr Helton, we too are sick, and growing more so at a frightful pace If we are to survive to the year 2000 we must be tough, writes Mr Helton. Behind those words is a world of thought. Does he mean a people who can go hungry, jobless, and hopeless that they may have the guns to protect their right to go on being hungry, jobless, and hopeless? France thought that, and in the foreboding lull of the long winter months her soldiers, her youth, weighed that concept and in the spring found it not worth the candle."

(3) De Saint Jean tells us how the French developed a highly efficient mechanized army in the '20's when discarded American tanks were in storage and the Germans were using cardboard imitations. Then the French sat down behind

their Maginot Line. They are like that, early to invent and discover,—the automobile, aniline dyes Then they leave it to the Germans to work out and the Americans to exploit The Frenchman has the logical mind. The German has the work habit and the need The American has the market and the desire for profit. The French mechanician made the automobile an individual work of art, expensive, at a time when we had nothing but horseless carriages. And when mass production came in to supply our great market, it was a long time before the French began to imitate us with their Citroen, then Citroen went bankrupt

(4) "The French had at least three million men under arms and most of them were put into action against the Germans at some time during the battle. Yet, the German Panzer divisions which smashed through them with apparent ease numbered hardly two hundred thousand men " (Gunther, *Look*, Aug. 27, 1940)

"In his now famous book—Vers l'Armée de Métier, published in 1934, General de Gaulle . argued for a professional long-service army of regular troops . ." expert "in the handling of multifarious and complicated mechanism of modern war . De Gaulle did not believe in the fureur de nombre, stating that a mere mass army becomes immobile, it cannot manoeuvre and therefore cannot win victories, it can only crush by sheer weight. Also the large army the more difficulty it is to feed and supply." (*Washington Diplomatic Letter*, Jan. 14, 1941)

(5) Kenneth T. Downs, chief of the Paris Bureau of International News Service, declares, "I can best explain what happened in France and what is happening right here in America this moment by saying that the French military intelligence knew, just as our intelligence department and our officers knew, what was going on in Germany They knew that Germany was building a great air force and panzer divisions. When the planes and tanks came streaming across the French plains, there was no surprise. French army leaders begged for planes, tanks and men, but in vain "

(6) "The monetary, financial and economic problem", Pertinax says, "was badly handled by the cartel of the left in 1924 and, when the prosperity era initiated by M Poincaré had come to an end, by the weak conservative leaders of 1931-32, as well as by the radical socialists of 1932-36. The British government had given up the gold standard in 1931, and, in March 1933, President Roosevelt had followed suit. The effect of the all-round lowering of world prices had been to increase by 50 per cent the purchasing power of the franc, as stabilized by Poincaré. "But the Banque de France, which neither conservatives nor radical socialists (those conservatives of the left) dared challenge, never realized that France could not stick to the gold standard and refuse to devaluate her currency without burdening national economy with production costs heavier than those of other states. The inescapable result was the exhaustion of French economy .. Blum was carried into office upon the wave of the masses' discontent, born of long-endured suffering. . . . Clenched fists never departed from the memory [of] the moneyed classes Those threats were in the front of their minds whenever problems of foreign policy claimed their attention."

Poincaré's part in all this Pertinax either overlooks or obscures. Eugene J

Young, who until his recent death had long been cable editor of the N. Y *Times*, in his "Looking Behind the Censorships" (Lippincott, 1938) tells the tale simply. America was up aganist the gold bloc. France then had $3,254,000,000, and the sterling bloc had over $1,500,000,000 of gold. "Poincaré and other shrewd Frenchmen did something for their country. . . . They took four-fifths of the gold value out of the franc but controlled values at home so that the franc retained most of its domestic buying power. As a result, France, by manufacturing cheaply, was able to undersell most of her competitors—even in their own markets—and by cheap living costs also attracted many tourists and foreign residents who left hundreds of millions of their money. Huge balances rolled up abroad."

We owed France more than she owed us Unexpectedly she demanded payment of the balance due her, in gold, which we didn't have then. So we had to sell stocks. "Our panic in 1929 was precipitated by a sudden cashing of French credit in New York followed by a demand for gold . . . When we started to recover from our depression in 1932 we were sent back to further depths by the sudden demand of the French for $700,000,000 gold based on the credits they had rolled up here. The profits France took from this country by her manipulations must be left to the imagination, but they were undoubtedly huge."

Britain under Neville Chamberlain as Chancellor of the Exchequer had long been aware of Poincaré's game, which was putting England at a disadvantage. It became necessary to lower the value of the pound in foreign exchange and to combine with France to "keep American money at a high value so they could retain their trade advantages"

At the same time Chamberlain prevented devaluation at home to save loss to the holders of "some twenty billion dollars' worth of loans and investments" which "were based on sterling" (Young, p 309). This was done by milking India of $4,000,000,000 in gold hoarded there. This was easily accomplished by putting India on the gold standard and demanding that all gold be surrendered in return for paper Having extracted all the gold possible from India, "Britain dropped the pound to about two-thirds of its old value, so British goods could be cheapened in world trade, but prevented inflation and consequent higher prices at home by limiting the currency." (Young)

This forced the British Commonwealths, the Scandinavian, many South American and Near and Far Eastern countries to tie their money to the pound, forming a sterling bloc, so that the devalued pound, though no longer backed by gold, remained the world's standard for business

"All this time America had been the champion of the traditional gold standard . . . still harboring the ideas her financiers and business men had absorbed from Britain . . in 1896 and 1900. All our bonds, here and abroad, carried the clause for payment in that standard and those who tried to point out that insufficient gold existed to carry on the world's great and growing business were treated as heretics. What France had started .   Britain, the sterling bloc   . completed. Foreigners found that with the low-priced pound, yen and franc they could buy more elsewhere . . . than they could buy in America when they had to acquire our dear dollars and use them for purchases here   Our foreign market was smashed, our domestic prices driven down to catastrophic levels. When Britain, having rolled up huge balances here in the former French way, demanded gold early in 1933, the strain became too great and the collapse of our banking system was hastened " (Young, pp 311-12).

(7) Maurois presents himself frankly, as his auditors expect, as a sophisticated but innocent participant. It was on a "beautiful summer night" that "negligently sipping champagne" at the ball at the Polish Embassy as war was about to break, Maurois heard Bonnet tell how the military had assured that there was no reason for postponement. Though Bonnet had promised Ciano delay, the English could not because the Chamberlain Government felt that it would fall unless at the assembling of Parliament on the morrow it could be told that an ultimatum had been sent   Maurois maintains it was lack of material, not treason, that caused France to fall in 37 days   He admits, however, there was corruption and defeatism among "the three thousand persons in Paris who, as Byron said, 'because they go to bed late believe they are the leaders of the world.' "

Maurois in *Life*, January 6, 1941, attempts to allay "American grievances against his country". "The war had been lost, it seemed to me, not on the battlefields of Flanders in May, 1940, but in the armament factories of France and England from 1931 to 1939. . .   It could of course, have been won, or altogether avoided, if, from 1931 onwards, France and England had prevented German rearmament; if, in 1936, they had opposed the fortification of the Rhineland; if, in 1937 and 1938, they had built masses of planes and tanks; France, in one year, had built less planes than Germany in one month."

Two years ago Maurois in "The Miracle of England", wrote "the English ruling class still remains in the saddle", and "it is the fear of what might follow the collapse of Hitler or Mussolini that accounts in large measure for the hesitation of the British ruling class to force a show-down with either of the Fascist dictators"

(8) Raymond Gram Swing, reviewing Armstrong in the New York *Herald-Tribune*, Nov. 24, 1940, says, "It may be good politics to tell people in this country that France fell only because of the mistakes of the Blum regime. The statement has some factual authenticity   But it is not truth, it is only a fragment of the truth, which is to say that it is untruth in its effect on the people to whom it is told."

(9) Most will think of Bryce as the best   Brogan covers the same ground up to date with more keenness, zest, humor, understanding. Those who know will proclaim as best the two-volume work to which Bryce wrote the preface (Macmillan, 1902), little known and much neglected in our universities, of Ostrogorski the Russian, who spent more than ten years in residence in both England and America studying the actual workings, the mechanics of the machinery of democracy in the small towns and the great cities,   a thing that doesn't so much interest the Anglo Saxon who finds opportunity to 'work' it for his own purposes.

Whereas the British Bryce was an optimist, the Russian Ostrogorski was a realist. Ostrogorski's study, though it did not appear in book form until 1902, was made simultaneously with that of Bryce and published as a series of articles in the Annales des Sciences Politiques of 1888 and 1889.

"In this book I investigate the working of democratic government", Ostrogorski tells us, "not institutions . . . political forms, it is on political forces that I dwell. Owing to the nature of the investigation which I undertook, the greater part of the materials had to be gathered from real life and not from libraries. . . . I found myself confronted with a void when, about fifteen years ago, I began my work. The facts relating to it were evidently not deemed worthy of the attention of historians and political thinkers."

In the conclusion to his single volume "Democracy and the Party System" (Macmillan, 1910) which is a condensation brought up to date of Volume II of his earlier work, Ostrogorski pays tribute to the wisdom of the founders. "But they could not foresee the destiny of their country, they had no idea of the course along which it was to be carried by its economic evolution. . . . The Fathers did not anticipate . . . the all-pervading development of Party, nor the coming of conquering Plutocracy. . . . These factors—Democracy, Party, and Plutocracy taken together, completely altered the direction of government and went far to reduce the Constitution of the United States to a paper constitution. Extra-constitutional forms developed, which have frequently superseded or encroached upon the constitutional order. It is impossible to understand the American government unless one has studied well those extra-constitutional forms. . . . The party Organization has served as a lever to all great private interests in their designs on the public weal."

No American has attempted any similar scientific study of our government. True, there have been journalistic books, of which perhaps the best is Frank Kent's "The Great Game of Politics". But the American has been relatively uninterested, willing to believe myths, to hide his head in the sand, to leave government control to the politician and his henchmen and the ward heelers and the plutocrats, who were subservient only to the finance capitalists who wanted franchises or protection. Ostrogorski explains this on the basis that Americans were wholly absorbed in making money, taming a continent, exploiting its resources, and that the plutocrats who came into control did not want political power, they aimed only at plunder.

The first knowledge I had of Ostrogorski came through the "Confessions of an Economic Heretic" by J. A. Hobson who called it "the first clear and comprehensive exposure of the corruption of democratic institutions in American States and cities". Hobson writes, "To present the appearance of democracy, without handing over the reality of government to the people, had long been the unchallenged achievement of the upper classes in Britain and America. The machinery of two-party politics was successfully devoted to this end."

Hoping to learn that the Social Science departments at Harvard had been better informed, I wrote to Prof. William Yandell Elliott of the Government

Department,—"I have just made the discovery of Ostrogorski. He has brought me great excitement. I have gone through his three volumes on the American government, and I have read what Bryce has to say about his writing, and am about to put in print, subject to your correction, that this is a scientific study that has been studiously avoided in our American universities, like so many other things, and for reasons which I shall not cite as brusquely as does Veblen, but which he made so clear. Tell me I am wrong, that Ostrogorski's work is well known to the teachers of government at Harvard. Of course, there have been some new developments in ways of manipulating democracies since his time. And in regard to that, I formed the impression along about 1900 from my own personal observation that Henry Cabot Lodge was perhaps one of the most fertile minded and capable men in inventing new ways of corrupting legislatures. That would make an interesting study for a doctor's thesis in government. Do you suppose that Lowell ever saw Ostrogorski's study before he wrote his rather stupid two volumes?"

This brought an interesting reply Elliott said his assistant Mims had been at work bringing Ostrogorski up to date "I think we do know and understand Ostrogorski's work. Our course in Party Politics has used it as a basic text. . . . As time goes on he seems more important. . . I know that Lowell knew of Ostrogorski's study, and I do not think he was as unconscious of these aspects of politics as you think I always had felt he was an obscurantist in his approach to these questions because he believed that a social myth should be built up in terms of preventing any reference to something like class war. He once said, I remember, that the ideal feature of the American party system was that it was perfectly calculated to obscure issues ! That is a shrewd kind of Tory philosophy which has its points, but one with which I think neither of us would agree."

(10) "The Second Empire" by Octave Aubry (Lippincott, 1940) gives a picture of moral rot and political catastrophe out of which came the Third Republic, —which gives us hope today It is a noble and patriotic piece of writing and as Albert Jay Nock remarks in January *Atlantic*, for Americans it has value in "the clear and steady light it throws" on "pseudo-ideas", "cant terms", "unquestioned beliefs", "superstitions", that demand examination and analysis "We are all republicans . only beginning to 'know what a republic means'. . . . We are all democrats, we believe in democracy",—but only "beginning to know what democracy means." But "Democracy has only just caught up with the United States", and may not stay with us.

"Not one of those dictators has seized power, not a single one The people want them. . . . Portugal is a dictator-bossed European country . . peaceful . . getting the best and cheapest government in Europe . . . and if the election was forced . . . the line between free and forced elections is pretty hard to draw. . . .

"M. Aubry tells us nothing, insists upon nothing, teaches us nothing, but he puts us in the way of teaching ourselves a great deal, and no service can be more salutary than this."

(11) André Morize, long professor at Harvard and recently Director of the

French Ministry of Information under Jean Giraudoux, speaks of that sensational book, "J'Accuse!" as written by a German refugee. Morize cast doubt on some of the details but it is quite apparent that he and his department were somnolent. For example, he writes, "We knew vaguely that Germany was building planes". He is now again at Harvard. (Boston *Herald*, Jan. 26, 1941)

(12) M. W. Fodor, Hungarian journalist, now professor at Northwestern University and said by the publishers to know the author personally, reviewing the book in the N. Y. *Times* claims that this is "dramatic proof that fear of Bolshevism and exaggerated class differences . . . can lead to the downfall even of as mighty a country as was Republican France". The *Chr Sci Monitor* reviewer remarks, "When one has finished the book one has long ceased to be surprised at the fall of France. One is even amazed that a regime so riddled with corruption, treason, and division could have withstood the mild test of Sitzkrieg." The *New Republic* review says, "No country on the European continent was closer to us, in spirit and institutions. At least a clear outline of the causes that led to the disaster is urgently needed here, particularly since dishonest and patently interested interpretations are already being circulated. . . . A great national heritage was ruined by treacherous politicians who began their nefarious work long before the war. . . . We are impressed not so much by their villainy as by their sordid mediocrity."

(13) *Le Temps, Le Journal des Débats, L'Information, La Journée Industrielle* were openly owned by big industrialists. Ten other newspapers received important financial support from the two hundred families. Three were owned by one paper manufacturer whom Reynaud appointed Minister of Information. The Socialist organ *Le Populaire* was subsidized by Reynaud when Paul Fauré, to get rid of Blum, induced provincial Socialists to discontinue support. "The rest of the papers, the so-called 'confidential sheets'—so called because of their extremely small circulation—lived from hand to mouth." Daladier testified before an examining committee that " 'eighty per cent of the French press is subsidized either by Government or private sources'. The 'envelopes' were made ready at the beginning of every month at the Quai d'Orsay and other Ministries, to be called for either by the business managers or the journalists of the various papers." (Simone, "J'Accuse!")

(14) "The French Army did not, of course, live in a vacuum. It was also infested with this vermin of corruption which marked the waning years of the Third Republic. . . . Gamelin, who headed the French Army from 1935 on, must have been aware of the demoralization in the officers' corps. The majority of officers sympathized with the dictators . . . Gamelin did nothing to purge the Army of even its most suspect elements. . . . He attained his post of supreme command by chance. . . . The most unimpressive of French Generals", it was difficult to weave a legend but the American press succeeded in presenting him as a strong man to rely on. "Never, unlike such of his fellow officers as Petain and Weygand, did he plot against the Republic." But he was "responsible for the gaps and lags in armaments . . . for the terrible neglect of the Little Maginot

Line." On the outbreak of the war the French army lacked blankets, shoes. "It was simply a complete lack of organization." Airplane factories "were producing less planes than before the war because of the lack of raw materials. . . . The Air Minister refused to place large orders, because the French manufacturers insisted that the money be spent in France."

"One wonders whether Weygand was really brought back from disgraceful retirement in the Near East to fight the already lost Battle of France or to help arrange for the establishment in power of the representatives of the 200 Families and the fascist groups to which, prior to the war, he had sold the rifles and ammunition of the French army that they might riot at the portals of the Ministry of State and shout for Petain." (Simone, "J'Accuse!")

(15) The Boston *Transcript,* June 18, editorialized, "There are times in the affairs of man when we must take the long look of things . . In 20 years a people, stripped of their wealth and manpower by war and inflation, have built for themselves one of the most powerful positions in the long history of Europe They made every sacrifice to do it, including that of freedom. . . . After the same interval, her neighbor victorious only 20 years ago, lies prostrate . . . Democracy had not been functioning efficiently in France . . . incompetency in government . . social unrest . national unit had reached a low ebb Democracy in America, also, has fallen into bad days. Our economic structure has been creaking We . have been living beyond our means, carelessly blinding ourselves to the day of reckoning. Ten million people have been unemployed. Incompetency of the highest order has held sway. Waste has been prodigious "

The much abused Petain Government, not popular in lower New York, has been trying to remedy abuses. "All abuses of the capitalistic system, Finance Minister Marcel Yves Bouthillier said, evolved around the 'irresponsibility of the chiefs of the corporations' The new legislation meant no more 'monkeying around with other people's money'. . . The president of a company must be an active participant in its management, and president and board are personally liable for all the company's debts" (*Time,* Sept 30, 1940).

July 22, *Time,* giving the "Obituary of a Republic" had said, "To some it seemed because of that final acquiescence, France, now brazenly fascist, must always have been unfaithful to democracy at heart. . . . By last week it was crystal clear that France's collapse had been preceded by a long, slow disintegration of the democratic and republican ideal, and in the process of disintegration was many a lesson for thoughtful U S. citizens to ponder. . . . The preservation of democracy requires all citizens vigilantly to exercise their democratic rights."

(16) M. Pierre Cot replied to Mr. Thompson in the *New Republic,* Jan. 20, "This is part of the same pro-fascist thesis intended to make me responsible for the bad state of French aviation at the beginning of the war. As the life of an army plane is at the most eighteen months, such propaganda must maintain that I directed the Air Ministry in 1938 I left the Air Ministry in January, 1938 " But in his main thesis, Mr Thompson "is right. At the beginning of the war the German aviation was about six times more powerful and numerous than the

French." His added explanation as to why this was is not very satisfactory.

(17) " 'The big war aim', wrote Edmund Taylor, quoting a French observer in mid-winter 'is not the smashing of Germany, but the smashing of Communism in France' ('The Strategy of Terror,' p 252). In the debacle the smashers joined the enemy in preference to any other course" (Schuman, "Night Over Europe").

Lloyd George: "From the start of the campaign, whilst blazoning liberty on their banners, the rulers of France constantly pursued a policy of repression in their decrees. Freely elected members of Parliament were thrown into prison for no breach of law, for no act or word of treason to the state. Of those who elected these persecuted members to the Chamber of Deputies and municipal councils there were at least 500,000 men who were actually enrolled in the armies defending the frontiers of their country. What a mockery it must have appeared to them in these circumstances to be called upon to face death for liberty, equality and fraternity, which were trampled underfoot by their own government!" (Lloyd George, quoted by Dreiser, "America Is Worth Saving", p 250)

WHY GERMANY WINS

Win what? The war? Churchill[1] and other English statesmen have believed and stated that the last war would better have ended in a stalemate. Today some, like President Wilson in his time, are discerning enough to see that what we should pray for is "peace, without victory". Victory certainly brought no peace.[2]

What does it mean to win? Halifax has just come to tell us that "every last vestige" of the ideas back of the present German regime "must be destroyed".[3] Of course, what the leaders in England want is security to enjoy past gains. They want to be left alone.

What can America win? What we can lose is more apparent. But the leaders of our Administration seek power and prestige. To them it seems more possible to gain these overseas than at home, and it is proving easier to get money to spend for overseas projects in the name of 'defense' than for more civic improvements, more swimming pools, whose upkeep the taxpayer will no longer support. (cf Bul #82)

'Defense'—that's a slave's passive attitude. Reliance on someone else to defend us is pusillanimous. If there is to be war, the American spirit will be to win. To win you have to know your opponent, his power, his tactics, his strategy. Otherwise, you cannot train to meet and counter, even in the ring. If you know the other's methods, you can anticipate his moves. You may be able to defeat him and win.

In football we have scouts. In the military we have Intelligence Officers who attempt to get something across to those in command. Mental tests eliminate the nitwits from the recruits.

"Brains for the Army" are cautiously advocated by Donald W. Mitchell in the *Nation,* January 25, 1941 We have 'em, he says, but they are mostly in the lower ranks. He asks, "Why .   . is our army now frantically aping the Germans?" and answers, "The men with the best brains do not hold the highest jobs". The Chief of Staff, General Marshall, has testified that "our army costs more than twenty times as much, in proportion to its size" as the German army. True, there is higher pay but much of this expense "is due to poor management and inefficiency".[4]

Intelligence, and particularly Military Intelligence, is needed for Defense. Any study that will throw light on the success thus far achieved by the Germans should be the meat and drink of patriotic Americans today.

"Why Hitler Wins. A Lesson in Technological Politics for Americans" presents some of these problems and considerations Carl Dreher tells of this with frank understanding in last October's *Harper's,* and writes me that he is now expanding this into a book. A radio engineer for RCA, Hollywood sound director, four years ago he retired and in *Harper's* told of his disgust with American business methods

"How Come France Collapsed" we entitled the last Bulletin, intending to imply that there was no design, no conspiracy, but that 'men of good will' through their lack of understanding brought about the events that preceded and made inevitable the fall With Germany there seems to have been modern scientific planning, deliberate design

'Why' implies planning,[5] design, a Great Artificer. A child asks mother or father 'why'. Those who like Buchman or Halifax are guided directly by a personal god may well ask 'why'. Those who believe that God helps him who helps himself don't whine 'why'.[6] They don't attribute design They don't complain about Fate or Kismet

The German industrial and economic system is no creation of Hitler's It is an historical development. Walter Rathenau tried to put it into practice. Dreher quotes one of Dorothy Thompson's four "simple, realistic reasons why Hitler has so far won this war". She says, "Hitler is winning the war because he has been fighting it with an industrial and engineering economy, while the democracies have been fighting it with a money or financial economy."[7]

German "capitalist technology" has developed faster in Germany "than in England, the land of its birth, or in America where technology had every natural advantage", Dreher tells us   "The early and middle German industrialists, men like Alfred Krupp and Werner Siemens, were technically trained."[8]

"These German technicians were no wizards.   Their engineering schools were no better than ours " American industry has enjoyed such advantages of material and labor that it should have outstripped German industry in every field, but it didn't, Dreher observes,—because in Germany there was an alliance between technology, business and the state, while in the United States business dominated all, profits were first.   Progress could be stopped when there was no profit in it.[9]

In America industrialists are stock gamblers and manipulators,— bankers we call them.   Edison in Germany would have been "more respected than bankers and promoters, although naturally not as much as Junkers and officers divinely ordained to protect the honor and commerce of the Fatherland".[10]   But in America he was kicked out in ten years and then a myth was built about him and his name exploited in innumerable Edison companies in which he had no share.

Technological advance in military history has been coincident with and dependent upon metallurgical advance and this has been due to the initiative and inventive capacity of civilians   This progress is interestingly traced by Waldemar Kaempffert, science editor of the N. Y. *Times,* in "War and Technology", in the remarkable issue on war of the *American Journal of Sociology* for January, 1941.   There is the same cultural lag in military history as in industrial, Kaempffert brings out   But the complete disarmament of Germany gave stimulus for subsidized technological research, and especially in aviation, as has been so warningly pointed out to us by Lindbergh and Al Williams

"German Planning for Total War" is described with brilliance and imagination in February *Harper's* by Fletcher Pratt.   He tells in detail of technical plans remade, criticized, tested,—every difficulty thought out, obstacles provided for, and time-tabled for future use.[11]   The German tactics which seem so startling to us are not new.   Pratt cites examples of how the same tactics have been successfully used for thousands of years. They consist, as genius is said to, in "the infinite capacity for taking pains".

Major General J. F C. Fuller, whose active mentality has long confused his more stolid British colleagues, is now being recognized as sound in his discernment. Years ago he urged that a staff officer "must study modern engineering journals and the old prints of hundreds of years ago depicting flamenwerfers and gas bombs. These will set vibrating brain-waves which will awaken new designs He must study the evolution of weapons—in fact, he must become an adept in war tool biology".

"There is a good deal more substance to be vibrated on this subject in the mind of the engineer than in that of the general", writes Bernard Brodie, discussing "Defense and Technology" in the *Technology Review*, January, 1941 [12] "Let the latter's mind be vibrated by contemplation of the instruments which the engineer produces so that the general may be stimulated to devise new tactics by which those instruments can be used to best advantage. Tardiness in doing so has been the traditional weakness of the military commander. The overcoming of this disability probably more than any other one fact accounted for the brilliant German victories in the fall of 1939 and the spring of 1940."

The strategy of the Germans that so startled us as to make 'blitz' an English word, is the result of the ancient method of planning for surprise and speed, which the Confederate cavalry raider early referred to as bringing the 'mostest there fustest'. Overlooked during the 19th century was the old strategy of first eliminating the conquerable and not risking defeat by attacking the stronger force till weakened. Revival of this old strategy may be due to Hitler.[13] But it would necessarily be adopted by the German army staff to insure tactical successes. They have also developed "the system Napoleon inherited from the French Revolution and expanded—that of living off the conquered, making war feed war". (Pratt)

"Does Hitler Represent Germany?" A. Whitney Griswold of Yale University, author and specialist on international affairs, answers this question in the *Atlantic* for March, 1941, reminding us that the doctrine of Lebensraum, the Kaiser's "Place in the Sun", filled the minds of the German people long before Hitler and the present war.

Surprise, the most important age-old element of strategy, General Braddock had to learn for the British from the North American Indians. To overwhelm, shock, terrorize, confuse, stampede and immobilize the enemy is the result to be attained to bring victory.

Killing is incidental and unnecessary. High ideals, moral preaching, righteousness, whether genuine or hypocritical, will not help. What will help will be unity among the people produced by a sense of common danger or a long established feeling of resentment. If the threat is ever present that they will continue to be deprived if they lose, and that they may have a cup of coffee when they want it if they win, that may help too.

"Educational Philosophy of the Third Reich", Ph.D. thesis by George Kneller, to be published by Yale University Press in 1941, without the usual prejudice and vilification to which the American taste has been accustomed, makes clear how such unity is established through the education of the young (cf Bul #1)

Secrecy insures surprise and saves lives by stampeding or immobilizing the enemy. Democratic ways interfere with secrecy. That's one reason why dictatorship is so essential to success in modern war. The surprise insured by totalitarian secrecy accounts, too, for the enormous results achieved with small numbers and with small loss of life as compared with the old warfare of position and attrition of the stupid brass hats of the last war, and by the naval blockade economic warfare which through disease and deprivation is more destructive than explosives.[14]

Psychology to this end has been scientifically used by the Germans,— how skilfully has been brought out in "The Strategy of Terror" by Edmund Taylor (Houghton Mifflin, 1940), which has served well for propaganda purposes But every new weapon is denounced The use of gunpowder was heinous to chivalrous knights, the use of gas horrified us in the last war, though Americans, largely through the researches of President Conant, are perhaps more advanced in its use than any other nation.

The 'war of nerves' has been denounced as "bluff or armed blackmail". But when was deception not a part of war? That this psychological warfare has been successful and has created fear is evident from the hatred.[15] Hoffman Nickerson makes these observations in "The Armed Horde, 1793-1939" (Putnam, 1940) in a striking study in which he shows that conscription arose with democracy in the French Revolution and advanced with democratic control. Now that again the technical professional army is proving superior to the armed horde, dictatorship under Hitler or Roosevelt replaces democracy in war. (cf Bul #85)

German economics "remains [even] more mysterious", and violates our university teaching. But aren't universities endowed by those who have recently made profits to perpetuate the profit system? German economics has grown out of their lack of resources and deprivation, necessitating that they eliminate waste and practice economy, material and political Deprived of gold, they had to devise a system without it. Doing away with gold as a symbol, they eliminate much of banking and its profits. This necessitates dealing with actual things, labor as the source of wealth and commodities as the result of wealth.

"The German Financial Revolution" is explained in February *Harper's* by Dal Hitchcock, with a following article in the March issue on the "dynamic use of government securities". The revolution consists in "changing capitalism" without "destroying it". The orthodox view has been that "a government which ran itself into debt was . . . headed for trouble. The debt was a true indication that the people were unwilling currently to pay the essential costs of government or that the government was extravagantly spending beyond its power to tax. . . . Debt merely represented deferred taxes".

Orthodox financiers have been waiting for Germany to go bankrupt. "Instead of being bankrupt, Germany has created vast public improvements, expanded her industry, and built . . [a great] war machine. . . . All this has been done in a nation that at the start was debt ridden, impoverished, and deep in depression." Hitler "began by strengthening the nation from within, working with the materials that then were available". Ways had to be devised to do this without money.[16]

Simple is the explanation given by Hitler to G. Ward Price, the English correspondent, in his "Year of Reckoning" (Cassell, 1939). "The fundamental difference between your economic policy and ours is that in England you work on a basis of capital, whereas the basis of the German system is productive labour. . . . After inflation and the world slump, practically no capital existed in Germany. . . . I had to devise new machinery for performing it. The effectiveness of that machinery can be judged by the results. As for your expectation of our collapse, I may say that the greatest economists in Germany have been foretelling it for the past six years, but they have given that up now because even experts cannot afford to go on being wrong forever."[17]

The German system of barter we have come to deride and fear, due to the promptings of British propagandists. But it is simplicity itself and has of necessity been extensively adopted by the British government and cautiously by our own administration in dealing with Britain.[18] Essentially it goes back to the most ancient, even primitive, mode of exchange of surplus for something needed. In the German system the nation as a whole considers what it has to sell and surveys what another nation produces. Then a financial agent, perhaps Dr. Schacht, works out a plan for exchange Propaganda has made of this simple thing a terror. But the turning back toward the primitive in this as in many other things is the inevitable way out, 'as the facades fall'.

"Big Business and Defense" in the February *Atlantic* explains how the German financial revolution is being brought to Washington.[18] Bronson Batchelor, the author, a New Yorker, formerly a Washington correspondent, accounts for the slowing down of 'defense' as an indication of the strain between big business and the government, as "men influential in directing government policy as A. A. Berle, Leon Henderson, and Lauchlin Currie, because of their own critical attitude toward the system of free enterprise, cannot quite bring themselves to entrust this full responsibility to business men"

Keynes' "Theory of Employment, Interest and Money" brought these ideas from Germany by way of England to President Roosevelt's advisers The war has resulted in his "Multiplier" thesis being tried in England and now in this country The President may not know whence came these ideas, but they serve his purpose admirably. The Schacht plan in Germany is based on this same theory, Batchelor recognizes, but he fails to see as Hitchcock does that there is something more basic in the German plan than anything that Schacht devised. So Schacht had to go But the plan has worked in Germany The English have had to apply it in part and now we are following along the same path that the Germans blazed from before the time of Hitler. The financial revolution is on in this country, though we lag behind for lack of centralized authority and clear understanding, and because of questioning, doubt and opposition from a "free press". But 'defense' gives every opportunity to accelerate the process.

The American people derived from the Nye investigation the idea "that 'profits must be taken out of war'. To achieve this, we see the government, despite billions of idle private capital, acting as banker for a large part of the defense activities. Even though industry protests, the RFC finances the purchase of vital raw materials and the building of new industrial plant facilities Any factory can be taken over summarily on Presidential edict while Congress rubberstamps the demand that wealth, along with manpower, shall also be conscripted. This drafting of wealth becomes, under present and prospective revenue acts, a near actuality Earnings are no longer a right of capital; they are merely a permissive return, now regulated by government. (cf Bul #88) When government becomes so big as to dominate half the economy, the transition from private enterprise to state capitalism is well on its way to completion. With governmental expenditures still rising toward an unpredictable total, America is rapidly approaching that danger point "

Seeking the intellectual pioneers in America for this revolution, Batchelor points to "John Dewey, Charles A. Beard, and Rexford Tugwell, of Columbia, Felix Frankfurter and James M. Landis, of Harvard; A. A. Berle, Jr., Assistant Secretary of State, Leon Henderson, of the Securities and Exchange Commission, and Dr. Lauchlin Currie, probably the President's most influential economic adviser; Lloyd Garrison, of the University of Wisconsin, and Paul Douglas, of the University of Chicago" and "the two great liberal dissenting justices of the United States Supreme Court, Oliver Wendell Holmes and Louis D. Brandeis.

"The intensity of conviction held by this group as to what is wrong with the present economic system" has been brought out in hearings, perhaps best in the statement of Assistant Secretary of State Berle before the Temporary National Economic Committee, — "The government will have to enter into direct financing of activities now supposed to be private, and a continuance of that direct financing must mean inevitably that the government will ultimately control and own those activities. . . Over a period of years the government will gradually come to own most of the productive plants of the United States."

"We may say that it is politically safe for the United States Government to continue financing by deficits until . . . the cost of living rises painfully; then they will have to stop", we are told in the February *Atlantic* by Harold M. Fleming, Wall Street correspondent for the *Chr Sci Monitor*. The art of "Living by Deficit" is another German contribution to economy. "Since 1932 modern governments have discovered vastly greater powers over economic activity than ever before . . control of production, consumption, prices, profits, and public opinion. . . . From mine and field, through processing and distribution, commodities are clocked by cautious bureaucrats who, if they don't know their business, at least know their powers. . . . Germany long ago abandoned all pretense of a balanced budget, and has hidden an incalculable deficit in a multitude of banking devices, without appreciable rise in the cost of living."

What is happening in the world is being commonly interpreted in emotional terms and abstractions which inhibit the use of the cerebrum.[20] The editors of *Harper's* and *Atlantic* are to be congratulated on presenting these remarkable, clear-sighted articles. Due to the present state of hysteria to which faculty and club members have been worked up, the editors or authors have felt it needful to throw in the usual emotional abstractions, "tyranny", "aggression", "slavery", which we have been conditioned to associate with things German,[21]—words that have nothing to do with their subject, which is the perfecting of a seemingly impossible intricate process as a result of necessity.

Those who have read these articles may care to go on a grade higher and read the January issue of the *American Journal of Sociology* where the scientific method is more fully applied to present day war problems, though scientists too have glands and react emotionally, as will be seen in some of the articles.

Behind the screen of ideologies, and behind the hopes to have and to hold or to gain plunder or territory, there is something even more basic to account for the present dissensions stirred up among the World's peoples. Though we have been confused by claims of self-righteousness, by the vilification of opponents, some are beginning to understand that there are deep implanted age long resentments that can only be removed by supplying the basic needs of people long deprived. This is the motive power that started once more the turning of the wheel. It is what we call revolution.

A people of vitality, deprived, will find compensations. The Scots, contemptible to the English even to Dr. Johnson's time, the Armenians, persecuted by the Turks for hundreds of years,—both in turn have come to positions of influence in British trade and empire.

Alertness, acute discernment, quick response are qualities that we find alike in the rat, the cur, and virile peoples like the Irish that have been downtrodden. We New England Yankees, regarded by those left behind in England as non-conforming outcasts, owe something of our thrift and shrewdness perhaps to that British despiciency, to which we still respond, as well as to the lack of lushness of the land we love. Dr. Holmes grossly attributed this to the east wind and our diet of salt cod

The German people, divided for centuries under hundreds of petty governments, reduced to a hundred by Napoleon, to forty by Bismarck, only within a few years have become one and felt the strength of national unity. Impoverished, their country ravaged by wars which made possible the survival of Protestantism at the time the Pope had declared a holy war against England and excommunicated her queen, Germany came too late to national maturity to share in the age of discovery and the plunder of the world [22]

To this still immature and retarded ugly duckling among the nations the industrial revolution and the thrill of national feeling came late The advance in technology has since been rapid. But still deep in the unconscious there lingers the memory of suffering and the sense of long-standing resentment. A disciplined people, with habits of work, they have the 'will to win' in workshop or laboratory. Encircled, they have adapted their technology to the immediate national need of a state besieged, and savage have been their sallies into trade, industry or buffer states.[23] If we don't like the result, Carl Dreher advises, "the thing to do is to see how it was accomplished. The process had a history, and the technological and economic phases of that concern us first of all."

January 30, 1941

NOTES

[1] "America should have minded her own business and stayed out of the World War. If you hadn't entered the war the Allies would have made peace with Germany in the Spring of 1917", Churchill declared in August 1936 (cf pp 261, 262, also 256, 257)

(2) "The minimum of peace and the maximum of anarchy", the brilliant French statesman Caillaux characterized the Versailles Treaty as promising. Sir Austen Chamberlain, writing of the Treaty of Locarno, said, "After the War, peace rested, not on goodwill or assent, but solely on the incapacity of the vanquished to renew the struggle Some day the wheel of fortune will turn. It will be possible for Germany to find an ally, and on that day, embittered by suffering, provoked by constant interference, seeing no other hope, however desperate the throw, she will stake her all on a new gamble, and Europe will be faced with another and yet more appalling Armageddon."

Jerome Frank in "Save America First" (Harper, 1938), notes that "As Englishmen like H. G. Wells and J M. Keynes pointed out at the time, [England and France] imposed impossible terms in the peace treaty of 1919. The new German republic, which had superseded the Kaiser, was at once compelled to confess that Germany was solely responsible for the war, although that, as we know now, was untrue. And then, using that forced confession as a pretext, there was wrested from Germany fifteen per cent of her total area, twelve per cent of her population, seventy-five per cent of her iron-ore supply, and much of her other resources, all her colonies, and, in addition, she had to agree to pay staggering reparations " (p 157-8)

Ambassador William E Dodd, historian, no friend of Hitler's, on his return to America, pointed out the selfish blunders of the nations since the war. He says, when "I remind you that we are more the cause of Hitler's rise to power than any other nation in the world, you may be a little bit sad—and I think you are. Anybody who has lived a long time in Germany and listened to the common man's talk, and watched events carefully since 1919, will see that Hitler himself is a product of our treatment of the scheme and the method which had defeated the Germany of the old Kaiser " (*Educational Record*, July, 1938)

(3) "In these days, when the disturbing factors are intangible ideas", Lord Halifax remarked in June, 1938, "it is realized that war is a very uncertain remedy" And in October, 1938, his Prime Minister Chamberlain had signed an agreement with Hitler "never to go to war with one another again. . . . Consultation shall be the method . . to deal with   . questions" (cf Editorial, Boston *Transcript*, Jan 28, 1941). Halifax, the ambassador, March 25, 1941, at the Pilgrim dinner in New York, urged the United States to join the war for four principles,—religious, moral, social and domestic.

(4) "The United States Army" is rather optimistically described by Frank C. Hanighen in *Harpers* for Dec , 1940. "That many officers believe that the present system stifles new ideas is evident from several recent articles and editorials in the *Infantry Journal* . . . One of these advocates selecting experts whose sole task will be to 'examine every possible development of science to determine its possible adaptation to the national defense of the future.' "

Major Malcolm Wheeler-Nicholson pleads for a modernized army in *Harpers*, March, 1941 He tells us that we have "had access to the same set of lessons from the last war as did the German General Staff Yet we find our own military control body at least twenty years behind the Nazi military leaders . . . Our Ordnance Department's record in the World War is remarkable for the manner in which it produced, at the end of the war, a variety of weapons badly needed at the beginning. . . .

"Every officer in the army, instead of being silenced as is the custom now, should be encouraged to write suggestions for improvement in tactics, material, and methods. . . . These would result in having the brains of the Army hitting on all six and would enormously stimulate energy and improvement Our present Army system is unfit for modern war. There is urgent need for modernization lest we be caught up and hurled suddenly into the hell of modern battle unprepared. If this be plain speaking, let it be said that there is no time for weasel words—better some brusqueness of speech than that our sons should be uselessly slaughtered in battle under unskilled leaders."

William Shirer, who has spent much time "With the German Armies: A War Diary", *Atlantic*, March, 1941, comments on "the youth that England neglected so criminally in the twenty-two post-war years when Germany, despite its defeat and the inflation and six million unemployed, was raising its youth in the open air and the sun. You have to have a body that will stand terrific wear and tear And then, especially in this war, you have to have all the machines of warfare . . While the French here and there fought valiantly and even stubbornly, their army seems to have been paralyzed as soon as the Germans made their first breakthrough."

(5) Planning, which is now in bad repute because of Stalin's and Roosevelt's ineptness, is still in good repute in industrial concerns in their own plants. George Washington planned the national capital. John Quincy Adams' losing fight against vested interests was for improvement and preservation of the public domain. War and preparation for war has always called for centralization of authority, as John T. Flynn points out in the *American Mercury*, February, 1941 In our Civil War, Washington was repeatedly threatened by rebel raids down the Shenandoah Valley into the Potomac. Our most successful cavalry general, Sheridan, to prevent these raids, planned for the destruction of everything in the valley. Today the chimneys of the old plantation houses still stand as monuments to such success that Sheridan could say "a crow traveling across it would have to carry its own rations". General Sherman's 'gone with the wind' expedition was planned to divide the Confederacy While there was only defense, Washington had been continually threatened. Planning stopped the raids.

Flynn sees "Pericles setting up his PWA's and his CCC's and his WPA's and his RRA's", and quotes Plutarch's "Pericles",—"Every year he sent out threescore galleys, on board which there were numbers of the citizens, who were in pay eight months, learning   the art of seamanship. He sent, moreover, a thousand of them into the Cherosonese as planters. That which gave most pleasure to the city of Athens . . . was his construction of the public and sacred buildings."

Loans from the Delian Fund supplied Pericles with the money. The little island of Delos was just about covered with banking houses, which are still

there, excavated by the French about forty years ago. "Against these extrava-
gances the propertied classes murmured", says Flynn, but Pericles replied, "With
their variety of workmanship and of occasions for service, which summon all
arts and trades and require all hands to be employed about them, they do actually
put the whole city, in a manner, into state pay . . . For as those which are of
age and strength for war are provided for and maintained in the armaments
abroad by their pay out of the public stock, so it being his desire and design that
the undisciplined mechanics that stayed at home should not go without their
share of public salaries, and yet should not have them given them for sitting still,
to that end he thought fit to bring in among them these vast projects."

(6) Buchman, we understand, receives guidance each midday, Halifax even
more frequently. As Viceroy of India, Halifax, then Lord Irwin, needed frequent guidance. During a conference Gandhi would retire for meditation, Halifax to communicate with God. "I always ask God's guidance before making
any important decision", said he, and Gandhi remarked "It's too bad God gives
him such bad advice". At that time the Viceroy had put in prison 47,000 Indian aspirants for freedom, liberty and democracy.

(7) The German system is no creation of Hitler. As Miss Thompson observed,
Veblen knew about it   Veblen's idea was that the engineers and technicians
ought to run things, throw over the financiers. A fantastic idea, but Hitler has
done it   The technicians now have a set of new bosses who "understand technics
better"   At any rate they must have production to hold their jobs,—profits won't
insure it. "Call it the revolution or nihilism or what you will . . Hitler . . . is a
success." He has done what we were afraid to do, and that's why we are afraid
of him now   "Men of good will could not." So, says Dreher, Miss Thompson
advocates turning the airplane production over to Ford   But then we would
have the same system as Germany, and nothing to fight about.

"Stability and peace will reign in the world economy only when the forces on
the side of technology and the forces on the side of politics have once more been
accommodated to each other. . . It is desirable that the forces of technology
should triumph, and that we should have a system of world-wide economic exchange rather than a collection of more or less closed national economies", writes
Eugene Staley, Associate Professor of International Economic Relations at
Fletcher School of Law and Diplomacy, in "World Economy in Transition:
Technology vs. Politics, Laissez Faire vs Planning, Power vs. Welfare" (Council
on Foreign Relations, 1939).

(8) "In the second quarter of the nineteenth century Germany was, industrially
and politically . . . at least a century behind England . . . trailing even the new
republic of the West with its vast agricultural areas and untapped natural resources. . . . All the nineteenth-century capitalisms fed the lower strata of their
populations to the machines . . . England by the eighties had a somewhat moss-
grown industry, drifting slowly toward obsolescence . . . and satisfied. . . The
new gentry depended for their incomes less on productive efficiency than on
foreign exploitation and money-lending based on the accumulations of the past

France had never given herself whole-heartedly to the industrial Moloch and, except in the northern areas, remained largely a peasant economy in which the machine worked at a slower tempo."

Germany and the U. S. developed industrially parallel about the same time, the last quarter of the 19th century. But how differently. The Germans had their promoters and speculators,—for the railroads for instance. But on the whole they were built under state supervision, with an eye to military strategy In the U. S. railroad building "involved colossal feats of engineering and thievery, inextricably mingled. After having been plundered in building, the roads were plundered again in stock operations, and they plundered industry, agriculture and one another in competition Parallel roads were built for pure blackmail, and the sky was the limit. This state of affairs could have only one end· bankruptcy And bankruptcy was the signal for fresh plundering The elder Morgan stepped in and averted complete chaos. . .

"German business imposed no such burden on Germany industry as American business on American industry German business was accustomed to small returns. . . There was less obsolescent equipment and less need to nurse it into old age by restricting production. . . . And the industrial machine, relatively free from graft and financial hamstringing, worked so well that after the dynasty and the war machine had taken their toll enough was left to keep the workers in old-age pensions and social security of a kind." (Dreher, *Harper's,* Oct. 1940)

(9) Dreher takes one example to prove it,—nitrogen from the saltpeter beds of Chile. In 1902, the supply getting short, Americans devised a method of fixing atmospheric nitrogen in commercial quantities, using Niagara Falls water power But the financial backers didn't find profit enough in it and it was stopped "Thirty-eight years after this exhibition of business statesmanship we discover that we lack a sufficient supply of nitrogen to fight a war. This is something that could never have happened in modern Germany, even before Hitler", says Dreher

About the same time, the Norwegians, who had tremendous water power, developed a similar process, but less expensively than in U S "Since water falls no harder from a given height in one place than in another, and since the Westinghouse turbo-generators at Niagara Falls were just as good as any that Europe could build, the power cost-differential must have been due to the application of the usual formulas of pecuniary logic in their extreme American form."

The Germans, however, having no water power, devised another method, which they perfected in 1912. Then they were ready for war All wars are fought with nitrogen today, and have been since the invention of gunpowder. We use the instability of the molecules built around nitrogen to destroy our enemies. The new process of making nitrogen made it possible for Germany to go to war.

"The War was nevertheless lost, or rather not won until 1940. . . . A British mission inspected the chemical industries of the Rhineland . . . reported, ' . . outstanding examples of German thoroughness and efficiency, fitted with the most perfect machinery for compressing and otherwise dealing with gasses .. they are great engineering workshops. . . Scientific insurance of industry-has never before been effected on so liberal a scale.' This generous appreciation was duly noted and filed by the leaders of British industry, after which business went on about as usual."

In the United States when the Muscle Shoals development was started "distinguished patriots in the Congress and the National Electric Light Association . . . traveled up and down the land, shouting .. 'Pin the red label on 'em!'" So in 1922 it was "almost sold to Henry Ford for a song", and later was to Commonwealth and Southern It had a capacity for only 40 thousand tons of nitrogen a year. Germany has an annual capacity of a million and a half metric tons (10% more than an American ton) Now we are to build nitrogen plants for war purposes, but meantime farmers have been kept from having fertilizer.

"Because we run our economics on a businesslike basis, one third of our population is ill-fed, and to keep them ill-fed we must avoid building nitrogen plants in time of peace, and so we don't have nitrogen when we decide to prepare for war. .. We are not prepared for war nor are we prepared for peace. We are prepared for nothing. And that is what is called good business" (Dreher, *Harper's,* Oct. 1940)

Stuart Chase in "Idle Money, Idle Men" (Harcourt, Brace, 1940) tells us "Germany, Italy, France, Britain, Russia, Japan, rolled into one do not approach our industrial potential." We have intelligence, technical skill, ability, resources, but in our aim at profits rather than production there is large waste. We sabotage scientific inventions because of investment in plant, of inventory that would be made obsolete and valueless if the new were introduced. (cf Kaempffert, *American Journal of Sociology,* January, 1941 on why we use antiquated and inefficient needles and disks when for forty years we have known how to produce sound electro-magnetically)

(10) "From the point of view of technology German pre-World War Junkerism was the counterpart of American business as a retarding force, but proportionately of lesser magnitude . . . The voice of reason is usually heard only when unreason has brought disaster, and it was not until after Germany's defeat that Rathenau regained influence. .. Under this 'New Economy' highly productive machinery, standardization, scientific division of labor between plants, the wide development of power, and the expropriation of the private owners .. Rathenau attacked conspicuous consumption, salesmanship, and the wastes of business 'Whoever squanders labor, labor-time, or the means of labor is robbing the community,' he declared" (Dreher, *Harper's,* Oct., 1940)

(11) "Any nation that will subject itself to military communism, and sacrifice every other consideration to military organization and armament, can go through its neighbors not so organized like a red-hot shot through a pound of butter", writes Bernard Shaw (*Living Age,* September 1940). "And that is what we are too sensibly happy-go-lucky to do under any leadership. We have just instituted, on paper, a military communism . . . placing our lives, our properties and our

liberties, such as they are, at the disposal of the brass hats. But it has got no further than paper."

"It never occurred to me that we were making an army too democratic to fight for democracy", said Hore-Belisha, perhaps thus coming closest to an explanation for his dismissal from the duties of War Minister. (Boston *Transcript*, Jan. 16, 1940)

(12) Dr. Brodie, at present engaged in research at the Institute for Advanced Study in Princeton, as a holder of a Carnegie Corporation fellowship, is working on a book soon to be published by the Princeton University Press on "Naval Inventions and World Politics, 1814-1918".

(13) This is the strategy not used in the first world war, as Lord Fisher wanted to when he proposed "attacking Germany through Denmark". "Their grand strategy was directed by public opinion, which in the total state is a synthetic product, manufactured to support decisions already taken on pure military grounds, in an atmosphere free of 'bourgeois morality'." (Fletcher Pratt, *Harper's*, Feb. 1941)

"The new military technique of Germany, so surprising to the outside world, is a direct offspring of the military restrictions imposed on Germany after the last war. . . . German industry, too, had been trained for war for many years, under dire restrictions before Hitler, and free of restrictions ever since the Nazis came into power. . . . The problems of transition and adjustment from peacetime methods to wartime methods of production and distribution, technical and otherwise, that cause so much friction and delay to democratic nations with a free economy, do not exist for Germany That country has been living on a war footing for several years. It was mobilized economically as well as militarily." ("German Economy 1870-1940", by Gustav Stolper, Reynal & Hitchcock, 1940)

"The first World War tested out the weapons of the machine gun, long-range artillery, airplane, tank, poison gas and submarine. And these are the weapons of 1940, carried to a climax of effectiveness and embroidered with the use of parachute troops The very tactics of 1940 are merely a logical development of the infiltration tactics that dominated the last year of the first World War. But above all, the prime antagonists are the same. . . ." (*Life*, June 3, 1940)

(14) Hanson W Baldwin in the N. Y. *Times*, July 8, 1940, gives the grand total of losses, "Killed", "Wounded", "Prisoners and Missing", for the war up to July 1 in thousands· Germany 243, Italy 5, France 1,988, Britain 90, Poland 620, Netherlands 331, Belgium 545, Norway 59 This is a total of over 4 million, of which nearly 3 million were "Prisoners and Missing".

(15) "The German 'war of nerves' however was decisive against England and France during the bloodless conquest of Czechoslovakia. How far the French and British governments of the moment deliberately acted a part by emphasizing to their peoples the horrors of conflict in order to discourage the war parties in their respective countries, we need not ask . . . The feeling of the Germans, although less conspicuously shown, was the same, they were well pleased at not having to fight. After all, during 1914-18 they had endured not only the war

but also the blockade which has been estimated to have killed nearly a million of their civilians for want of food The disappearance of the unstable Czechoslovak state did not ease international tension On the contrary, through the summer of '39 the expectation of war and the fear of it more and more darkly overshadowed Europe. Everywhere policy centered upon preparation by arms and alliances." (Nickerson, "The Armed Horde", p 358)

British and American propaganda in this war has chiefly been directed against their own people. In Wilson's time his propaganda, devised for not only his own people but the Germans, and promoted by H. G. Wells, was tremendously effective. The Germans actually believed in Wilson's Fourteen Points and surrendered on that basis. This time the British started out showering leaflets during the first year of the war on the Germans in the fond hope that they would create revolution and discontent. There is no evidence it has had any effect. Remember that they succumbed to enemy propaganda in the last war. They feel as the Irish do, that they have some acquaintance, less than the Irish it is true, with the methods of the British.

(16) "The result has been that the Nazi regime has had an inexhaustible supply of funds that could be used to produce or buy anything within the Reich. . . . The German financial system no longer places any limitation on rates of domestic production, as we feel ours still does They have achieved and sustained what the economist calls 'full employment' and they are not headed for the financial rocks, no matter how ardently we may hope and believe that such a fate must be their end. . . . While . . . perfecting their methods of safeguarding the currency and banking system against the effects of a growing government debt" they discovered something as yet little comprehended in "Great Britain, the United States, and the other capitalistic national economies." (Dal Hitchcock, *Harper's*, Feb. 1941)

The method prevents stagnation and keeps up a healthy circulation in the social organism and body politic. "When commercial investment opportunities are scarce" and do not absorb all savings, the government sells securities to the savers and then spends "the funds so obtained, thus returning them to the stream of commerce. . . . The savers force the government to go into debt."

(17) Vernon Bartlett, young British M P. and editor of the London *World Review*, quotes what a prominent Nazi said to him at the time of the Hitler-Chamberlain talk at Berchtesgaden. "Why Hitler will win is because he has realized that the wealth of a nation is not the amount of gold hidden away in the vaults of its national bank but is the brains and muscles of its citizens." (*Forum*, March, 1939)

(18) "In a warehouse in Boston the Government is preparing to store 82,000 tons of rubber which we are to get in a swap with Britain for 680,000 bales of cotton. . So far 160,000 bales of cotton have been sent to England but we have received only 1000 tons of rubber." (Boston *Transcript*, Jan. 17, 1940) We gave the destroyers and we gave 17 shiploads of munitions in return for leases (cf Bul #87), but the British are still bickering about the bases.

(19) Robert R Doane in "The Anatomy of American Wealth" (Harper, 1940), a study based on extended subsidized research, gives the total assets for 1938, including everything, "even our shirts!", as $388,421,000,000. Our total indebtedness, corporate, local, state, and federal is probably greater. In that case an orthodox banker would call us bankrupt So in the issue of "Liberty Bonds", forced loans to come, the inside finance boys of the Administration distract our attention from the balance sheet and assure us that we can borrow on our productive power. That is, we are going to spend first and destroy the wealth we may create if we live and have the opportunity.

"A system of forced savings is likely to be set up. A certain amount of a worker's earnings might be required for investment in government bonds. A new kind of liberty bond campaign will be started (Mr. Morgenthau has already promised this much) to sell baby bonds and thrift stamps" (Paul Mallon, Jan. 20, 1941) "Roosevelt administration has abandoned its New Deal theory of recovery for its present war panacea" (*Economic Notes, Oct., 1940*).

Stuart Chase, in "Idle Money, Idle Men", suggests that the government should, (1) decrease savings and hoardings or national income by increased income taxes above a certain limit, (2) invest this money in permanent public works, (3) thus utilizing our labor supply, (4) finance investment public and private through government banks at low interest rates.

(20) Like any other explanation, justification or excuse, "isms', 'ocracies', 'archies', are all abstractions after-the-fact, but they are effectively used to fool the people The appearance on paper or the sound of certain terms causes such an emotional reaction in most people that cerebration is blocked. In new situations, in times of stress, we get jittery, even hysterical.

The new ways of doing things that have arisen out of necessity are lumped together with old ideas of communism, of persecution, of Torquemada and Savonarola, and the autocratic methods of the old monarchs. We call the result 'fascism' or 'totalitarianism' or what you please. There are some new elements but it is not new, John Flynn tells us (*American Mercury*, Feb. 1941). Go East, thou sluggard, and learn from the wise men of the past. Christ learned of the elders and from the Buddhists, and John the Baptist dwelt among the Essenes.

(21) Even our standard reference books in their modern revisions must conform to the hysteria of the time and fall into the accepted patter Langer's revision of Ploetz' "Epitome", 1941, has absorbed something of the pro-British hysteria prevalent at Harvard where the manuscript was manufactured.

Shepardson and Scroggs, in the 1939 annual "The United States in World Affairs" (Council on Foreign Relations), write under similar compulsion "To win . . . Nazi Germany must free herself from the restrictions imposed on her by British sea power. . . Now it is not true to imply, as some do, that this navy, for a hundred years or so, has been spending a considerable part of its energies protecting the United States It has spent all its energies watching over the British Empire, and this country owes no obligation to that navy. A German victory would . . . substitute a dynamic, dissatisfied (and destructive) power in the strategic position hitherto occupied by a passive, satisfied (and constructive) power. It would crown with victory the program of the 'Have-nots' and put in jeopardy the interests of the 'Haves'—chief of which would thereafter be the United States. . . . Their genius and their imagination would be attracted to the task of trying to organize Europe under their domination into a powerful unit of production, manufacture and sale, (forcing) their next-door neighbors into a position where they would be bound to supply raw materials and take manufactured goods in exchange."

The emotion-rousing words, indicated by parentheses, are defensive but do not fully disguise that they know better.

(22) William Henry Chamberlin, in his disillusioned "Confessions of an Individualist" (Macmillan, 1940), "recalled the Thirty Years War, which had also started in Bohemia. By the time it was ended everyone had forgotten how it started, and the whole of Central Europe had been reduced to a dreary waste which it required generations to restore to relative prosperity. . . To my friends, who insisted that Hitler must be stopped, that war was better than surrender, I maintained that, on the basis of the very recent experience of the World War, war was far more likely to produce Hitlerism, communism, or some other denial of democracy and individualism in France and England than it was to make sweetness and light prevail in Germany."

"In the course of fifteen years, three catastrophes befell Germany. The first, the military catastrophe in 1918, gave birth to the Republic. From the second, the utter collapse of the currency in 1923, the young Republic seemingly recovered miraculously, but in reality the social repercussions and consequences of the inflation were a continual drain on its vitality. The third and final catastrophe, the economic crisis of the early 1930's, resulted in the downfall of the Republic." (Gustav Stolper, "German Economy 1870-1940", p 181)

Professor Arnold Toynbee said in 1931, "To a foreign observer, who visited Germany at this date, it was a strange and awful spectacle to see a whole nation—and this one of the greatest and most civilized nations in the world—wrestling heroically against fate, yet half paralysed in its titanic struggle by the conviction that all the time its feet are irrevocably set upon the paths of destruction." (Toynbee, "Review of International Affairs")

In the campaign of 1930, George W. Edwards reminds us in "The Evolution of Finance Capitalism" (Longmans, Green, 1938), "Hitler denounced all the past efforts of international security capitalism at solving Germany's difficulties in the following searing words: '. . . with lies our people were led into the Dawes Plan, with lies we were induced to sign Locarno, and lies, lies and yet more lies have now given us the Young Plan. Germany has been doped with illusion after illusion, Spa, Brussels, Versailles, Geneva, Paris, London, Locarno, the League of Nations, and now the Young Plan—all were illusions, and under the curse of these illusions Germany has lost her freedom, she has lost her moral prestige and, having no longer any political honour she has now even sacrificed her economic substance.' " (pp 112-113)

"The Athenians had sea-power with all its dangers and its blessings—'how great a thing is sea-power' (Thucydides). But, as a sea-power, they were vulnerable, as England is today." (F. A. Voigt, "Unto Ceasar", Putnam, 1938)

(23) "Role of Buffer States in International Relations" by Mary Barnes Gear, teacher of fifth and sixth grades in the Ideal Elementary School, La Grange, Illinois, now graduate student at University of Chicago, in the issue of March, 1941, is one of a series on world problems that have appeared in the *Journal of Geography.* If Mr. Roosevelt, Mr. Hull, or Mr. Welles could have studied geography under Miss Gear, our foreign policy would have been different. As an adviser of the State Department, Miss Gear on our present basis of expenditure for 'defense' should be worth several billions a year "Contrary to the reciprocal plan of Nature, Man, with his greed and feeling of self-importance, has worked relentlessly for centuries to hack the surface of the earth into small bits, politically Where the aggressive state has acquired all it dares to take . . . a boundary is needed, especially if the acquired territory extends close to the ecumene of a nearby state. Marches in the Middle Ages in Britain and what is now Germany were formed of newly conquered borderlands under marcher lords " Later buffer states were set up, natural like Afghanistan, Nepal and Bhutan to protect India Belgium, a state created after Napoleon's time, and the Netherlands, political buffer states, control the mouths of the Rhine and keep Germany off. "The British Empire seems to be the world's greatest buffer builder Great Britain and France have guaranteed the independence of the lowland passage countries. The security of a buffer state depends upon the security it affords its neighbors by its existence between them" and most "pursue a precarious policy of neutrality" "What is to be the future of the buffer states?"

THE ROAD WE FOLLOW

Defense is a euphemism today necessary with a democratic peaceful people preparing for offense.[1] Arming has but one purpose, to create a striking force, with modern weapons to develop superior fire power. The stimulus to kill a greater number quicker is fear. The English take a realistic view. Churchill wants to "smash Germany", Halifax to "destroy every vestige" (cf p 563) The President's purpose, which has now become the nation's, is simple, and reveals an animus against a personal devil,[2]—"I want to help England lick Hitler".[3]

Total war today involves psychological as well as technological preparation Economic factors however come first, the necessity for providing material and food,—tungsten as well as vitamin B. On the economic side, in wealth of natural resources, we are supreme. Technologically, we will in time prevail. But the psychological side of warfare, surprise to demoralize through shock and terror, we seem to be neglecting. Not only is that the most modern, but it is the most primitive means to success in war, as we British learned in Braddock's defeat by the North American Indians.

In all the modern applications of psychology,[4] in public relations, advertising and the creation of public opinion, we are today superior to the Germans But these psychological skills have not been turned to the building of national morale. To bolster morale we are endeavoring to put our effort on a moral basis, to make this seem a holy war, but to the man in the street it does not seem that morality, religion or civilization is about to be advanced by the proposed methods

Morale is of importance not only for the man who fights but for the greater number necessary to support him, greatly increased in modern technological war. The flying man requires 30 to 40 ground men to keep him and his plane in condition, and even more to produce and supply it. Failure anywhere along that line may result in a crash.

Morale is a matter of feeling, for something we may lose, against those who may take it. Fear and hatred of the enemy must be instilled in the people as well as in the fighting men that we may have the will to fight. Moreover, we must feel that we are protecting something that we cherish. Our fathers thrilled to the call, "Strike for your altars and your fires". They had a stake in the country. But Mark Twain must have known some who had not, to make him remark, "Almost any man worthy of his salt would fight to defend his home, but no one ever heard of a man going to war for his boarding house".[5]

"We are morally and intellectually unprepared . . . to intervene to support the moral order . . . to fight for 'the supremacy of human rights everywhere' ", declared President Hutchins in a radio address Jan. 23.[6] "Think of the sharecroppers, the Okies, the Negroes, the slumdwellers, downtrodden and oppressed for gain They have neither freedom from want nor freedom from fear. They hardly know they are living in a moral order or in a democracy where justice and human rights are supreme. We have it on the highest authority that one-third of the nation is ill-fed, ill-clothed, and ill-housed. . . . More than half the army which will defend democracy will be drawn from those who have had this experience of the economic benefits of 'the American way of life'."[7]

The morale of those who are fighting for a democracy they have never experienced, for a morality they have not seen exemplified, for a civilization that has brought them no benefits, will be low. Only faith in their leaders can compensate for the weakness of these abstractions.

In the face of "excessive and unequivocal" pledges of non-intervention from both presidential candidates, our entry into the war would "have the same unhappy effect upon American morale as we have seen produced abroad by similar acts of bad faith on the part of trusted men. ... The loss of confidence on the part of the French people in the good faith of their rulers in recent years contributed greatly to the dismal collapse of the republic", jointly declared professors Holcombe, Hocking and Shapley of Harvard.

The Administration has evidently felt it necessary to conceal from a people reluctant to go to war the steps it was taking. But immediately after election much was revealed that would have been inadvisable earlier. Attempt to repeal the Johnson Act would have roused the country, so a way round had to be found. As early as December 4 the Washington correspondent of the London *Times* told Britishers "with inspired vision" of a pending "major development in the (U.S.) programme of aid for Great Britain".[8] Sir Frederick Phillips, representing the British Treasury, was about to arrive in Washington December 6. Lord Lothian, December 11, made his last appeal for financial aid the day before his death. December 15 the President, returning from his inspection tour of the West Indian bases, told of his 'lease lend' plan. December 18 President Roosevelt "advised British officials to go ahead with their plan to order about $3,000,000,000 of additional war materiél without waiting for the completion of financial arrangements." (*Facts on File*)

The origin of this 'lease lend' bill, where and by whom it was written, was cloaked with secrecy in the House and Senate Committee hearings. It was what the British Foreign Office wanted and evidently they knew about it before the American people. The British government had complete confidence in the President, but not in Congress.[9] At the hearings, the pro-British pro-war Administration recruits who had been adopted from the Republican Party, Stimson, Knox, and Willkie, were pushed to the forefront. No question was raised as to how these men came to hold their views. Investigation as to their interests and connections would be revealing.

But never has there been a greater stake in maintaining tabus, in questioning men's motives and what makes them act as they do. But revealing facts are in the printed record, some given under oath. Stimson's law firm has beeen counsel for Commonwealth and Southern, a Morgan promotion for which Willkie had been selected by Thomas Lamont as front man Knox' Chicago *Daily News* is reported to be financed by bonds held by Kuhn Loeb The staff and foreign correspondents, the Mowrers and Stoneman, are as violently hate-promoting anti-nazi as Kuhn Loeb could wish.[10]

Senate hearings did bring out the confused hysteria of the members of the committee, of Congress and the American people. Major Al Williams, who like Col. Lindbergh knew and forecast from observation on the ground the superiority of German aviation, accused the Administration of "talking peace at home and shouting war abroad and meddling in the internal affairs not only of Europe but also of Asia". He charged that enactment of the bill would mean "virtual suicide of the American way of life". The Administration, he claimed, would not have stripped our defensive forces of all fighting planes[11] if they had had any fear of invasion, the imminent peril of which they used for "persistent promotion of hysteria".[12]

President Valentine of the University of Rochester testified that advocates of the bill "have succeeded in confusing and frightening the American people . . . by every form of propaganda. The only difference between a good dictator and a bad one is a matter of time." Gen. Robert E. Wood testified, "People have been scared to death" (Boston *Herald,* Feb 5, 1941). Col. Hanford MacNider, head of the American Legion, declared that "propaganda about imminent invasion" was "a vicious attempt to demoralize a great people into a breakdown of free government. Coming from high places, it cannot help but create hysteria and destroy sanity."

Efforts of senators on the committee to get Presidents Hutchins and MacCracken to testify were unavailing. None such were wanted. President MacCracken of Vassar, in a radio broadcast late in January, not generally reported in the press, had called upon educators to combat the conspiracy to get us into war "The outline of strategy is fairly clear. The slogans have been devised, the publicity offices are working night and day The psychologists have selected the emotions." "We are not agreed that invasion is near." "We want to know how our money is being spent . . . that it is not being wasted." "We want free discussion of the whole matter, not denunciation or intimidation." "We are not ready to sanction British rule of the black and brown races of the earth, or to enlarge her maritime tyranny." "For us to engage in a war to preserve one group of empires against another has no shadow of moral justification."

"What Issues Are At Stake in This War?" was discussed by four writers and publicists at New York's Town Meeting Feb. 6. The first clearheadedly showed that there were no stakes for America to gain, that all might be lost. The second emotionally and earnestly manifested his feeling of animosity against the powers that are now ruthlessly tearing up the Versailles map of Europe. The third, speaking for and to American business, advocated that we keep our skins whole and make money while we can.[13] The fourth, fresh from the battle front, in British uniform, demanded that we join in the melée. The discussion was characteristic of American confusion as to what is to be won or lost.

Morale, which will create the will to fight, the necessary military striking force, must depend upon objectives that will make widespread appeal as offering something intensely desired.[14] In that way unity can be achieved. Basic motives, primitive desires are still effective in war. To these Mohammed appealed in stirring people to religious war. Our President is filled with religious zeal, and hate, to fight, but it is doubtful if he can communicate this to the millions. The aggressor nations of Europe feel that they have everything to win, little to lose. They are resentful at being deprived and have hope of gaining necessities and opportunities by uniting under their gangster leaders,—of a cup of coffee when they wish without "Britannia's permission", as Goebbels puts it.[15] Our belief that German morale is maintained only by suppression may lead to disappointment.[16]

Moreover, the widespread suspicion must be removed that our defense program affords the Administration a means of winning support by dispensing largesse. And behind this there may remain a more sinister fear that the reports of enormous increase in corporation income and dividends conceal waste, extravagance and graft, than which "no aspect of the war effort of 1917-18 has brought more shame", as Frederick Lewis Allen puts it in *Harper's*, Sept., 1940, writing of the aftermath of twenty years ago. (cf Bul #81)

The President in his first election campaign pledged economy and one of his first steps was to cut all salaries 10%. No economist, he found that a difficult policy to maintain, and the New Deal embarked on a spending program. But eventually municipalities could no longer continue to raise taxes for the upkeep of swimming pools and playgrounds provided by the government. With his Party split, with "the rising tide of political antagonism", the bitter opposition of his 'economic royalists' and the hatred of his fellow Harvard alumni, the New Deal spending program was stalemated, and like Wilson twenty-two years before, in order to keep in power, Roosevelt was forced to turn to another kind of spending program. (cf Bul #82) [17]

The New Dealers had no choice. It was the only way they could possibly remain in the saddle to continue their internal reforms. This "will to live" applies not only to individuals but to groups, communities, states, governments. To live is the first purpose of anything living, louse, rat, human or a civilization. The government that does not take measures to perpetuate itself is soon overthrown [18] This 'defense' spending program has united the Democratic Party, reconciled the 'economic royalists' won the support of Harvard alumni.

At a conference in Washington Nov. 11, 1940, between New Deal economists and New York bankers, "ignored or meagerly treated in the press", Garner of Guaranty Trust challenged, "If the Administration knows how to create employment why hasn't it done so in the past eight years?" Tugwell answered, "It's always required from $12 billion to $15 billion of Government spending to do the job, not $2 to $3 billions." Thurman Arnold asked Tugwell, "Do you mean that from an economic point of view, it's a grand war?" "Yes, if we don't get into it." [19]

They think they can "ride the tiger", Frank Hanighen adds in "The War and the New Dealers", *Common Sense*, January, 1941. They "take an indulgent, if somewhat contemptuous attitude toward the President's Anglophile tendencies . . . believe that under the guise of defense, they can not only spend, but also prove the validity of spending." [20]

Spending, the essence of our defense program, affords opportunity to satisfy both labor racketeers and economic royalists, to bring employment to workers and prosperity to shopkeepers. But these are mere lubricants in the process of furthering new financial and economic trends. There are cool heads behind the New Deal, Berle, Frank, Henderson,

Currie, who give evidence of being more interested in these things than in satisfying personal hates or the urge for righteousness.

The principles of capitalism and socialism must be made to work together. There is ample room for private enterprise and initiative in our American economy under state control. It is unimportant what term we apply, social collectivism or reform capitalism or whatnot, so long as we continue in the right direction.[21] These fundamental beliefs of Adolf A Berle Jr. are put forth in his "New Directions in the New World" (Harper, 1940). Out of "The Failure of Marxism"[22] and other isms we may find a social conception "that is still stronger". "This dogma, whether we call it Communist or Nazi, or Fascist, has already failed.... The decay has already set in ... There is ... merely a shuddering wonder as to how long a dance of death can continue." --

In his socio-political analysis of our societal history, Berle sees throughout the "political contest between individualism held together by faith, duty and love, and the dictatorship held together by king, force and fear". He pays tribute to the achievement of our own country through the capitalistic system which is now so rapidly changing and perhaps ending.

A great crisis ahead is foreseen by Berle With demobilization in four or five years, social unrest will bring about an explosive situation.[23] "At least one-third of the life of Western Europe which is now devoted to making war and war supplies, will find itself without immediate purpose. The task of its readjustment into peaceful life and production of peacetime goods will be staggering. Dislocation will be at once commercial, financial, mechanical and spiritual." Failure of the economic system will be directly due to malorganization.

A planned program will have to immediately provide for employment. This, Berle tells us, "would give tools so that initiative and ideas could go to work, and so that our financial system could do what is expected of it, namely to permit materials and ideas to combine in satisfying the obvious needs of the country and in meeting the increased demands which the less fortunate part of our population properly makes on the system as a whole". Such a post war policy was announced by the Administration in the press the first week in February, 1941.

These semi-public enterprises would be based on a credit system which would apply to those seeking "profit, as monuments to themselves", as well as to those who wish to create something useful, "out of a purer spirit of public service or altruism". (cf Bul #97) "Long term capital credit is by no means a thing apart from money and credit." Berle cites Harold Moulton's revolutionary statement that "a considerable part of what we had called 'savings' consisted merely in an excess of money or bank deposits".

Berle does not fail to give the moral tone fashionable in America at this time "I am firmly of the view that the faith we have in each other and in the ultimate value, necessity and essential glory of a moral order is sufficient." Nor does he fail to sound an optimistic note. "The United States, like any other nation in the world, is well along in a great crisis. It is my conviction that this country, so far from being on the brink of disaster, is on the eve of one of the most amazingly magnificent periods in history. . . . It is likely to change its intellectual and economic habits in a manner which will release more of individual productivity and more of individual spiritual fertility than has been true for a century."

Hans Heyman, reviewing Berle (*Common Sense,* Jan 19, 1941) reminds us that "in 1921 I presented a somewhat similar plan for a national construction bank to Berle's European prototype, Walter Rathenau (then Minister of Reconstruction of the German Republic) in connection with the problem of reparations". (cf Bul #97) Lloyd George supported it against Briand, and a year later this was expanded by Heyman in his "Die Voelker Bank". Some of these features were later adopted in the Bank for International Settlements After Rathenau's assassination there were no further developments of these plans in Germany until recently. Berle's capital credit banks and Hemisphere Bank (cf Bul #69) follow some of these earlier proposals. Heyman further elaborates on this in a book soon to be published by Harper, "Plan for Permanent Peace, an American economic program based on a national credit and investment corporation".

The attributes of a people we personalize. We say France did this, or England wants that. In the last war we magnified the ingenuity of the Germans and the viciousness of the Kaiser. This brought us to the attitude of 'kill the Hun' and 'hang the Kaiser'. Today Hitler is the scapegoat. If removed, all will be well. "There is an idea among Americans that Adolf Hitler appeared upon the German scene with a brand-new doctrine and a new cause, completely upset the old Germany and set up a wholly new one   Nothing could be further from the truth and anyone who nurses this illusion would do well to read Dr. Gustav Stolper's 'German Economy', just published.   There is the story of how, over a period of years, German economic and social mechanisms were slowly shaped toward the corporative and totalitarian model." (John T. Flynn, *New Republic,* Sept. 9, 1940)

Necessity has compelled the people of Central Europe to adopt an economy wholly different from ours.   Without natural frontiers, their country has for centuries been the highway and the battle ground of conflicting armies.   Poor in natural resources, often in a state of seige, living on a rationed dietary, the people have been schooled in deprivation, trained in adversity.   Habits of work and application, elimination of waste, and utilization of meager resources have resulted in an efficiency which has prevailed in competition with republican France and soviet Russia.[24]   More recently blockaded and denied access to the world's resources, they have been obliged to operate without gold, reverting to a more primitive system   The millions of lives lost in the last war have led them to use mechanical and psychological methods to gain territory and plunder with less human loss.   Private initiative and enterprise have been preserved and stimulated but harnessed for the benefit of the whole. In the face of surrounding danger, the entrepreneur as well as the working man has been enslaved

We English, outlawed and excommunicated by the Pope, raided the seven seas, enslaved the peoples of the tropics, possessed ourselves of the world's gold, and built a quite different economy   With our far-ranging experience in meeting new conditions, we are adaptable and can do anything that others can, anything we want to.[25]   It would take a greater feeling of resentment at injustice than we have yet felt, generations of hunger and belt-taking-up to create in us the willingness to submit to the regimentation to which these people have been brought.   If we are superior in anything, it is in brains, but if we don't use them how can we demonstrate that superiority?   If we use our brains we will organize and prepare for what we have to meet, and that will not be for such war as we engaged in in 1917. It will be less wasteful for us if we know more about those whom we are to fight and conquer.   The misinformation presented in our public prints will not so equip us.

Americans have thought of the wealth of their country as inexhaustible, as it was apparently. The National Resources Board has taken account of the waste of our natural resources, the exhaustion of our coal, oil and metals, the fifth of our food-producing topsoil washed into the sea. But the government, foundations, and universities have been little interested in a complete inventory of our assets. Such an accounting would reveal something of ownership, and those who control prefer to have their holdings undisclosed. The privately subsidized Bureau of Economic Research of the University of Notre Dame has published such a study which has been drawn upon by Robert R. Doane for his "Anatomy of American Wealth" (Harper, 1940), a textbook for statesmen.

The most accurate estimate of our total assets, all our properties from our unmined mineral wealth to our last shirt, was in 1938 only 388 billions (cf p 580). Today it may be slightly more In 1929 our wealth was greater, but our indebtedness was then relatively higher, perhaps 500 billions. We were bankrupt then. But the government closed the banks, glossed it over, and saved us.

There are those who say that if we had gone through the wringer then we would be in a sounder condition now, for again we are bankrupt and forced to go to war to conceal it (cf p 58). Our mounting federal indebtedness conceals a huge state, municipal and local government indebtedness. Our corporate indebtedness is even greater. Every bond is a debt. Personal indebtedness through installment buying, personal finance companies, advances to sharecroppers, credits at company stores, is encouraged.

War is more expensive for America than other countries It costs us more than 20 times as much to put a man in the fields as in the European countries (cf p 337). In the last war our short experience cost us about the same as the longer experience for Great Britain and France. And we are wasteful and extravagant. In our loose legislative and administrative processes, favoritism and graft are by no means eliminated. Expenditures today run far ahead of estimates. Soon we will be spending at a higher rate than Great Britain, and the cost of the expeditionary force we are preparing for Col. MacCormick estimates at 400 billions, which is more than our total assets

'Your government' will finance this expenditure of hundreds of billions by the one way open to governments, by taking the earnings and savings of the people and giving them in exchange promises to pay, pieces of engraved paper Harry Scherman's "The Promises Men Live By" (Random House, 1938) explains all this. So long as there are savings or earnings to take, this can go on indefinitely, and as the government increases its armed forces, its secret police and its tax collectors, more money will be necessary to pay them and the propaganda to suppress discontent.

Governments tempt people to give up their savings and earnings by offering interest. Thus bond holders who receive interest become supporters of the government At present they are being subsidized to the extent of about a billion and a quarter dollars a year Confidential Washington financial authorities inform us of the plans being worked out within the government, announcement of which is being delayed as bad public psychology. Congress might shrink from measures pressed upon them if they were obliged to consider how the war was to be paid for. Taxes to the extent of a little over a billion will be levied this year which will bear specially, on the middle and well-to-do classes. Bonds of several kinds, but all bearing the 'defense' label to appeal to the sentiment of the public, will be offered this spring, gently leading up to high moral pressure methods later, as in the Liberty Bond campaigns. Laws to force people to buy bonds as in Germany will come later. Taxes levied now will be permanent.

As expenditure rises and more interest-bearing pieces of paper are put out, more taxes must be raised to pay the interest on the bonds Eventually the producer-consumer will be loaded with all kinds of indirect and concealed as well as income taxes An ever increasing proportion of salaries and wages will necessarily be taken, which will leave less for the living expenses of the individual [26] As the standard of living falls, with less to eat, more needs unsatisfied, discontent will rise Popular clamor may reenforce the government's need for higher taxes on profits and inheritances. Accumulations of wealth, the result of sweat of generations preceding, will be drawn upon. The money will have to come from where it is. There can be no question as to who will pay. It will be those who have.[27]

Bonds will decline in value as interest remains unpaid, and eventually be repudiated.[28] Has any government ever paid its debts except while there was more to be borrowed? But in the juggling of refunding and refinancing the thread is lost. Have the debts of the Venetian Republic, or of Byzantium been paid? "Assyria, Greece, Rome, Carthage, where are they?" Did they end in solvency? Britain hasn't yet paid for the Napoleonic wars. British consols, yielding 2%, represent that unpaid debt Twelve billions from other countries are still due us from money lent them in the last war. Uncle Sam has not paid back to the working man the wages forced from him in exchange for Liberty Bonds which furnished the money lent to Britain and her allies.

The debts to the past, bonds, mortgages, insurance policies, all have been liquidated from the Rhine to the Pacific. Little remains in France, much is lost in England, and we are following the same road. Inflation is a bogey that periodically is brought up to scare us. Starting the printing presses has been the final stage in those countries that stood against change, as in czaristic Russia and republican Germany [29]

The Administration's plan is to borrow on our 'productive power' [30] (cf Bul #97). But there is a limit to the number of hundreds of billions that can be taken out of the sweat of our millions of workers, and our children and our children's children can't sweat enough to wipe out the debt that will result from the squandering here and over seas of our natural heritage.

How is it we have come along this road? It's been easy down hill, but it's steep and rocky ahead. We who once were the ejected of Europe, the seed of many peoples, sifted to make this new nation, in a land endowed with resources as no other, "This fortress, built by Nature for herself, against infection and the hand of war", this land between two great oceans which serve it "as a moat defensive . . . against the envy of less happier lands",—how is it that we have wasted, squandered our inheritance?

How come that this idealistic people who once soundly resolved "never again" to be led through hate into foreign wars, who once saw clearly how they had been misled,—how can it be that they have come to such a state that they are incited with moral purpose to fight a religious war to destroy another people whose innovations, financial and governmental, they are themselves unconsciously following? And this in the name of civilization! [31]

The steps along this road, the stages in the process, the forces that have acted, the methods that have been used to change our direction,—if we

do not understand these how can we plan the way ahead? Our own motives and those of the chief actors we should examine.[32] Our President
once wisely warned us not to be "tempted for the sake of fool's gold",
"to resist the clamor of that greed if war should come". "We can keep
out of war if those who watch and decide have a sufficiently detailed
understanding of international affairs to make certain that the small decisions of each day do not lead toward war and if, at the same time, they
possess the courage to say 'no' to those who selfishly or otherwise would
let us go to war."[33]

Secrecy has cloaked these small decisions. At the turnings of the road
we have been blindfold. Now the momentum we have acquired on this
course may carry us like the Gadarene swine over the cliff. From whom
were they cast out? How did we become possessed of these devils?
Man's great mystery is himself. What makes us act as we do? How do
we get our opinions? How do we know we are right? In "What Makes
Lives" last year I endeavored to throw some light on these complex
problems of human behavior. Our feelings, which so largely determine
our actions, are based upon our mental content, the information that
comes to us. A study along these lines may be the approach to the solution of man's great mystery, himself.[34]

"I only know what I read in the papers", remarked our great American philosopher, Will Rogers. And so our news services determine our
feelings and reactions. Public opinion polls are supported by the newspapers. They originated with advertising agencies who knew what they
wanted to prove [35] Columnists are selected or eliminated by the newspapers to give us what somebody decides is good for us. Radio commentators at the suggestion of the President are coordinated by Wythe
Williams. The movies, financially controlled and centrally directed, are
even more effective in creating popular feeling. (cf "What Makes
Lives", p 167)

Congress, inequitably representing the population, controlled by the
President through patronage, submissive to other influences, is not oblivious to popular opinion if it is strongly expressed. The vote of the
House may be determined by a bloc of representatives elected by a small
percentage of the population of the states of the South they over-repre-
sent[36] (cf p 516). Few are the representatives or senators who have
knowledge which enables them to think for themselves, or if they do,
conscience or courage to speak out.

Our schools have their patterns set by our great universities, and these centers of learning are dependent for support upon legislatures, foundations, or wealthy donors, all in turn subject to control or influence. So they must play safe. There are fields of investigation they may not safely enter. Who owns what, what motives actuate those who control, such topics are tabu. Academic halls echo with the slogans that come from Whitehall, Washington or Wall Street. So in this war as in the last, when our diplomats and statesmen, finally frustrated, turn their failure over to the military for solution, our universities that from their historical learning might have reenforced sound public opinion, will have let us down.[87]

The selection, elimination and conditioning processes to which a university president has been subjected leaves him and his underlings subservient. Rarely is there a voice left free and bold enough to denounce, as did President MacCracken, the conspiracy that is bringing us into war, to declare, as did President Valentine, that the Administration is frightening the American people, or to utter the warning of President Hutchins,—"The American people are about to commit suicide."

Rushing as we are down the steep road to disaster, were the blindfolds stripped from our eyes there are still turnings in the road ahead that could be taken, level spots where we might still slow up, save lives and billions.

February 24, 1941

NOTES

[1] "Mere defense is negative. Antagonism to Fascism or Communism, to Stalin and Hitler, is in itself neither a doctrine nor a program. Democracy to survive must become a positive, not a negative force." (Carleton Beals, "Pan America", Houghton Mifflin, 1940)

[2] "Mr Roosevelt feels that extirpation of Hitler is the way out. So do innumerable Americans who think that it can be as easily done as was our defeat of the Kaiser", writes Oswald Garrison Villard (*Progressive*, Feb. 8, 1941) "Mr. Roosevelt's trouble is, unfortunately, that he does not face realities outside of the political field in which he is past-master. Money means nothing to him. Subordinating the entire life of America to the military machine is but an incident."

"It is easier to blame Hitler for our troubles than to fight for democracy at home. As Hitler made the Jews his scapegoat, so we are making Hitler ours", President Hutchins remarks "He sprang from the materialism and paganism of our times. In the long run we can beat what Hitler stands for only by beating the materialism and paganism that produced him." Yet many seem to believe that if Hitler is destroyed and Germany partitioned, all will be well.

For our own deficiencies we must find a scapegoat. The Western parent beats his child in righteous indignation. We go forth to slay those who interfere with our economic way of life armed with righteous indignation at what we consider a breach of morality. Mild intoxication is satisfying to one's ego. It justifies the most sadistic practices, but after we have recovered we are not so proud of ourselves. The President has taken tremendous punishment. But from frustration he has now passed to a state of righteous indignation. Hot hatred is displayed against Martin, Barton and Fish, Burton Wheeler, and Adolf Hitler.

"Even if Germany should collapse this week and Hitlerism should vanish blessedly from the earth", the Boston *Herald* editorially commented, Sept 16, 1940, "socially, economically, financially, educationally, politically and otherwise, England will undergo a historic transformation." An editorial in *Private School News*, Sept., 1940, quoting this, went on to observe, "Were perfect peace to descend upon the earth tomorrow and all the denounced evil influences eliminated, the loss that has already resulted would continue the suffering and poverty and deprivation for all of us for another generation. . . Caught in the tide of world revolution which we can not turn back and have not understanding enough to direct, we are swept helplessly toward totalitarianism But something of our social order, something of our accumulated capital, though slipping rapidly, may yet be saved."

"We have to remember that the present war grew out of a social upheaval the end of which is not yet in sight If we involve ourselves in this war, we might involve ourselves in a revolution as well", wrote Alvin Adey in *Events*, Sept , 1940. "That the drive to war already threatens America with so much disruption of our ordered ways ought to be a danger signal."

(3) House and Senate leaders met the President in the White House on his birthday, February 10. Joe Martin asked, "What's your objective, Mr President —what do you want?" The President replied, "Joe, I want to help England lick Hitler." "Mr President, what about the tremendous power this bill confers on you?" "Joe, this bill can't give me as much power as I already have. I am Commander in Chief of the Army and Navy. The power of that position frightens me sometimes I am not interested in more power. All I want is to get the job done . Suppose you simply voted two or three billion dollars and set up some kind of agency, or used the RFC Who do you suppose is going to administer it? Why, I am, of course. And I think we can do the job more efficiently this way." (*Time*, Feb 10, 1941)

Churchill's purpose on the other hand is realistic, imperialistic "Germany is getting too strong. We must smash her." That's the way he put it to Gen Robert E. Wood in November 1936, the latter testified at the hearing on the 'lease lend' bill.

(4) Morale is a matter of psychology in which the Germans early led To Wilhelm Wundt's first psychological laboratory in Leipzig went McKeen Cattell, G

Stanley Hall and Lincoln Steffens (cf "What Makes Lives", p 79). William James brought Munsterberg over to establish the first psychological laboratory at Harvard.

(5) This was quoted by Sen. Richard B. Russell Jr. of Georgia, after Sen. Lister Hill had stated that "42 percent of all the farmers of the Nation today are farm tenants; and in some States, like my own State of Alabama, we have a farm tenancy of about 65, or at least 64 per cent." Sen Chavez of New Mexico remarked that 2,865,000 families are farm tenants, "and the number of tenants has been increasing at the rate of 40,000 a year". While farm tenancy has been decreasing in other countries, it has been increasing in the United States, and today, some estimaters claim, more than 52% of the farmers are tenants In Ireland, the percentage is less than in the United States, though only a short time ago much higher. In Denmark farm tenancy, two generations ago general, is now almost eliminated.

Mark Twain says, "Vast material prosperity always brings in its train conditions which debase the morals and enervate the manhood of a nation—then the country's liberties come into the market and are bought, sold, squandered, thrown away, and a popular idol is carried to the throne upon the shields or shoulders of the worshipping people and planted there in permanency. . . . It is curious—curious that physical courage should be so common in the world, and moral courage so rare." ("Mark Twain in Eruption", Harper, 1940, De Voto's editing of hitherto unpublished papers)

(6) President Hutchins, seeing the 'lease lend' bill as an attempt "to underwrite a British victory", said "We have made some notable advances in the long march toward justice, freedom, and democracy. If we go to war, we cast away our opportunity and cancel our gains. For a generation, perhaps for a hundred years, we shall not be able to struggle back to where we were. . . . The latest figures of the National Resources Board show that almost precisely 55 per cent of our people are living on family incomes of less than $1,250 a year. This sum, says *Fortune* Magazine, will not support a family of four. On this basis more than half our people are living below the minimum level of subsistence"

While Hutchins was speaking, 125 of the 900 faculty members of the University of Chicago were issuing a statement (at Harvard 375 signed such a statement) which urged immediate enactment of the 'lease lend' bill and "set forth that Americans who say the war is of no concern to the nation 'practice a policy of appeasement' " (AP, Jan 24). Hutchins doesn't imply that the "war is of no concern", nor do most of the so-called "appeasers". On the contrary, he sees it as of great concern. "Its object is moral We are seeking, the President tells us, 'a world founded on freedom of speech, freedom of worship, freedom from want, and freedom from fear'. . . . Let us agree now that we want the four freedoms; we want justice, the moral order, democracy, and the supremacy of human rights, not here alone, but everywhere. The question is whether entrance into this war is likely to bring us closer to this goal."

When "friends of the 'lend lease' bill" tried to find someone to answer

Hutchins, President Conant of Harvard and Guy S. Ford of Minnesota "both gave excuses". Then they tried to get Governor Stassen of Minnesota, "but he, too, ducked". Finally they devised "a symposium of persons in various sections of the country, a farmer, laborer, a youth; Mayor Maury Maverick of San Antonio, a decorated war veteran, and Walter Wanger, brilliant liberal movie producer". (Pearson and Allen)

Nor has Conant in his two appearances to testify before the House and Senate committees dared to touch upon points raised by Hutchins. He and Willkie both apparently made as good a show as they could, as would hired counsel. Thomas Lamont would take exception to nothing they said, though he might well have felt that they could have done better. The Harvard president "described the present war as more 'religious' than 'imperialistic' " (Boston *Transcript*, Feb. 11). There followed an interesting colloquy with Sen. Gillette in which Conant agreed that he was a Christian, believed in the Christian doctrine of "love thy neighbor" rather than "an eye for an eye", but admitted he had not been "praying daily for Hitler and Mussolini" (*Chr Sci Monitor*, Feb. 11). Such a 'religious' attitude is a balm to a wounded spirit. Decision clears the mind, gives you certitude, particularly if you can make your decision on a religious basis.

Conant was almost the first to come out for 'religion and morality' as the purpose of this war, and now to advocate war. Harvard is a natural testing ground for any ideas favored by those who are symbolized by 'Thomas Lamont'. And Conant has been pushed forward as a spearhead to try these out. Overheated faculty members are constantly sending up hot air trial balloons which often win them a headline, and a pat on the back at the faculty club.

President MacCracken of Vassar, in a January radio broadcast, criticized religious leaders for preaching propaganda "to persuade the great Christian public of America that war is our inevitable course". He urged examination of all war propaganda, "especially when this propaganda gets into Christian churches and puts on the cloak of religion to preach hate and anger do we want to understand it and, understanding, to oppose it".

(7) "Our own worst Fifth Column is not that of disguised enemy aliens, but political incompetence and selfishness, poverty and ignorance. France was not stabbed in the back by Mussolini or by seditious Communists, aliens, and hooded Nazis, but by graft and treachery and incompetence of men in high places who sent soldiers without blankets or proper weapons to battle Hitler's scientific mechanized columns. Every Okie, starving in California labor camps, every sharecropper, every slum-dweller, every man on public relief, is a weak spot in the line which an alert enemy may break through. The physical and moral welfare of each and every citizen is quite as much a part of true national defense as the manufacture of a torpedo." (Carleton Beals, "Pan America")

(8) "There had previously been a meeting of Sec. of the Treas. Morgenthau, Sec. of War Stimson, Sec. of the Navy Knox, Under-Sec of State Welles, Under-Sec. of the Navy Forrestal, Asst Sec. of War Patterson, Chief of Staff Gen. Marshall, Defense Council Knudsen, and Herbert Feis, Economic Adviser to the State

Department. The President was not present at this meeting, but "it is to be noted that not one of these men holds his position through the gift of the people, but only by appointment". (*Commonwealth*, Feb. 1941)

"Great Britain maintains two ambassadors in the United States, one appointed by the Foreign Office, the other named by the London *Times*. Lord Lothian, Viscount Halifax—the Foreign Office envoys come and go, and many Americans do not know their names. But Sir Willmott Lewis, the emissary of the *Times*, stays. His detractors claim that Sir Willmott is a propagandist beside whom Goebbels is a lout with a toy horn. His admirers maintain that he is an interpreter of events the price of whose wisdom is above rubies", Maxine Davis tells us in "Britain's Ambassador Incognito" Lord Northcliffe "admired Lewis' adroitness as well as his penetration of American psychology and grasp of American techniques . . . sent for him, offered him the post of Washington correspondent of the *Times*, replacing Sir Arthur Willert, who was about to leave the *Times*." (*Sat Eve Post*, Jan. 25, 1941)

(9) Representative Hamilton Fish, in a radio address (Appendix, *Congressional Record*, Jan. 13) characterized the 'lease lend' bill as "totalitarian technique in its most brazen form, placing 90 per cent of the American people who oppose war 99 per cent of the way into Europe's and Asia's war. . . . If this bill is passed as proposed by the President, we would be no longer talking about dictatorship; it is dictatorship, complete and all embracing The 'lend lease' bill was conceived and written in the White House as a final consummation of the President's unceasing quest and passion for power. . . . The defense program has been stalled by the four deadly horsemen of the New Deal—brag, lag, drag, and snag—and not by Congress or Martin, Barton, and Fish."

(10) A geography class about sixth grade might well be established in Administration circles. Knox, who commands naval movements in the seven seas, when asked by Sen Nye "How far is Dakar from Gibraltar, about 500 miles?" replied, "Yes, about 500 miles". It is 2,000. Jesse Jones, when asked if the United States had made any loans to Central American countries said "I'm not so sure of my geography, but we're lending seven and a half million to Uruguay". Sir Willmott Lewis, on the Information Please program February 7, requested by Clifton Fadiman, "Name any British possessions in South America", rumbled "British Honduras". "But isn't that Central America?" No reply

(11) In response to Williams' charge that there was "not a single-seater, interceptor fighting plane in the United States today that is modern in any sense of the word, either in armor, fire power or performance", a letter from Stimson was read the next day which explained that they had planes "on order". Sen. George was criticized for introducing this testimony without the opportunity of cross-examining Some believe George is favoring this administration measure in every way, suppressing opposition wherever possible

In connection with the War Department's investigation of army camp site purchases (cf note Bul #42), Under-Secretary Robert Patterson "has also ordered a probe of 360,000 acres acquired in southern Georgia which include a large malarial swamp". Questions have been aroused by the fact "that Georgia Senators Walter F. George, chairman of the Foreign Relations Committee, and Richard B. Russell backed the choice vigorously", "that the purchase price will come to around twice the $2,500,000 originally allocated for the land", "that the Government will have to put out another $1,000,000 for drainage and malaria control". "The average cost of the land so far has been $14.50 an acre. But a survey by the Land Division last year indicated the land could be bought for around $8 an acre." (Pearson and Allen, Feb. 7) Sen. George, whom Roosevelt failed to purge, was reelected by 2.4% of 10.3% of the population of Georgia (cf pp 515, 516).

(12) The U. S. and the Soviets, because of geographical position and resources, are defensible. The U. S. and Germany excel in technological advance and in possibilities of supremacy in the air. Germany because of geographical position can utilize air supremacy to greater advantage than any other power. The U. S. sacrifices its ideal defense position by extending its lines across the Pacific to the Philippines and the East Indies, across the Atlantic to the continents of Europe and Africa. It will have to maintain and protect supply lines two-thirds way around the earth. It sacrifices its technological preeminence by shipping the output of its factories to where Germany and Japan can take them over, airplanes at Casablanca, all kinds of equipment at Dunkirk, airplanes and trucks at Hanoi. We are risking capture or destruction of our equipment overseas as did Britain in Flanders, and when we are denuded, whom shall we turn to? Australia?

(13) Hutchins in his radio address dissociated himself "from those who want us to stay out of war to save our own skins or our own property. . . . The principal end that we have hitherto set before ourselves is the unlimited acquisition of material goods. The business of America, said Calvin Coolidge, is business. We must now learn that material goods are a means and not an end. We want them to sustain life, but they are not the aim of life.

"The aim of life is the fullest development of the highest powers of men. This means art, religion, education, moral and intellectual growth. These things we have regarded as mere decorations or relaxations in the serious business of life, which was making money. . . . The path to war is a false path to freedom. A new moral order for America is the true path to freedom. . . . We must show the world a nation clear in purpose, united in action, and sacrificial in spirit. The influence of that example upon suffering humanity everywhere will be more powerful than the combined armies of the Axis."

(14) The American lacks clear objectives to fight for, Lawrence Dennis wrote in response to Frederic L. Schuman's letter in critical admiration of his book "The Dynamics of War and Revolution". "Intelligence and character in pursuing the wrong policy will merely accelerate the career to destruction", said Dennis. If Hitler wins, "we may embark upon long-range military adventures in the Far East or Latin America with disastrous consequences, or we may merely string along with the defense hysteria, raising taxes, lowering living standards, disrupting our traditional social order, accentuating class struggles, discouraging

private enterprise, paralyzing investor confidence, and generally demoralizing the people with the pursuit of a military policy intended to stop Hitler but calculated only to stop American progress. In either course of events we shall have disintegration and revolution."

Schuman evidently turned both letters over to his facile minded colleague, Max Lerner, who with a letter of his own to Schuman turned them over to his friend Freda Kirchwey, who published them in the *Nation*, January 11. An editorial introductory paragraph characterized Schuman, the former Leninist, as an "intellectual defeatist", Dennis, the prognosticator of the coming fascism, as a "champion of dictatorships", and Lerner, whose hopes were once all on the soviets, as a "democrat".

(15) "To free herself from economic rationing by the British Empire has been a long-standing German national aspiration." "We in America have had little conception of the hate growing up for generations against this British domination It is a muffled hate, similar to that long held by the people of Cuba, Mexico, Central America, and Colombia toward the United States " "Germany has increasingly felt with bitterness that its investments and trade in most parts of the world rested on an insecure basis so long as England controlled the seven seas. Whatever outsiders may have thought of the alleged crimes of the Prussian Junkers during World War I, the Germans saw their people reduced to near starvation by blockade and their investments and trade wiped out They, more than anyone else, know the disastrous story of oil, of potash, zinc, and copper, the story of their investments in Australia, the Balkans, Africa, the former colonies, and the Near East " (Carleton Beals, "Pan America")

(16) "Something of the reason for the stronger morale of the German forces is explained", Carleton Beals thinks, if to "adequate industrial organization, the maximum efficient use of man-power, and superior technical training" you add "a conviction instilled in the German masses that a new revolutionary order promises more bread and that they are fighting from under oppression and injustice due to a previous defeat, harsh peace terms and economic coercion by other powers." ("Pan America", Houghton Mifflin, 1940)

(17) William J. Baxter, Wall Street financial adviser, in his International Economic Research Bureau bulletin, writing Nov. 6, 1940, on the election, speaks of it as "the coming rape of private capitalism . . . at the ballot box in the 'American way' ". "First, we had the party in power using the crookedest political machines in the country to conduct a farce at a convention called a 'forced draft'. This was followed up by record spending in all the key political areas in the country in as bold an effort as was ever made to buy the vote." Having in mind Hague and Jersey City and others, he asked, "Is it the 'American way' to join with the cheapest gang of machine politicians in our history to loot the country, the one country in the world where private capital and democracy had a ghost of a chance?"

"There is no other way out for the present administration from its present position but a foreign adventure Outside of war there are only two ways to put the people to work and keep the economic machine busy", through the "confidence" of capital and labor or through public works. So we had to go to the war method, says Baxter

"As a student of foreign exchanges and international banking, I long admired the way the Bank of England, in indirect methods, quietly but effectively controlled the money markets of the world. In recent months I have marvelled equally at their control of the propaganda machines and news channels of the world. We are now about to see, in the next few months, the greatest propaganda drive of all to involve this country in Europe and Asia to 'Save Democracy' As an international service we have been amazed at the skilful job the English censors have done in the past month to create the impression that England is doing well in this war and that if America only intervened, the Fascist powers would last no time. The English public have been educated to expect certain intervention on the part of the American government as soon after Roosevelt's victory as 'politically practicable'. . .

"We are not far from a time when the United States will put into force the same system of 'blocked money' as exists in Europe, and it will be impossible to take money out of this country without getting a license from the government . . . all of which add up to a capital levy on the accumulated wealth of this country."

In his best seller, "Country Squire in the White House" (Doubleday Doran, 1940), John T. Flynn has made apparent how "the President's love of military and naval might and display, his truculence about the command of the seas, his well-known sympathies both by blood and sentiment with England", together with his growing power, has led to the development of his foreign policy. (cf Bul #82)

(18) The "will to live" is the underlying principle in "Biological Considerations About War", as Raymond Pearl pointed out in the remarkable special war issue of the *American Journal of Sociology*, Jan. 1941, perhaps the last thing written by Pearl before his untimely death. Anything that seems to threaten our existence stimulates us to fight,—the individual, the group, the nation. It isn't danger, it's the fear of danger, "real or fancied". "This menace to group survival, whether real or merely imagined, is then magnified by all possible applications of the arts of propaganda during a period of 'negotiations' preceding actual combat, with biological effects presently to be discussed. Eventually war ensues. At once all restrictions on group behavior of the sort normally associated with such terms as law and decency automatically go by the board, if, as, and when any belligerent finds such restrictions irksome."

(19) At this same meeting, Hanighen tells us, "on one side were ranged Richard Gilbert, Defense Commission consultant; Leon Henderson; Mordecai Ezekiel; Isador Lubin; Rexford Tugwell and other names prominent in the Government. On the other were Robert L. Garner, of the Guaranty Trust Company; Noel Sargent of the National Association of Manufacturers, Alexander Sachs of the Lehman Corporation; and other financiers and industrialists." Gilbert outlined a plan of keeping money and labor continuously in operation, without referring to its similarity to methods the Germans have of necessity invented.

At an earlier Washington conference in September, "the wild·men's branch of the New Deal met with the savings bank branch of the wolves of Wall Street in a generally unadvertised economic discussion . . . and no one was even scratched" (Paul Mallon, Sept. 20, 1940). Lawrence Dennis, invited, caused such "fireworks at the Mayflower" (*Time,* Sept. 30) that to obviate his being smeared Dennis beat *Time* to the draw by publishing his report in his *Weekly Foreign Letter* a day early Setting forth his response to the "all star cast of brainy experts", he remarked, "When the representatives of high finance and big business come up in conference against this New Deal battery of brains, it reminds one of a meeting between the student's council and the faculty in a very junior prep school." That we may eat our cake and have it too, spend a hundred billions and not go bankrupt,—Dennis "charged that the New Dealers were exploiting defense as a new W P.A. project to serve as a pump primer. The New Dealers admitted these charges though they resented the label of a W.P.A. project."

(20) "Wide-spread acceptance was found for the idea that government spending is a motive force absolutely necessary to keeping the productive economy running at even a moderate tempo; and in 1940 nearly all discretion and criticism in this respect were abandoned under the justification of national defense, perhaps on the hypothesis that enormous deficits for armaments are financially less dangerous than small deficits for housing, schools, and public works. With a political machine, a judicial machine, an industrial machine, and a military machine combined under his control, a President of dictatorial propensities could find ready instruments at hand for extending and entrenching his authority" (Charles A. Beard and George H. Smith, "The Old Deal and the New", Macmillan, 1940, p 278)

(21) "The language of modern economists is the language of enormously complicated cooperation. . . . It is not possible in a modern world to think in simple units. Indeed, if simple units are needed for the real development of human beings, a part of the contribution which must be made is the development of means by which they can once more be attained." (Berle)

"The so-called elite in the United States are not susceptible of a revolution, rather they are the result of a continuous revolution, since year by year the continuous struggle to think, to produce, to act, to command public confidence, weeds out the less able and tends to bring to the fore new groups. Practically every population has been led, during the past twenty-five years, into a blank impasse. There is scarcely a single great nation whose people have lived as they wished to live; who have seen any real hope of attaining what they most desire. The struggle to escape, to rebuild, will be almost universal." (Berle, p 1)

"The weakness of our situation will be that many of our economic institutions will no longer mesh with the institutions overseas Our financial system will still be, comparatively speaking, along classic lines, at a time when almost everywhere else in the world currency and credit will be on a wholly different basis. (p 3) The United States has been so fortunate, in the main, that instinctively we dislike to be disturbed Elsewhere, disturbance will have been so great that revolution will be accepted as probably a change for the better " (Berle, p 5)

"The real task, I take it, of diplomatic defense is to make military defense unnecessary The proper aim of the conduct of foreign relations should be to create a state of affairs in which the national interest of all parties is protected, the structure of international organization is preserved, and the use of military force is unnecessary " (Berle, p 20)

"Likewise, during the past decade, the work of Maynard Keynes had indicated the importance of capital financing in a national economy. This formula, sometimes call the 'Keynes Multiplier', can roughly be taken as multiplier of two and one-half to one, meaning that national income is increased by about two and a half times the amount spent on heavy capital construction. The theory of the 'Keynes Multiplier' has been both attacked and defended My own conclusion . is that .. Keynes' demonstration stands up There is evidence, based on the work of Schacht who put the theory into practice in Germany, that it stands up in practice as well." (Berle, p 100)

"We have not, anywhere in the banking world, that process of development which has been the life blood of the technical development of American industry There is no one looking for new financial methods, new theories of credit, new means of attacking financial and economic difficulties with the same persistence, freedom to explore ideas, and to state results which the chemical or technical research bureaus in any large industry continuously use in looking for new processes, new products, new developments, and new methods." (Berle, p 110)

"A bank today is a mechanism for creating currency It receives this privilege from the government, there is no more valid reason why a bank should make an unlimited profit for creating and applying currency than there is why taxes should be farmed out to the highest bidder, and tax collectors allowed to make a profit on their collection " But banks should serve to "keep an even flow of capital construction" rather than "for making profits for private shareholders". "Many of our largest and most successful financial institutions today are nonprofit, for instance, savings banks and mutual insurance companies. Apparently it is perfectly possible for large financial institutions to be organized and run without the necessity of a set of stockholders asking for profits " (Berle, p 113)

(22) "The Failure of Marxism" has in the last year become apparent even to its most devoted former disciples, and many have been the obituaries, none more effective than George S. Pettee's in the *Journal of Social Philosophy*, Jan 1941.

(23) "We sowed the dragon's teeth from which we will reap a terrible harvest through all time to come", declared former Sen Henry F. Ashurst from Arizona in opposing the conscription bill "Do not delude yourself into the belief that you can shackle and handcuff and gag yourselves under a military despotism and then throw off the shackles. It will not be done. If you put this draft on the people, this European and continental system, you will walk out of this chamber having taken from your people more liberty than you ever gave them. And mark me, mark me, at the first opportunity, with lips compressed and with hearts firm, they will march up in a phalanx to the ballot box, there to repudiate and forever repudiate those who fasten these shackles upon them if they can."

"When the war ends and this country—if it acts the fool—finds its economic machine damaged, jammed, all sorts of strange leaders will rise up with strange doctrines. And strange doctrines feed upon sick economic communities." (John T. Flynn, *New Republic,* June 16, 1940)

(24) Stalin has seen that he needs the initiative, the enterprise of the German engineers. To discover gold, which he considered worthless, he offered huge rewards, enormous profits (cf Bul #39, Littlepage)

(25) "Surely a man can do what he wills", said Schopenhauer, "but how can he determine what it is he wills?" We Americans can do anything we want to do, but we may have to suffer first before we will want to.

(26) Insistent on reducing the American standard of living is I. F Eliott of the British Purchasing Commission, who, addressing the Harvard Club in February 1941, in a Boston *Herald* interview, said, "I appeal for further realization of the value of time in aid to Britain. . . . Industry should resist customers asking for supplies of material not needed for defense"

"The vast sums of money now appropriated for armament have little meaning and lack all substance and efficacy unless definitely pointed to an absolutely specific necessity. We must agree upon just what we mean to defend. . . . Today we are working at the fringes of preparedness and national defense We have yet to establish what we are going to defend. . . . Whatever we recognize as the essential requirements of national preparedness, we have yet to tax ourselves for the cost of such rearmament, an omission all the more serious in view of our accumulated deficit of \$25,000,000,000 If, failing to achieve appreciable domestic recovery, we continue at our present low capacity employment of capital and labor, the cost of armament must come out of our standard of living . . . We must make doubly sure, therefore, that this expenditure is efficiently administered and in keeping with our actual rather than with supposed needs born of hysteria." (G K Howard, "America and a New World Order", Scribners, 1940, pp 84, 86)

(27) "Who's Going to Pay the Defense Bill?" John T. Flynn asks in the *New Republic,* June 10, 1940 "Of course I can hear our patriot friend rise to his full height and say—'The world is on fire and this man talks of cost'. The President himself has said that 'he is not interested' in the manner of paying the bill, as 'that is a minor detail'. . . You patriots want to pay it with bonds. That is, you do not want to pay for it at all. You want to hand the bill to your kiddies." July 15 Flynn continued, "Taxes will be resisted as long as possible and this job will be done with borrowed funds until we come to the end of that road." August 26, in "Defense on the Cuff", Flynn, recalling the "self-satisfying warm turkish baths of hate . . . the usual pious immersion in self-righteousness and—almost no taxes", notes that "the more the war is paid for on the cuff the worse the aftermath will be".

(28) "Continuation of Mr Roosevelt's theories and practices will bring us ultimately to a point at which free men will refuse to buy at par the bonds of their government. . . . Men will believe that the debt, so swiftly and so vastly

expanding, will go beyond all control and will become unpayable. When that hour comes, the prices of the government bonds will collapse. When they collapse, the value of assets in every bank and insurance company will collapse. . . . If nature shall be allowed to take its course, suffering will be so great that demand will inevitably arise for a government which will take charge of production and distribution, and the labor of men and women, in order that the masses of the people may be fed and clothed." (Editorial, Baltimore *Sun*)

"Surely as night follows day, there must come the final accounting. Defense material is wealth having no permanent benefit—wealth that does not add to the standards of living of the people. . . . The conditions the economy will face upon the liquidation of the program for national defense, superimposed upon the other economic problems that demand solution, will provide a challenge to our political and industrial leadership. . . . There is grave danger in the years ahead." (Alfred P. Sloan Jr., Chairman of General Motors, quoted by Ralph Robey, *Newsweek*)   —

(29) "In the U. S., which in many ways is socially about where Britain was a year ago, at least one capitalist has spoken plain words to his colleagues about the revolutionary aims of the world. He is Charles Edward Wilson, new President of General Electric, who said last month: 'The world, our nation included, is passing through what history may later record as the second stage of a revolutionary movement of the masses—a movement born during World War I and likely to last, with intermittent armistices of one kind or another, for two or three decades more. . . . Stalin, Mussolini, Hitler and the Japanese Army leaders are but symbols of this movement. .   As a world movement the scope of this conflict extends beyond . . . these symbols." (*Time*, Feb. 17, 1941)

(30) Robert L. Garner of Guaranty Trust asked, "You are going to have to pay back the fellows from whose wages you get the money. Who is going to pay them back?" (*Time*, Sept. 30, 1940)

(31) "After each actual war the surviving and disillusioned combatants . . . and the youths too young at the time of the war to have been combatants . . . exhibit almost invariably the psychological reaction epitomized in the phrases 'There must never be another war' and 'Never again so far as we are concerned'. . . .

"The explanation of this recurring volte-face is found in the effects of propaganda, referred to in the preceding section After examining realistically the historical facts as to the immediate causation of war and the 'organs of society in which the war-making power is lodged', as well as the considerations controlling the 'bellicose determinations' of those organs, Alvin Johnson ("War", Encyclopaedia of the Social Sciences, 1935) reaches the following conclusion: 'After war is on, the union of the great majority in support of the war is effected, mainly by the inherent force of the situation but in part by propaganda. It is by this ex post facto consent, given unavoidably, that wars inaugurated by minority interests or in response to traditional policies present a pseudo-popular character.' . . .

"The 'inherent force of the situation' derives its 'force' almost wholly as the result of propaganda, so far as concerns its effect upon the opinions and behavior of individuals. For the individual—the common man—is not in a position really to know anything about 'situations' of the sort under discussion, except from 'information' reaching him through so-called 'organs of public opinion' or through governmental pronouncements, specifically designed and intended to instill into the public mind a prefabricated set of ideas, attitudes, and emotions. The 'information' so received is always and inevitably colored by propaganda . . . Military men have come more and more to regard propaganda per se as one of the most effective direct agencies in bringing about and conducting war.

"Anyone doubting this needs only to read in the periods just preceding and during an actual war the accounts of the same identical objective events in the leading newspapers of different countries, in order to be convinced of the truth of the statement; always assuming, of course, that the reader is in a state of mind capable of being convinced by evidence." (Raymond Pearl, "Some Biological Considerations About War", *American Journal of Sociology,* Jan. 1941)

(32) "Tell us about the crooked man Who got his crooked pence By meeting people with a smile—And good hard business sense", we read in an up-to-date version of Mother Goose Then we open the *Sat Eve Post,* Feb 15, 1941 and learn that such tales are tabu With their three million readers they have to say it's tabu. Deploring "the weakness" of Rush Holt, they assert, "We have no right and it is indecent to impugn one another's motives "

(33) These quotations are from President Roosevelt's Chautauqua address of August 15, 1936, while a candidate for a second term June 10, 1940, at Charlottesville, while a candidate for a third term, pleading for war against the Central European peoples, he pictured "The nightmare of a people lodged in prison, handcuffed, hungry and fed through the bars from day to day by the contemptuous, unpitying masters of other continents." That's the most eloquent picture that could be drawn of the millions of Central Europeans, economically and territorially confined these past several hundred years, surrounded by buffer states built up after the Napoleonic wars, after the war to save democracy blockaded, bled, deprived of their own natural resources, stripped of their colonial resources. And yet our President's nightmare of self-pity was for 130 millions who stretch from sea to sea across the heart of a continent of boundless resources.

(34) That our feelings are based on our mental content, concepts sensorily derived, is a matter of scientific demonstration. Pavlov psychologists have by auditory or visual stimuli produced mental concepts in the cat or dog experimented on, so that they react as to danger where there is no danger. In the same way the Cannon physiologists have experimentally by stimulus of nerves or injection of hormones caused all the reactions of fear and anger where there is no situation to justify it. Similarly our Administration and British propagandists have injected false interpretations of events into the minds of our university faculties so that they show similar reactions. In the production, artificially, of

such emotional states, Pavlov, Cannon, and Vansittart, approaching from different directions, have produced enormous results which deserve careful study as to their social applications.

Raymond Pearl emphasizes, whether it is "real or fancied", if we believe there is danger of injustice, the result is the same. (cf p 602) Our hackles rise or our tails go between our legs as the result of feeling. Later with fuller knowledge we may learn that the situation we feared was not dangerous and might have produced a feeling quite opposite.

(35) Gallup with a British branch, *Fortune* with a Wall Street connection, have influence. Most of us have the herd instinct, we like to be with the majority and on the bandwagon.

(36) Texas, Carolina and Georgia senators and representatives have been of great aid in putting across the 'lease lend' bill. "Credit for getting the bill through the House is mainly Speaker Sam Rayburn's In his first big job he proved himself even sterner and stronger than Garner", his predecessor. "A picture few observers will forget revealed Rayburn backing Representative Voorhis of California into a corner, wielding his forefinger like a sword point because Voorhis had dared to offer an amendment limiting the President's powers to one year. Rayburn used not only his finger, but both feet on his Democrats to keep them in line. He had them so frightened, many declined to appear in some of the last minute voting on Republican amendments, but chose refuge in the cloakroom It was fairly well understood in the House that any Democrat who voted for amendments was a marked man." (Mallon, Feb. 11)

Paul Mallon as early as January 16 wrote, "There has never been as carefully planned a legislative movement as the one the administration organized behind the lend-lease bill for British aid So much fixing apparently was not needed, but not the slightest detailed opportunity to blanket the opposition was overlooked from the start "The administration leaders have been attempting to designate any opposition as 'unpatriotic' " "Mr. Roosevelt . . called Senator Wheeler's accusation that the bill 'would plow under every fourth American boy', 'the most untruthful, dastardly, unpatriotic thing that has ever been said.' The rage may have been livid but it was not unpremeditated."

March 11, Mallon told of the defeat of Senator Ellender's amendment to prevent American troops being sent outside the Western Hemisphere or U S possessions "He counted 56 votes sure, a majority of at least 8, a few days before the vote " But Secretary Hull and Chairman George "got busy", and other "administration leaders Barkley, Byrnes and Harrison worked on Mr Ellender . . changing the amendment so . . . the lease-lend bill did not change existing law except in the ways it changed existing law". The opposition held strong even after the bill passed, until one of the leading senators became infatuated, it is reported, with the beautiful widow of a British diplomat.

(37) "The destructive ignorance of the cultured and educated, university trained statesmen and leaders in education is what appalls . . Wells . . . Wilson took to the Peace Conference the best brain trust he could assemble from

the universities. . . . "They had unco-ordinated bits of quite good knowledge, some about this period and some about that, but they had no common understanding whatever. There were the universities, great schools, learned men, experts, teachers gowned, adorned, and splendid . . . this higher brain, this cerebrum, this gray matter of America was so entirely unco-ordinated that it had nothing really comprehensive, searching, thought-out, and trustworthy for him to go upon . . . He was a politician—of exceptional good-will. . . He showed himself extremely open and receptive to the organized information and guidance . . . that wasn't there. And it isn't there now.' " (cf Hdbk. of Private Schools, 1936-37, pp 77-8)

Viscount Esher, who died in 1930, had for 50 years been in the public service, as confidant and counsel of the monarchy for almost 40 years "Discreet, unobtrusive, influential, he was at the heart of the political system. . . . His whole position derived from the fact that he was the most secret confidant of the Crown." His Journals and Letters in four volumes were published under the title, "The Captains and the Kings Depart".

August 11, 1917, Esher wrote, "It is the intention at present that the resources of America shall not be dribbled into the field, so that the blow, when it comes, shall be delivered by a force thoroughly organized and trained. That there is another aspect of this question Mr. Morgenthau [Mr Henry Morgenthau Sr.] is aware, and he realizes the importance upon the morale of the French army and the French people of cementing the alliance by shedding American blood at the earliest possible moment."

After an interview with Mr. Henry Morgenthau Sr. he wrote, "I told Mr. Morgenthau that while full of sympathy with his ideals I had no great belief in their practical efficacy . . . that I did not believe that this was a war likely to end all wars, and that if we beat the Germans, England and France and the United States would be exceedingly foolish if they failed to get all the material guarantees they could get, so that when the next war comes, each of these nations would find themselves stronger and more self-supporting."

The next day, August 12, Esher wrote to Sir Douglas Haig, "It is curious to listen to a man, deep in Wilson's counsels, reflecting all his ideals, his hopes for the future, and his plans for their achievement, who lives when at home in the Mountains of the Moon. . . . I am not sure whether Wilson or Kerensky is the more dangerous." (From the cross examination of Secretary Morgenthau by Senator Nye at the hearings of the Congressional Committee, January 28, 1940. Cf Scribner's *Commentator*, April, 1941)

WHOSE 'NEW ORDER'?

There were other roads to follow, other objectives to attain. Today, in time of trouble, many prophets arise to proclaim their new order. Some are fakes, some lead to tank traps. Woodrow Wilson fought and died for his new world order, the League of Nations, which the great powers prostituted to perpetuate their rule, using little nations as blind contributors until the barefaced farce ended again in war.

Mankind has always sought an easy road to salvation. Still intrigued, man is ready to give his allegiance to a new order of things which promises something better.

Since Henry VIII broke with the Pope and Sir Thomas More brought forth his "Utopia", dreamers and schemers, fanatics and fakers have brought forth proposals and plans for putting down evil and bringing about "orderly processes everywhere" They have promised new freedoms. At times of discontent and disturbance, of suffering and sacrifices, such receive attention.

The old faith that "God's in his heaven, all's right with the world" does not satisfy, though as disaster comes, "hope springs eternal in the human breast". Whatever disappointment overtakes us, we still hope "man never is but always to be blessed". But today we sturdily believe that God helps them that help themselves, that we must improve the order about us, better homes, cleaner streets, happier lives for children.

Today all the blue-prints are rolled away.[1] "We have broken with our past. We have thrown away our New World", we Americans have given away "our geographical advantage" which the Lord had given us, Garet Garrett, "looking back" "to say farewell" without "misgivings", writes in his editorial "Toward the Unknown" (*Sat Eve Post*, March 29, 1941). "There was never in all human history a story like it. We began it unconsciously. . . . We did not know we were doing it. Indeed, we kept saying we were not. . . . It is too soon to be either critical or analytical. Hardly the first page of the new book has been written."

To bring the world again to a fighting, killing stage, we have followed the age-old pattern of making the opponent a hated scapegoat, a devil. We have been dosed with propaganda about 'gangsters'. We have heard still more about 'victims'. We ignore the fact that revolution chooses efficient rather than polite agents for its accomplishment. In the days of change, the gentle are not long remembered. Those we hear about have been rough and tough enough to survive.

Whitney Griswold of Yale in "Paving the Way for Hitler" in the *Atlantic* for March, 1941, reminds us of all this, but adds that we have heard little enough about the ideas, and those who developed them, that are behind the revolution which produces 'gangsters' and 'victims'.

We may have heard of the renegade Englishman, Houston Chamberlain, and of the Frenchman, Gobineau, who became "apostles of racism", but we know little about the great English geographer, Sir Halford Mackinder, who foresaw Russo-German collaboration in making Eurasia, the great mother continent of civilization, the " 'heartland of the old world reaching from the Elbe to the Amur' united in defiance of British sea power and pressing on the life lines of British empire." Nor are others than geographers aware of the great German, Ratzel, who after the Franco-Prussian War traveled over Europe and America and from 1876 was professor of geography at Munich. He saw the earth as the home of the human race and recognized "the political value of space". "The decay of every state is the result of a declining space conception."

Long before Hitler was born 'Lebensraum' had become a demand of the overflowing millions of Germans confined to an area smaller than Texas But it was a Swedish historian at Göteborg, Kjellen, who on Ratzel's death carried his "theories into the realm of politcal science, where he greatly expanded them and applied them to current world politics. . . . He saw and reemphasized the fundamental rivalry between Germany and England. 'England stands today as the last and greatest embodiment of the ancient idea that the oceans of the world must have one master and not several', he wrote in 1914; 'just as if the vast oceans were not better suited to divide rule than the land, since traffic can no longer be monopolized in one hand!' "

"The New Order" then for Europe is of German-Swedish origin, and for the greater Eurasia of earlier English origin. Japan's "New Order in Asia" is merely notice that it is time to accelerate the "Retreat of the West" (cf p 534) from the trading posts they have occupied these few hundreds years. India, too, cries out for freedom from the fetters that have been put upon her in recent time, that she may live her life as she did for 5000 years before the westerner came.

These demands of the great people of the historic cultures of the world, that they be freed from the fetters of usurpers, make trivial such 'new orders' as Streit's "Union Now",—that we come under British dominion, or Curtis' "World Order",—for a greater British Empire, or Luce's "American Century",—a hope that we may step into Britain's worn out imperialistic shoes.

All this talk of 'morality' as an excuse for killing one's fellows somehow falls flat to one of simian ancestry, conscious of his origin. And as for upholding 'religion' by destruction, we no longer uphold religion by burning heretics at the stake, and in the future religion may be even more merciful. There are those for whom religion is personal, who want it fresh every day with new hope, made to fit the occasion, not a threadbare medieval hand down.

The 'new world order' on which H. G. Wells has been harping for so long is less political, perhaps less practical, but takes a broader, more human view. Had it not been for his preaching in the wilderness these twenty years, it is doubtful if the bishops and churchmen and socially minded who met at the Malvern Conference (cf p 345) could have formulated so boldly their demands. They were conscious of England's dog in the manger continental policy of which in his "Save America First", Jerome Frank, now of the S. E. C., soon, it is rumored, to go to the Supreme Court, speaks of as the maintenance of "continental anarchy" which "has brought all Europe, including England, to the edge of destruction" (cf p 19). We hope it is not to preserve this system nor the old order of the British Empire that we are fighting.

Lord Lothian deprecated the continued attempt of Britain to maintain its hegemony over Europe. He wrote in the London *Observer*, Nov. 27, 1938,—

"Though few yet realize it, the old anarchy of multitudinous national sovereignties is about to dissolve, and quickly at that. It is not going to disappear through a revived League of Nations, for the League, in basing itself on national sovereignty, consecrated anarchy as a principle. It is going to disappear either through federation, which is the democratic way, or through an integration consequent on the rise of the great Totalitarian powers We can see the process going on in Europe and Asia under our eyes, whereby the great military powers, either by compulsion or by the magnetic attraction of their own strength, consolidate a group of otherwise autonomous units to whom they promise peace, security and prosperity in return for entering their orbit and for accepting mutually satisfactory arrangements for trade."

Lord Lothian knew intimately the system of indentured labor and tropic exploitation on which the Empire parasitically existed. He had lived for years with Cecil Rhodes' dream of Anglo-Saxon unity, with Lionel Curtis' hope of world unity under Anglo-Saxon domination.

But when driven from a sense of duty and loyalty to bring us in in order to save the Empire, he proved himself a master of all the means of propulsion and propaganda that are used to protect this system, and did not hesitate to drive himself to the full use of them. He promoted Streit's plan for "Union Now", based on Rhodes' and Curtis' ideas, against which he had warned.

"World unity is, of course, at present entirely out of sight. But that the world is going to fall into four or five main political and economic groups, each in great measure self-supporting, each under the leadership of a great state equipped with modern military and air power, at any rate for a time, seems certain. Nothing that we can do can prevent it The only issue is whether the process need involve world war, and whether when the consolidation is made the groups can live together in peace."

In "America and a New World Order", (Scribner, 1940) Graeme K. Howard, looks ahead much as did Lord Lothian Both knew their European world. Howard reminds us the transition from feudalism to capitalism was marked by "wars, economic levellings, and political integrations. City, states and feudal manors were forcibly absorbed into the authority of the king, and the nation stage of history appeared. Inevitably we must now witness another transition into a newer relationship of peoples. . . .

"Small states have rarely possessed complete sovereignty . . they have usually been . . . under the domination of a larger power", if not set up or maintained by a great power as a buffer state (cf p 582) "Any attempt to settle international disputes which neglects the element of power is unrealistic and doomed to failure Dissatisfied nations seek change; satisfied nations resist it. . . .

"Regional groups, however, will endure and prosper only so long as the dominant member makes life fuller and richer for the smaller members   . . The world of tomorrow may contain various major regions: Continental Europe, a British Empire, a Union of Soviet Republics, a Latin-Mediterranean Federation, an American Federation, and a New Order of Asia. . . .

"Cooperative regionalism, with each region having set its own house in order, offers the practical ideal and the idealistic practice for world peace and advancement." It "is the substitute for single or coalition power domination, for laissez-faire Darwinism, for international economic chaos, for revolution and conflict."

Most of these new orders and Utopias are more or less rearrangements of old conceptions, essentially political, devices for securing change for an individual or a group or a people. That is, they are based on who shall control and how. We still suffer from the idea of rule by divine right The future of the world belongs to those who realize that they are but advanced simians who can devise or make possible a way of life that is natural, that is organic.

Walter B. Cannon envisions a time when the body politic, the men who constitute the population of this globe, may so regulate their internal affairs that they too may live in harmony. "The Wisdom of the Body" is such that within our own skins diverse colonies of cells bathed in common fluids manufacture all that is needful for the life of man and regulate themselves and their activities so that he can live and function under great range of external physical conditions. This doctrine of biocracy, of control based on biological principles, working and sharing for the good of all, as do the elements that make up our individual bodies, he again preached in his address as retiring president of the American Association for the Advancement of Science, Philadelphia, December 27, 1940,—an elaboration of the idea first set forth by him in 1932 in the epilogue of his book, "The Wisdom of the Body".
March 28, 1941

NOTES

(1) "Communism and Fascism are now just historical concepts The Labour Party in England is going the way of the Liberal Party The New Deal here is over. . . . Both Churchill and Roosevelt are relevant and significant only as wartime dictators, just as are Hitler and Stalin Hitler and Stalin, however, are significant as builders of a planned new order. Roosevelt and Churchill have only a war purpose: to win. . . The Republican Party is dying just like the Labour Party. . . . In America the fact that F.D.R. has scrapped the New Deal is powerful reason why he must go to war. Only by doing so can he develop a plan of action—a plan, of course, to win the war. In Britain, as here, once war is in the air, the people emote rather than think, thus leaving the war dictator a free hand." (Dennis, *Weekly Foreign Letter*, Feb 27, 1941)

"The greatness of the British Empire is based, you may say, on English sportsmanship, English endurance, English guts, and the incorruptibility of English judges. All that is true, but there is a greater reason: the greatness of the British Empire is based on the English lack of cerebration. The lack of cerebration, or insufficient cerebration, produces moral strength. The British Empire exists because the Englishman is so cocksure of himself and his own superiority. No nation can go about conquering the world unless she is quite certain of her 'civilizing' mission The moment, however, that you begin to think and see something in the other nation or the other fellow and his ways, your moral conviction leaves you, and your empire collapses. The British Empire still stands today because the Englishman still believes that his ways are the only correct ways and because he cannot tolerate anybody who does not conform to his standards. The English maxim is—When you are traveling in Rome, do exactly as at home." (Lin Yutang, "With Love and Irony", John Day, 1940)

ADJUSTMENT AND CHANGE

"The world order which we seek is the cooperation of free countries, working together in a friendly, civilized society", the President declared in addressing Congress in his annual message January 6, 1941.

"Since the beginning of our American history we have been engaged in change—in a perpetual peaceful revolution—a revolution which goes on steadily, quietly adjusting itself to changing conditions."

President Roosevelt arrives at many things by intuitions and hunches as the result of his many contacts. An authority on the early American navy, the President has little time for reading solid books on economic and international affairs, what with detective stories and his stamp collection for relaxation. His close adviser Adolf Berle understands what is happening. When Germany invaded Poland, he remarked, "This is the beginning of the world revolution". (Pearson and Allen, July 8, 1940)

It is an American conception this idea of perpetual revolution, the continuous turning of the wheel and unending progress forward. Ely Culbertson in his brilliant autobiography, "The Strange Lives of One Man" (Winston Co., 1940) tells of his conversation as a young man interested in the Russian revolution with his Pennsylvania born father, who admonished, "and as for your being a revolutionist—well, dammit, we Americans are natural revolutionists! Only, Ely, if you must be one, then don't disgrace your poor old father: lead, and don't be led."[1]

Our nation was born of 'Revolution', but the word has been tabu. Only the 'Daughters' dared flaunt it, and with the implication that all that was past. When the repressed and resentful nations broke through the cordon of buffer states, they were looked upon as rebels, 'aggressors', just a nuisance to be suppressed.

In two years there has come general recognition that a great change is going on in the world,—that our economic system which has served well in a period of imperialistic expansion is undergoing fundamental modification,—that our social system has left large masses deprived, with growing resentment. Reluctantly we have come to admit that this is revolution, social and economic.[2]

Radical visionaries prophesying revolution we have had. But for this revolution, recognition came late. John Macmurray gave an inkling in "The Clue to History" (Harper, 1939). Peter Drucker in "The End of Economic Man" (John Day, 1939) made the thesis more familiar.[3] Wallace Deuel saw it in Berlin and radio-ed, May 29, 1940, "world economic revolution" win or lose M. W Fodor in "The Revolution Is On" (Houghton Mifflin, 1940) sees communism, fascism, and national socialism as part of a single revolutionary struggle for the social and economic freedom of the bottom strata of industrial societies.

Rauschning at first could see nothing but 'Nihilism' in this. Now he begins to see a pattern. Though he regrets any change, he confesses, "It would have been better if human insight, instead of letting things take their own course, had spared us the revolution by giving us peaceful evolution before it was too late, for much that was worth preserving has been destroyed with that which was not But as things now are, Hitler's attack upon the existing order has compelled us to face up to a reconstruction of our European world." (NNS, Nov 5, 1940)

The "perpetual peaceful revolution" had not been going on in Europe. The wheels had stopped turning. Now things have started with a jolt Some hope they will slide back in the old ruts, but there is so much of sacrificing and suffering ahead which now cannot be avoided that those who survive will not turn back to the old ways. When one sees how the London masses are now living in the underground tubes, it seems a little incongruous that since he came over here, the salary of Halifax should have been increased by £1800 to something like $70,000.

That is a little thing, only a grain of sand. But it is the little things that count. The hills, the mountains, are constantly rising due to the earth's internal strains. Drops of water move grains of sand down the slopes. Bending and uplift is resisted by the stiffness of the rocks. A condition of strain results in a sudden break so that far beneath the rocks slide. We call it an earthquake.

The processes of nature and of human affairs are generally slow, continuous, so gentle as to be imperceptible. Human tendencies are largely conservative, to hold what we have won and to prevent change. Traditions and institutions are conserving, like the grass, or the forests that prevent the washing away of the soil. But through the grass or from the forest undergrowth, a tree may struggle upward and win its share of sunlight. So from our human undergrowth, may rise new individuals or groups to win out.

There is nothing new about revolution. Change is constant and even evolution moves in mutations, jumps. Probably the greatest revolution in social and economic life that our ancestors underwent was when they were forced down from the treetops by the unprecedented drought. Some old man monkey probably said, "Oh, it's just a dry season. We will be back in the treetops next year" Later, when they lost their tails for lack of use among the trees, a wail went up, "What will we do without them? What will we put in their place?" A far-seeing old monk cracked, "Tails you lose, heads you win".

Adjustment is always a painful process. We like the old ways to which we react automatically. Under new conditions we have to use our heads. That's something we humans put off as long as possible.
April 4, 1941

NOTES

(1) Of his later revulsion Culbertson wrote, "The war finally opened my eyes to the shameless exploitation of all peoples by conservatives, liberals, and radicals alike Above all I was nauseated by the abject groveling of liberal and radical 'idealists' who overnight gave up their slogans of humanity for the shouts of command   Although the air was full of propaganda and slogans calling the world to fight for 'Democracy' and 'Justice', I knew that these nations had been hurled at each other by one of those inexorable historical cyclones in which only might can prevail."

(2) By January, 1940, *Fortune* Round Table admitted that an increasing number of "thinking men" are coming to see that this is a social revolution. But there are many who accept the propaganda conception denying this is revolution. It is only a disturbance. Throw the 'Gangsters' out   To Bruce Bliven, the idea is the "grimmest joke of the present day world". David Cort (*Life*, August 19, 1940), says it's time to give "the great American razzberry" to the "idiot mouthing . . that Nazism and Fascism and Communism are 'revolutions' ". The "true revolution" is "democracy". Raymond Gram Swing in the *Nation*, Dec. 21, 1940, excoriates "The Hitler 'Revolution' ", and "although the author did not offer it as such", the editors "submit the article as a reply to Anne Morrow Lindbergh".

[3] Reginald Phelps, Assistant Dean of Harvard, in *The Commonweal*, May 24, 1940, wrote, 'Some day the Nazi movement will be placed in its proper perspective, not simply as a product of Versailles and the depression, but as a revolt against the West, rooted in over a century of troubled and uncertain feeling that the liberal-bourgeois age is not the German Age. Then the forerunners of it may be as familiar as Hitler and Rosenberg are now, and names like Langbehn, Legarde, Klages may mean something, as Nietzsche's already does, in the world outside Germany. The thought of these men, and of many others like them, helped to stir a whole generation into the tumult of primitivism and sentiment that was called the German Youth Movement. The universal German cry was for a new humanity; the lament, that no pottering with surface symptoms would cure a sick world."

The revolutions that Crane Brinton examines in his "Anatomy of Revolution" (1938) are those that were incident to the final transition from the feudal to the capitalistic state They cover just one narrow phase of man's progress The revolutions that are ahead are of a different type Brinton's book was based on his Lowell lectures of that year. Robert Morss Lovett, reviewing the book and the lectures, remarked, "He doubtless afforded special relief to his Boston audience by his suggestion that revolutions do not occur in decadent societies." Brinton in his lectures skilfully dodged diagnosing the world of today, but by the end of 1939 it seemed to him "a safe bet" to say that the German system would "take more and more the sort of measures we ordinarily associate with socialism. . . . Some of the conditions which made possible the Nazi revolution are world-wide in their application." (Boston *Herald,* Oct. 28, 1939)

[4] What has happened in Europe brings home to us that we "can get nowhere by talking about democracy unless [we] are willing to break down the economic and national barriers that prevent the peoples of Europe from enjoying the benefits of a machine civilization. . . . Suppose Europe does achieve some kind of economic unity under Nazi leadership, is it fantastic to foresee an accelerating social revolution" such as "at the time of the Protestant Reformation and of the French Revolution? Not to recognize that such an upheaval has been taking place in Europe for the past twenty years is to miss the whole significance of contemporary events" (Quincy Howe, "After Munich—What?", *Common Sense,* Nov., 1938)

ERRATA

Hundreds will probably be discovered, these few already, too late to change. pp 98, 302, For "O. W. Reigel" read Riegel—132, For "D. A. Fleming" read D. F. Fleming—243, For "Albert Duff Cooper" read Alfred—248, For "Chatham House" read Wellington House—341, For "William Harding" read Warren G Harding—455, For "British Office" read British Foreign Office

INDEX

This is not a complete encyclopedic index which would have involved three times the 300 hours that were put into it. Names that occur only once in the text are seldom included. Authors are generally listed but not their books Publishers are given with addresses on page 636

Abbott, Beatrice, 240, 261
Abrams, Ray H.; 265
Abshagen, Karl H , 43, 120, 155-6
Abstractions, political, 490, 580
Acland, Sir Richard, 40, 345
Acton, Lord, 514
Adams, C. F., 365
John Quincy, 319, 394, 574
Adey, Alvin, 596
Adler, Julius Ochs, 78-9, 398, 400
Aeroplane, The, 240, 262
Agar, Herbert, 517
Aiken, Sen. George D., 281, 365
Alabama Claims, 235, 457
Aldrich, Winthrop, 297, 372
Aliens, registration of, 284
Allen, C. B , 550
Frederick Lewis, 58-9, 65, 77, 125, 416, 433-4, 586
Alsop and Kintner, 63, 288, 332-3, 349
American alliance with Britain, 150-1, 274, 305-12, 357, 380, 454, 504, 528, 543
financial revolution, 569-70, 580, 588, 593, 602-6
foreign policy, 62-3, 66, 118, 448, 451, 455, 526
government, 548, 558-60
gullibility, 44, 107, 111-12, 287
indebtedness, 591
invasion, 441, 511, 519
Legion, 49, 69, 377
morale, 399, 428, 583, 586
quarantine against foreign ideas, 276, 281, 510
relief to Europe, 269, 383
stake in the Orient, 107, 111, 527, 536, 541
technology, 576, 577
trade with China, 526, 541-2
trade with Japan, 526, 535, 541-2
Ameringer, Oscar, 372, 483-4
Anderson, Sir John, 199, 349

Angell, James Rowland, 109
Sir Norman, 186 ·
Anglo-Saxon responsibility for peace, 240, 263
Anti-alien bills, 282
Appeasement policy, 21-2, 24, 27-40, 64-5, 68, 84, 97, 100, 120, 233
Argentina, loan to, 116, 393-4, 414
Arithmetic, teaching of, 335
Armstrong, Hamilton Fish, 109, 174, 548, 558
Army, cost of maintaining, 337
Army and Navy Journal, 451
Army intelligence, 556, 564, 574
Army Recruiting News, 420, 454
Arnold, Matthew, 159
Thurman, 359, 397, 439, 587
Ashurst, Sen Henry F , 432, 444, 446,
Asquith, Lord, 166
Astor, Lady, 100, 116
Vincent, 177, 536
Viscount, 66, 126
Attlee, Clement, 375
Aubry, Octave, 560
Austin, Sen. Warren R., 353, 364
Australia, 117, 322, 505
Aydelotte, Frank, 71
Bacon, Robert, 117, 120
Baden-Powell, Robt. S., 492, 499
Balance of power, 19, 24
Balderston, John L., 81, 452, 457-9
Baldwin, Hanson, 364, 578
Stanley, 22, 25-7, 42, 87, 104, 114, 136, 159-60, 216, 575
Balfour, Lord, 22-3, 290, 506
Bank of England, 602
Barnes, Brig.-Gen G. M , 334
Harry Elmer, 134, 285
Barrie, Sir James M , 132, 136
Barton, Rep Bruce, 304, 368, 371, 404, 426, 512, 596, 599
Baruch, Bernard, 434
Batchelor, Bronson, 569

Batista, Col Fulgencio, 413
Baxter, James Phinney, 301
   William J., 601-2
Beals, Carleton, 299, 311, 331, 348, 391, 404, 410, 412, 414-5, 542, 548, 595, 598, 601
Beard, Chas. A , 14, 51, 55-6, 58-9, 67, 69, 103, 128, 156, 175, 176, 180, 186, 313, 336, 363, 377, 404, 570, 603
   Dan, 492, 499
Beaverbrook, Lord, 38, 47, 133, 154-5, 161, 181, 266, 287
Belgion, Montgomery, 23, 67, 555
Belgium, 116, 121, 257, 269-70, 283, 320, 582
Bell, Bernard Iddings, 405
   Eric T., 87, 497
Belloc, Hilaire, 383
Benes, Eduard, 214, 240
Bennett, Arnold, 308
Bergdoll, Grover Cleveland, 292
Berle, Adolf A. Jr , 63, 76, 297, 334, 395, 455, 468, 569, 570, 587, 588-9, 603-4, 613, 615
Bernays, E. L., 135
Bess, Demaree, 349, 431
Bessarabia, 203, 211, 239
Beston, Henry, 303, 404, 554
Bevin, Ernest, 426
Bidwell, Percy W., 399, 401-2, 419
Bigger, John D , 436-7
Bill of Rights, 275, 363
Billings, Josh, 237
Bingham, Alfred M , 117, 134
Black, Maj Percy, 197
Bloom, Rep. Sol, 123, 172, 312
Blum, Leon, 549, 552, 558, 561
Boaz, Franz, 272
Boeing Aircraft, 433
Bolinger, Dwight L , 402
Bolshevism, fear of, 20-6, 28, 190, 206, 217, 233, 546, 561
Bomb sight, 458
Boncour, Paul, 37
Bone, Sen. Homer T., 98, 151, 230
Bonnet, M., 200-1, 210, 310, 374, 549, 550, 558
Books, burned, 487

   suppressed, 102-3, 155, 163-4, 276, 281
Boothe, Clare, 548
Borah, Sen. Wm. E., 49, 98, 172, 230, 238, 274, 279, 284, 289, 304
Borchard, Edwin M , 134
Boston terrozied by Spanish, 350, 533
Bowman, Isaiah, 301, 405
Braddock, Gen., 567, 583
Brailsford, H. N , 26, 150
Brandeis, Louis D , 570
Brayman, Harold, 477, 482
Brazil, 387-8, 390, 392, 411
Breckinridge, Col., 354, 371
Brewer, Joseph, 134, 171
Brewster, Ralph O., 305
Briand, Aristide, 589
Briffault, Robert, 156
Brinton, Crane, 157, 618
Britain a "good risk", 116
   aid to, 74, 84, 111, 125, 128-9, 259, 335, 364, 443, 508, 605
   National Government, 240, 273
British Council, 48
   Blockade of Germany, 197, 206, 217, 222, 234-5, 269-72
   Empire, support of, 97, 108, 113, 115, 117, 127, 138-9, 180, 183, 199, 267, 270, 299, 372, 406, 454, 457, 505, 506, 519, 532, 535, 544
   Exports, 526
   Foreign Office, 43, 49, 74, 98-9, 104, 106, 126, 145, 245, 258, 264, 266, 294, 312, 324, 455,
   Intelligence Service, 43, 48, 243
   Investments in China, 527
   Ministry of Economic Warfare, 263-4, 266
   Ministry of Information, 45, 48, 66, 106, 126, 241
   Navy, 397, 407
   Trade with Japan, 115
   Trade with Latin America, 388
   West Indies, 325-6, 537
Brogan, Dennis W., 548, 558
Brody, Bernard, 566, 578
Bromfield, Louis, 38-9
Bromley, Dorothy Dunbar, 284, 303,

Brussels Conference, 56, 60
Bryan, William Jennings, 316, 516
Bryce, Lord, 135, 422, 558-9, 560
Buck, Pearl, 528
Buell, Raymond Leslie, 272, 369
Buffer States, 42, 85, 211, 535, 582
Bullitt, William; 37, 62, 130, 200, 209, 310, 334, 430
Bunyan, John, 283
Burgin, Leslie, 235
Burke, Kenneth, 16, 175
Burke, Sen Edward R , 397, 399, 420
Burma Road, 389
Burrow, J. R., 141, 360, 379
Butler, Nicholas Murray, 71, 76, 130, 171, 183, 311, 352, 354
  Samuel, 344
Bynner, Witter, 151, 154
Byrnes, Sen. James F., 35, 74, 130, 204, 468
Byron, Lord, 558
Cadogan, Sir Alexander, 47
Calloway, Congressman, 48
Camp Edwards, Mass., 482-4
Canada, 138, 144, 155, 247-53, 505
Canham, Erwin D , 62
Canning, 19, 388, 489
Cannon, Walter B , 336, 405, 607, 608, 614
Canterbury, Archbishop of, 265, 345, 399
Canton and Enderbury Islands, 53, 61, 306, 308, 455, 493
Capitalism, 489
Capper, Sen. Arthur, 304, 424
Carnegie, Andrew, 150
Carr, Katherine, 388
Carroll, Lewis, 474
Carter, Boake, 163, 185-7, 356, 368, 460, 469
Castlereagh, Viscount, 36
Cattell, J. McKeen, 596
C C.C., 401, 429, 492, 500-1, 574
Cecil, Lord, 87, 154
Censorship in America, 279
  Canada, 248-50
  England, 97, 105, 161, 376
  France, 277, 374, 549, 563
Chamberlain, Austen, 528, 573

Houston, 610
John, 262, 490, 497
Joseph, 149, 494, 526-7, 537
Neville, 25, 27-8, 34-6, 41-2, 53, 64, 66, 97, 106, 111, 115-6, 124, 125, 145, 160, 172, 190, 197, 199, 233, 253, 267, 352, 470, 557, 573, 579
Chamberlin, William H , 274-5, 348, 487, 537, 581
Change, adjustment and, 613-6
  resistance to, 497, 546
Chase National Bank, 110, 177
Chase, Stuart, 134, 393, 577, 580
Chavez, Sen Dennis, 597
Chiang Kai-Shek, 534
Childs, Marquis W., 453
China, 53, 107, 115-6, 140, 185, 296, 525-6, 531
Churchill, Winston, 19-20, 32-3, 38, 42, 44, 58, 65-6, 149-50, 155, 158, 183, 197, 256-7, 261-2, 264, 266, 270, 283, 310, 351, 451, 454, 458, 471, 493, 504, 506, 563, 573, 596
Civil Liberties in America, 82, 169, 187, 272-85, 345, 362, 364, 371, 398-9, 470, 494, 508, 510, 512, 533
  Canada, 247, 249-50, 252
  England, 105, 110, 198, 210, 245
  France, 201, 210-11, 245, 274
Clapper, Raymond, 391, 514
Clark, Sen. Bennett C , 104, 129, 146, 242, 244, 287, 436, 462, 487
  Sen D Worth, 357
  Evans, 518
  Grenville, 77-8, 81-2, 353, 359, 363, 397-8, 400, 425, 427, 430
Clausewitz, 427
Clemenceau, Georges, 24, 195, 240
Cless, George H Jr , 113, 152, 164, 381, 383
Close, Upton, 397, 404
Clugston, W. G , 367, 370, 379, 381
Cobb, Irvin S., 494
Coffee, 395
Colby, Bainbridge, 348
Committees

America First Committee, 384, 472, 474

American Civil Liberties Union, 274, 282, 293

American Friends Committee, 269

American Peace Mobilization, 384

American Union for Concerted Peace Efforts, 71

Civil Rights Federation, 283

Commission to Study the Organization of Peace, 71

Committee to Defend America by Aiding the Allies, 77, 79-84, 147, 349, 353, 357-60, 369, 371, 380-2, 419, 449, 452, 457-8, 469, 472, 474, 531

Council of Democracy, 279, 517

Council on Foreign Relations, 81, 108, 468, 551, 575, 580

English-Speaking Union, 76, 108

Foreign Policy Association, 457

France Forever, 171, 383

Institute of Propaganda Analysis, 385

Joint Committee on Foreign Relations, 281

Keep America Out of War Congress, 384

League of Nations Association, 71, 108, 154, 167, 354

National Committee to Keep America Out of War, 98

National Popular Government League, 370

No Foreign War Committee, 384, 474

Non Partisan Committee for Peace Through Revision of the Neutrality Law, 72, 84, 130

World Peaceways, 384

Writers' Anti-War Bureau, 384

Commonwealth College, 285

Commonwealth and Southern, 77, 367, 369, 371, 448, 450, 577, 585

Community Chest, 499

Conant, James B, 32, 38, 78, 80-2, 117, 119, 133, 165-6, 168, 170, 269, 353, 355-6, 358, 360, 363-4, 400, 519, 543, 567, 598

Congressional Record, 49, 61, 78, 80, 97, 102, 155, 185, 244, 284, 291, 300, 319, 346, 356, 410, 419, 455, 467, 470, 473

Connally, Sen Tom, 173, 184, 465

Conscientious objectors, 104

Conscription, 78, 82, 243, 282, 361-6, 396-402, 405, 415-21, 424-32, 442-7, 467, 488, 604

Coolidge, Calvin, 167, 218, 328, 381, 442, 600

Cooper, Duff, 111, 113, 116, 136, 153, 203, 243

Corwin, Edward S., 110, 514

Cost plus, 483-4

Cot, Pierre, 374, 551-2, 562

Coudert, Frederic René, 79-80, 352-3, 357, 368, 397

"Course of Human Events", 25, 100, 112, 160

Cox, George Clarke, 297

   Philip W L, 301, 524

Crawford, Kenneth, 157, 471, 526,

Creel Bureau, 162, 279-80, 502

Cripps, Sir Stafford, 194, 498

Croft-Cooke, Rupert, 100

Cromwell, James H. R., 321, 323, 332

Cross, Ronald H., 263-4

   Samuel Hazzard, 190, 192, 209

Crowe, Sir Eyre, 43, 145

Crozier, Gen., 398

Cudahy, John, 209

Culbertson, Ely, 615, 617

Cummings, E. E , 201

Curie, Eve, 251

Currie, Lauchlin, 569, 570, 588

Curtis, Lionel, 124, 126, 144

Curtiss-Wright Aircraft, 433, 436

Czechoslovakia, 22-3, 37, 51, 61-2, 66, 137, 214, 240, 549, 551, 578

Dakar, 495, 537, 599

Daladier, Edouard, 128, 190, 200-1, 205, 211, 246, 374, 376, 549, 552, 561

Daniels, Jonathan, 277, 300, 303, 404

Davenport, Russell, 368-71, 447-8

Davies, Ambassador, 212

Davis, Jerome, 303

Maxine, 599
Norman, 60, 287, 334
Saville, 214, 223
Dawes, Charles G , 483
Déat, Marcel, 552
Debs, Eugene V., 69, 283
De Chambrun, René, 550
Deeds, Col., 319
Defense, 406, 437, 477, 482, 563, 570,
    582, 586, 587, 595, 604, 605
    appropriations for, 187, 237-8,
    335-6, 339, 377, 487
    Advisory Commission, 436, 439,
    468, 493, 539
    orders, 488-9
De Gaulle, Gen., 383, 556
Democracy, 275, 331, 488, 497-8, 532,
    560, 595, 597
Democratic Party split, 51, 57, 227
Denmark, 257, 597
Dennis, Lawrence, 40, 66, 163, 285,
    319, 384, 386, 390, 428, 444,
    474, 525, 600-1, 603, 615
Denny, George V , 326
DeSaint Jean, Robert, 545, 555
Destroyer transfer, 81, 451-61, 471,
    503, 506
Deterding, Sir Henri, 20, 24, 156,
    158-9, 214, 268, 351
Deuel, Wallace R., 209, 349, 616
De Voto, Bernard, 597
Dewey, John, 103, 570
    Thomas, 227, 340, 368, 371
Diamonds, 299
Dictatorship in America, 129, 174,
    284, 290-5, 346, 430, 476-512
    England, 198, 486, 577
    France, 273
    Germany, 273
    Latin America, 279
Dies, Rep Martin, 104, 166, 282, 284,
    348-9, 516
Dies Investigation, 187, 280, 282
Disaffection Acts, 155, 199, 234, 249,
Disarmament, 240, 555
Divine, Father, 396
Doane, Robert R , 580, 591
Dobrudja, 203
Dodd, William E., 36, 209, 573

Domville-Fife, Charles, 97, 100
Donham, Wallace B., 163
Donovan, Col. William ("Wild Bill")
    400, 443, 545
Doob, Leonard W., 98
Dos Passos, John, 549
Dougherty, Cardinal, 343, 390
Douglas, Lewis, 78, 80-1, 352, 356-7,
    360
Downey, Sen Sheridan, 399, 479, 486
Drake, F. V., 237
Dreher, Carl, 330, 467, 470, 564, 565,
    572, 575, 576-7
Dreiser, Theodore, 36, 48, 516, 563
Drucker, Peter F., 133, 157, 272, 616
Dulles, Allen W., 174, 250
    Avery, 335
    John Foster, 47, 118, 133, 157
Dunkirk, 547
DuPont interests, 58, 110, 158, 166,
    173, 434
Durant, John, 328
    Will, 275, 303, 404
Duranty, Walter, 25, 316
Dutch East Indies, 532, 537, 542
Dykstra, Clarence, 172
Economic Notes, 313, 314, 318, 319,
    333, 339, 378, 379, 384, 438,
    462, 466, 580
Eden, Anthony, 53-4, 60, 98, 100, 136
Edison, Charles, 220, 230, 238, 288
    Thomas A., 565
Educational Orders, 291, 390
Edwards, George W , 162, 581
Ehrlich, Henry, 35, 39, 237, 305, 436,
    447, 473
Eichelberger, Clark M., 71-3, 79, 130,
    167, 170, 354, 457
Einstein, Albert, 135, 168
Eire, 231, 270
Elections, cost of, 340-1
Eliot, Major Fielding, 225, 237, 531
Elliott, Wm. Yandell, 461, 559, 560
Engel, Rep. Albert J., 482
England, evacuation of children, 198
    love of, 87, 142, 251
    rationing, 217, 234
    schools, 198
    technology, 575

Enlistment in Foreign Armies, 292
Ernst, Morris, 370
Esher, Viscount, 538, 609
Everts, William P., 393
Export-Import Bank, 116, 232, 259, 286, 314-15, 394, 409, 411
Ezekiel, Mordecai, 602
Fadiman, Clifton, 599
Fagen, Melvin M., 229, 438
Fairbank, John K, 543
Far East, U S. in, 59, 205, 221, 307
Farley, James, 237, 369, 490
Farm tenancy, 597
Fascism in America, 228, 238, 273, 275-6, 279, 362, 399, 448, 481, 487, 500
    roots of, 491-2
Fay, Sidney, 166, 170, 245
Federal Bureau of Investigation, 104, 243, 275, 279, 283-4, 293, 348, 469, 485, 512, 540
Federated Malay States, 148-9, 322
Fifth column, American, 84, 348, 598
    British, 111, 347, 356, 360, 371
    French, 549
    in Ulster, 231
Finnish flare-up, 130, 187-195, 202-3, 207, 211, 215-6, 239, 253, 320
    loans and debts, 189, 214, 232, 260, 286, 313-19
Firth, Sir William, 435
Fish, Rep. Hamilton, 214, 418-19, 443, 596, 599
Fisher, Lord, 578
Flandin, M, 212, 552
Fleming, D F, 132
    Harold M., 571
Fleury, Cardinal, 148
Flying fortresses, 240, 453
Flynn, John T., 48, 67, 284-5, 310, 409, 412, 415, 428, 437, 439, 442, 450, 472, 488, 509, 533, 574 5, 580, 590, 602, 605
Foch, Marshal, 20, 24, 216
Fodor, M. W, 374, 561, 616
Ford, Harvey S, 377
    Henry, 158, 263, 275, 390, 434, 472, 577
Foreign Policy Association, 108, 548

Fort Devens, Mass, 483
    Sill, Okla, 484
Fortune Round Table, 272-3, 617
Fosdick, Harry Emerson, 115
Foundations (cf Peace)
    Carnegie Endowment for International Peace, 71, 330
    Rockefeller, 109
    World Peace Foundation, 71
Four Power Pact, 20
France, aid to, 64, 125, 128, 129, 185
    arrogance of, 19, 20, 23
    expenditure on war, 221
    fall of, 68, 86, 149, 194, 200, 201, 211, 277, 374-6, 390, 407, 425, 434, 438, 545-63, 564
    grumbling of troops, 235
    love of, 545, 548, 553-4
Franco, Francisco, 140, 201, 204
Frank, Jerome, 19, 468, 498, 573, 587
Frankfurter, Felix, 284, 570
Franklin, Benjamin, 265, 329
Freedom of the seas, 544
    of the press (cf Newspapers)
    of speech, 510, 597
'Free elections', 493-4, 507-8, 516, 560
French-British pool, 201, 233
Friedrich, Carl J., 21, 121, 122, 518
Froelicher, F. M., 134
Fuller, Alvan T, 355
    Maj.-Gen J F C, 444, 566
    R. Buckminster, 250
Funk, Dr Walther, 299
Furlong, Rear Admiral W. R., 432, 436, 438
Gadarene swine, 594
Galileo, 235
Gallipoli, 257
Gallup, George (cf Public opinion polls), 419-20, 422
Galsworthy, John, 132, 136
Gamelin, Gen, 235, 547, 552, 561
Gandhi, 39-40, 270, 283, 575
Gannett, Frank, 340, 365, 517
Garner, John, 340, 608
    Robert L, 587, 602, 606
Garratt, Geoffrey, 59, 262
Garrett, Garet, 21, 26, 83
Gathorne-Hardy, G. M., 26

Gear, Mary Barnes, 582
General Semantics, 115
Geography, 582, 599
George, Lloyd, 21-2, 24, 28, 37, 116, 234, 240, 309, 563, 589
  Sen. Walter F., 178, 465, 516
Germany and the church, 344
  agreement with Russia, 102, 122,
  British loan to, 21-2, 24, 34-5
  economics, 568-9
  educational philosophy, 101
  effect of blockade, 271, 601
  embroiling with Russia, 22, 24-5, 97, 111, 120, 197
  expansion of, 100, 350
  expenditure on rearmament, 337
  financial revolution, 299, 337, 438-9, 569, 579, 590, 604
  immaturity, 572, 575
  morale, 209, 337, 567, 583, 596
  Nazi caches of gold, 132
  negotiations with Russia, 540
  reparations, 43, 216, 573
  Republican, 119, 273, 492, 581
  resources, 208
  revolt in, 197
  strategy, 195, 566
  technological advance, 564-6
  trade with Latin America, 388, 392, 394-5, 412, 414
  trade with Russia, 121
  unification of, 30
  why she wins, 563-81
Gibbs, Philip 22, 199
Gibson, Sen. Ernest W., 82
Gillette, Sen. Guy M, 341, 429, 520
Gilmour, Sir John, 289
Giono, Jean, 201
Girdler, Tom, 423, 466
Glass, Sen. Carter, 174, 232, 364, 495
Goebbels, Paul Joseph, 27, 132, 153, 272, 586, 599
Goering, Hermann, 27, 46, 100, 212
Gold, 24, 116, 218, 228, 238, 255, 258-9, 262, 263, 266, 267, 270, 295-301, 322, 325, 556, 557, 568, 590, 605
Goldenweiser, E A , 297
Gort, Gen , 233, 235, 261-2

Government, art of, 490, 497-8
  secrecy in, 61, 63, 290, 305-12, 450-61, 481, 493, 594
Grace, Eugene, 434
Graf Spee, 223-5
Graham, Frank D., 179, 238, 259, 263, 267, 296-7, 322, 336
Gras, N S B., 162
Grattan, C. Hartley, 163, 427
Graves, John Temple II, 382
Greece, 148, 515
Greene, Jerome, 135
Grew, Ambassador, 185, 544
Grey, Lord, 114, 148, 166, 182, 308
Gribble, Major Philip, 546-7
Griffin, Charles C., 392
  William, 261
Griswold, A. Whitney, 53, 54, 60, 107, 156, 160, 528, 535-6, 566
Guardia, Fiorello, La, 191
Gulbenkian, 214, 351
Gunther, John, 155, 546 556
Hacobian, 214, 352
Hague, Frank, 485, 507, 601
Halifax, Lord, 27, 34-6, 38-9, 41, 46, 56, 64, 85, 100, 168, 183, 197, 214, 217, 266, 270, 283, 312, 351, 470, 563, 564, 573, 575
Hall, G. Stanley, 597
Hamilton, Dr Alice, 271
Handley-Page Aircraft, 333, 376
Hanighen, Frank S., 58, 157, 203, 211, 374-5, 377, 573, 587, 602
Hankey, Lord, 264
Hanna, Mark, 340
Hapsburg Restoration, 211
Harding, Warren G., 167, 341
Haring, C H , 414
Hart, Capt. Liddell, 97, 99, 195, 234
Hartman, George, 524
Harvard Alumni Bulletin, 78, 82, 352, 353, 358, 372, 530
  Crimson, 165, 170, 300, 353, 358, 393, 446, 509, 513, 519, 543
  Guardian, 135, 169
  Progressive, 117, 266
  University, 77, 78, 122, 170, 171, 282, 355, 530, 543, 580, 598
Hate creating, 85, 98, 109, 115, 118-9,

131, 162, 255-6, 265, 274, 487
Hatry, Clarence C., 163
Havana Conference, 387, 389, 393, 395, 408, 410-14
Hay, John, 527-8, 538
Hayakawa, Dr. S. I., 115
Hearst, William Randolph, 350, 358,
Hedin, Sven, 100, 534
Heiden, Konrad, 210
Heindel, Richard H , 13, 149, 172, 281, 384, 537-8
Henderson, Leon, 468, 569, 570, 587
  Sir Nevile, 33, 38, 197
Herbert, A. P., 262
Herring, Hubert, 55, 60, 67, 112, 162, 294, 336, 357
Hertzberg, Sidney, 474
Heyman, Hans, 589
Himmler, Heinrich, 272
Hindenburg, Paul von, 24, 189
History, cultural approach to, 15
  interpretation of, 18
  what it is, 13-14
  written by victors, 16
Hitchcock, Dal, 568, 569, 579
Hitler, as an economist, 568
  British praise for, 28, 32, 38, 97, 100-1, 197
  conversation with Lansbury, 68
  does he represent Germany?, 566
  value to Roosevelt, 525
  who made, 573, 581, 589, 595
Hoag, Alden B , 317, 521
Hoare, Sir Samuel, 106
Hoare-Laval plot, 41, 62, 160
Hobson, J A , 559
Hocking, W. E., 170, 584
Hoffman, Rep. Clare, 423, 473
Hogben, Lancelot, 168
Holcombe, A. N , 170, 584
Holland, 114, 116, 121, 147, 202, 239, 257, 270
Holmes, John Haynes, 446, 506
  Justice Oliver Wendell, 570
Holt, Sen Rush D., 125, 129, 244, 277, 304, 355-6, 359-61, 365, 467, 522, 607
Honorary Degrees, 114
Hooton, E. A , 117, 134, 163

Hoover, Herbert, 61, 131, 135, 175, 232, 269, 317, 340, 364, 367, 370, 382, 484, 491
  J. Edgar, 104, 275, 280, 284, 348
Hopkins, Harry, 40, 58, 395, 492
Hore-Belisha, Leslie, 150, 195, 199, 201, 233-4, 344, 578
Horton, Robert, 493, 502-3
House, Col 24, 60, 162, 182, 227, 287, 308, 506, 539
Howard, Graeme K , 605, 613
  Roy, 82, 382
Howe, Quincy, 26, 49, 62, 69, 76, 108, 109, 125, 146, 156, 158, 207, 262, 376, 385
  Louis McHenry, 51-2
Hubbard, Elbert, 358
Hull, Sec Cordell, 36, 54, 61, 63, 69, 108, 114, 123, 174, 178, 235-6, 264, 274, 287, 290, 305, 307, 321, 334, 362, 387, 389, 391, 395, 407, 411-12, 536, 539, 542, 544
"Human Affairs", 81, 534
Hutchins, Robert M., 172, 405, 418, 583, 585, 595, 597, 600
Hutton, Graham, 22
Huxley, Aldous, 213
  Julian, 243
Ickes, Sec Harold, 348, 509, 517
Imperial Policy Group, 124
In Fact, 158, 209, 279, 349, 352, 360, 367, 370, 380, 384, 391, 469
Indentured Labor, 267, 270, 532
India, 144, 148, 165, 213, 247, 270, 283, 557, 575
Industrial Revolution, 275
Industry, patriotism of, 275
Inge, W R , 163
Ingersoll, Ralph, 435, 437
Inter-American Bank, 409, 411, 589
International Affairs, 100, 124, 125
International Finance, 556-7
Ironside, Com Gen., 199, 233, 235, 261-2
Italy, 204, 213
Jacks, G V , 328
Jackson, Robert H., 283, 293, 348, 469, 498, 503-4

Jamaica, 325, 460
James, William, 181, 351, 597
Janeway, Eliot, 172, 298
Japan, abrogation of 1911 trade treaty, 35, 123, 526, 542
alliance with Axis powers, 539
blockade of, 53, 310-11
'dangerous thought', 228, 274
embargo on, 530, 542
investments in China, 527
'New Order', 391
protest to Britain, 288, 325
relations with U. S, 525-45
scrap iron to, 115, 466, 529-30
Tokugawa shoguns, 276
trade with Latin America, 394
trade with U. S, 526
Jefferson, Thomas, 146, 478, 486, 503
Jews, 25, 38, 56, 99, 115-6, 161, 210, 255, 281, 351, 507, 595
Johnson Act, 113, 116, 176, 199, 259-60, 286, 333, 453, 584
Alvin, 606
Edwin C., 98, 365, 443
G Griffith Jr., 300
Sen. Hiram, 274, 378, 447, 516
Gen Hugh S., 248, 270, 276, 295, 316, 362, 364-5, 370, 375, 377, 395, 401, 419, 421, 427, 432, 455, 472, 477, 495, 511, 529, 543
Robert, 368, 371
Samuel, 67, 476
Johnston, Winifred, 109, 275
Johnstone, William C., 538
Jones, Jesse, 116, 315, 409, 411, 433, 544, 599
John Price, 73, 530
Jordan, David Starr, 488
Josephson, Matthew, 56-7, 121, 135
Kaempffert, Waldemar, 565, 577
Kennedy, Joseph P., 62, 111, 114, 116, 120, 127, 184-5, 206, 209, 212, 334, 441, 495, 511, 550
Joseph P. Jr., 550
Kent, C. S., 97, 155, 161, 181
Frank, 559
Raymond, 172, 405
Rockwell, 404

Kettering, C. F., 497
Keynes, John Maynard, 309, 322, 569, 573, 604
King, Judson, 370
MacKenzie, 248, 252
Kingdom, Pres. Frank, 80, 364
Kipling, Rudyard, 25, 132, 136, 226
Kiplinger *Washington Letter*, 76, 359, 373, 376, 377, 384, 385, 556
Kirchwey, Freda, 80, 272, 518, 601
Kluckhohn, Frank L., 259, 426, 453
Kneller, George F, 101, 164, 567
Knox, Col Frank, 78, 361, 394, 443, 539, 584, 585, 598, 599
Rev. Owen, 283, 427, 469-70
Knudsen, William S., 430, 434, 493, 544, 598
Krock, Arthur, 387, 507, 536
Kuhn-Loeb & Co , 177, 243, 359, 515
Labor unions, 484
La Chambre, Guy, 374, 551-2
LaFollette, Gov. Philip F., 423
Sen Robert M. Jr , 348, 426, 464, 472, 516
Lake Chaugogagog-manchaugagog-chaubunagungamaug, 388
Lamont, Thomas W., 20, 71, 73, 76-81, 130, 180-1, 183, 245, 262, 333, 352-3, 356-7, 360, 363, 367, 370, 372, 386, 397, 405, 430, 450, 530-1, 542, 585, 598
Land speculation, 319
Landis, James M., 530, 570
Landon, Alfred M , 362, 364, 366, 371, 421, 471, 517
Landone, Brown, 335, 357, 404, 414
Langer, William L., 56, 580
Langsam, Walter Consuelo, 393
Lansbury, George, 68, 100
Lansing, Robert, 60, 66, 290, 308, 316
Laski, Harold J., 293, 518
Lasswell, Harold D., 44-6, 48, 83, 97-8, 107, 156, 243, 275, 332
Latin America, attitude toward U. S, 223, 387, 389, 392, 411-14, cartel, 389, 395, 409, 412
expeditionary force to, 390, 415
loans to, 408-11
trade, 388, 392, 396, 414

Lattimore, Owen, 542
Laval, Pierre, 550, 552
Lavine, Harold, 76, 163, 191-3, 239, 262, 521
Lawrence, David, 227, 262, 350, 401, 429, 434, 468-9, 476, 479, 486, 495, 507-8
Layton, Sir Walter, 520
League of Nations, 26, 30, 54, 59, 87, 126, 182, 216
Leahy, Admiral, 543
'Lease Lend' Bill, 178, 276, 351, 394, 508, 584-5, 596, 597, 599, 608
'Lebensraum', 611
Leigh, Randolph, 113
Lerner, Max, 601
Lewis, H T, 270
 John L., 51, 284, 370, 424, 496, 509
 Sinclair, 517
 Sir Willmott, 153, 599
Liberty Bonds, 580, 592
Lindbergh, Anne Morrow, 265, 617
 Col. Charles A., 154, 346, 348, 382, 522, 550, 565, 585
Lindley, Ernest, 332
Lin Yutang, 615
Lippmann, Walter, 167, 370, 497, 511
Littlepage, J D., 24, 295
Lloyd, Lord, 39-40, 120, 145, 148, 190, 203, 213
Lobbyists, 157, 172, 176
Lodge, Henry Cabot, 560
 Sen. Henry Cabot, Jr., 285, 294, 418, 516, 524
London Economist, 22, 321, 538
 Observer, 75, 180, 289
 Times, 24, 28, 30, 47, 66, 97, 153, 155, 161, 198, 202, 227, 266, 372, 538, 584
Londonderry, Marquess of, 21, 27-8, 36, 100
Long, Huey, 228, 273, 276, 284, 367, 370, 480, 485, 493
Longworth, Alice Roosevelt, 367, 472
Lothian, Lord, 23, 27-32, 37-8, 64, 68, 71, 75-6, 85, 98, 100, 108, 120, 122, 124, 125-6, 130, 143, 164, 172, 180, 196, 202, 207, 235,

236-7, 244, 264, 269, 274, 296, 356, 360, 380, 453, 458, 515, 519, 539, 584, 613
Lowell, Abbott Lawrence, 71, 184, 394, 560
Lozada, Enrique de, 112, 396
Luce, Henry, 517
Ludendorff, 20, 99
Ludlow Referendum, 59, 69, 180, 415
Lumber, our surplus, 233, 260, 315
Lundberg, Ferdinand, 81, 323, 385
Lundeen, Sen. Ernest, 31, 185, 227, 264, 355, 360, 419, 426, 453-4, 460, 469, 522
McCarran, Sen Pat, 129, 365
McCormick, Col. Robt.-R , 365, 423, 431, 515, 533, 591
MacCracken, Henry Noble, 382, 418, 585, 595, 598
MacDonald, Ramsay, 27, 156, 160
McGowan, Lord, 158
Machiavelli, 35, 485, 497
Mackinder, Sir Halford, 611
McKinley, William, 293, 340, 481
MacLeish, Archibald, 58, 78, 158, 207, 262, 275, 348, 353, 498-9
Macmillan, Lord, 126, 131, 196, 234
Macmurray, John, 133, 157, 616
McNary, Sen Charles L., 76, 366, 513
MacNider, Col. Hanford, 365, 472
Madison, James, 146
Magna Carta, 207-8, 275
Mail, Seizure of, 174, 178, 207, 226, 233, 235, 264, 287, 290, 322,
Mallon, Paul, 62, 113, 208, 221, 227, 232, 279, 286, 321, 339, 367, 373, 376-7, 400, 412, 426, 432, 444, 453, 457, 462, 468, 470, 477, 485, 490, 493, 503, 509, 517, 519, 543, 580, 603, 608
Malvern Conference, 40, 345, 612
Manchester Guardian, 150, 277
Mandel, Georges, 374, 550
Mann, Erika, 97, 101, 136
Mannerheim, Baron Gustav, 188, 190, 191, 194-5, 215, 231, 316
Manning, Bishop William, 265, 343, 399, 401
Manton, Judge, 169, 277

Marshall, Gen. George C, 337, 417, 420, 431, 438, 539, 543, 564
Martin, Rep Joseph, 366, 442, 596
Martinique, 230, 392, 412, 495
Masefield, John, 136
Mass Observation, 210
Masterman, C F G, 43-4, 267, 308
Matheson, Walker, 107, 527
Maugham, Somerset, 147, 446
Maurois, Andre, 547, 558
May, Mark A., 309, 336
Mellett, Lowell, 280, 493, 502
Mellon, Andrew, 266, 340
Melo, Dr. Leopoldo, 394, 412-13
Mencken, H L, 67, 113, 134, 137, 140, 142, 164, 211, 276, 279, 285, 335, 340, 343, 352, 404-8, 423, 429, 456, 472-3, 475, 478, 485, 490, 510-11, 522
Merchant Marine, 527, 536
Messersmith, George S, 184-6, 334
Michelangelo, 46
Michelson, Charles, 366
Military Training Camps Ass'n, 78, 361-2, 397, 400, 444
Mill, John Stuart, 490
Miller, Clyde, 385
Francis P., 80, 81, 457
Millionaires, no new, 333, 372-9, 390
Millis, Walter, 98, 181
Milne, Lord, 197
Milner's 'Kindergarten', 117, 122, 145-6, 248
Mohammed, 586
Moley, Raymond, 58, 60, 63, 64, 310
Monroe Doctrine, 37, 146, 386-96, 412, 537-8
James, 394
Mooney, James, 489
Morality, 42, 46-7, 102, 118-20, 137, 142, 164-5, 168, 255-6, 372, 408, 542, 544-5, 584, 589, 597
Morgan, Anne, 371
House of, 20, 26, 57, 60, 99, 109, 121, 135, 154, 158, 161, 165-7, 174, 177, 180-1, 267, 316, 333, 356-7, 359, 367, 370, 390, 402, 424, 450, 529, 576
John (Laborite M. P.), 66

Joy Elmer, 186, 303
J. P., 76
Morgenthau, Henry Jr., 258-9, 295, 299, 317, 333, 462, 505, 539, 580, 598, 609
Morize, Andre, 560-1
Morley, Felix, 65
Motives, questioning, 15, 16, 96, 463, 585, 607
Moulton, Harold, 589
Mowrer, Edgar Ansel, 24, 160, 210, 374, 399, 545, 585
Muck, Dr. Karl, 348, 500
"Muckraking", 272
Muir, Ramsay, 486
Munich Settlement, 27, 36, 38, 61-3, 113, 116, 455
Munitions, international trade in, 49, 239, 549
investigation (cf Ny)
Munsterberg, Hugo, 597
Murphy, Frank, 220, 280, 291, 293
Murray, Adirondack, 499
Gilbert, 310
Muscle Shoals, 577
Mussolini, Benito, 20, 38, 140, 159, 204, 239, 288, 408, 494, 500
Myers, Gustavus, 162
Napoleon Bonaparte, 566, 572
National City Bank, 373, 378, 437
unity, 129, 187, 228, 273-4, 279, 293, 424, 491, 510, 513, 517
Naval bases, British, 205, 222, 311
cost of, 459-60
leased to U. S., 453-60, 503-4
Uruguayan, 393
Naval expansion (cf Neutrality Act), 219, 221, 230, 544
Nehru, 519
Neilson, William Allan, 71
Neutrality Act, 35, 53, 59, 62-3, 69-76, 113-4, 116, 122-3, 126-7, 129, 130, 170, 172-8, 199, 204-5, 228, 241, 245, 250, 259, 288, 306, 320-1
Belt, 205, 213, 219-31, 288, 325
Nevins, Allan, 23
"New Immoralities", 37
'New Order' in Asia, 541

News letters, 320, 383-6
Newspapers, control of, 97, 102, 104, 117, 131, 133, 386, 402-3, 503, 517, 561
Nichols, Beverley, 23
Nickerson, Hoffman, 444, 525, 567
Nicolson, Harold, 145, 546
Nitrogen, 576-7
Nixon, Larry A , 162, 213
Nock, Albert Jay, 560
Nordau, Max, 18
Norman, Montagu, 21, 42, 100
Norris, Sen George, 284, 347, 361, 363, 397, 426
Northcliffe, Lord, 33, 97, 101, 107, 111, 133, 155, 161, 356, 545
Norwegian Campaign, 77, 252
Nye, Sen. Gerald P., 49, 58, 68, 95, 97-9, 102-4, 117, 129, 134, 244, 274, 355, 360, 365, 420, 438, 539, 599, 609
    Investigation, 49, 58, 69, 121, 156, 158, 176, 229, 356, 375-6
O'Connell, Cardinal, 18, 83, 147, 343, 345, 390
O'Connor, Harvey, 185, 520
O'Flaherty, Liam, 231
Ogilvie, Margaret Stuart, 296, 304
Oil, 213-4, 267-8, 351, 359, 542
Open Door Policy, 156, 528, 539, 541
Opinion, American, 63-4, 66, 85, 108, 111, 115, 117, 120, 129-30, 267, 336, 419, 422, 446, 486
    made, 121, 227, 482
    what it is, 17, 96
O'Ryan, Gen. John F., 78, 431
Ostrogorski, 558-60
Page, Kirby, 274
    Walter Hines, 114, 118, 120, 162, 227, 308
Paish, Sir George, 48, 243
Palmer, Atty. Gen., 280, 345, 405
Palmerston, Lord, 24
Panama Conference, Sept. 1939, 221
Pareto, Vilfredo, 497
Park, No-Yong, 534
Parker, Sir Gilbert, 98, 107, 111, 132, 136, 162, 165, 168, 180, 308, 538, 545

Patiño, Don Simon, 112-3, 158
Patterson, Robert P., 78, 400, 598, 599
Pavlov, 607, 608
Pax Britannica, 372
Peace foundations, 71, 180, 183, 311
    proposals, 65-6, 68, 70, 75
Pearl, Raymond, 117, 134, 172, 602, 607, 608
Pearson and Allen, 83, 137, 150, 212, 215, 224, 231, 286-7, 319, 335, 355, 370, 382, 393, 423, 436-7, 454, 460, 462, 465, 469, 516, 540, 544, 598, 600
Pecora, Ferdinand, 157
Pepper, Sen. Claude, 335, 451, 480
Pericles, 574-5
Pershing, Gen., 425, 452, 456, 461
Pertinax (Andre Geraud), 86, 546, 555, 556
Petain, 374, 552, 561, 562
Peterson, H. C , 45, 97-9, 102, 132, 136, 155, 172, 243
Pettee, George S., 604
Phelps, Reginald, 618
Philippines, 221, 312, 492, 500, 528, 532, 536, 538, 543
Phillips, Sir Frederick, 54, 584
Phillips Exeter *Bulletin*, 359, 372
Pinchot, Amos, 509
Pittman, Sen. Key, 128, 465
Planning, 564, 574
Plant extensions subsidized, 238, 258, 263, 432-39
Ploetz's "Epitome", 56, 290, 580
Poincaré, Raymond, 545, 556, 557
Pol, Heinz, 374, 521, 549
Poland, 116, 133, 195, 214
Polk, Frank, 352, 357
Portugal, 323, 560
Pound, Dean Roscoe, 280, 284, 530
Pratt, Fletcher, 565, 566, 578
President, powers of (cf Roosevelt, Franklin D.)
Price, G. Ward, 100, 337, 350, 568
Priestley, J B., 136, 163, 165-6, 170, 198, 244, 383
Private School News, 359, 520, 596
Professors and propaganda, 99, 116, 119, 135-6, 162, 165, 168, 170,

179, 181, 183, 185, 196, 258, 309, 491, 543, 595

Profits, England, 376, 435, 438
  shipbuilding, 228-30, 435, 464
  steel, 466
  "take profits out of war", 49, 58-9, 69, 84, 98, 376-7
  tax, 376, 378, 415, 436-7, 461-7,
  war, 372-9, 433, 483-4, 570, 586

Propaganda, Administration, 98, 132, 332, 441, 446, 480, 492, 502, 508-9, 579, 585, 607
  British, 41-8, 58, 72, 97-104, 106-9, 113, 117-27, 130-7, 143, 155, 161-2, 165, 196, 207, 227, 236, 241-5, 249, 258, 316, 323, 327-8, 347, 349, 360, 381, 383, 385, 579, 602, 607
  countering, 384-5
  events as, 135
  expenditure on, 44, 48, 107, 111,
  German, 46, 104, 127, 134, 327
  improved technique, 43-5, 107
  movie, 105, 109, 275
  of the deed, 275
  peace, 69, 70, 167, 178-84, 205-6
  purpose of, 85-6, 101, 115, 498
  war, 97, 162, 606-7

Propaganda Analysis, 113, 241, 385
Propagandists, registration of, 241
  tricks of, 46, 118-9, 127, 131-2, 135, 167

Psychology, 567, 583
Public opinion polls, 62, 72, 77, 167, 416, 419-22, 424, 453, 479, 485, 594, 608
Pujo Investigation, 121
Rabelais, 330
Radio, control of, 105, 109
Rascoe, Burton, 48, 134, 293, 341, 404, 498-9, 540
Rathenau, Walter, 564, 577, 589
Rauschning, Hermann, 133, 135-6, 616
Red Cross, 232, 383
  drives, 280-5, 292-3, 345-9, 534
Reed, Douglas, 26, 118, 163, 178, 375
Regionalism, 613
Reith, Sir John, 234, 243

'Religion' and 'morality', 119, 139, 143, 164, 167, 254, 261, 265, 272, 320, 342, 490, 598
Remarque, Erich Maria, 289
Revolution, 26, 133, 135-6, 157, 162, 234, 444, 571, 603, 604, 606, 615-18
Reynaud, Paul, 365, 375-6, 451, 555
Rhodes, Cecil, 126, 143-5, 149, 186
Ribbentrop, Joachim von, 21, 27, 100, 350, 386, 540
Rickenbacker, Capt Eddie, 46-7, 331
Riegel, O. W., 98, 302, 384
Riverdale, Lord, 258
Roberts, Glyn, 24, 43, 156, 158, 214
  W. Adolphe, 413, 460
Robey, Ralph, 409, 606
Rockefeller, John D., Jr., 115
Rogers, Will, 594
Rogerson, Capt. Sidney, 19, 42, 45, 95, 97, 99, 101-3, 113, 119, 131
Romains, Jules, 359, 470, 546-7
Roosevelt, Eleanor, 20, 125, 151, 227, 285, 348, 468, 482
Roosevelt, Franklin D.
  advocates conscription, 415-6, 440, 443
  and royalty, 125, 505, 519
  Anglophilia, 114, 123, 151, 287, 311, 406, 587
  Chautauqua speech, 49-50, 58, 75, 84, 372, 594, 607
  course toward war, 34, 49-86, 107, 117, 122, 125, 132, 141, 162, 172, 178, 185, 187, 216, 227, 237, 244, 276, 306-7, 312, 332, 340, 349, 361, 364-6, 376-7, 386, 390, 441-2, 451, 453-4, 487, 496, 503, 509-10, 536, 580, 582
  fishing trips, 110, 493, 516
  good will, 609
  guarantees Canada, 61, 250, 307
  impeachment called for, 311
  intentions, 184, 196, 228, 239, 268, 305
  Messages to Congress, 61, 64, 227, 237, 277
  naval enthusiasm, 391-2, 440,

441, 615
on revolution, 615
opposition to, 228, 512-25
parallel with Wilson, 56-7, 59,
    60, 67, 120, 121
pledges against war, 69, 170, 228,
    268, 305, 334, 377, 393, 415,
    455, 493, 494, 495, 505, 510,
    511, 514, 584
plurality, 515, 518
powers, 105, 110, 128, 173, 215,
    220, 291, 293-4, 427, 430, 468,
    478-9, 484-6, 491, 496, 514,
    596
quarantine speech, 54-5, 59, 61,
    125, 310
removing the dollar sign, 116, 263
revolutionary, 439, 605-6
secrets, 305, 310, 386, 450-461,
    493, 504, 505
third term, 113, 205, 212, 221,
    339, 349, 351, 365, 377, 402,
    407, 418, 421, 429, 455, 463,
    471-7, 509, 512, 514, 518, 607
toward dictatorship, 129, 174,
    228, 273, 277, 279, 284, 346,
    428, 432, 468, 476-512, 599
Warm Springs farewell, 65, 120,
    121, 184
zeal for religion and morality, 59,
    66, 140, 164, 167, 185, 259,
    324, 339, 343, 595
Roosevelt, Kermit, 177, 536
    Quentin, 543
    Theodore, 22, 121, 182, 293, 340,
        391, 528, 537
Root, Elihu, 371, 383
    Elihu, Jr, 78, 400
Rosenstock-Huessy, Eugen, 429, 492,
Ross, Charles G, 79-80, 357, 457, 459,
    470, 474
    E A., 117, 134
Rothermere, Lord, 33, 38, 211
Roudybush, Franklin, 134, 212, 384,
    386, 451, 539-40
Round Table, 31, 35, 68, 74, 100,
    107, 122, 130, 191, 198, 200,
    204, 205, 212, 220-2, 306-7,
    311, 320, 471, 528

Royal Institute of International Affairs
    (Chatham House), 23, 26, 28-
    31, 66, 75, 124-5, 130
Royal Visit, 113-4, 123-5, 248, 251
Rubber, 532
Ruhr, 20, 23-4, 216
Rumania, 40, 148, 190, 193, 203,
    208, 213, 239, 268, 539
    Exports to Germany, 211-2, 214
Runciman, Walter, 51, 53, 61-2, 66
Russell, Bertrand, 331
    Sen. Richard B., Jr, 479, 486,
        597, 600
Russia, courted by Britain, 114
    embroiling with Germany, 97,
        111, 120, 197
    invasion of, 213-4
    trade with Germany, 121
Ryti, Risto, 194, 203, 215, 232, 314
St Louis Globe-Democrat, 239
    Post-Dispatch, 80, 81, 357, 366,
        402, 453, 457, 459, 470, 474,
        503, 509
Saint Pierre, Abbe de, 148
Salisbury, Lord, 167
Saltonstall, Leverett, 483
Sargent Bulletins, 11, 95-6, 244-7, 256,
    274, 285, 323
    Jane, 399
    Porter, 25, 37, 117, 170, 272, 300,
        385, 499, 500, 534, publications
        of (cf "Course of Human
        Events", "Human Affairs",
        "New Immoralities", Schools,
        Handbook of Private, Summer
        Camps, Handbook of, "What
        Makes Lives")
Scandinavia, 114, 116, 557
Scapegoats, 551, 589, 595-6
Schacht, Hjalmar, 21, 100, 569, 604
Scherman, Harry 300-1, 592
Scholarship, materials of, 181-2
Schools, Handbook of Private, 38, 48,
    82, 87, 98, 100-1, 140, 168-70,
    272, 330, 360, 372, 382, 497,
    500, 609
Schoonmaker, E D., 163
Schopenhauer, 605
Schuman, Frederick L., 18, 22, 24, 35,

56, 59, 66, 76, 86, 193, 195, 231, 319, 460, 506, 563, 600-1
Science, sabotage of, 577
Scroggs, William O., 65, 551, 580
Seldes, George, 158, 194, 209, 240, 349, 357, 367, 370, 379, 382
Seymour, Charles, 79, 80, 117, 119, 146, 164-5, 353, 446
Shapley, Harlow, 117, 134, 170, 584
Shaw, George Bernard, 136, 190, 195, 198, 271, 312, 344, 352, 577
Shearer, William B., 172, 175-6
Shedd, Brig.-Gen., 400, 417
Shepardson, Whitney H., 65, 551, 580
Sherwood, Robert E., 79, 80, 146, 383
Ships, cost of, 229
Shipstead, Sen. Henrik, 426, 516
Shirer, William, 574
Shotwell, James T., 71
Siberia, American troops in, 20, 24, 121, 158, 268, 481, 528
Silver, 322, 324
Simon, Sir John, 22, 37, 59, 124, 195, 199, 201, 321, 470
Simone, Andre, 548, 562
Singapore, 108, 115, 151, 280, 308, 311, 495, 505, 531, 533, 537,
Sloan, Alfred P., Jr., 606
Smith, Al, 494
  Edson B., 466
  George H. E., 51, 56, 67, 313
  Robert Aura, 112, 531, 533
Smuts, Gen. Jan Christian, 395
Smyth, Joseph Hilton, 107
Snowden, Philip, 160
Snubbery and snobbery, 238
Soil, exhaustion of, 328, 591
Southern Congressmen, 205, 260, 509, 516, 594, 600, 608
Spain, 49, 68, 70, 201, 292
Spanish refugees, 201, 210
Spengler, Oswald, 489
Spring-Rice, Cecil, 537
Squires, J Duane, 44, 98, 301, 405
S S. Athenia, 288, 290
  Bremen, 222, 225
  City of Flint, 226
  Columbus, 225-6, 231, 239, 288,
Staley, Eugene, 575

Stalin, Joseph, 25, 34, 97, 102, 108, 120, 140, 194, 197, 211, 605
Standard Oil, 59, 110, 158, 173, 176-7, 351, 541-2
Stanley, Henry M,, 538
Stark, Admiral, 220, 230, 457, 460
Starvation, 217, 256, 263-72
State Department, 63, 104, 173-4, 182, 223, 236, 242-3, 264, 287-90, 294, 323, 387-8, 391, 393, 409, 530, 539-40, 542, 545
Stead, W. T., 144, 149
Stettinius, Edward R, Jr., 544
Stimson, Henry L, 59, 78-9, 178, 352, 356-7, 360, 364, 368-9, 397, 400, 407, 417-18, 420-1, 427-8, 430, 434, 437, 443, 445, 454, 539, 542-3, 584, 585, 598
Stoddard, Lothrop, 208, 386
Stolper, Gustav, 578, 581, 590
Stone, I. F, 433, 466, 530, 539, 542
Stoneman, W. H, 115, 199, 233, 256, 375, 515, 519-20, 585
Strabolgi, Lord, 215, 217
Strakhovsky, Leonid I., 188-9
Strasser, Otto, 136
Streit, Clarence, 71, 103, 126, 143-4, 146-7, 150-1, 168, 174, 196, 218, 253, 287, 369, 380-1
Sullivan, John L, 437, 462
Summerall, Gen. Charles P, 50
Summer camp, 492, 499
Summer Camps, Handbook of, 499
Supreme Court debacle, 51, 57, 518
Swastika, origin of, 491
Swing, Raymond Gram, 263, 518, 558
Taft, Sen. Robert, 290, 339-40, 397, 409, 431
Taussig, Charles William, 176, 178
Taylor, Edmund, 348, 563, 567
  Myron, 343
Teeling, William, 40
Thirty Years' War (new), 121, 181
Thomas, Sen. Elbert, 129, 413
  Norman, 213, 303, 395, 399, 474-5, 488, 507, 515
Thompson, C. Bertrand, 552-3, 562
  Dorothy, 146, 184, 186, 193, 319, 370, 384, 472, 497, 564,

Thoreau, Henry David, 283, 499
Thucydides, 582
Thyssen, Fritz, 158
Tin, Bolivian, 108, 112-3, 393, 396,
    Malayan, 148, 532
Tinkham, Rep Geo. H., 61, 98, 103,
    114, 227, 242, 304-6, 308,
    311-2, 318, 387, 391, 451, 493
Tobacco, American sales to Britain,
    259-60, 286
Tobey, Sen. Chas. W , 173, 304
Tobin, Harold J., 104, 301, 399, 401-2,
    419, 468
Tory Crew, 83, 87, 251, 327, 333, 356,
Toynbee, Arnold, 21, 581
Transfer of Registry, 173, 176-7
Tugwell, Rexford Guy, 52-3, 518, 570,
    587, 602
Turkey, loan to, 191, 204, 213, 259
Twain, Mark, 278, 583, 597
Tweedsmuir, Lord, 145, 248, 289
Tyrrell, Lord, 43, 182
Uncensored, 47, 63, 72, 76, 81, 110,
    161, 167, 201, 215, 241, 284,
    290, 291, 293, 334, 354, 364,
    369, 373, 384, 416, 417, 430,
    453, 457, 474, 475, 505
'Union Now' (Federal Union), 71,
    103, 123, 126, 143-51, 167,
    196, 218, 287, 322, 380
United Eurasia, 528, 534, 541
United States of Europe, 121, 149
U. S , a debtor nation, 263, 296
Valentine, Alan, 171, 301, 405, 418,
    585, 595
Vandenberg, Sen. Arthur, 123, 209,
    286, 291, 295, 305, 340, 397,
    404, 417, 464, 513, 516, 522
Van Paassen, Pierre, 202
Vansittart, Sir Robert, 41-7, 97, 99-
    100, 104, 106, 111, 117, 120,
    155, 196, 227, 246, 253, 255,
    267, 309, 323, 540, 608
Van Zandt, James E , 304, 404
Van Zeeland, Paul, 372
Vargas, Getulio,387, 411
Vatican, 204
Veblen, Thorstein, 471, 559, 575
Versailles Treaty, 19, 23, 31, 37, 100-1,

    118, 197, 240, 324, 555, 573,
Villard, Oswald G , 147, 197, 208,
    261, 277, 285, 336, 339, 404,
Vinson Act, 435, 464
Voigt, F. A., 582
Voltaire, 18, 309, 383, 488
Von Schirach, Baldur, 111
Von Seeckt, Gen., 555
Vorys, Rep John M , 173, 184, 304
Walker, John Brisben, 316
Wall Street Journal, 366, 373, 378
    433, 438, 466
Wallace, Sec. Henry A., 36, 212, 269,
    468, 475, 509, 513
Waln, Nora, 45
Walsh, Sen David I., 98, 103, 104,
    117, 133, 134, 173, 184, 363,
    432, 456-7, 487, 516
War, betting when American gets in,
    74, 76, 130, 133, 204, 266,
    biology of, 602, 607
    casualties, 578
    cost of, American, 138, 218, 328-
    35, 591, 596
    English, 199, 321, 338
    French, 321
    debts, 263, 266, 328, 453, 456,
    essentials to success in, 567
    fever, 118, 260
    scares, 63, 67, 127, 130, 132,
    143, 172, 205, 237, 274, 281,
    290, 480
    who pays for, 591, 593, 605
Warbasse, James P., 186
Warburg, James P , 118
Washburne, Carleton, 135
Washington and Whitehall, 74, 113,
    119, 167
    Capitol, burning of, 129, 137, 395
    George, 472, 574
Watson, Goodwin, 15-16, 186, 301,
Wealth, conscription of, 294, 425,
    467-8, 592
    estimate of American, 580, 591
Webster, Daniel, 363, 476, 478
Wechsler, James, 76, 163, 191, 193,
Wecter, Dixon, 134, 152, 154
Week by Week, 161, 200, 203, 212,
    214, 217, 226, 384, 386, 415,

Weekly Foreign Letter, 40, 66, 161, 206, 285, 330, 384, 390, 418, 428, 474, 603, 615

Weir, Ernest T., 340, 423
   L. MacNeill, 156, 159, 160

Welles, Sumner, 63, 286, 288, 321, 334, 407-8, 411, 455, 540, 598

Wellington House, 43, 136, 221-2, 248, 267

Wells, H G, 33, 101, 111, 120, 132, 136, 143, 147, 162, 163, 192, 227, 244, 308-9, 405, 482, 573, 579, 608, 612

Weygand, Gen. Maxime, 213, 219, 374, 561, 562

Whaley Eaton Letter, 321, 336, 373, 384, 385, 395, 396, 425

"What Makes Lives", 20, 31, 41, 43, 48, 61, 78, 81, 99, 111, 112, 126, 135, 159, 168, 170, 353, 355, 358, 384-6, 442, 486, 488, 497, 594, 597

Wheeler, Sen. Burton K, 83, 119, 209, 244, 252, 255, 277, 284, 305, 319, 355, 360, 365, 370, 397, 404, 415, 417, 420, 427-8, 437, 454, 456, 479, 509, 516, 522, 524, 596

Wheeler-Nicholson, Malcolm, 573

Whitaker, John T., 115, 204

White, Henry, 22-3
      William Allen, 72, 77-82, 146, 208, 276, 354, 356-8, 360-1, 379, 381-3, 452, 459

Whitney, Richard, 166, 169, 276, 372

Whittlesey, Chas. R., 179, 238, 259, 263, 267, 296-7, 322

Whyte, Sir Frederick, 66

Willert, Sir Arthur, 105, 153, 599

William the Bastard, 87, 323, 385

Williams, Maj. Al J, 342, 384, 404, 565, 585, 599
      Wythe, 250, 594

Willkie, Wendell, 77, 81, 104, 140, 169, 276, 336, 339-40, 351-2, 356, 360, 364, 366-72, 380-1, 402, 418-19, 421-24, 426, 429-30, 443, 447-50, 455, 465, 467, 471, 473-5, 477, 479, 482, 489, 493, 495, 503, 507-9, 513-17, 520, 584, 585, 598

Wilson, Woodrow, 20, 24, 56-7, 59-60, 67, 69, 101, 105, 107, 120-1, 126, 158, 179, 182, 251, 276, 293, 308, 316, 332, 335, 432, 471, 475, 480, 486, 503, 505-6, 514-5, 528, 563, 579, 587, 608, 609, 610

Windsor, Duke of, 75

Wiseman, Sir William, 243

Wolfe, Bertram D., 213
      Humbert, 289

Wolfers, Arnold, 182-3

Wolsey, Cardinal, 22

Wood, Gen. Robert E, 65, 295, 472, 474, 585, 596

Woodring, Sec. of War Harry, 131, 356, 417, 420

Woodruff, Maj -Gen. James A., 484

Woodside, Willson, 28, 62, 66

Woollcott, Alexander, 146

"World Order", 124, 126, 144, 609

Wrench, Sir John Evelyn, 100

Wundt, Wilhelm, 596

Yarnell, Admiral, 54, 288

Ybarra, T. R., 395

Yeats-Brown, Maj. Francis, 197

York, Archbishop of, 265, 345

Young, Eugene J., 47, 263, 266, 305, 556-8
      Owen D., 372

Youth, American, 82, 290, 429, 554, Movement, 492

Yugoslavia, 203, 218

Zinoviev letter, 25, 159

Zinsser, Dr. Hans, 157

PUBLISHERS

Books Quoted or Reviewed

Bles, Ltd , Geoffrey, 22 Suffolk St , London, S W 1
Bobbs-Merrill Co , 724 N Meridian St , Indianapolis, Ind.
Cape, Jonathan, 30 Bedford Sq , London, W C 1
Carrick & Evans, Inc , 20 East 57th St , New York
Cassell & Co , Ltd , La Belle Sauvage, London, E C 4
Columbia Univ. Press, 2960 Broadway, New York
Cooperative Books, Norman, Oklahoma
Covici-Friede, Inc , 386 Fourth Ave., New York
Coward-McCann, Inc , 2 West 45th St , New York
Crofts & Co , F S , 41 Union Sq , New York
Day Co , The John, 40 East 49th St , New York
Dodd, Mead & Co , 449 Fourth Ave , New York
Doubleday, Doran & Co , Inc , 14 West 49th St , New York
Eyre & Spottiswood, Ltd , 6 Great New St , London, W C 4
Faber and Faber, 24 Russell Sq , London, W C 1
Flanders Hall, Scotch Plains, N J
Gollancz, Ltd , Victor, 14 Henrietta St , London, W C 2
Greystone Press, 40 East 49th St , New York
Harcourt, Brace & Co , Inc , 383 Madison Ave , New York
Harper & Bros , 49 East 33rd St , New York
Harvard Univ Press, 38 Quincy St , Cambridge, Mass
Heinemann, Ltd , William, 99 Great Russell St , London, W C 1
Holt & Co , Inc , Henry, 257 Fourth Ave , New York
Houghton Mifflin Co , 2 Park St , Boston, Mass.
Hutchinson & Co , 34 Paternoster Row, London, E C 4
Knopf, Alfred A , 501 Madison Ave , New York
Lippincott Co , J B , East Washington Sq , Philadelphia, Pa
Little, Brown & Co , 34 Beacon St , Boston, Mass
Longmans, Green & Co , 55 Fifth Ave , New York
Macmillan Co , The, 60 Fifth Ave , New York
Macrae-Smith Co , 1712 Ludlow St , Philadelphia, Pa
McBride & Co , Robert M , 116 East 16th St , New York
Messner, Inc , Julian, 8 West 40th St , New York
Modern Age Books, 432 Fourth Ave , New York
New York Univ Press, New York
Norton & Co , Inc , W W , 70 Fifth Ave , New York
Oklahoma Univ. Press, Norman, Oklahoma
Oxford Univ Press, 114 Fifth Ave , New York
Pennsylvania Univ. Press, 3622 Locust St , Philadelphia, Pa
Princeton Univ Press, Princeton, N J
Putnam's Sons, G P , 2 West 45th St , New York
Reynal and Hitchcock, Inc , 386 Fourth Ave , New York
Rich and Cowan, Ltd , 25 Soho Sq , London, W. 1
Scribner's Sons, Charles, 597 Fifth Ave , New York
Secker and Warburg, Ltd , 5 John St , Adelphi, London, W C 2
Seeley Service & Co , Ltd , 196 Shaftesbury Ave , London, W C 2
Sidgwick & Jackson, Ltd , 44 Museum St , London, W C. 1
Simon and Schuster, Inc , 1230 Sixth Ave., New York
Smith, Peter, 321 Fifth Ave , New York
Smith, Richard R , 120 East 39th St , New York
Stackpole, 250 Park Ave , New York
Stokes Co , Frederick A , 443 Fourth Ave , New York
Viking Press, Inc , 18 East 48th St , New York
Whittlesey House, 330 West 42nd St , New York
Yale Univ Press, 143 Elm St , New Haven, Conn.

A HANDBOOK OF PRIVATE SCHOOLS

by Porter Sargent

25th edition, May 1941, 1232 pages, $6.00

An Annual Guide and Survey of Private Schools and Colleges, lists and classifies geographically 4200 Private Schools, Day and Boarding, Junior and Senior Colleges, describes critically and statistically in geographical sequence 1500 Private Schools and Junior Colleges, reviews annually what's doing in education and in the intellectual world.

PARTIAL CONTENTS

THE INTRODUCTION, Current changes in education, English and American, public and private, university and secondary—Passing of England's public schools—School masters in the army—Why men behave so much worse than apes—The present mess—Myths, abstractions, and delusions—Other fetters—The Degradation of intellectual integrity—Worship of facts—No consistent body of information—Education piece-meal—Preparing seed beds for propaganda—Are we in a pre-revolutionary stage?—The American philosophy of "That's That"—The world has meaning—Biocracy

THE LEADING PRIVATE SCHOOLS—Statistical and Critical Descriptions.

SUPPLEMENTARY LISTS OF SCHOOLS AND JUNIOR COLLEGES—Of lesser or local importance—Secondary—Tutoring—Elementary Boarding—Student.

SCHOOLS CLASSIFIED BY TYPE—To meet special needs—Boys—Girls—Coeducational—Professional and Vocational

A BRIEF GUIDE TO PRIVATE SCHOOLS

6th edition, 1941, 176 pages. Illustrated. 25c.

Boarding Schools, Day and Country Day Schools, Junior Colleges, Schools for Specialized Training by Classification. Chapters on Selecting the School, What to Avoid, What to Look For.

THE SUMMER CAMP GUIDE

6th edition, 1941, 112 pages. Illustrated. 25c.

Describes and lists the 400 better private camps. Chapters on Pitfalls to Avoid, Selecting the Camp, What the Child Needs

WHAT MAKES LIVES

224 pages, silk cloth, $1.50

EXPLAINS—what makes you thing so—how the world has been brought to its present sorry state—at least it's an attempt.—EXAMINES—how personalities are shaped or misshaped by our changing environment, by persons of the past and present, seen and unseen, by misleading propaganda and teaching—resulting in maladjustment, hate, waste, and war.—INTERPRETS—domestic and foreign affairs—previously unpublished, not generally known—in terms of human motives.

WHAT THEY SAY
About the Handbook of Private Schools

John Erskine, New York—"Your review of education covers a wide field, and what you say is very sprightly If the parents who are choosing a school can digest all that you feed them, the education of the elder generation must have been remarkably good."

Douglas A. Thom, Boston—"Many stimulating discussions . . . so much that is pertinent to the problem of education that the book should be in the hands of every educator—in fact, everyone interested in problems of youth."

Harvard Educational Review—"Finding comments as earnestly honest and unafraid in a publication circulating primarily where special privilege is rampant is astonishing. The author strikes out in all directions with impartiality."

Charles C. Tillinghast, Horace Mann School—"You are rendering a real service by stimulating us to clarify our thinking. I find your Handbook of great interest and of tremendous informational value."

New York Sun—"A guide for parents and teachers, it serves that purpose without fear of treading on an occasional academic toe. Spicy comments on things pedagogic. Concise and critical information."

President Stanley C. Ross, Wayland Junior College—"Beyond a doubt the most reliable and pungent school directory that can be obtained anywhere in the United States."

The Nation's Schools—"This invaluable reference book for secondary school principals presents the most authentic and comprehensive information concerning private schools."

The Philadelphia Inquirer—"A wealth of comment on almost every phase of education and its history . . . the author has gone through his field thoroughly, attacking bogeys and fetishes, laying bare the varying degrees of bunk."

The New York Times—"The information about schools is compiled with care, sifted with judicial integrity and organized with such lucidity that it cannot help but be of immense assistance to the parent in search of a school."

O. L. Reiser, University of Pittsburgh—"Your appraisal of the academic situation is just and realistic Keep up the good work!"

Frank E. Gaebelein, The Stony Brook School—"Your Handbook always contains real ideas and is always a very valuable volume to have at hand."

Advance—"A great compendium . . . a most incisive and interesting critique of life, manners, current events, and practical philosophies."

Mrs. S Bolling Wright, Mexico—"Used in our household along with the Bible, the encyclopedia and the dictionary as a sure reference and guide."

Trigant Burrow, The Lifwynn Foundation, New York—"Marvel at the breadth of your educational interests and activities."

Carroll C Pratt, Rutgers Univ.—"Greatly impressed by your comments on the present academic situation. I wish your ideas could be spread"

THE NEW IMMORALITIES

by Porter Sargent

192 pages, black cloth binding, gold stamped, $2.00

Releasing the Dead Hand which has kept us from more rational and natural attitudes, the "New Immoralities" are those new modes of thought, lines of action, that violate the old established codes. A volume of short essays grouped informally as 'What's It All About', 'The Dead Hand Upon Us', 'The American Backdrop', 'Immoral School Teachings', 'Personal Ethics Revised', 'You Don't Have To'.

In straightforward, vigorous language the author clears away some of the outworn and antiquated moral rubbish and lays the foundation for a new freedom, a greater sanity and a more hopeful future for the race through natural and biologically sound modern ways of thinking and acting.

Claude M. Fuess, Phillips Academy—"Full of provocative sentences "

Boston Transcript—"Brief ethical squibs provide most amusing reading "

The Boston Globe—"A good deal of this window smashing needs to be done to let in light and air and I am elated to find you doing it."

President H N. MacCracken, Vassar College—"There are a great many pithy sayings in the volume, well worth remembering."

New Haven Journal Courier—"The sensational little essays are delightful in their moodiness, wit and psychiatry, irreverence and anti-war pleas The pithy bits that enliven the pages stab the complacent spirit awake "

SPOILS

by Porter Sargent

112 pages, black and burgundy cloth, gold stamped, $2.00

Poems From a Crowded Life reflecting many moods and experiences, with a preliminary essay on who writes poetry and why, and how they happened to—grouped under such titles as 'Rewards For Living', 'Personalia', 'Aspirations', 'Revolt of Youth', 'Pre-War Vintage 1913', 'Varia', 'Inspirations From the Bible', 'Baubles'.

Detroit Free Press—"It is a distinct surprise to find much of beauty, workmanlike skill and more than a touch of humor in his verses."

Frank S. Hackett, Riverdale Country School—"I find a depth and a breadth which is inspiring."

Alfred Machin, England—"I often have a dip in your works, but find my chief pleasure in your verse, strangely enough, because I have never had much use for poetry. But yours is a new kind, with no straining after rhyme etc "

The Boston Globe—"The poems represent loot from a rich and varied life, show a wide range of poetic expression, lyric, dramatic and facetious. There is understanding of the revolt of youth; the joy and thrill of mountain climbing; broad sympathy for all mankind. His style is virile and robust."

WHAT THEY SAY

About Recent Books by Porter Sargent

H. G Wells, London—"A very bright, clear summary."

John Dewey, Columbia University—"You are doing a unique work "

Arthur M Schlesinger, Harvard Univ.—"Read with attention and profit."

H W. Dodds, Princeton University—"I always enjoy your sharp comments."

Robert H. Jackson, Attorney General, D. C.—"Of great interest."

Lancelot Hogben, Aberdeen—"Many thanks for your interesting enclosure "

Lucien Price, The Boston Globe—"It's a gold mine."

Time—"The saltiest commentator on U. S education "

Harold D. Lasswell, University of Chicago—"Astonished and stimulated by the outspoken candor of your judgments "

W. Y. Elliott, Harvard University—"Pleases me to see an independent critic still among us—and one with your powers."

Sir Arthur Keith, England—"I wish every missionary of Science well and you are a missionary of a very live kind."

Laurence Housman, England—"It contains a lot of meat, serious and amusing; wherever I dip into it, I find it interesting."

Lord Stamp, London—"Contains an enormous amount of useful information, and I hope to make practical use of it."

Harvard Alumni Bulletin—"Many pungent remarks . . range of reading and criticism is nothing short of amazing "

Earnest Hooton, Harvard University—"This is the best and most brilliant collection of essays you have published."

Carleton Beals, Branford, Conn.—"Have enjoyed your frank utterances in a world where so few people have that sterling quality "

Quincy Howe, New York City—"As usual you have turned out an original and necessary interpretation."

The Christian Century—"Packed with pungent criticism and constructive suggestion about the education process."

Walter B. Cannon, Harvard Medical School—"The wit, the irony, the erudition of it have impressed me deeply."

E. W. Balduf, Director of Adult Education, Des Moines—"As refreshing as a welcome arctic breeze on a humid, stuffy, mid-summer Iowa day."

Charles Beard, New Milford, Conn.—"We always take delight in your writings for you are not afraid to look into the horse's mouth."

Edward C. Mack, New York City—"I wholeheartedly agree with your educational beliefs, knowing that it is profoundly true that only live and flexible minds can produce a decent society."

Edwin G Conklin, Princeton University—"Like your other writings it is full of pepper and salt and pithy sayings Indeed it is a modern treasury of wit and wisdom."

Lightning Source UK Ltd.
Milton Keynes UK
UKHW021824160223
417092UK00004B/417